# *Studies in Scripture*

## VOLUME ONE The Doctrine and Covenants

# *Studies in Scripture*

## VOLUME ONE The Doctrine and Covenants

Edited by Robert L. Millet and Kent P. Jackson

Salt Lake City, Utah

*Studies in Scripture* series

Vol. 1: The Doctrine and Covenants
Vol. 2: The Pearl of Great Price
Vol. 3: Genesis to 2 Samuel
Vol. 4: 1 Kings to Malachi
Vol. 5: The Gospels
Vol. 6: Acts to Revelation
Vol. 7: 1 Nephi to Alma 29
Vol. 8: Alma 30 to Moroni

Cover illustration: "Joseph Smith before the Nauvoo Temple" by Dale Kilbourn




First printing in hardbound by Randall Book Co. 1984
First printing in hardbound by Deseret Book Company 1989
First printing in paperbound by Deseret Book Company 2003

Visit us at deseretbook.com

ISBN 0-87579-274-X (hardbound)
ISBN 1-59038-257-9 (paperbound)

Printed in the United States of America 72076-018P
Publishers Printing, Salt Lake City, UT

10 9 8 7 6 5 4 3 2 1

# CONTENTS

# ABBREVIATIONS USED

*HC* . . . Joseph Smith, *History of the Church of Jesus Christ of Latter-day Saints,* ed. B. H. Roberts, 7 vols. (Deseret Book Co., 1957).

*JD* . . . . *Journal of Discourses,* 26 vols. (Liverpool: F.D. Richards, LDS Book Depot, 1855-86).

*TPJS* . . Joseph Fielding Smith, comp., *Teachings of the Prophet Joseph Smith* (Salt Lake City: Deseret Book Co., 1976).

*Ibid.* . . For the Latin *ibidem,* "in the same place," indicating that the quotation is taken from the same source as the reference which precedes it.

# PREFACE

In a revelation given through Joseph Smith, early missionaries were instructed concerning their callings. They were told to preach the gospel, "saying none other things than that which the prophets and apostles have written, and that which is taught . . . by the Comforter through the prayer of faith" (D&C 52:9). Similarly the Lord commanded: "You shall declare the things which have been revealed to my servant, Joseph Smith, Jun." (D&C 31:4). *Studies in Scripture Vol. 1—The Doctrine and Covenants* is the first in a series of volumes intended to enhance and supplement one's personal study of the revelations found in the Standard Works of the Church of Jesus Christ of Latter-day Saints. Recognizing that there is no substitute for a sincere and serious study of the scriptures themselves, this series, *Studies in Scripture*, is presented as a resource, an aid in pointing members of the Church toward the profound realities to be discovered in the books which comprise our scriptural canon.

This volume is a collection of essays written to give deeper insight into historical and doctrinal aspects of those revelations, epistles, and instructions which constitute the Doctrine and Covenants. These essays have been prepared by Latter-day Saints who are committed to the gospel and active in its service, while striving for excellence in research and scholarship. They are men and women who possess both a love for the Prophet Joseph Smith and his successors, and a devotion to the gospel truths which the Lord has revealed through his chosen servants. We make no apology for the fact that this book is written from the vantage point of faith in the Lord Jesus Christ. It is an expression of testimony, a statement of faith.

Each of the contributors is responsible for his or her own conclusions, and the volume is a private endeavor, and not a production of either Brigham Young University or the Church of Jesus Christ of Latter-day Saints. Although the writers and editors have sought to be in harmony with the teachings of the scriptures and the leaders of the Church, the reader should not regard this work as a primary source for gospel understanding but should turn instead to the scriptures and the words of modern prophets for authoritative doctrinal statements.

Grateful appreciation is expressed to a number of persons, without whose active involvement and support this undertaking would not have been possible. Colleagues and friends from around the country have offered helpful suggestions and given enthusiastic support from the beginning. Each of the contributors has been extremely cooperative during the months involved in writing, editing, and final preparation of the manuscript for publication. Thanks is also expressed to F. Warren Bittner, Linda Reber, Timothy J. LaVallee, Lanise Porter, Christine Purves, and Jeffrey W. Snow, for their assistance in the preparation of the book, as well as to the staff of Randall Book Company. The editors owe a special debt of gratitude to their wives and children, who have been generous with their husbands' and fathers' time.

We sincerely hope that this book will make a meaningful contribution in bringing Latter-day Saints to a greater understanding of the Doctrine and Covenants and an increased desire to study it. Many of the historical details given in the essays are based on recent research and draw from newly available primary sources. A number of the essays provide a fresh view into important principles of the gospel. We have sought to be consistent with the revelations of the Restoration, with the hope that readers may be edified and instructed by what is contained herein and further encouraged to study the revelations of the Lord in the Standard Works. It is our hope that all who use this book will find the same enjoyment in reading it that we have found in preparing it.

Robert L. Millet
Kent P. Jackson
1 September 1984

# 1
# THE DOCTRINE AND COVENANTS A HISTORICAL OVERVIEW

Robert J. Woodford

> Behold, I am God and have spoken it; these commandments are of me, and were given unto my servants in their weakness, after the manner of their language, that they might come to understanding.
>
> And inasmuch as they erred it might be made known;
>
> And inasmuch as they sought wisdom they might be instructed;
>
> And inasmuch as they sinned they might be chastened, that they might repent.
>
> And inasmuch as they were humble they might be made strong, and blessed from on high, and receive knowledge from time to time (D&C 1:24-28).

Joseph Smith desired that the revelations which he had received be printed; a council of high priests assembled in 1831 for the purpose of discussing the matter had the same desire; and now the Lord had spoken, saying that it was also his will. Thus the way was opened for this modern book of scripture to be published.

Our dispensation opened with the First Vision of the Prophet Joseph Smith, and from that beginning the Lord guided the Prophet whenever specific instruction was needed. By the fall of 1831, more than three score revelations had been received which were recorded; no one knows how many others were received but remained unrecorded. Understandably, these revelations were vital to the Church, and it was important that the instructions in them be observed. They contained moral prescriptions and details for organizing and administering the Church, yet they were oftimes not readily available to those who needed their guidance the most.

Manuscript copies were made, but that only allowed for limited circulation of the revelations, and it led to additional problems: errors brought about by inaccurate copying, poor penmanship, and misspelled words. There also must have been concern about the sacred revelations being read by those who were enemies to the work. Thus there were good reasons in this situation for both printing the revelations and not printing them. Joseph Smith did as he was accustomed to do when he desired an issue to be discussed freely: he called for a conference of high priests. These men met in Hiram, Ohio, over a twelve-day period in the forepart of November 1831 in several conference sessions.

## A Book of Commandments

During the first session the assembled priesthood holders decided that the revelations should be printed as *A Book of Commandments.* They also decided to publish ten thousand copies, and that they should be printed in Zion (Missouri).[1] The meeting was then dismissed. During the interlude Joseph Smith received the revelation known as "The Preface" to the Doctrine and Covenants (section 1), in which the Lord confirmed their decision that the revelations be published for all the world to read.

Back in session later the same day, Joseph Smith requested the brethren to place their testimony in the Book of Commandments, much the same as the testimonies of the three and eight witnesses were included in the Book of Mormon.[2] Most of them were willing to do so, but others made comments about the language in which the revelations were expressed.[3] Their objections appear to have been over the poor spelling and grammar used in the revelations. Because these men did not consider the revelations to be word-for-word dictations from the Lord, they were not accusing the Lord, through the Prophet, of having a poor grasp of the English language.[4] Instead they were attacking the Prophet's ability to write what the Lord had given him and, therefore, making a not-too-subtle attempt to show themselves "better men" than the Prophet. Joseph Smith received some inspiration during the ensuing discussion which places the objector in a defensive position:

> And now, I, the Lord, give unto you a testimony of the truth of these commandments which are lying before you.
>
> Your eyes have been upon my servant Joseph Smith, Jun., and his language you have known, and his imperfections you have known; and you have sought in your hearts knowledge that you might express beyond his language; this you also know.
>
> Now, seek ye out of the Book of Commandments, even the

> least that is among them, and appoint him that is the most wise among you;
>
> Or, if there be any among you that shall make one like unto it, then ye are justified in saying that ye do not know that they are true;
>
> But if ye cannot make one like unto it, ye are under condemnation if ye do not bear record that they are true (D&C 67:4-8).

William E. McLellin took the challenge to write a revelation and attempted to do so before the next session of the conference the following morning. Joseph Smith made this comment about his vain attempt: "William E. M'Lellin, as the wisest man, in his own estimation, having more learning than sense, endeavored to write a commandment like unto one of the least of the Lord's, but failed; it was an awful responsibility to write in the name of the Lord."[5] The next morning, section 67, written the day before, was read by Oliver Cowdery to the conference and, "the brethren then arose in turn and bore witness to the truth of the Book of Commandments."[6]

Joseph Smith later observed: "The Elders and all present that witnessed this vain attempt of a man to imitate the language of Jesus Christ, renewed their faith in the fulness of the Gospel, and in the truth of the commandments and revelations which the Lord had given to the Church through my instrumentality; and the Elders signified a willingness to bear testimony of their truth to all the world."[7]

The Prophet then wrote by inspiration a statement concerning the truth of the revelations to which the high priests were willing to sign their names. This testimony was found in earlier editions of the Doctrine and Covenants in the Explanatory Introduction, but it was excluded in the 1981 edition. It is a similar statement to the Testimony of the Twelve Apostles which is found in all editions.

How could the revelations be published if there were errors in them? In the next conference session, held 8 November, Sidney Rigdon spoke concerning this matter, and the conference voted: "Resolved by this conference that Brother Joseph Smith Jr correct those errors or mistakes which he may discover by the holy Spirit while reviewing the revelations & commandments & also the fulness of the scriptures."[8] Oliver Cowdery was assigned at the same time to assist.

Before the conference ended there were other decisions made which were either resolutions passed by those attending, or were given them by the Lord. John Whitmer was to accompany Oliver Cowdery to Missouri with the revelations (D&C 69). Certain brethren, under the law of consecration, were given the publication of the scriptures as a stewardship (D&C 70). And others, who had assisted materially in the publication of the scriptures, were to be "remembered to the Bishop in Zion as being worthy of an inheritance."[9]

Plans for the publication of the Book of Commandments went forward until Saturday, 20 July 1833, when a mob destroyed the printing establishment in which the book was being printed. The mob was seeking to put the *Evening and Morning Star* out of circulation, but most of the uncut pages of the Book of Commandments were lost in the fire and destruction. Some very brave Latter-day Saints risked harm from the mob in order to secure a relatively few copies of the incomplete book's pages, scattered around the building. All that had been printed to that date were five signatures of 32 pages each, or a total of 160 pages. William W. Phelps noted that the book was not yet finished at the time of the mobbing.[10]

The surviving incomplete copies of the book were bound by various parties and circulated among the members.[11]

## 1835 Edition

Shortly after the failure to publish the Book of Commandments, plans were made to publish the revelations in Kirtland, Ohio. In April 1834 Sidney Rigdon was set apart to assist Oliver Cowdery in publishing the reprint of the *Evening and Morning Star*, and to arrange the Book of Covenants. Oliver Cowdery was also set apart to assist Elder Rigdon in arranging the Book of Covenants, and do the work of printing in the Church.[12] On 24 September 1834 the high council at Kirtland recorded in their minutes:

> The council then proceeded to appoint a committee to arrange the items of the doctrine of Jesus Christ for the government of the church of Latter Day Saints which church was organized and commenced its rise on the 6th of April 1830. Those items are to be taken from the bible, book of Mormon, and the revelations which have been given to the church up to

> this date or shall be, until such arrangement is made. Brother Samuel H. Smith then nominated brethren Joseph Smith Jun., Oliver Cowdery, Sidney Rigdon and Fredrick G. Williams, to compose said committee, which was seconded by brother Hyrum Smith. The counsellors then gave their vote, which was also agreed to by the whole conference. The council then decided that said committee, after arranging and publishing said book of covenants, have the avails of the same.[13]

This committee was composed of almost the same members which had made preparations for the Book of Commandments.[14] The labors of the committee and those assisting them lasted for almost a year.

A conference of the Church in Kirtland was called for 17 August 1835. In this conference the Saints were to vote on this edition of the revelations and accept them as scripture. Prior to this conference, reference was made to the compilation by title, section, part, and paragraph by the Prophet Joseph Smith.[15] Since the book did not return from the bindery at Cleveland until mid-September, the Prophet must have been using unbound pages from the book itself. Such copies also must have been given to priesthood quorum leaders to peruse; for in the conference several of them testified of the truth and correctness of the revelations and the "Lectures on Faith," because they had read them all or in part. Based on these testimonies, the whole conference assembled voted as quorums and as general church membership in favor of accepting the book as arranged. Two other documents were voted on by the congregation to be put into the publication, and unanimously accepted. The original minutes of this conference are found in the Kirtland Council Minute Book. These minutes were then published in the *Latter-day Saint Messenger and Advocate*, and they were also included in the Doctrine and Covenants.[16]

The whole compilation was then sent to Cleveland, Ohio to be bound. William W. Phelps recorded that the book was available by the second week in September.[17] Shortly after that, Orson Pratt and others, as missionaries, distributed them in the branches of the Church.[18]

**Title and Contents**

The change in name from "A Book of Commandments" to "Doctrine and Covenants" reflected a change in content. Unlike the

Book of Commandments, which contained revelations only, the Doctrine and Covenants was divided into two parts: seven theological treatises commonly known as the "Lectures on Faith," and the revelations. The title page to the "Lectures on Faith" stated that they were: "On the Doctrine of the Church of the Latter Day Saints."[19] The second part was entitled: "PART SECOND Covenants and Commandments."[20] It seems, therefore, that the title, "Doctrine and Covenants," reflected the subtitles of these two parts of the book: the Doctrine (seven "Lectures on Faith") and Covenants (one hundred-three revelations).

In addition to the "Lectures on Faith," there were other changes in content. Some revelations were combined: i.e., chapters 17-21 in the Book of Commandments were combined into what is now section 23 of the Doctrine and Covenants; chapters 31-33 became what is now section 30; and chapters 44 and 47 became section 42. Chapter 28 was combined with another revelation that was not even in the Book of Commandments, creating what is now section 27.

Additional revelations were also included. Some of these may have been intended for inclusion in the Book of Commandments, but others were received after the destruction of the press in Missouri.

The minutes of the 24 September 1834 high council meeting in which the Doctrine and Covenants was authorized and the 17 August 1835 assembly in which the book was approved were also included in the first edition, along with a brief preface by the committee.

## The Second, Third, and Fourth American Editions 1844, 1845, and 1846

### Second American Edition, 1844

During the conference of the Church in October 1840, the Prophet announced that a new edition of the Doctrine and Covenants would be published in Nauvoo.

According to Ebenezer Robinson, he began stereotyping the Doctrine and Covenants and hymn book sometime between the spring of 1841 and August of the same year.[21] Willard Richards was given the responsibility to arrange the Doctrine and Covenants, the Book of Mormon, and the New Translation of the Bible into their new format.[22] On 4 February 1842 the Twelve, with Joseph Smith as principal, purchased the book bindery, printing office, stereotype foundery, and paper fixtures of Elder Robinson.[23] Wilford Woodruff became one of the employees following this purchase, and he recorded in his journal under the dates of 1-4 February 1843: "Spent my time as usual in the Printing Office. We commenced this week on Monday to sterrotype the Doctrine and Covenants of the Church of Jesus Christ of Latter Day Saints."[24] As the Doctrine and Covenants was being stereotyped, Joseph Smith and William W. Phelps read the proofsheets.[25]

By November, 1843 the Quorum of the Twelve voted on means to raise money to buy paper to print the Doctrine and Covenants,[26] and on 5 December 1843 Joseph Smith instructed them to send money to Orson Hyde, who was in the East, in order for him to purchase the paper.[27]

On 12 June 1844 a notice was placed in the *Nauvoo Neighbor* that the new edition of the Doctrine and Covenants would be ready in about one month.[28] This same notice ran in later issues from 30 June to 30 October 1844. The assassination of Joseph Smith on 27 June 1844, and the severe wounds suffered by John Taylor, who was the publisher, obviously delayed the work.

Eight additional sections were incorporated into this edition, including one written by John Taylor after the death of Joseph Smith. These sections are now numbered 103, 105, 112, 119, 124, 127, 128, and 135 in the current edition.

The minutes of the conference in which the 1835 edition was sustained as scripture were included in that edition but deleted in the 1844 edition. Also, no action was taken in conference to accept the new edition as scripture. Unlike the earlier edition, this one, and the profits from its sale, were considered to be the property of the Church.[29]

**Third American Edition, 1845**

The second American edition of the Doctrine and Covenants had been stereotyped. Using this system of printing, metal plates were cast that could be used again; therefore, the third and fourth American editions in Nauvoo were duplicates of the 1844 edition. By April, 1845 a decision was made by the Quorum of Twelve to again print copies of the Doctrine and Covenants.[30] Further details concerning this edition are not known.

**Fourth American Edition, 1846**

In October, 1845 Wilford Woodruff was in Pennsylvania to (among other things) purchase paper for the printing of yet another edition of the Doctrine and Covenants.[31] When this edition was printed and circulated is not known, nor the number of copies involved.

**The Stereotype Plates**

When the Latter-day Saints left Nauvoo, the Church leadership considered it important to continue its printing operations, even on the prairies. Therefore, an appeal by Brigham Young was made to Almon Babbitt, Joseph Heywood, and John Fullmer (who had been appointed trustees for the Church in Nauvoo) to bring the printing fixtures to Winter Quarters.[32] Brigham Young also wrote later: "Be sure and have a watchful eye to the stereotype plates of the Book of Mormon and Doctrine and Covenants, that no evil befall them, and that they be forewarded to us with all safety, this season, also the rule machine that was left in the printing office."[33]

This letter was written on 1 April, and Brigham Young's company of pioneers left Winter Quarters on 7 April. No more correspondence has been found on this subject, and what eventually happened to the plates is not known. They were never used again, since all other editions of the Doctrine and Covenants were published in England, until a greatly revised and enlarged edition was published in 1876 at Salt Lake City.

## The First European Edition, 1845

In August, 1844 Brigham Young wrote in his journal: "Br. Wilford Woodruff is going to England to take charge of all the Churches Printing and emegration Business. Br. H. Clark goes with him."[34] Wilford Woodruff was in England on this mission by February, 1845 and wrote a lengthy epistle to the Latter-day Saints about his purposes for being there, including: "We shall probably publish the 'Book of Doctrine and Covenants' in England, as soon as circumstances will permit."[35] His plans were indefinite as to a date for publication, but he was soon forced into a decision, as he recorded in his journal:

> I received a letter to day from a friend containing a copy of a letter Dated Pittsburgh Jan. 30, 44 written by John Greenhow at Pittsburgh to his father in Kendel Stating that he was getting the doctrine & covenants in that place & was going to bring the plates to England to Print the work here & get the copyright secured so that the Church of Jesus Christ of Latter Day Saints couldn't Print them. This certainly is a bold move for an apostate or apostates to undertake to Print the works of the Church & rob them out of it. I view it nothing more than the mercy of God in Putting the knowledge of this thing into my hands. I spent the day examining the Law to see what I could learn concerning securing copyrights. Walked 8 miles. . . .
>
> I also informed Br. Young of the deep laid plot of our enemies John Greenhow Samuel Bennett & others of trying to rob the Church in England of the Copyright of the doctrine & covenants &c.
>
> I wrote a letter to M__________ [left blank] Secretary at Stationers Hall London requesting information concerning securing the Copyright of any work.
>
> I received another letter from my friend to day stating that Mr. Greenhow had written to his son John Greenhow of Pittsburgh.
>
> I wrote a letter to Br. Coredon to send me the copy of Doctrine and Covenants which he has.[36]

This new edition was in the process of printing by mid-April, and the plans were to publish 3,000 copies.[37] On 12 May Elder Woodruff wrote to Heber C. Kimball and said that he expected the new Doctrine and Covenants would be: "out of press in about ten days."[38] On 18 May 1845 Elder Woodruff was in a conference at Carlisle and preached on buying the new Doctrine and Covenants.[39] By 5 June Elder Woodruff was making preparations to leave Liverpool for London to secure the copyright;[40] on 7 June he recorded in his journal: "I this day secured the copyright in my own name at the Stationers Hall in London carrying one copy according to Law to the British Museum & got my receipt for it."[41] The *Millennial Star* for 15 June 1845 announced the book ready for sale,[42] and the following issue gave some information about the value of the work and the index.[43]

The plans of those in the United States to secure the copyright of the Doctrine and Covenants in England in order to prevent the Church from publishing it had been thwarted by the quick action of Wilford Woodruff. Less than a month after the book was offered for sale, one of the apostate group made his appearance in England as a missionary. In writing to his parents about this man, Wilford Woodruff finally revealed that it was Sidney Rigdon's group that was behind the plot.[44]

### Second European Edition, 1849

The historical background on this edition is not well known, due to the fact that there is no journal available for Orson Pratt, the publisher, for the year 1849. The manuscript History of the British Mission has no entry about the Doctrine and Covenants except what is found in the *Millennial Star.* The 15 May 1849 issue contained this notice: "The Book of Doctrine and Covenants are all gone, but soon will be reprinted."[45] This notice ran in all issues until 15 November 1849, when the following was printed: "The 'DOCTRINE AND COVENANTS' are now ready. An additional index has been formed in the order of the date in which the several revelations were given."[46]

### Third European Edition, 1852

On 12 October 1849, the First Presidency issued a general epistle to the Church in which Elder Franklin D. Richards of the Quorum of Twelve was called to assist Orson Pratt in England.[47] Shortly thereafter he was called to succeed Elder Pratt and preside over that mission.[48] He served as president of that mission until the spring of 1852.

In May of 1851, Elder Richards had reported that nearly all copies of the Doctrine and Covenants were gone, but with help, a new edition could be published "by the opening of next emigration season."[49] Unlike the previous two European editions, this one was made into stereotype plates so that future editions could be printed from them. Elder Richards reported in a letter to Brigham Young on 24 February 1852 that the Doctrine and Covenants was in the process of stereotyping.[50] By April, when he was preparing to leave for Utah, the work was not yet completed; however, he arranged to have Elder

Samuel W. Richards finish it.[51] Elder Samuel Richards and others had already been helping with the publication by reading the proofsheets as they came from the printer.[52]

In a letter written by Samuel W. Richards and George A. Smith, dated 3 September 1852, a report was made on the work accomplished by Franklin D. Richards: "He had just closed a bargain for the printing and stereotyping of the Book of Doctrine and Covenants, which I immediately went to work upon, and had it through the press some time since."[53]

## Fourth European Edition, 1854

Orson Pratt was called in a special conference held on 28 August 1852 to preside over the Church in the eastern part of the United States.[54] Part of his mission was to raise money to finance the printing of the Book of Mormon and the Doctrine and Covenants. It is not clear if the plans called for him to publish them in the United States or in England. From the correspondence, it seems that it was left up to Elder Pratt.[55]

Orson Pratt spent much of his time in the remainder of 1852 preparing articles for a monthly paper called *The Seer*, that he published in Washington, D.C. But Brigham Young wrote to Elder Pratt in October that he wanted the new edition of the Doctrine and Covenants published as quickly as possible. Orson Pratt then went to work investigating costs and reported that it would be less expensive to have the books printed in England and shipped to the United States.[56] The Journal History for 4 March 1853 records that Elder Pratt was then preparing to leave for England to print the Doctrine and Covenants.

By September, 1853 Orson Pratt was back in Washington, D.C. He reported by letter to Brigham Young that the books were printed and on their way to the United States.[57]

The date of the arrival of the books into the Salt Lake Valley is not known, but they must have been greatly appreciated, since it had been over eight years since any had been made available to the Saints in the United States in a large quantity.

## Fifth European Edition, 1866

This edition of the Doctrine and Covenants was published by

Brigham Young, Jun. while he served as the mission president in Europe. He kept a journal when in England, but he made no mention of publishing the Doctrine and Covenants with the exception of this: "I have been compelled to expend considerable in buying paper for Books Mormon, Doc. & Cov. Spencers Letters Voice of Warning and also to send money to New York."[58] The *Millennial Star* and the Manuscript History of the British Mission are also silent on the events that led to this edition. It was, of course, a stereotype copy of the 1852 edition with no change in content.

## Sixth European Edition, 1869

This edition is another stereotype copy of the 1852 edition. It was published by Elder Albert Carrington while he served as mission president. All records are silent on the events leading to its publication, including the journal kept by Elder Carrington. When it was finished, this notice was placed in the *Millennial Star:* "The new edition of the *Doctrine and Covenants* is now ready, bound in morocco extra, calf, gilt edges or roan."[59]

## 1876 Edition

January of 1875 found Orson Pratt laboring on a project to revise substantially the text of the Doctrine and Covenants. Acting under the counsel of Brigham Young, he divided the sections into verses and added several sections not previously found in this volume of scripture. The Historian's Office Journal records:

> Elder Orson Pratt has been engaged, at times, for several days, in recopying and arranging the order in which the revelations are to be inserted in the edition of the Book of Doctrine and Covenants, now in the hands of the printer. By the counsel of President B. Young, Elder Pratt has divided the various revelations into verses and arranged them for printing, according to the order of date in which they were revealed. Elder Pratt has also, in a few cases, restored the original names as they were first given in the manuscripts, enclosing them in parentheses immediately following the fictitious names that were, for a wise purpose, substituted in the preceding editions.[60]

This new edition (the first one published in the United States since the 1846 Nauvoo edition) was published by the *Deseret News* in Salt Lake City.

The additional revelations in this edition included what are now sections 2, 13, 77, 85, 87, 108-11, 113-18, 120-23, 125, 126, 129-32, and 136—a total of twenty-six.

## 1879 and 1880 Editions

Orson Pratt went to England late in 1878 to print a new edition of the Book of Mormon using electrotype plates. While there, he considered the possibility of doing the same for a new edition of the Doctrine and Covenants. Permission to do so would have to come from Salt Lake City, and so correspondence on the subject began. Fortunately, many of the letters have survived to this date and tell the complete historical background to this proposal. President John Taylor approved the project with the provision that this new edition include an index and footnotes. An appeal by Orson Pratt to include the Books of Moses and Abraham and eliminate the Lectures on Faith was not approved.[61]

Orson Pratt arrived in Salt Lake City from England on 2 September 1879,[62] and the electrotype plates arrrived sometime later. The book was offered for sale in England by mid-October, 1879,[63] but it was not printed in Utah until 1880. In the October General Conference of the Church in 1880, the new edition of the Doctrine and Covenants was accepted officially by the Church in the following conference resolution:

> President George Q. Cannon said: I hold in my hand the Book of Doctrine and Covenants, and also the book, The Pearl of Great Price, which books contain revelations of God. In Kirtland, the Doctrine and Covenants in its original form, as first printed, was submitted to the officers of the Church and the members of the Church to vote upon. As there have been additions made to it by the publishing of revelations which were not contained in the original edition, it has been deemed wise to submit these books with their contents to the conference, to see whether the conference will vote to accept the books and their contents as from God, and binding upon us as a people and as a

> Church.
>
> President Joseph F. Smith said: I move that we receive and accept the revelations contained in these books, as revelations from God to the Church of Jesus Christ of Latter-day Saints, and to all the world.[64]

The vote was carried by the conference, and the new edition became accepted as one of the Standard Works of the Church.

### 1882-1920 Editions

During the interval of 1882 to 1920, no less than twenty-eight printings of the Doctrine and Covenants were made. Most of these were printed from the two sets of electrotype plates made in 1879, and the others in a similar format. Some of these were made into double or triple combinations with others of the Standard Works of the Church. Some were "vest pocket" size, and the later ones printed in Salt Lake City had a concordance added. All of these, however, maintained a constant text; i.e., the same material could be found on the same page in each text. The footnotes also remained unaltered.

In 1908, the Official Declaration by Wilford Woodruff of 1890 ending polygamy (and more commonly known as the Manifesto) along with a motion by Lorenzo Snow in conference that the Church support President Woodruff in the declaration, were incorporated into the text of the Doctrine and Covenants. When the 1908 edition came from the press, the following announcement was made in the *Deseret News:*

> A new edition of the Doctrine and Covenants has just been prepared and is for sale at the Deseret News Book Store. It contains for the first time, the concordance compiled by Prof. Keeler. The "News" has made arrangements with the author to have this inserted in the book hereafter. It ought to enhance its value considerably, but no increase will be made in the selling price. The edition also contains the official declaration generally known as the Manifesto of President Woodruff. We call special attention to this edition of one of the four standard works of the Church.[65]

## The 1921 Edition

On 18 March 1920 Elder George F. Richards was appointed chairman of a committee to revise and correct the Book of Mormon. The other members of the committee were Anthony W. Ivins, James E. Talmage, and Melvin J. Ballard.[66] The committee met frequently over the months and by June had expanded in size to include six members of the Quorum of Twelve.[67] The two additional members were not named by Elder Richards in his journal at that time but later events show Joseph Fielding Smith to be one of them.[68] The other might have been Anthon H. Lund, even though he was at that time a member of the First Presidency, and therefore, not one of the Twelve.[69] The work of the committee continued until the new edition of the Book of Mormon came from the press in December, 1920. In early 1921 the committee continued to meet to discuss Book of Mormon geography and associated subjects; by February, a new assignment was being planned for them. James E. Talmage intimated that a complete revision of the Doctrine and Covenants was to be undertaken. He reported:

> Preliminary steps have already been taken toward a thorough revision of the Doctrine and Covenants, and we all know that the current editions, as printed in this country and in Liverpool, contains [sic] many errors by way of omission. Moreover there are certain improvements by way of Section Headings, amplification of notes, and rearrangement of text in the double column style to be made, if the present tentative plans are carried into execution.[70]

By March, 1921 the Book of Mormon committee was given the assignment to revise the Doctrine and Covenants. George F. Richards, still chairman of the group, wrote in his diary: "I attended a committee meeting of what has been known as the Book of Mormon Committee to whom has been delegated the labor of revising the Doctrine & Covenants which I may now properly style the Doctrine & Covenants Committee. Later we went before the Presidency with certain recommendations."[71]

Again, the committee met frequently until the edition was published in December, 1921. On 29 July 1921 Elder Richards wrote this interesting item in his journal: "I attended D&C Committee meeting from 9 to 12 o'clock with other members of the Twelve when we read the revelations which do not appear in the present edition of the Doctrine and Covenants, about twenty in number with the view of recommending to the First Presidency certain of them to be included in the edition we are just now preparing."[72] The First Presidency obviously never approved the addition of those revelations, and Elder Richards made no mention again of it in his journal.

In the 1921 edition extensive changes were made in the footnotes, the introductory statements at the beginning of the revelations were expanded, the text was divided into double columns, and the "Lectures on Faith" were deleted.

On 17 December 1921, the First Presidency of the Church made an official announcement of the new edition:

> OFFICIAL ANNOUNCEMENT
>
> We have pleasure in announcing new issues of the Doctrine and Covenants and the Pearl of Great Price, with double-column pages, index and other helps, all conforming in general to the style and arrangement of the latest edition of the Book of Mormon.
>
> The text of the Doctrine and Covenants is preceded by an "Explanatory Introduction" comprising in concise form the essential facts relating to the history of this sacred volume of latter-day revelation. Another introductory feature is the "Chronological Order of Contents" in which the several Sections are listed with date and place relating to each. Each Section is introduced by a comprehensive heading, in which are stated the circumstances under which the particular Section was given, and a brief summary of its contents. An extended "Index and Concordance" is included. . . .
>
> We recommend these new issues of the three distinctive standard works of the Church for thoughtful and prayerful study.
>
> Heber J. Grant,
> Charles W. Penrose,
> Anthony W. Ivins
> First Presidency[73]

This edition was the one used by the Church until 1981, when our latest edition was published.

### Early Non-English Editions

As the missionary work of the Church expanded, the need for copies of the modern scriptures in languages other than English became a necessity. These were generally translated by missionaries or local converts and printed in the same country. The early non-English editions of the Doctrine and Covenants, printed outside of the United States, are listed below:

| | |
|---|---|
| 1851 | Welch |
| 1852 | Danish |
| 1876 | German |
| 1888 | Swedish |
| 1908 | Dutch |
| 1914 | Hawaiian |
| 1919 | Maori |

At the time of this writing the Doctrine and Covenants is published in twenty-two languages with one additional edition in Tahitian in the process of translation. Recent studies by the Translation Department of the Church show that if the Church could have the scriptures in 193 select languages, ninety percent of the world's population could read them in their own tongue. There are plans to publish the Book of Mormon, whole or in part, in all of these languages, and to publish the Doctrine and Covenants in at least some of them. And so the ideal given by the Lord to the Church in 1833 comes closer to reality, wherein the promise was given that "every man shall hear the fulness of the gospel in his own tongue, and in his own language" (D&C 90:11).

## Notes

[1]Donald Q. Cannon and Lyndon W. Cook, eds., *Far West Record* (Salt Lake City: Deseret Book Co., 1983), p. 27. The most complete history of the

Doctrine and Covenants to date is Robert J. Woodford, "The Historical Development of the Doctrine and Covenants" (unpublished Ph.D. dissertation, Brigham Young University, 1974).

[2]*Ibid.*

[3]*HC* 1:224.

[4]*Ibid.*; see also Cannon and Cook, *Far West Record*, p. 29.

[5]*HC* 1:226.

[6]Cannon and Cook, *Far West Record*, p. 28.

[7]*HC* 1:226.

[8]Cannon and Cook, *Far West Record*, p. 29.

[9]*Ibid.*, pp. 31-32.

[10]*Latter-day Saints Messenger and Advocate*, August 1835, p. 170.

[11]Journal History of the Church, 2 January 1834, Church Archives, Historical Department of The Church of Jesus Christ of Latter-day Saints, Salt Lake City (hereafter cited as Church Archives).

[12]*HC* 1:51.

[13]Kirtland Council Minute Book, pp. 74, 76, Church Archives.

[14]*Millennial Star*, 30 April 1853, p. 283.

[15]Joseph Smith Letterbook, 22 November 1832-4 August 1935, Church Archives; see also *HC* 1:239.

[16]Kirtland Council Minute Book, pp. 98-106, Church Archives; see also *Latter-day Saints Messenger and Advocate*, August 1835, pp. 161-64; and Doctrine and Covenants (Kirtland, Oh.: The Church of the Latter-day Saints, 1835), pp. 255-57.

[17]William W. Phelps to Sally Phelps, 16 September 1835, Church Archives.

[18]Orson Pratt Journal, 1835-1837, forepart of November 1835, Church Archives.

[19]1835 edition of D&C, p. 5.

[20]*Ibid.*, p. 75.

[21]*The Return*, July 1890, p. 302.

[22]*Times and Seasons*, 15 January 1842, p. 667.

[23]*HC* 4:513, 514.

[24]Wilford Woodruff Journal, 1-4 February 1843, Church Archives.

[25]*HC* 5:264, 273.

[26]*HC* 6:100.

[27]*Ibid.*

[28]*Nauvoo Neighbor*, 12 June 1844, p. 235.

[29]Joseph Smith Journal, 18 September 1844, Church Archives.

[30]*HC* 7:345.

[31]Wilford Woodruff to Phoebe Woodruff, 8 October 1845, Church

Archives.

[32]Journal History of the Church, 28 September 1846, pp. 2, 3, Church Archives.

[33]*Ibid.*, 1 April 1847, p. 3.

[34]Brigham Young Journal, July 1837-March 1845, p. 51, Church Archives.

[35]Manuscript History of the British Mission, February 1845, p. 4, Church Archives.

[36]Wilford Woodruff Journal, 1-3 March 1845, Church Archives.

[37]Wilford Woodruff to Brigham Young, 1 April 1845, Church Archives.

[38]Wilford Woodruff to Heber C. Kimball, 12 May 1845, Church Archives.

[39]Manuscript History of the British Mission, 18 May 1845, p. 1, Church Archives.

[40]Wilford Woodruff Journal, 5 June 1845, Church Archives.

[41]*Ibid.*, 7 June 1845.

[42]*Millennial Star*, 15 June 1845, p. 14.

[43]*Ibid.*, 1 July 1845, p. 30.

[44]Wilford Woodruff to his parents, 22 July 1845, Church Archives.

[45]*Millennial Star*, 15 May 1849, p. 160.

[46]*Ibid.*, 15 November 1849, p. 351.

[47]*Ibid.*, 15 April 1850, pp. 118-22.

[48]James R. Clark, ed., *Messages of the First Presidency*, 6 vols. (Salt Lake City: Bookcraft, 1965-75), 2:47.

[49]Manuscript History of the British Mission, 15 May 1851, p. 1, Church Archives.

[50]Journal History of the Church, 24 February 1852, Church Archives.

[51]Manuscript History of the British Mission, 7 April 1852, Church Archives.

[52]Samuel W. Richards Journal, 10, 11, 22, 24 March 1852, Marriott Library, University of Utah, Salt Lake City, Utah.

[53]*Deseret News*, 25 December 1852, p. 10.

[54]Clark, *Messages of the First Presidency*, 2:100.

[55]Orson Pratt to Brigham Young, 31 January 1853, Church Archives.

[56]Orson Pratt to Brigham Young, 30 January 1853, Church Archives.

[57]Orson Pratt to Brigham Young, 3 April 1854, Church Archives.

[58]Brigham Young, Jr. Journal, 7 March 1866, Church Archives.

[59]*Millennial Star*, December 1869, p. 789.

[60]Historian's Office Journal (7 July 1874-14 November 1875), p. 70, Church Archives.

[61]See William Budge to John Taylor, 25 February 1879; Orson Pratt to John Taylor, 1 March 1879; and John Taylor Letterbook (16 August 1878-27

May 1879), pp. 612-16, 658, 710-13, Church Archives.

[62]Historian's Office Journal (1 March 1879-31 December 1880), p. 79, Church Archives.

[63]William Budge to Charles C. Rich, 16 October 1879, Church Archives.

[64]*Deseret News*, 11 October 1880, p. 2.

[65]*The Deseret Evening News*, 18 December 1908, p. 4.

[66]George F. Richards Journal (1918-1920), 18 March 1920, Church Archives.

[67]*Ibid.*, 8 June 1920.

[68]*Ibid.*, 4, 12 October 1920.

[69]Anthon H. Lund Journal, 15 April 1920 and 27 May 1920, Church Archives.

[70]James E. Talmage to George Albert Smith, 23 February 1921, Church Archives.

[71]George F. Richards Journal (1921-1934), 11 March 1921, Church Archives.

[72]*Ibid.*, 29 July 1921.

[73]Clark, *Messages of the First Presidency*, 5:207, 208.

# 2
# USING THE 1981 EDITION OF THE DOCTRINE AND COVENANTS

Robert J. Matthews

## Background

In 1972 the First Presidency of The Church of Jesus Christ of Latter-day Saints appointed a committee with the charge to produce a new publication of the King James Version of the Bible with study helps arranged in a manner that would assist the Latter-day Saints to better understand and use the Bible. This group was composed primarily of Elders Thomas S. Monson, Boyd K. Packer, and Bruce R. McConkie and was identified as the "Bible Aids Committee."[1] This committee selected others to help.[2] As work progressed on the Bible aids, it became apparent that the use of latter-day scriptures would be facilitated also if they were updated and improved in format. Therefore the assignment to the Bible committee was extended to include the Book of Mormon, Doctrine and Covenants, and Pearl of Great Price. At about this same time the name was changed from "Bible Aids Committee" to "Scriptures Publications Committee" to accommodate the enlarged assignment. The Bible came off the press in 1979, the new triple combination in 1981. A slightly corrected reprint of the modern scriptures was issued in 1982.

This article will center on the features of the new edition of the Doctrine and Covenants, so as to point out what is different from earlier editions and how one can benefit from the new materials.

Special features of the new edition of the Doctrine and Covenants include a newly-written "Explanatory Introduction," two new sections (137 and 138), material by President Wilford Woodruff explaining the Manifesto of 1890 (Official Declaration 1), and the official announcement by the First Presidency of the June 1978 revelation on priesthood (Official Declaration 2). There are also improved footnotes and cross-references, improved section headings, new subject-matter summaries for each section, four maps showing major geographical locations, and an index.

There is only one reason for publishing the Doctrine and

Covenants, and that is to make the information readily available to people for their instruction. If the material can be presented in a form more usable and accurate than before, or if new information is available, a new edition serves to underwrite and facilitate the basic purpose for which the revelations are printed. It is, therefore, an important investment in scripture study to have a copy of the new editions of the standard works, because they contain information and a reference system not found in earlier editions.

If we obtain a new edition but do not use the headnotes or the footnotes, the doctrinal summaries, the index, the Topical Guide, or the maps, then we are no better served than we were before. A major purpose of this discussion is to show the reader what kind of new information is available and also to offer suggestions about how to use the study aids. In reality, the Doctrine and Covenants constitues a *data bank* (a storehouse) of useful, necessary, revealed information important to the spiritual health of every person. But it is stored on the pages of a book, and it is sometimes hard to find the right pages. The headnotes, footnotes, index, Topical Guide, summaries, maps, and supplementary materials constitute an *information retrieval system* that makes it possible for the average scripture student to find what he needs or wants in a minimum of time. It also enables him to interpret correctly what he finds through comparison with other related passages on the same subject. This later case is where the index, the Topical Guide, and the Dictionary perform a very unique and valuable service. The Topical Guide (abbreviated TG) and the Bible Dictionary (BD) are published in the LDS publication of the Bible. However, these were prepared with the new edition of the Doctrine and Covenants in mind and hence are vital supplementary aids to a study of the Doctrine and Covenants.

It would not be feasible in a summary article such as this to include every variant, but we will present a few to show the type of thing that has been done. We will also attempt to give the rationale behind the corrections in the new edition, so the reader will know why it has been done. Information for corrections and additions was drawn from many sources, the most significant of which are Robert J. Woodford's "The Historical Development of the Doctrine and Covenants," Ph.D. dissertation, Brigham Young University, 1974; and Lyndon W. Cook's prepublication manuscript for his book *The Revelations of the Prophet Joseph Smith,* Seventy's Mission Bookstore, Provo, Utah, 1981. In addition, many of the faculty of Religious Education at Brigham Young University contributed individual items and made helpful suggestions.

## Explanatory Introduction

The new "Explanatory Introduction" is designed (1) to inform the reader why the Doctrine and Covenants exists, (2) to present a short history of various printings, (3) to present the "Testimony of the Twelve Apostles [of 1835] to the Truth of the Book of Doctrine and Covenants," and (4) to explain how this new edition is different from earlier ones. It closes with the explanation that various errors have occurred and have been perpetuated in previous editions, especially in dates and geographical place-names given in the historical portions of the headnotes; therefore, some minor corrections were in order in this 1981 edition.

## Section Headings

In the earlier editions of the Doctrine and Covenants, the headnotes contained two types of material: historical background and a content summary. These were printed across the entire page, covering the space of two columns. In the new edition, the headnotes still reach across the entire page but contain only background information. The content summaries are now separated from the headnote and are placed in italics at the top of the left-hand column, consistent with the format used in the chapter summaries of both the Bible and the Book of Mormon. This new format places the content summary, which is generally doctrinal in nature, in a paragraph by itself and is thus in a more conspicuous position than formerly. They are interpretive as well as comprehensive and summatic. A reader is benefited and often receives a new insight or catches a new relationship by reviewing these summaries while studying a section.

The headnotes containing background information are significantly different from the earlier headings for sixty-six different sections. A discussion of some of these and the reasons why they needed to be improved follows in the numerical order of the sections.

*Section 1.* Beginning with the 1921 edition, the heading read:

"Revelation given through Joseph Smith the Prophet, during a special conference of Elders of the Church of Jesus Christ of Latter-day Saints, held at Hiram, Ohio, November 1, 1831." The 1981 edition omits the phrase "of Jesus Christ of Latter-day Saints."

When the Church was organized on 6 April 1830, it was officially called the Church of Christ (see D&C 20:1). This is evident from many early documents, including the title page of the Book of Commandments printed in 1833. The complete title of the Church as we know it today was not revealed until 1838 (see D&C 115:3-4). Therefore it would be anachronistic to refer to the Church in 1831 by a title it did not receive until 1838. This minor but historically accurate adjustment was also made in the headings of Sections 21, 22, and 102.

*Section 3.* The former heading "REVELATION given to Joseph Smith the Prophet, at Harmony, Pennsylvania, July, 1828, relating to the loss of certain manuscripts of the first part of the Book of Mormon . . ." is enlarged to read: ". . . relating to the loss of 116 pages of manuscript translated from the first part of the Book of Mormon, which was called the 'Book of Lehi." A similar clarification mentioning the "Book of Lehi" occurs in the heading to section 10. A footnote to D&C 10:42 explains the source for the information: "In the Preface to the first edition of the Book of Mormon, the Prophet explained that the material in the 116 pages had been translated from a portion of the plates called the 'Book of Lehi.'"

*Section 11.* This revelation was given through Joseph Smith the Prophet to his brother Hyrum and carries a date of May 1829. Its placement in the Doctrine and Covenants (as section 11) tends to suggest a time prior to the restoration of the Aaronic Priesthood on 15 May 1829 (section 13). However, in the *History of the Church,* compiled from data dictated or approved by the Prophet, the revelation to Hyrum is placed *after* the restoration of the Aaronic Priesthood.[3] Consequently, the headnote of the new edition indicates that section 11 possibly was received "after the restoration of the Aaronic Priesthood."

*Section 30.* This is a revelation to David Whitmer, Peter Whitmer, Jr., and John Whitmer. The heading is essentially the same in both the former and new editions for the date, place, and recipients. However, the new edition adds the following historical comment: "Originally this material was published as three revelations; it was combined into one section by the Prophet for the 1835 edition of the Doctrine and Covenants." In the Book of Commandments (1833), this material appeared as chapters 31, 32, and 33.

*Section 34.* The forepart of the heading is essentially unchanged except for a comment that Parley P. Pratt is an "older brother" to Orson Pratt. However, at the end of the heading the new edition adds: "This revelation was received in thePeter Whitmer, Sen., home."[4]

*Section 35.* The former editions read:

> REVELATION given to Joseph Smith the Prophet, and Sidney Rigdon, December 1830. As a preface to his record of this revelation the Prophet worte: "In December, Sidney Rigdon came to inquire of the Lord, and with him came Edward Partridge; the latter was a pattern of piety and one of the Lord's great men."

The new edition alters this considerably:

> Revelation given to Joseph Smith the Prophet and Sidney Rigdon, at or near Fayette, New York, December 1830. . . . At this time the Prophet was engaged almost daily in making a translation of the Bible. The translation was begun as early as June 1830, and both Oliver Cowdery and John Whitmer had served as scribes. Since they had now been called to other duties, Sidney Rigdon was called by divine appointment to serve as the Prophet's scribe in this work (verse 20). As a preface to his record of this revelation the Prophet wrote: "In December Sidney Rigdon came [from Ohio] to inquire of the Lord, and with him came Edward Partridge. . . . Shortly after the arrival of these two brethren, thus spake the Lord."

In order to show the context of this revelation, it seemed necessary to provide information about the work of revising the Bible in which the Prophet was engaged. The close relationship that exists between Joseph Smith's revision of the Bible and the revelations in the Doctrine and Covenants is shown in the new edition of the Doctrine and Covenants in the headnotes to sections 35, 45, 71, 73, 76, 77, 86, and 91; and in the footnotes to D&C 9:2; 35:20; 37:1; 42:56; 45:60; 49:21; 73:3; 76:17; 84:14; 93:53; 94:10; 104:58; and 124:89.

*Section 49.* This revelation was given to Sidney Rigdon, Parley P. Pratt, and Leman Copley about the religious group known as the

Shaking Quakers. The new edition explains that the correct name of the Shakers was "United Society of Believers in Christ's Second Appearing."[5] It also adds useful information about some of the major doctrinal concepts held by the Shakers, without which the reader cannot get the perspective to understand the force of the doctrinal statements in the revelation. The new edition thus adds the following to the heading:

> Some of the beliefs of the Shakers were that Christ's second coming had already occurred and he had appeared in the form of a woman, Ann Lee; baptism by water was not considered essential; the eating of pork was specifically forbidden, and many did not eat any meat; and a celibate life was considered higher than marriage. In prefacing this revelation, the Prophet wrote: "In order to have a more perfect understanding on the subject, I inquired of the Lord, and received the following."

When the reader has some idea of the beliefs of the Shakers, he can see the intent of the revelation. Without a knowledge of those beliefs, the revelation appears to be only of general application. The headnote shows the revelation to be specific and of strong intent.[6]

*Section 78.* Most students of Church history are aware that sections 78, 82, 92, 96, 103, 104, and 105 carried a number of code names and words used to disguise the identity of the persons, places, and concepts mentioned. The original drafts of these revelations did not contain these code words but used rather the real names of the persons and places. These code words began with the 1835 edition of the Doctrine and Covenants. Many readers have not understood why these unusual names were used. Some have supposed they represented a divine or revealed name of the persons and perhaps pertained to a past or future existence. This was not the case. The code names were used in 1835 so as not to expose to the enemies of the Church the identify of the persons, places, or concepts. The 1876 edition of the Doctrine and Covenants printed the real names in brackets after the code words. This practice was continued until the 1981 edition. Since there exists no present need to have the code names, the 1981 edition uses only the names in the original manuscripts. This procedure is expalined in the new headnote to sections 78 and 82.

*Section 82* has some additional interesting factors requiring further discussion. Prepublication handwritten manuscripts are available for all of the revelations containing code words except for section 82. Since the printed editions of section 82 have four code names not found in the other sections, the people to whom they refer remained unidentified, even in the 1981 edition. This was explained in a footnote to v. 11: "Alam was probably Edward Partridge. See *HC* 1:363. The other unusual names in this verse are not identifiable at this time." Since the printing of the 1981 edition, new evidence is available, due to the research of David Whittaker of Brigham Young University, and so the newest printing of the Doctrine and Covenants (1982) has even these four names identified. Alam *is* Edward Patridge; Mahalaleel is Sidney Gilbert; Horah is John Whitmer; and Shalemanasseh is W. W. Phelps.[7]

Much of what we have known about the origin of the unusual names was given in an article by Elder Orson Pratt, longtime Church Historian and a member of the Twelve. He explained the circumstances that gave rise to the names, and he also identified some of the persons. But he was writing from memory and made some errors.[8] Some of the words, such as Baurak Ale (formerly in D&C 105:16) and Baneemy (in 105:27), resemble Hebrew words.

*Section 86.* This revelation clarifies some aspects of the parable of the wheat and the tares contained in Matthew 13. The former heading read, "REVELATION given through Joseph Smith the Prophet, at Kirtland, Ohio; December 6, 1832." The new heading adds by way of explanation: "This revelation was received while the Prophet was reviewing and editing the manuscript of the translation of the Bible." There are interesting historical items that contribute to the foregoing statement. The Prophet had already "completed" the translation of the New Testament by March 1832, eight months before he received the revelation recorded as section 86. In his journal for 2 February 1833, the Prophet said that he had that day completed the "translation and review" of the New Testament.[9] Apparently there were two steps. The "translation" was done by March 1832; the "review" by February 1833.

In his initial translation, the Prophet did not alter Matthew 13:30, which in the King James Version places the gathering of the tares before the gathering of the wheat. However, the Joseph Smith Translation manuscript has a note pinned over the passage rephrasing the sentence so that the wheat is gathered first. This sequence corresponds with the order given in D&C 86:7, and the correction apparently was added on 6 December 1832 while the Prophet was reviewing the manuscript for publication. Although this entire "review" of the New Testament was not completed until February 1833, it is clear that the previous December the Prophet was working with Matthew 13.

A note in the Prophet's journal for 6 December 1832 reads: "December 6th translating and received a revelation explaining the Parable of the wheat and the tears &c—."[10] The activity referred to by the Prophet in this case apparently was his review of the Bible manuscript. This also illustrates that during the process of the Bible translation the Prophet received light and inspiration, not only correcting errors but also providing additional information. In this instance, section 86 not only corrects an error in the modern text of the Bible but also interprets the parable in terms of latter-day fulfillment. It also demonstrates the close relationship that existed between the translation of the Bible and the reception of many revelations now contained in the Doctrine and Covenants.

*Section 87.* The former editions have the following headnote: "REVELATION AND PROPHECY ON WAR, given though Joseph Smith the Prophet, December 25, 1832." The new edition adds the following: "This section was received at a time when the brethren were reflecting and reasoning upon African slavery on the American continent and the slavery of the children of men throughout the world." This background information is attributed to President Brigham Young.[11]

*Section 89.* The heading in former editions read: "REVELATION given through Joseph Smith the Prophet, at Kirtland, Ohio, February 27, 1833, known as the Word of Wisdom." The 1981 edition adds the following background information: "As a consequence of the early brethren using tobacco in their meetings, the Prophet was led to ponder upon the matter; consequently, he inquired of the Lord concerning it. This revelation, known as the Word of Wisdom, was the result. The first three verses were originally written as an inspired introduction and description by the Prophet."

When the Word of Wisdom was first printed, originally as a separate tract and later in the 1835 edition of the Doctrine and

Covenants, the material now contained in vv. 1-3 consisted of an introductory paragraph that was not part of the text. It became a regular part of the text in the 1921 edition.

*Section 102.* The headings in the former editions of this section have read: "Minutes of the organization of the first High Council of the Church of Jesus Christ of Latter-day Saints, at Kirtland, Ohio, February 17, 1834." The 1981 edition contains several significant differences. To avoid an anachronistic reference to the present name of the Church, the words "the Church" are used instead of the complete title (see discussion of section 1 above).

Other additions in the headnote include the following: "The original minutes were recorded by Elders Oliver Cowdery and Orson Hyde. Two days later, the minutes were corrected by the Prophet, read to the high council, and accepted by the council. Verses 30-32, having to do with the Council of the Twelve Apostles, were added by the Prophet Joseph Smith in 1835 when he prepared this section for publication in the Doctrine and Covenants." This addition was appropriate and necessary since the Council of the Twelve was organized in February 1835, a year after the Kirtland high council came into being, and a clarification between the two was needed.

*Section 107.* This extensive revelation on priesthood is dated in the 1921 edition as 28 March 1835. However, it is clear from the text itself that this is not the correct date for the entire section. The 1981 edition adds this explanation: "Although portions of this section were received on the date named, the historical records affirm that various parts were received at sundry times, some as early as November 1831."

The records referred to tell us that when first published in the 1835 edition of the Doctrine and Covenants, this revelation was identified as Section III and captioned "On Priesthood" with no date given. Later, when the 1876 edition was prepared by Elder Orson Pratt, he placed this revelation as Section CVII with the explanation: "the fore part, or first fifty-eight verses, being given March 28, 1835; the other items were revealed at sundry times." Since the entire document appeared in the 1835 edition, the "sundry times" spoken of by Elder Pratt had to be earlier than 28 March 1835.

The material that is now vv. 59-100 is cited in the "Kirtland Revelation Book," with the explanation that it was revealed in

November 1831. This information clarifies D&C 107:58, which refers to an earlier but unspecified revelation on Church government. Likewise, v. 93, which speaks of a "vision showing the order of the seventy," clearly refers to an earlier revelation. There are other evidences that parts of section 107 were received earlier than the traditional date. For example, vv. 53-55 about Adam and his family occur verbatim in a blessing given by the Prophet to his father on 18 December 1833, sixteen months before the popular date (28 March 1835) for section 107.

The realization that section 107 is a compilation of revelations rather than a single revelation is helpful to understanding the Doctrine and Covenants. It says something about how revelation comes and how it is used, and it indicates that the Prophet received some revelations earlier than the dates under which they appear formally in the Doctrine and Covenants.

*Section 108.* This revelation is directed through the Prophet Joseph Smith to Lyman Sherman. The former editions of the Doctrine and Covenants have not presented enough background material in the heading to enable the reader to understand the content of the revelation correctly; consequently, there has been some misunderstanding concerning it. Former editions have interpreted the revelation as a promise to Brother Sherman that he would be ordained to the office of elder (see the heading to the 1921 edition and subsequent printings). However, since Brother Sherman was already a seventy and a high priest at the time of the revelation, some additional background is needed.

On 26 December 1835, Lyman Sherman came to the Prophet and said he was "wrought upon" and troubled and desired a revelation through the Prophet as to his (Sherman's) duties. Just what was bothering him is not specified. The direction in D&C 108:2-4 (26 December 1835) is that Brother Sherman should let his "soul be at rest concerning your spiritual standing" and that he would be "remembered with the first of mine elders, and receive right by ordination with the rest of mine elders whom I have chosen." This is not intended to mean an ordination to the office of elder in the Melchizedek Priesthood (as the 1921 edition states), since he was already a high priest, but seems to mean something like, "You shall be one of the first [leading] elders in the Church, etc." In 1837 he was released from the office of seventy (since at that time high priests could not be seventies) and was subsequently called as a member of the Twelve (16 January 1839). He died (February 1839) before he was ordained. The headnote and content summary to this section in the new edition of the Doctrine and Covenants are worded in a manner to guide the reader toward a proper context and interpretation. This section is a clear example of the need for adequate historical information if we are to understand what a revelation really says.

*Section 119.* This section presents a revelation that was given to the Prophet Joseph Smith at Far West, Missouri, on 8 July 1839. Earlier in the Church, the United Order had been practiced, wherein those who belonged to the Order deeded their entire property to the Church. Due to severe persecution and the failure of many to comply with the requirements of the Order, this procedure was changed by revelation and a system of tithing instituted. The revelation known as section 119 was given in response to the Prophet's supplication: "O Lord! Show unto thy servant how much thou requirest of the properties of thy people for a tithing."[12] Without knowing this background, one could easily misunderstand the revelation. The word tithing itself means "a tenth"; however, the Prophet was not asking the Lord simply to show him how much a tenth was. It is evident that he was using the word "tithing" in a different context than we do today. In the transition from the United Order there needed to be some guidelines. Furthermore, it is evident that the word tithing as used in the earlier revelations and as commonly spoken of by the Brethren in those days was not limited to a tenth, but it was a more inclusive term covering all contributions and consecrations of property. Thus, in the 1981 edition the following is added to the headnote:

> The law of tithing, as understood today, had not been given to the Church previous to this revelation. The term "tithing" in the prayer just quoted and in previous revelations (64:23; 85:3; 97:11) had meant not just one-tenth, but all freewill offerings, or contributions, to the Church funds. The Lord had previously given to the Church the law of consecration and stewardship of property, which members (chiefly the leading elders) entered into by a covenant that was to be everlasting. Because of failure

> on the part of many to abide by this covenant, the Lord withdrew it for a time, and gave instead the law of tithing to the whole Church. The Prophet asked the Lord how much of their property he required for sacred purposes. The answer was this revelation.

Not only is the clarification valuable to understanding this section, but it also enables us to get the proper insight to a previous revelation known as section 64 in which is found the statement "he that is tithed shall not be burned" at the Lord's coming (D&C 64:23). When we understand what tithing meant in that day (1831), we can appreciate that it is not a mere ten percent that guarantees protection against the fire. The true sense of the revelation is that he who is wholly consecrated and dedicated shall not be burned. As a footnote to 64:23, the new edition tells the reader to "see note on tithing in heading to section 119." Having this foreground information is essential to gaining a correct understanding of both section 64 and section 119.

*Section 129.* This section presents "three grand keys by which the correct nature of ministering angels and spirits may be distinguished." In earlier editions of the Doctrine and Covenants, this section was described as a revelation "given to Joseph Smith the Prophet [on] February 9, 1843," conveying the impression that it was on this date the Prophet himself learned of these keys. However, there is documentary evidence he had given a similar explanation to the First Presidency and the Twelve on 27 June 1839.[13] The written source used for the Doctrine and Covenants was from a later occasion (1843) on which the Prophet explained the same concepts and on which date his scribe William Clayton recorded it. Thus the material now identified as section 129, although the product of revelation, was not a *new* revelation received in 1843. We do not know when the Prophet first received this knowledge, but we know that it was at least by 27 June 1839. Accordingly, the headnote to the 1981 edition reads: "Instructions given by Joseph Smith . . . February 9, 1843," rather than "REVELATION given to Joseph Smith . . . February 9, 1843." This is an important matter, for it contributes to the accuracy of the new edition and relieves the awkward inference that the Prophet himself did not receive the keys to angelic identification until late in his ministry after most of the heavenly ministrants had already appeared to him.

*Sections 137, 138.* These two sections are new to the Doctrine and Covenants with the 1981 edition. Both documents are known to students of Church history and have been published in Church literature. They were first made part of the standard works by the sustaining action of the general conference of 3 April 1976 and were published as an insert to the Pearl of Great Price. They were then transferred to the Doctrine and Covenants in the 1981 edition. Section 137 is a record of a vision of the celestial kingdom given to the Prophet Joseph Smith at Kirtland, Ohio, 21 January 1836; section 138 is an account of a vision of the Savior's ministry in the world of spirits given to President Joseph F. Smith, 3 October 1918. Both of these documents are fundamental to the doctrine of salvation for the dead and are therefore invaluable additions to the Doctrine and Covenants, especially at this time when genealogical research, temple building, and ordinance work for the living and the dead are reaching unprecedented activity.[14]

*Supplement to Official Declaration—1.* Official Declaration—1, the Manifesto, has been published as part of the Doctrine and Covenants since 1908 and remains unchanged in the new edition. However, there have now been added "Excerpts from Three Addresses by President Wilford Woodruff Regarding the Manifesto," which give detailed explanation as to why the Manifesto was issued. President Woodruff tells of the role of the President of the Church and of the revelations which he himself had received leading to the discontinuance of plural marriage. This material from President Woodruff had been published previously, but this is the first time it has appeared in a standard work. This not only makes it more accessible, it gives it a well-deserved aura of authority.

*Official Declaration—2.* In June 1978 the First Presidency announced that a revelation had been received by President Spencer W. Kimball extending priesthood and temple blessings to all worthy male members of the Church. The First Presidency subsequently sent a letter to the leaders of the Church throughout the world informing them of this revelation. Official Declaration—2 consists of (1) an introductory statement, (2) the letter, and (3) a concluding note to the effect that the letter was unanimously sustained by the vote of the general conference on 30 September 1978 as the "word and will of the Lord."[15]

## Footnotes and Cross-references

The cross-references refer the reader, by scriptural citation, to similar passages, or to the Topical Guide, without explanation, text, or comment. The reference itself is to the most direct verse in a corollary passage; then a longer passage is cited in parentheses to show the reader the context. Hence, D&C 88:30 speaks of the terrestrial glory. The footnote 30a directs the reader to 76:71(71-80), meaning that the specific key reference is v. 71, but the discussion of the terrestrial glory in section 76 continues from v. 71 to v. 80. This feature often helps to avoid a text-proof, out-of-context interpretation. Repeated use of these parentheses rewards the reader for his extra effort. The user should also understand that the association of ideas in the cross-references reflects the opinions of the compilers and might not always be the official position of the Church on items wherein official pronouncements have not been made.

Footnotes (in contrast to cross-references) are intended to be content-centered and supplementary. They do not offer a scriptural citation but rather an explanation. They thus differ in their service from a cross-reference. Examples of explanatory or directive footnotes are found in D&C 1:36f; 5:3b; 9:2a; 10:42a; 13:1g; 76:39a; 93:53b; and 103:29a.

## Maps

The 1981 edition of the Doctrine and Covenants is the first to contain maps showing significant locations having to do with the rise of the church in this dispensation. Not every place mentioned in the Doctrine and Covenants is shown, but the four maps make it possible to locate the most significant cities, rivers, and other sites having to do with the contents of the Doctrine and Covenants. These maps were specially prepared by the Department of Geography at BYU for publication in the new edition.

## Conclusion

As every reader of the Doctrine and Covenants soon learns, there is much in this book that pertains to the Bible, the Book of Mormon, and the Pearl of Great Price. Although separate books, these all pertain to the same gospel, the same plan of salvation, and the same Messiah.

There is a prophecy of Joseph in Egypt, preserved in JST, Gen. 50:30-31 and quoted also in 2 Ne. 3:12, that the words of Judah and the words of Joseph would "grow together" in the establishment of truth, peace, sound doctrine, and the confounding of error and contention. The study aids of the new editions of the standard works (including the Doctrine and Covenants) are contributing to the fulfillment of this prophecy by bringing the student of the Doctrine and Covenants to a clearer realization of the essential unity, harmony, and correctness of the scriptures and showing how the latter-day revelations clarify and restore the meaning to many biblical passages that have become shrouded in darkness, misconception, incompleteness, and error. Every Latter-day Saint should eagerly welcome the opportunity to search the new edition of the Doctrine and Covenants and to benefit from its contents.

## Notes

[1]Elders Howard W. Hunter and Marvin J. Ashton also served for a brief period on this committee. Daniel H. Ludlow, then Director of Correlation Review, served as a valuable advisor throughout the entire project. William James Mortimer, Director of Church Printing Services, served as the executive secretary for the committee.

[2]Many persons assisted in the production of the new editions, among whom were Ellis T. Rasmussen, Robert C. Patch, and Robert J. Matthews.

[3]*HC* 1:39-46.

[4]*JD* 7:311, from a discourse by Elder Orson Pratt, 18 September 1859.

[5]The material concerning the Shakers' beliefs was obtained from Milton V. Backman, Jr., of the Brigham young University Religious Education faculty, and several written sources, notably Frederick William Evans, *Compendium of the Origin, History, Principles, Rules and Regulations, Government, and Doctrines of the United Society of Believers in Christ's Second Appearing* (New York: D. Appleton and Co., 1859).

[6]See Keith W. Perkins, "The Ministry to the Shakers," found herein.

[7]See David J. Whittaker, "Substituted Names in the Published Revelations of Joseph Smith," *BYU Studies*, Winter 1983, pp. 103-12, for a full account of these and other names.

[8]Discourses by Orson Pratt, 16 August 1873, *JD* 16:156; see also Orson

Pratt, *The Seer* (1853-54), reprint ed. (Salt Lake City: Eugene Wagner, n.d.), pp. 227-29.

[9]*HC* 1:324.

[10]Dean C. Jessee, ed., *The Personal Writings of Joseph Smith* (Salt Lake City: Deseret Book Co., 1984), p. 17.

[11]*JD* 8:58; discourse on 20 May 1860.

[12]*HC* 3:44.

[13]Lyndon W. Cook, *The Revelations of the Prophet Joseph Smith,* pp. 286-87; see Bruce A. Van Orden, "Important Items of Instruction," found herein.

[14]See Robert L. Millet, "Salvation Beyond the Grave," found herein.

[15]See Richard O. Cowan, "Official Declarations 1 and 2," found herein, for further discussion.

# 3
# "KNOWING THE CALAMITY"
## (D&C 1)

George A. Horton, Jr.

### A Modern Parable

They were singing, shouting, laughing, and talking about their personal victories and adventures as the boat carried them peacefully down the slow-moving river. In their merriment they did not notice a quiet quickening of the current. Their preoccupation with each other kept them from paying much attention to one who appeared on the nearby shore waving excitedly for them to make their way to safety. A few waved back with curious smiles but continued on with their immediate interests.

"Rapids! Rapids! Falls! Change your direction! Come to shore quickly!" was the man's urgent call repeated over and over; but they were unconcerned until they happened to observe the faster current and looked ahead to see a short stretch of white-capped waves dashing around and over jagged rocks. An increasing roar indicated that suddenly the river would drop from sight, spilling into a roaring chasm of churning, foamy water.

With screams of horror they lunged for the oars and began to row frantically for shore. But it was too late—they had waited too long. The power of the current was too strong, and into the rapids they plunged—tossing, turning, shreiking, and cursing; finally over the falls they went to a watery grave.

Knowing that the world is largely preoccupied with material and physical pleasures as it drifts faster and faster toward the coming calamities, a loving Lord has called special servants to raise a resounding voice of warning—"Repent! Repent! Change your patterns of living before it is too late. 'Row' diligently toward the shore of the loving grace of Jesus Christ, follow the counsel of his prophets, and avoid the rocks and shoals of calamity and judgment that are just ahead."

## The Lord's Preface

When the revelation that became known as section 1 of the Doctrine and Covenants was given in November 1831, the Lord designated it as "my preface unto the book of my commandments" (D&C 1:6). In this way he placed a sacred stamp of approval on these divinely authored revelations which would be published to the world to help mankind avoid impending judgments and gain eternal salvation. Section 1, an important outpouring of the Spirit, came during a conference at Hiram, Ohio at a time when there were probably less than one thousand members in the fledgling Restored Church. The young, newly-called disciples were charged with the responsibility not only to be true to their own covenants, but to share the new and everlasting covenants—the fulness of the gospel of Jesus Christ—with all the "inhabitants of the earth" (D&C 1:6). At the least, it was a superhuman task. After all, it was a time of no television, telephones, radios, or other means of modern mass communication except newspapers with limited circulation. There were no automobiles, airplanes, or even railroads available. Transportation was basically limited to horseback, carriages, riverboats, or ships, and often great distances had to be covered on foot.

Could such a monumental challenge—taking the message of the Restored kingdom of God to every nation, kindred, tongue, and people—be accomplished by such a small band of disciples? The Lord knew that it could, for his servants would "go forth and none shall stay them, for I the Lord have commanded them" (D&C 1:5). It was his work, and he would sustain it. As Joseph Smith, Jr., his chosen prophet to head this last dispensation, boldly declared: "No unhallowed hand can stop the work from progressing; persecutions may rage, mobs may combine, armies may assemble, calumny may defame, but the truth of God will go forth boldly, nobly, and independent till it has penetrated every continent, visited every clime, swept every country, and sounded in every ear, till the purpose of God has been accomplished, and the great Jehovah shall say the work is done."[1]

The reception of section 1 on 1 November 1831 places it chronologically between sections 66 and 67. It was received when publication of the Book of Commandments was being proposed, and it was designated by the Lord to be the "preface" to the revelations (v. 6).

The Book of Commandments, printed in 1833, contained 65 sections—similar in content and arrangement to the first 64 sections of our present Doctrine and Covenants. Only a few copies were preserved after a mob ransacked the W. W. Phelps Printing Co. at Independence, Missouri. Section 1 has retained its position in the front of the collection of revelations in all successive editions of the Doctrine and Covenants.[2]

Most of the revelations to Joseph Smith (representing over ninety percent of the sections) were received during the light of day, generally in the presence of other people. Many persons saw and heard him pray, and the answers received were spoken aloud or dictated by him to his clerk as they listened.[3]

## Notes and Quotes

*Hearken (v. 1).* To "hearken" is not only to hear, but to obey as well. The injunction to do so is directed "unto all men" (v. 2).

*The voice of the Lord (v. 2).* Jesus Christ is the Author and source of all true revelations given to the inhabitants of this earth. "All revelation since the Fall," taught President Joseph Fielding Smith, "has come through Jesus Christ, who is the Jehovah of the Old Testament. In all of the scriptures, where God is mentioned and where he has appeared, it was Jehovah who talked with Abraham, with Noah, Enoch, Moses and all the prophets. He is the God of Israel. . . . The Father has never dealt with man directly and personally since the Fall, and he has never appeared except to introduce and bear record of the Son. . . . In giving revelations our Savior speaks at times for himself; at other times for the Father, and yet it is Jesus Christ, our Redeemer who gives the message."[4] All the revelations given in the Doctrine and Covenants were given by Jesus Christ (e.g., D&C 10:57; 27:1; 29:1; 62:1) or under his immediate direction.

*There is none to escape (v. 2).* Joseph Smith stated, "You cannot go anywhere but where God can find you out."[5]

*The rebellious (v. 3).* This refers to "every soul who rejects the everlasting Gospel."[6]

*The voice of warning (v. 4).* To the righteous it is a voice of hope, but to the wicked it is a notice of judgment and woe unless they repent.

*Unto all people (v. 4).* In the words of Joseph Fielding Smith, this book "belongs to all the world, to the Catholics, to the Presbyterians, to the Methodists, to the infidel, to the non-believer. It is his book if he will accept it, if he will receive it. . . . It belongs to all the world, not only to the Latter-day Saints. . . . They will be judged by it, and you will be judged by it."[7]

*Mine authority (v. 6).* Section 1 contains "the credentials given by our Lord to the Prophet Joseph and his associates in the ministry, and by them transmitted to others, regularly called and ordained, giving them divine authority to preach the gospel and warn the world."[8]

*My preface (v. 6).* A preface summarizes in advance the message of the author and prepares the reader to receive the content of the book in a proper perspective. This is "the only book in existence which bears the honor of a preface given by the Lord himself. . . . It was not written by Joseph Smith, but was dictated by Jesus Christ, and contains his and his Father's word to the Church and to all the world."[9]

*Power given them to seal (vv. 8-9).* By the Holy Priesthood, power is given to perform those ordinances or other acts that have binding force unto salvation. Likewise, under the direction of the Holy Spirit, when covenants are broken or sacred truths have been flaunted, power is given to loose the binding ties and place "a seal" of disapprobation upon those who persist in unbelief and rebellion. The unrepentant transgressor will suffer the wrath of God.

*Recompense unto every man according to his word (v. 10).* For the full elaboration of the meaning of this verse, consider the whole of section 76.[10]

*Prepare ye (v. 12).* This is a major theme of the Doctrine and Covenants with the injunction appearing about ninety times. It reflects the Lord's great desire to encourage his people to so live that they will be able to escape many of the impending judgments and be ready for his Second Coming. "Even today," wrote President Smith, "the cleansing process is going on, but eventually it will come with dreadful suddenness, and none who work iniquity shall escape."[11] The Lord has said, "If ye are prepared ye shall not fear" (D&C 38:30).

*The anger of the Lord (v. 13).* God is infinitely patient and long-suffering, but the world has now exceeded the limits of justice, and even in love God can no longer forbear.

*His sword (v. 13).* The sword is a metaphor that symbolizes powerful judgments and destruction upon the wicked (see Isa. 34:5-6).

*The arm of the Lord (v. 14).* This represents the power of the Lord used either to protect or punish as the case requires (see Ex. 6:6; Ps. 136:12; Jer. 27:5).

*Cut off (v. 14).* This includes being severed from the community of believers, or excommunicated.

*"For" (vv. 15-16).* This is one of the most helpful key words used throughout the scriptures. What follows it usually reveals the specific reasons for an attitude or action. In this case the Lord's anger is expressed because his children have (a) strayed from his ordinances, (b) broken the everlasting covenant, and (c) succumbed to the worship of idols.

*After the image of his own god (v. 16).* President Spencer W. Kimball has taught: "Idolatry is among the most serious of sins. There are unfortunately millions today who prostrate themselves before images of gold and silver and wood and stone and clay. But the idolatry we are most concerned with here is the conscious worshipping of still other gods. Some are of metal and plush and chrome, and of wood and stone and of fabrics. They are not in the image of God or of man, but are developed to give man comfort and enjoyment, to satisfy his wants, ambitions, passions and desires. Some are in no physical form at all, but are intangible." President Kimball continued:

> Many seem to "worship" on an elemental basis—they live to eat and drink. They are like the children of Israel who, though offered great freedoms associated with national development under God's personal guidance, could not lift their minds above the "flesh pots of Egypt." . . . They cannot seem to rise above satisfying their bodily appetites. . . .
>
> Modern idols or false gods can take such forms as clothes, homes, businesses, machines, automobiles, pleasure boats, and numerous other material deflectors from the path of godhood. What difference does it make that the item concerned is not shaped like an idol? Brigham Young said: "I would as soon see a man worshipping a little god made of brass or of wood as to see him worshipping his property" (*JD* 6:196).
>
> Intangible things make just as ready gods. Degrees and letters and titles can become idols. Many young men decide to attend college when they should be on missions first. The

> degree, and the wealth and the security which come through it, appear so desirable that the mission takes second place. Some neglect Church service through their college years, feeling to give preference to the secular training and ignoring the spiritual covenants they have made.
>
> Many people build and furnish a home and buy the automobile first—and then find they "cannot afford" to pay tithing. Whom do they worship? Certainly not the Lord of heaven and earth, for we serve whom we love and give first consideration to the object of our affection and desires. Young married couples who postpone parenthood until their degrees are attained might be shocked if their expressed preference were labelled idolatry.[12]

*Babylon (v. 16).* Throughout the scriptures, this ancient capital of the Babylonian Empire is used as the symbol for wickedness and depravity among men and nations. Thus the Lord has admonished his Saints in modern times: "Go ye out of Babylon" (D&C 133:7). This Babylon shall fall, as did the ancient city from which it derives its name.

*Knowing the calamity which should come (v. 17).* Because the Lord loves all men he has raised his voice and has sent his servants to encourage them to prepare, so that their chances of escaping the impending judgments will be greatly increased. The warning voice is one of hope and reassurance—a reminder that the Lord has never allowed a major calamity of judgment to come without forewarning. There is sufficent time to prepare, organize, and change our lives if we do not procrastinate. We must actively bring our lives into harmony with the great principles of eternal salvation in order to be ready for the judgments that will come upon an erring world. Can the Saints of the latter days learn any lessons from the experiences of Enoch's city, Noah's family, Jared and his brother, Lot and his daughters, Moses and Israel on passover night, Nineveh at Jonah's time, Lehi and his family, Christians fleeing Jerusalem before the Roman destruction, and perhaps others who have heeded prophetic calls? Now the call is to this generation, to each one of us—to every living soul. How is today's world drifting toward troubled waters with catastrophies almost sure to follow? Who will hearken to the warning voice soon enough to be saved by making their way to the shore of salvation—through faith in the Lord Jesus Christ, repentance, keeping the commandments, and through a life of love and service?

Many judgments are mentioned by the prophets that will occur before the Second Coming.[13] They are horrible to contemplate. Jesus wept over Jerusalem as he thought of the destruction that awaited it (Luke 19:41-44), and the Prophet Joseph also wept[14] as he instructed the early Church leaders about the corruption and destruction that would come upon the wicked world.[15] Surely it is not the Lord's desire that his children would have to suffer these judgments.[16]

Most prophecy is conditional. Many scriptural cases could be cited to illustrate this point. The language of the text is usually something like this: IF you keep the commandments, THEN you will be blessed; BUT IF you do not keep the commandments, THEN the judgments will come upon you (cf. Lev. 26:3-4, 14, 24; Deut. 4:25-40; 28:1-2, 15; 2 Ne. 1:9-10; D&C 5:16-24). Thus we see that in the case of prophesied judgments they are usually contingent on whether a person or a people repent and change their iniquitous ways. A case in point is the wicked city of Ninevah which heeded Jonah's call to repent and was spared destruction (Jonah 3:10).

Recently an American President raised the question as to whether all the difficulties and wars in the Middle East were an inevitable prelude to the last great battle of Armageddon. To this query a Jewish newspaper correspondent made the following observation: "When the future is foreseen and foretold, it's not an unconditional, inevitable future. The outcome, whether redemptive or destructive, is always conditional—for it is dependent on human behavior in response to God's word."[17] Indeed, most prophecies recorded in holy writ appear to be contingent on how people and nations live the covenants and commandments of the Lord. Is it possible, then, that the calamities that have been prophesied for the last days prior to the Second Coming of the Lord could be avoided? President Ezra Taft Benson, who shares in the call to provide the warning voice, spoke of these calamities: "These particular prophecies seem not to be conditional."[18] He clarified the assertion by adding: "The Lord, with his foreknowledge, knows that they will happen. Some will come about through man's manipulations; others through the forces of nature and nature's God, but that they will come seems certain."[19] This inevitability seems to be an outgrowth of man's failure to keep the commandments and his calculated willingness to persist in spiritual rebellion against his Lord and Savior, Jesus Christ. Therefore the Lord is able to declare that these calamities will come because he knows that the disposition of men—caught up in the priorities of the world—leaves no room for repentance in their hearts. Joseph Fielding Smith taught: "Men are rebellious. . . . They are not willing to receive the good things of the earth as the Lord would give them in abundance; but in their narrow-mindedness, shortsightedness, and in their greed and selfishness, they think they know better than the Lord does. And so, they pursue another course, and the result is that the blessings of the Lord are withdrawn, and in the place thereof come calamity, destruction, plagues, and violence. Men have themselves to blame."[20]

President Smith explained: "We have been taught how we might avoid them. . . . Hear the counsels that come to us, heed the testimony of truth. . . . *We may escape these things through faithfulness.*"[21] The Lord has offered hope: "Zion shall escape if she observe to do all things whatsoever I have commanded her. But if she observe not to do whatsoever I have commanded her, I will visit her according to all her works" (D&C 97:25-26). During the impending wars, as the wicked slay the wicked, the situation will be so severe that "the saints also shall hardly escape" (D&C 63:34). They are admonished to "gather together, and stand in holy places," e.g., stakes of Zion (D&C 101:22).

Another aspect of this question is reflected in the Prophet Joseph's statement that "it is a false idea that the saints will escape all the judgments, whilst the wicked suffer; for all flesh is subject to suffer. . . . Many of the righteous shall fall prey to disease, to pestilence, etc., by reason of the weakness of the flesh, and yet be saved in the Kingdom of God."[22] As another writer has explained, "It would be wrong to assume that the more righteous one is . . . the less he will suffer. . . . He will be blessed even though his blessings may be strength to endure suffering. . . . The difference is that the wicked must suffer the consequences of their sins in addition to the suffering that is part of life. . . . Those who live faithful to their covenants can be assured that they will not have to suffer in vain."[23] Elder Bruce R. McConkie has further declared: "We do not say that all the Saints will be spared and saved from the coming day of desolation. But we do say there is no promise of safety . . . except for those who love the Lord and who are seeking to do all that he commands. It may be, for instance, that nothing except the power of faith and the authority of the priesthood can save individuals and congregations from the atomic holocausts that surely shall be."[24]

President Joseph F. Smith gave additional perspective: "Severe natural calamities are visited upon men by the Lord for the good of his children, to quicken their devotion to others, and to bring out their better natures. . . . They are the heralds and tokens of his final judgment, and the schoolmasters to teach the people to prepare themselves by righteous living for the coming of the Savior."[25] On another occasion he taught that "judgment is not an end in itself. Calamities are only permitted by a merciful Father, in order to bring about redemption. Behind the fearful storms of judgment, which often strike the just and the unjust alike . . . there arises bright and clear the dawn of the day of salvation."[26] In summary: "All through the ages some of the righteous have had to suffer because of the acts of the unrighteous, but they will get their reward,"[27] for "the Lord receiveth them up unto himself, in glory" (Alma 14:11).

The Lord knows what is coming. Through his servants and these revelations he has forewarned all men in order that they might gain strength, exercise faith, enter into covenants, and be prepared for whatever comes. Thus, "knowing the calamity which should come upon the inhabitants of the earth," the Lord has called upon his servant Joseph Smith and others and has opened the heavens to them, revealing to the Saints and to the world the things of eternity. Thereby the people of God can prepare for the day of judgment and blessing. The Doctrine and Covenants contains many of those revelations.

*My servant Joseph (v. 17).* The Lord chose him! Of the millions out of every nation who could have been called to head this last and greatest of all gospel dispensations—the fulness of times and the period of the restitution of all things—the Lord chose a New York farm boy. But Joseph was more than that. Was he not one of the "noble and great ones" in the premortal councils? (Abr. 3:22; D&C 138:53). Was not his ministry foreseen by ancient prophets? (JST, Gen. 50:27, 33; Isa. 11:1; 29:12; 2 Ne. 3:11, 15). Was he not foreordained? "Every man who has a calling to minister to the inhabitants of the world was ordained to that very purpose in the Grand Council of heaven before the world was," Joseph said. "I suppose I was ordained to this very office in the Grand

Council."[28] Joseph magnificently fulfilled his calling as First Elder, Apostle, Prophet, Seer, Revelator, and Translator in an unsurpassed mortal ministry climaxed by martyrdom. The statement that he had "done more, save Jesus only, for the salvation of men in this world, than any other man that ever lived" was merited (D&C 135:3). Elder Stephen L Richards said, "My grandfather [Willard Richards] was a close friend and companion of this man. He knew him as intimately as one man may know another. He had abundant opportunity to detect any flaws in his character and discover any deceit in his work. He found none, and he has left his testimony to his family and to all the world that this man was true, that he was divinely commissioned for the work he had to do, and that he gave his life to the fulfillment of his mission."[29]

*"That" (v. 18).* This is another important word in scriptural interpretation because it alerts us to the desired consequences of an action. The Lord called Joseph and others in order *that* (a) they could proclaim this message, (b) the message would be fulfilled, (c) men would know the Lord and could speak in his name, (d) faith would increase, and (e) the fulness of the gospel would be proclaimed before the great and the humble. All of these purposes are now in the process of fulfillment.

*Trust in the arm of flesh (v. 19).* Refers to the weakness and imperfections of man when trusting in his own power.

*The weak and the simple (v. 23).* As Joseph Fielding Smith taught, "The Lord's ways are not man's ways, and he cannot choose those who in their own judgment are too wise to be taught. Therefore he chooses those who are willing to be taught and he makes them mighty even to the breaking down of the great and the mighty."[30]

*After the manner of their language (v. 24).* One Latter-day Saint writer has observed:

> The word of the Lord can be only in the language of the prophet when the ideas received are clothed in the prophet's own words. If the prophet's language is faulty and he is subject in his speech to the grammatical errors common to most of us, we may expect grammatical mistakes in the written revelation until they are discovered and eradicated. The mistakes are not the mistakes of God. In all the revelations received by men from God, as portrayed in the Bible, this human element is present.

> The poet clothes the message of God in beautiful phraseology and sets in to meter; the psalmist sets it to music, while the writer of prose stamps it indelibly with his own style. Thus the writings of Moses, Isaiah, Jeremiah, Micah, Amos, and Habbakuk are different in style and perfection of expression, but all are the word of God spoken through prophets in their language that mankind might come to understanding.[31]

What was the status of Joseph Smith's English during the period of the late 1820s and 1830s when the majority of these revelations were given? During this time Noah Webster was proposing many spelling changes in order to have a somewhat unique "American" English. In 1828, when he introduced his big "American Dictionary of the English Language," there were already five other dictionaries being used in the United States with variant spellings. Phonetic spelling (i.e., words spelled as they are pronounced) was very common, and some of Webster's 'new' spellings with a phonetic emphasis were accepted. This reflects a continually changing language. Therefore, the grammar also was not as standardized as it now is. Despite all of this, people were able to communicate effectively with each other, contributing to the Lord's objective—"that they might come to understanding"of his revelations given through the Holy Spirit to his chosen prophet.

In what language do the revelations of God come? Do they come in the pure Adamic language? Ancient Hebrew? Aramaic? Greek? Reformed Egyptian? No! They come to the prophet like they do any other humble disciple—in his own language: "These comandments are of me, and were given unto my servants in their weakness, after the manner of their language, that they might come to understanding" (D&C 1:24). Elder George A. Smith suggested that "when the Lord reveals anything to men, he reveals it in language that accords with their own. If any of you were to converse with an angel, and you used strictly grammatical language, he would do the same, but if you used two negatives in a sentence, the heavenly messenger would use language to correspond with your understanding."[32]

When Joseph was criticized in 1834 for "glaring errors" in a published revelation, he replied that shades of meaning or literary mechanics were not as important as the general message: "We did not think so much of the orthography [spelling], or the manner, as we did the subject matter; as the word of God means what it says."[33]

The words are abundantly clear! The message given through his chosen prophet to a drifting world needs little explanation. The voice of warning, coming, as it were, from the nearby shore is clear: Hearken! Repent before it is too late! "Prepare ye, prepare ye for that which is to come. . ." (D&C 1:12). "Search these commandments, for they are true and faithful, and the prophecies and promises which are in them shall all be fulfilled. What I the Lord have spoken, I have spoken . . . and though the heavens and the earth pass away, my word . . . shall all be fulfilled, whether by my own voice or by the voice of my servants, it is the same" (D&C 1:37-38).

*Inasmuch as (vv. 25-28).* Several conditions are mentioned which would keep a person consciously or unconsciously alienated from the Lord and what must be done to overcome such problems—instruction, repentance, and humility would allow one to receive knowledge, be made strong, and receive the Lord's blessings.

*Having received the record (vv. 29-30).* It would be difficult to overestimate the key role played by the Book of Mormon in the restoration of the true Church of Jesus Christ. Its self-professed objectives include being another witness of Jesus Christ and the confounding of false doctrines. Elder Bruce R. McConkie has said:

> The Prophet's expression that "the Book of Mormon is the keystone of our religion" means precisely what it says. The keystone is the central stone in the top of the arch. If that stone is removed, then the arch crumbles, which, in effect, means that Mormonism so-called—which actually is the gospel of Christ, restored anew in this day—stands or falls with the truth or the falsity of the Book of Mormon. . . .
>
> The Book of Mormon—which has come forth to prove that God inspires men and calls them to his holy work in this age and generation—establishes the verity of these great truths which comprise the message of the restoration. If the Book of Mormon is true, our message to the world is truth; the truth of this message is established in and through this book. . .
>
> This book is a witness of the divine mission of the Prophet Joseph Smith and of the divinity of the Church set up under his instrumentality. It establishes and proves to the world that Joseph Smith is a prophet for he received the book from a

resurrected personage and translated it by the gift and power of God. And since the Book of Mormon came by revelation, which included the ministering of angels, then obviously Joseph Smith also received other revelations and was ministered to by other heavenly beings. Among those revelations was the command to organize the Church. The Church is thus the one true Church because it was set up by a prophet acting under command of god. Thus the truth of the message of the restoration is established in and through and by means of the Book of Mormon."[34]

Brigham Young taught, "There is not a man or a woman who on hearing the report of the Book of Mormon, but the Spirit of the Almighty has testified to them of its truth; neither have they heard the name of Joseph Smith but the Spirit has whispered to them, 'He is a true prophet.'"[35] Similarly, President Ezra Taft Benson said, "The Book of Mormon was written for us today. God is the author of the Book. It is a record of a fallen people, compiled by inspired men for our blessing today. Those people never had the book—it was meant for us. Mormon, the ancient prophet after whom the book is named, abridged centuries of records. God, who knows the end from the beginning, told him what to include in his abridgment that we would need for our day."[36]

*Speaking unto the Church (v. 30).* Elder James E. Talmage observed: "I have no concern for the Church as a whole; its destiny is foretold, it is going on to a glorious victory [sec. 65]. But that does not say that each of us who are members of the Church will go on to glorious victory. . . . What are we doing individually?"[37]

*With the least degree of allowance (vv. 31-32).* This verse is a solemn reminder to the sinner that he cannot be justified in sin (cf. 2 Ne. 28:8-9) but through sincere repentance can receive loving forgiveness. President Harold B. Lee taught:

> If the time comes when you have done all that you can to repent of your sins, whoever you are, wherever you are, and have made amends and restitution to the best of your ability; if it be something that will affect your standing in the Church and you have gone to the proper authorities, then you will want that confirming answer as to whether or not the Lord has accepted

> of you. In your soul-searching, if you seek for and you find that peace of conscience, by that token you may know that the Lord has accepted of your repentance. Satan would have you think otherwise and sometimes persuade you that now having made one mistake, you might go on and on with no turning back. That is one of the great falsehoods. The miracle of forgiveness is available to all of those who turn from their evil doings and return no more."[38]

As the Prophet Joseph Smith said, "Our Heavenly Father is more liberal in his views, and boundless in his mercies and blessings, than we are ready to believe or receive; and, at the same time, is more terrible to the workers of iniquity, more awful in the execution of his punishments, and more ready to detect every false way, than we are apt to suppose him to be."[39]

*My Spirit shall not always strive (v. 33).* "The Spirit He has withdrawn from the world is not the Holy Ghost (for they never had that!)," explained Joseph Fielding Smith, "but it is the light of truth, spoken of in our scriptures as the Spirit of Christ, which is given to every man that cometh into the world. . . . Not because the Lord desires to withdraw that Spirit, but because of the wickedness of mankind, it becomes necessary that this Spirit of the Lord be withdrawn."[40]

*No respecter of persons (v. 35).* The Lord is not partial and "grants to each man, if he will repent, the same privileges and opportunities of salvation and exaltation."[41]

*Peace shall be taken from the earth (v. 35).* The First Presidency in the days of Brigham Young stated: "We know that the revelations of Jesus Christ are true, and that peace is taken from the earth, and that those who will not receive and obey the Gospel of Jesus Christ, when they hear it, will grow worse and worse, in evil passions, strife, war, and blood, until the wicked shall have overthrown the wicked and destroyed themselves from the face of the earth."[42] "The beginning of the fulfillment of this day when peace was taken from the earth appears to be at the commencement of the Civil War."[43] President Wilford Woodruff wrote:

> When I have the vision of the night opened continually before my eyes, and can see the mighty judgments that are about to be poured out upon this world, when I know these things are

> true . . . and while I am holding this position before God and this world, can I withhold my voice from lifting up a warning to this people, and to the nations of the earth? . . . God has held the angels of destruction for many years, lest they should reap down the wheat with the tares. But I want to tell you now, that those angels have left the portals of heaven, and they stand over this people and this nation now, and are hovering over the earth waiting to pour out the judgments. And from this very day they shall be poured out. Calamities and troubles are increasing in the earth, and there is a meaning to these things. . . . If you do your duty, and I do my duty, we'll have protection."[44]

*The Lord shall come down (v. 36).* From President Harold B. Lee: "One of the ways by which 'he comes down among his people' is clearly explained in the revelation in which he defines certain gifts of the Spirit . . . which men might enjoy," i.e., D&C 46.[45]

*Idumea, or the world (v. 36).* "Idumea or Edom," noted Bruce R. McConkie, "was a nation to the south of the Salt Sea, through which the trade route (called the King's Highway) ran between Egypt and Arabia. The Idumeans . . . were a wicked non-Israelitish people; hence, traveling through their country symbolized to the prophetic mind the pilgrimage of men through a wicked world; and so, Idumea meant the world."[46]

*Search these commandments (v. 37).* Read? Study? Indeed even more—search! "Search the scriptures—search the revelations which we publish," Joseph Smith pleaded, "and ask your Heavenly Father, in the name of his Son Jesus Christ, to manifest the truth unto you, and if you do it with an eye single to his glory nothing doubting, he will answer you by the power of His Holy Spirit. You will then know for yourselves and not for another. You will not then be dependent on man for the knowledge of God; nor will there be any room for speculation."[47] "All members of the Church are commanded to search and obey these commandments. . . . If we fail to do so and remain ignorant of the doctrines, covenants, and commandments, we shall stand condemned."[48]

## Conclusion

Dear Reader: This voice of warning is also a voice of love and reassurance. It is like the voice of one calling from the shore to "row" to safety before it is too late. Let those who love the Lord rejoice and let them sing: "In faith we'll rely on the arm of Jehovah to guide through these last days of trouble and gloom; and after the scourges and harvest are over, we'll rise with the just when the Savior doth come."[49]

## Notes

[1]*HC* 4:540.

[2]For the history of the Doctrine and Covenants, see Robert J. Woodford, "The Doctrine and Covenants: A Historical Overview," found herein. For more information on the seven "Lectures on Faith" which appeared in all printings of the Doctrine and Covenants between 1835 and 1921, refer to *HC* 2:175-76 (and note), 180; Joseph Fielding Smith, *Doctrines of Salvation*, comp. Bruce R. McConkie, 3 vols. (Salt Lake City, Bookcraft, 1954-56), 2:303-4; Bruce R. McConkie, *Mormon Doctrine*, 2nd ed. (Salt Lake City: Bookcraft, 1966), p. 439.

[3]For additional information on the process of revelation, see sections 8, 9, 18, and 68; see also Joseph F. McConkie, "The Principle of Revelation," found herein.

[4]Smith, *Doctrines of Salvation*, 1:27; cf. Ex. 6:3 and D&C 110:1-4.

[5]*HC* 6:366.

[6]Hyrum M. Smith and Janne M. Sjodahl, *Doctrine and Covenants Commentary*, revised ed. (Salt Lake City: Deseret Book Co., 1965), p. 5.

[7]Joseph Fielding Smith, *Conference Report*, October 1919, p. 146.

[8]Smith and Sjodahl, *Commentary*, p. 5.

[9]Joseph Fielding Smith, *Church History and Modern Revelation*, 2 vols. (Salt Lake City: The Council of the Twelve Apostles of the Church of Jesus Christ of Latter-day Saints, 1953), 1:252.

[10]See Larry E. Dahl, "The Vision of the Glories," found herein.

[11]Smith, *Church History and Modern Revelation*, 1:254.

[12]*The Miracle of Forgiveness* (Salt Lake City: Bookcraft, 1969), pp. 40-1; see also "The False Gods We Worship," *Ensign*, June 1976, pp. 3-6.

[13]The judgments most prominently mentioned by the prophets that will occur before the Second Coming include the following: pestilence, overflowing rain, great hailstones, fire and brimstone (Ezek. 38:22); the abomination that maketh desolate (Dan. 11:31); wonders in the heavens, and in

the earth, blood, and fire, and pillars of smoke (Joel 2:30); the fire of the Lord's jealousy (Zeph. 3:8); a plague that will consume eyes, tongue, mouth, feet, and flesh (Zech. 14:12); famines, pestilences, and earthquakes (Matt. 24:7); a desolating scourge or sickness (D&C 5:19; 45:31); desolations (D&C 29:8; 35:11; 45:19, 21, 31, 33; 84:114, 117; 88:85; 112:24); the destruction of the great and abominable church (D&C 29:21; 88:94); the darkening of the sun, the moon turning to blood, and stars falling from heaven (D&C 29:14; 34:9; 45:42; 88:87; 133:49); flies and maggots eating the flesh, a great hailstorm to destroy the crops, flesh falling from the bones, eyes from their sockets; beasts of the forest devouring people (D&C 29:16-20); lightnings, thunderings, and earthquakes wreaking havoc (D&C 43:25; 45:33; 87:6; 88:89-90); wars upon the face of the earth (D&C 45:26; 63; 63:33; 87); the sea heaving itself beyond its bounds (D&C 88:90); a sore affliction, pestilence, the sword, vengeance, and a devouring fire (D&C 97:25-28); and a very destructive whirlwind (D&C 112:24). To the foregoing, modern prophets have added floods, withdrawal of the Spirit from the earth, bands of Gadianton robbers infesting every nation, immorality, murder, and crime increasing, and the assurance that every man's hand is against his brother. See Smith, *Doctrines of Salvation,* 3:29, 34; Bruce R. McConkie, *Conference Report,* April 1979, pp. 131-32.

[14]Smith, *Doctrines of Salvation,* 3:29.

[15]*TPJS*, pp. 47-49, 87, 161-63, 252-53.

[16]Smith, *Doctrines of Salvation,* 3:28.

[17]Yehezkiel Landau, "Presidents and Prophets," *Jerusalem Post,* 4 November 1983.

[18]*Ensign,* January 1974, p. 68.

[19]*Ibid.*, p. 69.

[20]Smith, *Doctrines of Salvation,* 3:28.

[21]*Ibid.*, pp. 32, 34.

[22]*HC* 4:11.

[23]*Book of Mormon 121-122 Student Manual,* 2nd ed. (Salt Lake City: The Church of Jesus Christ of Latter-day Saints, 1981), p. 185.

[24]*Conference Report,* April 1979, pp. 132-33.

[25]*Gospel Doctrine,* 13th ed. (Salt Lake City: Deseret Book Co., 1963), p. 55.

[26]*Improvement Era* 9 (June 1906):651.

[27]Smith, *Doctrines of Salvation,* 3:37.

[28]*TPJS,* p. 365.

[29]*Conference Report,* October 1951, p. 117.

[30]*Church History and Modern Revelation,* 1:255.

[31]William E. Berrett, *Teachings of the Doctrine and Covenants* (Salt Lake City: Deseret Book Co., 1968), pp. 4-5.

[32]*JD* 12:335.

[33]Letter to Edward Partridge, William W. Phelps, et al., 30 March 1834, from Oliver Cowdery's Letter Book, pp. 30-36. Quoted in Dean C. Jessee, ed., *The Personal Writings of Joseph Smith* (Salt Lake City: Deseret Book Co., 1984), p. 315.

[34]*Conference Report*, April 1961, pp. 39-40.

[35]Brigham Young, quoted by B. H. Roberts, *Ibid.*, April 1905, p. 45.

[36]Ezra Taft Benson, *Ibid.*, April 1975, p. 94.

[37]James E. Talmage, *Ibid.*, October 1928, p.118.

[38]Harold B. Lee, *Ibid.*, April 1973, pp. 177-78; cf. Mosiah 4:2-3.

[39]*TPJS*, p. 257.

[40]"The Predicted Judgments," *Speeches of the Year* (Provo, Ut.: Brigham Young University Extension Publications, 1967), pp. 5-6; an address delivered at Brigham Young University, 21 March 1967.

[41]Smith, *Church History and Modern Revelation*, 1:255.

[42]The First Presidency, Brigham Young, Heber C. Kimball, and Willard Richards, *Millennial Star* 15 (9 July 1853): 437.

[43]Smith and Sjodahl, *Commentary*, p. 10.

[44]*Young Woman's Journal* 5 (24 June 1894): 512-13.

[45]*Conference Report*, October 1960, p. 16.

[46]*Mormon Doctrine*, p. 374.

[47]*TPJS*, pp. 11-12.

[48]Smith, *Church History and Modern Revelation*, 1:256.

[49]*Hymns of the Church of Jesus Christ of Latter-day Saints* (Salt Lake City: The Church of Jesus Christ of Latter-day Saints, 1948), Hymn no. 118, v. 3.

# 4

# TURNING THE HEARTS OF THE FATHERS AND THE CHILDREN

## (D&C 2)

CHARLES R. HARRELL

As Joseph Smith knelt in his father's house on the evening of 21 September 1823 to inquire concerning his standing before the Lord, "God ministered unto him by an holy angel, whose countenance was as lightning, and whose garments were pure and white above all other whiteness" (D&C 20:6). Moroni, the resurrected prophet from the fifth century A.D. in the Americas, stepped forward and gave his significant message. In addition to delivering a sacred charge regarding the translation of the Book of Mormon, Moroni quoted numerous passages from the Bible. After first quoting from the third chapter of Malachi, Joseph recounted, Moroni "quoted also the fourth or last chapter of the same prophecy, though with a little variation from the way it reads in our Bibles" (JS-H 36). Moroni's variant rendering of Mal. 4:5-6 constitutes what is now section 2 of the Doctrine and Covenants. It emphasized one of the ways in which Elijah would turn the hearts of the fathers to the children, and the children to the fathers. The Prophet Joseph himself made additional modifications to Malachi's prophecy, drawing attention to other aspects of its fulfillment. From his and other Church leaders' teachings, we gain an appreciation for the extent to which the hearts of the fathers and children are to be turned to each other.

### Turning the Hearts of the Living

Because of an occasional haste to associate Elijah's mission primarily with work for the dead, President Harold B. Lee reminded us that "it applies on this side of the veil as well as on the other side."[1] Recognizing the importance of turning the hearts of living parents and children to each other, Joseph Smith admonished that elders should "commence their labors with parents, or guardians; and their teachings should be such as are calculated to turn the hearts of the fathers to the children, and the hearts of the children to the fathers."[2] The Lord has placed the responsibility for bringing children up in light and truth squarely upon the heads of the parents. Upon receiving the saving ordinances of the gospel for themselves, their immediate obligation is to turn their hearts to their children in making the blessings of the gospel available to them. After the fathers and children are given opportunity to turn their hearts to each other in embracing the gospel, the Prophet Joseph warned that "the destroying angel will commence to waste the inhabitants of the earth."[3] This destruction has reference to the second part of Malachi's prophecy that if the hearts are not turned, the entire earth will be smitten and wasted.[4] The Prophet further taught that one reason this destruction would occur would be precisely because parents and children would be turned against each other.[5] Joseph Smith was graphic in his description of the horrible warfare to be waged within families, saying: "I saw men hunting the lives of their own sons, and brother murdering brother, women killing their own daughters, and daughters seeking the lives of their mothers."[6]

Another way in which the hearts of the living fathers and children are turned to each other, thus avoiding the curse with which the earth is to be smitten, is by the sealing power of Elijah. Joseph Smith clarified Malachi's prophecy saying, "the word *turn* here should be translated *bind* or *seal*."[7] In answer to the question, "How shall God come to the rescue of this generation?" the Prophet responded, "He will send Elijah the prophet . . . [who] shall reveal the covenants to seal the hearts of the fathers to the children, and the children to the fathers."[8] Although, as will be discussed subsequently, this includes children being sealed to their kindred dead, while parents are living they have a specific charge to see that their children are sealed to them. "The first thing you do," said Joseph Smith, is to "go and seal on earth your sons and your daughters unto yourself."[9] By so doing, families "may be sealed and saved, that they may be prepared against the day that the destroying angel goes forth."[10]

## Turning the Hearts of the Living to the Dead

To expand the Saints' thinking regarding Elijah's mission to turn the hearts of the fathers and children toward each other, the Prophet asked: "Now was this merely confined to the living, to settle difficulties with families on the earth? By no means. It was a far greater work."[11] One of the manifestations of the spirit of Elijah is to have those on earth turn their hearts to their deceased fathers. This occurs in at least three ways.

First, as used in D&C 2, the word "fathers" seems to refer to the ancient fathers—Abraham, Isaac, and Jacob. Those living must emulate the works and seek after the blessings of the fathers pertaining to the fulness of the everlasting gospel. In this sense the hearts of the children are turned to the fathers for their own sakes. It is a turning of "the hearts . . . of the disobedient to the wisdom of the just" (Luke 1:17), and "the hearts of the Jews unto the prophets . . . lest [the Lord] come and smite the whole earth with a curse, and all flesh be consumed before [him]" (D&C 98:17).

Second, the righteous living are turned to their fathers through their concern for the welfare of their kindred dead. Joseph emphasized that this concern is manifested "by building their temples, erecting their baptismal fonts, and going forth and receiving all of the ordinances . . . in behalf of their progenitors who are dead."[12] In essence, every effort of the living to make the blessings of the gospel available to their deceased ancestors is a manifestation of the spirit of Elijah. The Prophet warned that "those saints who neglect it in behalf of their deceased relatives, do it at the peril of their own salvation."[13]

Third, in addition to children performing saving ordinances for the dead, they must also be turned to the fathers who are dead by being sealed to them. The Prophet made it clear that the living cannot be made perfect without being sealed to their deceased ancestors adding, "I wish you to understand this subject, for it is important; and if you receive it, this is the spirit of Elijah, that we redeem our dead, and connect ourselves with our fathers which are in heaven."[14] Everyone who is exalted must be connected through the sealing ordinances into the extended celestial family of God.

## Turning the Hearts of the Dead to the Living

There are several ways in which the hearts of the righteous dead are turned to their living descendants. In most instances where this occurs, both the living and the dead are blessed.

First, the living receive revelation and guidance, which are vital to their salvation, through their righteous ancestors. In speaking of the righteous who have departed this life, Joseph Smith observed, "These men are in heaven, but their children are on the earth. Their bowels yearn over us."[15] These noble progenitors "are not far from us, and know and understand our thoughts, feelings, and emotions, and are often pained therewith."[16] Their mission is to "come down, combine together to gather their children, and gather them."[17] This is accomplished through inspiration, revelation, and other forms of influence exerted by these concerned parents. Even the Book of Mormon was written largely by loving fathers whose hearts were turned to their posterity in hope of bringing them to a knowledge of the gospel (see Enos 13-18). "We cannot be made perfect without the fathers," said the Prophet. "We must have revelation from them."[18]

Second, it is through the ministration of the fathers that the restoration of the keys of the priesthood was effected. In a revelation the Lord declared, "the keys of the dispensation, which ye have received, *have come down from the fathers*" (D&C 112:32, italics added). The extent of the involvement of the fathers in this restoration should not be overlooked. "Had it not been for the fathers that are dead," Orson Pratt reminded, "where would have been the priesthood? Is there any possible way by which the people calling themselves Latter-day Saints could have been benefitted by the authority and priesthood of heaven, unless it were through our fathers who were sent from heaven, holding the authority and conferring it upon the children?"[19]

Third, the dead have been influential in guiding the living to perform genealogical and temple work for them. Indeed, one of the main reasons why the dead exert such a strong influence to save their living descendants is so the living will, upon embracing the gospel, perform this work in their behalf. The late apostle, Elder Melvin J. Ballard, made the following remark in this regard: "Why is it that sometimes only one of a city or household received the Gospel? It was made known to me that it is because of the righteous dead who had received the Gospel in the spirit world exercising themselves, and in answer to their prayers elders of the Church were sent to the homes of their posterity that the Gospel might be taught to them and through their righteousness they might be privileged to have a descendant in the flesh do the work for their dead kindred. I want to say to you that it is with greater intensity that the hearts of the fathers and mothers in the spirit world are turned to their children than that our hearts are turned to them."[20]

Remarkable stories have been related of how loved ones from the other side of the veil have interceded, often in miraculous ways, to aid their offspring in the search of genealogical records. Elder Ballard testified that "the spirit and influence of your dead will guide those who are interested in finding those records. If there is anywhere on the earth anything concerning them, you will find it."[21]

Fourth, the fathers "plant in the hearts of the children the covenants made to the fathers" (D&C 2). Commenting on this phrase, Elder Bruce R. McConkie has explained: "The fathers involved are Abraham, Isaac, and Jacob. Each of them for themselves and for their seed received the promise that through celestial marriage they and their seed after them would have posterity as numerous as the sands upon the seashore and as the stars of the heavens."[22] Elder McConkie further observed that to plant these promises in the hearts of the children, "Elijah conferred upon men the sealing power, the power by which the promises made to the fathers could be made operative in the lives of men."[23]

When couples receive the promises made to the fathers by entering into the new and everlasting covenant of marriage, and then eventually prove worthy of the ratifying seal of the Holy Spirit of Promise (D&C 132:26), they will be preserved so that certain inhabitants of the earth will not be utterly wasted at the Lord's coming. It is this sealing power, which is also a manifestation of the spirit of Elijah,[24] that Joseph apparently had in mind in referring to John's vision (Rev. 7:1-3) of "four destroying angels holding power over the four quarters of the earth until the servants of God are sealed in their foreheads, which signifies sealing the blessings upon their heads, meaning the everlasting covenant, thereby making their calling and election sure."[25]

### Summary

Through the teachings of the Prophet Joseph Smith and other Church leaders, it is evident that Elijah's mission to turn the hearts of the fathers to the children and the children to the fathers is comprehensive in nature—from uniting their hearts in embracing the gospel and building eternal family units to turning their hearts toward each other through the veil in performing work aimed at saving one another. Finally, it is through Elijah that the family of Adam is organized under the patriarchal order and sealed up unto eternal life. "The spirit and power of Elijah," explained Joseph Smith, is to hold "the keys of power, building the Temple to the capstone [i.e., performing all of the ordinances for the living and the dead, and organizing them under the patriarchal order], placing the seals of the Melchizedek Priesthood upon the house of Israel [i.e., sealing them up to eternal life], and making all things ready . . . before the coming of the great day of the Lord."[26]

## Notes

[1]*Church News,* 11 August 1973, p. 14.

[2]*TPJS*, p. 86.

[3]*Ibid.*, p. 87.

[4]The earth being *wasted* is often interpreted as the earth having failed to fulfill its divine destiny; i.e., the work of God having been wasted. Additionally, Joseph Smith consistently implied that the word "wasted" in this prophecy referred to the destruction of the wicked wherein the earth would be *laid* wasted at the Lord's coming. "In the days of Noah," he explained, "God destroyed the world by a flood, and he has promised to destroy it by fire in the last days: but before it should take place, Elijah should first come and turn the hearts of the fathers to the children, etc." (*TPJS*, p. 337).

[5]*TPJS*, pp. 160-61.

[6]*Ibid.*, p. 161.

[7]*Ibid.*, p. 330.

[8]*Ibid.*, p. 323.

[9]*Ibid.*, p. 340.

[10]*Ibid.*, p. 330.

[11]*Ibid.*, p. 337.

[12]*Ibid.*, p. 330.

[13]*Ibid.*, p. 193. Although Joseph Smith had specific reference to baptism for the dead in making this statement, he later mentioned, "It is not only necessary that you should be baptized for your dead, but *you will have to go through all the ordinances for him*, the same as you have gone through to save

yourselves" (*TPJS*, p. 336, italics added).

[14]*Ibid.*, pp. 337-38.

[15]*Ibid.*, p. 159.

[16]*Ibid.*, p. 326.

[17]*Ibid.*, p. 159.

[18]*Ibid.*, p. 338.

[19]*JD* 7:81.

[20]Briant S. Hinckley, *Sermons and Missionary Services of Melvin Joseph Ballard* (Salt Lake City: Deseret Book Co., 1949), p. 249.

[21]*Ibid.*, p. 230.

[22]Bruce R. McConkie, "A New Commandment: Save Thyself and Thy Kindred," *Ensign*, August 1976, p. 9.

[23]*Ibid.*, p. 11.

[24]See *TPJS*, p. 338.

[25]*Ibid.*, p. 321.

[26]*Ibid.*, p. 340.

# 5

# THE WITNESSES OF THE BOOK OF MORMON

## (D&C 3, 5, 17, 20)

Monte S. Nyman

The significance of the Book of Mormon for the organization of The Church of Jesus Christ of Latter-day Saints is often overlooked. Sections 20 and 21 of the Doctrine and Covenants were given in conjunction with the organization of the Church. These sections are cited most often with regard to the date of the organization, the role of the prophet Joseph, and the other offices of the priesthood. However, thirty-two of the eighty-four verses (vv. 5-36) of section 20 deal with the significance of the Book of Mormon, how it was translated, what it contains, its purposes and importance, and the doctrines it teaches. It seems apparent that the Lord chose the occasion of the organization of the Church to reveal those things about the Book of Mormon in order that its importance to the Church might be emphasized. This emphasis also points out the importance of the Book of Mormon in giving people an opportunity to come into the Church and gain eternal life: "Therefore, having so great witnesses, by them shall the world be judged, even as many as shall hereafter come to a knowledge of this work. And those who receive it in faith, and work righteousness, shall receive a crown of eternal life; But those who harden their hearts in unbelief, and reject it, it shall turn to their own condemnation" (D&C 20:13-15).

This same emphasis was given by the prophet Joseph later (21 April 1834) when he told a conference of elders about the translation of the Book of Mormon, the organization of the Church, the revelations of the priesthood, and the gift of the Holy Ghost. On that occasion he is quoted as saying: "Take away the Book of Mormon and the revelations, and where is our religion? We have none."[1]

A common reaction of people when they are told about the Book of Mormon is that they would believe it if they could see the plates from which the book was translated. Such people probably would not believe even if they were shown, as shall be evidenced later. The Lord does not give this kind of evidence but uses another system of conveying information. This system is the furnishing of witnesses. This the Lord declared when he organized the Church: "For the Lord God has spoken it; and we, the elders of the church, have heard and bear witness to the words of the glorious Majesty on high, to whom be glory forever and ever. Amen" (D&C 20:16). Furthermore, the Lord does not operate with a single witness, but furnishes several witnesses. In an earlier revelation (D&C 5) the Lord had talked about four witnesses to the Book of Mormon. Each of these witnesses is unique. Collectively they will leave all who come to a knowledge of the Book of Mormon without excuse if they reject the sacred record.

## The Prophet's Witness

The Lord instructed Joseph Smith to tell Martin Harris that he (Joseph) had been commanded to stand as a witness of the plates of the Book of Mormon. He was commanded further to show them to no one except those designated by the Lord (D&C 5:2-3). This further verifies that the Lord uses a system of witnesses rather than personal observation.

Joseph Smith's first calling was the gift to translate the Book of Mormon (D&C 5:4). Those who honestly examine the book have sufficient evidence that Joseph fulfilled his calling and that the Book of Mormon is indeed the word of God (see D&C 17:6).

Following the translation, Joseph Smith was to deliver the Book of Mormon to others (D&C 5:5-6). The Lord again confirmed his system of witnesses. He declared that if the people would not accept the Book of Mormon, they would not believe Joseph Smith even if he did show them all the things in his possession (see D&C 17:1 for an enumeration of "all these things"). While the Lord had reserved the sealed portion of the plates for future generations, this generation (possibly from the time of the restoration until the time of the Second Coming) was to have the Lord's word, or the Book of Mormon, through Joseph Smith. Joseph's calling was not restricted to the publication of the Book of Mormon. His ministry was to expound "all scriptures unto the Church" as well as to warn the world (D&C 24:1-9). The Prophet repeatedly expounded the scriptures. The importance of his comments should be strengthened when one considers that he was called of God to do so. Joseph Smith and his translation of the Book of Mormon stand as the first witness to this generation.

That those who desire a physical sign or evidence would not believe anyway, as mentioned above, is verified in the New Testament parable of Lazarus and the rich man. Lazarus, a beggar, died and was carried into Abraham's bosom. The rich man died also and in hell asked for Lazarus to bring him a drop of water. When told this was impossible, the rich man said:

> I pray thee therefore, father, that thou wouldest send him to my father's house:
>
> For I have five brethren; that he may testify unto them, lest they also come into this place of torment.
>
> Abraham saith unto him, They have Moses and the prophets; let them hear them.
>
> And he said, Nay, father Abraham: but if one went unto them from the dead, they will repent.
>
> And he said unto him, If they hear not Moses and the prophets, neither will they be persuaded, though one rose from the dead (Luke 16:27-31).

The sealing of Joseph's testimony with his blood makes that testimony even more significant. Although referring to Jesus Christ, the book of Hebrews has application here. "For where a testament is, there must also of necessity be the death of the testator. For a testament is of force after men are dead; otherwise it is of no strength at all while the testator liveth" (Heb. 9:16-17). Joseph Smith knew that someday he would be required to seal his testimony with his blood. The Lord had possibly suggested this to him as early as March 1829 (D&C 5:21-22). He knew, however, as did Abinadi (Mosiah 13:3-4), that it would not be until he had completed his mission. "I know what I say; I understand my mission and business. God Almighty is my shield; and what can man do if God is my friend? I shall not be sacrificed until my time comes; then I shall be offered freely."[2]

Since he sealed his testimony, the witness of Joseph Smith is given to everyone who comes in contact with the Book of Mormon.

## Other Witnesses

Joseph's testimony was not to stand alone, in keeping with the law revealed to Moses and also taught by Jesus during his earthly ministry, "at the mouth of two witnesses, or at the mouth of three witnesses," was a matter to be established (Deut. 17:6; Matt. 18:16). The Lord revealed to Joseph that others would be called "in addition to your testimony, the testimony of three of my servants, whom I shall call and ordain, unto whom I will show these things, and they shall go forth with my words that are given through you" (D&C 5:11).

The Book of Mormon had also foretold these three witnesses. Moroni, while abridging the record of the Jaradites, spoke to the future translator, Joseph Smith, and told of "those who shall assist to bring forth this work" (the Book of Mormon) being shown the plates. Of those who did assist, three would "be shown by the power of God" (Ether 5:2-4). Nephi, probably quoting the original text of Isaiah (see Isa. 29:17-19), recorded that three witnesses would behold the book "by the power of God," and no others except "a few according to the will of God" (2 Ne. 27:12-14). Others were to bear testimony also, "those who shall assist to bring forth this work," as stated by Moroni, or the "few according to the will of God," as stated by Nephi. These phrases probably refer to the eight special witnesses and possibly to some others as well.[3]

The three special witnesses, Oliver Cowdery, David Whitmer, and Martin Harris, are probably—with Joseph Smith—the elders of the Church mentioned in D&C 20:16. Earlier, Cowdery and Whitmer had been given promises or premonitions of their opportunities. To the former the Lord had said: "Look unto me in every thought; doubt not, fear not. Behold the wounds which pierced my side, and also the prints of the nails in my hands and feet; be faithful, keep my commandments, and ye shall inherit the kingdom of heaven. Amen" (D&C 6:36-37). If or when Oliver Cowdery actually saw what he was here invited to see is not known.[4] However, to behold such would certainly qualify him as a special witness of Christ and would also prepare him for other miraculous manifestations. To David Whitmer the Lord had promised, on the condition of his asking in faith, that he would stand as a witness of the things he would "both hear and see" (D&C 14:8). He was further promised that through his calling to assist Joseph in the work he would be blessed both spiritually and temporally, and great would be his reward (D&C 14:11). Whether he comprehended what these promises entailed is not known, but certainly there is evidence of the Lord preparing him to be a special witness.

The case of Martin Harris is somewhat different. He was desirous of a physical wintess (D&C 5:1), but the Lord admonished him that he needed to make some corrections in his life before he could receive it (D&C 5:24). It is unlikely that he comprehended the type of witness he would receive.

Harris already had received evidence of Joseph's work. The Prophet had allowed him to take the manuscript of the first 116 pages that had been translated. He had lost this manuscript through his failure to keep the conditions of his taking it. This brought severe chastisement from the Lord upon Joseph, who lost his privilege of translation for a short period. At this same time, the Lord had called Martin Harris a wicked man (D&C 3:12). Section 5 was given about eight months later, yet Harris still had not humbled himself sufficiently, in spite of his sin in losing the manuscript. The character of Martin Harris is revealed further by the Lord's admonition to him concerning his role as a special witness: the Lord told Martin what to say and to say "no more" (D&C 5:25-29). As he had gone beyond his covenant to show the manuscript to only five people, it appears that his nature was to say more than was wise. About three months later, in June of 1829, Martin Harris had still not taken this last commandment to repent seriously enough. Following the completion of the translation, he was again warned. The Prophet's mother described the occasion:

> The next morning, after attending to the usual services, namely, reading, singing and praying, Joseph arose from his knees, and approaching Martin Harris with a solemnity that thrills through my veins to this day, when it occurs to my recollection, said, "Martin Harris, you have got to humble yourself before God this day, that you may obtain a forgiveness of your sins. If you do, it is the will of God that you should look upon the plates, in company with Oliver Cowdery and David Whitmer."[5]

Following Joseph's admonition to Harris, the Three Witnesses and the Prophet were shown the things which had been promised them

(D&C 17:2). The testimony itself shows the power of God that was manifest.

> Be it known unto all nations, kindreds, tongues, and people unto whom this work shall come, that we, through the grace of God the Father, and our Lord Jesus Christ, have seen the plates which contain this record, which is a record of the people of Nephi, and also of the Lamanites, their brethren, and also of the people of Jared who came from the tower of which hath been spoken; and *we also know that they have been translated by the gift and power of God, for his voice hath declared it unto us;* wherefore we know of a surety that the work is true. And we also testify that we have seen the engravings which are upon the plates; and *they have been shown unto us by the power of God, and not of man.* And we declare with words of soberness, that *an angel of God came down from heaven, and he brought and laid before our eyes, that we beheld and saw the plates,* and the engravings thereon; and we know that it is by the grace of God the Father, and our Lord Jesus Christ, that we beheld and bear record that these things are true. And it is marvelous in our eyes. Nevertheless *the voice of the Lord commanded us that we should bear record of it;* wherefore, to be obedient unto the commandments of God, we bear testimony of these things. And we know that if we are faithful in Christ, we shall rid our garments of the blood of all men, and be found spotless before the judgement-seat of Christ, and shall dwell with him eternally in the heavens. And the honour be to the Father, and to the Son, and to the Holy Ghost, which is one God. Amen.[6]

Thus these three men became special witnesses of the Lord Jesus Christ and the Book of Mormon in fulfillment of the prophecies of Isaiah, the Book of Mormon, and of the promises given by the Lord in the Doctrine and Covenants. Further evidence of their being special witnesses of Jesus Christ is their later commission to search out the twelve apostles who were also to be special witnesses (D&C 18:37). These twelve were also ordained under the hand of these three special witnesses.

Much more signficant than the history of the choosing of these three special witnesses is the purpose for which they were chosen. In the revelation given to them prior to their viewing the engraved plates, the Lord said that witnesses were necessary to preserve the life of Joseph Smith (D&C 17:4). The spiritual life of Martin Harris was also protected through his becoming a witness (D&C 5:32). The witnesses were a tremendous blessing to the Prophet. The pressure which had been borne by him prior to the viewing of the plates by the Three Witnesses was described by his mother:

> On coming in, Joseph threw himself down beside me, and exclaimed, "Father, mother, you do not know how happy I am; the Lord has now caused the plates to be shown to three more besides myself. They have seen an angel, who has testified to them, and they will have to bear witness to the truth of what I have said, for now they know for themselves, that I do not go about to deceive the people, and I feel as if I was relieved of a burden which was almost too heavy for me to bear, and it rejoices my soul, that I am not any longer to be entirely alone in the world."[7]

An additional purpose for the calling of witnesses was to bring about the Lord's righteous purposes (D&C 17:4). This was to help fulfill the promise made by the Lord to the Nephite prophets that the Lamanites might come to a knowledge of their fathers and of the gospel of Jesus Christ (D&C 3:16-20; 10:46-52; Enos 16-18). The Book of Mormon was also to go to all the house of Israel, the Gentiles, and to all the ends of the earth (Morm. 3:17-22; 5:9-24). The power manifest through witnesses since the Restoration began has been and will still be felt greatly throughout the world.

### The Witness of the Spirit

Perhaps the power of a witness can be comprehended more easily in light of the Lord's promise of a third kind of witness to the truthfulness of the Book of Mormon: a personal witness of his Spirit to those who accept the book. The Lord has said, "And behold, whosoever believeth on my words, them will I visit with the manifestation of my Spirit; and they shall be born of me, even of water and of the Spirit" (D&C 5:16). There is no refutation of a testimony borne and accompanied by the Holy Spirit. For this reason Alma resigned his judgeship to preach among his people "seeing no way that he might reclaim them save it were in bearing down in pure testimony against them" (Alma 4:19).

This type of pure testimony, accompanied by the Spirit of God, will save those who accept it; but it will also condemn those who reject it: "And their testimony shall also go forth unto the condemnation of this generation if they harden their hearts against them" (D&C 5:18). As one contemplates the thousands who have received this personal testimony and the thousands more to whom they have borne testimony, we see the power of witnesses reaching to all people.

## The Witness of Destruction

The Lord's fourth and final witness will be *de*structive rather than *con*structive. Destructions will be periodic until the final destruction of all the wicked through the Second Coming of Christ: "For a desolating scourge shall go forth among the inhabitants of the earth, and shall continue to be poured out from time to time, if they repent not, until the earth is empty, and the inhabitants thereof are consumed away and utterly destroyed by the brightness of my coming" (D&C 5:19; see also D&C 88:88-90). The Lord has given and will continue to give witness to the world. As one receives a witness, one becomes able to influence others. Rejection of the witnesses subjects one to both temporal and spiritual destruction.

The Book of Mormon will go forth to all nations to bring about the work of the Lord. Just as the Lord, through his fore-knowledge, had prepared another record to replace the manuscript lost by Martin Harris (the first 116 pages translated) and thus frustrated the work of those "wicked men" who had obtained it with the intent to destroy Joseph Smith and his work, future efforts to destroy the Lord's work are foreknown by him. He has provided defenses against them (see D&C 10): "The works, and the designs, and the purposes of God cannot be frustrated, neither can they come to naught" (D&C 3:1).

The Lord has provided ample witness for his work. Those who receive those witnesses and follow the teachings of the Book of Mormon will obtain eternal life. Those who reject it do so to their own condemnation against the testimony of divinely designated witnesses. To this the Doctrine and Covenants testifies.

## NOTES

[1]*HC* 2:52.

[2]*TPJS*, p. 274.

[3]Richard Lloyd Anderson, *Investigating the Book of Mormon Witnesses* (Salt Lake City: Deseret Book Co., 1981), pp. 21-34, 123-49.

[4]See Dean C. Jessee, comp., *The Personal Writings of Joseph Smith* (Salt Lake City: Deseret Book Co., 1984), p. 8.

[5]Lucy Mack Smith, *History of Joseph Smith*, ed. Preston Nibley (Salt Lake City: Bookcraft, 1958), pp. 151-52.

[6]"The Testimony of the Three Witnesses," Book of Mormon, emphasis added.

[7]Lucy Mack Smith, *History of Joseph Smith*, p. 152.

# 6

# A GREAT AND MARVELOUS WORK

## (D&C 4, 11-12, 14-17)

Monte S. Nyman

### By the Gift and Power of God

In February of 1829 the Lord told Joseph Smith, Sr. through his son, the Prophet Joseph Smith: "A marvelous work is about to come forth among the children of men" (D&C 4:1). In April, May, and June of that same year, Oliver Cowdery, Hyrum Smith, Joseph Knight, and David Whitmer were also informed of this same event through the same medium, Joseph Smith the Prophet, but with added emphasis—calling it "a great and marvelous work" (D&C 6:1; 11:1; 12:1; 14:1). This marvelous work had been foretold much earlier by Isaiah, as a work which would be necessary because of the spiritual state of the Christian world. The Christian people would do lip service to the Lord but would not be worshiping him correctly; they would be taught by the precepts of men (Isa. 29:13-14; 2 Ne. 27:25-26). The announcement of the Christian world being in this condition—and thus ready for the fulfillment of the marvelous work to commence—was made in the spring of 1820 to the boy Joseph Smith in what is commonly referred to as the First Vision (JS-H 19).

In describing the overall readiness of the people of the nineteenth century to receive the gospel, the Lord explained that "the field is white already to harvest" (D&C 4:4). Such an intellectual and spiritual preparation consisted of a general dissatisfaction with existing organized religion, as well as an anticipation of a restoration of the "ancient order of things." Ralph Waldo Emerson, in his famous Divinity School Address at Harvard—shortly after the Restoration—stated that "the need was never greater of new revelation than now." Further, "the Church seems to totter to its fall, almost all life extinct." Continuing, "I look for the hour when the supreme Beauty, which ravished the souls of those eastern men, and chiefly of the Hebrews, and through their lips spoke oracles to all time, shall speak in the West also."[1]

A number of later Latter-day Saint leaders spoke of their own quest for truth and the frustrations they felt before they encountered Joseph Smith. Brigham Young stated: "My mind was open to conviction, and I knew that the Christian world had not the religion that Jesus and his Apostles taught. I knew that there was not a Bible Christian on the earth within my knowledge."[2] Wilford Woodruff said: "I did not join any church, believing that the church of Christ in its true organization did not exist upon the earth."[3] Willard Richards became "convinced that the sects were all wrong, and that God had no church on earth, but that he would soon have a church whose creed would be the truth."[4]

This marvelous work and wonder, to which the Lord referred, was heralded by the coming forth of the Book of Mormon. The Lord, in speaking to Nephi, foretold the time when he would remember his covenants to the house of Israel and recover them a second time (2 Ne. 29:1). When the Savior visited among the Nephites, following his resurrection in Jerusalem, he referred to the coming forth of the Book of Mormon and the great and marvelous work which was to come among the Gentiles (3 Ne. 21:9). He said "there should be among [the Gentiles] those who would not believe it, although a man shall declare it unto them." The Lord promised Nephi and his father Lehi that God's word would proceed forth through their seed to all the ends of the earth for a standard to the house of Israel (2 Ne. 29:2). This promise was an extension of the promise made to Joseph who was sold into Egypt "that his seed should never never perish as long as the earth should stand" and that "the nations who shall possess them shall be judged of them according to the words which are written" (2 Ne. 25:21-22). The Book of Mormon serves as a "standard" of another kind as well, since it is closely associated with "the ensign," as translated in the KJV, which the prophet Isaiah foretold would be lifted up to the nations in the last days (Isa. 11:12; 18:3). This concept is used throughout the KJV book of Isaiah but is sometimes translated "banner" (Isa. 13:2), or "standard" (Isa. 49:22; 62:10). All of these are translated from the same Hebrew word, *nēs*. These revelations show that the coming forth of the Book of Mormon, as a great and marvelous part of the restoration of all things, was long anticipated by both Nephite and biblical prophets.

As a great and marvelous work, the Book of Mormon was a major part of the restoration of all things. This conclusion is justified in several ways. First, it is a work which was done by or through the Father (3 Ne. 21:9) and a work which the learned Gentiles of the day could not do on their own (2 Ne. 27:19-20; cf. JST, Isa. 29). Second, it was translated through the medium of the Urim and Thummim by the gift and power of God.[5] The Urim and Thummim was an instrument which was furnished by God and worked by the power of God (D&C 3:12). The language from which the book was translated was a language neither known nor understood by man at the time when the plates were revealed (Morm. 9:32-34). Third, the book was translated in a miraculous period of time, no more than ninety days, but probably closer to a sixty-day time period. This was a much shorter time period than the six months it took the printers to set the type and print the book, August 1829 to March 1830.

## "Give Heed Unto My Word"

The above justifications are dependent upon the validity of the work of Joseph Smith. The Doctrine and Covenants confirms this validity. The Lord repeatedly verified that Joseph the Prophet did fulfill his role as translator and thus qualify the translation as a marvelous work and a wonder. The Lord reminded Oliver Cowdery, at the time that he began to act as scribe for the translation process (April 1829), "the words or the work which thou hast been writing are true" (D&C 6:17). Following the completion of the translation, the Lord affirmed in the words of an ancient Hebrew oath to Oliver Cowdery, David Whitmer, and Martin Harris—the three selected to be special witnesses of the Book of Mormon—that Joseph had "translated the book, even that part which I commanded him, and as your Lord and your God liveth it is true" (D&C 17:6). These three witnesses have declared to the world in written testimony that they knew that the Book of Mormon had been "translated by the gift and power of God, for his voice has declared it unto us, wherefore we know of a surety that the work is true."[6] Following the completion of the translation, Oliver was again reminded by the Lord: "Behold, I have manifested unto you by my Spirit in many instances, that the things which you have written are true; wherefore you know that they are true." He was commanded to "rely upon the things which are written" (D&C 18:2-3). Thus, four times the Lord verified, through revelation, that the work of Joseph Smith was valid.

In the earlier revelations concerning the marvelous work and wonder which was about to come forth, the Lord had declared that his hand would be in the work. To Oliver Cowdery, Hyrum Smith, Joseph Knight and David Whitmer, the Lord said: "Behold, I am God; give heed unto my word, which is quick and powerful, sharper than a two-edged sword, to the dividing asunder of both joints and marrow; therefore give heed unto my words" (D&C 6:2). "I am God" confirms that the Book of Mormon was to come forth under his supervision and power. "Give heed to my words" also confirms that the Book of Mormon would contain his words as revealed to the Nephite prophets. The defining of his word as sharper than a two-edged sword is using a symbolic comparison of truth (his word) and the sword of the warrior of ancient times. The two-edged sword will cut regardless of which way it may be swung. There is no place that a person may touch it without feeling the effect it does or could do. Likewise, the word of God will have a positive or a negative affect upon whomever it contacts. This is illustrated in a comment made by Nephi to Laman and Lemuel when they complained that he declared hard things to them which seemed to be more than they could bear. Nephi responded: "I knew that I had spoken hard things against the wicked, according to the truth; and the righteous have I justified, and testified that they should be lifted up at the last day; wherefore, the guilty taketh the truth to be hard, for it cutteth them to the very center" (1 Ne. 16:2).

God's word is described further as having the power to divide asunder both joints and marrow. While a sword will cut flesh easily, it takes a forceful blow to sever a joint or cut to the center of the bone. The joint is the point of coordination of the parts of the body. With it being severed, or injured, that part of the body is lost or ceases to function. Likewise the word of Christ can and does penetrate to the coordination and organization of our lives in the Church, home, and community. When one resists the power of the word of God, it may lead to being isolated from the Church, being severed from the family, and being out of harmony with the community—depending on the degree of the resistance. The marrow of the bone is the innermost part and an essential factor for health. An injury of this depth requires a great healing process. The word of Christ also has the ability to penetrate to the marrow of our souls and thus affect our physical and spiritual health for good or evil.

A further insight into the Lord's involvement in this marvelous work may be shown in a revelation to both John Whitmer and Peter Whitmer, Jr. Christ revealed to them: "I speak unto you with sharpness and with power, for mine arm is over all the earth. And I will tell you that which no man knoweth save me and thee alone" (D&C 15:2-3; 16:2-3). Just as the marrow is the innermost ingredient of the bone and cannot be discerned externally, even if the flesh is cut away, the innermost thoughts of man are hidden to others but are known to Christ. Just as medicines or proper diet can influence physical health, the Lord's word can and will penetrate to the very center of one's soul for a healing effect or, if rejected, will leave a person sick and troubled. According to the Doctrine and Covenants, the word of God contained in the Book of Mormon, which was to come forth through a marvelous work of the Lord, was to have a quick and powerful effect on a world which was sick and out of coordination with him. It also was to have a healing effect on the honest in heart, which would "cause a great division among the people" (2 Ne. 30:10), separating the righteous from the wicked.

The commencement of this great division would be through the fulness of the gospel contained in the Book of Mormon (JS-H 34). That the word of God in its fulness was not available to the world prior to its publication was made evident to Hyrum Smith in the revelation directed to him in May of 1829. He was told to wait a little while before commencing to preach the gospel "until you shall have my word, my rock, my church, and my gospel, that you may know of a surety my doctrine" (D&C 11:16). Hyrum was told further that he would have the opportunity to assist in the translation of the Book of Mormon. The Lord then gave this timely advice:

> Seek not to declare my word, but first seek to obtain my word, and then shall your tongue be loosed; then, if you desire, you shall have my Spirit and my word, yea, the power of God unto the convincing of men. But now hold your peace; study my word which hath gone forth among the children of men, and also study my word which shall come forth among the children of men, or that which is now translating, yea, until you have obtained all which I shall grant unto the children of men in this generation, and then shall all things be added thereto (D&C 11:21-22).

While the Book of Mormon is an essential part of the marvelous work to which the Lord referred in these revelations, the subsequent events which led to the establishment of the Church and restoration of the fulness of the gospel are also a continuation of that great work and may collectively be referred to as the great and marvelous work. In this context, President David O. McKay observed:

> When [D&C 4] was given to the Prophet Joseph Smith, he was only twenty-three years of age. The Book of Mormon was not yet published; no man had been ordained to the priesthood. The Church was not organized; yet the statement was made and written without qualification that ". . . a marvelous work is about to come forth among the children of men." Another significant feature of this revelation, and others given about the same period, is the naming of essential qualifications of those who were to participate in the bringing about of this marvelous work. These qualifications were not the possession of wealth, not social distinction, not political preferment, not military achievement, not nobility of birth; but a desire to serve God with all your "heart, mind, and strength"—spiritual qualities that contribute to nobility of soul. I repeat: No popularity, no wealth, no theological training in church government—yet a marvelous work was about to come forth among the children of men. Manifestly, some higher power was operating to bring about this marvelous work other than mere human and material means.[7]

## The Challenge of the Book of Mormon

The culmination of this great and marvelous work was to be the building of Zion. This was implied when the Lord commanded Oliver Cowdery, Hyrum Smith, Joseph Knight, and David Whitmer to "seek to bring forth and establish the cause of Zion" (D&C 6:6). The Lord later identified Zion as "an ensign unto the people," to which people from every nation would come; "the nations of the earth shall tremble because of her, and shall fear because of her terrible ones" (D&C 64:41-43). Thus the bringing forth of the Book of Mormon initiated a marvelous work and a wonder among the inhabitants of the earth which will not be completed until Zion is established in preparation for the Second Coming of the Lord. All of these early revelations, to which reference has been made, give the requirements to serve in this great work. They further declare that those who follow those requirements will understand the mysteries of God and will become rich, in that they will obtain eternal life (D&C 4:2-7; 6:3-7).

Two and one-half years after the Book of Mormon was translated, the Lord declared that in times past the minds of the elders of the Church had "been darkened because of unbelief, and because you have treated lightly the things you have received [the Book of Mormon]." The Lord further declared that such "vanity and unbelief have brought the whole church under condemnation." This condemnation would remain, according to the Lord "until they repent and remember the new covenant, even the Book of Mormon and the former commandments [the Bible] . . . , not only to *say*, but to *do* according to that which I have written" (D&C 84:54-57, emphasis added). What would the Lord say today if he gave a revelation about our use of the Book of Mormon? Is the Book of Mormon being utilized as the Lord intended? The condemnation will not be lifted collectively from the Church until the majority of the individuals in the Church are using the Book of Mormon by speaking and living as it teaches. The work will continue until Zion is built in preparation for the Lord's Second Coming. Those who come in contact with this marvelous work must choose to become a part of it or be found fighting against it. It will result in our glory or our condemnation (cf. D&C 20:13-16).

## Notes

[1]Ralph Waldo Emerson, "The Divinity School Address," delivered before the senior class at the Harvard Divinity School, Cambridge, Massachusetts, 15 July 1838; in Sidney E. Ahlstrom, ed., *Theology in America* (Indianapolis: Bobbs-Merrill, 1967), pp. 306, 315-16.

[2]*JD* 5:75.

[3]*Ibid.*, 4:99.

[4]*HC* 2:470.

[5]*HC* 4:537. See also the Title Page of the Book of Mormon.

[6]"The Testimony of Three Witnesses," Book of Mormon. See also Monte S. Nyman, "The Witnesses of the Book of Mormon," found herein.

[7]*Conference Report,* April 1954, pp. 22-23; *Improvement Era,* June 1954, p. 390.

# 7

# THE PRINCIPLE OF REVELATION (D&C 6, 8, 9, and 11)

JOSEPH FIELDING MCCONKIE

When revelation ceased—not long after the death of Christ and the Apostles—the knowledge of how revelation comes was lost also. Christ, the son of a carpenter, came to be viewed by later Christians something like a hillbilly preacher, who having never finished grammar school, takes the pulpit one Sunday, and to everyone's surprise opens the Bible, takes a text at random, proceeds to preach a discourse of pure scripture in Shakespearean English, and by the power of the Spirit converts everyone present. To such (even some within the Church today) revelation is thought of as a state of spiritual ecstasy, a state in which bodily powers are suspended and might, mind, and soul, surrendered to heavenly powers.

Similarly, it is held by such that when the word of God is to be written, man is but the pen, for the power, the thought and the expression all must be God's. Every vowel point and accent of the Hebrew Bible are attributed to him.

Many, Jew and Christian alike, worshipped the scripture with such exaggerated zeal that they lost contact with the giver of the word and thus betrayed him with the kiss of false devotion. In their professed reverence for that which God had spoken in the past, they denied him the right to continue to speak. They lost themselves in the smoke of their own offerings. Their God had spoken and need speak no more, and their records of what he had said must be regarded as both inerrant and infallible.

As marvelous as the Bible is, those proclaiming its infallibility and total sufficiency ought to remind themselves that the Church of Christ existed long before a single Gospel or Epistle had been written. The apostasy was complete before the New Testament as the Christian world now has it ever came into existence.[1] No member of the Church established by Christ in the meridian dispensation ever read it. The life-giving force of the ancient Saints was not the echo of the past as it was found in scriptural records or in someone else's revelation; it was in the living voice of personal revelation. Theirs was a faith that centered in the spirit of revelation.

Yet it remained for Joseph Smith to announce to a disbelieving world that that same God who spoke so freely in times past not only could, but *had* spoken again, and that the promise of James that any who sought the wisdom of heaven in faith still had claim upon it (James 1:5).

This being the setting of the restoration of the gospel in our day, it seems both natural and appropriate that among the early revelations of this dispensation are those that describe, define, and explain the spirit of revelation. Let us turn to these revelations and briefly review the principles they teach.

## The Voice of Peace

While teaching school in Palmyra, Oliver Cowdery learned about the work of translating the Book of Mormon, in which Joseph Smith was then engaged. By this time Joseph and his wife Emma had been forced to flee to Harmony, Pennsylvania, in order to escape the continued attempts to interrupt the work and steal the plates containing the ancient records.

Having learned of the matter, Oliver found himself constantly reflecting on it. "It worked on my very bones," he said.[2] Following his impressions he went to Harmony and offered his services to Joseph Smith. His offer to help was gratefully accepted and in a matter of days after his arrival he was busy recording the Prophet's words. Still Oliver had some feelings of uncertainty. In a desire to obtain a more sure witness that the work he was involved in was the work of God, he requested the Prophet to inquire of the Lord in his behalf. Joseph Smith did so, the result being what we know today as D&C 6. In that revelation the Lord commended Oliver for what he had done in following his impressions to come and offer his services to Joseph. The Lord also told Oliver that as often as he had sought divine instruction he had received it (D&C 6:14).

Thus we find Oliver Cowdery being given a revelation, the primary purpose of which was to assure him that he had been receiving revelation! As an evidence that he had been responding to the Spirit, the Lord told him, "If it had not been so, thou wouldst not have come to the place where thou art at this time" (D&C 6:14).

Oliver had been responding to the promptings of the Spirit without consciously realizing that he was doing so. By way of additional explanation the Lord said, "Thou knowest that thou hast inquired of me and I did enlighten thy mind; and now I tell thee these things that thou mayest know that thou hast been enlightened by the Spirit of truth" (D&C 6:15). So that Oliver would be without reason to doubt this revelation, the Lord continued: "Verily, verily, I say unto you, if you desire a further witness, cast your mind upon the night that you cried unto me in your heart, that you might know concerning the truth of these things. Did I not speak peace to your mind?" Then to emphasize his point, the Lord asked, "What greater witness can you have than from God?" (D&C 6:22-23). The reference to the earlier experience known only to Oliver assured him that his prayers had been answered and that he was involved in the work of the Lord.

As Oliver grew into his understanding of the spirit of revelation, the first great lesson he had to learn was the unobtrusive, quiet nature of that Spirit. The witness of the Spirit always involves feelings, and chief among those feelings is that of peace. No other word is as consistently used in scriptural descriptions of the presence of angels, the Lord, or his Spirit, than "peace." It was also important for Oliver to learn how easily the spirit of revelation can be overlooked or missed if we do not learn to pay attention to it. Oliver was being prompted, directed, and enlightened, without even being conscious of it. These quiet operations of the Spirit provide a marked contrast with the feelings of spiritual ecstasy so often professed in spiritual counterfeits.

## The Necessity of Effort and Study

In the revelation just cited, Oliver Cowdery received the promise that he could labor as a translator even as Joseph was doing (D&C 6:25-27). The blessing was greatly to be desired, and it was with the greatest of expectations that Oliver approached the work of translation when the opportunity was extended to him. Yet to his surprise he was unable to decipher the characters before him.

There is much in Oliver's experience that is profitable for our instruction in obtaining an understanding of the spirit of revelation. First, let us consider the instruction given him before his attempt to translate. That Oliver might have the assurance that he was translating by the spirit of revelation, the Lord said: "I will tell you in your mind and in your heart, by the Holy Ghost, which shall come upon you and which shall dwell in your heart." This Oliver was told was the "spirit of revelation" (D&C 8:2-3). We observe that neither he nor Joseph was to experience any suspension of their natural faculties in the process of obtaining revelation. Quite to the contrary, their hearts and minds were to be the very media through which the revelation came. Prophets are not hollow shells through which the voice of the Lord echoes, nor are they mechanical recording devices; prophets are men of passion, feeling, and intellect. One does not suspend agency, mind, or spirit in the service of God. It is only with heart, might, mind and strength that we have been asked to serve, and in nothing is this more apparent than the receiving of revelation. There is no mindless worship or service in the kingdom of heaven.

"You have not understood," the Lord told Oliver. "You have supposed that I would give it unto you, when you took no thought save it was to ask me" (D&C 9:7). But the revelations of heaven are not granted to one in mindless stupor; rather, they embrace the complete use of all heavenly given endowments. Man, who has been created in the image of God, has been given heart and mind, both divine attributes, as sources of knowing the divine heart and mind.

"You must study it out in your mind," the Lord said to Oliver. "Then [that is, after you have labored to your utmost, after you have pondered, and searched and sought] you must ask me if it be right." And now, having paid the tuition of effort, you have claim upon an answer, and now the promise is yours that if your conclusion is right, the Lord "will cause that your bosom shall burn within you; therefore, you shall feel that it is right" (D&C 9:8). The understanding comes not with the blare of heavenly trumpets but as a feeling. Truth is a feeling! As Joseph Smith subsequently said, "It tastes good."[3] Further the Lord added, "If it be not right you shall have no such feelings, but you shall have a stupor of thought that shall cause you to forget the thing which is wrong; therefore, you cannot write that which is sacred save it be given you from me" (D&C 9:9).

The same principles are immediately identifiable in the revelation given to Hyrum Smith as he began to awaken to the things of the Spirit. To him the Lord said, "Put your trust in that Spirit which leadeth to do good—yea, to do justly, to walk humbly, to judge righteously; and this is my Spirit" (D&C 11:12). Thus we are assured that we can find the Spirit of the Lord by doing the works of the Lord. For by so doing the Lord promised Hyrum that his mind would be enlightened and his soul filled with joy. Through such a procedure the Lord said he could know "all things" that pertained to righteousness (D&C 11:14). Again we see the quiet proddings of the Lord. It was earlier observed that no word is more frequently associated with the presence of the Lord's Spirit than "peace." Let it now be observed that "peace" is closely rivaled in that distinction by the word "joy."

The Lord instructed Hyrum: "Seek not to declare my word, but first seek to obtain my word, and then shall your tongue be loosed; then, if you desire, you shall have my Spirit and my word, yea, the power of God unto the convincing of men" (D&C 11:21). Once more we are emphatically taught that the Holy Ghost does not work in a vacuum. One does not mindlessly or thoughtlessly approach the throne of God. Even submissive ignorance is not flattering to God. If the desire of Hyrum Smith, one of the best-living men to ever grace the earth, to labor in the kingdom, was refused because he needed first to "study" the word of the Lord (D&C 11:22), then how much more need have we to labor and prepare to be worthy companions of the spirit of revelation?

## Greater Promises to Follow

These principles enunciated with such power and clarity in the early revelations were but the foundation upon which greater promises were to stand. To the early missionaries, and in principle to all who labor in faith in the Church, the Lord said: "It is your privilege, and a promise I give unto you that have been ordained unto this ministry, that inasmuch as you strip yourselves from jealousies and fears, and humble yourselves before me, for ye are not sufficiently humble, the veil shall be rent and you shall see me and know that I am—not with the carnal neither natural mind, but with the spiritual" (D&C 67:10). In the great revelation on the degrees of glory the Lord again promised those that feared him and served him in righteousness and truth that they would be greatly rewarded and that he would reveal "all mysteries" to them: "Yea, all the hidden mysteries of my kingdom from days of old, and for ages to come, will I make known unto them the good pleasure of my will concerning all things pertaining to my kingdom. Yea, even the wonders of eternity shall they know, and things to come will I show them, even the things of many generations" (D&C 76:5-10).

Revelation has always been an identifying characteristic of the Children of God. And as for our day the Prophet declared: "As well might man stretch forth his puny arm to stop the Missouri river in its decreed course, or to turn it up stream, as to hinder the Almighty from pouring down knowledge from heaven upon the heads of the Latter-day Saints" (D&C 121:33).

---

## Notes

[1]The generally acknowledged date for the acceptance of the twenty-seven books that now constitute the New Testament is A.D. 367. At least this is the earliest reference we have to them together as a group. Athanasius, a bishop of Alexandria, was the man who first so named them in an annual letter he wrote to the churches of his diocese. Though we do not know when the authority of Christ's Church was lost and the apostasy complete it would have to have been an appreciable time before Athanasius' day.

[2]Lucy Mack Smith, *History of Joseph Smith*, ed. Preston Nibley (Salt Lake City: Bookcraft, 1958), p. 139.

[3]*TPJS*, p. 355.

# 8

# THE RESTORATION OF THE PRIESTHOOD

## (D&C 13 and 27)

CHARLES R. HARRELL

In the angel Moroni's appearances to Joseph Smith in September 1823, he foretold of the restoration of the Aaronic and Melchizedek Priesthoods in connection with the translation of the gold plates. "When they are interpreted," said the angel, *"the Lord will give the holy priesthood to some,* and they shall begin to proclaim this gospel and baptize by water, and *after that they shall have power to give the Holy Ghost* by the laying on of their hands."[1] As the translation of the Nephite record commenced, the Lord began preparing the minds of the early Saints to receive the priesthood, outlining the qualifications for labor in the ministry (D&C 4, 6, 11, 12). In a revelation dated March 1829, the Lord declared: "For *hereafter you shall be ordained* and go forth and deliver my words unto the children of men" (D&C 5:6, italics added).

### The Aaronic Priesthood Restored

#### The Visit From John the Baptist

It was mid-May of 1829 in Harmony, Pennsylvania where Joseph Smith and Oliver Cowdery had been engaged almost incessantly since April 7th on the translation of the Book of Mormon. As they came to the instructions of the Savior to the Nephites (probably 3 Nephi 11) on the necessity of authority and baptism, Oliver relates that it became apparent to them that "none had authority from God to administer the ordinances of the Gospel."[2]

On Friday, 15 May 1829, Joseph and Oliver retired to a nearby wooded area near the banks of the Susquehanna River in fulfillment of the prophecy of Joseph of old, the son of Jacob, that the lesser priesthood would be restored in the latter days by the administration of an angel in the bush. According to Joseph Smith, this ancient patriarch prophecied of blessings that "should come upon the seer of the last days and the scribe that should sit with him, and that should be ordained with him, *by the hands of the angel in the bush,* unto the *lesser* priesthood."[3] In this natural surrounding they knelt in humble prayer to "inquire of the Lord respecting baptism for the remission of sins, that [they] found mentioned in the translation of the plates" (JS-H 68).

It was not a casual interest to know "the Lord's position on this issue" that drove them into the woods that day, but a heartfelt personal desire to know "His will concerning [them]."[4] As Oliver Cowdery recollected, "our souls were drawn out in mighty prayer, to know how we might obtain the blessings of baptism and of the Holy Spirit according to the order of God; and we diligently sought for the right of the fathers, and the authority . . . to administer the same; for we desired to be followers of righteousness, and the possessors of greater knowledge, even the knowledge of the mysteries of the kingdom of God."[5]

In answer to their petition, John the Baptist, now a resurrected being, was sent to restore the Aaronic Priesthood on the earth. Oliver Cowdery eloquently captured the grandeur of this heavenly manifestation that followed their humble supplication:

> . . . after we had called on Him in a fervent manner, aside from the abodes of men, [He] condescended to manifest to us His will. On a sudden, as from the midst of eternity, the voice of the Redeemer spake peace to us, while the veil was parted and the angel of God came down clothed with glory, and delivered the anxiously looked for message, and the keys of the Gospel of repentance. What joy! what wonder! what amazement! While the world was racked and distracted—while millions were groping as the blind for the wall, and while all men were resting upon uncertainty, as a general mass, our eyes beheld, our ears heard, as in the "blaze of day"; yes, more—above the glitter of the May sunbeam, which then shed its brilliancy over the face of nature! Then his voice, though mild, pierced to the center, and his words, "I am thy fellow-servant," dispelled every fear. We listened, we gazed, we admired! 'Twas the voice of an angel from glory, 'twas a message from the Most High! And as we heard we rejoiced, while His love enkindled upon our souls, and we were wrapped in the vision of the Almighty! Where was room for doubt? Nowhere; uncertainty had fled, doubt had sunk no more to rise, while fiction and deception had fled forever![6]

Joseph Smith's less vivid but more informative account (although omitting the "voice of the Redeemer" that Oliver said spoke peace to them at the outset of the angel's visit[7]) related:

> A messenger from heaven descended in a cloud of light, and having laid his hands upon us, he ordained us, saying:
>
> Upon you my fellow servants, in the name of Messiah, I confer the Priesthood of Aaron, which holds the keys of the ministering of angels, and of the gospel of repentance, and of baptism by immersion for the remission of sins; and this shall never be taken again from the earth until the sons of Levi do offer again an offering unto the Lord in righteousness.
>
> He said this Aaronic Priesthood had not the power of laying on hands for the gift of the Holy Ghost, but that this should be conferred on us hereafter; and he commanded us to go and be baptized, and gave us directions that I should baptize Oliver Cowdery, and that afterwards he should baptize me. Accordingly we went and were baptized. I baptized him first, and afterwards he baptized me—after which I laid my hands upon his head and ordained him to the Aaronic Priesthood, and afterwards he laid his hands on me and ordained me to the same Priesthood—for so we were commanded.
>
> The messenger who visited us on this occasion, and conferred this Priesthood upon us, said that his name was John, the same that is called John the Baptist in the New Testament, and that he acted under the direction of Peter, James and John who held the keys of the Priesthood of Melchizedek, which Priesthood he said would in due time be conferred on us, and that I should be called the first Elder of the Church, and he (Oliver Cowdery) the second (JS-H 68-72).

## Authority and Keys Restored

Although John is loosely mentioned as having conferred "the Aaronic Priesthood," Joseph was specific in outlining the twofold nature of this confirmation saying, "he laid his hands upon my head, and *ordained me to a Priest* after the order of Aaron, *and to hold the keys* of this Priesthood."[8] Differentiating between the authority and the keys conferred on this occasion, Elder Bruce R. McConkie noted, "When John came, he did two things: He conferred upon Joseph and

Oliver the Aaronic Priesthood—he gave them authority. The second thing that he did was to give them the keys of the priesthood, the keys of presidency, the right to preside in the Aaronic Priesthood, and the right to authorize either themselves or someone else to use the priesthood, within the field and scope that people are entitled to use that particular priesthood."[9] As keys are not always conveyed when priesthood is conferred, President Joseph F. Smith emphasized that, "a distinction must be carefully made between the general authority, and the directing of the labors performed by that authority [i.e., keys]."[10]

## Authority of John the Baptist

For John to have conferred the authority and keys of the Aaronic Priesthood on Joseph and Oliver, he had to have possessed them himself. These powers he received in mortality, being the firstborn son in the lineage of Aaron (see D&C 84:27-28). While the tribe of Levi had a hereditary right to the Aaronic Priesthood, only the firstborn of the sons of Aaron had a legal right to the presidency or the keys of this priesthood. In speaking of the presidency of this priesthood a revelation in our day states: "No man has a legal right to this office, to hold the keys of this priesthood, except he be a literal descendant and the firstborn of Aaron" (D&C 68:18; cf. 107:16). In reference to John's authority, President Joseph Fielding Smith observed that "by divine right of descent, he was the rightful presiding priest of the Aaronic order in Israel. This authority had come to him by lineage. . . . Had the Church of God been in existence with the Jews in that day, instead of the Jews being in a dreadful state of apostasy, then John the Baptist would have taken his proper place as the presiding priest of the Aaronic order."[11] With the coming of John the Baptist, Joseph and Oliver received all of the rights of the Aaronic Priesthood that were vested in Aaron and were thus literally "called and ordained even as Aaron" (D&C 27:8).

## The Keys Held by the Aaronic Priesthood

In stating that the Aaronic Priesthood "holds the keys" of the gospel of repentance, etc., reference is being made to the rights and privileges associated with the authority of the Aaronic Priesthood and not to the *directing* keys of the priesthood. This is a second and more general usage of the word "key" as used in the scriptures. It is with this broader sense of the word "key" in mind that, in response to the question "What is a key?" Joseph F. Smith explained, "It is the right or privilege which *belongs to and comes with the Priesthood.* . . . It is the right to enjoy the blessing of communication with the heavens, and the privilege and authority to administer in the ordinances of the gospel of Jesus Christ, to preach the gospel of repentance, and of baptism by immersion for the remission of sins. That is a key. . . . We ordain boys . . . to that Priesthood which holds the keys of the ministering of angels and of the gospel of repentance and baptism by immersion for the remission of sin."[12] Thus every holder of the Aaronic Priesthood has certain rights and privileges (i.e., keys) according to his calling in that priesthood.

## Eternal Nature of the Aaronic Priesthood

The record of Joseph Smith that the Aaronic Priesthood is to remain on the earth "*until* the sons of Levi do offer again an offering unto the Lord in righteousness" (D&C 13, italics added) may suggest to some that the Aaronic Priesthood is only temporary. Oliver Cowdery's earlier account[13] is perhaps a bit more precise, using the word "that" instead of "until." In a special conference held 21 October 1848 in Kanesville, Iowa (now Council Bluffs), Oliver Cowdery, who had been excommunicated 11 April 1838, arose to seek forgiveness of the Church and bore this testimony: "I was present with Joseph when an holy angel from God came down from heaven and conferred on us, or restored the lesser or Aaronic Priesthood, and said to us at the same time, that *it should remain upon the earth while the earth stands.*"[14] This statement is consistent with the Lord's declaration that the Aaronic Priesthood "continueth and *abideth forever* with the priesthood which is after the holiest order of God" (D&C 84:18, italics added).

There are several ways in which the Aaronic Priesthood may be considered eternal in duration. In one respect everyone who holds the Melchizedek Priesthood also holds the Aaronic Priesthood for the following reasons:

(1) The greater comprehends the lesser so that all who hold the Melchizedek Priesthood *ipso facto* hold the Aaronic Priesthood.

(2) When a person receives the Aaronic Priesthood and

subsequently receives the Melchizedek Priesthood, none of the former authority is taken away.

In another respect it has been taught that the Church on earth, down to the office of Deacon, has been organized after the pattern of the Church which exists in Heaven.[15] This would imply that somewhere in our Father's house, there is a place for the ministration of this lesser order of the priesthood. At least one realm in which this priesthood will minister is in the earths that will always be passing through a temporal existence. With respect to the functioning of the Aaronic Priesthood on *this* earth after it has "passed away" and become celestialized, Joseph Fielding Smith has explained, "As long as we have temporal things on the earth this priesthood is necessary. Eventually, when the earth is celestialized, I suppose all priesthood will be of the higher order."[16]

### Fulfillment of Malachi's Prophecy

The promise that the sons of Levi would offer again an offering unto the Lord in righteousness is an allusion to the prophecy found in Malachi which the angel Moroni quoted to Joseph Smith saying, "Behold, I will send my messenger, and he shall prepare the way before me: and the Lord whom ye seek shall suddenly come to his temple. . . . And he shall sit as a refiner and purifier of silver: and *he shall purify the sons of Levi*, and purge them as gold and silver, *that they may offer unto the Lord an offering in righteousness*" (Mal. 3:1, 3, italics added). It was in partial fulfillment of this promise that, according to Joseph Fielding Smith, "John the Baptist came to Joseph Smith and Oliver Cowdery and gave them his priesthood, *thus preparing the way for the coming of the Lord.*"[17] When the Lord suddenly comes to his yet future temple in Jackson County, Missouri, he will purify the sons of Levi so that all of their offerings will be done in righteousness.

Section 84 of the Doctrine and Covenants reveals that all who receive and honor the Aaronic and Melchizedek Priesthoods "become the sons of Moses and Aaron" (v. 34), thereby becoming in effect the sons of Levi (Moses and Aaron were of the tribe of Levi). These sons of Levi, whether they be literal sons who receive the priesthood by right of descent or sons "according to the Holy Priesthood" (v. 6), "shall be filled with the glory of the Lord, upon Mount Zion in the Lord's house" (v. 32) where they "shall offer an acceptable offering and sacrifice in the house of the Lord" (v. 31).

Joseph Smith taught that the sacrifice to be offered by the sons of Levi will be, at least initially, an offering of the firstlings of the flock such as was practiced prior to the law of Moses. "These sacrifices," he observed, "as well as every ordinance belonging to the priesthood, will, when the Temple of the Lord shall be built, and the sons of Levi be purified, be fully restored and attended to in all their powers, ramifications, and blessings."[18] Joseph envisioned that the temple to be reared in the city of Zion would be a complex consisting of twelve temples, some of which would be dedicated to the lesser priesthood where ordinances such as blood sacrifice might be performed.[19] As to whether blood sacrifices will be permanently reinstated, Joseph Fielding Smith has explained: "blood sacrifices will be performed long enough to complete the restoration in this dispensation. Afterwards sacrifice will be of some other character."[20]

## The Melchizedek Priesthood Restored

### Date of Melchizedek Priesthood Restoration

The exact date of the restoration of the Melchizedek Priesthood is unknown. The Prophet records that he and Oliver "were forced to keep secret the circumstances of having received the priesthood . . . owing to a spirit of persecution which had already manifested itself in the neighborhood" (JS-H 74). In 1878, Orson Pratt and Joseph F. Smith visited David Whitmer, one of the three witnesses who was closely associated with the Prophet during this period. The first question Pratt asked Whitmer was, "Can you tell the date of the bestowal of the Apostleship upon Joseph, by Peter, James, and John?" David's answer was, "I do not know, Joseph never told me."[21]

The earliest explicit reference to the priesthood having been restored is found in D&C 18, given in June 1829. Joseph mentioned that this revelation was intended to "illustrate the nature of our calling to this priesthood, as well as that of others who were yet to be sought after."[22] In this revelation directed to Oliver Cowdery and David Whitmer the Lord said: "I speak unto you, even as unto Paul mine apostle, for you are called even with that same calling with which he was called" (D&C 18:9).

Because this revelation is dated simply *June 1829*, it has been difficult to establish the date of the restoration with any more precision than sometime between 15 May and the end of June, 1829. Recent research[23] shows evidence, however, that this event very likely occurred sometime between the 15th and 29th of May, 1829. The evidence in support of this conclusion is as follows:

> (1) Oliver Cowdery wrote a letter to Hyrum Smith dated 14 June 1829 which contained a considerable amount of wording identical to that found in section 18, strongly suggesting that the revelation contained in section 18 had been given by that time.
> (2) David Whitmer affirmed that Joseph and Oliver spent the month from 1 June to 1 July 1829 at the Whitmer farm, which is about three days journey from where the Melchizedek Priesthood was restored. Being busily occupied in the translation of the Book of Mormon, it is unlikely that they would have taken nearly a week sometime between the 1st and 14th of June to make a round-trip journey to Harmony.
> (3) With the likelihood that the priesthood was restored before Joseph and Oliver moved to Fayette where they arrived approximately 1 June, coupled with the fact that the distance was about three days, the probable time of the restoration is narrowed to between 15 May and 29 May.

## The Appearance of Peter, James, and John

Regrettably, there exists no detailed first-hand account of the restoration of the Melchizedek Priesthood other than to mention that it was restored by the two resurrected beings Peter and James, together with John the Beloved who had been translated. An interesting second-hand description of what transpired comes from Addison Everett in a letter he wrote in 1881. Brother Everett relates that he overheard a conversation between Joseph and his brother Hyrum a few days before their martyrdom in which Joseph told how he and Oliver had been arrested at Colesville for preaching and were being held at the home of the Justice of the Peace. Their attorney, Mr. Reid, helped them escape through a window as a mob had begun to gather in front of the house. Everett goes on to say, "it was night and they traveled through brush and water and mud, fell over logs, etc., until Oliver was exhausted; then Joseph helped him along through brush and water, almost carrying him. They traveled all night, and just at the break of day Oliver gave out entirely and exclaimed, "O Lord! Brother Joseph, how long have we got to endure this thing?" They sat down on a log to rest and Joseph said that at that very time Peter, James, and John came to them and ordained them to the Apostleship. They had 16 or 17 miles to go to get back to Mr. Hales, his father-in-law's, but Oliver did not complain any more of fatigue."[24]

Elder Erastus Snow gave a similar account of Joseph and Oliver's experience in a conference address delivered in 1882: "It was at a period when they were being pursued by their enemies and had to travel all night, and in the dawn of the coming day when they were weary and worn who should appear to them but Peter, James, and John, for the purpose of conferring upon them the Apostleship, the keys of which they themselves had held while upon the earth, which had been bestowed upon them by the Savior."[25]

## Adam's Role in the Restoration

Enlarging on the events attending the restoration of this priesthood, Joseph Fielding Smith has suggested (alluding to D&C 128:20) that Satan "appeared on the banks of the Susquehanna River to oppose the restoration of keys, and was detected by Michael, and his plans were thwarted."[26] That Michael, or Adam, played a major role in the restoration of both the Aaronic and Melchizedek Priesthood is evidenced by the fact that he holds "the keys of salvation" (D&C 78:16) for this earth. According to the Prophet's teachings,[27] whenever messengers are sent from heaven to establish a gospel dispensation and restore the priesthood it is by Adam's authority.

## Confirming the Priesthood on Each Other

Similar to the procedure followed in the restoration of the Aaronic Priesthood, in which Joseph and Oliver were commanded to ordain each other to the Aaronic Priesthood after having received it from John the Baptist, Oliver Cowdery testified, "I was also present with Joseph when the Melchizedek Priesthood was conferred by the angels of God . . . *which we then confirmed on each other by the will and commandment of God.*"[28] While repeating the ordination of the Aaronic Priesthood preserved the order of the kingdom which requires baptism to precede ordination, in the case of the Melchizedek Priesthood, Joseph and Oliver's confirmation of the priesthood on each other was apparently essential to comply with the law of common consent and possibly had reference to the occasion of the organization of the Church on 6 April 1830, at which time they ordained each other Elders by the common consent of the Church. This ordination was in fulfillment of John the Baptist's instruction that, after receiving the higher priesthood, Joseph was to be called the first Elder in the Church and Oliver the second Elder. This ordination was also in accordance with "the voice of God in the chamber of old Father Whitmer, in Fayette" (D&C 128:21), instructing Joseph and Oliver that the promise to receive the priesthood would not be fully realized until they ordain each other elders. Writing on the events occurring the latter part of June, 1829 (presumably after the visit from Peter, James, and John), and Prophet records:

> *We now become anxious to have that promise realized to us,* which the angel that conferred upon us the Aaronic Priesthood had given us, viz., *that provided we continue faithful, we should also have the Melchizedek Priesthood,* which holds the authority of the laying on of hands for the gift of the Holy Ghost. We had for some time made this matter a subject of humble prayer, and at length we got together in the chamber of Mr. Whitmer's house, in order more particularly to seek of the Lord what we now so earnestly desired; and here, to our unspeakable satisfaction, did we realize the truth of the Savior's promise—"Ask, and it shall be given you; seek, and ye shall find; knock, and it shall be opened unto you"—for we had not long been engaged in solemn and fervent prayer, when *the word of the Lord came unto us in the chamber, commanding us that I should ordain Oliver Cowdery to be an Elder in the Church of Jesus Christ; and that he also should ordain me to the same office;* and then to ordain others, as it should be made known unto us from time to time. We were, however, commanded to defer this our ordination until such times as it should be practicable to have our brethren, who had been and who should be baptized, assembled together, *when we must have their sanction to our thus proceeding to ordain each other,* and have them decide by vote whether they were willing

> to accept us as spiritual teachers or not; when also we were commanded to bless bread and break it with them, and to take wine, bless it, and drink it with them; afterward proceed to ordain each other according to commandment; then call out such men as the Spirit should dictate, and ordain them; and then attend to the laying on of hands for the gift of the Holy Ghost, upon all those whom we had previously baptized, doing all things in the name of the Lord.[29]

It appears puzzling that, in response to Joseph and Oliver's petition to receive the Melchizedek Priesthood, the Lord told them to proceed and ordain each other as soon as they obtained the consent of the other brethren without mentioning anything about waiting for Peter, James, and John to come. Accepting the premise that Peter, James, and John had already conferred the Melchizedek Priesthood on Joseph and Oliver, but that their ordination was not complete until they ordained each other, may help explain why the Lord gave these instructions.

## Authority and Keys Conferred

The revelations and accounts frequently speak of Joseph and Oliver as having been ordained to the *apostleship* under the hands of Peter, James, and John. The Lord told Joseph, "I have sent [Peter, James, and John] unto you, by whom I have *ordained you and confirmed you to be apostles*, and especial witnesses of my name, and bear the keys of your ministry and of the same things which I revealed unto them" (D&C 27:12). Regarding Joseph and Oliver's ordination to the Apostleship, Joseph Fielding Smith made this clarification: "These men were not ordained to the specific office in the priesthood, but received the priesthood itself out of which the offices come."[30] Since the offices are appendages to and grow out of the priesthood (D&C 107:5, 8), there would be no need for these messengers to ordain them to the office of apostle.

With the Melchizedek Priesthood restored, Joseph and Oliver could administer the higher ordinances of the gospel which communicate the spiritual blessings of the Church by which members can ultimately become sanctified and inherit eternal life (see D&C 84:20 and 107:18-19). In addition to the authority of the Melchizedek Priesthood which was restored, there were special keys and powers which the Lord gave Peter, James, and John and which were subsequently conferred by them on Joseph and Oliver. The Lord revealed, "I have committed [unto Peter, James, and John] the keys of my kingdom, and a dispensation of the gospel for the last times; and for the fulness of times" (D&C 27:13). Thus when these ancient apostles appeared to Joseph and Oliver, they declared themselves "as possessing the keys of the kingdom, and of the dispensation of the fulness of times" (D&C 128:20). Having received the keys of the kingdom, Joseph and Oliver could preside in the Melchizedek Priesthood and build up the Church or Kingdom upon the earth. The conferral of the keys of the dispensation of the fulness of times was an appointment for Joseph and Oliver to preside jointly over this last and most glorious dispensation. Aside from these keys being taken from Oliver when he lost his standing in the Church and given to Joseph's older brother Hyrum, these keys were not passed on to others, but continue to reside with Joseph and Hyrum. Presiding under Adam, who holds the keys of all dispensation under the direction of Jesus Christ, they will stand throughout eternity at the head of this dispensation.

## Conclusion

With the coming of John the Baptist to restore the Aaronic Priesthood, and Peter, James, and John to restore the Melchizedek Priesthood, the Lord declared: "The keys of the kingdom of God are committed unto man on the earth, and from thence shall the gospel roll forth unto the ends of the earth" (D&C 65:2). The impact that these priesthoods are destined to have on the earth has only begun to be realized. In a letter to his brother-in-law while yet out of the Church, Oliver Cowdery wrote this sober confession:

> I have cherished a hope, and that one of my fondest, that I might leave such a character as those who might believe in my testimony, after I should be called hence, might do so, not only for the sake of the truth, but might not blush for the private character of the man who bore that testimony. I have been sensitive on this subject, I admit, but I ought to be so; you would be, under the circumstances, had you stood in the presence of John with our departed brother Joseph, to receive the lesser priesthood, and in the presence of Peter, to receive the

> greater *and looked down through time, and witnessed the effects these two must produce*—you would feel, what you have never felt, were wicked men conspiring to lessen the effects of your testimony to man, after you have gone to your long sought rest.[31]

The restoration of the priesthood was more than simply one small part of the overall restoration "of all things, which God hath spoken by the mouth of all the holy prophets since the world began" (Acts 3:21). It established the channel through which the Lord will continue to bring to pass all of his holy purposes until the earth and all therein that are righteous are ultimately restored to the glory from which they fell.

---

## Notes

[1]Oliver Cowdery in *Messenger and Advocate,* 2 (October 1835): 199.

[2]*Ibid.*, 1 (October 1834):15.

[3]Cited in Joseph Fielding Smith, *Doctrines of Salvation,* comp. Bruce R. McConkie, 3 vols. (Salt Lake City, Bookcraft, 1954-56), 3:101. Oliver Cowdery testified of the fulfillment of this promise in 1835, stating: "We repaired to the woods, even as our father Joseph said we should, that is, to the bush, and called upon the name of the Lord" (*Ibid.*, p. 100).

[4]*TPJS,* p. 335.

[5]Smith, *Doctrines of Salvation,* 3:100.

[6]*Messenger and Advocate,* 1 (October 1834): 15.

[7]*Ibid.*, p. 16.

[8]*TPJS,* p. 335, italics added.

[9]Bruce R. McConkie, "The Keys of the Kingdom" (address to Wilford Stake Priesthood Meeting, 21 February 1955), p. 3, typescript, Special Collections, Harold B. Lee Library, Brigham Young University.

[10]Joseph F. Smith, *Gospel Doctrine,* 5th ed. (Salt Lake City, Deseret Book Co., 1939), p. 136.

[11]*Doctrines of Salvation,* 3:89.

[12]*Gospel Doctrine,* p. 142, italics added.

[13]*Messenger and Advocate,* 1 (October 1834):16.

[14]Journal of Reuben Miller, 21 October 1848 (Church Historian's Library), italics added.

[15]This view was widely taught by Church leaders up until about 50 years

ago (see *JD* 17:375; 18:138-39; 22:308-9, 333-34; *Conference Report*, April 1912, p. 51; *Ibid.*, October 1928, pp. 59-60; *Ibid.*, April 1933, p. 76). The teaching at least partially originated from a statement attributed to Joseph Smith that the Church on earth has been organized "according to the heavenly vision, and the pattern shown me from heaven" (Parley P. Pratt in *Millennial Star*, 5 [March 1845]:15).

[16]*Doctrines of Salvation*, 3:92.

[17]*Ibid.*, 3:12. The messenger spoken of by Malachi has also been interpreted as having reference to the mission of John the Baptist in mortality, Joseph Smith (*Ibid.*, 1:193), and even the Gospel (D&C 45:9).

[18]*TPJS*, p. 173. Although some have concluded that the Prophet had reference to the offering of the sons of Levi when he spoke all Church members presenting genealogical records to the Lord in the temple (D&C 128:24), it may be that the Prophet was merely using Malachi's prophecy as an analogy; i.e., just as the sons of Levi are to offer an acceptable offering unto the Lord, Joseph admonished Latter-day Saints to compile genealogical records likewise worthy of acceptation.

[19]*HC* 1:357-59.

[20]*Doctrines of Salvation*, 3:94.

[21]"Report of Elders Orson Pratt and Joseph F. Smith," *Deseret Evening News*, 11.302 (16 November 1878).

[22]*HC* 1:61-62.

[23]Larry C. Porter, "Dating the Restoration of the Melchizedek Priesthood," *Ensign*, June 1979, pp. 5-10.

[24]Letter of Addison Everett to Oliver B. Huntington, reproduced in *Young Woman's Journal*, 11 (November 1890): 75-76.

[25]*JD* 23:183.

[26]Joseph Fielding Smith, *Answers to Gospel Questions*, 5 vols. (Salt Lake City: Deseret Book Co., 1957-66), 1:177.

[27]*HC* 3:386; 4:207-8.

[28]Journal of Reuben Miller, October 21, 1848, italics added.

[29]*HC* 1:60-61, italics added.

[30]*Doctrines of Salvation*, 3:147. Brigham Young held the view that Joseph's ordination to the Apostleship signified that he was given the keys of the kingdom which are inherent in the Apostleship (*JD* 1:134-35).

[31]Letter of Oliver Cowdery to Phineas H. Young, Tiffin, Ohio, 23 March 1846, Church Archives.

# 9

# JESUS CHRIST AND THE COMMAND TO REPENT

## (D&C 18 and 19)

RODNEY TURNER

The dominant theme of sections 18 and 19 reflects the central message of the Book of Mormon: the divine mission of Jesus Christ and mankind's imperative need to repent and receive him by covenant. That such should be the case is understandable since sections 18 and 19 of the Doctrine and Covenants were received some nine months apart, during the period in which the translation of the Book of Mormon was completed and subsequently printed by E. B. Grandin.[1] The following month, on 6 April 1830, the Church of Christ[2] was organized and instructed to carry the message of the Book of Mormon to "both the Gentiles and also the house of Israel" (D&C 18:6).

Section 18 stresses the Lord's gentle but firm command to all mankind to repent by taking upon them his name so that they might inherit "the kingdom of my Father" (D&C 18:25, 46). Section 19 underscores this commandment by vividly describing the fate of those who ignore it. Thus, the first revelation is essentially positive in its approach while that of the second is somewhat negative. It reveals the dual mission of the Redeemer with great clarity. On the one hand he is a merciful Savior who has assumed the moral burden of every soul. On the other hand he is a just but demanding Judge whose wrath will be poured out without measure upon those who reject his sacrifice and refuse to repent.[3] Nowhere in all scripture is the atonement so graphically described, nor the need for repentance emphasized with more power and directness.

### The One True God

There is but one true God. All other deities worshipped by the myriad denominations, sects, and cults are mere phantoms fashioned from nothing in the minds of men and devils. But just as a mirage is a deceptive distortion of a distant reality, so are the false gods of this world multiple caricatures of the one true God. As such, they reflect—whether with crudity or sophistication—the once-possessed, but now lost key to all revealed religion. That key was given to Joseph Smith in his First Vision. He affirmed it again shortly before his martyrdom when he stated: "It is the first principle of the Gospel to know for a certainty the character of God, and to know that we may converse with him as one man converses with another."[4] The ministry of Jesus confirmed this statement, for he was God manifest in the flesh (see John 1:1, 14; D&C 93:3, 4). Only those who come to know "the only true God, and Jesus Christ" whom he sent will inherit eternal life (see John 17:3). The revelations of Joseph Smith make this knowledge available to all.

## The Only Name Given

Just as there is but one true God, so is there but one true name endowed by him with saving power: Jesus Christ. That name—first spoken in eternity—was reconfirmed in the days of Adam as "the only name which shall be given under heaven, whereby salvation shall come unto the children of men" (Moses 6:52). All other names, titles, and epithets applied to other supposed deities are spiritually impotent.

The restoration of the gospel of necessity involved the restoration of the saving name of Jesus Christ. Not, of course, the literal name familiar to all Christians, but the correct understanding of the personality behind that name, together with that authority and those doctrines and ordinances encompassed by it. For just as there are false gods, so are there false Christs or, rather, false concepts associated with him. Christ condemns those "who use the name of the Lord, and use it in vain, having not authority" (D&C 63:62). Therefore, we cannot receive Christ and validly take his name upon us without committing ourselves to the gospel as restored through Joseph Smith. The Lord made this clear to James Covill, a Baptist minister: "He that receiveth my gospel receiveth me; and he that receiveth not my gospel receiveth not me" (D&C 39:5).

The uniqueness of the name of Christ was understood by the Nephites in ancient America (see 2 Ne. 25:20; Mosiah 3:17; 5:8) and is emphatically reaffirmed in D&C 18:21-25. This revelation calls upon Oliver Cowdery and David Whitmer to "search out the Twelve" who were to function as special witnesses of Christ and his gospel throughout the world (see D&C 18:26-42).[5]

Thus the Church—those called out of the world into the kingdom of God—consists of those who, in taking upon themselves his name, become his spiritual children (see Mosiah 5:7) or, in the aggregate, the bride of Christ (see Isa. 62:5; Matt. 9:15; John 3:28, 29; Rev. 19:7, 8). They have entered into a binding and eternal covenant with him. In doing so, they pledge to replicate within their own characters and lives those attributes and principles he personifies. In other words, the acceptance of the name is nothing less than a commitment to eventually becoming perfect as he is perfect. This is why the resurrected Savior asked his Nephite disciples the rhetorical question: "What manner of men ought ye to be? Verily I say unto you, even as I am" (3 Ne. 27:27). And this is why he, in speaking of the Latter-day Saints, said: "I will raise up unto myself a pure people" (D&C 100:16). "Holiness to the Lord" has ever been the watchword and shibboleth of those who would attain unto the presence of the Father, the "Man of Holiness" (see Moses 6:57; 7:35). Indeed, in his intercessory prayer, Jesus prayed that all who believed on his name "may be one; as thou, Father, art in me, and I in thee, that they also may be one in us" (John 17:21).

This divine unity is the grand objective of the restored gospel of Jesus Christ. For while men may, of themselves, achieve a measure of goodness as the world defines the term, no one can achieve *holiness* in any other way than by lawfully taking upon himself the redeeming name of Christ in the only church on earth authorized by him to act in his behalf (see D&C 1:30; 23:7). Those who do so will inherit a mansion in the celestial kingdom. For they have become sanctified through "the law of Christ" (D&C 88:21). Becoming holy, they are prepared to dwell with the "Man of Holiness." Those who fail to do so, yet who are capable of receiving a lesser glory (see D&C 88:21-24), will eventually repent in terms of terrestrial or telestial law and acknowledge the name designated by the Father for the salvation of his children. For in due time every knee shall bow and every tongue confess that Jesus is the Christ, that all were saved through him (see Isa. 45:23; Phil. 2:10, 11; Mosiah 27:31; and D&C 88:104).[6]

**The Word of My Power**

The eternal plans and purposes of God the Father become

accomplished realities through Jesus Christ, the living embodiment of the Father's will. Thus the Only Beogtten is referred to as "the word of my power" (Moses 1:32, 35), meaning that the Father conferred his spiritual powers upon his Son, so that he might be capacitated to fulfill those vital missions which lie at the very heart of the plan of salvation.[7] "And he received all power, both in heaven and in earth, and the glory of the Father was with him, for he dwelt in him" (D&C 93:17).

The unending work and ever-increasing glory of the Father is centered in the immortality and eternal life of man (see Moses 1:39). The atonement and resurrection wrought by Jesus Christ, "the Word, even the messenger of salvation—the light and the Redeemer of the world; the Spirit of truth" (D&C 93:8, 9) is indispensible to the Father, who is added upon in glory by and through his Son (see D&C 45:4; 76:24; 132:63; and John 13:31, 32). However, each needs the other: as the Father is glorified through the Son, so is the Son glorified through the Father (see John 17:1). In like manner worthy Saints will be glorified through their children and their children through their parents (see D&C 88:60).

## Judge of the Quick and the Dead

The Father appointed Christ to be the final judge of both the living and the dead (see D&C 76:68; 77:12; Acts 10:42). This right is his by virtue of his perfect obedience to the Father's will, including the bitter cup of the atonement. Jesus drank that cup to its dregs so that "I might subdue all things unto myself—retaining all power, even to the destroying of Satan and his works at the end of the world, and the last great day of judgment, which I shall pass upon the inhabitants thereof" (D&C 19:2, 3). Having "bought" the human family with his own blood, the Redeemer is justified in "judging every man according to his works and the deeds which he hath done" (D&C 19:3; see 1 Cor. 6:19, 20).

Paradoxically, it is the judgment of Christ which enables him to save all mankind with the exception of the sons of Perdition. For had it not been for his sacrifice, there would have been no resurrection of the body, and the spirits of all men would have become angels to the devil (see 2 Ne. 9:7-9). Clearly, the Savior sacrificed himself to become our Judge in order to save us from endless physical and spiritual death. He willingly laid down his life so that he might exercise the power of immortality vested in him by his Father and take that life up again (see John 10:17, 18). In doing so, Christ broke the bands of physical death for all mankind; his resurrection assures our resurrection as well (see John 5:28, 29; 12:24, 32; 1 Cor. 15:20-23)

Those who accept and are faithful to the gospel covenant will stand at the Lord's "right hand"—the hand of mercy. "Having been cleansed by the blood of the Lamb" (Morm. 9:6), they enjoy a fulness of the remission of sins and are spared the demands of eternal justice (see D&C 29:27; Mosiah 5:8, 9). However, "weeping, wailing and gnashing of teeth" await those who, having failed to repent, "are found on my left hand" (D&C 19:5; Mosiah 5:9-12). These hapless souls must suffer the relative demands of justice—described by the Lord in deliberately fear-provoking terms as "endless torment" and "eternal damnation" so "that it might work upon the hearts of the children of men" to their ultimate salvation (D&C 19:6, 7; see 43:25).

## Eternal Punishment

The Lord's explanation that such terms as endless, eternal and everlasting punishment are to be interpreted qualitatively rather than quantitatively is a marked departure from the widespread belief of many Christians that the wicked are doomed to suffer in a hell of infinite duration. Happily, such is not the case. Divine justice recognizes the fact that no sin committed by *finite* man warrants an *infinite* punishment. Therefore, the expression eternal punishment is in contradistinction to those punishments meted out by men. The quality of God's punishment is transcendently superior to that of men, being truly redemptive in nature. Its purpose is not only to meet the demands of injured justice but to allow mercy, on conditions of repentance, to claim its own. Salvation through reformation is the grand goal of eternal punishment.

When repentance is not forthcoming, however, either in this world or the next, mercy is rendered helpless and justice has full sway. This is why the Lord commands all men to repent lest they suffer the fulness of his wrath and those "exquisite" sufferings attendant thereto. Nothing Satan can inflict on any sinner can begin to compare with the pains resultant from God's wrath (see D&C 19:15-17; Mosiah 2:38; Alma

12:13-15; Morm. 9:3-5).

## The Atoning Sacrifice

The Savior's own description of the sufferings he endured in his atoning sacrifice is totally unique to the Doctrine and Covenants (see D&C 19:16-19; Luke 22:44). His words constitute his personal witness to the reality of that awesome event which cannot be gainsayed. They also reveal the fact that those who never repent will "suffer even as I" (D&C 19:17).

Since Jesus suffered in "both body and spirit," it follows that the unrepentant will do likewise.[8] And this can only occur after their spirits and bodies have been reunited in the resurrection. While the unjust who are heirs of the telestial kingdom will be obliged to pay for their sins prior to their eventual salvation, it is questionable if their sufferings will equal those of the Savior.[9] In time they *do* repent. Such is not the case with the resurrected sons of Perdition (such as Cain) who "willeth to abide in sin, and altogether abideth in sin" and who, therefore, "must remain filthy still" (D&C 88:35, 102). These will suffer the fulness of the wrath of God in both body and spirit.

While heirs of the telestial kingdom will partake of a portion of the second spiritual death prior to their redemption (see D&C 63:17, 18; 76:84, 104-6), only those termed "the filthy still" will suffer its fulness—not because God refuses to forgive them, but because "they repent not" (D&C 29:44; see also 29:27, 28; 76:44). Satan has sealed them unto himself (Alma 34:35). Yet the sufferings of even these lawless souls may eventually come to an end; their ultimate fate is unknown (see D&C 29:29, 30; 43:33; 76:45-48).

### A Divine Sacrifice

"I, God, have suffered these things for all" (D&C 19:16), removed all doubt as to the nature of Jesus Christ. He was God incarnate, in the flesh. It was God who agonized in body and spirit, who sweat blood and who was crucified on Golgotha. Jesus was no mere mortal man. "For in him dwelleth all the fulness of the Godhead bodily" (Col. 2:9). Therefore, as Amulek testified, "it shall not be a human sacrifice; but it must be an infinite and eternal sacrifice" (Alma 34:10).

Only a God can fully comprehend the things of God (see Isa. 55:8,

9). Consequently, the depths of the atonement are unfathomable to us mortals. Yet it seems that since the Son was one with the Father, serving as his surrogate and messenger, he represented the Father in the atonement as in all other things. Jesus did for his Father that which his Father could not do himself. The Father could not shed his blood for the sins of mankind, for he had no blood to shed. Nor could he lay down his life in the manner Jesus did. The Father was a resurrected being whose spirit and flesh were "inseparably connected" (D&C 93:33) and "never to be divided" (Alma 11:45).

Such was not the case with Jesus at that time. Thus the great atoning sacrifice was a supreme, vicarious ordinance in behalf of both the Father and his children. The Father sent his Beloved Son because he could not come himself; he gave his Only Begotten because he could not give himself. And this was in accordance with the plan of redemption which had been formulated by the gods before the foundation of the world was laid. The atonement was an ordinance of God, and God alone.[10]

## The Pains of All Men

The mystery of the atonement, whereby the Son of Man took upon himself the sins of the world, is unrevealed. We know *what* he did, but we do not know *how* he did it. The Lord testified, "I, God, have suffered these things for all" (D&C 19:16). Joseph Smith stated that "the scriptures say what they mean, and mean what they say."[11] Christ atoned for every soul born into mortality. The number, however large, is still finite. The atonement, being infinite, easily encompasses all the sins of this world and all other worlds which look to him for salvation (see D&C 76:24).[12]

The question as to whether the Redeemer atoned for the specific sins of each soul, or whether mankind was granted a general amnesty for its collective sins on conditions of individual repentance cannot be answered with certitude. Jacob declared: "He suffereth the pains of all men, yea, every living creature, both men, women, and children, who belong to the family of Adam" (2 Ne. 9:21). As each ordinance of salvation is necessarily performed on an individual basis, so may the Savior have possessed an awareness of each soul for whom he was being sacrificed. While this may seem an incredible feat even for the Lord, through the power of the Holy Ghost, Moses was given a vision in which he "beheld the earth, yea, even all of it, and there was not a particle of it which he did not behold, discerning it by the spirit of God. And he beheld also the inhabitants thereof, and there was *not a soul* which he beheld not; and he discerned them by the Spirit of God" (Moses 1:27, 28).

Having ascended above all things after having descended below all things, Christ—the embodiment of the "light" or "Spirit" of truth—is "in all things and through all things" (see D&C 88:6-13, 41; 93:20, 26). As his Spirit permeates all reality, so did his atonement permeate all reality. For when he suffered, creation itself responded (see 1 Ne. 19:12; Moses 7:48, 56). If Moses was empowered to discern every individual soul on the earth at a given time, may not the Son of Man have been aware of the sins of each of his brothers and sisters for whom he was laying down his very life? The apostle Paul identified himself with the Savior in a most personal way: "I am crucified with Christ: nevertheless I live; yet not I, but Christ liveth in me: and the life which I now live in the flesh I live by the faith of the Son of God, who loved me, and gave himself for me" (Gal. 2:20).

Who can measure the worth of a human soul? Brigham Young stated: "The least, the most inferior spirit now upon the earth, in our capacity, is worth worlds."[13] Who can doubt it? The greatest evidence of the value of each child of God is the fact that the Redeemer "suffered the pain of all men, that all men might repent and come unto him. . . . And how great is his joy in the soul that repenteth!" (D&C 18:11, 13). Such is the glorious message of sections 18 and 19 of the Doctrine and Covenants.

## Notes

[1]A letter from Oliver Cowdery to Hyrum Smith, dated 14 June 1829, contains extracts from section 18. See Robert J. Woodford, "The Historical Development of the Doctrine and Covenants" (unpublished Ph.D. dissertation, Brigham Young University, April 1974), p. 264.

[2]The original name of the LDS Church was the Church of Christ. In May 1834, the name was changed to the Church of the Latter-day Saints, which was retained until a revelation given on 17 April 1838 confirmed its present name

(see *HC* 2:62-63; D&C 115:3).

[3]Joseph Smith wrote: "Our heavenly Father is more liberal in His views, and boundless in His mercies and blessings, than we are ready to believe or awful in the executions of His punishments, and more ready to detect every false way, than we are apt to suppose Him to be" (*TPJS*, p. 257). Martin Harris (D&C 19:15, 20) experienced this fact for himself.

[4]*TPJS*, p. 345.

[5]Martin Harris joined Cowdery and Whitmer in February 1835 in fulfilling this assignment.

[6]The term, saved, is usually employed in scripture in a relative rather than an absolute sense. The plan of salvation encompassed all three kingdoms of glory as described in D&C 76. Joseph Smith taught: "There is a salvation for all men, either in this world or the world to come. . . . Every spirit in the eternal world can be ferreted out and saved. . . . Jesus will save all except the sons of perdition" (*TPJS*, pp. 356-58).

[7]In D&C 29:30 the "word of my power" is equated with the "power of my Spirit." Jesus enjoyed a fulness of the Spirit (see JST, John 3:34; D&C 93:15-17; and *TPJS*, p. 188).

[8]Inasmuch as the fall of Adam involved the transgression of both spiritual and physical law, the atonement was likewise spiritual and physical in nature. Hence, Jesus suffered in "both body and spirit"—first in Gethsemane and, thereafter, in all that he endured in connection with his crucifixion.

[9]This does not mean that the wicked who are eventually saved will escape God's wrath. Alma described his own spiritual agony in terms identical to those found in D&C 19:15: "Yea, I say unto you, my son, that there could be nothing so exquisite and so bitter as were my pains" (Alma 36:21).

[10]The Book of Mormon speaks of "Christ, the Son, and God the Father, and the Holy Spirit, which is one eternal God" (Alma 11:44; see also D&C 20:28 and the Testimony of the Three Witnesses in the Book of Mormon).

[11]*TPJS*, p. 264.

[12]See Bruce R. McConkie, *Mormon Doctrine*, 2nd ed. (Salt Lake City: Bookcraft, 1966), p. 65.

[13]*JD* 9:124.

# 10

# THE ORGANIZATION REVELATIONS

## (D&C 20, 21, and 22)

RICHARD LLOYD ANDERSON

What is the "most distinguishing feature of The Church of Jesus Christ of Latter-day Saints"? President David O. McKay gave a succinct answer: "divine authority by direct revelation."[1] The three revelations surrounding church organization give the same answer. The longest is section 20, prepared as a declaration of doctrine and practice. Its two important satellites are section 21, given on the founding day to clarify the position of the Prophet, and section 22, given soon afterward to explain the need for rebaptism by the power of the restored priesthood. All these revelations can be called the "constitution" of the Restored Church. But by length and intent, this title really belongs to section 20, with the following sections as valuable amendments. Section 20 is one of the few long revelations in the Doctrine and Covenants, a sure indication of its importance. Nothing longer had been given before the Church was formally established.[2]

The first page of the first Latter-day Saint periodical printed section 20 with the title, "The Articles and Covenants of the Church of Christ."[3] Because section 22 is appended there, some historians feel that this title applied to both sections. But evidence does not bear this out, since only one other primary manuscript includes section 22 with section 20.[4] Otherwise "The Articles and Covenants" is applied solely to section 20. That is the case in its June, 1833 reprint in *The Evening and Morning Star,* in its heading in the 1833 *Book of Commandments,* and in the 1835-36 Kirtland reprints of the June, 1832 and June, 1833 issues of the *Star.* Was section 22 included at first in "The Articles and Covenants," dropping out later? More probably, the first printers in Missouri were away from the Prophet and included the short message on baptismal authority as a matter of logic. A year later the same editors printed "Articles and Covenants" above section 20 in the Book of Commandments, with section 22 printed separately. Thus when early journals, minutes, and priesthood licenses mention "The Articles and Covenants of the Church," they are likely referring only to section 20.[5] In 1835 and 1844, the chronological arrangement of the Book of

Commandments was altered by placing the main doctrinal and priesthood revelations directly after the revealed preface. Then section 20 appeared as the second document in the Doctrine and Covenants, consistent with its prominence from the beginning.[6] The first general conference after organization was 9 June 1830, and the minutes read: "Articles and Covenants read by Joseph Smith, Jr. and received by unanimous voice of the whole congregation." This emphasis was repeated in the next conference of 26 September 1830: "Articles and Covenants read by Br. Oliver Cowdery."[7]

There are more eloquent revelations in the Doctrine and Covenants. After all, America's Declaration of Independence is more vibrant than its Constitution. But few revelations will repay study with so many spiritual dividends as section 20. Its main parts are a review of the historical revelations of the restoration, followed by a statement of distinctive beliefs, and concluded by the longer section of sacred ordinances and priesthood government. These last two subjects need less discussion here because section 20 treats them with full detail.[8]

## The Restoration Revelations

The opening segment (D&C 20:1-16) stresses the visions that brought about the Book of Mormon. The angel's coming to Joseph Smith is seen in a brilliant verbal photograph (D&C 20:6-8), fully explained later in the motion pictures of the Prophet's historical narratives.[9] Likewise, the vision of the Book of Mormon witnesses is glimpsed: "Confirmed to others by the ministering of angels, and is declared unto the world by them" (D&C 20:10).[10] The First Vision is also identified in a most important historical reference. Joseph Smith fell into transgression "after it was truly manifested unto this first elder that he had receive a remission of his sins" (D&C 20:5). So the sequence is clearly a revelation of forgiveness, further transgression, and then "after repenting . . . God ministered unto him by an holy angel" (D&C 20:6). Joseph Smith's vision narratives detail his repentance before the 1823 coming of Moroni, but the "Articles and Covenants" tells that God's pardon was earlier "manifested," a term generally synonymous with "revealed" in the Doctrine and Covenants. There is no doubt about Joseph's thinking on the subject, for in his diary accounts of 1832 and 1835, he personally related the glorious First Vision as including divine assurance of forgiveness of sins, followed by lapsing into transgression, and then the 1823 coming of the angel revealing the Book of Mormon.[11] Thus the First Vision was briefly noted from the beginning of the Church, but in terse language that those informed would understand.

The review of revelations closes with the testimony that "we, the elders of the Church, have heard and bear witness to the words of the glorious Majesty on high" (D&C 20:16). Literalism just seen in listing the other supernatural experiences goes against interpreting these words allegorically. The presiding elders are named in the opening language, and they stood together in the woods when "the voice of the Lord commanded us" to bear record of the revelation and translation of the Book of Mormon.[12] In a similar setting they had prayed for priesthood authority, when "the voice of the Redeemer spake peace to us," followed by the angelic ordination by John the Baptist.[13] And after the similar coming of ancient apostles, they were authorized to use the restored apostleship by "the voice of God in the chamber of old Father Whitmer," where Joseph and Oliver were translating the Book of Mormon (D&C 128:21).[14] In summary, the 1830 Articles and Covenants surveyed the same events that the Prophet gave in his 1832 journal and also in his history, which he began in 1838 specifically to review his calling as a Prophet. All three accounts begin with some form of "the rise of the Church of Christ," followed by the story of how it was set up by God and not man. These three histories review the First Vision, the revelations resulting in the Book of Mormon, and the restoration of priesthood authority to establish the modern Church. Thus in phrases compressed with meaning, the founding document consciously paraphrases Paul's review of revelation that would bring "so great salvation" because it was based on divine "signs and wonders," and many "miracles" (Heb. 2:3-4). Just as the apostles' authority was validated by the miraculous events of the Gospels and Acts, modern apostles testified together of the revealed reality of "so great witnesses" (D&C 20:13) in calling a world to God's renewed work.

## Articles of Faith and Doctrine

The next segment of section 20 presents articles of faith. Like the fuller Articles of Faith done in Nauvoo, they can be better understood by agreements and disagreements with the prevalent Protestant creeds. Joseph and his family were involved with the Methodist and Presbyterian churches. So their statements of belief are points of departure for the Latter-day Saint Articles and Covenants. The LDS format has marked similarities, though content deeply differs. Protestant creeds generally began with God and moved to the fall, Christ's redemption, the saving ordinances, and the believer's moral duties. That also summarizes D&C 20:17-26. But this simple LDS credo eliminates all language about the God "without body" and "parts" as well as the strong descriptions that the Father and Son are together "one substance."[15] Indeed, these phrases come from the later Christian councils, not the scriptures. Joseph said that in 1820 the First Vision taught him the error of Christian creeds, and in 1830 he avoided their nonscriptural language in the first statement of Latter-day Saint beliefs.

Is "Mormonism" Christian? Fully half of its first articles of faith (D&C 20:17-26) concentrate on the reality of Christ's mission and how one gains the benefits of his atonement. The oldest continuous test of Christian belief is the Apostles Creed, a blending of convictions about Christ known to have circulated from the early second century.[16] Since section 20 repeats most of these basics on Christ's mission (vv. 21-24), Latter-day Saints should clearly be classed as early Christian. Section 20 then sets out to wash away the later sediments that formed on the bedrock of Christ's saving work.

The doctrines of "justification" and "sanctification" through Christ's grace are affirmed, a necessity because they are prominent in the apostles' letters. They explain that all are considered forgiven or "just" through their acceptance of Christ's plan of salvation, and that by continued faithfulness they may become holy, the literal meaning of "sanctify." New Testament letters are not primarily letters of rejoicing but of exhorting—asking believers in Christ to retain their holiness of life and increase in it.[17] Thus in the Articles and Covenants, "there is a possibility that man may fall from grace" (D&C 20:32). This negates the Presbyterian formula that those "effectually called and sanctified by his Spirit can neither totally nor finally fall away from the state of grace."[18] But in Latter-day Saint doctrine, human agency chooses, and even God's decree cannot modify it. In the Articles and Covenants, man's choice links with God's grace but is not a mere result of it. Protestant theory generally defines the moral life as a desirable result of the Holy Spirit but does not insist that salvation hangs on tough decisions of self-control. Thus in section 20, salvation demands the grace of Christ, but also baptism, followed by individual performance to "endure in faith to the end" (D&C 20:25).[19]

Section 20 also attacks traditional theology on the idea of complete statements of belief. The Westminster Confession freezes "the whole counsel of God"—meaning "all things necessary for . . . man's salvation, faith, and life"—into the cubicle of the listed 66 books of the Bible, "unto which nothing at any time is to be added, whether by new revelations of the Spirit, or traditions of men."[20] Echoes of a completed canon and closed system also come in the Methodist articles, where existing scriptures "contain all things necessary to salvation."[21] But the Prophet told an inquirer that "the first and fundamental principle of our holy religion is, that we believe that we have a right to embrace all, and every item of truth, without limitation or without being circumscribed or prohibited by the creeds or superstitious notions of men"—provided it comes "by any manifestation, whereof we know that it has come from God."[22] This became a major theme of Joseph's striking Nauvoo discourses, but it was just as clear at the foundation, when the Articles and Covenants declared faith both in past "holy scriptures" and also in the call of new prophets "in this age and generation, as well as in generations of old" (D&C 20:11). John's warning not to add (Rev. 22:18-19) was seen as cautioning men and not shackling God, whose revelations would "come hereafter by the gift and power of the Holy Ghost, the voice of God, or the ministering of angels" (D&C 20:35).

## The Expansion of Section 20

Critics ridicule later additions in section 20, but they have not faced the open-ended principle of continuing revelation. As a basic statement of doctrine and practice, section 20 has been rephrased far more than other revelations. And some additions, principally vv. 65-67, update the expanding priesthood offices of the Church. Thus the first high priests were ordained in 1831, so reference to this office was later inserted in the 1830 Articles. Yet there was no attempt to mislead, for the earliest printing of this revision was subtitled, "With a few items from other revelations," meaning the changes to section 20, for no parts of any other sections were printed then.[23] Indeed, section 20 had grown with the Church, for Aaronic Priesthood restoration made baptism operative after 15 May 1829,[24] as described by Joseph Smith, though he also said that the full use of the Melchizedek Priesthood was not authorized until some time later.[25] A document giving 1829 Church practice was written by Oliver Cowdery and is the forerunner of Section 20. It remarkably fulfilled his blessing of section 8 to receive a "knowledge of the ancient records," for by the spirit of revelation he compiled and explained church ordinances from the Book of Mormon, opening with "A commandment from God unto Oliver how he should build up his Church." Instructions on baptism and the sacrament were given, and directions on ordaining teachers and priests. It closed: "Written in the year of our Lord and Savior 1829—a true copy of the Articles of the Church of Christ. O.C."[26] In his aged years, David Whitmer expended much ink in arguing that "high priests" had been added to section 20, not remembering that "elders" had to be added to an earlier draft after that priesthood was authorized by the voice of God.[27]

Thus the basic format of section 20 preceded the formal organization of the Church, as Joseph Smith wrote in indicating that the Lord gave a revelation that "pointed out to us the precise day" of incorporation.[28] The 1833 Book of Commandments gave June, 1830 as the date of the revelation, though this could be the final form. Yet there is no proof of a late revision, so it is safer to follow Joseph Smith's chronology, for his history arranged the revelations in sequence, and he approved listing section 20 before the March, 1830 revelation (D&C 19). The Book of Commandments was published over 800 miles from Joseph Smith's residence and is not necessarily accurate in its headings, since several locations and dates were corrected in the Kirtland edition of the Doctrine and Covenants. One interesting dating problem within the revelation concerns the meaning of the Church organized "one thousand eight hundred and thirty years since the coming of our Lord and Savior Jesus Christ in the flesh" (D&C 20:1). Does this give the exact year of Christ's birth? That calculation places too much weight on what may have been an elaborate phrase of dating or an incidental statement. The first edition of the Doctrine and Covenants Commentary cautioned against using this to prove that Christ was born at the exact beginning of the Christian Era; so have Bible scholars J. Reuben Clark and Bruce R. McConkie.[29] Part of the problem is that Christ was alive at the death of Herod the Great, an event of 4 B.C. in careful chronologies.

## D&C 21: The Prophet's Position

Joseph Smith's 1838-39 recollections of church organization seem clearly superior to David Whitmer's, made almost 50 years after that time. The latter rationalized his "congregational" position by minimizing the Prophet's authority, claiming that the main reason the young church organized was to obtain legal status for marriages and holding of church property.[30] That is evidently part of the picture, since the Articles mention "being regularly organized . . . agreeable to the laws of our country" (D&C 20:1). But the same preface stresses the "will and commandments of God," similar phraseology to Joseph Smith's history of the founding day. Was there a divine purpose transcending the attempt to establish a legal corporation? Section 21 was given the day of organization and gives an organizational answer. Before 6 April 1830, there were believers, some baptized, in three major areas, Manchester-Palmyra, Fayette, and Colesville, just north of the Pennsylvania border. Whitmer argued that these branches functioned well with cooperative priesthood direction. Certainly Joseph had led by the prestige of his revelations, but where was his position specifically defined? By the revelation known as section 21, Joseph was designated to be ordained by Oliver Cowdery as "a seer" and "a prophet," the "first" elder in relationship to fellow-founder Oliver Cowdery (D&C 21:1, 11).[31] Thus Joseph Smith was authorized to give "commandments" to the Church, which it was obligated to receive "as if from my own mouth" (D&C 21:4-5). So like the Constitutional Convention of the United States, the founding meeting of the Church established central executive government, a presiding prophet as head.

As Joseph's leadership was challenged in later situations, it was reinforced in further revelations. But the doctrinal constitution of section 20 has the important organizational supplement of section 21, showing that the church membership approves presiding priesthood, which is the proper agency for originating official doctrine. Section 21 was sealed with the power of the Spirit, for the recollections of that day report harmony and inspiration. The Prophet remembered the setting for the revelation: "The Holy Ghost was poured out upon us to a very great degree—some prophesied, whilst we all praised the Lord and rejoiced exceedingly."[32] Joseph Knight, Sr., added in reference to the same revelation: "They all kneeled down and prayed, and Joseph gave them instructions how to build up the Church and exhorted them to be faithful in all things, for this is the work of God."[33]

## D&C 22: Rebaptism Required

The founding documents link the power of prophecy with the power of a presiding Prophet, the blending of divine revelation and divine authority. The new Church was unschooled in these principles, for section 22 soon came to explain what restored priesthood meant in relationship to baptism. Joseph's history gives the setting of applications for membership right after the organization meeting. His mention of his mother is intriguing. In her early marriage she was miraculously healed after a personal revelation assured her she would not die. Disagreeing with any church she knew, she nevertheless found "a minister who was willing to baptize me, and leave me free in regard to joining any religious denomination."[34] Whether or not she was one who raised the question concerning rebaptism, her case illustrates the sincerity of baptisms performed by other churches. The heading of section 22 is not just the surmise of commentary but rephrases the heading printed in the Book of Commandments, Kirtland Doctrine and Covenants, and the Prophet's history: "Given . . . in consequence of some desiring to unite with the Church without rebaptism, who had previously been baptized." It is instructive to see the Prophet's history agree with earlier versions of the circumstances of section 22, but change the location from Fayette to Manchester. This conscious correction of data in Joseph's history shows a care which should lead historians to favor the sequence of revelations there also. This requirement of rebaptism is placed in his history in a five-day space after church organization, showing the immediate need to rule on the exclusive nature of priesthood ordinances of the restoration.

Section 22 ties to a passage in the book of Acts that puzzles commentators. On Paul's last eastern missionary journey, he rebaptized those who were already "disciples" (Acts 19:1-6). This last term in Acts indicates that they already believed in Jesus, so rebaptism "in the name" logically means not mere use, but proper employment of Christ's name, or its authorized use.[35] Roger Williams was typical of American restorationists who considered Christian baptisms invalid until new authority should be sent from God. And the first harvest of converts to the restored Church in Northern Ohio was great because many seekers agreed with Latter-day Saint testimony that biblical ordinances were invalid without restored authority.[36] After church organization, New York converts learned the same lesson as new revelation outdated old baptisms. From the beginning Joseph was consistent in claiming that no other church could validly perform gospel ordinances. Specifically, his history places section 22 between Tuesday, the church organization day, and the following Sunday, when a number of others were baptized.[37]

Churches lax on the necessity of baptism would naturally not stress divine authority in administering it. However, baptism stands out in modern revelation as the foundation covenant for salvation. And to bring about this eternal result, the following conditions must be met: full repentance as measured by a worthy life before baptism (D&C 20:37),[38] a condition that makes infant baptism unnecessary (D&C 20:71); the proper form of immersion (D&C 20:73-74); and performance by the true priesthood, a condition important enough to be stressed in words of the ceremony (D&C 20:73). Christian churches regularly use the trinitarian formula, since it is commanded by the Savior (Matt. 28:19-20), but Latter-day Saints are distinctive in adding words of authority to the baptismal prayer: "Having been commissioned of Jesus Christ" (D&C 20:73).[39]

Theologians have resisted baptism as an essential element of salvation because a ceremony would thus be valued higher than inner faith or righteousness. But since Latter-day Saints view baptism as a covenant expressing faith and a means to virtue, ritual and reality are designed to blend. This covenant is a profound causal factor, a personal and social commitment, the specific obligations of which continue in the covenant of the Lord's Supper (D&C 20:37 and 20:77). Because the latter is the most visible and oft-repeated of all sacraments, it is for

Latter-day Saints *the* Sacrament. But for them it is not the mystical sacrifice of the Roman Catholic Mass, or the focus on Communion that gives the Protestant hope for divine companionship. For the Latter-day Saint the Sacrament is an inspired personal promise for growth. Thus "the duty of the members after they are received by baptism" is overall "works and faith" (D&C 20:68-69). This "duty" of modern disciples matches the challenge in New Testament epistles to desert the old "conversation" (Gal. 1:13; Eph. 4:22), a Greek term *(anastrophē)* meaning a way of life and not merely communication. Thus baptism commits one to a lifetime of being inspired by Christ and living up to his standards "by a godly walk and conversation" (D&C 20:69). These last two nouns are synonymous, since "conversation" is there used in the older sense of the King James Bible.

### Summary

In perspective, the three revelations associated with church organization proclaim neither revelation only nor authority only, but the bonding of the two. New revelation restored lost knowledge and the authority to reestablish the divine organization and ceremonies so fully described in the Book of Mormon (Moro. chapters 1-6). This first priesthood handbook, the Articles and Covenants, is supplemented by the next two sections clarifying the presiding keys of the Prophet, and the only valid priesthood of the Restored Church. The modern Church of Christ began with a commission from him that invalidated "all old covenants" of Christian churches, whether based on tradition or reformation (D&C 22:1). This astonishing message came with the credentials of a loving God interested in the salvation of all people of all generations (D&C 20:25-27), a foreshadowing of the later sweeping revelations on degrees of glory and salvation for the dead. And whether in the words of the organization statement of doctrine, of the revealed preface given a year later (D&C 1:30), or of a later presiding prophet, Spencer W. Kimball, "There is just one church which Jesus Christ, himself, organized by direct revelation; just one church that teaches *all* of his doctrines; just one church which has all of the keys and authorities which are necessary to carry on the work of Jesus Christ."[40]

## Notes

[1]David O. McKay, *Gospel Ideals* (Salt Lake City: *Improvement Era*, 1953), p. 98 (1937), p. 533 (1952). Cf. Wilford Woodruff's report of an 1843 Joseph Smith discourse: "Whenever men can find out the will of God and find an administrator legally authorized from God, there is the kingdom of God." Andrew F. Ehat and Lyndon W. Cook, eds., *The Words of Joseph Smith* (Provo, Ut.: Brigham Young University Religious Studies Center, 1980), p. 158, also *TPJS*, p. 274.

[2]No earlier revelation begins to approach the length of section 20 except section 10, given in the crisis of the loss of the 116 pages of Book of Mormon manuscript. Even that section is about twenty percent shorter than section 20.

[3]*The Evening and the Morning Star* 1:1 (June 1832). But the earliest known copy appeared in the non-Latter-day Saint press just a year after church organization, antedating known Latter-day Saint printings and manuscripts by about a year: *Painsville* [Ohio] *Telegraph,* 19 April 1831, p. 4. The editor said that his document came "from the hand of Martin Harris," and it begins with the same heading quoted above from the 1832 *Evening and Morning Star.* The text is nearly exactly that later published in the Book of Commandments, but see n. 26, below. LDS archives holds a letter from Lucy Mack Smith to her brother Solomon Mack, written from Waterloo, New York, 6 January 1831, published by Ben E. Rich in his *Scrapbook of Mormon Literature.* Lucy quoted D&C 20:6-8 quite closely, so all evidence points to the identity of the 1830 text and that which was published from 1831 on.

[4]For a table of early mss. and printings, see Robert J. Woodford, "The Historical Development of the Doctrine and Covenants" (Ph.D. dissertation, Brigham Young University, 1974), Table 20. Out of five copies dated 1832-34, only one manuscript includes section 22 with section 20. Since another includes most of the revelation giving the law of the Church (D&C 42), the tendency is evident for section 20 to attract other revelations that had different titles or circumstances. The earliest known copy of section 20 is printed in the *Painesville Telegraph*, 19 April 1831, and it appends section 22 and also section 27 in its early Book of Commandments form. However, the "Articles and Covenants" heading applies only to section 20, since the added sections have their own titles. Section 22 is headed: "A commandment unto the Church of Christ, which was established in these last days A.D. 1830, on the 4th month and the 6th day of the month which is called April." Section 27 is headed: "A commandment given unto Joseph, concerning the Sacrament." Cf. n. 3.

[5]Early priesthood licenses refer to the proper authorization outlined in section 20, and Joseph Smith referred to the opening part of section 20 in

alluding to his youthful weaknesses. On the latter point see *Messenger and Advocate,* December, 1834, conveniently printed in Dean C. Jessee, *The Personal Writings of Joseph Smith* (Salt Lake City: Deseret Book Co., 1984), p. 337. No known quotation from "The Articles and Covenants" refers to any other revelation than section 20.

[6]Section 22 appeared as section 47 in the 1835 Kirtland edition and in the 1844 Nauvoo edition of the Doctrine and Covenants.

[7]Both minute entries quoted appear under the dates given in the Far West Record. See Donald Q. Cannon and Lyndon W. Cook, *Far West Record* (Salt Lake City: Deseret Book Co., 1983), pp. 1, 3.

[8]For additional discussion of Book of Mormon references in section 20, see Monte S. Nyman, "The Witnesses of the Book of Mormon," found herein.

[9]See the Prophet's principal vision narratives in Jessee, *The Personal Writings,* pp. 4 ff.; 74 ff.; 196 ff.; 212 ff. Cf. Richard Lloyd Anderson, "Confirming Records of Moroni's Coming," *Improvement Era* 73 (October 1970): 82-89.

[10]Doctrine and Covenants quotations in this chapter are from the current edition, but they have been checked carefully against the earliest copies. In the case of section 20, there are verbal variations, none of which affect meaning in the quotations used. The quoted sentence from section 20 clearly reflects the language of the Three Witnesses, who "declare" that they saw the angel and the plates in their printed testimony in the Book of Mormon. See also Monte S. Nyman, "The Witnesses of the Book of Mormon," found herein.

[11]See Jessee, *The Personal Writings,* p. 6: "I saw the Lord, and he spake unto me, saying Joseph, my son, thy sins are forgiven thee." And see *ibid.*, p. 75: "Another personage soon appeared like unto the first—he said unto me, 'thy sins are forgiven thee.'" My spelling and punctuation is used here.

[12]Book of Mormon, The Testimony of Three Witnesses. Cf. D&C 128:20.

[13]Oliver Cowdery to William W. Phelps, in *Messenger and Advocate* 1 (October 1834): 15-16, also JS-H 71, n. Cf. the summary phrase concerning "the certainty that we heard the voice of Jesus."

[14]Cf. *HC* 1:60-61; see also Charles R. Harrell, "The Restoration of the Priesthood," found herein.

[15]Quoted phrases appear in both the Westminster Confession of Faith (1647), chapter 2, and the Methodist Articles of Religion (1784), article 1, cited in the edition of Philip Schaff, *The Creeds of Christendom* (Grand Rapids, Mich.: Baker Book House, 1983 reprint) 3:606-8, 807. Section 20 has language of the unity of the persons of the Trinity, but not their essential identity. Section 20 is verbally close to the individual statements of faith on the records of each congregational church of the time. These retained much Calvinism.

[16]For known background and text of the Apostles Creed, see John H. Leith, *Creeds of the Churches*, rev. ed. (Atlanta: John Knox Press, 1973), pp. 22-25.

[17]For a survey of the above issues, see Richard Lloyd Anderson, *Understanding Paul* (Salt Lake City: Deseret Book Co., 1983), pp. 158-68; pp. 177-83.

[18]Westminster Confession, chapter 17, cited in Schaff, *The Creeds*, 3:636.

[19]Easy grace is not possible in the formula of D&C 20:31, where Christ's offer is only completed by the disciples' total and lifetime devotion. This high standard is evidently a criticism of simplistic regaining of grace, as in irresponsible practice of the Methodist view, "We may depart from grace given, and fall into sin, and by the grace of God, rise again and amend our lives." Methodist Articles, article 12, cited in Schaff, *The Creeds*, p. 809-10. Cf. Joseph Smith's later label of this as a half-truth: Ehat and Cook, *The Words of Joseph Smith*, pp. 333-34; also *TPJS*, pp. 338-39.

[20]Westminster Confession, chapter 6, cited in Schaff, *The Creeds*, p. 603. Cf. chapter 2.

[21]Methodist Articles, article 5, cited in Schaff, *The Creeds*, p. 808.

[22]Joseph Smith to Isaac Galland, 22 March 1839, Liberty Jail, cited in Jessee, *The Personal Writings*, p. 420.

[23]*Evening and Morning Star*, 1835 Kirtland reprint of June, 1832 issue, 1:2. Doctrine and Covenants editions from 1876 to 1920 carried a note that these verses had been added later, the same procedure in all printings of *HC* 1:68.

[24]*HC* 1:39, 44, 51.

[25]*Ibid.*, pp. 60-1.

[26]A full transcription of the Cowdery document is printed in Woodford, Historical Background to section 20. The continued interdependence of section 20 and the Book of Mormon is indicated in the major variant in the earliest present form of the revelation in the 1831 *Painesville Telegraph*, cited in n. 3, above. There the instructions on baptism and the Sacrament do not appear (D&C 20:72-79), but in their place is this sentence: "And the manner of baptism and the manner of administering the Sacrament are to be done as is written in the Book of Mormon."

[27]*HC* 1:60-1. Cowdery's 1829 document indicates that he had the higher priesthood, since he speaks of himself as "an apostle of Jesus Christ by the will of God the Father and the Lord Jesus Christ." Instructions were given on ordaining priests and teachers, the pattern of elders doing so in the Book of Mormon (Moro. 3:1) or apostles in D&C 18:31-32. But since the higher office of elder was evidently restricted at this time (after June, 1829, since D&C 18 is quoted liberally), David Whitmer overstated that elders were as operative

before 6 April 1830 as afterward. This does not appear to be true in the Cowdery document, so David may also be inaccurate in his claim of pre-organization confirmation. He remembered the 1829 circulation of a document that might be the same as the Cowdery revelation: "The Book of Mormon was still in the hands of the printer, but my brother, Christian Whitmer, had copied from the manuscript the teachings and doctrine of Christ, being the things which we were commanded to preach." See David Whitmer, *An Address to All Believers in Christ* (Richmond, Mo.: David Whitmer, 1887), pp. 32-33, and cf. pp. 59-60.

[28]*HC* 1:64.

[29]Hyrum M. Smith and Janne M. Sjodahl, *The Doctrine and Covenants* (Salt Lake City: Deseret News Press, 1923), p. 138. Cf. J. Reuben Clark, Jr., *Our Lord of the Gospels* (Salt Lake City: Deseret Book Co., 1954), pp. vi-vii. See also Bruce R. McConkie, *The Mortal Messiah,* 4 books (Salt Lake City: Deseret Book Co., 1979-81), 1:349-50.

[30]Whitmer, *An Address,* pp. 32-33. Statutory requirements for church incorporation were met except filing—see Larry C. Porter, "Was the Church Legally Incorporated at the Time It Was Organized in the State of New York?" *The Ensign*, December 1978, pp. 26-27. This summarizes Porter's fuller treatment in his Brigham Young University doctoral dissertation, "A Study of the Origins of the Church of Jesus Christ of Latter-day Saints in the States of New York and Pennsylvania, 1816-1831."

[31]Though the 1835 Doctrine and Covenants originally designated "first" and "second" elders in D&C 20:2-3, Joseph Smith is called the "first elder" in the early versions of D&C 20:5, perhaps written before the explicit language on 6 April 1830 that Joseph Smith was "first" (D&C 21:11).

[32]*HC* 1:78.

[33]Joseph Knight, Manuscript of the Early History of Joseph Smith; also cited in Dean C. Jessee, "Joseph Knight's Recollection of Early Mormon History," *BYU Studies* 17 (Autumn 1976): 37. The context is also given in Lyndon W. Cook, *The Revelations of the Prophet Joseph Smith* (Provo, Ut.: Seventy's Mission Bookstore, 1981), pp. 32-33. Spelling and punctuation are edited in my quote. Whitmer later disagreed with the Prophet's presiding position, but he wrote of the harmony of members at the time of organization: "We had all confidence in Brother Joseph, thinking that as God had given him so great a gift as to translate the Book of Mormon, that everything he would do must be right" (Whitmer, p. 33).

[34]Lucy Mack Smith, *Biographical Sketches* (Liverpool: Orson Pratt, 1853), p. 48, the same thought of the preliminary manuscript, though worded differently.

[35]Cf. Anderson, *Understanding Paul,* pp. 59-63. Cf. the related incident (Acts 19:13-16), where Jesus' name was ineffectual in casting out evil spirits when used by an unauthorized individual.

[36]See the recollections of restored authority as the key issue in the conversions of John Murdock and Edward Partridge: Milton V. Backman, Jr., *The Heavens Resound: A History of the Latter-day Saints in Ohio, 1830-1838* (Salt Lake City: Deseret Book Co., 1983), pp. 5-6, 16. Cf. Richard Lloyd Anderson, "The Impact of the First Preaching in Ohio," *BYU Studies* 11:480-83.

[37]*HC* 1:79-81.

[38]See also *ibid.*, pp. 104-5.

[39]The earliest manuscripts and printings followed the Book of Mormon language here: "Having authority given me of Jesus Christ" (cf. 3 Ne. 11:25). The shift of synonyms was made in the 1835 Kirtland printings. Cf. n. 26.

[40]Edward L. Kimball, *The Teachings of Spencer W. Kimball* (Salt Lake City: Bookcraft, 1982), p. 421.

# 11

## "WHERE I AM YE SHALL BE ALSO" (D&C 25 and 27)

LEON R. HARTSHORN

### An Elect Lady

Emma Smith was a most remarkable lady. She married Joseph Smith knowing that if she became his wife, she would share in the persecution. She was a woman of faith and courage. Doctrine and Covenants, section 25, is given to Emma. The section is unique because it is the only section that is addressed to a woman. The section begins: "Hearken unto the voice of the Lord your God, while I speak unto you, Emma Smith, my daughter" (D&C 25:1).

In this revelation we learn that all who receive the Gospel are sons and daughters of Jesus Christ by adoption (v.1). Emma Smith was admonished to be faithful and virtuous. The Lord said that she was an "elect lady" whom he had called. The meaning of the term "elect lady" was given by the Prophet Joseph Smith several years later on 17 March 1842 in Nauvoo, Illinois. Emma Smith was chosen to be the president of the newly-formed women's organization in the Church. When the prophet found that Emma had been chosen as president of the Relief Society, the following took place: "Joseph read to his wife the revelation given in July 1830, wherein she was called an elect lady and told the sisters that this appellation meant that she was to be elected to a certain work; this revelation was fulfilled in her election to the presidency of the Society."[1]

Verses 3 and 4 of section 25 apparently refer to the fact that Emma Smith would have liked to have seen the Book of Mormon plates, but they were to be shown to specified witnesses only: "Murmur not because of the things which thou hast not seen, for they are withheld from thee and from the world." Emma was admonished to accept the Lord's will in this matter.

In v. 5 the Lord affirmed that the prophet's wife was called to comfort and console her husband. Through the Prophet Joseph Smith, the fulness of the Gospel of Jesus Christ was being restored to the earth. While he was engaged in this sublime work, he continually had to fend off the ignorant and the vicious. How needful, how wonderful, to have a wife—his closest friend and companion—to help, comfort, and console him.

We have noticed that this is the apparent role of the wives of other presidents of the Church. Camilla Kimball in our own day served as an excellent example of one who comforted and consoled her husband. Like Joseph Smith, President Spencer W. Kimball always served the Lord gladly, but he also knew challenges in his labors, including fatigue, disappointment, suffering, and sorrow. The pattern for future wives of the Lord's prophets was apparently established when the Lord spoke to Emma Smith in July 1830.

Verse 6, which refers to Emma as a scribe, apparently has reference to her brief role as a scribe to her husband in his revision of the Bible. Emma had served for a while as a scribe on the Book of Mormon, which had been published the previous March. It was not intended that she be a permanent scribe, but a substitute while the Prophet's regular scribes were unavailable. On this occasion and on later occasions, Emma assisted Joseph in this way. Emma Smith was a very intelligent person and was a gifted writer.

The promise contained in v. 7, "Thou shalt be ordained . . . to expound scriptures, and to exhort the church," was fulfilled at the same time the promise in v. 3 was fulfilled, when Emma Smith was set apart as the President of the Relief Society. The word "ordained" is used in this verse. Presently, the word "ordain" pertains to priesthood offices and the words "set apart" are used when one is called to a church position.

The revelation to Emma Smith includes many elements that we might find in a patriarchal blessing. Some of the instructions, admonitions, and promises to Emma pertain to the present and others to the future. The promised opportunities and blessings are predicated upon faithfulness and obedience.

Emma Smith had previously been baptized; it was shortly after this time that she was confirmed by her husband and had the gift of the Holy Ghost bestowed upon her. The Lord has asked all of us to lay aside the things of the world and seek eternal life. In the revelation directed to her, Emma was told to do so. Her heart and mind were to be on those things which are of lasting substance and value—the eternal, not the earthly; that which is endless, not that which is fleeting. People who lose sight of the transcendent value of the eternal lose perspective and may lose their way.

Verse 12 probably contains the best one-verse statement in the scriptures pertaining to the importance of music in the Lord's Church. The Lord "delighteth in the song of the heart" and "the song of the righteous is a prayer unto me." Such prayers will be answered with a blessing. Emma Smith was given a very sacred and important assignment (v. 11). She completed the assignment in an excellent manner; she selected hymns and prepared the first hymn book of the restored Church. It was a book small in size and included the words of the hymns, but not music.

Verses 13-15 contain concluding counsel and admonitions to the Prophet's wife. The Lord told Emma to rejoice. She had much to cause her to rejoice: she was a daughter of God, a member of the Lord's kingdom on the earth, the wife of the Lord's chosen prophet, and an elect lady. In addition, she had the promise that the Lord was with her. He would be her strength in trials and be near to strengthen and comfort her.

The Lord knows each of us better than we know ourselves. He knows our strengths and weaknesses. We each have our free agency; he loves us and wants us to use it wisely. Emma Smith was counseled by God to continue in the spirit of meekness and beware of pride. She was to continually keep God's commandments.

The Lord is no respecter of persons. No one is given the greatest gift of all, the gift of eternal life, because of the good deeds of someone else. Ancestry, family name, church position, or the faithfulness of loved ones cannot guarantee eternal life. Eternal life can only be obtained by one who abides the covenants made personally by the Lord (2 Ne. 26:23-33; 30:2; Acts 10:34-35). This principle was stated very clearly by the Lord to Emma in v. 15: "Keep my commandments continually, and a crown of righteousness thou shalt receive. And except thou do this, where I am you cannot come."

We note, as we read the concluding verse of section 25, that the wonderful counsel given is not just for Emma Smith but to all. We love Emma Smith, and recall her noble deeds and honor her for them.

Emma Smith was by the Prophet Joseph Smith's side until his death at Carthage Jail on 27 June 1844. She married Lewis Bidamon in December 1847. Emma Smith lived the remainder of her life in Nauvoo. She was 75 years old when she died in the mansion house on 30 April 1879.

## The Whole Armor of God

Joseph Smith and Sidney Rigdon beheld the glory of the Lord Jesus Christ, on the right hand of his Father (D&C 76:20-24). This glorious vision took place on 16 February 1832 in Hiram, Ohio. The next vision opened to them on that day presented not only a warning to them but to all of us: they saw Lucifer or Satan cast out of heaven to the earth. The scripture records: "Wherefore, he maketh war with the saints of God, and encompasseth them round about" (D&C 76:29).

Elder Bruce R. McConkie has written: "Satan is a formal Hebrew name for the devil and means adversary, signifying that he wages open war with the truth and all who obey its principles."[2] The Prophet Joseph Smith experienced continued persecution against himself and the Church and said: "The enemies of this people will never get weary of their persecution against the Church, until they are overcome. I expect they will array everything against me that is in their power to control, and that we shall have a long and tremendous warfare. He that will war the true Christian warfare against the corruptions of these last days will have wicked men and angels of devils, and all the infernal powers of darkness continually arrayed against them."[3]

Joseph Smith and Sidney Rigdon both saw Satan and knew of his mission of destruction. In 1844, Joseph Smith died in full faith, a valiant death, with the name of the Lord upon his lips. Sidney Rigdon, who served as the Prophet's first counselor for many years, failed in his attempt, after the death of Joseph Smith, to persuade Church members to follow him as the self-proclaimed guardian of the Church. He continued on the road to complete apostasy and never returned to the Church. The Church continued successfully under the guidance of the Lord's authorized leadership, the Quorum of the Twelve.

How could it happen? How could Sidney Rigdon, David Whitmer, Thomas B. Marsh, and others be lost, when Joseph Smith, Brigham Young, Heber C. Kimball, and others were such stalwarts? We ask the same questions of those about us today. How can one fall while others exercise remarkable strength and cope successfully with many trials? A key to answering these questions is found in the 27th section of the Doctrine and Covenants.

Let us consider briefly the historical setting and the first part of the section. The Prophet Joseph Smith recorded: "Early in the month of August [1830] Newel Knight and his wife paid us a visit at my place in Harmony, Pennsylvania; and as neither his wife nor mine had been as yet confirmed, it was proposed that we should confirm them, and partake together of the Sacrament, before he and his wife should leave us. In order to prepare for this I set out to procure some wine for the occasion, but had gone only a short distance when I was met by a heavenly messenger, and received the following revelation."[4] The above is Joseph Smith's introduction to section 27. The angel instructed Joseph that elements other than bread and wine could be used for the sacrament. The angel emphasized the vital importance of always partaking of the sacrament with an eye single to the Lord's glory.

The revelation then noted that when the Savior returned to the earth in glory, Joseph would have the privilege of partaking of the sacrament with the Lord and many great leaders of the past. Several of their names are mentioned in this section of the Doctrine and Covenants. If we desire, and if we are faithful, we may also be present on that marvelous occasion and partake of the sacrament with the Savior (D&C 27:14).

Each Sabbath day when we partake of the sacrament, if we are worthy, we are renewing our covenants, but are also foreshadowing a time when we will be with the Savior. John Taylor taught: "We have met to partake of the Sacrament of the Lord's Supper, for in partaking of the Sacrament we not only commemorate the death and sufferings of our Lord and Savior Jesus Christ, but we also shadow forth the time when he will come again and when we shall meet and eat bread with him in the kingdom of God. When we are thus assembled together, we may expect to receive guidance and blessings from God."[5]

We now come to the "key" or the specific counsel that if followed faithfully will permit us to "stand" as Joseph Smith did and not "fall" as Sidney Rigdon did. All of us who want to be faithful and stand against the enemies of truth and right should internalize vv. 15-18 of section 27 and also study Eph. 6:10-18 in the New Testament. We may all stand faithfully and overcome the things of this world, and be saved at the Lord's coming and partake of the Sacrament with him, if we will put on God's whole armor, and keep it on. No one can escape the battle; Satan makes war upon each servant of the Lord. To stand successfully and come off conqueror, we must wear the armor of the Lord.

The six parts of the spiritual armor that we are to wear are enumerated. The first part of the armor mentioned is the girdle of armor that goes about the loins, the armor of truth. An ancient soldier wore a girdle of physical armor about his loins to protect vital parts of his body. A servant of the Lord wears the spiritual armor of "truth" to protect his virtue. Elder Harold B. Lee wrote: "Truth is to be the substance of which the girdle about your loins is to be formed if your virtue and vital strength is to be safeguarded."[6]

The next part of the armor mentioned is the "breastplate of righteousness." One of the beatitudes says: "Blessed are the pure in heart: for they shall see God" (Matt. 5:8). We cannot build Zion without being pure in heart; to be pure in heart we must keep inpurities out. That is done by wearing the breastplate of righteousness. Righteousness means meeting the standards of that which is morally right and just.

The Saints are next admonished to have their feet shod with the preparation of the gospel of peace. Again, Elder Lee, commenting upon this part of God's armor, said: "Your feet, which are to represent your goals or objectives in life, are to be shod. Shod with what? With the preparation of the gospel of peace. . . . He [Apostle Paul] knew that preparedness is the way to victory and that 'eternal vigilance is the price of safety.' Fear is the penalty of unpreparedness and aimless dawdling with opportunity."[7]

The Latter-day Saint who would ward off Satan's fiery darts (flaming arrows) takes the shield of faith. When persecution, heartbreak, temptation, disappointment, illness, etc., comes into the life of a Latter-day Saint, the first thing he should do is get behind the shield of faith. He must let the Lord help him; if he does not, then Satan's fiery darts may wound him spiritually. Some have sustained so many wounds that their recovery is lengthy, and there are some who have never recovered.

That which is to protect our mind, our ability to think properly, is the "helmet of salvation." Wilford Woodruff said that Oliver Cowdery at one time had a powerful testimony, but he "yielded to the temptation of the evil one." Oliver began to think that he was smarter than Joseph Smith and wanted to direct the prophet; thus Oliver apostatized.[8] We are all grateful to Oliver Cowdery for the great contributions he made to the Church. It is tragic that he did not keep the helmet of salvation in place. His thinking deviated from the truth first, and soon his actions followed.

The sword of the Spirit, which is the word of God, is another part of the armor which we are to wear. The Lord never intended that his servants, his soldiers, fight only a defensive battle. He desires that we be on the offensive and help overcome evil, free mankind from the terrible effects of evil, and prepare the earth for the return of the Savior. The sword is primarily an offensive weapon. We are to take the sword of the Spirit, the word of God. Thus we are to study the scriptures, listen to the voices of the living prophets, and have the companionship of the Holy Ghost as we move forward in God's service.

One who wears God's whole armor is happy and confident in the battle against evil. One who does not is devastated by the struggle. We must wear the armor always throughout life, keep it polished through service, and keep it in good repair through repentance.

Picture mentally two missionaries or a husband and wife dressed in God's whole armor: the shining helmet, the beautiful breastplate, the glistening shield, the powerful sword, the girdle about the loins, and the footwear appropriate for the battle. It is difficult for honest-in-heart people to resist missionaries who come to their door dressed in the Lord's armor. It is also difficult for children to resist the teachings, admonitions, and examples of parents who wear God's whole armor.

On the other hand, picture mentally two missionaries or a father and mother wearing a tarnished helmet, a corroded breastplate, a rusted shield, a broken sword, a girdle about the loins that has slipped downward, and tattered footwear. How effective would two missionaries be in persuading someone to live gospel principles and become a member of the Lord's Church? How effective would a father and mother be in convincing a son or daughter to give allegiance to the Lord and his gospel if they were dressed in such armor?

If we are to follow the Lord, resist evil, and build the kingdom of

God on earth, we must follow the counsel of the Lord as given in section 27: "Wherefore, lift up your hearts and rejoice, and gird up your loins, and take upon you my whole armor, that ye may be able to withstand the evil day, having done all, that ye may be able to stand" (D&C 27:15).

If we accept the Lord's invitation to put on his whole armor, we will joyfully succeed in the battle and accomplish the Lord's work. Regardless of the manner of the attack, regardless of the tactics used, we will be protected, overcome all, rejoice in the Lord's goodness, and stand. We will have the privilege of partaking of the sacrament with the Lord Jesus Christ and all of the faithful in his kingdom after his triumphant return to the earth.

---

## Notes

[1]Ivan J. Barrett, *Joseph Smith and the Restoration* (Provo, Ut.: Brigham Young University Press, 1973), p. 506. Citing *HC* 4:552-53.

[2]Bruce R. McConkie, *Mormon Doctrine,* 2nd ed. (Salt Lake City: Bookcraft, 1966), p. 677.

[3]*TPJS*, p. 259.

[4]*HC* 1:106.

[5]*JD* 14:185.

[6]*Stand Ye in Holy Places* (Salt Lake City: Deseret Book Co., 1975), p. 331.

[7]*Ibid.*, p. 333.

[8]*Millennial Star* 57 (30 May 1895): 339-40.

# 12

# JOSEPH SMITH'S TRANSLATION OF THE BIBLE AND THE DOCTRINE AND COVENANTS

Robert L. Millet

The Lord instructed Moses anciently concerning a time when precious truths would be restored through a mighty prophet: "And in a day when the children of men shall esteem my words as naught and take many of them from the book which thou shalt write, behold, I will raise up another like unto thee; and they shall be had again among the children of men—among as many as shall believe" (Moses 1:41). This chapter will deal with the role of Joseph Smith as a translator, and particularly with the relationships between Joseph Smith's Translation of the Bible (JST) and the book of Doctrine and Covenants.

It is not uncommon in the Church to encounter books and lessons on the Doctrine and Covenants with little or no mention of this standard work's tie to the JST. In reality, the full history of the Church—the line upon line unfolding of sacred matters in the last dispensation—cannot be told appropriately without at least some awareness of the Prophet's work of inspired revision of the King James Version of the Bible. The first part of this article will concentrate upon the nature of the JST (methods and details), while the second part will discuss the critical relationship of the JST to the Doctrine and Covenants. Before moving ahead, however, it is vital that the reader recognize the fact that Joseph Smith and the Lord himself viewed this "branch of his calling"—his work as Bible translator—as a key element in the grand Restoration. The translation of the Bible was not a gospel hobby, a parlor game, or a prophetic whim. In the nineteenth century Joseph's work with the Bible was undertaken and received as a labor and a product of profound gravity. In the words of the Lord, Joseph was called "to do a great work and hath need that he may do the work of translation for the salvation of souls."[1]

## Restoring Plain and Precious Truths

Joseph Smith had learned early in his translation of the Book of Mormon that theological darkness and spiritual stumblings of the Christian world were due in large measure to a wilful tampering with some of the earliest Bible texts; plain and precious truths, including many covenants of the Lord, had been "taken away" or "kept back" by designing individuals in the periods incident to and following the original compilations of the Old and New Testaments (1 Ne. 13:23-34). "From what we can draw from the scriptures relative to the teaching of heaven," Joseph observed in 1834, "we are induced to think that much instruction has been given to man since the beginning which we do not possess now."[2] More specifically: "From sundry revelations which had been received, it was apparent that many important points touching the salvation of men, had been taken from the Bible, or lost before it was compiled."[3] Though we do not have in our possession a specific revelation instructing Joseph Smith to begin a careful study of the Bible (as a means of restoring many of the plain and precious parts), yet we do have numerous statements by the Prophet and the Lord indicating its value and overall import. Joseph and his scribes acknowledged that this specific assignment was a sacred mission appointed unto him (D&C 76:15).

There was nothing particularly unusual about a new translation of the Bible in the 1830s. Religious revivalism reached a peak in the New York area in the early nineteenth century, and with it came a heightened awareness of the need for the Bible as a divine standard for living. In fact, New England was not the only section of the country which manifested an intense interest at this time in a study and scrutiny of the biblical record; from 1777 to 1833 more than 500 separate editions of the Bible (or parts thereof) were published in America.[4] Many of these represented new translations or "modern translations," often with an attempt to prepare paraphrased editions or alternate readings based upon comparisons with Hebrew and Greek manuscripts.

Joseph Smith's translation of the scriptures was, however, highly unusual. Joseph had no background or training in ancient languages until later in life, when he did study Hebrew with a number of the leaders of the Church. Nor did he work with manuscripts written in the biblical languages in undertaking this study. What, then, was the nature of his "translation," and how was it effected? The Prophet Joseph began a careful reading and study of the King James Bible in June of 1830. He acted under divine direction according to his appointment as "a seer, a revelator, a translator, and a prophet, having all the gifts of God which he bestows upon the head of the church" (D&C 107:92). He sought to harmonize himself with the Spirit of God, as well as the mind and will of the ancient writers, so as to convey (as nearly as possible) not only that which was written, but also that which was intended. In one sense, then, Joseph was "translating" the Bible in attempting to interpret it, to explain it by the use of clearer terms or a different form or style of language. In another sense Joseph was "translating" the Bible inasmuch as he was restoring in the English language ideas and events and sayings which were originally recorded in Hebrew or Greek.

On 8 October 1829 Joseph Smith and Oliver Cowdery purchased a large pulpit-style edition of the King James Bible (containing the Old and New Testaments and Apocrypha) from E. B. Grandin in Palmyra, New York for $3.75. It was this Bible which was used in the translation. June of 1830 is the earliest date of translation given on any of the Prophet's records. From his own journal history we find the following entry: "I will say . . . that amid all the trials and tribulations we had to wade through, the Lord, who well knew our infantile and delicate situation, vouchsafed for us a supply of strength, and granted us 'line upon line of knowledge—here a little and there a little,' of which the following was a precious morsel."[5] Joseph then recorded some "selections from the Book of Moses" (Moses 1) containing the "words of God, which he spake unto Moses at a time when Moses was caught up into an exceedingly high mountain" (Moses 1:1).

Joseph Smith and his scribe continued their study of the book of Genesis for many months. Work on the Old Testament continued until 7 March 1831. On that date Joseph received a revelation in which he was instructed to begin a translation of the New Testament (D&C 45:60-62). The manuscript of the work with Matthew, chapter 1 is dated 8 March 1831. To that point a translation of the Old Testament had progressed through Genesis 19:35.[6] For a period of about one month, work with Matthew and Genesis was undertaken concurrently, but by early April the Old Testament was put aside temporarily in order that the New Testament might receive full attention. During the months that followed, Joseph continued the translation of the New Testament and labored as time would permit. As was so often the case, the problems associated with administering a growing church as well as providing the necessities of life for his own family, precluded more frequent work with the Bible.

Early in 1833 the Prophet wrote: "I completed the translation and review of the New Testament, on the 2nd of February, 1833, and sealed it up."[7] At this point, work with the Old Testament resumed. By 8 March 1833 the translators had progressed through the Old Testament to the Prophets (D&C 90:13). On the very next day—9 March—Joseph inquired of God concerning the Apocrypha and received what is now section 91 of the Doctrine and Covenants. Essentially, Joseph was instructed that there were many truths to be found within the collection of Old Testament apocryphal writings (those books of questionable authorship or antiquity), as well as interpolations of men. He was told not to take the time to translate the Apocrapha. The Old Testament Apocrypha was contained in the particular 1828 edition of the King James Bible being used in the translation and was located in the middle of the Bible, between the Old and New Testaments. The Prophet Joseph's journal entry from 2 July 1833 is as follows: "We are exceedingly fatigued, owing to a great press of business. We this day finished the translating of the Scriptures, for which we returned gratitude to our Heavenly Father."[8]

Joseph Smith was assisted with his translation during the three-year period by a number of persons, but three men in particular were of greatest service as his amenuenses. John Whitmer, one of the Eight Witnesses of the golden plates, assisted the Prophet early in the translation; the Lord explained to Joseph: "Behold, it is expedient in me that my servant John should write and keep a regular history, and assist you, my servsant Joseph, in *transcribing*[9] all things which shall be given you, until he is called to further duties" (D&C 47:1). Oliver Cowdery, one of the Three Witnesses of the Book of Mormon, had served faithfully as the scribe for Joseph in the translation of the Nephite record. The Lord explained to Oliver in a revelation given in April of 1829 that following the completion of the Book of Mormon translation, further labors lay ahead: "Behold, other records have I, that

I will give unto you power that you may assist to translate" (D&C 9:2). Both John Whitmer and Oliver Cowdery were given new assignments after assisting the Prophet for a short while, and the bulk of the scribal activity was accomplished by Sidney Rigdon. Sidney entered the Church in Ohio and joined Joseph Smith and the Saints in New York in December of 1830. Rigdon became involved immediately in the work with the Bible and labored consistently until the formal work of translation ceased in July of 1833.

The work of the scribe seems to have consisted in writing on sheets of paper that which was dictated by Joseph Smith. Joseph would read directly from the Bible and through the spirit of inspiration note the need for a revision of a text. An examination of the original manuscripts reveals different approaches or methods to the work of translation. For example, the biblical text is written out in full (longhand) on the manuscripts for Gen. 1-24 and Matt. 1-John 5. A shorter method was also employed, whereby only the passages to be revised were noted by the scribe on the manuscript pages. Of equal importance in the process of translation was Joseph's marking of the large Bible. Before or after many of the passages that were altered one may note a check or an X or some other symbol. Additional marks in the Bible (e.g., dots, slanted lines, circled words, or lined-out words) were discovered to be essential (in conjunction with the manuscripts) in discerning exactly what Joseph intended about particular passages.[10]

A total of 3,410 verses in the printed JST differ in textual construction from the King James Bible. Of this number 25 verses compose the visions of Moses (Moses 1), 1,289 changes are in the Old Testament, and 2,096 in the New Testament. Of the books in the Old Testament, all received revision except Ruth, Ezra, Esther, Lamentations, Haggai, Malachi and The Song of Solomon. It is interesting to note that at the bottom of one of the Old Testament manuscript pages is the following: "The Songs of Solomon are not Inspired Writings." Hence, the Song of Solomon is not contained in the printed edition of the JST. Of the books of the New Testament, only the second and third epistles of John received no revisions. In glancing over the Bible as a whole, some of the books which received more revisions than others were (the number indicates the number of verses which differ from the King James text):[11]

| Old Testament | | New Testament | |
|---|---|---|---|
| Genesis | 662 | Matthew | 483 |
| Exodus | 66 | Mark | 349 |
| Psalms | 188 | Luke | 563 |
| Isaiah | 178 | John | 159 |
| | | Romans | 118 |
| | | 1 Corin. | 68 |
| | | Hebrews | 47 |
| | | Revelation | 75 |

Although the formal work of translation ceased in July of 1833, Joseph spent his remaining years (until the time of his death in 1844) reviewing and revising the manuscripts—seeking to find appropriate words to convey what he had come to know by revelation. Joseph Smith's Translation of the Bible was never published in full during the Prophet's lifetime. The manuscripts were held by Joseph's widow, Emma, and eventually came into the possession of the Reorganized Church of Jesus Christ of Latter Day Saints. The RLDS Church published the JST in full in the year 1867.[12]

## The JST and the Doctrine and Covenants

Not infrequently in our day the question is posed: "Wasn't Joseph Smith simply 'Mormonizing' the Bible in his work with the King James text?" In other words, wasn't the Prophet making his way through the scriptures and changing verses so as to make them agree with Mormon doctrine? Certainly the work with the Bible was not begun (in June of 1830) in an intellectual vacuum; the Prophet had gained a significant amount of knowledge and doctrinal insight from his experience with the Book of Mormon. In addition, there can be no doubt but that Joseph learned by revelation valuable lessons, the details of which he may never have disclosed to the Saints. At the same time, to suppose that the whole or even the bulk of the 3,410 verse alterations represent a type of prophetic paraphrase or modern *midrash* based upon what Joseph Smith already knew, is to miss a critical point as to the grand purpose of the translation. Robert J. Matthews has explained:

> The Lord had Joseph Smith make a translation of the Bible because of the good it would do Joseph Smith as well as the good

> it would also do the Church. This was the way in which the Prophet Joseph Smith learned many things about the gospel. He did not read through the Bible looking for errors, looking for ways to correct it. He studied the scripture for what he could gain. Then when it was inadequate, either because of loss of material or because of faulty translation, by inquiring of the Lord and studying and pondering and thinking about it, he was able to perceive by revelation what the intention of that passage really was.[13]

In short, "through the experience of translating the Bible Joseph Smith was to come into possession of knowledge he did not previously have. . . . The labor was to be its own reward and would result in the spiritual education of the Prophet."[14]

In a very real sense, to speak of the JST as a process of 'Mormonizing' the Bible is historically anachronistic. Not only were a large percentage of the revelations now contained in the Doctrine and Covenants (77 sections or approximately 56 percent of our present total) received during the June 1830-July 1833 time period, but, more significant, key revelations containing singular doctrinal matters came to the Prophet directly or indirectly as a result of the Bible translation.

## The JST and the D&C: Direct Ties

A number of revelations now found in our Doctrine and Covenants came as a direct result of Joseph Smith's translation of the Bible. For example:

*D&C 76, the "Vision of the Glories," received by Joseph Smith and Sidney Rigdon on 16 February 1832, came as a result of prayerful pondering of John 5:29.

*D&C 77 is a question and answer session with the Lord, wherein Joseph learned valuable insights regarding the Apocalypse of John the Beloved.

*D&C 91 (as already mentioned) is a set of instructions regarding the collection of noncanonical records known today as the Old Testament Apocrypha.

*D&C 132 is a revelation on eternal (including plural) marriage.

Though it does not seem to have been recorded finally in its present form until July of 1843, there is evidence to suggest that it was received as early as 1831, at the time that Joseph was translating the Old Testament.

A number of other revelations in the Doctrine and Covenants are tied to the work with the Bible directly because of instructions within the revelations regarding the JST. Information regarding scribes (D&C 25:6; 35:20; 47:1), the interruption and resumption of translation activities (D&C 37:1; 45:60-61; 73:3; 93:53), facilities for translating (D&C 41:7; 94:10; 104:58; 124:89), and related matters (D&C 26:1; 42:56-61; 90:13) are found throughout the Doctrine and Covenants. Without at least some background in and appreciation for the place of the JST in the overall history of the Church, many revelations and activities of the Prophet Joseph Smith will remain enigmatic and unintelligible.

## The JST and the D&C: Indirect Ties

As noted earlier, over 50 percent of the revelations in the Doctrine and Covenants were received during the time period associated with the inspired revision of the Bible. It is my observation that this is not without significance. We have in the translation activities of Joseph Smith a living lesson in the matter of how to receive revelations; as the Prophet immersed himself in the scriptures, issues and curiosities and questions surfaced, eventuating in many cases in further light and knowledge to the Latter-day Saints in the form of contemporary revelations.

It is important also that we recognize that revelation in the form of biblical revisions was being received at the same time that revelation in the form of the Doctrine and Covenants was being received; the same spirit of inspiration was at work with Joseph the Seer. For example, a number of the doctrinal matters revealed in the early chapters of Genesis—agency, accountability, pre-mortal existence, the Fall of Adam, the revelation of the gospel to Adam and his posterity—are to be found as well in D&C 29, a revelation received at about the same time as the inspired revisions were being made to the early chapters of Genesis. Another example is the proximity of the Enoch material in the JST of Genesis (November-December of 1830) and the number of revelations in early 1831 which deal with the establishment of Zion. The Lord identified himself to Joseph Smith in a revelation given 2 January 1831 in an interesting manner: "I am the same which have taken the Zion of Enoch into mine own bosom" (D&C 38:4). In February of 1831 the Lord revealed the "Law of the Church" (D&C 42), in which particular details of the law of consecration and stewardship—the economic pattern by which the Saints were able to be "of one heart and one mind," and by which there would be "no poor among them" (Moses 7:18)—were made known.

A final note of comparison might prove helpful. The significant doctrinal statement concerning the age of accountability of children (D&C 68:25-26) was given by revelation in November of 1831. This, however, was not the first time in our dispensation where such information was made known. While translating the 17th chapter of Genesis in the Old Testament (sometime between February and April, 1831), Joseph Smith recorded the following regarding the Abrahamic covenant and the token of circumcision:

> And I will establish a covenant of circumcision with thee, and it shall be my covenant between me and thee, and thy seed after thee, in their generations; that thou mayest know for ever that *children are not accountable before me until they are eight years old.*
>
> And thou shalt observe to keep all my covenants wherein I have covenanted with thy fathers; and thou shalt keep the commandments which I have given thee with my own mouth, and I will be a God unto thee and thy seed after thee (JST, Gen. 17:11-12, italics added).

Thus we see that the concept of an age of accountability of children was known by the Prophet through his work of Bible translation some six to nine months before D&C 68 was received.

When the full picture of the Restoration is unveiled, perhaps then we will come to appreciate an even greater impact of the JST on the final dispensation. In the meantime, we can only surmise concerning other sections of the Doctrine and Covenants and their possible relation to the translation of the Bible. For example:

*D&C 7 as contained in the 1835 edition and subsequent editions of the Doctrine and Covenants is an expanded version of the same revelation recorded in the 1833 Book of Commandments. What impact, if any, did the Prophet's work with the Bible have upon his later inspired editorial labors?

*D&C 46 is an important revelation regarding the gifts of the Spirit. Is there any tie to Paul's sermon in 1 Cor. 12?

*D&C 84 has a number of themes (oath and covenant of the priesthood, the rest of God, etc.) similar to themes found in the book of Hebrews in the New Testament.

*D&C 88 has language and concept found in the book of John, as does D&C 93.

We could go on and on regarding possible indirect ties between the JST and the Doctrine and Covenants, but the point seems to have been made clearly enough.

## Summary

What can we say by way of conclusion? First of all, Joseph Smith the Prophet received a commandment and commission to undertake a serious study of the Bible. In doing so, he and his scribes were privileged to be a part of the restoration of plain and precious truths, doctrines, and covenants which had been lost, taken away, or kept back through the centuries prior to the dispensation of the fulness of times. Further, the work of Bible translation proved to be of inestimable worth in the preparation and education of the great latter-day Seer, the means by which (1) Joseph Smith became intimately acquainted with the Bible and its teachings, and (2) a veritable flood of truth and intelligence were given to the Latter-day Saints, in many cases through revelations now a part of the book of Doctrine and Covenants. Robert J. Matthews, the world authority on the JST, made the following remarks at the 1984 Sidney B. Sperry Symposium regarding the relationship of the JST to the Doctrine and Covenants:

> What then is the conclusion to the whole matter? That the Prophet's work with the Bible was a primary source for much of the doctrinal content and the instructional information of the D&C. Consequently, one could not adequately understand either the background or the content of those parts of the D&C without an acquaintance with the history and content of the

> JST. The two volumes, when placed in tandem, enable the student to gain a clearer picture of how the gospel was restored in this dispensation, and gives the reader an insight as to how divine revelation comes. Underlying the whole process is the bold demonstration that revelation comes through a careful study of the scriptures. As the Prophet labored with the translation of the Bible, additional revelation was given to him. That this is one of the purposes of the JST is stated in D&C 45:60-62, wherein the Lord said in effect, if you want more knowledge, translate the New Testament, for in it "all these things shall be made known." Thus, we see enacted a gospel truth: that when we study the revelations already given, new revelation comes to enlarge our spiritual understanding. And that is, after all, our reason for searching the scriptures.[15]

It is indeed a serious matter to be selective with the labors and products of a prophet of God. To do so is tantamount to being choosy about what we will receive from the Lord and what we will not. The same prophet who was the means by which the truths of the Book of Mormon and the Doctrine and Covenants were made available to the Saints received literally hundreds of priceless gems in his work of Bible translation. That the work with the Bible was not alone a mental exercise but also a revelatory experience is shown in a simple entry at the top of page one of the manuscript for the book of Matthew: "A translation of the New Testament translated by the power of God."[16] In a revelation to Sidney Rigdon—the primary scribe for the translation—Jesus Christ gave to his people his own perception of the nature and scope of the Bible translation: "And a commandment I give unto thee—that thou shalt write for him; and *the scriptures shall be given, even as they are in mine own bosom, to the salvation of mine own elect*" (D&C 35:20). It is abundantly clear, therefore, that the work of translation was critcally important to the Lord as well as to Joseph Smith. Because of its doctrinal and historical ties to the Doctrine and Covenants, a closer and more ponderous study of this exciting "branch of his calling" would certainly seem to be appropriate and necessary for those who continue to sustain Joseph as a Prophet, a Seer, a Revelator, and a Translator.

# Notes

[1]From a revelation to Frederick G. Williams, 5 January 1834 in Joseph Smith Collection, Letters, 1834, Church Historian's Office, Salt Lake City.

[2]*HC* 2:18.

[3]*Ibid.*, 1:245.

[4]See Margaret T. Hills, *The English Bible In America* (New York: The American Bible Society, 1961); cited in Robert J. Matthews, *A Plainer Translation: Joseph Smith's Translation of the Bible, A History and Commentary* (Provo, Ut.: Brigham Young University Press, 1975), p. 9. Matthews' work is the definitive treatment of the background and significance of the JST.

[5]*HC* 1:98.

[6]Matthews, *A Plainer Translation*, p. 96.

[7]*HC* 1:324.

[8]*Ibid.*, 1:368.

[9]It is interesting to note an earlier record of this verse: "Behold, it is expedient in me that my servant John should write and keep a regular history, and assist you, my servant Joseph, in *translating* all things which shall be given you, until he is called to further duties" (Kirtland Revelation Book, p. 12).

[10]See Matthews, *A Plainer Translation*, chapters 3 and 4.

[11]See *ibid.*, pp. 424-25.

[12]*Ibid.*, chapters 4, 7, and 8.

[13]Robert J. Matthews, "Using the Scriptures," in *1981 Brigham Young University Speeches* (Provo, Ut.: Brigham Young University Publications, 1981), p. 123.

[14]Matthews, *A Plainer Translation*, p. 53.

[15]Robert J. Matthews, "The Joseph Smith Translation: A Primary Source for the Doctrine and Covenants," *Hearken, O Ye People*, Proceedings of the 1984 Sidney B. Sperry Symposium, BYU Campus (Salt Lake City: Randall Book Co., 1984), pp. 90-91.

[16]Matthews, *A Plainer Translation*, p. 267.

# 13

# THE LAW OF COMMON CONSENT
## (D&C 26)

WILSON K. ANDERSEN

### Background of Section 26

In early July of 1830 the fledgling Church was barely ninety days old. There were, at that time, no wards or stakes, no seventies, high priests, or bishops. There were no quorums. There was not as yet a First Presidency, or general authorities. The only executive or presiding officers were the First and Second Elders of the Church.

The Prophet Joseph had just returned to Harmony, Pennsylvania from Colesville, New York. The main body of the Church—if we call the small handful of members a body—was still in New York and now growing mostly in and around Colesville. Persecution was on the rise. Joseph's missionary work aroused the ire of some in Colesville; he was tried and acquitted of disorderly conduct and for setting the country in an uproar by preaching the Book of Mormon. But the foundation had been laid, and the first thirteen members of a vital and historic branch of the Church had just been baptized.

Section 26, just two verses long, was one of three revelations which came to the Prophet shortly after his return from Colesville. In this short message, the Lord told Joseph how he should spend time until the next conference. "And then it shall be made known unto you what you shall do." The Prophet was to continue his study and translation of the Bible,[1] as well as build up and strengthen the members of the Colesville Branch (v. 1). Then he was reminded that "all things shall be done by common consent in the church" (v. 2).

### Common Consent in the Church

It seems from the brevity of the language that the Lord (or the Prophet Joseph) was presuming a previous understanding of what "common consent" is. This was true. Though the Church had been in existence for only three months, the basic principle of common consent had been given one year earlier, in June of 1829. It was such an

Oct. 1994 Ensign

impressive experience, even among all the great revelations that came, that the Prophet mentioned it in his sublime letter on baptism for the dead where he listed the glad tidings that had come in the new dispensation (see D&C 128:21).

The original commandment on common consent was evidently closely connected with the great visitation by Peter, James, and John and their restoration of the higher priesthood.

The Prophet Joseph wrote:

> We now became anxious to have that promise realized to us, which the angel that conferred upon us the Aaronic Priesthood had given us, viz., that provided that we continued faithful, we should also have the Melchizedek Priesthood, which holds the authority of the laying on of hands for the gift of the Holy Ghost. We had for some time made this matter a subject of humble prayer, . . . and more particularly to seek of the Lord what we now so earnestly desired; and here, to our unspeakable satisfaction, did we realize the truth of the Savior's promise—"Ask, and it shall be given you; seek, and ye shall find; knock, and it shall be opened unto you"—for we had not long been engaged in solemn and fervent prayer, when the word of the Lord came unto us in the chamber [of father Whitmer in Fayette], commanding us that I should ordain Oliver Cowdery to be an Elder *in the Church* of Jesus Christ; and that he should also ordain me to the same office; and then to ordain others, as it should be made known unto us from time to time. *We were, however, commanded to defer this our ordination until such times as it should be practicable to have our brethren, who had been and who should be baptized, assembled together, when we must have them decide by vote whether they were willing to accept us as their spiritual teachers or not;* when also we were commanded to bless bread and break it with them, and to take wine, bless it, and drink it with them; afterward to proceed to ordain each other according to the commandment; then call out such men as the Spirit should dictate, and ordain them; and then attend to the laying on of hands for the gift of the Holy Ghost, upon all those whom we had previously baptized, doing all things in the name of the Lord.[2]

When these instructions were carried out the following April, the law of common consent was actuated as one of the basic procedures of the new Church. The Lord both honored and safeguarded the agency of his children from the very beginning of this dispensation.

It is, on the basis of this consistent practice, that the First Presidency said in 1907: "We deny the existence of arbitrary power in the Church; and this because its government is moral government purely, and its forces are applied through kindness, reason, and persuasion." And then, in one of the clearest statements ever made regarding the law of common consent, they added:

> It is a law that no person is to be ordained [or set apart] to any office in the Church, where there is a regularly organized branch of the same, without the vote of its members. . . . The ecclesiastical government itself exists by the will of the people; elections are frequent, and the members are at the liberty to vote as they choose.[3]

Why is the Church of Jesus Christ operated on the basis of such a patently theo-democratic principle? Consider the following:

1. The law of common consent *teaches us God's attributes* of love and patience, and his desire that his children have their agency that they might thereby become truly free.

2. The law of common consent, being basic to the polity of the kingdom, *safeguards our agency* in his kingdom and under the priesthood.

3. The law of common consent *keeps discipleship*, and membership in his kingdom *"a voluntary association."* Both real obligation (D&C 82:10) and real volition are essential to salvation.

4. The law of common consent *keeps leaders accountable* to the members they serve, as well as to God who calls them.

5. The law of common consent *makes the members accountable* and responsible, both for and to the Church. This is not only Christ's Church, it is also the Church of the Latter-day Saints. The members are accountable both for faith in their divinely called leaders and for sustaining those leaders in what the Lord calls them to do.

6. Our participation in the law of common consent *places us in a position where the Holy Spirit can bestow confirming witness* when we act in spirit and in truth. None of the Father's children who act in true faith go unrewarded.

7. The law of common consent *protects the Church* against

deception, it restricts false aspirants and autocrats, and brings to account those who might exercise unrighteous dominion.

8. The law of common consent *requires public knowledge and individual member decision* for the regular and continued operation of the Church. Common consent *precludes any secret ordinations or bestowals of authority* (see D&C 42:11). The members know to whom to look for proper direction, according to the order of the kingdom (D&C 28:2-7, 13; 43:3-6; 50:2-4, 7-9, 15-20).

9. The uplifted hand in the operation of the law of common consent is both a vote and *a token of a sacred covenant.* As one votes in our sustaining constituent assemblies, he is evidencing before God, angels, and those witnessing that he will sustain, or that he refuses to sustain, the chosen one in what he is called of God to do. President N. Eldon Tanner explained at a solemn assembly in 1974: "Everyone is perfectly free to vote as he wishes. There is no compulsion whatsoever in this voting. When you vote affirmatively, you make a solemn covenant with the Lord that you will sustain, that is, give your full loyalty and support, without equivocation or reservation, to the officer for whom you vote."[4] That vote does count, though the Church is so united that rarely is there the necessity for counting the votes.

10. President John Taylor asked: "Is there a monarch, potentate or power under the heavens, that undergoes a scrutiny as fine as this? No, there is not; yet this is done twice a year."[5] In effect, there are general elections every six months.

This consistent and unruffled operation of the law of common consent *sets an example to the world* and for the new members. How grateful we ought to be for this blessed and eternal principle!

---

## Notes

[1]See Robert L. Millet, "Joseph Smith's Translation of the Bible and the Doctrine and Covenants," found herein.

[2]*HC* 1:60-61, italics added.

[3]Joseph F. Smith, John R. Winder, and Anthon H. Lund, *Improvement Era* 10 (May 1907): 487-88.

[4]*Conference Report,* April 1974, p. 55.

[5]*JD* 1:230.

# 14

# THE PROPHET, SEER, AND REVELATOR

## (D&C 28 and 43)

A. Gary Anderson

### In All Patience and Faith

The very foundation of the Church of Jesus Christ of Latter-day Saints is the principle of present-day revelation. From the prophet Amos came the declaration that "surely the Lord God will do nothing, but he revealeth his secret unto his servants the prophets" (Amos 3:7). President Spencer W. Kimball declared: "Man never needs to stand alone. Every faithful person may have the inspiration for his own limited kingdom. But the Lord definitely calls prophets today and reveals his secrets unto them as he did yesterday, he does today, and will do tomorrow: that is the way it is."[1] The idea of continuous revelation in our present day seemed consistent with the word of God to many early converts to the gospel. One early lesson that needed to be taught to the members of the restored Church was the relationship of the members to the appointed prophet. Thus, on the very day the Church was organized, 6 April 1830, the Lord gave instruction to the early Church members:

> Wherefore, meaning the church, thou shalt give heed unto all his words and commandments which he shall give unto you as he receiveth them, walking in all holiness before me;
>
> For his word ye shall receive, as if from mine own mouth, in all patience and faith.
>
> For by doing these things the gates of hell shall not prevail against you; yea, and the Lord God will disperse the powers of darkness from before you, and cause the heavens to shake for your good, and his name's glory (D&C 21:4-6).

This revelation seems to point out very clearly the special role of the prophet and the responsibility of Church members to look to that prophet; this, however, was a difficult lesson for Church members to learn and a test of their faith. The Lord warned in a later revelation that enemies would prevail against the Church as long as they did not give heed unto his commandments through his prophet (D&C 103:4-8). Even in more modern times President Harold B. Lee brought this to the attention of the Church in these words:

> We have some tight places to go before the Lord is through with this church and the world in this dispensation, which is the last dispensation, which shall usher in the coming of the Lord. . . .
>
> Now the only safety we have as members of this church is to do exactly what the Lord said to the Church in that day when the Church was organized. We must learn to give heed to the words and commandments that the Lord shall give through his prophet, "as he receiveth them, walking in all holiness before me: . . . as if from my own mouth, in all patience and faith." There will be some things that take patience and faith. You may not like what comes from the authority of the Church. It may contradict your political views. It may contradict your social views. It may interfere with some of your social life. But if you listen to these things, as if from the mouth of the Lord himself, with patience and faith, the promise is that "the gates of hell shall not prevail against you; yea, and the Lord God will disperse the powers of darkness from before you, and cause the heavens to shake for your good, and his name's glory. . . .
>
> Your safety and ours depends upon whether or not we follow the ones whom the Lord has placed to preside over his church. He knows whom he wants to preside over this church, and he will make no mistake. . . . Let's keep our eye on the President of the Church.[2]

## The Key Against Deception

One of the early members of the Church who was present at the organization of the Church and had shared many revelatory experiences with the Prophet Joseph Smith was Oliver Cowdery. He was one who struggled to understand the role of the prophet in giving revelation to the Church. Just months after the organization of the Church, Joseph Smith received a letter from Oliver Cowdery which gave him both "sorrow and uneasiness." The contents of the letter were as follows, as recorded in the *History of the Church:*

> He wrote to inform me that he had discovered an error in one of the commandments—Book of Doctrine and Covenants:

> (D&C 20:37) "And truly manifest by their works that they have received of the Spirit of Christ unto a remission of their sins."
>
> The above quotation, he said, was erroneous, and added: "I command you in the name of God to erase those words, that no priestcraft be amongst us!"
>
> I immediately wrote to him in reply, in which I asked him by what authority he took upon him to command me to alter or erase, to add to or diminish from, a revelation or commandment from Almighty God.
>
> A few days afterwards I visited him and Mr. Whitmer's family, when I found the family in general of his opinion concerning the words above quoted, and it was not without both labor and perseverance that I could prevail with any of them to reason calmly on the subject. However, Christian Whitmer at length became convinced that the sentence was reasonable, and according to Scripture; and finally, with his assistance, I succeeded in bringing, not only the Whitmer family, but also Oliver Cowdery to acknowledge that they had been in error, and that the sentence in dispute was in accordance with the rest of the commandment.[3]

Joseph had returned to Harmony, Pennsylvania after this event, but persecution was beginning to develop there as it had in the Palmyra-Manchester area earlier. Peter Whitmer, Sr., having heard of the persecutions against the Prophet, invited him and Emma to live with him in Fayette, New York. Newel Knight had taken his wagon from Colesville to Harmony to move the family. They arrived at Fayette during the last week of August, 1830—as Joseph said, "amidst the congratulations of our brethren and friends." The Prophet then recorded:

> To our great grief, however, we soon found that Satan had been lying in wait to deceive, and seeking whom he might devour. Brother Hiram Page had in his possession a certain stone, by which he had obtained certain "revelations" concerning the upbuilding of Zion, the order of the Church, etc., all of which were entirely at variance with the order of God's house, as laid down in the New Testament, as well as in our late revelations. As a conference meeting had been appointed for the 26th day of September, I thought it wisdom not to do much more than to converse with the brethren on the

> subject, until the conference should meet. Finding, however, that many especially the Whitmer family and Oliver Cowdery, were believing much in the things set forth by this stone, we thought best to inquire of the Lord concerning so important a matter; and before conference, we received the following."[4]

Doctrine and Covenants 28 was then recorded. Joseph had been quick to recognize that this whole affair was contrary to the New Testament and previous revelations he had received. This revelation recognized the Prophet as the man like unto Moses, which is also affirmed in later revelations (D&C 103:15-16; 107:92). Newel Knight described the events connected with this matter in his personal journal:

> [Page] had managed to get up some discussions of feeling among the brethren by giving revelations concerning the government of the Church and other matters, which he claimed to have received through the medium of a stone he possessed. . . . Even Oliver Cowdery and the Whitmer family had given heed to them. . . . Joseph was perplexed and scarcely knew how to meet this new exigency. That night I occupied the same room that he did and the greater part of the night was spent in prayer and supplication. After much labor with these brethren they were convinced of their error, and confessed the same, renouncing [Page's] revelations as not being of God.[5]

The Lord then commanded Joseph in the revelation to "take thy brother, Hiram Page, between him and thee alone, and tell him that those things which he hath written from that stone are not of me and that Satan deceiveth him" (D&C 28:11). This then becomes a key against deception for the Church. Oliver was recognized by the Lord as the second Elder in the Church, but the Church must learn this important lesson as reiterated by Joseph Smith in these words: "I will inform you that it is contrary to the economy of God for any member of the Church, or anyone, to receive instructions for those in authority, higher than themselves; therefore, you will see the impropriety of giving heed to them; but if any person have a vision or a visitation from a heavenly messenger, it must be for his own benefit and instruction, for the fundamental principles, government, and doctrine of the church are vested in the keys of the kingdom."[6]

The proposed conference of the Church was convened on 26

September 1830, in which Hiram Page's revelation was discussed: "The subject of the stone previously mentioned was discussed, and after considerable investigation, Brother Page, as well as the whole Church who were present, renounced the said stone, and all things connected therewith, much to our mutual satisfaction and happiness."[7] The Spirit of the Lord was strongly felt at the conference and several revelations were given.

The Lord showed further concern in these revelations that members of the Church remember the lessons learned from these events in Fayette. He cautioned David Whitmer in these words: "You have not given heed unto my Spirit, and to those who were set over you, but have been persuaded by those whom I have not commanded" (D&C 30:2). And again to the missionaries who were sent out to preach the gospel to the Lamanites the Lord said: "And they shall give heed to that which is written, and pretend to no other revelation; and they shall pray always that I may unfold the same to their understanding" (D&C 32:4). These were all gentle reminders to look to the Lord and his prophet for guidance and direction in order to avoid confusion and deception. Later missionaries were cautioned to preach "none other things than that which the prophets and apostles have written" (D&C 52:9, 36).

The Church was slow to learn this lesson concerning revelation for the Church coming only to the Prophet. It was less than six months later in Kirtland, just after the Lord had revealed his law to the Church (D&C 42), that the following transpired, as recorded in the *History of the Church:* "Soon after the foregoing revelation was received, a woman came making great pretensions of revealing commandments, laws and other curious matters; and as almost every person has advocates for both the various notions and projects of the age, it became necessary to inquire of the Lord, when I received the following."[8] Section 43 was then recorded, in which the Lord referred to Joseph as "him whom I have appointed unto you to receive commandments and revelations from my hand" (v. 2). The Lord continued: "There is none other appointed unto you to receive commandments and revelations. . . . And this shall be a law unto you, that ye receive not the teachings of any that shall come before you as revelations or commandments; And this I give unto you that you may not be deceived, that you may know that they are not of me" (D&C 43:3, 5-6).

This woman's name, according to the history of the Church kept by John Whitmer, was Hubble. "She professed to be a prophetess of the Lord, and professed to have many revelations, and knew the Book of Mormon was true, and that she should become a teacher in the church of Christ. She appeared to be very sanctimonious and deceived some who were not able to detect her in her hypocrisy; others, however, had the spirit of discernment and her follies and abominations were manifest."[9]

Ezra Booth, an early apostate to the Church, gave us added insight with respect to the purported Hubble revelation:

> A female, professing to be a prophetess, made her appearance in Kirtland and so ingratiated herself into the esteem and favor of some of the Elders that they received her as a person commissioned to act a conspicuous part in Mormonizing the world. Rigdon, and some others, gave her the righthand of fellowship, and literally saluted her with what they called the 'kiss' of charity. But [Joseph] Smith . . . declared her an imposter, and she returned to the place whence she came. Her visit, however, made a deep impression on the minds of many, and the barbed arrow which she left in the hearts of some, is not as yet eradicated.[10]

Continual reference has been made to these revelations to prevent members of the Church from being deceived. In 1972 President Harold B. Lee reminded the Saints of these early events as he warned the Church by quoting a statement of the First Presidency given in 1913:

> From the days of Hiram Page at different periods there have been manifestations from delusive spirits to members of the Church....
>
> When visions, dreams, tongues, prophecy, impressions or an extraordinary gift or inspiration convey something out of harmony with the accepted revelations of the Church or contrary to the decisions of its constituted authorities, Latter-day Saints may know that it is not of God, no matter how plausible it may appear. Also, they should understand that direction for the guidance of the Church will come, by revelation, through the head. All faithful members are entitled

> to the inspiration of the Holy Spirit for themselves, their families, and for those over whom they are appointed and ordained to preside. But anything at discord with that which comes from God through the head of the Church is not to be received as authoritative or reliable. In secular as well as spiritual affairs, Saints may receive Divine guidance and revelation affecting themselves, but this does not convey authority to direct others, and is not to be accepted when contrary to Church covenants, doctrine or discipline, or to known facts, demonstrated truths, or good common sense. No person has the right to induce his fellow members of the Church to engage in speculations or take stock in ventures of any kind on the specious claim of Divine revelation or vision or dream, especially when it is in opposition to the voice of recognized authority, local or general. The Lord's Church "is a house of order." It is not governed by individual gifts or manifestations, but by the order and power of the Holy Priesthood as sustained by the voice and vote of the Church in its appointed conferences.
>
> The history of the Church records many pretended revelations claimed by imposters or zealots who believed in the manifestations they sought to lead other persons to accept, and in every instance, disappointment, sorrow and disaster have resulted therefrom. Financial loss and sometimes utter ruin have followed.[11]

The Lord in section 43 promises protection against deception as the Saints meet together and are instructed and edified by inspired leaders and are admonished to bind themselves to these things and thus be sanctified (D&C 43:8-11). They are to support the Lord's prophet both temporally and by the prayer of faith (D&C 43:12-14). The Lord concludes this revelation by admonishing the elders to teach the truth to the world and prepare for his Second Coming (D&C 43:15-28). He also reminds them that at the day of the Second Coming there will be none to deliver them if they have not believed the prophet (cf. D&C 133:71). The warning seems clear that proper preparations for the Second Coming consists in looking to and obeying his servants, the prophets.

## The Power of God Unto Salvation

When the decision was made in the November conference of the Church in 1831 to compile the revelations given to the early Church, the Lord gave another revelation which was to be the Preface to the Book of Commandments. Again the Lord stressed the importance of listening to and obeying the words of his prophet and other leaders in these words:

> And the arm of the Lord shall be revealed; and the day cometh that they who will not hear the voice of the Lord, neither the voice of his servants, neither give heed to the words of the prophets and apostles, shall be cut off from among the people . . . . What I the Lord have spoken, I have spoken, and I excuse not myself; and though the heavens and the earth pass away, my word shall not pass away, but shall all be fulfilled, whether by mine own voice or by the voice of my servants, it is the same (D&C 1:14, 38).

Perhaps this is why President Harold B. Lee said: "That person is not truly converted until he sees the power of God resting upon the leaders of this Church, and until it goes down into his heart like fire."[12]

The Lord in another revelation given in November 1831 further emphasized the importance of the inspired words of his living servants: "And this is the ensample unto them, that they shall speak as they are moved upon by the Holy Ghost. And whatsoever they shall speak when moved upon by the Holy Ghost shall be scripture, shall be the mind of the Lord, shall be the word of the Lord, shall be the voice of the Lord, and the power of God unto salvation" (D&C 68:3-4). When the servants of the Lord, speaking within their assigned stewardship, are moved upon by the Holy Ghost, then we have received scripture. President Spencer W. Kimball made these remarks at the conclusion of a general conference: "Let us hearken to those we sustain as prophets, and seers, as well as the other brethren, as if our eternal life depended upon it, because it does!"[13] Certainly our salvation is at stake if we fail to be in tune with the Holy Ghost which enables us to know when our leaders are moved upon by the Holy Ghost.

When Frederick G. Williams was called as a counselor in the First Presidency of the Church in 1833, the Lord again emphasized the importance of his word given to his prophet: "Verily I say unto you, the keys of this kingdom shall never be taken from you, while thou art in the world, neither in the world to come; Nevertheless, through you shall the oracles be given to another, yea, even unto the church. And all they who receive the oracles of God, let them beware how they hold them lest they are accounted as a light thing, and are brought under condemnation thereby, and stumble and fall when the storms descend, and winds blow, and the rains descend, and beat upon their house" (D&C 90:3-5). This revelation is certainly a key in interpreting what the Lord was trying to say when he concluded the Sermon of the Mount with the story of the man who built his house on sand (Matt. 7:24-27). His children are on shaky ground when they take lightly the words of his prophet.

In the midst of apostasy in the trying Kirtland years, the Lord reminded the Church of the importance of the First Presidency: "Whosoever receiveth me, receiveth the First Presidency" (D&C 112:20). President Marion G. Romney said, "What they say as a presidency is what the Lord would say if he were here in person."[14] The Saints again in Nauvoo were told that they could not be blessed if they did not hearken unto the voice of his servants (D&C 124:45-46). And in the same revelation Alman W. Babbitt was rebuked for rejecting the counsel of the First Presidency (D&C 124:84). The warning of the Lord to those who were responsible for the martyrdom of the Lord's prophet, Joseph Smith, should not go unnoticed (D&C 136:34-36). President Ezra Taft Benson stated: "The prophet and the presidency—the living prophet and the First Presidency—follow them and be blessed—reject them and suffer."[15] President Benson further stated that the prophet is the only man who speaks for the Lord in everything. He substantiated this thought with D&C 132:7: "There is never but one on the earth at a time on whom this power and the keys of this priesthood are conferred."

## Conclusion

From the day of the organization of the Church in 1830 the Lord has taught and emphasized the importance of his servants; he has carefully defined the special role of the Prophet and President of the Church in receiving guidance and revelation for the entire Church.

That theme has been echoed and re-echoed throughout the revelations in the Doctrine and Covenants. The Lord even said that all that his Father promised to him could be shared by the Saints if they were true to the covenant of the priesthood. Notice, however, that this is predicated upon these words: "And also all they who receive this priesthood receive me, saith the Lord; For he that receiveth my servants receiveth me; And he that receiveth me receiveth my Father" (D&C 84:35-39). Certainly our happiness and exaltation depend on following the Lord through his prophets.

## Notes

[1]*Conference Report*, April 1977, p. 115; *Ensign*, May 1977, p. 78.

[2]*Ibid.*, October 1970, pp. 152-53; *Improvement Era*, December 1970, pp. 126-27.

[3]*HC* 1:105.

[4]*Ibid.*, 1:108-10.

[5]Lyndon W. Cook, *The Revelations of the Prophet Joseph Smith* (Provo: Seventy's Mission Bookstore, 1981), pp. 39-40.

[6]*HC* 1:338.

[7]*Ibid.*, p. 115.

[8]*Ibid.*, p. 154.

[9]*Ibid.*, footnote.

[10]Cook, *The Revelations*, pp. 61-62.

[11]*Conference Report*, October 1972, pp. 125-26; *Ensign*, December 1972.

[12]*Ensign*, July 1972, p. 103.

[13]*Conference Report*, April 1978, p. 117; *Ensign*, May 1978, p. 77.

[14]*Ibid.*, April 1945, p. 90.

[15]"Fourteen Fundamentals in Following the Prophet," *1980 Devotional Speeches of the Year* (Provo, Ut.: Brigham Young University Press, 1980), p. 29.

# 15

# CALLS TO PREACH THE GOSPEL

## (D&C 30-36)

Richard O. Cowan

Most of the eleven individuals addressed in the revelations contained in D&C 30-36 are well known. The three Whitmer brothers had received earlier revelations (sections 14-16) and were included among the special witnesses to the Book of Mormon. Five others—Thomas B. March, Parley P. Pratt, Orson Pratt, Sidney Rigdon, and Edward Partridge—later became General Authorities. In several ways the instructions received in these sections would have a far-reaching impact on the Church.

### The Mission to the Lamanites

Early revelations had emphasized the Church's responsibility to the Lamanites, descendants of the people from whom the Book of Mormon had come (see, for example, D&C 3:16-20). Latter-day Saints therefore felt a responsibility to help the Lamanites "blossom as the rose" (D&C 49:24) and to achieve their prophesied destiny.

At the same time that the Lord had cautioned Oliver Cowdery against Hiram Page's claims to revelation, he also called him to "go unto the Lamanites and preach my gospel unto them" and to "cause my church to be established among them" (D&C 28:8, cf. Alma 17:11). This commission has become the foundation for the Church's efforts among the Lamanites ever since. The revelations in sections 30 and 32 called three additional individuals—Peter Whitmer, Jr., Parley P. Pratt (a recent convert who had followed Sidney Rigdon), and Ziba Peterson—to join Oliver Cowdery on this mission. Their assignment, received in the fall of 1830, is generally recognized as the first formal mission in the history of the Church.

The Lamanite missionaries commenced their work with the Catteraugus Tribe near Buffalo, New York. Here their message was well received, and after leaving copies of the Book of Mormon, they continued their journey west. Near Kirtland, Ohio, Parley P. Pratt and his associates preached to Sidney Rigdon and his congregation. Although this may have seemed like a diversion from the missionaries' major objective, it resulted in one of their most significant accomplishments. Because Reverend Rigdon had taught the need for a restoration of Christ's Primitive Church, he and most of his congregation readily accepted the missionaries' message and joined the restored Church. Within a short period of time, 130 people were baptized, making this the largest single group of Latter-day Saints then on the earth.[1]

As the missionaries continued their westward journey, they were joined by a fifth companion, Frederick G. Williams, a convert just baptized in Kirtland. They visited the Wyandot Tribe near Sandusky, Ohio. From here they embarked on the most difficult part of their journey, trudging through winter snows in the wilderness to the frontier village of Independence, Missouri. They appeared to be enjoying success as they testified concerning the Book of Mormon to the Delaware Indians living just across the Indian frontier in what is now the state of Kansas. Their hopes were dashed, however, when other Christian missionaries brought pressure on the Indian agent to evict the Mormons from Indian territory. At this point, Parley P. Pratt was selected to return east, visiting the newly-baptized converts in Kirtland and reporting the missionaries' work to Joseph Smith. The other missionaries remained in Independence, teaching the gospel to the non-indian residents of that area.[2]

What had the mission accomplished? Although probably no Indians had been baptized, the work of preaching to the Lamanites had nevertheless begun. A large number of other converts had been baptized, including such future leaders as Sidney Rigdon and Edward Partridge. The missionaries had also provided the first Latter-day Saint contacts with Kirtland and Independence, both of which were to become important centers in the later history of the Church.

## Revelations to Individuals

The revelations in D&C 30-36 illustrate how the Lord knows his children well enough to suit commandments, cautions, and counsel to individual needs. Although the three Whitmer brothers addressed in section 30 all were to continue in the Lord's service, David was to remain at the family home, Peter was to go with Oliver Cowdery to the Lamanites, while John was to preach in the area of Philip Burrough's home at nearby Seneca Falls, New York. The Whitmers had been among those believing in Hiram Page's revelations. This is reflected in the Lord's reminding David that he must give heed to "those who were set over you" (v. 2) and in his insistence that Peter should follow the counsel of Oliver Cowdery, who in turn was to receive direction from the prophet Joseph Smith (vv. 5-7).

Thomas B. Marsh, a native of Massachusetts, happened to be visiting in Palmyra at the time the Book of Mormon was being printed. From Martin Harris he received a large printer's sheet containing the first sixteen pages of the book. When he and his wife read it, they gained a testimony. A short time later, upon learning that the Church had been organized, they moved to Fayette in order to become part of the latter-day work. Here they were baptized, just before the time section 31 was received. In 1835 Marsh would be called as one of the original Twelve Apostles and would serve as that quorum's first president. In 1838 he fell from this lofty calling when he refused to follow the counsel of local Church leaders relative to some questionable dealings of his wife.[3] Apparently he needed but failed to heed the Lord's counsel to "govern your house" (v. 9), to remain "faithful unto the end," and to "pray always" in order to avoid temptation which could lead to his losing his reward (vv. 12-13). Eventually Marsh returned to the Church, but never again to his standing among the Twelve.[4]

Parley P. Pratt, who had friends in northeastern Ohio, was an inspired choice for the mission that would take him through that very area. Before leaving on his mission to the Lamanites, however, he taught the gospel to his younger brother Orson, baptizing him on his nineteenth birthday. Less than two months later this young convert received the revelation in D&C 34. The Lord's comparison of Orson Pratt's preaching to the sound of a trumpet which is both "long and loud" (D&C 34:6) was truly prophetic. Orson became one of the original Twelve Apostles, lived longer than any of his colleagues, filled a total of seven missions, and earned a life-long reputation as one of the most capable defenders of the faith.[5]

In the revelation recorded in section 35 the Lord addressed Sidney Rigdon, the former Protestant minister. Referring to Sidney's future service as a "*greater* work" (v. 3, emphasis added), the Master suggested that he—like clergymen in other churches—had already accomplished good. Verse 4 suggests that Reverend Rigdon had labored in the same spirit as John the Baptist, who had been sent to prepare the way for the coming of the Savior. Now it was necessary for him and for his congregation to join the true Church for which they were prepared. Prior to his conversion and reception of the priesthood, Rigdon had baptized—but without evidence of divine acceptance; now he could perform this ordinance with authority, and the gifts of the Spirit would follow (vv. 5-6). Somewhat later the Lord similarly called James Covill, a Baptist minister, to "a greater work," promising that following his baptism into the restored Church he could preach the gospel with power (D&C 39:10-12).

Sidney Rigdon was called to assist Joseph Smith in at least two ways. He was to serve as a scribe, the Lord promising that "the scriptures shall be given, even as they are in mine own bosom" (D&C 35:20). Rigdon would provide substantial help in the Prophet's recently commenced inspired revision or "new translation" of the Bible.[6] He also was called to draw on his background as a minister to "preach [the] gospel and call on the holy prophets to prove [Joseph Smith's] words as they shall be given him" (D&C 35:23). A later revelation would explain that while Rigdon would be a spokesman for the Prophet, the latter would be a revelator to him (D&C 35:22 and 100:9-11).

After hearing the gospel from the Lamanite missionaries in November 1830, Edward Partridge traveled to New York the following month with Sidney Rigdon, in order to meet the prophet Joseph Smith. On this occasion the Lord revealed through the Prophet section 36, addressed to Edward Partridge. The Lord promised him: "I will lay my hand upon you by the hand of my servant Sidney Rigdon" in order to confirm him a member of the Church (v. 2). This suggests that ordinances performed by the authority of the priesthood should be accepted as though the Lord had performed them in person. The Master indicated that all who accepted the gospel "with singleness of heart" were to be sent forth to share the glad tidings with others (cf. D&C 36:5-7 and 88:81). Partridge did accept his calling in this spirit and only two months later was found worthy to become the first bishop in the Church (see D&C 41:9).

## The Missionaries' Message

Most of the men addressed in these revelations were called to go out and teach the gospel. Only a few months had passed since the organization of the Church, so the work of these missionaries in spreading news about the latter-day restoration was vital. As the Lord called Ezra Thayre and Northrop Sweet in section 33, he specifically defined the principles they were to teach: faith in the Lord Jesus Christ as the only means of salvation, repentance and preparation for that which is to come, baptism in water for the remission of sins, and reception of the purifying and sanctifying baptism of the Holy Ghost. This latter gift was to be received by the laying on of hands at the time converts were confirmed as members of the Church. To them the Lord solemnly affirmed: "This is my gospel" (D&C 33:10-12; note a similar but more abbreviated definition of the gospel message in D&C 39:6). Compliance with these precepts provides the foundation for all future growth toward the utlimate goal of exaltation in the celestial kingdom; hence they may be called the *first* [but surely not the only] principles and ordinances of the gospel.

The Doctrine and Covenants clearly teaches the central role of Jesus Christ in the plan of salvation. For centuries Christians have cherished the truth that because of God's great love he "gave his only begotten Son, that whosoever believeth in him should not perish, but have everlasting life" (John 3:16). In a latter-day revelation the Savior expanded on this concept: Christ "so loved the world that he gave his own life, that as many as would believe might become the sons of God" (D&C 34:3). All people are the begotten sons and daughters of the Father in the spirit but become his children in another sense as they accept and live the gospel of Jesus Christ. They thereby become the children of deity through spiritual rebirth (see Mosiah 5:7). Subsequent revelations explain how his voluntary and love-inspired sacrifice enabled Christ to become the advocate with the Father, pleading for those who have faith in him and who comply with the requirements of his gospel plan (D&C 38:4; 45:3-5).

The Master reminded the early missionaries of the Church that they could receive instruction from the Book of Mormon, the "holy scriptures" (i.e., the Bible), as well as from his Spirit (D&C 33:16). The "church articles and covenants" which the missionaries were to observe

(D&C 33:14) were what we now know as sections 20 and 22; they had been accepted formally as binding at the Church's first conference the previous June.

### Urgency of the Work

As the Savior called these individuals to the minstry, he clearly communicated to them a sense of urgency in their assignment. To Thomas B. Marsh he did not describe the field as being "white already to harvest," but rather he suggested a much more advanced state of affairs with his surprising declaration that the field was now ready to be burned (contrast D&C 31:4 with 4:4). The Lord described Ezra Thayre's and Northrop Sweet's calls as coming during the "eleventh hour" (the twelfth hour being the end), and hence "the last time" he would be calling servants into his vineyard (D&C 33:3). He reminded Sidney Rigdon of the parable of the fig-tree and affirmed that "even now already summer [the time of his coming] is nigh" (D&C 35:16). The Redeemer ended sections 33-35 with the same declaration: "I come quickly."

If the Lord sent his servants out with a sense of urgency in 1830, how much more eager should we be to be prepared and to accomplish his purposes in our day over a century and a half later.

## Notes

[1]See Milton V. Backman, Jr., *The Heavens Resound: A History of the Latter-day Saints in Ohio 1830-1838* (Salt Lake City: Deseret Book Co., 1983), pp. 1-19.

[2]For an eye-witness account of the missionaries' labors, see Parley P. Pratt, *Autobiography* (Salt Lake City: Deseret Book Co., 1966), chaps. 7-8.

[3]See Gordon B. Hinckley's analysis of this incident in "Small Acts Lead to Great Consequences," *Ensign*, May 1984, pp. 81-83.

[4]See Lyndon W. Cook, *The Revelations of the Prophet Joseph Smith* (Provo, Ut.: Seventy's Mission Bookstore, 1981), pp. 42-43.

[5]*Ibid.*, pp. 49-51.

[6]For an in-depth consideration of this subject, see Robert J. Matthews, *"A Plainer Translation": Joseph Smith's Translation of the Bible, A History and Commentary* (Provo, Ut.: Brigham Young University Press, 1975). See also Robert L. Millet, "The Joseph Smith Translation and the Doctrine and Covenants," found herein.

# 16

# HEEDING THE LORD'S CALL

## (D&C 37-41)

LEAUN G. OTTEN

### Introduction

In the revelation recorded in D&C 37, the Lord instructed Joseph Smith to cease temporarily the translation of the Bible (see D&C 37:1). The reason for this cessation is indicated in the same verse when the Lord said: "Behold, I say unto you that it is not expedient in me that you should translate any more until ye shall go to the Ohio, and this because of the enemy and for your sakes" (D&C 37:1).

Not only was Joseph Smith instructed to move to Ohio, but the Lord also commanded the Church membership in the New York area to assemble in Ohio (D&C 37:3). One reason for this move and the gathering of the Saints in Ohio was because enemies of the Church were plotting the deaths of the members (see D&C 37:1; 38:13, 28, 31-33). Shortly after section 37 was received, a conference of the Church was convened. At this conference, the Lord gave a revelation (section 38) in which he reaffirmed the importance of the Church's move to the Ohio (see D&C 38:31-33). This revelation also contained counsel and instructions that would assist the Saints to make this move with greater faith and confidence in the Lord.

### The Great I AM

The commandment to move to Ohio was the first time in this dispensation that the Lord's people were asked to move and gather. It would be natural for some of them to have had feelings of hesitancy about moving from already-established homes and leave friends and family in order to be obedient to the Lord's commandment. In section 38 the Lord gave the Saints sufficient reason to dispel doubt and place their confidence and trust in him and his judgment. He explained who he is and why he is able to give his Saints and all others correct counsel and direction. In the first eight verses of this section we learn the following truths about Jesus Christ:

1. He is the Great I AM, the Jehovah of the Old Testament (vv. 1, 4).
2. He knows all things (v. 2).
3. He made the world (v. 3).
4. He has power and control over the wicked (vv. 5-6).
5. He presides in the midst of the Saints, and the righteous will see him in due time (vv. 7-8).

The words "I AM" constitute a title that was another name for Jehovah, the God of the Old Testament people (see Exod. 3:14). The beautiful truth given in this revelation is that Jesus Christ is the same God that has directed the affairs of his Father's Kingdom since the world began. He is the Great Jehovah, the Great I AM.

Another eternal truth revealed by the Lord about himself is that he knows all things. All that God has ever revealed to mankind is supportive of this declaration. There is a multitude of scriptural references that declare this same doctrine (see 2 Ne. 9:20; Ether 3; Moses 1:8-28; D&C 88:41; etc.). The Savior and his prophets have declared and taught the omniscience of the Great I AM. Why is it necessary that he knows all things? And why does it matter that we know that he does? As an answer to both of these questions, Joseph Smith taught:

> The great Jehovah contemplated the whole of the events connected with the earth, pertaining to the plan of salvation, before it rolled into existence, or ever "the morning stars sang together" for joy; the past, the present, and the future were and are, with him, one eternal "now"; he knew of the fall of Adam, the iniquities of the antediluvians, of the depth of iniquity that would be connected with the human family, their weakness and strength, their power and glory, apostasies, their crimes, their righteousness and iniquity; he comprehended the fall of man, and his redemption; he knew the plan of salvation and pointed it out; he was acquainted with the situation of all nations and with their destiny; he ordered all things according to the council of his own will; he knows the situation of both the living and the dead, and has made ample provision for their redemption, according to their several circumstances, and the laws of the kingdom of God, whether in this world, or in the world to come.[1]

The Prophet also taught:

> By a little reflection it will be seen that the idea of the existence of these attributes in Deity is necessary to enable any rational being to exercise faith in him; for without the idea of the existence of these attributes in the Deity men could not exercise faith in him for life and salvation; seeing that without the knowledge of all things, God would not be able to save any portion of his creatures; for it is by reason of the knowledge which he has of all things, from the beginning to the end, that enables him to give that understanding to his creatures by which they are made partakers of eternal life.[2]

## The Savior's Love and Concern

From the revelation in section 38 we learn that there are several dimensions of the Lord's love and concern for his people:

1. Their temporal welfare and salvation (vv. 16-20, 34-38)
2. Just laws and freedom (vv. 21-22)
3. Unity of the Lord's people (vv. 23-27)
4. Intent of the hearts of men (vv. 29-30)
5. Obtaining and properly using riches (v. 39)

For every law that is kept, there is a blessing attached that comes from the Lord. Obedience has its own reward. When the Saints were commanded to go to Ohio, the Lord promised them: "That ye might escape the power of the enemy, and be gathered unto me a righteous people, without spot and blameless—Wherefore, for this cause I gave unto you the commandment that ye should go to the Ohio; and there I will give unto you my law; and there you shall be endowed with power from on high" (D&C 38:31-32). Not only would the Saints escape their enemies by going to Ohio, but they would be able to be gathered unto the Lord as a righteous people. Through their obedience to his will, they would establish a relationship of unity with him. The Lord also promised to give his Church additional laws and commandments that were needed in order to govern his people properly and carry out the functions of his kingdom. The fulfillment of that promise was begun in the revelation of the Lord's law as found in section 42 of the Doctrine and Covenants.

Still further, the Lord promised to endow his Saints with power from on high. There are several ways the fulfillment of this promise can be seen in the Ohio history of the Church. A few are listed:

1. The first temple of this dispensation was built in Ohio.
2. Keys of the priesthood were restored by angelic messengers in the temple.
3. The Savior appeared to many of the Saints.[3]
4. The offices of Bishop, Quorum of Twelve Apostles, First Presidency, etc., were revealed to the Church.

## A True Disciple of Jesus Christ

A disciple is usually defined as "a follower," "a student," etc. The Lord revealed his definition of discipleship as follows: "He that receiveth my law and doeth it, the same is my disciple; and he that saith he receiveth it and doeth it not, the same is not my disciple" (D&C 41:5). It is a sacred privilege to be designated as a disciple of the Master. It is likewise a serious and sacred step to enter into covenants with him. Those who intend to receive the rewards of discipleship need to be aware that willful failure to comply with the conditions of the covenants is hypocrisy and brings the displeasure of the Lord and can result in serious consequences. Self-inventory of one's discipleship with the Savior is vital in measuring progress. This inventory should include some of the following questions:

1. Since I have received the Lord's law of tithing, am I obeying it?
2. Since I have received the Lord's law of the Sabbath, am I keeping it?
3. Since I have received the Lord's law of marriage, am I living it?

There are many areas of our covenant commitments with the Savior that should be evaluated from time to time. Such evaluations will provide us with a barometer of our true discipleship to the Lord.

## A Call to Serve

In D&C 41, Edward Partridge received a call from the Lord to serve as the first bishop of the Church in this dispensation (D&C 41:9-11).

This calling of Bishop Partridge illustrates the process by which people are called to serve in the Kingdom. The process involves the following:

1. The Lord calls through his authorized representatives.
2. The individual called is presented to the Church membership for their sustaining vote.
3. The individual called is given the authority to act in the office of his calling.

## The Lord Calls

It needs to be emphasized that this process pertains to a calling to serve in the Savior's Church, not in any organization of men. Anyone who serves is entitled to know, and should be aware, that he serves not alone, but he can and should rely upon the Lord, from whom the call comes. With such an awareness, one can then go forth and serve with confidence and conviction, being especially careful to be sensitive to the wishes and prompting directions of the Lord. Thus, a sacredness is associated with the call that provides a greater depth of responsibility to the call and serves as a quiet reminder of the sacred responsibility conveyed to those who serve the Lord.

## Voice of the Church

As revealed in section 26 the Lord's law to this Church requires that those who are properly called must be presented to the membership of the Church and sustained by them.

## Authority to Act

Who has the right to assume authority? Even the laws of man do not permit such an assumption. Yet, some sincere people have mistakenly assumed that a desire to serve the Savior is sufficient authority to act in his name. There is no scriptural support for such a course of action.

In section 41 the Lord revealed the necessity of receiving authority through authorized and designated servants. Only through such authority are actions valid in the sight of the Lord: "We believe that a man must be called of God, by prophecy and by the laying on of hands, by those who are in authority, to preach the Gospel and administer in the ordinances thereof" (Article of Faith 5).

## Notes

[1]*HC* 4:597.

[2]Joseph Smith, *Lectures on Faith*, Fourth Lecture, paragraph 11; comp. N.B. Lundwall (Salt Lake City: N. B. Lundwall, n.d.), p. 43.

[3]For these, see Milton V. Backman, Jr. and Robert L. Millet, "Heavenly Manifestations in the Kirtland Temple," found herein.

# 17

# UNITED UNDER THE LAWS OF THE CELESTIAL KINGDOM CONSECRATION, STEWARDSHIP, AND THE UNITED ORDER, 1830-1838

## (D&C 42, 51, 78, 82, 83, 104, etc.)

Milton V. Backman, Jr. and Keith W. Perkins

Temporal welfare has been a major concern of people in all ages. Early in this dispensation the Prophet Joseph Smith became concerned about this problem; partly because of these concerns the Prophet went to the Lord. Subsequently, the law of consecration or the United Order (as called in some revelations) was unfolded.[1]

Like many other principles of the gospel, the law of consecration and stewardship of property was gradually made known to the Prophet Joseph Smith, who in turn gradually disclosed these principles to Latter-day Saints, line upon line, precept upon precept. Some members of the Church were granted an opportunity to live this higher law, but most failed. The law was misinterpreted, misunderstood, neglected, and eventually replaced by a less comprehensive law, the law of tithing (D&C 119).

In one of the revelations instructing the Saints to move to Ohio (see D&C 38:32), Joseph was told that the Lord would reveal to him a new divine law in that state. Upon his arrival, Joseph learned that serious problems were plaguing members of "the Family." A group of people, seeking to organize themselves according to the pattern in the New Testament ("all things in common"), had established a "common stock" social order on the Isaac Morley farm. They called themselves "the Family." The pooling of property had led some to believe that everything should be shared, including clothes; it was felt that what belonged to one belonged to all.[2] On 9 February 1831, twelve elders approached Joseph Smith and inquired if the time was ripe for the unfolding of the "law" that had been mentioned in the New York revelation. In their presence, the Prophet sought divine instruction and recorded most of what is today section 42 of the Doctrine and Covenants.[3]

Section 42 of the Doctrine and Covenants contains a series of laws and policies, including such matters as preaching the gospel, moral laws and commandments (including a number of the ten commandments), administering to the sick, location of the New Jerusalem and other mysteries of the kingdom to be revealed, and punishment for transgression. This revelation, along with a number of others, also contains a partial description of what is sometimes called the United Order or the law of consecration.

## Guiding Principles of the United Order

The revelations of the Lord pertaining to consecration or the United Order, contain six major categories that are the guiding principles under which this law was to operate. These six categories are: (1) the earth is the Lord's, (2) all people are children of God, (3) free agency, (4) management by a central agency, (5) specified behavior patterns, and (6) private ownership of property.

Let us examine (in outline form) some details from the Doctrine and Covenants and Joseph Smith's *History of the Church* under these six general categories. In doing so, we may gain a much clearer understanding of how the law of consecration or the United Order was to be lived, and also the principles which guided it.

### I. The Earth is the Lord's

A. Lord created the earth (14:9; 104:14).
B. Earth is rich; there is enough and to spare for all people (38:17; 104:17).
C. Riches of eternity promised by the Lord (38:39).
D. Goods given to the poor are given to the Lord (42:31).
E. Poor provided for in the Lord's own way (104:15-16).
F. Lord is no respector of persons, rich or poor (38:16).

### II. All People Are Children of God

A. Esteem brother as self (38:24-25).
B. Be one or not the Lord's (38:27).
C. We are responsible for the poor, needy, widow, and orphan so there will be no suffering (38:35; 83:1-6).

D. To be equal spiritually we must be equal temporally (78:6).
E. Poor will be exalted and the rich humbled (104:16-17).

## III. Free Agency

A. Free agency is basic to the law (104:17).
B. Stewardships were received according to just wants, needs, family, and circumstances (51:3; 82:17).
C. A person leaving the order retained his stewardship (51:5).
D. Saints had the privilege of organizing according to the Lord's law (51:15).
E. If the bishop and an individual did not agree on the amount the individual received as a stewardship, the contributor had the right of appeal (*HC* 1:364-65).

## IV. Management by a Central Agency

A. Properties were consecrated to the Lord through the Lord's agents, the bishop and his two counselors, with a covenant and deed which could not be broken (42:30-31; 58:35-36).
B. Stewardships received by written deed from a bishop (51:4).
C. Surplus property, money, and food were placed in a bishop's storehouse (42:33-35; 51:13).
D. Surpluses provided food and clothing for poor and needy and were used to purchase additional property (42:33-35; 58:37, 49; 83:1-6).
E. Deeds conveyed according to the laws of the land (51:6).
F. Two treasuries in Order: the sacred treasury and "another treasury" (104:60-72).

## V. Specified Behavior Patterns

A. Labor with own hands (38:40)
B. Deal honestly and receive alike (51:4).
C. Avoid pride (42:40).
D. Avoid idleness (42:42; 56:17).
E. Pay for what was received (42:54).

F. Pay debts (104:78).
G. Improve talents and gain additional talents for the benefit of all (82:18).
H. Be faithful, just, and wise (51:19).
I. Give an accounting of stewardships to the Bishop (42:32; 72:16-18; 104:11-13).
J. Seek interest of neighbor and glorify God (82:19).

VI. **Private Ownership of Property**

A. Pay for what was received from another branch of the Order (51:11).
B. System not communal (*HC* 1:146-47; 3:28; 4:33; 6:37, 38).
C. Surpluses given to Church after the needs and wants of an individual or family are provided for (42:32-34).
D. Everyone to provide for own needs (75:28).
E. Saints to stand independent of all other creatures (78:14).
F. Initiative rewarded (82:17-18).
G. If individual left the order, he had no claim on original consecration, but the stewardship was retained by individual (42:37; 51:5).

The law of consecration and stewardship, or the United Order, was unfolded in the 1830s as the Welfare Program has been revealed in our day for similar reasons: to provide for the poor, needy, widows, and orphans, and to help the Saints obtain unity.

On 4 February 1831 Edward Partridge had been called by revelation as the first bishop of the Church. He was commanded to sell his property and devote full time to the "labors of the church" (see D&C 41:9). Sections 42 and 51 provided Bishop Partridge with instructions regarding his responsibilities.

### Problems in Implementing the Law

A variety of problems interfered with the immediate application of the law of consecration in Ohio in 1831. John Whitmer, who had been called by revelation on 8 March 1831 as Church Historian (see D&C 47:1-4), wrote that the time had not yet come for the law to be fully established. The disciples, he explained, were scattered and were small in number, and many did not understand and would not accept this law.[4] There were other reasons, however, that should be considered. Between the end of October and December 1830 approximately nine families living in Kirtland joined the Church. These individuals owned 132 acres of land in that township. Most of these converts were living on the Isaac Morley farm. If all of the land owned by the Kirtland Saints had been divided among these nine families, each family would have received less than fifteen acres. Although Newel K. Whitney owned a profitable mercantile store and did not need as much land as most, a majority of the Kirtland converts were farmers; fifteen acres were not sufficient to support an average family.[5] One problem encountered in organizing communal societies was a tendency for poor people to be attracted to such movements and for the wealthy to shun such enterprises. For example, one possible problem encountered by the Family was that some took advantage of Isaac Morley, who had undoubtedly contributed more than others. That which belonged to one was considered the property of all, arousing jealousy and bitter feelings.[6] In the revelation that Joseph Smith received on 9 February 1831, members learned that they were not to live in a communal type order, but they were to be stewards over their own property (see D&C 42:32). However, as explained, one of the probable reasons that the United Order was not immediately put into use in Kirtland was because members did not own sufficient land in that town for a satisfactory redistribution to have occurred.

## Arrival of New York Saints in Ohio

The problem of applying this law was compounded by the migration of about two hundred Latter-day Saints to Ohio between January and June of 1831. At the call of a Prophet, these converts had sold their farms, disposed of much of their property, and traveled to Ohio (see D&C 37:3; 38:32). In the initial publication of section 42 in the Book of Commandments, there was a reference to members in Ohio assisting Bishop Partridge in locating places for these immigrants (see Book of Commandments 44:57). Some of the first Saints to arrive settled in Kirtland, including members of the Joseph Smith, Sr., family and the Peter Whitmer family. Apparently there was not enough money nor land available in that township to care for the needs of the New York Saints. John Whitmer observed that because of the lack of preparation to receive the Saints from the east, Bishop Partridge sought advice from Joseph concerning where they should settle. Whitmer added that some Easterners believed that Kirtland was the "place of gathering, even the place of the New Jerusalem spoken of in the Book of Mormon." Therefore, John Whitmer recorded that the "Lord spake unto Joseph Smith," resulting in what is today section 48 of our Doctrine and Covenants.[7] Members were told that the place of the New Jerusalem had not yet been revealed and the Ohio Saints were to share their surplus property with the "eastern brethren." If needed, the immigrants were to purchase additional property (see D&C 48:2-5).

Some of the economic problems of the Ohio Saints seemed to be alleviated when Leman Copley, a former Shaker who lived in Thompson—located about twenty miles east of Kirtland—joined the Church. Copley granted the immigrants the right to settle on his farm. Consequently, most of the New York Saints established their homes there.[8]

## The Thompson Saints

As the New York Saints continued to arrive, Bishop Partridge sought additional advice from Joseph concerning the United Order. The Prophet again inquired of the Lord and in mid-May, shortly after most of the Eastern Saints had settled in Ohio, received additional information regarding stewardships. While visiting the Saints in Thompson, the Prophet learned that the bishop of the Church was to receive the property of the people and was to divide the "inheritances" among the stewards according to their "circumstances," "wants," and "needs" (see D&C 51:3). Therefore, under this law, everyone was not to have exactly the same thing. "The 'equality' was to vary as much as the man's circumstances, his family, his wants and needs, may vary."[9] Or as Brigham Young said, "How could you ever get a people equal with regard to their possessions? They never can be, no more than they can be in the appearance of their faces."[10]

When Leman Copley left the Order, the Saints were in a difficult situation. After initiating a building program in Thompson, they were ordered by the legal owner of the property to leave. They had sacrificed economically while complying with the commandment to move to Ohio. Some had sold farms at a loss, and all had spent part of their money during the move westward. Undoubtedly, they lacked the necessary funds to buy suitable property in Ohio, and members did not own sufficient land in Kirtland to accommodate the needs of all these converts.[11] After seeking advice from the Prophet, they were instructed to move to western Missouri (see D&C 54:8, 9). Consequently, during the summer of 1831 most of the New York Saints settled in the American frontier, where they sought to live in harmony with the law of consecration.[12]

The New York Saints were not the only members to move West. Most of the converts, including those who are known to have been members of "the Family" and had been living in Kirtland in the fall of 1830, also migrated to Jackson County, Missouri. Morley sold his farm in Kirtland and received an inheritance in the West. Some of the Saints, including Bishop Edward Partridge, Titus Billings, and A. Sidney Gilbert (Newel K. Whitney's business partner), emigrated in harmony with revelations received by the Prophet. Members in Kirtland were instructed by revelation to assist financially in the building of the land of Zion (see D&C 63:40; 64:26). Meanwhile, developments in and near Kirtland had brought on questions that prompted the Prophet to seek counsel from the Lord. Therefore, all major revelations relating to the law of consecration or the United Order were unfolded in northeastern Ohio.

## Gathering at Kirtland

But Kirtland was not abandoned. After returning from Missouri in late August 1831, Joseph Smith received several revelations regarding Kirtland's future (see D&C 63 and 64). Joseph learned from the Lord that the Frederick G. Williams farm (consisting of approximately 150 acres) was not to be sold and that Newel K. Whitney and Sidney Gilbert were not to dispose of their store or possessions, that a "strong hold" might be retained in Kirtland "for the space of five years" (see D&C 64:21, 26). Frederick G. Williams, Newel K. Whitney, most members of the Smith family, and a few other Saints continued to reside in that township. Although Joseph Smith, Sidney Rigdon, and their families moved to Hiram, Ohio, in mid-September 1831, they left that community in the spring of 1832. Fleeing from their oppressors, Joseph, Sidney, and their families relocated in Kirtland by September 1832. For the second time, Kirtland became the home of the Prophet; furthermore, while most emigrating Latter-day Saints were moving to Missouri, Kirtland became a second gathering place and headquarters of the Church. Joseph continued to reside in Kirtland until January 1838. Then in the midst of apostate mobocracy, the Prophet sought refuge in Far West, Missouri.

Meanwhile, Kirtland did not become a major gathering place for the Saints until members began building a temple in the summer of 1833. After selling their farms, immigrants from the East brought money to Kirtland, but instead of buying farms and building homes that compared with their former residences, many sacrificed and contributed generously to building a House for the Lord.[13]

## Failure of United Order in Missouri

Developments in Missouri helped to bring about a quick demise of the United Order there. Lack of a correct understanding of this law, lack of money and land, selfishness, covetous desires, persecution, and expulsion from Jackson County all contributed to the failure of the Saints in Missouri to live this higher law (D&C 101:6-8; 103:4; 105:2-6).[14] To be more specific, after the Saints in Thompson had been frustrated in their attempt to comply with the provisions of this law, a second attempt to institute the United Order was made in Jackson County, Missouri. Within six months of the initial settlement of that community (by the end of 1831), Bishop Edward Partridge had established a storehouse for the reception and distribution of consecrated goods, and one year after the gathering had commenced most of the three to four hundred converts living there had consecrated their property to the bishop and were living on inheritances. But the implementation of this law was again impeded by problems. Some members did not comply or did not learn of the recommendations of leaders in Kirtland, who instructed others not to gather unless they took with them money, seeds, cattle or other contributions to the system. Evidently, there was not sufficient property to give every Latter-day Saint family an adequate inheritance. A number of families crowded in homes that were meant to support a single family.

Apparently, some became lazy while they were waiting for an inheritance or the anticipated Second Coming. Others left the Church, taking with them their inheritances. As early as the fall of 1832, Bishop Edward Partridge began leasing land (rather than conveying deeds) to the Saints. Under the provision of these contracts, stewards were not permitted to transfer their inheritances to their wives, children, or heirs, or to sell their property.[15]

On several occasions, the Prophet wrote to Church leaders in Missouri informing them that their adaptation of the law of consecration was not correct. In a letter to William W. Phelps, dated 27 November 1832, Joseph Smith stated that he was displeased because the Saints who had gathered in Zion had not received "their inheritance by consecrations, by order of deed from the Bishop."[16] The Prophet eventually resolved this problem and in harmony with divine guidance edited section 51 (in the current edition of the Doctrine and Covenants) by adding the following instructions to this revelation: a transgressor who left the Church was to retain that which had been deeded to him but had no claim on the surplus that he contributed to the Church (see D&C 51:5).[17]

Commenting on Bishop Partridge's modification of the United Order in Missouri, President J. Reuben Clark, Jr., former member of the First Presidency, said that the "lease-lend" principle was not in accordance with the revelations which Joseph Smith received regarding the United Order. Basic to this principle, he added, was the private ownership of property. "Every man owned his portion, or inheritance, or stewardship, with an absolute title." This inheritance was to be used for the support of himself and his family. "There is nothing in the revelations that would indicate that this property was not freely alienable at the will of the owner. [And] it was not contemplated that the Church should own everything." Moreover, "life under the United Order was not a communal life, as the Prophet Joseph, himself, said (*HC* 3:28). The United Order is an individualistic system, not a communal [nor communistic] system."[18]

After experiencing frustrations and failures for almost a decade, in 1838 members throughout the Church were given a less comprehensive law, the law of tithing (see D&C 119).

## The United Order in Kirtland

Meanwhile, some members in Kirtland were striving to live the law of consecration or the United Order, although the practice was not precisely the same as the basic principles that were revealed. During the brief period the United Order was practiced in Missouri, Kirtland, and Utah, there were no practices that were identical. It is one thing to receive a revelation and another to implement it. Since the Lord has stated that we must be united under the principles of consecration and stewardship or we cannot inherit the Celestial Kingdom, one day we must live these principles (D&C 88:22; 105:5).

All attempts to live the principles outlined by the Lord to unite the Saints and provide for the poor are simply examples of learning to live the gospel, line upon line and precept upon precept. Welfare Services today, for example, is another effort to live these principles outlined by the Lord.

> Thus . . . in many of its great essentials, we have [in] the welfare plan . . . the broad essentials of the United Order. ([J. Reuben Clark,] *Conference Report*, October 1942, pp. 57-58) . . .
>
> It is thus apparent that when the principles of tithing and the fast are properly observed and the welfare plan gets fully developed and wholly into operation, we shall not be so very far from carrying out the great fundamentals of the United Order. The only limitation on you and me is within ourselves.[19]

It is not clear when early Latter-day Saints began to lived the United Order (or as it is called in other documents, the "United Firm"). In a revelation (4 December 1831) making known the duties of Newel K. Whitney, second bishop of the Church, the Lord declared that while the Saints in Missouri were to operate the United Order under the direction of Bishop Edward Partridge, the Order in Kirtland was to be under the direction of Bishop Whitney (D&C 72:5). Not only were members to give an accounting of their stewardship to him, but he was to keep the Lord's storehouse, receive Church funds, take account of the elders, and administer to the wants of the elders and the poor through the consecration of the Saints (D&C 72:9-12). He was, however, to operate under the direction of Bishop Partridge in Missouri (vv. 13-18).

## Section 78

By March 1832 the United Order was organized not only in Missouri but in Kirtland as well (D&C 78:3-8). Bishop Newel K. Whitney, in conjunction with Joseph Smith and Sidney Rigdon, sat in council with the Saints in Missouri (v. 9). In their organization of the United Order they were to organize by a "bond or everlasting covenant that cannot be broken." If any were to break this bond, they would lose their office and standing in the Church (vv. 11-12). It was through the United Order, despite the tribulation that would come upon them, that they would be able to stand independent of "all other creatures beneath the celestial world" and ultimately obtain exaltation, inheriting all things (vv. 13-22).

According to the minutes of the United Order for 30 April 1832, two agents were appointed for the Order, A. Sidney Gilbert in Missouri and Newel K. Whitney in Kirtland. It was the duty of the United Firm, by their branches at Jackson County, Missouri, and Geauga County, Ohio, to regulate their business by these two agents.[20] On the same day another part of the Order met, the Literary Firm. This firm was responsible for printing various writings, e.g., the revelations, the new translation of the Bible, the Church hymn book, and other Church publications.[21]

These early days in the Order must have been days of inquiry and searching for the best way to implement the program among the Saints. In a letter from the Prophet Joseph Smith to Oliver Cowdery, in response to inquiries regarding the procedures to be followed in the United Order, the Prophet gave this advice: "I have nothing further to say on the subject than to recommend that you make yourself acquainted with the commandments of the Lord, and the laws of the state, and govern yourselves accordingly."[22]

The original members of the United Order were ten leaders of the Church.[23] Under the direction of the Lord the group was increased by two members. On 15 March 1833 Frederick G. Williams was added to the group (D&C 92:1-2). Two months earlier it had been decided to pay him $300 annually for his services as assistant scribe for the Order.[24] On 4 June 1833 John Johnson, Sr. was selected to be a member of the Order (D&C 96:6-9).

The United Order continued to purchase land and operate the

Newel K. Whitney Store in Kirtland and the A. Sidney Gilbert Store in Missouri, until 10 April 1834. At that time the United Order was dissolved and each individual received his own stewardships.[25]

## Section 104

Thirteen days later the Lord gave specific direction on the division of stewardships. It must be remembered that some very dramatic events had made this move necessary. The Saints in Jackson County, Missouri, had been driven from their inheritances and therefore it was impossible to continue functioning as a united group. It is also obvious that the Lord never intended that the Saints participate in a communal order; while the Prophet was requesting information on what action should be taken, he received a reaffirmation of how to implement the Lord's economic order.

In this revelation the Lord reminded the Saints that it was he who commanded the United Order to be organized as an everlasting order until he returns (D&C 104:1). Those who had been obedient to the Order had obtained great blessings, while those who had transgressed their covenants were cursed (vv. 5-10).

The Lord again clarified the correct procedure in implementing the United Order. Individual stewardships were allocated to the various members of the Order and each would be responsible for giving an accounting of this stewardship to the Lord (vv. 11-13). First, Sidney Rigdon received his place of residence and the tannery (v. 20).

Second, Martin Harris received a lot from John Johnson and was to devote his money for the purpose of proclaiming "my words" (vv. 24, 26).

Third, Frederick G. Williams was given as a stewardship the place where he lived (v. 27).

Fourth, Oliver Cowdery received Lot One of the Kirtland Plat and also his father's lot (v. 28). Jointly Oliver and President Williams received the printing office. This was the beginning of the stewardship appointed unto them and their descendants (vv. 29-31).

Fifth, John Johnson had allocated to him his residence and the one hundred plus acre French Farm which had been purchased on 10 April 1833, except the temple lot and the lots assigned to Oliver Cowdery (v. 34). Lots were to be layed out and sold "for the building up of the city of my saints" as it would be made known to Brother Johnson by the voice of the Spirit and by the voice of the Order (v. 36).

Sixth, Newel K. Whitney received the houses and lots where he resided, the store, the lot directly south of the store, and the ashery (v. 39). Bishop Whitney was to continue to play a major roll in "*my* order which I have established for *my* stake in the land of Kirtland" (v. 40, italics added). In addition to the property and the building, the entire mercantile establishment was his stewardship, along with his agent (v. 41). The identity of this agent is not clear, although it could have been Orson Hyde; he worked for Bishop Whitney and later had the store deeded to him for a short period of time.[26]

Seventh, Joseph Smith, Jr. received as a stewardship the temple lot and the inheritance where his father resided. The Joseph Smith, Sr. stewardship was to be reckoned with the Prophet's (vv. 43, 45).

As a part of the individual stewardships, the United Order between Missouri and Kirtland, as we have seen, was dissolved and they were to become two separate orders: "the United Order of the Stake of Zion, the City of Kirtland" and "the United Order of the City of Zion" (vv. 47-48). This allowed them to be organized "in their own name, and in their own names." In other words, they were to have their individual stewardships. This action was necessary since the Saints in Missouri had been driven out (v. 49, 51). The Order in Kirtland and the Order in Missouri were not to be bound together except by loan, as agreed between them (v. 53).

This reorganization by the Lord really was implementing the principles already given by the Lord, for as he had said in this revelation, the properties were his and the Saints were his stewards (vv. 55-56).

One purpose for the organization of the Order was to print Joseph Smith's translation of the Bible and the Doctrine and Covenants. This would help prepare the Saints for the time when Christ would come and dwell among his people (v. 59). In addition, they were to prepare two treasuries and appoint a treasurer over each. The first was the "sacred treasury of the Lord." The funds in this treasury were for the purpose of printing the scriptures and other Church works. The profits acquired from this treasury were only to be used by consent of the Order and the Lord (vv. 60-66).

The other treasury was for the purpose of receiving all the improvements resulting from their individual stewardships. These could be of many types: houses, lands, cattle, money, everything except the "sacred writings" (v. 68). Once these items were placed in the treasury they no longer were a part of an individual's stewardship but belonged to the Order; none could be removed without the approval of those in the Order (vv. 70-71). If an individual in the United Order needed anything in this "other treasury" to assist him in his stewardship, with the approval and the common consent of the Order, the treasurer could give him what was required. He was forbidden to withhold anything approved by the common consent of the Order (vv. 72-75).

When this reorganization of the United Order in Kirtland came to an end is difficult to determine. However, the word of the Lord in D&C 105:34 removed from the Saints in Missouri the responsibility of living the law of consecration and stewardship of property until after the redemption of Zion.

By 1837 the United Order in Kirtland had definitely come to an end when a financial crisis struck. This economic plight was one of many factors that led to an apostasy in the Church, and forced Joseph to flee from Kirtland to save his life. In January 1838, seven years after he had initially settled in that community and five years after he had returned from his short stay in Hiram, the Prophet left Kirtland for the last time. Meanwhile, through the application of the principle of stewardship, which includes manifestations of love and sacrifice, Latter-day Saints made Kirtland into a stronghold for exactly five years. During this remarkable period, this religious community experienced an unusual outpouring of the blessing of God. Many Kirtland Saints experienced a memorable spiritual feast that was in the words of Oliver Cowdery too "[glorious] to be described. I only say," he added, "the heavens were opened to many, and great and marvelous things" were unfolded to Latter-day Saints.[27]

Efforts to live the principles of the United Order were attempted later in Utah. Like the various attempts in Kirtland and Missouri, there were different orders. Eventually they also failed.[28] Today we are living many of these same principles revealed by the Lord as we participate in welfare services and other programs of the Church. As explained by

President Marion G. Romney, "We as Latter-day Saints should live strictly by the principles of the United Order insofar as they are embodied in present Church practices, such as fast offering, tithing, and welfare activities. Through these practices we could as individuals, if we were of a mind to, implement in our own lives all the basic principles of the United Order."[29]

## Notes

[1]"These principles of union, which the Latter-day Saints in former times ignored, and in consequence of disobedience of them were driven from Missouri, are called by different names—united order, order of Enoch, the principles of union of the celestial law, etc. When we search the revelations of God in regard to them, we see that wherever the gospel of the Son of God has been revealed in its fullness, the principles of the united order were made manifest, and required to be observed" (Lorenzo Snow, *JD* 19:342). Although today many use the term "law of consecration and stewardship" to describe certain principles that are designed to bring about unity, support Church programs, and care for the poor, and United Order to describe the implementation of these principles, the scriptures and most Church leaders have used "United Order" to describe both.

[2]John Whitmer, *An Early Latter Day Saint History: The Book of John Whitmer Kept by Commandment*, ed. F. Mark McKiernan and Roger D. Launius (Independence, Mo.: Herald Publishing House, 1980), p. 37.

[3]*HC* 1:148; Whitmer, *Book of John Whitmer*, p. 38.

[4]Whitmer, *Book of John Whitmer*, p. 42.

[5]Milton V. Backman, Jr., *The Heavens Resound: A History of the Latter-day Saints in Ohio 1838-1838* (Salt Lake City: Deseret Book Co., 1983), p. 319. Clarence H. Danhoff, *Change in Agriculture: The Northern United States, 1820-1870* (Cambridge, Mass.: Harvard University Press, 1969), p. 114; Lee Soltow, "Inequality Amidst Abundance: Land Ownership in Early Nineteenth Century Ohio," *Ohio History* 82 (Spring 1979); Percy W. Bidwell and John I. Falconer, *History of Agriculture in the Northern United States, 1620-1860* (Washington, D.C.: Carnegie Institution, 1925), pp. 37, 115.

[6]*The Levi Hancock Journal*, n.p., n.d., p. 28.

[7]Whitmer, *Book of John Whitmer*, p. 54.

[8]*Ibid.*, p. 74.

[9]J. Reuben Clark, Jr., *Conference Report*, October 1942, pp. 54-59.

[10]Cited by Albert E. Bowen, *The Church Welfare Plan* (Salt Lake City: Deseret Sunday School Union, 1946), p. 25.

[11]*HC* 1:180; Newel K. Knight, *Scraps of Biography: The Tenth Book of the Faith-Promoting Series* (Salt Lake City: Juvenile Instructor, 1883), chapter 6.

[12]For a more complete discussion of the Leman Copley problem and the Thompson Saints, see Keith W. Perkins, "The Ministry of the Shakers," found herein.

[13]Backman, *Heavens Resound*, p. 16.

[14]For a discussion of the application of the United Order in Missouri during the 1830s, see Leonard J. Arrington, Feramorz Y. Fox, and Dean L. May, *Building the City of God: Community and Cooperation Among the Mormons* (Salt Lake City: Deseret Book Co., 1976), p. 22.

[15]Joseph Smith to William W. Phelps, 27 November 1832, cited in *HC* 1:297-99.

[16]Robert J. Woodford, "The Historical Development of the Doctrine and Covenants," unpublished Ph.D. dissertation, Brigham Young University, 1974. Compare Book of Commandments, chapter 44 vv. 26-29 with Doctrine and Covenants (1835), chapter 17 vv. 8-10.

[17]Woodford, "Historical Development," p. 672.

[18]J. Reuben Clark, Jr., *Conference Report*, October 1942, p. 57.

[19]Marion G. Romney, *Look to God and Live*, comp. George J. Romney (Salt Lake City: Deseret Book Co., 1973), pp. 227-28.

[20]Donald Q. Cannon and Lyndon W. Cook, ed., *Far West Record* (Salt Lake City: Deseret Book Co., 1983), pp. 47-8.

[21]*Ibid.*, p. 46.

[22]*HC* 1:341.

[23]The original members of the United Order were Joseph Smith, Sidney Rigdon, and Jesse Gause of the First Presidency; Bishops Edward Partridge and Newel K. Whitney; Oliver Cowdery and William W. Phelps, printers of the Church; A. Sidney Gilbert, agent in Zion; John Whitmer, the Lord's clerk; and Martin Harrris, one of the three witnesses (see D&C 70:1-5; 82:11-12; 104:19-46; *Far West Record*, p. 47).

[24]Kirtland Council Minute Book, located in Historical Department of the Church, 9 January 1833.

[25]Dean C. Jessee, comp. and ed., *The Personal Writings of Joseph Smith* (Salt Lake City: Deseret Book Co., 1984), p. 32.

[26]Geauga County, Ohio Land Records, 1835 and 1839.

[27]Oliver Cowdery, Sketch Book 21 January 1836, Archives of The Church of Jesus Christ of Latter-day Saints, Salt Lake City, Utah.

[28]Leonard J. Arrington, *Great Basin Kingdom: An Economic History of the Latter-day Saints 1830-1900* (Lincoln, Neb.: University of Nebraska Press, 1970), pp. 323-27.

[29]*Look to God and Live*, p. 227.

# 18

# THE SIGNS OF THE TIMES "BE NOT TROUBLED" (D&C 29, 43-45, 116, 133)

Kent P. Jackson

"Wherefore, I the Lord, knowing the calamity which should come upon the inhabitants of the earth, called upon my servant Joseph Smith, Jun., and spake unto him from heaven, and gave him commandments" (D&C 1:17). So states the Lord in his preface to the revelations that comprise the Doctrine and Covenants. Because the Lord knows the things which will transpire for the remainder of the history of the earth, and because he desires that his children experience peace—not only in their hearts but in their physical realities as well—he opened the heavens and sent forth revelations through his servant Joseph Smith. Among those revelations are many that speak of events that will transpire before the earth has finished her appointed mission as the home for God's mortal children and assumes her eternal role as their celestial dwelling place. With the revelations available to all who would read them and heed their message, the Lord's moving admonition invites all to share in the light and knowledge that can come from them: "Hearken ye to these words. Behold, I am Jesus Christ, the Savior of the world. Treasure these things up in your hearts, and let the solemnities of eternity rest upon your minds" (D&C 43:34).

In the Church today there is considerable interest in the events that will transpire in the latter days of the earth's history. Since the beginning of the Restoration, the Saints have been taught that they are in the last days—the period which will usher in the Second Coming of the Lord. Because of this, some have been involved in distracting speculations concerning prophesied events, even to the point of predicting the specific time of the Second Coming or other last-day occurrences, or placing such unnecessary emphasis on final things that they incite alarm or fear in the hearts of those who should find peace in the anticipation of the Savior's return. In all of this, the counsel of Church leaders has been to stay with the revealed truths of the scriptures. Concerning speculative writings about the last days, President Harold B. Lee taught in 1973, "Are you . . . aware of the fact that we need no such publications to be forewarned, if we were only conversant with what the scriptures have already spoken to us in plainness?"[1] More recently, President Ezra Taft Benson gave similar counsel "because of rumors, writings, and tape records that have recently circulated among the Saints and that have created among some of our Church members a feeling of uncertainty."[2] Wisdom would dictate that the Latter-day Saints become acquainted with what the *scriptures* say on the topic of the last days, for in them is revealed what the Lord would have us know about the grand events of the future.[3]

The Lord has seen fit not to announce to the world the date of his coming in glory. In 1831 he made known to the young Church that not even the angels in heaven knew "the hour and the day" of his coming, nor would man nor angel know "until he comes" (D&C 49:7). The deliberate suspense that is generated by anticipation and uncertainty in the hearts of the Saints serves an important function in the Lord's training of his people. While we wait, not knowing the day of his coming, we prepare. If we knew, some would find occasion to procrastinate their repentance. But keeping the uncertainty of the future in focus enables us to prepare continually—not only individually, but collectively as a Church as well.

There are some things that the Lord *does* want us to know concerning his coming; these are called in the scriptures the "signs of the times." They have been revealed so the Saints and the world can prepare for the events to come. Once again, personal and collective readiness are the keys; as the Lord said, "Therefore be ye also ready" (JS-M 48).

## Revelations Concerning the Last Days

Section 29 of the Doctrine and Covenants was revealed in September 1830 to the Prophet Joseph Smith, in the company of several others.[4] It appears from v. 33 that the revelation was received in response to specific questions that Joseph or other Church members had. It is the first large revelation dedicated to eschatological themes.[5] It is likely that prophetic passages in the recently published Book of Mormon (published six months earlier) and in the inspired revision of Genesis (which was in progress at the time) led the Prophet to inquire of the Lord for more revelation concerning the last days.

Section 45 was received several months later, in March of 1831.[6] In this revelation the Lord instructed his Prophet to begin the revision of the New Testament. Section 45 may have been a prelude to the New Testament revision, since it is itself an inspired expansion of the account of an event in the mortal ministry of the Savior.

Just three days before his crucifixion, Jesus sat on the Mount of Olives with his disciples and delivered the powerful discourse that is recorded in Matt. 24. In response to their questions he spoke of the last days of the temple and the Early Church, as well as the last days of the world and the signs that would precede his coming in glory. Doctrine and Covenants 45 expands on Matthew's account, as the Lord revealed to his latter-day Church additional insights concerning his Olivet discourse and its end-of-the-world subject. It is one of the most powerful views into the future that is available in all of our recorded scripture.

Section 133 was received on 3 November 1831.[7] It was intended to be the "Appendix" to the revelations, to be placed at the end of the Book of Commandments. The "Preface," section 1, had been received only two days before.

## The Coming Forth of the Gospel

One of the major signs of the times, foreseen long ago, is the restoration and spreading of the gospel prior to the coming of the Lord (see Acts 3:20-21; D&C 45:28; 133:37; JS-M 31). The Lord said that the coming forth of the gospel and its covenants would constitute "a standard for my people, and for the Gentiles to seek to it, and to be a messenger before my face to prepare the way before me" (D&C 45:9). It is necessary for the Church to be established and prepared before the Lord's return, for it is his kingdom from which he will rule. Anciently, Daniel foresaw that God would "set up a kingdom, which shall never be destroyed" (Dan. 2:44). This kingdom would fill "the whole earth" (Dan. 2:35), and it would be prepared to receive him who at his coming would be proclaimed its king (see Rev. 19:15-16). The Lord announced in 1831: "The keys of the kingdom of God are committed unto man on the earth, and from thence shall the gospel roll forth unto the ends of the earth, as the stone which is cut out of the mountain without hands shall roll forth, until it has filled the whole earth" (D&C 65:2).[8]

The restoration of the gospel and other related events were prophesied to take place in a period of time called in revelation the "times of the Gentiles" (D&C 45:28). In Jesus' Olivet discourse, the Lord spoke of things that would transpire shortly after his own day and of things that would transpire in the distant future. In section 45, vv. 16-25 pertain to the earlier period of time. Verses 26-59 deal with the "times of the Gentiles." The times of the Gentiles, our own day, refers to the time in which the gospel would be taken in force to the Gentile nations of the earth. Its major opening event would be the restoration of the gospel: "And when the times of the Gentiles is come in, a light shall break forth among them that sit in darkness, and it shall be the fullness of my gospel" (D&C 45:28). The fulfillment of the times of the Gentiles will be when the Gentile nations no longer accept the gospel, shortly before the Lord's coming (D&C 45:29-30; cf. JST, Luke 21:25-28). Then will be the great day of Jewish conversion. President Ezra Taft Benson stated: "The phrase *times of the Gentiles* refers to that period of time extending from when the gospel was restored to the world (1830) to when the gospel will again be preached to the Jews—after the Gentiles have rejected it."[9]

One of the major characteristics of the times of the Gentiles would be the preaching of the gospel to the nations of the earth. The missionary emphasis that is so strong in the Church, and has been since its beginning, is part of the Lord's time-table for our dispensation. The gospel must be taken to the ends of the earth before the Lord's return. In one of the most important discourses since the restoration of the gospel, President Spencer W. Kimball challenged the Latter-day Saints to take literally the divinely received commission to deliver the gospel to *all* the earth:

> It seems to me that the Lord chose his words when he said "every nation," "every land," "uttermost bounds of the earth," "every tongue," "every people," "every soul," "all the world," "many lands." Surely there is significance in these words! . . . I feel that when we have done all in our power that the Lord will find a way to open doors. . . . Is anything too hard for the Lord? . . . If he commands, certainly he can fulfill. . . . I believe the Lord can do anything he sets his mind to do. But I can see no good reason why the Lord would open doors that we are not prepared to enter.[10]

With these historic words, President Kimball showed the members of the Church that they could not be satisfied with their previous efforts at taking the gospel to God's children. He taught us that when the Lord commands that the "gospel shall be preached unto every nation, and kindred, and tongue, and people" (D&C 133:37), he expects his Saints to obey. With the gospel still not available in the 1980s to the vast majority of the people of the world, including the three most populous nations on earth, Latter-day Saints still have much to do, collectively and individually, before the Second Coming of the Lord. Increased missionary preparation, increased education regarding the peoples of the world, increased language training, and the overcoming of prejudice will help prepare members of the Church to enter doors as the Lord sees fit to open them.

## The Signs of the Times

While terrifying things have been foretold for the people of the earth prior to Jesus' return, the Lord has not left his faithful Saints without warning. Those events that are called "signs of the times" are given precisely for the purpose of warning, preparing, and letting those who would observe them know what is coming. They are the Lord's merciful efforts to announce to his Saints that his coming approaches and that the day of accountability is near. They are warnings to the people of the world that God is in control and that they must repent or be destroyed. But they develop in such a way that only those who observe with faith, listen to the voices of the Lord's servants, have the Spirit, and know the scriptures will recognize what they are (see D&C 45:57). Those who do not will find other explanations for the Lord's signs. Paul taught that the day of the Lord would come to the world "as a thief in the night"—that is, unexpectedly (1 Thess. 5:2). Yet he warned the believers to prepare and to look forward in faithfulness and anticipation: "But ye, brethren, are not in darkness, that that day should overtake you as a thief. Ye are all the children of light, and the children of the day: we are not of the night, nor of darkness. Therefore let us not sleep, as do others; but let us watch and be sober" (1 Thess. 5:4-6; cf. D&C 106:4-5). While those who disbelieve or disobey will be overtaken by the Lord's coming, those who are in tune with the signs of the times will be ready and will not be taken by surprise. The Saints have an obligation to recognize those signs—and will do so if they prepare: "And unto you it shall be given to know the signs of the times" (D&C 68:11).

The Lord told the Prophet Joseph Smith that the times of the Gentiles would end when the Gentile nations would no longer be receptive to the gospel (D&C 45:29-30; cf. JS-M 31). When the testimony of the Lord's messengers will cease to be heard because of the hardened hearts of the people of the world, then the Lord will speak to the world through another kind of testimony:

> And after your testimony cometh wrath and indignation upon the people.
>
> For after your testimony cometh the testimony of earthquakes, that shall cause groanings in the midst of her, and men shall fall upon the ground and shall not be able to stand.
>
> And also cometh the testimony of the voice of thunderings, and the voice of lightnings, and the voice of tempests, and the voice of the waves of the sea heaving themselves beyond their bounds.
>
> And all things shall be in commotion; and surely, men's hearts shall fail them; for fear shall come upon all people (D&C 88:88-91).

There is little doubt about the fact that the prophesied calamities of the last days will have terrible consequences for the people of the world. All of the standard works of the Church contain prophecies of terrifying things that will take place on earth before the return of the Prince of Peace. These include: "an overflowing scourge," "a desolating sickness," "earthquakes also in divers places," "many desolations," people "will take up the sword, one against another, and they will kill one another" (D&C 45:31-33).

We do not know the duration or the extent of the calamities that are foretold for the world, but it appears from the scriptures that they will increase in intensity as the coming of the Lord approaches. Included among these signs of the end of the world, "or the destruction of the wicked, which is the end of the world" (JS-M 4), are those that are called "signs of the coming of the Son of Man" (D&C 45:39; cf. 68:11). Section 45 provides the key for understanding these. Following a listing of some of the signs that would come upon the world, including natural and man-made disasters (vv. 32-33), the Lord then told how the righteous would look toward the "signs of the coming of the Son of Man," which would follow (v. 39): "And they shall see signs and wonders, for they shall be shown forth in the heavens above, and in the earth beneath. And they shall behold blood, and fire, and vapors of smoke. And before the day of the Lord shall come, the sun shall be darkened, and the moon be turned into blood, and the stars fall from heaven" (D&C 45:40-42). "And there shall be greater signs in heaven above and in the earth beneath" (D&C 29:14). These are signs on a cosmic scale; they will begin the change of the earth that must take place to prepare it to become the millennial home of the resurrected and glorified Lord.

The earth must be cleansed of all wickedness, wicked things, and wicked people, for God will come down to it to be with his Saints. Thus it must undergo a purification, which will include the destruction and death of evil people and their evil ways. Whereas the early signs of the times would be given to warn and to invite all to repent, there must come later signs of the Lord's coming that will punish and cleanse: "And it shall come to pass, because of the wickedness of the world, that I will take vengeance upon the wicked, for they will not repent; for the cup of mine indignation is full" (D&C 29:17). Wickedness must be removed from the earth, whether it be through repentance or through destruction. It can have no place in the Lord's millennial kingdom.

## Standing in Holy Places

When Jesus spoke of these things to his ancient apostles, they were concerned. The Savior comforted them with these words: *"Be not troubled*, for, when all these things shall come to pass, ye may know that the promises which have been made unto you shall be fulfilled" (D&C 45:35, italics added). The disciples could experience the distant calamities, trials, and destructions of the last days only through the words of their Master and through the power of the Spirit. But modern disciples can see the signs already developing—as the events of the world's end draw near and as the frightful specter of potential devastation is felt. No other generation in the history of the world has had the capacity to destroy itself as does the generation in which we now live. No other generation has had the ability to ruin the earth and all that is in it. Though thoughts of potential nuclear disaster are frightful beyond imagination, and world unrest is common, still today the Lord's word to his faithful Saints is one of internal peace. President Ezra Taft Benson has said: "You will live in the midst of economic, political, and spiritual instability. When you see these signs—unmistakable evidence that his coming is nigh—*be not troubled*, but 'stand . . . in holy places, and be not moved, until the day of the Lord come' (D&C 87:8)."[11] Peace, security, well-being, and happiness in the uncertain times of the last days can only come by living the gospel of Jesus Christ—by standing in holy places. President Benson continued, "Holy men and holy women stand in holy places, and these holy places include our temples, our chapels, our homes, and the stakes of Zion, which are, as the Lord declares, 'for a defense, and for a refuge from the storm, and from wrath when it shall be poured out without mixture upon the whole earth' (D&C 115:6)."[12]

## The Council at Adam-ondi-Ahman

In addition to the Lord's appearance in glory to the world as a whole, in which all will be made aware of his coming (JS-M 26; D&C 133:20-21), he will make an appearance to the faithful in a great gathering of Saints and priesthood leaders from all generations of the earth's history.[13] This is the topic of section 116.[14] The ancient prophet Daniel foresaw this event and recorded his vision of it in Daniel 7. Daniel told how the kingdoms of the world would lose their dominions, to be replaced utltimately by the kingdom of God. Then a great gathering would convene in which Christ (the Son of Man) and Adam (the Ancient of Days) would be the major participants. Daniel wrote:

> I beheld till the thrones were cast down, and the Ancient of days did sit, whose garment was white as snow, and the hair of his head like the pure wool. . . .
>
> Thousand thousands ministered unto him, and ten thousand times ten thousand stood before him. . . .
>
> I saw in the night visions, and, behold, one like the Son of man came with the clouds of heaven, and came to the Ancient of days, and they brought him near before him.
>
> And there was given him dominion, and glory, and a

> kingdom, that all people, nations, and languages, should serve him: his dominion is an everlasting dominion, which shall not pass away, and his kingdom that which shall not be destroyed (Dan. 7:9-10, 13-14).

Commenting on this passage in 1839, the Prophet Joseph Smith said:

> Daniel in his seventh chapter speaks of the Ancient of Days; he means the oldest man, our Father Adam, Michael, he will call his children together and hold a council with them to prepare them for the coming of the Son of Man. He (Adam) is the father of the human family, and presides over the spirits of all men, and all that have had the keys must stand before him in this grand council. . . . The Son of Man stands before him, and there is given him glory and dominion. Adam delivers up his stewardship to Christ, that which was delivered to him as holding the keys of the universe, but retains his standing as head of the human family.[15]

This great meeting will take place at a location called Adam-ondi-Ahman, in what is now Daviess County in northwestern Missouri. In it, all who have held keys will make an accounting of their service and deliver their keys to Adam, who serves under Christ as the presiding priesthood leader of the human family (D&C 78:16; 107:54-55). Elder Bruce R. McConkie asked concerning those who will be in attendance, "Are they not the ones who are called to report their stewardships and to give an accounting of how and in what manner they have exercised the keys of the kingdom in their days? Will not every steward be called upon to tell what he has done with the talents with which he was endowed? Truly, it shall be so; and those who minister unto the Ancient of Days are indeed the ministers of Christ reporting their labors to their immediate superiors, even back to Adam."[16]

With the keys of the ministries of all men in the hands of their patriarch, the crowning event of the great gathering will then take place. The Lord Jesus Christ will appear, and Adam, in his capacity as president and representative of all the human race, will make our collective accounting to the Lord, returning to him all keys, powers, and glories that had been entrusted to the hands of mortal men. Thus in the fullest sense it will be such that "the kingdoms of this world are become the kingdoms of our Lord, and of his Christ; and he shall reign for ever and ever" (Rev. 11:15).

The time when this event will happen has not been made known in the scriptures. Perhaps it will take place after the Lord has already returned in glory to cleanse the earth. But it is not unreasonable to suggest that this great gathering, in which the Lord will be acknowledged formally as king by his Saints—in which the keys of the kingdom held by his servants will be accounted for and returned to their rightful owner—will be the final event that will take place before the Lord will appear in royal glory and majesty to the world to be acknowledged by *all* people as "KING OF KINGS, AND LORD OF LORDS" (Rev. 19:16).

## The Coming of the Lord in Glory

The description that the revelations give of the Second Coming of Jesus Christ is truly awe-inspiring:

> And it shall be said: Who is this that cometh down from God in heaven with dyed garments; yea from the regions which are not known, clothed in his glorious apparel, traveling in the greatness of his strength?
>
> And he shall say: I am he who spake in righteousness, mighty to save.
>
> And the Lord shall be red in his apparel, and his garments like him that treadeth in the wine-vat.
>
> And so great shall be the glory of his presence that the sun shall hide his face in shame, and the moon shall withhold its light, and the stars shall be hurled from their places (D&C 133:46-49).

The glorious return of the Lord Jesus Christ will be an event unparalleled in the history of the earth. Perhaps only the atonement can be compared to it in its drama. Whereas Christ in mortality took upon him the nature of man to fulfill the mission for which the Father sent him (Heb. 2:16-17), now he will come as God and King—in glory and honor—to receive eternal praise from all of the Father's creations. Whereas in his mortal mission only those of pure heart recognized him to be their Master, now every knee shall bow and every tongue "confess that Jesus Christ is Lord, to the glory of God the Father" (Philip. 2:10-11). His coming will be no ordinary occurrence, and all will experience it (JS-M 26; D&C 133:20-21).

A major event of the Lord's Second Coming will be his appearance to the Jews in Jerusalem. To this event ancient prophets and modern revelation attest (see Zech. 14:1-9). The clearest account is found in D&C 45:43-53. The Lord declared that the Jews would be "scattered among all nations" (v. 24). "But," he continued, "they shall be gathered again; but they shall remain [i.e., remain scattered among the nations] until the times of the Gentiles be fulfilled" (D&C 45:25). As noted earlier, the "times of the Gentiles" will end when missionary work ceases among the nations and the testimony of calamities replaces that of the Lord's messengers (see D&C 88:88-91; JST, Luke 21:24-28). Perhaps this will be shortly before the Second Coming of the Lord. A remnant of the Jews will be found in Jerusalem, and to these the Lord will appear: "And they shall see me in the clouds of heaven, clothed with power and great glory; with all the holy angels" (D&C 45:44). As Jesus told his ancient apostles on the Mount of Olives,

> And then shall the Lord set his foot upon this mount, and it shall cleave in twain, and the earth shall tremble, and reel to and fro, and the heavens also shall shake. . . .
>
> And then shall the Jews look upon me and say: What are these wounds in thine hands and in thy feet?
>
> Then shall they know that I am the Lord; for I will say unto them: These wounds are the wounds with which I was wounded in the house of my friends. I am he who was lifted up. I am Jesus that was crucified. I am the Son of God (D&C 45:48, 51-52).

With words that can only evoke sorrow and compassion in the hearts of readers, the Lord foretold the reaction of those of Judah who would witness their Master's return: "And then shall they weep because of their iniquities; then shall they lament because they persecuted their king" (D&C 45:53). With this event the great millennial day of Jewish conversion and gathering will begin. Truly, those who had been first to hear their Savior speak in mortality—but rejected his pleas—will be last to accept his words in the final dispensation. But the end of the day of the Gentile will herald the dawn of a different day—the day of the Jew, in which those who had been first and last will share in the blessings of the gospel with their brethren of Israel. It is not unlikely that those who will have already gathered to the covenants of the Lord—the members of the Church of Jesus Christ of Latter-day Saints—will be sent to their brethren of Judah throughout the earth to teach them, baptize them, ordain them, endow them with temple blessings, and give them a millennial inheritance in their promised land. In this the prophesied gathering of Judah will find fulfillment.[17]

## The Millennium

Many scriptures tell us of the glorious Millennium, but few give us concrete insights into what life will be like during that extraordinary period of time. Perhaps we can imagine it to some degree if we consider having those things that are dearest to our hearts in an environment of complete peace and love. Most people of the present generation have been raised in a world where internal and international conflict, crime, and hatred are common realities. Imagine a world in which none of those exist. How different it will be when "the Lord, even the Savior, shall stand in the midst of his people, and shall reign over all flesh" (D&C 133:25). So powerful will be the presence of the Lord and his righteous Saints that Satan shall be bound, for he will have "no power over the hearts of the people, for they dwell in righteousness, and the Holy One of Israel reigneth" (1 Ne. 22:26; cf. D&C 45:55; 101:28). "For the Lord shall be in their midst, and his glory shall be upon them, and he will be their king and their lawgiver" (D&C 45:59). How inspiring to imagine a world without the influence of the adversary, who seeks "the misery of all mankind" (2 Ne. 2:18). Satan, sin, misery, and evil will not be here (D&C 101:26-29).

When the Lord returns and the Millennium begins, the earth will be populated with mortals who will have been found worthy to remain. Joining them will be the righteous Saints who have lived and died on earth since the ascension of Christ (see D&C 88:96-98; 133:56; 1 Thess. 4:13-18); these will be resurrected at his coming. Concerning those mortals who will live in the Millennium, the revelation states: "And the earth shall be given unto them for an inheritance; and they shall multiply and wax strong, and their children shall grow up without sin unto salvation" (D&C 45:58). Parents who are faced with the responsibility of training children today can contemplate the glorious reality of that day—when Satan's power will be gone, and children who are born will know neither sin nor its sorrows. In a revelation to Joseph Smith the Lord said, "In that day an infant shall not die until he is old; and his life shall be as the age of a tree; and when he dies he shall not sleep, that is to say in the earth, but shall be changed in the twinkling of an eye, and shall be caught up, and his rest shall be glorious" (D&C 101:30-31). Isaiah reported that those born in the Millennium will live to be one hundred years old (Isa. 65:20). Then they will be resurrected and will receive their celestial inheritance. How glorious will be that time! As President Joseph Fielding Smith wrote, "We are looking forward to that time. We are hoping for it; we are praying for it. *The righteous will rejoice when he comes*, because then peace will come to the earth, [and] righteousness to the people."[18]

## The Price of Our Future Blessings

It is a privilege and a blessing for us to live in the last days of the world. Our challenges are great, and our responsibilities are heavy, but the Lord has called us, and he will give us the means to do his will. Perhaps at some future time, those who have overcome the world, its sorrows, and its influences, and have received an inheritance in the celestial realm will look back on the trials of mortality and will consider them of small moment compared to the riches and glories of the Father's kingdom. Though our efforts and sufferings may be nothing compared to the Father's wages for our obedience (see Rom. 8:18), still our celestial inheritance will not have been purchased without a price of incomprehensible worth. That price was the suffering and atoning blood of Jesus Christ. He purchased for us the glories of the Millennium and the splendor of the celestial kingdom and offered them to us, as undeserving as we are and ever will be, as an act of infinite grace. Thus he reminds us:

> Listen to him who is the advocate with the Father, who is pleading your cause before him—
>
> Saying: Father, behold the sufferings and death of him who did no sin, in whom thou wast well pleased; behold the blood of thy Son which was shed, the blood of him whom thou gavest that thyself might be glorified;
>
> Wherefore, Father, spare these my brethren that believe on my name, that they may come unto me and have everlasting life (D&C 45:3-5).

We may have happiness now, peace in the midst of present and future calamities, and glory in the world to come—all because of him who has "abolished death, and brought life and immortality to light through the gospel" (2 Tim. 1:10).

## Notes

[1]*Ensign*, January 1973, p. 106.

[2]"Prepare Yourselves for the Great Day of the Lord," *Brigham Young University 1981 Fireside and Devotional Speeches* (Provo, Ut.: Brigham Young University Publications, 1981), p. 64.

[3]The best and certainly the most comprehensive treatment of the topic of latter-day events and the signs of the times is Bruce R. McConkie, *The Millennial Messiah* (Salt Lake City: Deseret Book Co., 1982).

[4]See Lyndon W. Cook, *The Revelations of the Prophet Joseph Smith* (Provo, Ut.: Seventy's Mission Bookstore, 1981), p. 41.

[5]Eschatology (from the Greek *éschatos*, "last") is the study of final things, i.e., things that pertain to the end of the world.

[6]See Cook, *The Revelations*, p. 63.

[7]*Ibid.*, p. 295.

[8]For a more detailed discussion of D&C 65 and the prophecy of Daniel, see Kent P. Jackson, "'May the Kingdom of God Go Forth," found herein.

[9]"Prepare Yourselves," p. 66.

[10]"When the World Will Be Converted," *Ensign*, October 1974, pp. 5-7.

[11]"Prepare Yourselves," p. 68.

[12]*Ibid.*

[13]See McConkie, *Millennial Messiah*, pp. 578-88.

[14]For the historical background of section 116 and Adam-ondi-Ahman, see Cook, *The Revelations*, pp. 228-29, 333-34.

[15]*TPJS*, p. 157.

[16]McConkie, *Millennial Messiah*, pp. 584-85. See also Joseph Fielding Smith, *Doctrines of Salvation*, comp. Bruce R. McConkie, 3 vols. (Salt Lake City: Bookcraft, 1954-56), 3:13-14.

[17]This appears to be what both Nephi and Jacob had in mind with their discussions of the fulfillment of the prophecy recorded in Isaiah 49:22-23. Nephi wrote that the house of Israel's being carried in the arms and on the shoulders of the Gentiles has to do with the Gentiles "making known of the covenants of

the Father of heaven" to Israel in the last days—"in bringing about his covenants and his gospel unto those who are of the house of Israel" (see 1 Ne. 22:8-12). Jacob's interpretation deals specifically with the Jews: after they accept the gospel of Jesus Christ, they will "be gathered in from their long dispersion." It will be the Gentiles—clearly the Church, those who have the gospel—who will carry them "forth to the lands of their inheritance. Yea, the kings of the Gentiles shall be nursing fathers unto them, and their queens shall become nursing mothers" (see 2 Ne. 10:7-9). That this will be a millennial event is seen in the fact that the day of Jewish conversion will be after the Second Coming, and that the gathering will take place following that conversion. See 3 Ne. 20:29-33; also 1 Ne. 19:15-17; 2 Ne. 6:10-11, 14-15; 25:16-17; 3 Ne. 5:26.

[18]Joseph Fielding Smith, *Doctrines of Salvation*, 3:14.

# 19

# "AND NOW COME . . . LET US REASON TOGETHER"

## (D&C 46, 50-52)

James R. Christianson

### Introduction

Even before he knew of the Lord's plan for him, Joseph Smith was made aware that the adversary would not allow God's work to go uncontested. The morning quiet of the spring day that ushered in the First Vision was shattered by a brazen but futile attempt to dissuade and, if possible, prevent the words of the prayer that would impact the destiny of all mankind everywhere. On this occasion and again during his initial visit to the Hill Cumorah, Joseph learned firsthand of the purpose and the powers of Lucifer.

As one who "was from the beginning" (Moses 4:1), Lucifer claimed a position of some influence among the pre-existent hosts. As his name implies, he was a bearer of light or truth, perhaps one entrusted with the teaching of the Plan of Salvation. In time, he betrayed that trust and taught something other than that ordained of God for the eternal well-being of the Father's children. Lucifer's duplicity ripened into rebellion and a frenzied attempt to exalt his "throne above the stars of God" (Isa. 14:13).

Whatever its nature, the confrontation between heavenly hosts resulted in the banishment of the rebellious from the presence of God. But the war goes on; the battlefield is the earth, and it has been from the days of Adam.

The deception practiced by Satan in that distant era has been used widely as an instrument for distorting truth and destroying faith throughout all dispensations. As might be expected, its focus on this the final, crowning dispensation has been intense. This was abundantly evidenced during the lifetime of the Prophet Joseph Smith.

### Background to Sections 46, 50-52

By mid-1830, with the Book of Mormon published and the Church organized, the attention of some faithful members had turned to two issues of major interest: the conversion of the Lamanites, and the building of the City of Zion or New Jerusalem.[1] Eager to see the Church fulfill its destiny but ignorant of the time and sacrifice that such would require, they persisted in their request that Joseph inquire of the Lord as to when and where they might begin. The answer that came in September 1830 was partly in response to an attempt by the adversary to introduce disharmony among the young Prophet's few proselytes and to undermine his role as the Latter-day spokesman for the Lord (see D&C 28).

Hiram Page, who was numbered among the Eight Witnesses to the Book of Mormon plates and was brother-in-law to David Whitmer, had acquired a stone which Hiram felt had some revelatory powers. Concerning the matter, Joseph noted: "To our great grief, however, we soon found that Satan had been lying in wait to deceive, and seeking whom he might devour. Brother Hiram Page had in his possession a certain stone, by which he had obtained certain 'revelations' concerning the upbuilding of Zion, the order of the Church, etc., all of which were entirely at variance with the order of God's house as laid down in the New Testament, as well as in our late revelations."[2] Among those persuaded by Page's declarations and who attempted to convince Joseph of their authenticity were the Whitmers and Oliver Cowdery. In response to this challenge, the Prophet asked the Lord for and received a directive which, in addition to naming him as the undisputed source of revelation for his Church, chastized Oliver for his obtrusive behavior, and directed that he apprise Hiram Page of the true source of his divinations. Oliver was further called to undertake a mission to the Lamanites with the added suggestion that the as yet unnamed site for the City of Zion "shall be on the borders by the Lamanites" (D&C 28:9).

Obedient to the charge given him, Oliver, along with Peter Whitmer, Parley P. Pratt and Ziba Peterson, made his way to western Missouri and the frontier settlement of Independence. En route, the four preached the Gospel, especially in and about Kirtland, a community in northern Ohio. As they passed through Ashtabul and Geauga counties they "became the topic of conversation in that section of the country . . . and excited the curiosity of the people."[3] While some mounted bitter attacks against them, others were persuaded that they were hearing the truth for the first time. Led by Sidney Rigdon, a prominent minister in the area and a former acquaintance of Parley P. Pratt, the number of converts grew to 127 within three weeks.[4]

Among those who responded favorably to the missionaries' message were some of Rigdon's disciples who, at his urging, had established a small communitarian order on the Isaac Morley farm near Kirtland. Known as "the Family," the group of some one hundred individuals was struggling to pattern their lives after the New Testament Church of Christ. Though in a state of decline due to a lack of direction and understanding as to how such a unit should function, its presence would shortly have a profound effect on the Restored Church.

Even though the missionaries soon left for Missouri, the newly-organized branches continued to grow. A visit to New York by Sidney Rigdon succeeded in convincing Joseph Smith that with the strength of the Church now in Ohio, its future would best be served by moving there. When a subsequent revelation confirmed this, the Prophet began preparation for the move.

In the meantime, however, the converts in Ohio, numbering several hundred, were virtually leaderless. Since all had joined the Church with little preparation except for their personal witness of its truthfulness, considerable baggage—a variety of prior religious experiences—came with them. In the absence of a tempering, authoritative influence, the newnesses of the Latter-day Saint faith acted as a catalyst and, like an organism gone wild, overt behaviors, both traditional and unique, became epidemic. Unaware of the extremes that had overtaken the Church in Ohio, Joseph sent John Whitmer to preside there. After a short time, John wrote an urgent message to the Prophet that, in summary, consisted of but one word: Help!

## Reasoning Together — Discerning the Spirit

When Joseph arrived in Kirtland on the last day of January, 1831, he was immediately aware that the Ohio branches were in trouble. The leadership vacuum created when Cowdery and his companions departed was quickly filled by the Prophet, whose pleas to the Lord received answers that had a profound impact.

Within days of his arrival, directives were received "embracing the

Law of the Church" (D&C 42).[5] Among the several subjects dealt with was the question posed by "the Family." Those of that group who were baptized wished to continue the common stock experiment while others wondered if the whole Church should accept their communitarian life-style. In his response, the Lord made clear that "the Family" was a confusing deception and was to be replaced by his own program, the Law of Consecration and Stewardship (D&C 42:29-36). In section 51 of the Doctrine and Covenants specifics of the program were revealed which, if followed, were designed to prepare a world community wherein justice, equality, peace, and mutual love and respect would predominate.[6]

A more pressing challenge for the Prophet was the seemingly unrestrained spiritual exercises manifest in all the Ohio branches and the manner in which they were viewed by an already hostile press and public. Most of the revelations received during Joseph's first five months in Ohio were in part a result of or dealt in some way with this problem. As reported by John Whitmer, the situation was one where

> Some had visions and knew not what they saw, some would fancy to themselves that they had the sword of Laban, and would wield it as expert as a light dragon, some would act like an Indian in the act of scalping, some would slide or scoop on the floor, with the rapidity of a serpent, which they termed sailing in the boat to the Lamanites, preaching the gospel. And many other vain and foolish manoevers that are unseeming and unprofitable to mention. . . . These things grieved the servants of the Lord, and some conversed together on this subject, and others came in and we were at Joseph Smith, Jr. the Seer, and made it a matter of consultation, for many would not turn from their folly, unless God would give a revelation.[7]

Parley P. Pratt, who returned to Kirtland in the early summer of 1831, wrote that "some very strange spiritual operations were manifested, which were disgusting, rather than edifying. Some persons would seem to swoon away, and make unseemly gestures, and be drawn or disfigured in their countenances. Others would fall into ecstasies, and be drawn into contortions, cramps, fits, etc. Others would seem to have visions and revelations, which were not edifying, and which were not congenial to the doctrine and spirit of the gospel. In short, a false and lying spirit seemed to be creeping into the Church."[8]

Obvious though it was to Whitmer and Pratt that the excesses they observed were not of God, there were others who were not easily convinced. Jared Carter, himself a New York convert, related how following his arrival in Kirtland he

> began to be tried with certain transactions that took place in the Church, and especially certain exercises which they called visions. The first instance of this kind, that I witnessed, was at the house of a Mr. Barna, in Amherst. On seeing these manifestations, I was doubtful concerning them, and did not know what to do. I felt that I could not depend upon my own views as well as upon those of some of the others, who were present who were more experienced than myself. But I proposed that we engage in prayer. In this, however, I could not obtain a union with the spirit that prevailed in the meeting. At last I concluded to kneel down and pray openly, and it seemed to me that I could pray in faith that any false spirit present should depart from the meeting. After I arose from my prayer, I found that quite a change in the meeting had taken place for when I began my prayer, two of the members laid prostrate in what some of them called a vision, but after I had prayed a few minutes, they suddenly came out of them and were clothed in their right mind. On seeing this, I felt pretty well convinced in my own mind that these exercises were not good; but after meeting, I conversed with some of the Elders, whom, I found to be fully of the belief that these visions were from a good source, in fact so united were the members of the church in their belief that these manifestations were from God, that I almost concluded that I had been mistaken. . . . I was led to conclude that these exercises were of the spirit of the Lord, though at other times I was very much concerned about them.
>
> On a certain occasion I attended a meeting together with Sylvester Smith, at Amherst, where, just as we were about to administer the sacrament, a young woman was taken with an exercise that brought her to the floor. I doubted the propriety of such an experience in a public meeting and suggested to Bro. Sylvester that we should try that Spirit according to the revelation that God had given. Complying with my suggestion, we kneeled down and asked our Heavenly Father in the name of

> Christ, that if that spirit which the sister possessed was of him, he would give it to us. We prayed in faith, but we did not receive the Spirit. After Bro. Sylvester had made some communication which was not proclaiming against the spirit, I arose and proclaimed against it with a loud voice, but this was very trying to the brethren present, as nearly all of them believed that the manifestations were of God and now after this I had some sore conflicts with Satan, for he told me I had lost all my influence in the Church, and sure enough that seemed to be the case for a while, but after contemplating for a time, I received assurance that I had the approbation of my Heavenly Father, which was better than the good will of many deceived brethren.[9]

Section 42 had, in effect, set the Church in order. In section 45 the faith of the Saints was reinforced in the face of the dibilitating criticism and sarcasm expressed by some non-Latter-day Saint neighbors. The matter of spiritual excesses and Satanic influences which had such a mesmeric effect on some members was approached directly in D&C 46, given 8 March 1831. Admonished to petition God in all things and respond to the resultant influence of the Spirit with holiness of heart, upright conduct, prayer, and thanksgiving, the Saints were informed that in this way they could overcome the seductions of evil spirits and the deceptions of men who were agents of the adversary. To further avoid such calamities they were counseled to seek the best gifts and to know why they were doing so.

The revelation further detailed the sacred nature of gifts of the Spirit and the manner in which they are dispensed. Emphasis was placed on the importance of understanding, of properly discerning, and of profiting from that which was given. To further guard against the abuse of sacred experiences and in order to detect satanic counterfits, the bishop and other ecclesiastical leaders were named as having the power of discernment (D&C 46:7-9, 27).

Throughout the spring of 1831, the strange behavior of some members continued. Though all were awed and some were repulsed by such actions, there was a hesitancy to resist them openly. Finally, as Parley P. Pratt, who felt compelled to act, noted: "Feeling our weakness and inexperience, and lest we should err in judgement concerning these spiritual phenomena, myself, John Murdock, and several other Elders, went to Joseph Smith, and asked him to inquire of the Lord concerning these spirits or manifestations."[10] The response to the Prophet's query was section 50 of the Doctrine and Covenants. As was so often the case when Joseph took a matter to the Lord, the answer became a means of teaching that went far beyond the question asked.

After making plain the Satanic nature of that which was plaguing the Church and acknowledging that the actions of some had given the adversary power among them, the Lord in patient and fatherly fashion bid Joseph and his fellow petitioners to "come, . . . let us reason together, that ye may understand; let us reason even as a man reasoneth one with another face to face" (D&C 50:10-11). The verses that follow suggested to the brethren a simple procedure for knowing if a thing be of God or of some other source. The basis for judging was their own growing certitude as they had been taught the gospel and had gained testimonies and, as teachers, had born witness of its truthfulness. On those occasions they were first given and then themselves gave of the Spirit of Truth. Whereas, that which is of God gives light and continues to enlighten until one knows with perfect assuredness, they were told, that which is of the evil one is a devourer of light and neither edifies nor magnifies the mind of the individual (D&C 50:13-25).

Thus, sound reasoning based on personal spiritual awareness was their key to discernment. If, however, they faced a unique situation wherein the true nature of an event was so camouflaged as to be undetectable, they should ask in the name of Christ that such be revealed to them; if they still perceived not its truthfulness it could be taken with certainty that such was of the adversary. With these directions they were to go forward with confidence and a voice of authority in proclaiming "against that spirit . . . that is not of God" (D&C 50:31-32).

Joseph Smith's concern for the power and influence Lucifer might exercise among the Saints continued throughout his lifetime. A warning to this effect that appears in section 52 was repeated on numerous other occasions.[11] An extensive treatment of the subject by the Prophet appeared in the 1 April 1842 edition of the Church publication *Times and Seasons*, entitled "Try the Spirits." The following paragraphs of that address summarize both the subject and its Kirtland episode as he viewed them.

> The Church of Jesus Christ of Latter-day Saints has also had its false spirits; and as it is made up of all those different sects professing every variety of opinion, and having been under the influence of so many kinds of spirits, it is not to be wondered at if there should be found among us false spirits.
>
> Soon after the Gospel was established in Kirtland, and during the absence of the authorities of the Church, many false spirits were introduced, many strange visions were seen, and wild, enthusiastic notions were entertained; men ran out of doors under the influence of this spirit, and some of them got upon the stumps of trees and shouted, and all kinds of extravagances were entered into by them; one man pursued a ball that he said he saw flying in the air, until he came to a precipice, when he jumped into the top of a tree, which saved his life; and many ridiculous things were entered into, calculated to bring disgrace upon the Church of God, to cause the Spirit of God to be withdrawn, and to uproot and destroy those glorious principles which had been developed for the salvation of the human family. But when the authorities returned, the spirit was made manifest, those members that were exercised with it were tried for their fellowship, and those that would not repent and forsake it were cut off.
>
> At a subsequent period a Shaker spirit was on the point of being introduced, and at another time the Methodist and Presbyterian falling down power, but the spirit was rebuked and put down, and those who would not submit to rule and good order were disfellowshipped. We have also had brethren and sisters who have had the gift of tongues falsely; they would speak in a muttering unnatural voice, and their bodies be distorted like the Irvingites before alluded to; whereas *there is nothing unnatural in the Spirit of God.*"[12]

## Conclusions

The very strange and seemingly clumsy actions of the adversary that were in part responsible for the circumstances that gave rise to sections 46 and 50-52 draw smiles and cause wonder 150 years later. We are ill-at-ease with such "goings on" and feel comfortable in the assurance that such has not and could not occur in our day. Even the

Lord's warning that Satan seeks "to deceive you, that he might overthrow you" (D&C 50:3) often falls on busy, bemused, and untuned ears. Our perspective through time assures us that, like Moses, we would not be fooled by a deception as transparent as the pretension, "I am the Only Begotten, worship me" (Moses 1:19).

Nonetheless, Joseph Smith was deeply concerned, as have been all his successors. Perhaps we have further need to "come and reason together"—not that we might successfully disclaim the obvious, but that we might detect and in wisdom identify the hand of him whose modern deceptions are perhaps beyond one's grasp of reality, being cunningly blended with our sophisticated perception of modern life and of wholesome living.

As we view our lives, rich and blessed in countless ways, is there need to seriously review the music to which we and our children listen, the words we choose to read and the filmed images with which we share time, both in and out of our homes? In our abundance, are we able to generate feelings for and take action concerning those who are desperately poor and in need throughout the earth? Have Satan's modern deceptions claimed us to the degree that love of and pride in physical possessions has clouded our vision and dimmed our memory of blessings promised and covenants entered into? In our worship,our payment of tithes and offerings, our scurrying to and from meetings, are we so concerned with and motivated by being right that we have no time for nor interest in being genuinely good?

The adversary is no less active in his efforts to deceive the Saints today than he was in the days of Joseph Smith. As we take this long view do we catch our breath in the awareness that our own foolishness, though different, is nevertheless akin to that of the Kirtland Saints of 1831? Such questions certainly seem worthy of our serious consideration.

## Notes

[1]See the Title Page of the Book of Mormon; 2 Ne. 12:2-4; 3 Ne. 5:23; 20:22; 21:20-25; Ether 13:2-11.

[2]*HC* 1:109-10.

[3]John Corrill, *Brief History of the Church of Christ of Latter-day Saints* (St. Louis: 1839), p. 34.

[4]Parley P. Pratt, *Autobiography of Parley Parker Pratt* (Salt Lake City: Deseret Book Co., 1964), p. 48.

[5]*HC* 1:148.

[6]Two years later in Missouri when the ideal of the revealed word was confronted with the frailty of its mortal practitioners, it became necessary to add verse five which allows for an individual's inheritance or stewardship to become his personal property. This was not originally the case. Formerly all that was consecrated as well as the portion deeded back remained in the name of the Church or as was the case in Missouri, in the name of Bishop Partridge (see Lyndon W. Cook, *The Revelations of the Prophet Joseph Smith* [Provo: Seventies Mission Bookstore, 1981], pp. 69-70).

[7]Cook, *Revelations of the Prophet Joseph Smith,* p. 134.

[8]Pratt, *Autobiography*, p. 61.

[9]Cited in Max H. Parkin, "The Nature and Cause of Internal and External Conflict of the Mormons in Ohio Between 1830 and 1838," unpublished master's thesis, Brigham Young University, 1966, pp. 73-75.

[10]Pratt, *Autobiography*, p. 62.

[11]D&C 52:12-21; 61:19; 63:28; 93:25; 123:4-8; 129:1-9; Andrew F. Ehat and Lyndon W. Cook, *The Words of Joseph Smith* (Provo: Religious Studies Center, Brigham Young University, 1980), pp. 20-21. Ehat and Cook quote Parley P. Pratt as stating, "There was no point upon which the Prophet Joseph dwelt more than the discerning of Spirits" (p. 21).

[12]*Times and Seasons*, 3 (1 April 1842): 747.

# 20

# THE MINISTRY TO THE SHAKERS

## (D&C 49, 51, 54)

KEITH W. PERKINS

In May 1831 a new convert to the Church, Leman Copley, came to the Prophet Joseph Smith asking that missionaries be sent to his former associates, the Shakers. This interesting people resided in a communal group at North Union, Ohio, fifteen miles from Kirtland. The Prophet Joseph Smith relates the event: "At about this time came Leman Copley, one of the sect called Shaking Quakers, and embraced the fulness of the everlasting Gospel, *apparently* honest-hearted, but still retaining the idea that the Shakers were right in some particulars of their faith. In order to have more perfect understanding on the subject, I inquired of the Lord, and received [D&C 49]."[1]

### Brief History of the Shakers

The Shakers had their beginning as a breakoff from the Quakers. The Quakers (Society of Friends) had been founded in England in the 1640s, believing that the scriptures were only a portion of God's revelation and that new revelation was to be expected. Two English Quakers, James and Jane Wardley, stated that God's spirit of revelation was frequently manifested to them in Quaker meetings through a violent shaking of their bodies. They broke off from the Quakers, and their group became nicknamed "Shaking Quakers." The Shaking Quakers gave equal place to women and men in church organization and predicted that since Christ had first appeared in the form of a man his second appearance would be in the form of a woman. When Ann Lee joined their group, the Wardleys became convinced that she had fulfilled this prediction.

Mother Ann, as she came to be called, believed that sexual relations were the root of all the evil she saw in the world, and therefore she advocated celibacy for both men and women, even though she herself had been married and had given birth to four children, who had died at birth. After severe persecution in England, Mother Ann claimed to have a revelation directing her to America to establish the Church of the United Society of Believers in Christ's Second Appearing

(Shakers).[2]

Some of the leading practices and beliefs of this unique group were:

1. The leading authority of the Shakers was vested in a committee, usually four persons, two females and two males.

2. Private ownership of property was eliminated and several communal groups were established throughout the United States.

3. God was both male and female.

4. God first made his appearance in the form of a male, Jesus Christ. In Ann Lee the female principle of God was manifested, and in her the promise of the Second Coming was fulfilled.

5. Confession was all that was necessary for forgiveness of sins, and, therefore, outward ordinances (baptism and laying on of hands) were unnecessary.

6. It was possible for people to live without sin.

7. Although the Shakers did not forbid marriage, they believed that those who lived a celibate life abided a higher law; they called this "the cross," probably having reference to the cross they had to bear.

8. Pork was forbidden in their diet and many ate no meat.

9. The resurrection consisted of the resurrection of the spirit but not the physical body.[3]

## Mission to the Shakers

As we have seen, when Leman Copley asked the Prophet to inquire of the Lord concerning the Shakers, the result was section 49. This revelation called the three missionaries that would labor among them, namely, Sidney Rigdon, Parley P. Pratt, and Leman Copley (D&C 49:1). According to the Church Historian at the time, John Whitmer, Copley desired that missionaries be sent to the Shakers. "He also feared to be ordained to preach himself, and desired that the Lord direct in this and all matters."[4] A few months earlier, Elder Pratt, and the other Lamanite missionaries had stopped at North Union for two nights and one day laboring among the Shakers, leaving seven copies of the Book of Mormon.[5]

It appears that immediately following the reception of the revelation, Elders Rigdon and Copley left Kirtland for North Union, arriving Saturday evening, 7 May 1831. They spent much of the evening discussing the doctrines of both faiths. Just before the Shaker meeting started Elder Pratt arrived and inquired if the Elders had delivered their message. It appears that the older missionaries were quietly waiting for an opportunity to deliver their message, but the young and vigorous Parley told them "they had come with the authority of the Lord Jesus Christ, and they must hear [the revelation]."[6] However, the missionaries went with the believers to their meeting and quietly waited for the opportunity to speak. After the services were dismissed Sidney Rigdon arose and told the still assembled congregation that they had a message from the Lord Jesus Christ and asked permission to read the revelation, which was granted. Elder Sidney Rigdon arose and read to the congregation of Shakers the entire contents of section 49. One can only imagine the reaction building in the minds of the Shakers as they heard a document read which the Mormon elders claimed to be from God—a revelation in which the Lord rejected their basic beliefs, one by one.

## Analysis of Section 49

Let us now analyze this revelation. The Lord acknowledged that the Shakers desired to know the truth "*in part*, but not all, for they are not right before me and must needs repent" (v. 2, italics added). The revelation next directed that Leman Copley be ordained a missionary to the Shakers; as he labored among the Shakers he was not to reason with them in the manner he was taught by them but he was to avail himself of the missionary methods taught him by "my servants." If he did this, he would be blessed by the Lord, otherwise he would not prosper (v. 4). How often the Lord has told us that when we keep the commandments, we would be blessed and prosper, but if not, we could not claim such promises (see 2 Ne. 1:9 and D&C 130:20-21).

The revelation then denounced the very foundation of Shaker doctrine. The Lord will *not* come in the form of a woman (v. 22). Christ *will* descend on the earth but the hour and the day no one knows, nor will they know until he comes (vv. 6-7). As we have seen, one of the basic doctrines of the Shakers was that in Ann Lee the female principle of God was manifested and in her the Second Coming was fulfilled.

Although the Shakers believed people could live without sin, the Lord taught in this revelation that "all men shall repent, for all are under sin" (v. 8). Further, the Shakers believed that confession alone was necessary for forgiveness and that no outward ordinances were necessary; the Lord stated that the first principles and ordinances of the gospel were: belief (faith) in Jesus Christ, repentance, and baptism in order to receive the gift of the Holy Ghost by the laying on of hands (vv. 11-14).

Another fundamental teaching of the Shakers, as we have seen, was that celibacy was a higher law than marriage. This doctrine was strongly denounced by the Lord: "Whoso forbiddeth to marry is not ordained of God, for marriage is ordained of God unto man" (v. 15). Not only is celibacy wrong, but without marriage God's children do not fulfill their very purpose in coming to earth, "and all this that the earth might answer the end of its creation; And that it might be filled with the measure of man, according to his creation before the world was made" (vv. 16-17). The end of creation, of course, was the commandment given to Adam and Eve in the Garden of Eden to multiply and fill the earth (Gen. 1:28). To forbid marriage is thus to deny the very purpose of the creation of the earth and mankind: "Adam fell that men might be; and men are, that they might have joy" (2 Ne. 2:25). "For behold, this is my work and my glory—to bring to pass the immortality and eternal life of man" (Moses 1:39).

The proper use of meat was next clarified by the Lord. Contrary to what the Shakers taught and believed—that pork was forbidden, and many ate no meat—the Savior explained that to forbid the use of meat is not pleasing in his sight, for he has appointed the use of meat for man, not only for clothing but for food. However, the Lord gave two cautions: that one person should not possess more than another, and that we must not waste nor shed blood when there is no need (vv. 18-21). Two years later the Lord further clarified in the Word of Wisdom the place of meat in our diet (D&C 89:12-15). One can plainly see why over the years the prophets have taught that all life is sacred and the blood of animals must not be shed except for food and raiment.

> I exhorted the brethren not to kill the serpent, bird, or an animal of any kind during our journey [Zion's Camp] unless it became necessary in order to preserve ourselves from hunger.[7]

> I do not believe any man should kill animals or birds unless he needs them for food, and then he should not kill innocent little

> birds that are not intended for food for man. I think it is wicked for men to thirst in their souls to kill almost everything which possesses animal life. It is wrong, and I have been surprised at prominent men whom I have seen whose very souls seemed to be athirst for the shedding of animal blood. They go off hunting deer, antelope, elk, anything they can find, and what for? "Just for the fun of it!" Not that they are hungry and need the flesh of their prey, but just because they love to shoot and to destroy life.[8]

> We do not kill. We are even careful about killing animals, unless we need them for food. When I was a boy . . . I would see boys there with a flipper flipping the birds in the trees. . . . Isn't that a terrible thing, to take life just for the fun of it?[9]

## Reaction of the Shakers

At the conclusion of his reading of the revelation, Elder Rigdon asked the Shakers if they were willing to be baptized for the remission of their sins and receive the laying on of hands for the gift of the Holy Ghost, Ashbel Kitchell, the leader of the group of Shakers, responded: "The Christ that dictated that, I was well acquainted with, and had been from a boy, that I had been much troubled to get rid of his influence, and I wished to have nothing more to do with him; and as for any gift he had authorized them to exercise among us, I would release them & their Christ from any further burden about us, and take all the responsibility on myself."[10]

But Sidney was not that easily dissuaded from his purpose. "This you cannot do," said Elder Rigdon, "I wish to hear the people speak." In response, Kitchell gave permission for the congregation of Shakers to speak forthemselves. Their response was very similar to their leader's; they were fully satisfied with their faith and wanted nothing to do with them or "their Christ." This seemed to satisfy Sidney, and he put the revelation back into his pocket. Young Parley P. Pratt, however, would not let the meeting come to a close without a further witness against the Shakers. He arose and shook his coattails: "He shook the dust from his garments as a testimony against us, that we had rejected the word of the Lord Jesus."[11]

This greatly angered Kitchell, a much larger man than Elder Pratt, and he severely rebuked him: "You filthy Beast, dare you presume to come in here, and try to imitate a man of God by shaking your filthy tail; confess your sins and purge your soul from your lusts, and your other abominations before you ever presume to do the like again, &c."[12] It is clear why the Lord found it necessary later to clarify to those early missionaries that any physical witness performed against those who reject the gospel should not be done "in their presence, lest thou provoke them, but in secret" (D&C 60:15). We can also discern why the Brethren today instruct us that such actions not be undertaken at all.

Not only did Kitchell vent his anger on Elder Pratt, but also upon Leman Copley. This experience was so upsetting to Copley that it caused him to reevaluate his membership in the restored Church. To make matters worse, when he arrived back at his farm in Thompson, Ohio, where the Colesville Branch of the Church had settled after arriving from New York, he found them very upset with him for what had happened. They had rejected him and "could not own him for one of them, because he had deceived them with the idea of converting [the Shakers]."[13] Having been rejected by members of the Church, he returned to North Union and begged for membership again with the Shakers. This mission, intended originally to bring people to Christ, resulted in more problems for the Saints.

Parley's reaction to the Shakers Mission was short but to the point. "We fulfilled this mission, as we were commanded, in a settlement of this strange people, near Cleveland, Ohio; but they utterly refused to hear or obey the gospel."[14]

## Other Doctrine Taught

In addition to the number of important items taught in D&C 49 that we have examined thus far, there are a number of other important doctrines that are taught in this revelation.

### Holy Men

As we have seen, the Lord said that all are under sin, *except* "those which I have reserved unto myself, holy men that ye know not of" (v. 8). According to Joseph Fielding Smith, these are "translated persons such as John the Revelator and the Three Nephites, who do not belong to this generation and yet are in the flesh on the earth performing a special ministry until the coming of Jesus Christ."[15]

## Nations Shall Bow to the Gospel

The knowledge that nations shall bow down to the gospel (v. 10) must have been interesting information to this small group of Saints living in Ohio and Missouri, but it is doubtful that they fully comprehended what we now know today to be reality. This is simply another way of stating that Saints will be gathered out of all nations (see D&C 45:69; Zech. 2:11). The Lord further stated, however, that they may not do this voluntarily, but bow down they must, "for that which is now exalted of itself shall be laid low of power" (v. 10; see also Matt. 23:12).

## Importance of Having Children

Having children assists the Lord in bringing about the "immortality and eternal life of man." Certainly this is one of the important purposes of marriage. President Spencer W. Kimball taught:

> Supreme happiness in marriage is governed considerably by a primary factor—that of the bearing and rearing of children. Too many young people set their minds, determining they will not marry or have children until they are more secure. . . . They have forgotten that the first commandment is to "be fruitful, and multiply, and replenish the earth, and subdue it." (Gen. 1:28). . .
>
> I am not sorry for women who sacrifice their lives for children. I am not sorry for those women who have many children. But I am sorry . . . for women who come to the Judgment Day who have never assumed the responsibility of rearing children, who have been afraid of pain, resistant to sacrifice. They are the one whose hearts will be heavy. . . .
>
> I know there are many women who could not have children—God bless them![16]

## Great Changes in the Earth before the Millennium

In this revelation the Lord indicated great changes were coming upon this earth. Much of that which is familiar to us will be changed. The heavens shall shake, the earth shall tremble and "reel to and fro as a drunken man," and the valleys and mountains shall change places (v. 23).

## Lamanites to Blossom as a Rose

The Lord explained that before these terrible events will usher in the great day of the Second Coming of Christ, "Jacob shall flourish in the wilderness, and the Lamanites blossom as the rose" (v. 24). This promise made over 150 years ago is finally beginning to see fulfillment. President Spencer W. Kimball, and many other prophets have longed for this day. President Kimball said:

> Wilford Woodruff, the President of the Church, in an oft-quoted statement said:
>
> I am looking for the fulfillment of all things that the Lord has spoken, and they will come to pass as the Lord God lives. Zion is bound to rise and flourish. The Lamanites will blossom as the rose on the mountains. I am willing to say here that, although I believe this, when I see the power of the nation destroying them from the face of the earth, the fulfillment of that prophecy is perhaps harder for me to believe than any revelation of God I ever read. . . . but notwithstanding this dark picture, every word that God has ever said of them will have its fulfillment, and they, by and by, will receive the Gospel. It will be a day of God's power among them, and a nation shall be born in a day (*Journal of Discourses* 15:282).
>
> The day of the Lamanite is surely here, and we are God's instrument in helping to bring to pass the prophecies of renewed vitality, acceptance of the gospel, and resumptions of a favored place as part of God's chosen people. The promises of the Lord will all come to pass; we could not thwart them if we would. But we do have it in our power to hasten or delay the process by our energetic or neglectful fulfillment of our responsibilities.[17]

## Saints to Gather Upon the Mountains

Even though the building of Zion in Jackson County, Missouri would soon be an anticipated dream for the Saints of that day, this revelation indicated that before that day could come "Zion shall flourish upon the mountains, and rejoice upon the mountains, and shall be assembled together unto the place which I have appointed" (v. 25). A few years later the Prophet Joseph Smith prophesied "that the Saints would continue to suffer much affliction and would be driven to the Rocky Mountains, . . . [but] some of you will live to go assist in making settlements and build cities and see the Saints become a mighty people in the midst of the Rocky Mountains."[18]

### Christ's Promise to His Saints

Finally, Christ gave this great promise to his people: "I will go before you and be your rearward; and I will be in your midst, and you shall not be confounded" (v. 27). What a marvelous promise to his Saints!

### Result of the Revelation

The Colesville Saints, upon their arrival in Ohio from New York in May of 1831, settled on a 759-acre plot owned by Leman Copley.[19] Here they entered into an agreement with Copley to reside on his farm, and according to commandment they entered into the Law of Consecration. They immediately went to work improving the farm by fencing the property and planting crops. However, with the problems that arose over the Shaker mission, Copley broke his agreement. This caused a major split with the Thompson Saints which had to be resolved with two revelations, sections 51 and 54. Section 51 clarified how the Saints in Thompson, as well as Saints in other places and all branches of the Church (v. 18), should live the United Order. With the confusion that resulted from Copley's wavering faith, Bishop Edward Partridge was told in this revelation that he would receive the direction he needed in organizing the Thompson Saints. Everyone was to be given his portion or inheritance by written deed; the inheritance belonged to the individual unless he should transgress the laws of the Church. In such a case he would not have power to claim the portion of property he had originally consecrated but should have claim only on that portion deeded to him—his stewardship (D&C 51:4-5). The property division in Thompson was to be "made sure, according to the laws of the land." To ensure a fair treatment, not only of Leman Copley, but also of the rest of the Thompson Saints, the instruction was given that that which belonged to the newly-arrived Colesville Saints should be appointed to them (D&C 51:6-7). Above all, everyone should be treated alike and receive alike "that ye may be one, even as I have commanded you" (D&C 51:9). What belonged to the Thompson Branch should not be taken and given to another branch of the Church. If another branch received money from the Thompson Branch, they must reimburse them as they previously had agreed through the Bishop or an agent (vv. 6-12). However, the Lord seemed to be preparing the Thompson Saints for what was about to come, for he warned them that the land in Thompson was only for "a little season" until he made other provisions (v. 16). Although the settlement in Thompson was not permanent, the Lord reminded them that the day and hour of their departure was not yet to be revealed. They were to live upon the land as though they would remain in Thompson for many years, that it "shall turn unto them for their good" (v. 17). What a settling effect such a message has upon all people who practice this principle: if they act like they will reside wherever they live as though they would reside there forever, it brings a peace and contentment that cannot be found otherwise. Finally, the Lord seemed to be directing v. 19 of section 51 to Leman Copley: "And whoso is found a faithful, a just, and a wise steward shall enter into the joy of the Lord, and shall inherit eternal life" (v. 19).[20]

Unfortunately, Leman did not heed the counsel of the Lord. When Copley was finally excommunicated, he demanded that the Colesville Saints residing in Thompson vacate his property. This put the Saints in Thompson in a serious dilemma; what do they do now? The Lord responded with another revelation, section 54. Newel Knight was commanded to "stand fast" in the office to which he had been called—he was the Presiding Elder at Thomspon (v. 2). Since the covenant had been broken with Leman Copley, it was now "void and of none effect" (v. 4). "And wo to him by whom this offense cometh [Leman Copley], for it had been better for him that he had been drowned in the depth of the sea" (v. 5). The Thompson Saints were told to leave "lest your enemies come upon you." They were to go to the land of Missouri, "unto the borders of the Lamanites" (vv. 7-8). Here they were to seek a living "like unto men" until the Lord prepared another place for them (v. 9). This seemed to instruct them not to live the United Order in Missouri until he commanded them.

What a difficult experience this must have been for the Saints in Thompson, for according to Joseph Knight they had made fences and planted fields, and yet "Copley took the advantage of us and we could not get any thing for what we had done."[21] His son, Newel Knight, was a little more resigned to what happened.

> We now understood that this was not the land of our inheritance—the land of promise, for it was made known in a revelation, that Missouri was the place chosen for the gathering of the Church, and several were called to lead the way to that State.
>
> A revelation was also given concerning the gathering, on the receipt of which we, who constituted the Colesville branch, immediately set to preparing for our journey, and . . . I took passage with the Colesville company at Wellsville, Ohio, [and departed for Missouri].[22]

Thus came to a close the short stay of the Colesville Saints in Thompson, Ohio. Here they lived a few weeks, but were forced to relocate because of the Shaker/Copley episode.

As we have seen, these three revelations, D&C 49, 51, and 54, become much clearer when we know their background and history. We must not leave this episode without commenting that Leman Copley did leave the Church. Even though in 1834 he took another stand against the Church by testifying against the Prophet Joseph Smith in a court case brought about by another apostate, Philastrus Hurlburt, in 1836, he asked for forgiveness and was rebaptized.[23] What subsequently became of Copley, however, is not fully clear. We do know he did not go West with the Saints to Missouri, Illinois, or Utah, but like many before and since he died in oblivion.

The Shakers, like many other "honorable men of the earth" (D&C 76:75), wanted "to know the truth in part, but not all" (D&C 49:2), and thus withheld from themselves the fulness of the gospel and its blessings. There are some Latter-day Saints who "are not valiant in the testimony of Jesus" (D&C 76:79), who accept the truth of the gospel and their responsibilities "in part, but not all."

Therefore, there are some serious questions that we should ask ourselves as we go about our daily labors. Am I willing to accept *all* the truth of the gospel or just part of it? Do I strive to keep *all* the commandments or just the more convenient ones? Do I want *all* the blessings available or just part of them?

We conclude with these thoughts from Elder Bruce R. McConkie:

> We are either for the Church or we are against it. We either take its part or we take the consequences. We cannot survive spiritually with one foot in the Church and the other in the world. We must take the choice, it is either the Church or the world. There is no middle ground. And the Lord loves a courageous man who fights openly and boldly in his army.
>
> Members of the Church who have testimonies and who live clean and upright lives, but who are not courageous and valiant, do not gain the celestial kingdom. Theirs is a terrestrial inheritance. Of them the revelation says, "These are they who are not valiant in the testimony of Jesus; wherefore, they obtain not the crown over the kingdom of our God" (D&C 76:79).
>
> What does it mean to be valiant in the testimony of Jesus? . . .
>
> To be valiant in the testimony of Jesus is to bridle our passions, control our appetites, and to rise above carnal and evil things. It is to overcome the world as did he who is our prototype and who himself was the most valiant of our Father's children. It is to be morally clean, to pay our tithes and offerings, to honor the Sabbath day, to pray with full purpose of heart, to lay our all upon the altar if called upon to do so.
>
> To be valiant in the testimony of Jesus is to take the Lord's side on every issue. It is to vote as he would vote. It is to think as he thinks, to believe what he believes, to say what he would say and do what he would do in the same situation. It is to have the mind of Christ and be one with him as he is one with his Father.[24]

## Notes

[1]*HC* 1:167.

[2]Cavin Green and Seth Y. Wells, *A Summary View of the Millennial Church or United Society of Believers Commonly Called Shakers* (Albany: C. Van Benthuysen, 1848), pp. 12-20 and Caroline B. Piercy, *The Valley of God's Pleasure: A Saga of the North Union Shakers* (New York: Stratford House, 1951), pp. 25-48).

[3]*A Summary View*, pp. 239-373 and *Testimony of Christ's Second Appearing, Exemplified by the Principles and Practice of the True Church of Christ* (Albany: Van Benthuysen, Printer, 1856), pp. 390-614.

[4]John Whitmer, *An Early Latter Day Saint History: The Book of John Whitmer Kept by Commandment*, ed. by F. Mark McKiernan and Roger D. Launius (Independence, Mo.: Herald Publishing House, 1980), p. 60.

[5]Ashbel Kitchell Journal, copied by Elisha D. Blakeman, pp. 1-3, The Shaker Museum Foundation, Inc., Old Chatham, N.Y.

[6]*Ibid.*, p. 6.

[7]*HC* 2:71-72.

[8]Joseph F. Smith, *Gospel Doctrine* (Salt Lake City: Deseret Book Co., 1963), p. 266.

[9]Edward L. Kimball, ed., *The Teachings of Spencer W. Kimball* (Salt Lake City: Bookcraft, 1982), p. 191.

[10]Kitchell Journal, p. 12.

[11]*Ibid.*, p. 13.

[12]*Ibid.*

[13]*Ibid.*, p. 15.

[14]Parley P. Pratt, *Autobiography of Parley Parker Pratt* (Salt Lake City: Deseret Book Co., 1950), p. 61.

[15]Joseph Fielding Smith, *Church History and Modern Revelation*, 2 vols. (Salt Lake City: The Council of the Twelve Apostles of the Church of Jesus Christ of Latter-day Saints, 1953) 1:208-9.

[16]*Teachings of Spencer W. Kimball*, pp. 328-29.

[17]Spencer W. Kimball, *Faith Precedes the Miracle* (Salt Lake City: Deseret Book Co., 1973), pp. 345, 349.

[18]*TPJS*, p. 255.

[19]Geauga County, Ohio Land and Tax Records, 1827-1832.

[20]For a more detailed discussion of the United Order, see Milton V. Backman, Jr. and Keith W. Perkins, "Consecration, Stewardship, and the United Order 1830-38," found herein.

[21]Dean Jessee, "Joseph Knight's Recollection of Early Mormon History,"

*BYU Studies* 17.1 (Autumn 1976): 39.

[22]"Newel Knight's Journal," *Scraps of Biography; The Tenth Book of the Faith-Promoting Series* (Salt Lake City: *Juvenile Instructor*, 1883), p. 70.

[23]*HC* 2:433.

[24]Bruce R. McConkie, "Be Valiant in the Fight of Faith," *Ensign*, November 1974, pp. 33-34.

# 21

# TO DO THE WILL OF THE LORD
## (D&C 53-56)

Richard D. Draper

## Introduction

Four revelations were received by Joseph Smith between the first and third weeks of June 1831. It was during this period that the Prophet and others were making preparations to fulfill the instructions given by the Lord to "let my servants Joseph Smith, Jun., and Sidney Rigdon take their journey as soon as preparations can be made to leave their homes, and journey to the land of Missouri. And inasmuch as they are faithful unto me, it shall be made known unto them what they shall do; and it shall also, inasmuch as they are faithful, be made known unto them the land of your inheritance" (D&C 52:3-5).

The idea that the Lord would designate a land to be an inheritance for the Saints, as he had done anciently with Israel, caused great excitement among them. Of the four revelations to be studied here, three (D&C 53, 54, and 56) were either a direct or an indirect outgrowth of the instructions given in section 52. The other one became directly tied to it. Therefore, to understand the setting and expectations of the Saints is most helpful in interpreting the message of these sections.

## The Importance of Zion

### Preparations for the Second Coming

Early members of the Church were conscious of living in the latter days. They understood fully that they were living during that era when the earth would be prepared for the return of the Savior. They also understood that they would be responsible, to a large extent, to bring about those preparations. Summarizing what the Saints were expected to do, Orson Pratt at one time asked, "Is it reasonable to suppose that Christ will return to the earth to reign upon it for a thousand years without preparing the way before-hand, for this most wonderful of all eras?" His implied answer was "No" and so the necessary steps were enumerated. First the gospel, which had been lost, must be restored fully and preached to all the world. This necessitated setting up the kingdom of God, in this case the Church, which would govern this operation. Second, the Saints had to be prepared through living the Celestial law on earth to meet him. Third, the kingdom would have to be spread to fill all the earth until it would reign supreme. Finally, the Saints must be gathered together and establish Zion. This ordering was not to be taken as a chronological sequence, for most of these events would be proceeding at the same time.[1] Nevertheless, all elements had to be completed before the Lord would come in glory.

## The Central Place of Zion

The central theme of Latter-day Saint millennial preparation was the establishment of Zion. This thought dominated much of the early history of the Church. Joseph Smith, under divine inspiration, yearned to establish it. As the Lord declared, "Him have I inspired to move the cause of Zion in mighty power for good, and his diligence I know, and his prayers I have heard. Yea, his weeping for Zion I have seen, and I will cause that he shall mourn for her no longer" (D&C 21:7-8). He had seen the grand vision and inspired others with it. "I intend to lay a foundation that will revolutionize the whole world," he declared.[2]

The plan was very vast, but the Prophet knew the whole of it, and under his direction with continual righteousness the Saints could effect it. Thus, many of Joseph Smith's revelations dealt with the idea of Zion. In the early revelations of the Church it is one of the major themes. Time after time men were instructed to "bring forth and establish the cause of Zion" (e.g., D&C 6:6; 11:6; 12:6; 14:6; 39:13; 103:11). From the moment a person joined the Church, he was to do all he could to bring Zion again to the Earth. The Latter-day Saint view was not world revolution. Joseph Smith taught that Zion would not come by the sword or gun.[3] However, what the Saints were trying to do was just as radical—to build a city, a state, a nation and eventually a world where all would live in harmony, peace and righteousness.

The reason that Zion was seen as so important was that the Saints believed that Christ would not come a second time until Zion had been established fully on the Earth. Taking Ps. 102:16 quite literally, the Saints believed that "When the Lord shall build up Zion, [then] he shall appear in glory."[4] The mission of the Church was to bring forth and establish Zion upon the Earth. Those who headed that organization and governed the Saints continually tried to motivate this large group of people to the end that the perfect society might be realized.[5]

In order to appreciate fully how the early Saints felt about Zion, one must keep in mind that the theology of the Church is one of the most literal and materialistic of all the Christian religions. The scriptures teach that even spirit is matter (D&C 131:7-8). Thus, when the Savior speaks through his prophet he does so in reference to real time and space. There is little room for metaphysical interpretation of scripture. When the Saints were instructed by their prophet to build a city, a kingdom, or Zion, it was an actual thing they were to realize.

This sense of literal reality is most strongly reflected in Latter-day Saint eschatology and may be demonstrated clearly from the tenth Article of Faith: "We believe in the literal gathering of Israel and in the restoration of the Ten Tribes; that Zion (the New Jerusalem) will be built upon the American continent; that Christ will reign personally upon the earth; and, that the earth will be renewed and receive its paradisiacal glory." This Article is particularly demonstrative in that it not only deals with time and space, but with very specific time and space, and also with the concept in which the Saints were highly interested—the millennial reign of Christ. It set forth the steps by which God would consummate his great latter-day work. Five steps were outlined: first, "the literal gathering of Israel"; second, "the restoration of the Ten Tribes"; third, that Zion was to be "built upon the American continent" (note how specific the statement is); fourth, "Christ will reign personally upon the earth," as a real king over an actual kingdom, not spiritually over some undefined realm; fifth, "the earth will be renewed and receive its paradisiacal glory."

Analyzing the importance of this Article of Faith, one Latter-day Saint scholar noted, "In each of these steps earthly time and place are implicit. The statement does not pinpoint either, but it leaves no doubt at all that things are going to happen in a definite temporal order involving people living in a definite place on this particular planet."[6] Zion then was a concrete place. For many of the early Saints what was necessary was to find the place, and then build the society upon it.

## Locating the Place of Zion

Even before the official organization of the Church, the leaders were anxious to find out where Zion was to be located. The Church was more than a religious body. It was an organization by which Zion would be established upon the earth, and so interest in the place of Zion was high after its organization. At one point Joseph Smith declared, "The land of Zion was the most important temporal object in view."[7] The location, he was instructed, would be revealed from heaven when the Lord saw fit. In June 1831 the Lord indicated that the time was near.

The excitement of finding out where Zion was to be located had already led to one of the first altercations within the Church. Hiram Page purported to have received a revelation concerning the location of Zion. This immediately brought a response from Joseph Smith. By revelation he declared, "And now, behold, I say unto you that it is not revealed, and no man knoweth where the city of Zion shall be built, but it shall be given hereafter. Behold, I say unto you that it shall be on the borders by the Lamanites" (D&C 28:9).

This incident helps one realize to what extent this concept was on the minds of the Saints at this early date. It is interesting to note that in this same revelation, Oliver Cowdery, along with three others, were assigned to go to the "borders of the Lamanites" to preach to them. Since it was learned that Zion would be somewhere in this area, it would appear that this mission was in preparation for the location of that land. Meanwhile Joseph Smith continued to await further revelation as to its exact location. Finally, a revelation stated that the location would soon be revealed but only on condition that the Saints "seek it with . . . [their] hearts" (D&C 38:18-19).

Based on this assurance, Joseph Smith and others left for the West on 19 June 1831. During the two weeks before his departure the four revelations under discussion here were given.

## Counsel to Individuals

These sections are not full of great doctrinal detail. Nevertheless, there are clear examples which give insights as to how the Lord works with his prophet, the individual Saint, and Saints in general.

Interest in the land of Zion and how it would affect each individual was high during this era. One of those individuals who sought information on how it would affect him was Algernon Sidney Gilbert.

**Counsel to A. Sidney Gilbert**

This man, prior to joining the Church, had been a successful merchant in Painsville, Ohio. When he heard the testimony of the Elders he believed and moved to Kirtland. There he joined Newel K. Whitney in opening up what proved to be a very successful merchandise store. For some time he had been concerned with his "calling and election in the Church" (D&C 53:1). This term, as used here, seems to mean his duty or responsibility in the Church. He was told that his talents would be used for the kingdom but that he must forsake the world and that salvation came only by enduring in righteousness (vv. 2, 4, 7).

That he took this admonition seriously is seen by the fact that when Joseph Smith departed for Missouri, Sidney Gilbert, with his wife and five others, went with him and labored in that land as an agent assisting the bishop. Further, during the persecutions in Missouri he not only sacrificed all his goods but also offered his life with six others in an attempt to free his friends.[8] Though he shrank from public speaking, he had a clear and lucid mind, as is shown in his correspondence during this period of persecution with Governor Dunklin on behalf of his brethren. In 1834 he was attacked by cholera, and the disease proved fatal.[9]

**Counsel to Newel Knight**

Though this revelation (D&C 54) was given to Newel Knight, it was meant for all those who were associated with him in Thompson, Ohio. These people were those known as the Colesville Saints. They had traveled from New York to Ohio in a body. Here they settled in Thompson and were directed by revelation to live the law of consecration and stewardship, as noted in section 51.

This required the cooperation of those Saints who already lived in the area and owned much of the land. These Saints agreed to share their holdings on the basis of the law of consecration and stewardship. Leman Copley was one of those who had large land holdings and agreed to share on the basis of this law. Just what happened at Thompson has not been preserved, but it would seem there was pettiness and selfishness. The Lord gave insight into the problem when he rebuked these Saints saying, "You seek to counsel in your own ways. And your hearts are not satisfied. And ye obey not the truth, but have pleasure in unrighteousness." He then condemned both the wealthy for not sharing of their substance and the poor for not curbing their greed (D&C 56:14-17).

Leman Copley and Ezra Thayre partook of, and perhaps even generated, this spirit of contention. The result was that Copley took back his land. This threw the Church members in that area into disorder. There was a good deal of antagonism against the Saints already from nomembers in the area. One of the consequences of the action by Laman Copley was that the Saints were placed in a position where they were dependent upon those who were less than friendly toward them. So they appointed Newel Knight to seek counsel from Joseph Smith.[10] In order to protect them the Lord commanded them to once again move—but this time to Missouri (D&C 54:8). Here they were no longer to practice the law of consecration and stewardship but to support themselves like other people (D&C 54:9).

The Lord revealed his anger toward those who had broken the covenant and gave a strong warning not only to those who did so but also to all those who would do so (vv. 4, 5). There are areas in which the Lord refuses to be mocked. One of these is in the area of making covenants. These sacred agreements are to be entered into with the full intention of keeping them no matter what circumstances may come to bear.

The purpose of making covenants is to put one in a position to receive the highest rewards that God can give. This pertains to covenants which may seem to have only temporal importance as well as those whose spiritual implications are obvious. When one then refuses to live up to an agreement either by open rebellion or through inaction he expresses no faith in God and so mocks him. From one who has entered into holy agreements of his own free will and choosing, the Lord will not allow such without severe judgments.

**Counsel to William W. Phelps**

During the hectic time of preparation, W. W. Phelps with his family arrived in Kirtland. He was from New York, where he had been a newspaper editor and also active in politics. There he had heard of the restoration of the Gospel and so went to Kirtland for one purpose: "to do the will of the Lord."[11] As with Sidney Gilbert, the Lord told W. W. Phelps that his talents would be used. This, however, would come only after baptism and the reception of the Holy Ghost. Then it would be his job, with Oliver Cowdery, to prepare texts for the education of the children of the Saints (v. 4).

## Quiet Miracles

It is interesting to note from these examples how the Lord used the talents of those men and women who were coming into the Church to meet the needs of the Church. Here we see one way that the Lord often chooses to meet the needs of his Church both on the individual level as well as on group levels. So often people want the Lord to meet their needs with a demonstration of divine force. Though the Lord does do this on occasion, and we speak of miracles, it would seem that the Lord has another way of working which often fits his economy better. This is the quiet working of the Holy Spirit on the souls of men and women who keep themselves in tune with him. To the sensitive souls of these individuals he reveals the needs of others. They then reach out to help.

These quiet miracles actually serve a dual purpose. If the Lord answered all prayers and needs directly, only one person would be blessed—the receiver. But choosing to answer one person's needs through inspiration to another allows two to be blessed: the individual who has the need because his need is fulfilled and the individual who responds because he becomes a partner in the saving work of God. Therefore, through the spirit of inspiration and revelation the Lord can have men and women use their natural as well as God-given abilities to push his work along. This is, as he says, "to bring to pass the immortality and eternal life of man" (Moses 1:39). Thus, by not doing all the work himself, he gives others practice in doing the work of gods and by so doing helps them to prepare for eternity.

## The Lord Commands and the Lord Revokes

Thomas B. Marsh had been assigned to go to Missouri during the conference held in Kirtland in June, 1831. His traveling companion was to be Ezra Thayre of Thompson. Thomas Marsh quickly put his affairs in order in preparation for the journey. Ezra Thayre, however, dallied. Part of the reason was because of his concern for his land holdings which he no longer wished to share with the Saints at Thompson. As the time grew long, Marsh became impatient and sought direction from Joseph Smith, and a revelation was received.[12]

Through this revelation the Lord took occasion to instruct the Saints in a gospel principle which had been broached in section 54 where the Lord had revoked a commandment which he had previously given. Many see the laws of God as immutable, arguing that he is the God "with whom is no variableness, neither shadow of turning" (James 1:17). "Hath he said, and shall he not do it? Or hath he spoken, and shall he not make it good?" (Num. 23:19). These scriptures and many others would suggest that the commands of God cannot be changed or modified. But in this revelation the Lord explained that he can both command and revoke as he sees good.

This is not done capriciously but only for good and sufficient reasons. "God is a *free agent.* We must not suppose that His immutability deprives Him of free agency. And because He is a free agent, He can command and revoke at will. But those who make it necessary for God, because of rebellion, to revoke laws given for the benefit of His children, will be held responsible."[13]

The revelation had special warning to Ezra Thayre, for he lost temporarily the privilege of going to Missouri. Thayre seems to have taken to heart momentarily the warning, for he later became a member of Zion's Camp and not long after was chosen among those worthy to be ordained to the office of Seventy. His devotion, however, did not last and he later apostatized.[14]

## Conclusion

These revelations serve to show that the Lord is conscious of the needs of his children. However, he has set criteria through which his blessings come. Sometimes it is the responsibility of individuals to bring his work to pass. When this is so, he expects obedience and devotion. When men are selfish or rebellious, they bring judgment upon themselves. However, if they work, "with an eye single to my glory, you shall have a remission of your sins and a reception of the Holy Spirit" (D&C 55:1). All is based on the condition of the heart; if it is pure, broken, and contrite, "they shall see the kingdom of God coming in power and great glory unto their deliverance; for the fatness of the earth shall be theirs" (D&C 56:18).

## Notes

[1]Orson Pratt, *A Series of Pamphlets by Orson Pratt, One of the Twelve Apostles of the Church of Jesus Christ of Latter-day Saints* (Liverpool, England: R. James, 39 South Castle St., 1851), pp. 239-54, Church Archives, Historical Department of The Church of Jesus Christ of Latter-day Saints, Salt Lake City, Ut.

[2]*HC* 6:365.

[3]*Ibid.*

[4]Note the emphasis given by Charles W. Penrose, once a member of the Twelve: "The time is close at hand. . . . God will cut his work short in righteousness. The day and the hour are not revealed; but 'when the Lord hath built up Zion, then will he appear in his glory.'" Quoted in Doxey, *Zion in the Last Days*, p. 81.

[5]See Monte S. Nyman, "The Redemption of Zion," found herein.

[6]Hugh W. Nibley, "To Our Glory or Our Condemnation," *Last Lecture Series* (Provo, Ut.: Brigham Young University Press, 1972), p. 1.

[7]*HC* 1:207.

[8]Roy W. Doxey, *The Latter-day Prophets and the Doctrine and Covenants* (Salt Lake City: Deseret Book Co., 1964), p. 216.

[9]Lyndon W. Cook, *The Revelations of the Prophet Joseph Smith* (Provo, Ut.: Seventy's Mission Bookstore, 1981), p. 84.

[10]*HC* 1:180-81.

[11]*Ibid.*, 184-86.

[12]*Ibid.*, 186-88.

[13]Hyrum M. Smith and Janne M. Sjodahl, *Doctrine and Covenants Commentary* (Salt Lake City: Deseret Book Co., 1953), p. 322.

[14]Cook, *Revelations*, p. 48.

# 22

# THE REDEMPTION OF ZION

## (D&C 57-62)

Monte S. Nyman

On 20 July 1831 the Prophet Joseph Smith asked three poignant questions of the Lord as he observed the degenerate conditions which existed in Missouri, in which he and other elders had recently arrived. These three questions were: "When will the wilderness blossom as a rose? When will Zion be built up in her glory, and where will thy Temple stand unto which all nations shall come in these last days?"[1] All three of these questions are associated with the writings of Isaiah, the Old Testament prophet. He had prophesied that the desert would blossom as a rose (Isa. 35:1), he had foreseen the glory of the Lord upon Zion (Isa. 60:1-2), and he had foretold concerning the temple in the last days unto which all nations would flow (Isa. 2:2). It is reasonable to assume that Joseph had been reading the prophet Isaiah and was contemplating the fulfillment of these prophecies in these latter days.

The Lord revealed what is now section 57 as an answer to his apparently disappointed prophet. Although he did not directly answer all three questions, he did answer the last question directly and indirectly gave instructions which, as we will see, led to the answers to the first two questions. The Lord concluded with a promise to reveal further directions later.

### Where Will Thy Temple Stand?

The place for the temple was designated in Independence, Missouri (D&C 57:3). On 2 August 1831, Sidney Rigdon, acting under the Prophet's direction, dedicated the area "for an inheritance for the Saints." The next day, Joseph Smith dedicated the site for the temple.[2] These events reaffirmed an earlier revelation that Missouri was indeed a land consecrated to the Lord's chosen people (D&C 52:1-2). The Lord's instructions were to buy land and divide it among the incoming Saints, and to print materials to further the preaching of the gospel for the gathering of the people. This would lead to the eventual building of Zion.

On 1 August 1831, the Lord kept his promise to give further directions by revealing what is now designated as section 58. In this revelation, the first two questions asked by the Prophet were answered. The second question, "When will Zion be built up in her glory?" was answered first.

## When Will Zion be Built?

The wording of the revelation (section 58) seems to have been chosen very carefully, as, undoubtedly, is that of all revelations. It is emphasized here to illustrate that the Saints did not read the revelation as carefully as the Lord gave it. The Saints were first told that Zion was not to be built up at this time but would be built after they had experienced much tribulation. They were assured, however, that their eternal reward would be just as great as though they had built Zion. The Lord then referred to the future glory which was to come after much tribulation, which glory was beyond their comprehension. He then reaffirmed that tribulation was to come before the glory of Zion and cautioned them to consider carefully ("lay it to heart") what he had told them (D&C 58:2-5). Whether or not they comprehended this part of the revelation cannot be determined for sure, but it seems that the Saints anticipated that they would build Zion immediately.

### Purposes for Going to Missouri

In the next part of the revelation, the Lord outlined the cause, or the purposes, for which he had at that time sent the Saints to Missouri. These purposes were introduced with the admonition for them to receive this stewardship (D&C 58:5), again implying that they would not build Zion. There are four basic purposes outlined by the Lord. The first was a test of obedience for those Saints. They had already been obedient to revelation in coming to Missouri. In a later revelation, the Lord revealed that all his people must be "tried even as Abraham" (D&C 101:1-4). The trial of Abraham was to receive with obedience all things by the revelation of the Lord (D&C 132:29). The trial of these Saints would come through their obedience to the other purposes which the Lord was now revealing to them concerning the land of Zion. They were to prepare their hearts so that they could bear testimony of what was to come—the building of Zion. One can bear testimony more assuredly when one has personal knowledge and experience upon which to base that testimony. These people would be so prepared, having been residents of the area. This was the second purpose for which the Lord had brought them to Missouri. The third purpose for their coming to Missouri was to lay the foundation for the city of the Zion of God. This was an honor that the Lord gave them, but it also enhanced their ability to bear testimony of the land. Their last prupose for being in Missouri was one which probably was not understood by the Saints then nor by many today. It was to prepare a feast for the poor.

As stated earlier, the Prophet Joseph may have been studying Isaiah's prophecies when he asked the questions leading to these revelations. After referring to the wording found in another prophecy of Isaiah which was linked with the establishment of Zion (Isa. 25:6), the Lord affirmed that the revelations of the prophets shall not fail (D&C 58:8).

It is my opinion that the "feast of fat things" for the poor was the law of consecration. The Lord had revealed this law as a part of the law of the Church (D&C 42:30-34). This revelation and subsequent revelations show that the purpose for the law of consecration was to benefit and even eliminate the poor (D&C 42:30; 78:3; 82:12). Although all nations were to be invited (D&C 58:9), there was a sequence to be followed. The first ones to be invited were "the rich and the learned, the wise and the noble" (D&C 58:10). The poor, the lame, the blind, and the deaf would then be invited. That the first group may represent the Gentiles and that the poor may represent the house of Israel was verified in the revelation outlining the law of consecration: "I will consecrate of the riches of those who embrace my gospel among the Gentiles unto the poor of my people who are of the house of Israel" (D&C 42:39). From the Savior's words given to the Nephites, the Gentiles—represented as "mighty above all"—had scattered the house of Israel and had been "a scourge unto the people of this land [the Americas]" (3 Ne. 20:27-28). The Gentiles had been the last to receive the gospel in the Meridian of Time but were to be the first to receive it in this dispensation. It is consistent with past and present prophecies that they were also to be given the first opportunity to participate in the establishment of Zion (Matt. 19:30; 20:16; 1 Ne. 13:42; D&C 29:30).

This opportunity for the Gentiles is the "day of calling," which the Lord referred to in a later revelation (D&C 105:35), the day when the Gentiles are offered the opportunity to use their might, power, and intellect to build Zion. However, the prophecies also foretell that instead of accepting this opportunity, they would not only reject it but would be the ones who would bring the tribulation upon the Saints who were laying the foundation of Zion (3 Ne. 16:8-10). Following this rejection, and the failure of the Gentiles to use their power, the Lord said that he will bring about the day of *his* power. Through the Lord's power, the poor, the lame, the blind, and the deaf would participate in the marriage of the Lamb—the covenant between Israel and Christ—and partake of the supper of the Lord—the law of consecration—prepared for the great day to come, the Second Coming (D&C 58:11).

The house of Israel's opportunity to establish Zion is the "day of choosing" which follows the "day of calling" (the opportunity of the Gentiles referred to above; D&C 105:35). The law of consecration is the law which will be lived in the day of the choosing of the house of Israel to go and build Zion (D&C 105:3-5, 34). The Colesville, New York, Saints were among the first members of the Church to settle in Missouri. They previously had been designated to practice the law of consecration at Thompson, Ohio, on a tract of land donated by Leman Copley.[3] Copley broke his agreement and left the Colesville Saints in distress. The Prophet Joseph sent them on to Missouri, where they would be given another opportunity to enter into the law of consecration. Those who will live there in the "day of chosing" will live in accordance with that law.

## The Accomplishment of God's Purposes

After stating the purposes for the gathering to Missouri, the Lord gave further instructions regarding how to accomplish these purposes. As a further clarification of their second purpose, to bear testimony of the land from "the city of the heritage of God" (D&C 58:13), the Lord outlined the stewardship of the bishop in Zion, Edward Partridge, or his successor if he did not repent (D&C 58:14-16). His stewardship was to be a judge in Israel, as in ancient days. His responsibilities were twofold: to divide the lands of the heritage of God (the city of Zion), and to "judge his people by the testimony of the just, and by the assistance of his counselors, according to the laws of the kingdom which are given by the prophets of God" (D&C 58:17-18). The Lord cautioned that the leaders in Zion were not to consider themselves as rulers but reminded them that God should rule the judges. The Lord also gave instructions concerning the Saints keeping the laws of the land. These instructions correspond to the 12th Article of Faith, which declares that the Church and its members are to be subject to the leaders and the laws of the land. The Lord then gave instruction concerning Edward Partridge and other leaders in Zion. Zion was to be the land of their residence; therefore, they were to "bring their families to this land as they shall counsel between themselves and me" (D&C 58:24-25). This seems to be an affirmation of the same principle revealed in section 9 of the Doctrine and Covenants regarding the process of the translation of the Book of Mormon. Oliver Cowdery was told to study it out in his mind and then go to the Lord for confirmation of the correctness of the translation (D&C 9:8-9). Similarly, the families were to discuss and determine the best time and way to come to Zion and then seek the Lord's approval on their decision.

Following these instructions, the Lord explained further why he expected the families first to use their own resources and thinking before consulting him. Throughout the years, these verses often have been taken out of context and greatly misunderstood by some members of the Church. Some have justified their failure to consult the Lord when making major decisions with the excuse that the Lord does not want them to bother him in matters which they have the ability to think through themselves. They base this justification upon verses 26 and 27. Those who so reason have failed to read carefully all that the Lord says on the matter. Verse 28 declares that men have the power in them to be their own agents. This power is the power of the Spirit, as is shown in v. 38 of the same revelation. All people are born with the light of Christ, which enables them to choose or discern good from evil (Moro. 7:12-16). This principle is implied at the end of verse 28, where it is stated that men who "do good [use the Spirit to discern their actions] shall in nowise lose their reward." The Lord is not pleased with those who do nothing but expect him to tell them what to do. On the other hand, he expects his children to confirm their well-pondered decisions with him—so as not to make mistakes—rather than proceeding without consulting him. The Lord had told Joseph Smith earlier, "you cannot always judge the righteous, or . . . you cannot always tell the wicked from the righteous" (D&C 10:37). If the Prophet Joseph Smith was unable to so tell, then certainly we today must rely on the Lord for confirmation of our decisions. The Lord also reminded the Saints, in this same context, that if men do not obey, the blessings connected with the commandments are revoked. The Lord further cited Martin Harris as an example for the Church in laying his moneys before the bishop. He gave further instruction concerning William W. Phelps' calling as the printer for the Church. Both Harris and Phelps were called to repent, and the Lord took that opportunity to enlarge on the principle of repentance (D&C 58:42-43).

## When Will the Wilderness Blossom?

Having sufficiently answered the second question for the time being (concerning the time of the building of Zion), the Lord turned to the first question asked by the Prophet, "When will the wilderness blossom as a rose?" In answering the question, the Lord addressed the next part of the revelation to the rest of the elders of the Church, telling what they must do in the many years before the time of the redemption of Zion (D&C 58:44). In a previous revelation the Lord apparently had paraphrased Isa. 35:1-2 in declaring that "before the great day of the Lord shall come, Jacob shall flourish in the wilderness and the Lamanites shall blossom as the rose" (D&C 49:24). Perhaps this revelation was also on the Prophet's mind prior to the revealing of sections 57 and 58, as he contemplated "the state of the Lamanites and the lack of civilization, refinement, and religion among the people generally" in the wilderness where Jacob was to flourish.

### The Gathering to America

Again using Old Testament prophecies, the Lord declared that the assignment of the Saints was to "push the people together from the ends of the earth" (D&C 58:45). Students of the Old Testament will recognize this phrase as a blessing of Moses on the descendants of Joseph (Deut. 33:13-17). The land given to Joseph's descendants was America (3 Ne. 15:12-13). In order for the wilderness to blossom, the children of Ephraim and Manasseh must be gathered together on the entire land of the Americas, not only in Missouri. This was to be accomplished through the preaching of the gospel in the regions round about. Since the house of Israel had been scattered among the Gentiles (Hos. 8:8-10; Amos 9:8-9), the preaching of the gospel among the Gentiles in the surrounding regions would be the process of gathering together "the ten thousands of Ephraim and . . . the thousands of Manasseh" (Deut. 33:17). Ephraim, being the birthright holder of all of Israel, would of necessity be gathered first. But included also would be thousands of the children of Manasseh, Joseph's other son, because America was given to all of Joseph's children.

As these people were assembled, they were to "build up churches" (D&C 58:48), as the people repented and made covenants with the Lord. The elders were to preach for a limited time and then return to their homes. They were to preach and bear record as they came and went, so that the gospel would be preached to everyone. Again drawing from the words of Isaiah, the Lord reminded the Saints that the gathering of the latter days was not to be done "in haste, nor by flight" (D&C 58:56; cf. Isa. 52:12), as the exodus from Egypt under Moses had been accomplished. The extent of the gathering was to be governed through direction given by the elders of the Church, as given at the conferences of the Church (D&C 58:56). A look at church history will certainly verify that this has been followed. Earlier in the history, people who accepted the gospel were advised to gather to the established stakes of Zion, while later they were admonished to remain in their own areas and there build up the stakes of Zion. The commandment to look to the conferences is still in effect, and if there are to be different or further instructions given, it will be given through this procedure. For instance, when the day of calling to redeem Zion comes, as outlined in D&C 105, the Church will be advised collectively, though the calling will be on an individual basis as declared in that revelation.

The next four revelations (sections 59-62) also concern Zion and the surrounding regions. Space does not allow a full treatise of these, but they are an extension of what was revealed in sections 57 and 58. Section 59 gives instructions regarding the laws which must be lived by those coming to Zion and particularly how the Sabbath was to be observed. Sections 60-62 are instructions to the elders who were traveling to and from Zion regarding how they should best travel to preach the gospel more effectively.

## Conclusion

Three years after sections 57-62 were received, the Lord told the Saints that they would have to wait "for a little season" for the redemption of Zion. He then outlined several things which had to happen before Zion would be redeemed (D&C 105). When that will take place is another subject, but by this time the Saints' obedience had been tested, they had been prepared to bear testimony of Zion, they had laid the foundation of Zion by designating and dedicating the site for the temple, and the Lord had revealed to them the law of consecration, which they had lived temporarily. Their cause was met, the regions have been and are still being built up, and the wilderness has begun to blossom. Today we wait for the decree to return to build Zion, as the further requirements outlined in section 105 are met.

---

## Notes

[1]*HC* 1:189-90; see also the preface to D&C 57, 1981 edition.

[2]*HC* 1:196.

[3]See the preface to D&C 49 (1981 edition) for background on Leman Copley, and D&C 51 for the commandment to establish the law of consecration.

# 23

# THE LORD REQUIRES OUR HEARTS

## (D&C 63 and 64)

ANN N. MADSEN

The first revelations given to the Prophet after his 1831 return to Kirtland from Missouri were the two lengthy ones we now have as sections 63 and 64 of the Doctrine and Covenants. The sixteen-month-old Church was built on revelations requested and receive regularly. Line upon line the Lord constructed a foundation designed to endure. In the first six verses of section 63 the awesome power of God is described. There is no pleading here. The facts of the Lord's role as righteous judge are made clear. There is no selfishness nor whim in his decrees. His avowed work is to bring about our immortality and eternal life. The day will come when all flesh shall know that he is God.

### The Choice: Obey or Rebel

In the beginning verses of section 63 the Lord distinguishes between the rebellious and the obedient. Obedience is the affirmation of our faith in a loving, caring Father. When we come to know the Lord we find him absolutely trustworthy and are completely willing to obey him. Rebellion indicates our lack of understanding of our relationship to him. We are his children. The ancient prophets recorded in many places their amazement at discovering this relationship. To Moses he said with absolute clarity, "Thou art my son." To the brother of Jared he showed himself. To Enoch he revealed his compassion for all his children (see Moses 1:3-11; Ether 3:4-20; Moses 7:29-36). Knowing the Lord is a necessary prerequisite to obedience. Those who have not come to know him do not understand that his promises can be trusted. They murmur and refuse to obey. They rebel. A ready example is found in the Book of Mormon account of the two brothers, Laman and Lemuel: "And thus Laman and Lemuel, being the eldest, did murmur against their father. And they did murmur because *they knew not the dealings of that God who had created them*" (1 Ne. 2:12, italics added). Although God *was* trustworthy he was unknown to them and therefore they would not obey him. The commandments are clear, and living prophets faithfully urge us to obey. The path to happiness is a straight and narrow one with the word of God solidly spanning its entire length. But whether we choose to hold on to that rod is up to each one of us. The choice is always before us to obey or rebel.

## Signs, But Not Unto Salvation

Warnings of pitfalls come regularly. In vv. 7 and 8 of section 63 the Lord begins to explain the folly of sign-seeking. Verse 7 teaches us a significant truth: "He that seeketh signs shall see signs, *but not unto salvation*" (italics added). In other words, we *will* find what we are seeking. We will one day possess what we prize. Where your heart is there will your treasure be also. We must decide with utmost care what is truly valuable to us. We have been wisely admonished, "Seek ye first the kingdom of God and his righteousness and all these things shall be added unto you" (Matt. 6:33). In earnestly seeking that kingdom we develop faith. One does not seek a kingdom which he does not believe to exist. Interestingly enough, the Lord goes on to teach us, that faith *does not* come by signs; rather, "signs *follow* those that believe" (D&C 63:9, italics added). Miracles abound among the Latter-day Saints and have since the earliest days of the restoration. This is partial evidence of the faith which has been generated among us. "Signs and miraculous manifestations prove the genuineness of man's faith; they do not produce it."[1]

The Lord makes it clear that he is not pleased with faithless sign-seekers. Often the ones seeking a sign are those who have lost their faith and become alienated from the Church—those who say, in effect, "I dare you to prove the truth to me." This is, of course, an impossible task before it is even begun. Concerning this the Prophet Joseph explained:

> I will give you one of the Keys of the mysteries of the Kingdom. It is an eternal principle, that has existed with God from all eternity: That man who rises up to condemn others, finding fault with the Church, saying that they are out of the way, while he himself is righteous, then know assuredly, that that man is in the high road to apostasy; and if he does not repent, will apostatize, as God lives. The principle is as correct as the one that Jesus put forth in saying that he who seeketh a sign is an

> adulterous person; and that principle is eternal, undeviating, and firm as the pillars of heaven; for whenever you see a man seeking after a sign, you may set it down that he is an adulterous man.[2]

What is an adulterous person? What is meant by that term? The Bible records instances of literal adultery, but it also provides many examples of marriage and adultery used to symbolize the relationship of the Lord with his people. In these examples the Lord is often characterized as the bridegroom or husband while his people, or the Church, are symbolized as the bride or wife. When the symbol of the adulterous wife is used, it is often combined with the idea of an unfaithful breaker of covenants, one who chases after other gods, leaving behind the true Lord and master.[3] Perhaps an adulterous person is an uncommitted person, one who is unfaithful to covenants already taken or unwilling to commit to offered covenants—a person who chases after other gods ignoring the one relationship that could save. Surely, the committing of adultery would be symptomatic of a wicked and adulterous generation, but this aspect of being unfaithful, especially in one's heart (see D&C 63:16; Matt. 5:28; 3 Ne. 12:28) has tremendous application to our own relationship with the Lord. As the Lord explains to Enoch concerning the people living at the time of Noah, "In the Garden of Eden, gave I unto man his agency. And unto thy brethren have I said, and also given commandment, that they should love one another, and that they should *choose me, their Father;* but behold, they are without affection and they hate their own blood (Moses 7:32-33, italics added). A few verses later we read, "Satan shall be their father and misery shall be their doom" (Moses 7:37). Our choices, that which we earnestly seek, will determine our ultimate destiny.

Sign-seeking is not a modern phenomenon. Anciently signs were sought by many. Moses and Aaron were warned by the Lord that Pharaoh would ask for a sign. When he did they were to cast the rod before him and it would become a serpent (Ex. 7:9). Thereafter, Pharaoh had his fill of signs, "but not unto salvation." Elijah's famous confrontation with the prophets of Baal on Mt. Carmel was another instance of a sign-seeking generation. Elijah set the stage when he challenged all the people, "How long halt ye between two opinions? if the Lord [Jehovah] be God, follow him: but if Baal, then follow him" (1

Kgs. 18:21). There had been a terrible famine and everyone in the land looked for rain; many gods had been implored to end the drought. Elijah urged the people to choose between the true and living God who made them and other impotent gods, including Baal, whom Elijah chided as either asleep or busy as his prophets pled before him, in a frenzy of gushing blood. Finally the truth was known. No matter what these false prophets did, no one answered, no voice was heard; in fact, Baal's prophets were left bleeding but unheeded. Then Elijah cried out, "Lord God of Abraham, Isaac, and of Israel, let it be known this day that thou art God in Israel and that I am thy servant, and that I have done all these things at thy word. Hear me, O Lord, hear me, that this people may know that thou art the Lord God, and that thou hast *turned their heart back again*" (1 Kgs. 18:36-37, italics added).[4] The prayer was answered when the fire of the Lord consumed the sacrifice and the people saw it, fell on their faces and said, "The Lord [Hebrew = Yahweh or Jehovah], he is the god" (1 Kgs. 18:39). Significantly, a few verses later the rains came, a consumate sign.

Several hundred years later, Jesus taught that "a wicked and adulterous generation *seeketh* after a sign" (Matt. 16:4). Signs themselves were not evil, but seeking signs with no regard for faith, which precedes the true sign, was condemned. Many times he, himself, was prodded to show the people a sign (Luke 11:16). Certainly the most dramatic moment was when sign-seekers challenged him to come down from the cross, the inference being that surely all would believe at such a sign (Luke 23:35-37). The temptation was subtle and came at such a significant time, when the Lord was finishing an eternal mission that could only be completed as he overcame death. The plan did not include avoiding death by showing his power in coming down from the cross. Suppose he had? Suppose the multitudes standing by had seen him yet alive though mortally wounded. Would they have rushed to believe anymore than they did after Jesus raised Lazarus?[5] Jesus' reclaiming of his body on the third day signalled a true resurrection: the greatest sign of all time, signifying that all men everywhere will reclaim their bodies in a literal resurrection. The sign followed the faith of the few.

## Faith Engendered Through Persuasion, Not Force

After Jesus' Second Coming, the promise that "at the name of Jesus every knee should bow" (Philip. 2:10-11) and every tongue confess that Jesus is divine provides an interesting backdrop for the sign-seekers who may remain at that time. The question might well be asked, "Will constraint produce this great confession of all living things?" And further, "Having seen so great a sign, how will anyone escape belief?" The answers are simple and relevant to us. His actual appearance, a truth too obvious to be spurned, will persuade all that Jesus Christ is indeed the Redeemer of the world. No amount of force could illicit such universal assent. Will this glorious resurrected Christ then confront a sea of adoring faces, determined to do his will forever? That supernal sign will no more result in faith in the faithless than the miracles he wrought in life convinced all to follow him. Signs are to be for men's good and God's glory. Not long after the multiplication of loaves and fishes, those who had witnessed the miracle began to go away. Soon Jesus asked his apostles, who had left all to follow him, if they were about to leave him also. Peter answered with tender faith, "Lord, to whom shall we go? thou hast the words of eternal life. And we believe and are sure that thou art that Christ, the Son of the living God" (John 6:68-69). Such an affirmation of faith emerged from daily contact. Brave and true as it sounded at the time, Peter was to know sooner than he could have guessed that there would be further testing of this commitment. Significantly, as he became solid in his faith as the rock his name signified, his concern was to strengthen those around him, preparing them for like commitment. He urged them to obey, aligning themselves with the life-style of Jesus.

## Learning the Lord's Pattern for Living

What is obedience to the Lord's commandments if it is not a pattern for aligning ourselves with Jesus' life-style? His pattern included healing. How often and freely he healed the sick. To what did he liken sickness as he taught? He compared sickness to sin. With that metaphor in mind, healing would be likened to the giving away of our sins—which we often label repentance, a recovery from sin. How beautifully Elder Bruce R. McConkie described this process as he urged us to pray, "O thou God of healing, wilt thou cause him who came with healing in his wings also to heal us spiritually. We would be clean: we desire to be a pure people; we need and desire and seek above all, the companionship of thy Holy Spirit."[6]

Having explained the fruitlessness of sign-seeking, the Lord turned to specific sins which we note have been connected to seeking for signs. Adulterers are addressed directly, and speedy repentance is advised (D&C 63:15). The gradual approaches to sin are outlined and the penalties revealed: they shall not have the Spirit, they shall deny the faith, and they shall fear. Fear, denying the faith, and absence of the Holy Ghost are dire rewards for the liar, adulterer, and unbeliever. Verses 20 and 21 of section 63 offer hope to the obedient who endure in faith: "the same shall overcome, and shall receive an inheritance upon the earth when the day of transfiguration shall come; when the earth shall be transfigured, even according to the pattern which was shown unto mine apostles upon the mount; of which account the fulness ye have not yet received." Add to that promise the one made in v. 23 concerning the mysteries of the kingdom. It will be noted that in much the same manner as signs follow faith, knowledge of mysteries follows obedience. Thus those who would find out the mysteries must learn obedience. When this is mastered, the "mysteries of my kingdom . . . shall be in him a well of living water, springing up unto everlasting life" (D&C 63:23). Compare to D&C 93:1: "Every soul who forsaketh his sins and cometh unto me, and calleth on my name, and obeyeth my voice, and keepeth my commandments, shall see my face and know that I am." Surely such promises contribute to a determination to endure and obey faithfully.

## Other Insights

Among the following verses which include instructions to individuals we can discover insights to enlarge our understanding. Verses 32-34 seem timely indeed in our day. Certainly wars and the fear of war are part of our environment. Verse 37 reiterates in beautiful imagery how we may save ourselves from the fear and desolation to come: "Every man should take righteousness in his hands and faithfulness upon his loins, and lift a warning voice unto the inhabitants of the earth; and declare both by words and by flight, that desolation shall come upon the wicked" (D&C 63:37). Ten verses later a comforting promise is added: "He that is faithful and endureth shall overcome the world" (D&C 63:47). Perhaps this could also be written, "shall NOT be overcome by the world."

Section 63 ends as it began with a short description of God's power and glory and a solemn warning to repent or be cut off (see D&C 63:58-63). The closing lines are wise counsel to any who have received revealed truth. "Remember that that which cometh from above is sacred, and must be spoken with care, and by constraint of the Spirit; and in this there is no condemnation" (D&C 63:64). In a sense this closes the discussion on signs, answering the last question that might be asked after a sign is given from heaven: When should we speak of such things? Only when constrained by the Spirit and "ye receive the Spirit through prayer," a formula we can all utilize.

## The Privilege of Learning To Forgive

Those who have responded to the need for repentance understand the sweetness of forgiveness. The devils believe and tremble but do not repent. Knowing about a Savior is not enough. Repentance is our only true affirmation of the Atonement of Jesus Christ. Faith in a compassionate Redeemer leads one to repent, and knowing the joy of having one's own sins forgiven opens wide the door to forgive others. In section 64 the Lord teaches us the requirements of forgiveness. What better way to understand than having one's own sins forgiven? The Lord explains, "I will that ye should overcome the world; wherefore I will have compassion upon you" (D&C 64:2). Analyzing these two ideas one might ask if feeling compassion is a prerequisite for overcoming the world. So much is spoken and written today about self-esteem: how to get it, keep it, give it to your children. Was the Lord teaching us a basic lesson here concerning our own feelings of worth and adequacy? What is compassion? Lehi's dying declaration to his sons may give a working definition: "The Lord hath redeemed my soul from hell; I have beheld his glory, and *I am encircled about eternally in the arms of his love*" (2 Ne. 1:15, italics added). What a glorious feeling for any man, woman, or child—encircled eternally with love! It is with this background of the unconditional love of the Lord that we can begin to understand forgiving: first, as one who has tasted the sweetness of having been forgiven and then as one who has the godly privilege to extend personal forgiveness to others.

In D&C 64:3 the example is given. The Saints are told that there are those among them who have sinned but "for this once, for mine own glory, and for the salvation of souls, *I have forgiven you your sins.*" The Lord sought for the fledgling Church an environment of acceptance and unconditional love of one another, a goal rarely achieved but beautifully set forth in this revelation. It is an ideal family pattern.

In D&C 64:7 we learn the principles on which the Lord will forgive us: if we confess our sins before him, ask his forgiveness, and have not sinned unto death (see D&C 76:32-37). It is well to remember that the only one capable of just judgment is the Lord, who himself is without sin and yet has experienced what we experience. No one of us can see clearly enough through the eyes of our selfishness and prejudices to judge another. This is why we are admonished not to judge but to leave judgment to God.

The Lord points out that his ancient apostles were troubled by jealousy and "forgave not one another *in their hearts;* and for this evil they were afflicted and sorely chastened " (D&C 64:8). The hope is that his modern Saints will learn from this negative example. It is significant to note that the requirement entails the heart, not just the mind, for, as we learn in v. 22, the Lord requires our hearts. If the heart is not right, the outward show means nothing. Every meaningful act involves a change of heart, not merely of mind. Conversion, testimony, faith, repentance, and forgiveness all require our whole-hearted focus. Forgiveness requires our hearts to change. We must be willing to encircle one another in the kind of love the Lord has offered each of us.

Two striking conclusions can be drawn from vv. 9 and 10:

1. If we do not forgive one another, there remains in us the greater sin.
2. We are required to forgive ALL men.

There are no qualifiers. Though our brother's sin be terrible or tiny, we will not be measured against its enormity, but we will be judged on our forgiveness or hardheartedness. We should have no problem deciding which of all those who have sinned against us to forgive. No formula is to be applied. It is required (not requested) that we forgive ALL.

These were lessons well fitted to the early Saints who struggled to forgive one another. And they are equally fitted to us. Satan desires to destroy us. How he must laugh when we will not forgive and forget so that a brother or sister may continue to progress unimpeded. Our lack of forgiveness may slow another's progress, while our compassion may speed another on his way.

The Lord explains to his people, "Ye are on the Lord's errand. . . . Wherefore, be not weary in well-doing, for ye are laying the foundation of a great work. And out of small things proceedeth that which is great" (D&C 64:29, 33). How would the nineteenth-century Saints have felt if they could have seen the Church even in our day? Some did see it. That vision gave them courage to continue in doing the Lord's business. We, too, must have a vision of the future. Ours includes the return of a risen Redeemer.

"Behold, the Lord requireth the heart and a willing mind; and the willing and obedient shall eat the good of the land of Zion in these last days (D&C 64:34).

## Notes

[1]Hyrum M. Smith and Janne M. Sjodahl, *Doctrine and Covenants Commentary* (Salt Lake City: Deseret News Press, 1941), p. 270.

[2]*TPJS*, pp. 156-57; *HC* 3:385.

[3]E.g., Hos. 2:2; Jer. 3:6-14; see also Kent P. Jackson, "The Marriage of Hosea and Jehovah's Covenant with Israel," pp. 57-73 in *Isaiah and the Prophets*, ed. Monte S. Nyman (Provo, Ut.: Religious Studies Center, Brigham Young University, 1984).

[4]It is interesting to note the phrase "turned their heart back again" in connection with the words of Malachi regarding Elijah's mission. See Mal. 4:5-6; D&C 2.

5The three days in the tomb were essential to the convincing of the Jews of Jesus' time that the body and spirit were indeed separated. Their belief was that a spirit remained near its body for three days and at that time left forever.

[6]Bruce R. McConkie, *Ensign*, May 1984, p. 34.

# 24
# "MAY THE KINGDOM OF GOD GO FORTH" (D&C 65)

Kent P. Jackson

## The Dream of Nebuchadnezzar

Among Latter-day Saints, one of the most well-known of the prophecies of the Old Testament is the remarkable dream of King Nebuchadnezzar in Daniel 2.[1] From the days of the Prophet Joseph Smith to the present, it has been understood to be a prophecy that foretells the growth and divinely established destiny of the latter-day Kingdom of God on earth, identified today as The Church of Jesus Christ of Latter-day Saints.[2] Doctrine and Covenants 65 is the key modern revelation that provides not only a powerful commentary on Daniel 2 but makes certain its interpretation as well.

The book of Daniel records that Nebuchadnezzar, the king of Babylon, had a dream in which he saw a large statue in the shape of a man, constructed of various substances: "This image's head was of fine gold, his breast and his arms of silver, his belly and thighs of brass, his legs of iron, his feet part of iron and part of clay" (Dan. 2:32-33). As the dream unfolded, Nebuchadnezzar saw "that a stone was cut out without hands, which smote the image upon his feet that were of iron and clay, and brake them to pieces. Then was the iron, the clay, the brass, the silver, and the gold, broken to pieces together, and became like the chaff of the summer threshingfloors; and the wind carried them away, that no place was found for them: and the stone that smote the image became a great mountain, and filled the whole earth" (Dan. 2:34-35).

Daniel explained the vision. The head of gold represented Nebuchadnezzar and his kingdom. Daniel told how Nebuchadnezzar's empire would be succeeded by another, represented in the dream as the breast and arms of silver, and then by another, characterized as the brass (Aramaic, "bronze") belly and thighs of the image. This kingdom would be followed in turn by another, represented as legs of iron. The last kingdom was represented as the feet of the image, "part of iron and part of clay."

Nebuchadnezzar's dream clearly represents a historical time-line—

a list of successive developments in the history of the world. In Daniel's inspired interpretation we can trace a succession of kingdoms from the days of Daniel to a later time when the kingdoms of the world would be replaced by the one kingdom established by God. As the main points of the history of the world since Daniel's day are well known, a reasonably sure reconstruction of the content of the vision can be made.

### The Head of Gold

The empire over which Nebuchadnezzar ruled is referred to technically as the Neo-Babylonian empire. Its power over Mesopotamia and surrounding areas lasted approximately from 610 B.C. to 539 B.C. Nebuchadnezzar, its chief architect, controlled almost the entirety of the Near East. His domain extended from southern Mesopotamia in the east to Upper Egypt in the southwest.[3] As Daniel explained, this empire was the golden head of the image. It is of interest to note that each succeeding power is characterized by a metal of lesser value than the one mentioned before it. On the other hand, each succeeding metal listed is stronger than the previous one. The division of time periods into gold, silver, bronze (KJV, "brass"), and iron is not unique to Daniel's prophecy. It is found in other ancient literature as well. For example, in the mythology of the first-century-A.D. Roman poet Ovid, time is divided into four ages: gold, silver, bronze, and iron. Ovid makes the point that each period was less glorious than that which it followed, but that each was characterized by increasingly greater strength.[4] It is well known that each of the succeeding empires that ruled the Near East and Mediterranean regions was more powerful than that which preceded it. But it cannot be said necessarily that they decreased in wealth or glory, as the decreasing value of the metals may lead some to conclude. All that can be said on the matter of the choice of materials is that a *sequence* is being represented in the substances from which the image is made. The purpose of the dream was not to show relative strength or value but to outline a succession from one to the next.

### The Breast and Arms of Silver

The second world power envisioned by Daniel was the Persian empire, which lasted from 539 B.C. to 330 B.C. When the city of Babylon was conquered by Cyrus in 539 B.C., the Persian monarch assumed control of the vast territory that had been ruled by Nebuchadnezzar and his successors.[5] For most people of the Near East, the Persian conquest was heralded as an act of liberation from the oppressive policies of Babylon. The Achemenid Persian empire, which lasted for approximately 200 years, employed vastly different imperial policies than those of the Babylonian and Assyrian realms that preceded it. Whereas the territories controlled by Assyria and Babylon amounted to little more than plundering and tribute-collecting grounds for those powers, the Persians developed an empire-wide state structure that involved a hierarchy of local rulers and an extensive bureaucracy. The Persians also extended the borders of their empire beyond the boundaries acquired by the Babylonians before them. In Daniel's visionary view, their kingdom constitutes the silver breast and arms of the image in Nebuchadnezzar's dream.

## The Belly and Thighs of Brass

The next great kingdom in Nebuchadnezzar's dream represented the empires of Alexander the Great and his successors (330-63 B.C.). When Alexander of Macedonia set out in the year 334 B.C. to reconquer the Ionian Greek cities from Persian rule, no one could have imagined either the scope of his future conquests or their lasting impact on the future of the world. In a series of massive battles against Persian forces, Alexander took control of the vast territory held by the Achemenids and extended far beyond it, creating the largest empire that had existed in the world to that time. This was the kingdom characterized as the belly and thighs of brass in the Babylonian king's vision. Alexander was not successful in creating a dynasty of his own descendants. At his death at age 32, his kingdom was divided among his generals. It was ruled by their descendants and others until they in turn were overthrown by an even stronger power.

## The Legs of Iron

The kingdom characterized as the image's legs of iron was the Roman empire (63 B.C.-A.D. 636).[6] The Romans conquered the territories of the Greeks that had succeeded Alexander the Great. Rome remained in power—not only over much of the Near East, but over the entire Mediterranean area as well—for several centuries. In the eastern

Mediterranean region, the Roman empire remained until the Muslim conquest of the seventh century A.D.

## The Feet of Iron and Clay

In Daniel's day the entire world, as known to Daniel and his Babylonian contemporaries, was under the control of the king of Babylon. His was truly a world empire from the perspective of that time. The realm of Persia, which followed, was similarly a kingdom that ruled the entire world, as were the empires of Alexander the Great and the Romans in succeeding centuries. Daniel saw in a later time a period in which the earth would no longer be under the domination of one state. With the fall of the Roman empire, the world entered into a phase of its history in which one world power would no longer rule over all. Instead, an era began in which numerous regional nations competed for the territories once held by the world powers of the past. Nebuchadnezzar's dream and Daniel's prophetic interpretation are conveyed in the metaphor of the great statue. As with any prophetic metaphor, the imagery is not meant to be interpreted in detail, but in major concepts. The details are often not important, but the larger picture is intended to be understood well. In Daniel's prophetic view of the future, the message is taught clearly that one world power would supersede another until there came a time in which smaller nations would be the pattern of world government. With the demise of Roman control over the then-known world, no longer was there one nation that ruled the earth. Out of the fall of the Roman world came a world of *many* nations. This is the world envisioned by Daniel, a kingdom "part of iron, and part of clay, so the kingdom shall be partly strong, and partly broken" (Dan. 2:42). "And whereas thou sawest iron mixed with miry clay . . . ," he continued, "they shall not cleave one to another, even as iron is not mixed with clay" (Dan. 2:43).

## A Great Mountain

It would be in the context of the world situation described above that a new kingdom would be established. This kingdom would be different than all others. Whereas the other kingdoms described would each grow out of the ruins of kingdoms that had come before, the new kingdom that Daniel envisioned would be "cut out without hands"

(Dan. 2:34), meaning that it would be of *divine* construction, rather than human. This kingdom would subdue the nations of the world and over the course of time would be transformed from a small stone into an immense mountain that would fill the entire earth. Daniel concluded: "And in the days of these kings shall the God of heaven set up a kingdom, which shall never be destroyed: and the kingdom shall not be left to other people, but it shall break in pieces and consume all these kingdoms, and it shall stand for ever" (Dan. 2:44).

A modern prophet, Spencer W. Kimball, provided an interpretation consistent with the revelation of Joseph Smith: "The Church of Jesus Christ of Latter-day Saints was restored in 1830 after numerous revelations from the divine source; and *this is the kingdom, set up by the God of heaven, that would never be destroyed nor superseded, and the stone cut out of the mountain without hands that would become a great mountain and would fill the whole earth.*"[7]

Doctrine and Covenants section 65 is scriptural substantiation of the role of the Church as God's kingdom, established in the last days of world history to prepare the way for the coming of him who is the rightful king of Israel and the earth, the Lord Jesus Christ. In Hiram, Ohio, in October 1831, the Prophet Joseph Smith uttered the following words of prayer, received by revelation:[8]

> The keys of the kingdom of God are committed unto man on the earth, and from thence shall the gospel roll forth unto the ends of the earth, as the stone which is cut out of the mountain without hands shall roll forth, until it has filled the whole earth. . . .Call upon the Lord, that his kingdom may go forth upon the earth, that the inhabitants thereof may receive it, and be prepared for the days to come, in the which the Son of Man shall come down in heaven, clothed in the brightness of his glory, to meet the kingdom of God which is set up on the earth. Wherefore, may the kingdom of God go forth, that the kingdom of heaven may come. . . (D&C 65:2, 5-6).

The Church of Jesus Christ of Latter-day Saints is the kingdom of God on earth. Its president holds "the keys of the kingdom," by the authority of which he presides over all of God's work on earth, under the direction of Jesus Christ. Among the primary goals of the Church is that of establishing itself ready to receive its master at his glorious coming. When the time is right, the Savior will return, take personal charge of his kingdom (the Church), and will reign on earth for a thousand years. At that time, in fulfillment of Daniel's prophecy, the Church will be the only kingdom that will survive. It will not only survive the calamities that will precede the Second Coming of Christ, but it will remain as his kingdom while he is on earth. Elder Bruce R. McConkie has stated: "During the millennium the kingdom of God will continue on earth, but in that day it will be both an ecclesiastical and a political kingdom. That is, the Church (which is the kingdom) will have the rule and government of the world given to it."[9]

President Brigham Young taught:

> The Lord God Almighty has set up a kingdom that will sway the sceptre of power and authority over all the kingdoms of the world, and will never be destroyed, it is the kingdom that Daniel saw and wrote of. It may be considered treason to say that the kingdom which that Prophet foretold is actually set up; *that* we cannot help, but we know it is so, and call upon the nations to believe our testimony. The kingdom will continue to increase, to grow, to spread and prosper more and more. Every time its enemies undertake to overthrow it, it will become more extensive and powerful; instead of its decreasing, it will continue to increase, it will spread the more, become more wonderful and conspicuous to the nations, until it fills the whole earth. If such is your wish, identify your own individual interest in it, and tie yourselves thereto by every means in your power. Let every man and every woman do this, and then be willing to make every sacrifice the Lord may require; and when they have bound up their affections, time, and talents, with all they have, to the interest of the kingdom, then have they gained the victory.[10]

## Notes

[1]Scholars have long argued for a late date for the book of Daniel, based on certain characteristics of it (language, vocabulary, historical references, etc.) that seem to be at home in the 3d/2d century rather than the 6th century B.C. (e.g., Louis F. Hartman and Alexander A. Di Lella, *The Book of Daniel*, Anchor

Bible 23 [Garden City, N.Y.: Doubleday, 1978], pp. 3-18, 29-54). Although some feel that the book in its present composition may date from long after Daniel's time—and thus include elements added by centuries of editorial work that reflect a Hellenistic-period date of final editing—the words of D&C 65 offer striking evidence for the prophetic content of Daniel 2 and the authenticity and inspiration of its prophecies. For a recent prophetic reference to Daniel 2, see President Gordon B. Hinckley's dedication of the Boise, Idaho Temple: "Father, the little stone which thou didst cut out of the mountain without hands is rolling forth to fill the earth. Guide and strengthen the messengers of the truth" (*Church News*, 27 May 1984, p. 7). See other references cited from latter-day prophets, below.

[2]Especially D&C 65; see also Joseph Fielding Smith, *Doctrines of Salvation*, vol. 1 (Salt Lake City: Bookcraft, 1954), pp. 229-46; and notes 7, 9, and 10 below.

[3]For a convenient survery of Nebuchadnezzar, his kingdom, and time period, see Georges Roux, *Ancient Iraq* (Harmondsworth, England: Penguin Books, 1964), pp. 338-68.

[4]*The Metamorphoses* 1.89-414.

[5]The standard history of Persia in this period is A. T. Olmstead, *History of the Persian Empire* (Chicago: University of Chicago Press, 1948). See also R. Girshman, *Iran* (Harmondsworth, England: Penguin Books, 1954).

[6]The date 63 B.C. does not represent the beginning of Roman conquests, nor the beginning of what is called technically "The Roman Empire." It is the date of Pompey the Great's conquest of Palestine and its subjugation to the Roman state. Though much of Alexander's realm had fallen already to Roman rule, most of Syria and Mesopotamia were conquered only later. The areas east of the Tigris never were conquered by Rome. The date A.D. 636 is used to identify the time in which Roman control ceased in the eastern Mediterranean.

[7]*Conference Report*, April 1976, p. 10, italics added; also *Ensign*, May 1976, pp. 8-9.

[8]*HC* 1:218; Lyndon W. Cook, *The Revelations of the Prophet Joseph Smith* (Provo, Ut.: Seventy's Mission Bookstore, 1981), p. 105.

[9]*Mormon Doctrine*, 2nd ed. (Salt Lake City: Bookcraft, 1966), p. 416.

[10]*JD* 1:202-3.

# 25

# REVELATIONS RESULTING FROM IMPORTANT CHURCH CONFERENCES (D&C 66-70)

MELVIN J. PETERSON

This article deals with revelations which were given to conferences of the Church during October and November of 1831. Elder Bruce R. McConkie has written of Church Conferences: "Conferences are far more than religious conventions in which views are expressed, differences resolved, and policies adopted. Rather they consist of a series of meetings at which the mind and will of the Lord is manifested to the people by the mouths of his servants. The Church being a Kingdom, not a democracy, instruction and direction comes from above; it does not originate with the citizens but with the king."[1]

As news of Joseph Smith and the work in which he was engaged began to spread, a number of persons became interested and made an effort to meet the Prophet and learn more of his activities.

On 25 October 1831, a general Church Conference was held in Orange, Ohio at the home of Sirenes Burnett.[2] William E. McLellin, a member of the Church for three months, requested Joseph Smith to inquire of the Lord in his behalf.[3] The revelation that is now section 66 was received as a result of that inquiry.

Such requests had been made previously by many who approached the Prophet, and as their requests were acted upon by him, those seeking information were invited to become active participants in the great proselyting work of the new Church (D&C 31:3-6; 33:1-3; 34:6; 35:4-6). It was no different with McLellin; he was told to "proclaim my gospel from land to land, and from city to city, yea in those regions round about where it has not been proclaimed" (D&C 66:5). The Lord's instructions to McLellin were somewhat detailed as to what McLellin should do in the ministry. He was to send money to Zion (66:6), work with his missionary companion Samuel H. Smith, and help instruct him (66:8). He was told to "lay your hands upon the sick, and they shall recover" (66:9); he also was to push people to Zion (66:11), and to "be patient in affliction" (66:9). His mission was to the eastern lands, and he was told to "ask" and to "knock" and he would receive.

## You Are Clean But Not All

McLellin's promises for ministerial success were not absolute guarantees. The Lord instructed him concerning his personal life. He was commended for turning away from his iniquities to receive the truth, "even the fulness of my gospel" (66:2), but he was warned of past influences with which he still needed to contend. He was warned of adultery, a temptation that had troubled him in the past. There is no evidence that McLellin had been an adulterer. President Joseph Fielding Smith has written, "He was not accused of committing such a sin, but the dangers, because of his failings, which lay in this direction."[4] The Lord counseled him, "Seek not to be cumbered" (D&C 66:10). Dictionaries define "cumber" as "to burden in a troublesome way." McLellin was troubled with adulterous thoughts, which the Lord warned him needed to be eliminated. "Forsake all unrighteousness" was the Lord's counsel to him, and while his thoughts were uncontrolled he was "clean but not all" (D&C 66:3).

President Kimball wrote of a man who refused to control his thoughts because he rejected the concept that his actions were endangered by lustful thoughts:

> In a community in the North, I visited a man who had above the desk in his printing establishment a huge picture of a nude woman. He laughed at the idea of its being destructive to his morals. But one day years later he came to me with a stained soul—he had committed adultery. His house had fallen in on him. Certainly the thoughts provoked by the things always before his eyes must have had a deteriorating effect on him. There may have been other factors, but surely this one played its part.[5]

It is significant that in this revelation given for William McLellin the Lord revealed what McLellin could accomplish; he also indicated the conditions he had to meet to be successful in obtaining the potential reward. If faithful, "you shall have a crown of eternal life at the right hand of my Father, who is full of grace and truth" (D&C 66:12).

As Church membership grew, the need to instruct the members increased. Instruction sessions were primarily Church Conferences, and so on 1 November 1831 the Church convened at Hiram, Ohio in a special conference to consider publishing the revelations which had been given through the Prophet Joseph Smith.[6]

The conference lasted two days. During the morning of the first day, the brethren were united in their desires to publish the revelations and set the number of copies at ten thousand. This expression of faith brought a revelation now identified as section 1, or the Lord's preface to the commandments. After the preface was received the Prophet recorded: "Some conversation was had concerning revelations and language."[7]

The Prophet wrote little concerning a challenge to the revelations. Richard O. Cowan discussed the problem: "There followed a discussion on the language in the revelations about to be published. Criticisms of Joseph Smith's imperfections aroused doubts in the minds of some of the brethren present. These concerns may have been related to the popular belief that God had dictated the scriptures word for word; thus, questions about the language represented a lack of faith in the divine origin of the revelations."[8]

A revelation given concerning the challenge of the language of the revelations stated: "Your eyes have been upon my servant Joseph Smith, Jun., and his language you have known, and his imperfections you have known, and you have sought in your hearts knowledge that you might express beyond his language; this you also know" (D&C 67:5). The Lord then challenged the critics as follows: "Now seek ye out of the Book of Commandments, even the least that is among them, and appoint him that is the most wise among you; Or, if there be any among you that shall make one like unto it, then ye are justified in saying that ye do not know that they are true; But if ye cannot make one like unto it, ye are under condemnation if ye do not bear record that they are true" (D&C 67:6-8).

The brethren were then taught a great principle concerning judgment. The Lord revealed that none were able to abide God's presence or the presence of angels except they be quickened by the Spirit of God. The revelation read: "And when ye are worthy, in mine own due time, ye shall see and know that which was conferred upon you by the hands of my servant Joseph Smith, Jun." (D&C 67:14). The Lord also taught, "inasmuch as you strip yourselves from jealousies and fears, and humble yourselves before me, . . . the veil shall be rent and you shall see me and know that I am—not with the carnal neither the natural mind, but with the spiritual" (D&C 67:10).

Lacking the spiritual preparation to know by the Spirit that the revelations were true, William E. McLellin sought to throw more doubts upon the divinity of the revelations by writing one himself.[9] As McLellin failed to produce a revelation, the Prophet castigated him when he wrote: "The Elders and all present that witnessed this vain attempt of a man to imitate the language of Jesus Christ, renewed their faith in the fulness of the Gospel, and in the truth of the commandments and revelations which the Lord had given to the Church through my instrumentality; and the Elders signified a willingness to bear testimony of their truth to all the world."[10] Thus the Lord turned a seeming crisis into a period of instruction and growing for the inexperienced Church members.

## The Power of God Unto Salvation

At the end of the first two days of the November 1831 Conference, four brethren—Orson Hyde, Luke Johnson, Lyman E. Johnson, and William E. McLellin—were desirous "to know the mind of the Lord concerning themselves."[11] Joseph Smith inquired of the Lord and received what is now section 68. There is some question as to whether the entirety of section 68 was received at one time.[12] The brethren mentioned were called to preach the gospel with the promise that "whatsoever they shall speak when moved upon by the Holy Ghost shall be scripture, shall be the will of the Lord, shall be the mind of the Lord, shall be the word of the Lord, shall be the voice of the Lord, and the power of God unto salvation" (D&C 68:4). Such broad latitude to the missionaries was to be received in connection with an earlier revelation for Oliver Cowdery wherein the Lord revealed: "And if thou art led at any time by the Comforter to speak or teach, or at all times by way of commandment unto the Church, thou mayest do it, but thou shalt not write by way of commandment, but by wisdom" (D&C 28:4-5). None were to receive revelations for the Church except Joseph Smith, Jr. (D&C 28:2). One's safety lies in obeying the Lord without assuming the role of revelator to the Church, which role belongs only to the President of the Church.[13]

Another item of concern related to the calling of the future bishops in the Church. Edward Partridge had been ordained a bishop by Sidney

Rigdon on 4 February 1831.[14] The concept that all future bishops be High Priests unless they be literal descendants of Aaron was revealed (D&C 68:15). At the time this revelation was given there was no First Presidency in the Church, and information about bishops was meager. When more was revealed, therefore, and increased organization occurred, section 68 was edited to harmonize with that increased understanding.[15]

According to section 68, should a person qualify as a literal descendant of Aaron he must also meet the qualifications of being called by the First Presidency, be worthy to be a bishop, and be ordained by proper authority (D&C 68:20). All bishops serving in the Church today are High Priests, as none have yet qualified to be a bishop due to their lineage. Further, President Joseph Fielding Smith has written regarding the priesthood office that a literal descendant of Aaron might claim:

> The office of *Presiding Bishop* of the Church is the same as the office which was held by Aaron. It is the highest office, holding the Presidency in the Aaronic Priesthood. It was this office which came to John the Baptist, and it was by virtue of the fact that he held the keys of this power and ministry that he was sent to Joseph Smith and Oliver Cowdery to restore that Priesthood, May 15, 1829. The person who has the legal right to this presiding office has not been discovered; perhaps he is not in the Church, but should it be shown by revelation that there is one who is the firstborn among the sons of Aaron, and thus entitled by birthright to this Presidency, he could "claim" his "anointing" and the right to that office in the Church.[16]

The Lord further revealed: "There remain hereafter, in the due time of the Lord, other bishops to be set apart unto the Church, to minister even according to the first" (D&C 68:14). In the General Conference of April 1984, Church statistics through the year 1983 were given. At that time it was reported that there were 9,329 wards in the Church,[17] each being presided over by a bishop.

### Responsibilities to Children

At the November Conference of 1831, the Lord placed directly upon parents the responsibility of teaching children faith in Christ, the doctrine of repentance, and of baptism and the gift of the Holy Ghost by the time they are eight years old (D&C 68:25). It is sin not to do so (D&C 68:25). While working on his inspired revision of Genesis, the Prophet Joseph Smith had learned that children are not accountable before the Lord until they are eight years old (JST, Gen. 17:11). Now, some seven to ten months later, the Lord reaffirmed through his Prophet the doctrine associated with the age of accountability.[18] Thus parents have an opportunity to teach their children both about the gospel and how to apply the gospel during the years of their lives in which they are not accountable to God for their actions. In another revelation the Lord revealed, "But behold, I say unto you, that little children are redeemed from the foundation of the world through mine Only Begotten; wherefore, they cannot sin, for power is not given unto Satan to tempt little children, until they begin to become accountable before me; For it is given unto them even as I will, according to mine own pleasure, that great things may be required at the hands of their fathers" (D&C 29:46-48). To understand that Satan cannot tempt little children during the years in which they are not accountable to God for their actions identifies the significance of the role of parents and the home in the training of children.

President Spencer W. Kimball has written:

> There is no guarantee, of course, that righteous parents will succeed always in holding their children, and certainly they may lose them if they do not do all in their power. The children have their free agency. But if we as parents fail to influence our families and set them on the "strait and narrow way," then certainly the waves, the winds of temptation and evil will carry the posterity away from the path. "Train up a child in the way he should go; and when he is old, he will not depart from it" (Proverbs 22:6). What we do know is that righteous parents who strive to develop wholesome influences for their children will be held blameless at the last day, and that they will succeed in saving most of their children, if not all.[19]

As the Conference came to a close some important decisions concerning the revelations were made. The Lord revealed that John Whitmer should accompany Oliver Cowdery to the land of Zion (Missouri) and share the trust of transporting the commandments and money to that area (D&C 69:1, 2). In the same revelation John

Whitmer was to "continue in writing and making a history of all the important things which he shall observe and know concerning my Church. . . . Let my servant John Whitmer travel many times from place to place, and from church to church, that he may the more easily obtain knowledge—preaching and expounding, writing, copying, selecting, and obtaining all things which shall be for the good of the church, and for rising generations that shall grow up on the land of Zion, to possess it from generation to generation, forever and ever. Amen" (D&C 69:3, 7, 8). As John Whitmer had been called in March of 1831 to "write and keep a regular history and assist you, my servant Joseph, in transcribing all things which shall be given you" (D&C 47:1), the instruction given at the November conference emphasized the importance of his assignment. The Lord also taught him and the Church that his servants "abroad in the earth should send forth the accounts of their stewardships to the land of Zion; for the land of Zion shall be a seat and a place to receive and do all these things" (D&C 69:5, 6).

Having decided that Oliver Cowdery and John Whitmer were to carry the manuscripts of the revelations to Missouri, the Prophet Joseph Smith requested that "the sacred writings which they have entrusted them to carry to Zion be dedicated to the Lord by the prayer of faith."[20] He also suggested that certain of the brethren who had labored with him from the beginning in writing be recompensed for their labors from the Church.[21] Certain of the brethren were then assigned as stewards to manage the revelations (D&C 70:5)[22] and receive compensation from the "benefits thereof" (D&C 70:5).[23] After receiving what "is needful for their necessities and their wants" the surplus should be given to the storehouse (D&C 70:7).

In an earlier revelation the Lord taught that Church business should be done in conferences (D&C 20:62). The November Conference of 1831 was a significant conference, in that much important Church business was done which has had great and lasting results in the growth and effectiveness of the restored Kingdom of God.

## Notes

[1]*Mormon Doctrine*, 2nd ed. (Salt Lake City: Bookcraft, 1966), pp. 156-57.

[2]Donald Q. Cannon and Lyndon W. Cook, eds., *Far West Record: Minutes of the Church of Jesus Christ of Latter-day Saints, 1830-1844* (Salt Lake City: Deseret Book Co., 1983), p. 19.

[3]*HC* 1:220.

[4]*Church History and Modern Revelation*, 2 vols. (Salt Lake City: The Council of the Twelve Apostles of the Church of Jesus Christ of Latter-day Saints, 1953), 1:245.

[5]*The Miracle of Forgiveness* (Salt Lake City: Bookcraft, 1969), p. 114.

[6]*HC* 1:222.

[7]*Ibid.*, 224.

[8]*Doctrine and Covenants: Our Modern Scripture* (Provo, Ut.: Brigham Young University Press, 1978), pp. 103-4.

[9]*HC* 1:226.

[10]*Ibid.*

[11]*Ibid.*, 227.

[12]Lyndon W. Cook, *The Revelations of the Prophet Joseph Smith* (Provo: Seventy's Mission Bookstore, 1981), pp. 108-9.

[13]*Doctrines of Salvation*, 3 vols., comp. Bruce R. McConkie (Salt Lake City: Bookcraft, 1954-56), 1:186; see also J. Reuben Clark, Jr., "When Are the Writings and Sermons of Church Leaders Entitled to the Claim of Being Scripture?" Address to Seminary and Institute Personnel at Brigham Young University, 7 July 1954, in David H. Yarn, Jr., ed., *J. Reuben Clark: Selected Papers* (Provo, Ut.: Brigham Young University Press, 1984), pp. 95-112.

[14]Cook, *The Revelations of the Prophet Joseph Smith*, p. 131.

[15]Robert J. Woodford, "The Historical Development of the Doctrine and Covenants," unpublished Ph.D. Dissertation, Brigham Young University, 1974, p. 854.

[16]*Church History and Modern Revelation*, 1:259.

[17]Francis M. Gibbons, "Statistical Report 1983," *Ensign*, May 1984, p. 20.

[18]See Robert J. Matthews, *A Plainer Translation: Joseph Smith's Translation of the Bible, A History and Commentary* (Provo, Ut.: Brigham Young University Press, 1975), p. 260.

[19]*Conference Report*, October 1974, p. 160.

[20]Cannon and Cook, *Far West Record*, p. 31.

[21]*Ibid.*, p. 32.

[22]*Ibid.*

[23]Cook, *The Revelations of the Prophet Joseph Smith*, pp. 112-17.

# 26

# NEW TESTAMENT ITEMS IN THE DOCTRINE AND COVENANTS

## (D&C 7, 74, 77)

KEITH H. MESERVY

"There are many things in the Bible," observed Joseph Smith the Prophet, "which do not, as they now stand, accord with the revelations of the Holy Ghost to me."[1] On a later occasion Joseph said: "I thank God that I have got this old book [German Bible]; but I thank him more for the gift of the Holy Ghost. I have got the oldest book in the world; but I [also] have the oldest book in my heart, even the gift of the Holy Ghost."[2] By means of the sacred endowment of the Spirit, the Modern Seer was able to discern and make known to the Latter-day Saints the true meanings and intentions of numerous scriptural passages; Joseph the revelator and translator frequently served as scriptural exegete, and the flood of intelligence that has come to the Church as a result of his serious contemplation of the Bible is among his greatest gifts to the dispensation of the fulness of times. This article will consider three specific sections of the Doctrine and Covenants, each of which contains prophetic insights into particular segments of the New Testament.

### Section 7

This revelation makes known John's fuller explanation of the enigmatic words contained in his Gospel account (John 21:20-23) of a promise Jesus made to him. Jesus had responded to John's unexpressed desire to continue to live on the earth in order that he might carry out an extended ministry for the Lord. John had an intense desire to continue to bring souls to him (D&C 7:2). Jesus assured John that he would be able to remain on the earth until the Second Coming, at which time John, along with the Three Nephites, would be changed instantaneously, "in the twinkling of an eye from mortality to immortality" (3 Ne. 28:8) when their "earthly" mission was completed. Comments made by Jesus and Mormon (3 Ne. 28) provide excellent resource material to help us understand what Jesus was promising to

John, because Jesus explicitly stated that the three Nephites had "desired the thing which John, my beloved, . . . desired of me" (3 Ne. 28:6).

## Power Over Death

Although the time would come when John and the Three Nephites would make the transition from mortality to immortality, Jesus promised them that they would never "taste of death" or "endure the pains of death." For them the transition from the one state to the other would occur as quickly as the twinkling of an eye (3 Ne. 28:8), this at the time of the Second Coming.

In addition to not tasting death, they were also promised that the hurtful effects of the fall would not be felt by them. Each of these four men, of course, came into a fallen world, subject to the conditions common to everyone else. But, once they had proven themselves and once the Lord had given them permission to remain on the earth beyond the normal time of testing, it would be unthinkable to believe they would be required to endure the problems incident to a fallen mortal world—sickness, disease, and temptation—during the approximately two thousand more years that they would be here on the earth. Thus, the promises made to the Three Nephites are very significant for understanding what happened also to John, because for them and, supposedly for John, the basic effects of the fall were circumvented.

*1. Mortality.* At a certain point in the lives of these men the natural aging process was stopped. This effect of the fall of Adam is being held in abeyance for them until Christ comes again, at which time they will be made immortal instantly.

How little effect the normal deadly powers of mortality had on their transformed bodies is vividly illustrated by Mormon when he wrote of the various attempts made to kill them by irate contemporaries. Though they were cast into prison, buried in the depths of the earth, cast into fiery furnaces or thrown into dens of wild animals, none of these could harm them. They were delivered in turn from each threat to their mortal lives (3 Ne. 28:19-22).

*2. Pain and Sorrow.* A change was made in their bodies so they no longer felt pain or sorrow, except for the sins of the world (3 Ne. 28:9).

*3. Temptation.* Their transformed bodies were no longer subject to the power of Satan: "He could not tempt them" (3 Ne. 28:39).

*4. Sanctification in the Flesh.* "And they were sanctified in the flesh, that they were holy, and that the powers of the earth could not hold them" (3 Ne. 28:39). Such men—sanctified in the flesh, removed from temptation, not subject to sickness or death, wholly committed to God's service, and not subject to the powers of this earth or the netherworld, would be ideal ministers for the Lord. Of the transfigured John it is said that he became "as flaming fire and a ministering angel" (D&C 7:6).

### A Greater Work

Concerning the duration of the Three Nephites' ministry the Lord said, "Ye shall live to behold all the doings of the Father unto the children of men, even until all things shall be fulfilled according to the will of the Father, when I shall come in my glory with the powers of heaven" (3 Ne. 28:7). Then shall they be "changed in the twinkling of an eye from mortality to immortality; and then shall [they] be blessed in the kingdom of my Father," said Jesus to the Three Nephites (3 Ne. 28:8).

The Three Nephites were called to minister not only to the Nephites but also to the gentiles, Jews, and all the scattered tribes of Israel. God would give them great convincing power (3 Ne. 28:27-29), as they would preach to whomever he would send them. When the time comes to listen to their missionary stories, will there be any others any more choice?

## Section 74

This section provides an interpretive revelation that helps us understand a difficult passage in 1 Cor. 7:12-16. It concerns Paul's answers to a question put to him by the Corinthian Saints. The revelation came to Joseph Smith as he was working on the inspired revision of the Bible.

The specific problem in 1 Cor. 7 concerned the tension between a husband and wife over the rearing of children. Often the husband was a Jew, who believed in the Abrahamic covenant of circumcision (Gen.

17:1-14), while the wife was a Christian. For the Jew, any male child of eight days was required to be circumcised as an indication of the fact that he was a son of Abraham and a member of God's covenant community. God had told Abraham that "the uncircumcised man child whose flesh of his foreskin is not circumcised, that soul shall be cut off from his people; he hath broken my covenant" (Gen. 17:14). What could be more serious for a believing Jew than to have his son grow up uncircumcized? On the other hand, the Christian wife believed that the necessity for such things was done away in Christ (Acts 15:1-29; 21:21).

Whereas there was a feeling among many Jews that little children were unholy without circumcision, this revelation reconfirms the principle that through Christ, little children are whole and sinless (see Moro. 8:8; Gen. 17:3-7, 11-12; JST, Gen. 17:11-12; JST, Matt. 18:11; 19:13).

To avoid such problems, Paul gave personal counsel that a believer in Christ ought not to marry a Jew "except the law of Moses should be done away among them, that their children might remain without circumcision; and that the tradition might be done away, which saith that little children are unholy; . . . but little children are holy, being sanctified through the atonement of Jesus Christ" (D&C 74:5-7). The counsel is not unlike what modern Saints would receive regarding the problem of marrying outside the Covenant.

## Section 77

### The Revelation of John

D&C 77 provides interpretive keys for understanding certain aspects of the Book of Revelation. These were revealed to Joseph Smith in March 1832. Reference to the Book of Revelation brings to most people's minds a sense of the vivid, dramatic symbols which permeate it, and also an uneasy feeling that while the symbols are vivid, the meaning seems to be obscure, as though the brilliant, vivid symbols were meant to dazzle rather than enlighten. The form and the content of the message seem to be in tension, so that the name of the book, *Revelation* (Greek: *apokalypsis,* "uncovering"), seems to belie its content. Rather than uncover, what is written seems to cover up.

Clearly when one interprets the prophecies, he must have the spirit of prophecy. This is why it is so significant that a prophet has provided us with interpretive keys for studying these revelations. The Book of Revelation is no more subject to private interpretation than any other book of prophecy is. All prophecies come through the revelations of the Holy Ghost (1 Cor. 2:9-16; 2 Pet. 1:20-21; D&C 50:17-20), and must, in order to avoid making a private interpretation, be interpreted by the light of the Holy Ghost, i.e., the same Spirit that inspired them originally.

One may yearn to understand, as Joseph Smith did, when he said that "the book of Revelation is one of the plainest books God ever caused to be written."[3] In saying this, he also taught: "I make this broad declaration, that whenever God gives a vision of an image, or beast, or figure of any kind, He always holds Himself responsible to give a revelation or interpretation of the meaning thereof, otherwise we are not responsible or accountable for our belief in it. Don't be afraid of being damned for not knowing the meaning of a vision or figure, if God has not given a revelation or interpretation of the subject."[4] Again, speaking of his interpretation of Revelation, Joseph said: "We cannot comprehend the things of God and of heaven, but by revelation. We may spiritualize and express opinions to all eternity; but that is no authority."[5] He advised the elders not to preach from Revelation but to preach repentance. The gospel must be established on a simpler foundation than Revelation affords, for the book of Revelation is really a book to confirm the faithful in their faith—not convert the unfaithful to have faith.

It is significant that section 77 came while Joseph Smith was working on the translation of the scriptures. As he recorded, "In connection with the translation of the Scriptures, I received the following explanation of the Revelation of St. John."[6]

One thing that dominates so much of the attention of Revelation is a sense of the titantic struggle that goes on between the forces of light and those of darkness. In a world—much like ours is today—where violence, apostasy, hate, contention, lieing, stealing, murder, adultery, war, etc., are too much in evidence and the devil seems to triumph, it is absolutely essential that the Saints know that it is God who is in absolute control and not the devil; God triumphs. It is critical to know that God does and will reign, and that his work cannot be frustrated, neither will it come to nought. So, when persecution inevitably comes to the faithful in a world that loves darkness rather than light, where the world shouts out that carnal and sensual values are what really produce happiness, then the Saints must know that what they believe represents reality—God's world, as it really is; they must endure to the end to be crowned as faithful with God. For his work does not fail. This triumph of God and his works over Satan is the major theme of John's revelation.

In that day to come, men will see how God was at work in each individual life as well as in the affairs of the nations to cause his work to succeed, this despite satanic and human wills to the contrary. The book of Revelation graphically demonstrates this truth. It teaches that history has a vertical dimension with God at work on earth from his residence in heaven, as well as a horizontal dimension, as men seek to carve out spheres of influence and accomplishment. And though it is difficult for the Saints to understand heavenly truths unseen by human eyes and ears (most especially when they are dressed in earthly garb), somehow, by the Holy Spirit, they are expected to understand something of the better world that awaits them where God reigns and his Saints dwell with him. The keys given by Joseph Smith fit within this overall framework.

**Interpretive Keys**

*D&C 77:1.* Before this earth is sanctified and prepared for its celestial order of life, it will melt (Isa. 24:19; cf. 3 Ne. 26:3; Morm. 5:23; 2 Pet. 3:10-12; Rev. 20:11) and become like glass or crystal, i.e., it will become a gigantic Urim and Thummim, "whereby all things pertaining to an inferior kingdom, or all kingdoms of a lower order, will be manifest to those who dwell on it" (D&C 130:8-9). For revelations "pertaining to a higher order of kingdoms" than those beneath the celestialized earth (D&C 130:10; Rev. 2:17), each inhabitant of that sanctified sphere will possess a personal Urim and Thummim (D&C 130:10). The Saints who love the truth in this world are assured by this revelation that they will possess the fullest means to acquire and utilize truth in the hereafter.

*D&C 77:2.* The question in this verse is specific but the answer is general, providing a fuller background for understanding an important principle. John's vision shows that spirits of beasts, creeping things, and fowls, as well as man, are in the likeness of their physical, temporal bodies. While other revelations make it clear that all life in this world has a spiritual counterpart (see Moses 3:4-5, 9) and that the one looks like the other—the physical like the spiritual body (see Ether 3:16)—what is explicit in D&C 77:2 is that all God's creatures live beyond the grave. The reference to fowls, beasts, creeping things (those categories of life identified in the various creation accounts) and "every other creature which God has created," provides inclusive enough language to show that all of God's creations are eternal in nature. God's concern for the well-being ("happiness") of all of his creatures is another truth revealed in this revelation. His work is not superfluous. The end toward which he works for his creatures as well as his children is their happiness, which, obviously, they are capable of experiencing. It is well known that animals possess intelligence. Current research is being done on the extent to which creatures "speak" or communicate with each other. This revelation says nothing about whether animal spirits have volition. What we do not learn, for example, is what it means to say that the devil "put it into the heart of the serpent [for he had drawn away many after him,]" when reference is made to the fact that Satan spoke to Eve through the mouth of the serpent (Moses 4:5-6). Neither is anything said about accountability, degree of intelligence, whether "laws" are given to other creatures, whether merit is involved in assigning animals to various degrees of glory, or even whether there are varying degrees of glory for God's other creatures. This revelation explaining what John saw in heaven suggests at least that they are not restricted to a separate kingdom of their own, but co-inhabit with man the glory prepared.

As the Prophet Joseph taught, "Says one, 'I cannot believe in the salvation of beasts.' Any man who would tell you that this could not be, would tell you that the revelations are not true. John heard the words of beasts giving glory to God, and understood them. God who made the beasts could understand every language spoken by them."[7]

*D&C 77:3.* John saw four specific, individual beasts. "The four beasts were four of the most noble animals that had filled the measure of their creation, and had been saved from other worlds, because they were perfect: they were like angels in their sphere. We are not told where they came from, and I do not know; but they were seen and heard by John praising and glorifying God."[8] Although each of these was a specific creature, nevertheless it seems that each in turn represented a particular class or order. What this means may be evident from another revelation, in which God taught Joseph Smith that three individual men—Abraham, Isaac, and Jacob had been exalted. While three specific men are identified, the revelation is meant to show that all others who belong to their particular "class" of men, i.e., those who show themselves willing to do "none other things than that which they were commanded" (D&C 132:27), may also be exalted.

The revelation showed John that animals are among those who enjoy the fullness of God's blessings for them in the world to come.

*D&C 77:4* Eyes are means of seeing and knowing and wings represent the power of mobility.

*D&C 77:5.* John actually saw twenty-four specific men from seven specific churches.

*D&C 77:6.* The seven thousand years of the earth's temporal existence are understood to be the six thousand years from the fall of Adam to the Millennium, plus the thousand years of the Millennium. Any book containing the will, mysteries, and works of God over the seven thousand years of the earth's temporal existence—his hidden "economy"—would provide readers with an insight into the grandeur and greatness of God. Adam, the Brother of Jared, and some others have had the privilege of "reading" parts of such a "book," but unless sanctified, men cannot behold either God or the fullness of his works and glory and remain in the flesh (Moses 1:5).

While immortality is gained for everyone by the Son of God's voluntary death and resurrection in a once-and-for-all-time act, that which God "works at" the rest of the time is to help his children to qualify for exaltation. The scriptures provide a partial picture of God at work doing this. They show us his reaching out, sending angels, calling prophets, teaching, calling to repentance, offering mercy, warning of impending judgments, answering prayers, testing, etc. It is a partial story of God at work in the affairs of the nations to advance his cause and frustrate the work of the Adversary.

*D&C 77:7* .The book that is sealed into seven parts representing 1,000-year blocks of the earth's temporal existence contains the full story. Opening one seal opens up one-seventh of God's story for scrutiny by those sanctified to see it. After the revelation of one-seventh of the story is completed, then the next portion will be unveiled.

*D&C 77:8.* The four angels have power to hurt the earth (Rev. 7:2) and thus may be identified with the angels referred to in the Parable of the Wheat and the Tares (Matt. 13:24-43 and D&C 86:1-7). That is, they have divine power to open or close the heavens, to bless with life or curse with destruction (cf. Hel. 10:4-11). They will not hurt anyone until God has finished his work of preparing his people for those days, until the angels (messengers of God) have sealed up the servants of the Lord—placed the seal of eternal life—against that destruction that is coming.

*D&C 77:9.* A seal of God is a sign of belonging to the Lord and being under his protection (see Ezek. 9:4-6). Joseph Smith taught: "Four destroying angels holding power over the four quarters of the earth until the servants of God are sealed in their foreheads, which signifies sealing the blessing upon their heads, meaning the everlasting covenant, thereby making their calling and election sure. When a seal is put upon the father and mother, it secures their posterity, so that they cannot be lost, but will be saved by virtue of the covenant of their father and mother."[9] Judgments are not to occur before the sealing of those who belong to God is complete. Since those whom the angels are sealing are the "servants of God," i.e., high priests, it is clear that they have received the gospel and the priesthood. So restoration of the gospel and gathering has preceded their sealing. Thus, the angel is logically involved in restoration preparatory to sealing.

*Elias* is a code name, a title given to anyone whose assignment from God is of a preparatory nature. It is used of numerous people in various ages—Abraham's day, Jesus' day, and the last days. The role of this latter-day Elias, as defined in chapter 7 of Revelation, is to preach the gospel, restore priesthood, gather the elect, and seal them up *before* the earth is hurt. He is a forerunner, a preparer of the way.

Since the title is applied to many individuals in the various revelations, Elias must be a "composite personage. The expression must be understood to be a name and a title for those whose mission it was to commit keys and powers to men in this final dispensation."[10] Thus, Elias in this revelation identifies each of the many keyholders who came to Joseph Smith to transmit keys. Moroni, John the Baptist, Peter, James, John, Moses, Elijah, Elias, Gabriel, Raphael, and Michael are known examples (see D&C 13; 110; 128:19-21).[11] From them Joseph Smith received the keys of gathering, and every priesthood key necessary for individuals on this earth to receive every ordinance and power to make their calling and election sure.

*D&C 77:11.* Elder Bruce R. McConkie wrote: "One of the ordained offices in the Melchizedek Priesthood is that of a *high priest* (D&C 20:67). This office grows out of and is an appendage to the higher priesthood (D&C 107:5). Beginning in Adam's day, whenever the Church has been organized and the fullness of the gospel has been had by men, there have been high priests (D&C 107:53; Alma 13). These brethren have been called to minister in spiritual things (D&C 107:18), to travel and preach the gospel (D&C 84:111), and to perfect the saints and do all the things that a seventy, elder, or holder of the Aaronic Priesthood can do (D&C 68:19)."[12]

The high priests referred to in D&C 77:11 fit this description. They are seasoned men who are redeemed and stand before the throne of God without fault (Rev. 14-15); subject to the key-holder's direction, they are capable of presiding over the Lord's work, wherever they are called. They are ordained as God's ambassadors to preach and administer the Gospel to the nations of the earth. That is, they are missionaries of the Lord Jesus Christ, who carry the gospel of peace, the message of redemption, the Hope of Israel to the nations of the earth. Thus, they will be privileged to stand as saviors on Mount Zion with the Lord when he comes again (D&C 133:18).[13]

Since they come from all the tribes of Israel, major movements in the gathering of Israel will have occurred by the time they are called to serve. Thus, this revelation makes it clear that the authority given to Joseph Smith and Oliver Cowdery to restore the Ten Tribes to their former high status in Israel and to lead them from "the land of the north" (D&C 110:11) will have been used to gather them before the events described in this revelation can take place. Elder McConkie has stated: "These keys now reside in the President of The Church of Jesus Christ of Latter-day Saints. That the remnants of Israel shall be restored before the Second Coming of the Son of Man is evident from the fact that 12,000 from each tribe are to receive the restored gospel, and that though the ordinances of the Lord's house they are to become kings and priests, who shall administer the blessings of the everlasting gospel to the Lord's elect (D&C 77:9-11)."[14]

These 144,000 will not act independently of the Church. There is one prophet, seer, and revelator for the whole earth. These 144,000 will serve as missionaries under the power and authority of the President of the Church of Jesus Christ of Latter-day Saints.[15]

*D&C 77:12-13.* Regarding these verses Elder McConkie wrote: "Thus our Lord is not destined to return when the seventh thousand years first commences. Plagues, destruction, fire, bloodshed, war, and desolation—all of incomparable power and degree—are to sweep the earth after the opening of the seventh seal and before the Second Coming. These are announced in the eighth and ninth chapters of Revelation."[16]

*D&C 77:14.* Ezekiel also was asked to open his mouth and eat the book that was given to him. The writing on both sides contained "lamentations, and mourning, and woe. Moreover he said unto me, Son of man, eat that thou findest; eat this roll, and go speak unto the house of Israel. So I opened my mouth, and he caused me to eat that roll. And he said unto me, Son of man, cause thy belly to eat, and fill thy bowels with this roll that I give thee. Then did I eat it. . . . And he said unto me, Son of man, go, get thee unto the house of Israel, and speak *with my words* unto them" (Ezek. 2:8-10; 3:1-4, italics added). Eating the roll seems to have symbolized the Lord's way of causing Ezekiel to absorb the message written on the roll which he was then to give to the people. Thus, the initial charge: "Eat this roll, and go speak unto the house of Israel" (Ezek. 3:1). Similarly, John's book seems to contain the mission that he would undertake. As Elder McConkie stated, "That John labors in fulfilment of this commission is evident from the statement of the Prophet Joseph Smith, made by the spirit of inspiration in June, 1831, 'that John the Revelator was then among the Ten Tribes of Israel who had been led away by Shalmaneser, king of Assyria, *to prepare them* for their return from their long dispersion, to again possess the land of their fathers' (*HC* 1:176)."[17]

*D&C 77:15.* These prophets fight in defense of Jerusalem and the Jews during their final battle—the Battle of Armageddon. They have power like Enoch, Moses, and Nephi to shut up the heavens, to smite the earth with plagues, to change water to blood, and to testify for the

Lord (Rev. 11:6). As with Abinadi, no one can hurt them until their testimony is finished. Whoever tries will be destroyed by fire from their mouths (Rev. 11:5). According to Elder McConkie:

> Their ministry will take place after the latter-day temple has been built in Old Jerusalem, after some of the Jews who dwell there have been converted, and just before Armageddon and the return of the Lord Jesus. How long will they minister in Jerusalem and in the Holy Land? For three and a half years, the precise time spent by the Lord in his ministry to the ancient Jews. The Jews, as an assembled people, will hear again the testimony of legal administrators bearing record that salvation is in Christ and in his gospel. Who will these witnesses be? We do not know, except that they will be followers of Joseph Smith; they will hold the holy Melchizedek Priesthood; they will be members of the Church of Jesus Christ of Latter-day Saints. It is reasonable to suppose, knowing how the Lord has always dealt with his people in all ages, that they will be two members of the Council of the Twelve or of the First Presidency of the Church.[18]

## Notes

[1]*TPJS*, p. 310.
[2]*Ibid.*, p. 349.
[3]*Ibid.*, p. 290.
[4]*Ibid.*, p. 291.
[5]*Ibid.*, p. 292.
[6]See *HC* 1:253-55; see also Robert J. Matthews, *A Plainer Translation: Joseph Smith's Translation of the Bible, A History and Commentary* (Provo, Ut.: Brigham Young University Press, 1975) for discussion of the significance of Joseph Smith's Bible revisions as an important aid to his receiving significant revelation; see also Robert L. Millet, "Joseph Smith's Translation of the Bible and the Doctrine and Covenants," found herein.
[7]*TPJS*, pp. 291-92.
[8]*Ibid.*, p. 292.
[9]*Ibid.*, p. 321.

[10]Bruce R. McConkie, *Doctrinal New Testament Commentary,* 3 vols. (Salt Lake City: Bookcraft, 1966-73), 3:491-92; see also Joseph Fielding Smith, *Doctrines of Salvation,* comp. Bruce R. McConkie, 3 vols. (Salt Lake City: Bookcraft, 1954-56), 1:170-74.

[11]See McConkie, *ibid.*

[12]*Mormon Doctrine,* 2nd ed. (Salt Lake City: Bookcraft, 1966), p. 356.

[13]*TPJS*, p. 366.

[14]McConkie, *New Testament Commentary,* 3:494.

[15]See McConkie, *The Millennial Messiah* (Salt Lake City: Deseret Book Co., 1982), pp. 217, 325-26.

[16]*New Testament Commentary,* 3:498.

[17]*Ibid.*, p. 506.

[18]*Millennial Messiah,* p. 390.

# 27

# THE VISION OF THE GLORIES
## (D&C 76)

LARRY E. DAHL

### A Significant Doctrinal Communication

"It is full of light; it is full of truth; it is full of glory; it is full of beauty. It portrays the future of all the inhabitants of the earth, dividing them into three grand classes or divisions—celestial, terrestrial, and telestial, or as compared to the glory of the Sun, the glory of the Moon, and the glory of the Stars. It shows who will be redeemed, and what redemption they will enjoy; and describes the position the inhabitants of the earth will occupy when they enter into the future state."[1]

"Section 76 of the Doctrine and Covenants in its sublimity and clearness in relation to the eternal destiny of the human family, has not been surpassed. It should be treasured by all members of the Church as a priceless heritage. It should strengthen their faith and be to them an incentive to seek the exaltation promised to all who are just and true. So plain and simple are its teachings that none should stumble or misunderstand."[2]

### Historical Context

The Prophet Joseph Smith had been engaged "somewhat regularly"[3] in making an inspired translation of parts of the Bible since June of 1830. That work was periodically interrupted by other duties. One such interruption was a conference of the Church held in Amherst, Ohio, 25 January 1832. Concerning his return from that conference and the reception of the revelation known to us as D&C 76, the Prophet wrote:

> Upon my return from Amherst conference, I resumed the translation of the scriptures. From sundry revelations which had been received, it was apparent that many important points touching the salvation of man, had been taken from the Bible, or lost before it was compiled. It appeared self-evident from what truths were left, that if God rewarded every one according to the deeds done in the body the term "Heaven," as intended

> for the Saint's eternal home must include more kingdoms than one. Accordingly, on the 16th of February, 1832, while translating St. John's Gospel, myself and Elder Rigdon saw the following vision.[4]

At this time Joseph and his family were living in the home of John Johnson in Hiram, Ohio, about 30 miles southeast of Kirtland. It was in this home that the vision was received.

The only description that has surfaced thus far of the event, in addition to the Prophet's brief introduction cited above, is the following remembrance of Philo Dibble published in the *Juvenile Instructor*, 15 May 1892:

> The vision which is recorded in the Book of Doctrine and Covenants was given at the house of "Father Johnson," in Hyrum [sic], Ohio, and during the time that Joseph and Sidney were in the spirit and saw the heavens open, there were other men in the room, perhaps twelve, among whom I was one during a part of the time—probably two-thirds of the time,—I saw the glory and felt the power, but did not see the vision.
>
> The events and conversation, while they were seeing what is written (and many things were seen and related that are not written,) I will relate as minutely as is necessary.
>
> Joseph would, at intervals, say: "What do I see?" as one might say while looking out the window and beholding what all in the room could not see. Then he would relate what he had seen or what he was looking at. Then Sidney replied, "I see the same." Presently Sidney would say "what do I see?" and would repeat what he had seen or was seeing, and Joseph would reply, "I see the same."
>
> This manner of conversation was repeated at short intervals to the end of the vision, and during the whole time not a word was spoken by any other person. Not a sound nor motion made by anyone but Joseph and Sidney, and it seemed to me that they never moved a joint or limb during the time I was there, which I think was over an hour, and to the end of the vision.
>
> Joseph sat firmly and calmly all the time in the midst of a magnificent glory, but Sidney sat limp and pale, apparently as limber as a rag, observing which, Joseph remarked, smilingly, "Sidney is not used to it as I am."[5]

Ten years earlier (1882), "Philo Dibble's Narrative," an autobiographical sketch, was published by the *Juvenile Instructor* office. Concerning D&C 76 the narrative states:

> On a subsequent visit to Hiram, I arrived at Father Johnson's just as Joseph and Sidney were coming out of the vision alluded to in the book of Doctrine and Covenants, in which mention is made of the three glories. Joseph wore black clothes, but at this time seemed to be dressed in an element of glorious white, and his face shone as if it were transparent, but I did not see the same glory attending Sidney. Joseph appeared as strong as a lion, but Sidney seemed as weak as water, and Joseph noticing his condition smiled and said, "Brother Sidney is not as used to it as I am."[6]

If both of these accounts are accurate remembrances, Philo Dibble must have arrived in time to observe the latter portion ("probably two-thirds of the time," "which I think was over an hour") of the vision. No mention is made of the names of the "other men in the room, perhaps twelve." Whether any of those men wrote of the experience is not known.

## Reaction of the Saints and Early Publication of the Vision

Some of the Saints had difficulty accepting the doctrine in the vision, as it was different from their traditional view of life after death. Brigham Young wrote of his own struggle with it:

> After all, my traditions were such, that when the Vision came first to me, it was so directly contrary and opposed to my former education, I said, wait a little; I did not reject it, but I could not understand it. I then could feel what incorrect traditions had done for me. Suppose all that I have ever heard from my priest and parents—the way they taught me to read the Bible, had been true;—my understanding would be diametrically opposed to the doctrine revealed in the Vision. I used to think and pray, to read and think, until I knew, and fully understood it for myself, by the visions of the holy Spirit. At first, it actually came in contact with my own feelings, though I never could believe like the mass of the Christian world around me; but I did

> not know how nigh I believed as they did. I found, however, that I was so nigh, I could shake hands with them any time I wished.[7]

"Eventually, as this revelation was published in the periodicals of the Church and taught to the members over the pulpit, the Saints were able to overcome their prejudice, and section 76 is now held in high regard by the members of the Church."[8] The revelation was first published in the Church publication *The Evening and Morning Star* in July 1832, and was included in the 1835 edition of the Doctrine and Covenants.

It should be noted that in the vision itself Joseph and Sidney were told what they were to write and what they were *not* to write (D&C 76:28, 49, 80, 113, 114-16).

Eleven years after the vision (May 1843) Joseph Smith said: "I could explain a hundred fold more than I ever have of the glories of the kingdoms manifested to me in the vision, were I permitted, and were the people prepared to receive them."[9] It is possible that by then he already had revealed more than is recorded in D&C 76. Robert Woodford has suggested: "His later writings on the resurrection, . . . pre-earth life, . . . astronomy, . . . and the degrees within the celestial kingdom . . . may all have reflected some of the things he learned in this vision."[10]

If we have but a hundredth part, it seems obvious that the recorded revelation, as marvelous as it is, will not answer all the questions we may have about our eternal destinies. From what we do have, however, it is abundantly clear that there is an eternal reward comensurate with every level of obedience—rewards that range from godhood to perdition.

## An Overview

The revelation contained in D&C 76 is a series of visions on the following topics:

1. The Son of God (vv. 1-24)
2. Satan and his Followers (vv. 25-49)
3. The Celestial Kingdom (vv. 50-70, 92-96)
4. The Terrestrial Kingdom (vv. 71-80, 91, 97)

5. The Telestial Kingdom (vv. 81-90, 98-112)

The sequence is interesting. It must have been a profound lesson in contrast for Joseph and Sidney to *see* and *converse* with Christ (v. 14), hear "the voice bearing record that he is the Only Begotten of the Father" (v. 23), then to be shown the darkness of rebellion and perdition, and then again to bask in the glory and power attending the celestial kingdom.

## The Vision Of The Son of God (vv. 1-24)

After being assured that God's purposes do not fail and that he delights to honor the faithful with wisdom and understanding through his Spirit, Joseph and Sidney were privileged to *see* and *converse* with the Son of God in heavenly vision. The details of that conversation, or even by what means it was carried out, are not stated. The effect of it, however, is clearly stated in vv. 22-24. "Last of all" (v. 22) does not mean there will be no future testimonies born of him, rather that these brethren could now add their personal witness to all former testimonies that had been born to that time.

Note that John 5:29 is rendered somewhat differently in v. 17 than in the Bible—"just" and "unjust" replacing "life" and "damnation." Note, too, that the new rendering "was given" to them (v. 15). A careful examination of the words and their theological meanings will show that the new rendering is more in keeping with the idea of varied levels of eternal reward than are the words "life" and "damnation."

The vision came as a prophet and his scribe were *marveling* and *meditating* upon a gospel truth, which in this case they had just learned through the spirit of revelation. This seems to be a pattern. It is interesting to note how many of the great recorded visions through the ages came while prophets were engaged in "pondering," "reflecting," or "meditating" upon some principle brought to their attention by the scriptures and the Spirit. Examples include Joseph Smith's First Vision (JS-H 12), Nephi's vision of the tree of life (1 Ne. 11:1), Joseph F. Smith's Vision of the Redemption of the Dead (D&C 138:1, 2), Enos and Nephi (son of Helaman) being reasurred by the voice of God of their spiritual standing (Enos vv. 3, 4; Hel. 10:2, 3), and Spencer W.

Kimball's revelation on priesthood (OD 2). No doubt all of us could have revealed to us deeper understanding by devoting ourselves more to "pondering" and "reflecting" upon eternal truths. Perhaps that is why we are continually reminded to "search" (D&C 1:37), "treasure" (JS-M 37), "ponder" (Moro. 10:3), and "feast" (2 Ne. 31:20) upon the words of the Lord.

Verse 24 contains a powerful statement about the infinite nature of Christ's atonement. Citing this verse and the Prophet Joseph Smith's poetic version thereof (see below), Elder Bruce R. McConkie has written: "Now our Lord's jurisdiction and power extend far beyond the limits of this one small earth on which we dwell. He is, under the Father, the creator of worlds without number (Moses 1:33). And through the power of his atonement the inhabitants of these worlds, the revelation says, 'are begotten sons and daughters unto God' (D&C 76:24), which means that the atonement of Christ, being literally and truly infinite, applies to an infinite number of earths."[11]

## The Vision Of Satan and His Followers (vv. 25-49)

"The heavens wept over him" (v. 26), and with good reason! He was an "angel of God who was in authority in the presence of God" (v. 25). He was Lucifer, which means torch-bearer, or bringer of light. He was a "son of the morning," which could mean either "son of light" or an early-born spirit child of our Father in the pre-earth life. Obviously he had great capacity and promise and influence. But in his case pride ruled predominant. He rebelled against God. By his power and influence he convinced "a third part of the hosts of heaven" to rebel with him "because of their agency" (D&C 29:36). Satan, along with his followers, was "thrust down" (v. 25) "into the earth" (Rev. 12:9), "to deceive and to blind men, and to lead them captive at his will, even as many as would not hearken unto [the Lord's] voice" (Moses 4:4). The revelation (v. 29) states that "he maketh war with the Saints of God, and encompasseth them round about." Joseph Smith said, "The devil will use his greatest efforts to trap the Saints."[12] He also told Heber C. Kimball that "The nearer a person approaches the Lord, a greater power will be manifest by the adversary to prevent the accomplishment of His purposes."[13]

Just as those who completely follow Christ become sons of God (D&C 76:58; Moses 6:68), those who suffer "themselves through the power of the devil to be overcome" (v. 31) become sons of perdition, "Perdition" being another name for Satan (D&C 76:26). In both cases those involved make decisions with their eyes wide open—it is "impossible . . . to be saved in ignorance" (D&C 131:6), and those who become sons of perditions must:

- *know* God's power (v. 31)
- have been made *partakers* thereof (v. 31)
- *have suffered themselves* to be overcome (v. 31)
- *deny* the truth (v. 31)
- *defy* God's power (v. 31)
- deny the Holy Spirit after having received it (v. 35)
- deny the Only Begotten Son (crucify him unto themselves) (v. 35)
- deny the Son after the Father has revealed him (v. 43)

The question is often asked, "Just how much does one have to know before one could become a son of perdition?" The following quotations from Joseph Smith and Spencer W. Kimball may help:

> All sins shall be forgiven, except the sin against the Holy Ghost; for Jesus will save all except the sons of perdition. What must a man do to commit the unpardonable sin? He must receive the Holy Ghost, have the heavens opened unto him, and know God, and then sin against Him. After a man has sinned against the Holy Ghost, there is no repentance for him. He has got to say that the sun does not shine while he sees it; he has got to deny Jesus Christ when the heavens have been opened unto him, and to deny the plan of salvation with his eyes open to the truth of it; and from that time he begins to be an enemy. This is the case with many apostates of the Church of Jesus Christ of Latter-day Saints.
>
> When a man begins to be an enemy to this work, he hunts me, he seeks to kill me, and never ceases to thirst for my blood. He gets the spirit of the devil—the same spirit that they had who crucified the Lord of Life—the same spirit that sins against the Holy Ghost. You cannot save such persons; you cannot bring them to repentance; they make open war, like the devil, and

> awful is the consequence.[14]
>
> The sins unto death may be thought of as somewhat difficult to define and limit with precision. From the words of Joseph Smith quoted above we note that "... many apostates of The Church of Jesus Christ of Latter-day Saints" will fall into this category. We cannot definitely identify them individually since it is impossible for us to know the extent of their knowledge, the depth of their enlightenment, and the sureness of their testimonies before their fall....
>
> The sin against the Holy Ghost requires such knowledge that it is manifestly impossible for the rank and file to commit such a sin. Comparatively few Church members will commit murder wherein they shed innocent blood, and we hope only few will deny the Holy Ghost.[15]

The consequence of becoming sons of perdition is the "second death" (v. 37). They are the "only ones who shall not be redeemed in the due time of the Lord" (v. 38). Through the power of the atonement, Christ "saves all the works of his hands, except those sons of perdition" (vv. 43, 44). "They cannot be redeemed from their spiritual fall because they repent not; for they love darkness rather than light" (D&C 29:44, 45). Their determined lawlessness and its result is described in another revelation: "That which breaketh a law, and abideth not by law, but seeketh to be a law unto itself, and willeth to abide in sin, and altogether abideth in sin, cannot be sanctified by law, neither by mercy, justice, nor judgment. Therefore, they must remain filthy still" (D&C 88:35).

The Lord explained to Joseph and Sidney in the vision that though some are permitted to catch a brief glimpse of perdition, no one except the sons of perdition themselves truly understand the nature, extent and duration of the suffering there (vv. 44-48). In an earlier revelation the Lord said: "Wherefore I will say unto them—Depart from me, ye cursed, into everlasting fire, prepared for the devil and his angels. And now, behold, I say unto you, never at any time have I declared from my own mouth that they should return, for where I am they cannot come, for they have no power. But remember that all my judgments are not given unto man" (D&C 29:28-30). The "but remember" portion of that revelation has led some to speculate that eventually the sons of perdition may be restored, recycled, or redeemed. Concerning those who were advocating such an idea in the early Church, the First Presidency (Joseph Smith, Sidney Rigdon, and Fredrick G. Williams) wrote in 1833:

> Say to the brother Hulet and to all others, that the Lord never authorized them to say that the devil, his angels or the sons of perdition, should ever be restored; for their state of destiny was not revealed to man, is not revealed, nor ever shall be revealed, save to those who are made partakers thereof; consequently those who teach this doctrine, have not received it of the Spirit of the Lord. Truly Brother Oliver declared it to be the doctrine of devils. We therefore command that this doctrine be taught no more in Zion. We sanction the decision of the Bishop and his council, in relation to this doctrine being a bar to communion.[16]

Speculation, then, about the ultimate destiny of the sons of perdition—something that was not, is not, and will not be revealed—seems fruitless.

Some have wondered if the words "for all the rest shall be brought forth by the resurrection of the dead" (v. 39) means that sons of perdition will not be resurrected. We are assured by scripture and by modern prophets that they will be resurrected (see 1 Cor. 15:22; D&C 29:26; D&C 88:32, 102; Alma 11:41-45).[17] The sense of v. 39 then, is that all the rest (all except sons of perdition) will be "brought forth" (i.e., redeemed or brought out of hell) by the resurrection of the dead (see D&C 29:44; 88:16, 32).[18]

Satan and his unembodied followers, along with his resurrected but unredeemed followers, inherit a "kingdom which is not a kingdom of glory" (D&C 88:24), suffering "everlasting," "endless," "eternal" punishment (v. 44—explained to mean "God's punishment" in D&C 19:6-12), "where their worm dieth not, and the fire is not quenched" (v. 44). The "worm" and "fire" represent "guilt and pain, and anguish" (Mosiah 2:38). Joseph Smith said: "The torment of disappointment in the mind of man is as exquisite as a lake burning with fire and brimstone."[19] What a sad end. It is no wonder that the heavens wept!

## The Vision Of The Celestial Kingdom (vv. 50-70, 92-96)

A careful reading of the verses pertaining to the celestial glory shows that they refer to those who are *exalted* in that kingdom (see v. 55, "into whose hands the Father has given *all things*"; v. 56, "received of his fulness"; v. 58, "they are gods"). Later (see D&C 131:1-4) the Prophet explained that there were "three heavens or degrees" in the celestial glory; whether this fact was made known during the vision or whether he learned of it later is not stated. However, it seems clear that the focus of this part of the vision is upon the highest heaven or glory within the celestial kingdom.

Requirements include:

- a testimony of Jesus (v. 51)
- belief—faith? (v. 51)
- baptism (v. 51)
- receiving the Holy Ghost (v. 52)
- keeping the commandments (v. 52)
- overcoming by faith—overcoming *sin*? or the *world*? or whatever trial or obstacle "the Lord seeth fit to inflict upon him" (Mosiah 3:19), proving to himself and to God that he is "determined to serve God at all hazards"[20] (v. 53)
- sealing by the Holy Spirit of Promise (v. 53)

> *The Holy Spirit of Promise* is the Holy Spirit *promised* the saints, or in other words the Holy Ghost. This name-title is used in connection with the sealing and ratifying power of the Holy Ghost, that is, the power given him to ratify and approve the righteous acts of men so that those acts will be binding on earth and in heaven. "All covenants, contracts, bonds, obligations, oaths, vows, performances, connections, associations, or expectations," must be sealed by the Holy Spirit of Promise, if they are to have "efficacy, virtue, or force in and after the resurrection from the dead; for all contracts that are not made unto this end have an end when men are dead" (D&C 132:7).
>
> To seal is to *ratify*, to *justify*, or to *approve.* Thus an act which is sealed by the Holy Spirit of Promise is one which is ratified by the Holy Ghost; it is one which is approved by the Lord; and the person who has taken the obligation upon himself

> is justified by the Spirit in the thing he has done. The ratifying seal of approval is put upon an act only if those entering the contract are worthy as a result of personal righteousness to receive the divine approbation. They "are sealed by the Holy Spirit of promise, which the Father sheds forth upon all those who are *just* and *true*" (D&C 76:53). If they are not just and true and worthy, the ratifying seal is withheld.[21]

Nothing specific is said in this revelation about the necessity of eternal marriage in order to achieve exaltation in the celestial kingdom. That requirement is made clear in D&C 131:1-4 and D&C 132:15-25. Also, we learn from D&C 84:33-44 that faithfulness to the oath and covenant of the priesthood is a requirement.

Those who attain this glory are members of the "Church of Enoch, and of the Firstborn" (vv. 54, 67), and "are come unto Mount Zion" (v. 66). These are simply other ways of saying that they are exalted.[22]

"Just men made perfect through Jesus the mediator of the new covenant" (v. 69) is a reminder that even though someone learns to live in perfect harmony with the laws of God (i.e., becomes a just man) he must be absolved from his earlier mistakes before he is considered perfect. The blood of Christ remits those sins of which one has repented, and thus he is "made perfect."

Verse 94 (see also 1 Cor. 13:12) carries a powerful thought: exalted souls "see as they are seen, and know as they are known." How marvelous to consider the idea of living in such an open society, where there are no hidden agendas, where motives, thoughts, words, and actions are pure, so that there is nothing of which to be ashamed and therefore nothing to try to hide. It is an interesting experience to try to live that way for one day, or even one hour.

Verse 95 indicates that those who achieve this glory will be made "equal in power, and in might, and in dominion." What is probably meant is that *ultimately* "all that My Father hath" will be given to those who qualify for exaltation (D&C 84:38). This blessing will not necessarily be *conferred* simultaneously upon all at the resurrection. Joseph Fielding Smith has said: "To be 'made equal in power, and in might, and in dominion,' does not mean that all shall advance with equal rapidity and perfection, but that means are given to them as sons of God by which they may obtain this fulness."[23] And the Prophet

Joseph Smith taught in 1844:

> When you climb up a ladder, you must begin at the bottom, and ascend step by step, until you arrive at the top; and so it is with the principles of the Gospel—you must begin with the first, and go on until you learn all the principles of exaltation. But it will be a great while after you have passed through the veil before you will have learned them. It is not all to be comprehended in this world; it will be a great work to learn our salvation and exaltation even beyond the grave.[24]

Applying the principles contained in D&C 130:18-19, it will take some people less time than others to achieve a "fulness." Surely as we contemplate dwelling "in the presence of God and his Christ forever and ever" (v. 62), with all the blessings attendant thereto, we can understand Alma's declaration: "And my soul did long to be there" (Alma 36:22).

### The Vision Of The Terrestrial Kingdom (vv. 71-80, 86-89, 91, 97)

Those who are to receive the terrestrial glory are described as:

- those who died without law (v. 72)
- the spirits of men kept in prison, who received not the testimony of Jesus in the flesh, but afterwards received it (vv. 73-74)
- honorable men of the earth, who were blinded by the craftiness of men (v. 75)
- those who are not valiant in the testimony of Jesus (v. 79)

It seems clear that these categories are not absolutely definitive. For instance, *all* those who die without law will not end up in the terrestrial kingdom—those who would have received the gospel had they heard it are heirs of the celestial kingdom (D&C 137:7-9). And what better way is there of knowing whether they would have received it than seeing what they do with it when they do receive it, in the post-earth spirit world? Similarly *all* those who are "not valiant in the testimony of Jesus" will not receive terrestrial glory—some will be so "not valiant" (i.e., liars, sorcerers, adulterers, etc.) that they will be consigned to the telestial kingdom. Hence, it appears that these categories qualify one another, and taken together give us a profile of terrestrial personality.

That personality is capsulized in vv. 75 and 79—"honorable men" who have a testimony of Jesus, but who are not valiant in that testimony. Some, evidently, settled themselves into that mold in the pre-earth life and simply maintain it through this earthly probation. Elder Melvin J. Ballard suggested:

> Now those who died without law, meaning the pagan nations, for lack of faithfulness, for lack of devotion in the former life, are obtaining all that they are entitled to. I don't mean to say that all of them will be barred from entrance into the highest glory. Any one of them who repents and complies with the conditions might also obtain celestial glory, but the great bulk of them will only obtain terrestrial glory.[25]

Others, like some of the disobedient in the days of Noah, reject the gospel on earth, but through repentance and suffering in the post-earth spirit world raise themselves to a terrestrial level of obedience and qualify for a terrestrial reward (Moses 7:36-40; 1 Pet. 3:18-21, 4:6; D&C 138:32, 58). Still others accept the testimony of Jesus on earth or in the Spirit world and live honorable lives, but permit the craftiness of men to blind them to the higher gospel principles. Neither celestial laws nor telestial wickedness appeals to them.

By the time of the resurrection and judgment, the accumulated effect of all our decisions in the pre-earth life, mortality, and the post-earth spirit world will be an unmistakable demonstration of what we *really are*, what law we can and will obey, and therefore what measure of truth and light and glory we can abide (D&C 88:22-24, 40). In regard to those spoken of in D&C 76:72-74, discussion sometimes focuses upon whether rejecting the fulness of the gospel at one point in time disqualifies them from receiving it later. Perhaps more emphasis should be placed upon the idea that it is not so much a matter of God denying *opportunity* as it is a matter of our unwillingness or inability to repent fully and respond to higher levels of light and truth.

Those who receive the terrestrial glory will enjoy "the presence of the Son, but not the fulness of the Father" (v. 77). Their bodies differ from celestial bodies in glory "as the moon differs from the sun" (v. 78). They will be governed by "the ministrations of the celestial" (v. 87) kingdom, and have a part in governing the telestial kingdom (vv. 86, 88).

## The Vision Of The Telestial Kingdom (vv. 81-90, 98-112)

Just as there are souls who love and obey the truth with all their hearts and receive *celestial* rewards, and as there are souls who are honorable but not valiant and who receive *terrestrial* rewards, there are those who live wickedly, rejecting the gospel and Christ and the prophets. These receive *telestial* rewards.

The word "telestial" is a uniquely Latter-day Saint term. It does not appear in the Bible and even in Latter-day scripture only appears in D&C 76 and D&C 88. *Webster's Third New International Dictionary* defines "telestial glory" as "The lowest of three Mormon degrees or kingdoms of glory attainable in heaven."[26] Although Paul speaks of three glories of the sun, moon, and stars, and names the first two as celestial and terrestrial, he does not name the third. That name, telestial, comes from this vision to Joseph Smith and Sidney Rigdon (see 1 Cor. 15:40, 41; see also JST, 1 Cor. 15:40).

Those who will enter the telestial kingdom, where they will differ in glory from one another as one star differs from another star (v. 98), are described as:

- they who received not the gospel of Christ, neither the testimony of Jesus (v. 82)
- they who deny not the Holy Spirit (v. 83)[27]
- they who *say* they are some of one, and some of another—some of Christ and some of John, and some of Moses—*but* received not the gospel, neither the testimony of Jesus, neither the prophets, neither the everlasting covenant (vv. 99-101)
- they who are liars and sorcerers, and adulterers, and whoremongers, and whosoever loves and makes a lie (v. 103; Rev. 22:15 adds murderers)

Verse 82 has an interesting thought-seed in it. By speaking of "the gospel of Christ" and "the testimony of Jesus" as two factors, it appears that a person could have one, or both, or neither. In the context of this revelation, such an idea harmonizes with the concept that terrestrial-type souls receive a testimony of Jesus but are not valiant enough in that testimony to receive the fulness of the gospel; celestial personalities receive a testimony of Jesus *and* baptism and the Holy Ghost and a cleansing from all sin (i.e., the fulness of the gospel); telestial people do not receive either a testimony of Jesus or the gospel.

However, "these *all* shall bow the knee, and every tongue shall confess . . . that Jesus Christ is Lord" (v. 110; Philip. 2:9-11). This obeisance and confession will come sometime during the process of preparing to be "heirs of salvation" (v. 88).[28] This cleansing process involves their spirits' being called up and judged unworthy of resurrection at the beginning of the Millennium (D&C 88:100-1), then spending one thousand years in hell suffering for the sins they earlier refused to repent of, and learning to obey at least a telestial law (vv. 84-85, 105-7). Once they are cleansed and prepared, they shall be resurrected and placed in the telestial kingdom, the glory of which "surpasses all understanding" (v. 89).[29] No longer liars, sorcerers, whoremongers, adulterers, "they shall be servants of the Most High; but where God and Christ dwell they cannot come, worlds without end" (v. 112). Charles W. Penrose, later to become an apostle and counselor in the First Presidency, wrote in 1897:

> While there is one soul of this race, willing and able to accept and obey the laws of redemption, no matter where or in what condition it may be found, Christ's work will be incomplete until that being is brought up from death and hell, and placed in a position of progress, upward and onward, in such glory as is possible for its enjoyment and the service of the great God.
>
> The punishment inflicted will be adequate to the wrongs performed. In one sense the sinner will always suffer its effects. When the debt is paid and justice is satisfied; when obedience is learned through the lessons of sad experience; when the grateful and subdued soul comes forth from the everlasting punishment, thoroughly willing to comply with the laws once rejected; there will be an abiding sense of loss. The fullness of celestial glory in the presence and society of God and the Lamb are beyond the reach of that saved but not perfected soul, forever. The power of increase, wherein are dominion and exaltation and crowns of immeasurable glory, is not for the class of beings who have been thrust down to hell and endured the wrath of God for the period allotted by eternal judgment. . . .
>
> Those who were cast down to the depths of their sins, who

> rejected the gospel of Jesus, who persecuted the Saints, who reveled in iniquity, who committed all manner of transgressions except the unpardonable crime, will also come forth in the Lord's time, through the blood of the Lamb and the ministry of His disciples and their own repentance and willing acceptance of divine law, and enter into the various degrees of glory and power and progress and light, according to their different capacities and adaptabilities. They cannot go up into the society of the Father nor receive of the presence of the Son, but will have ministrations of messengers from the terrestrial world, and have joy beyond all expectations and the conception of uninspired mortal minds. They will all bow the knee to Christ and serve God the Father, and have an eternity of usefulness and happiness in harmony with the higher powers. They receive the telestial glory.[30]

Joseph Smith and Sidney Rigdon saw that the inhabitants of the telestial world were "as innumerable as the stars in the firmament of heaven, or as the sand upon the seashore" (v. 109). Though denied access to where God and Christ dwell, they will enjoy the presence "of the Holy Spirit through the ministration of the terrestrial" (vv. 86, 112).

## The Prophet's Poetic Version of the Vision

On 1 February 1843 there appeared in the *Times and Seasons* (pp. 81-85) a short poem by W. W. Phelps addressed to Joseph Smith, entitled "Go With Me." With it was a much longer poetic response by the Prophet. The Prophet's piece is a poetic re-phrasing of D&C 76, with some interpretive commentary. It is interesting to compare the verses from D&C 76 with Joseph Smith's poetic version of the same vision. The verse numbers from D&C 76 are given in parentheses following the corresponding verse in the poem.

## FROM W. W. PHELPS TO JOSEPH SMITH: THE PROPHET.

VADE MECUM, (TRANSLATED.) GO WITH ME.

Go with me, will you go to the saints that have died,—
To the next, better world, where the righteous reside;
Where the angels and spirits in harmony be
In the joys of a vast paradise? Go with me.

Go with me where the truth and the virtues prevail;
Where the union is one, and the years never fail;
Not a heart can conceive, nor a nat'ral eye see
What the Lord has prepar'd for the just. Go with me.

Go with me where there is no destruction or war;
Neither tyrants, or sland'rers, or nations ajar;
Where the system is perfect, and happiness free,
And the life is eternal with God. Go with me.

Go with me, will you go to the mansions above,
Where the bliss, and the knowledge, the light, and the love,
And the glory of God do eternally be?—
Death, the wages of sin, is not there. Go with me.
Nauvoo, January, 1843.

---

## THE ANSWER.
## TO W. W. PHELPS, ESQ.
*A Vision.*

1. I will go, I will go, to the home of the Saints,
Where the virtue's the value, and life the reward;
But before I return to my former estate
I must fulfil the mission I had from the Lord.

2. Wherefore, hear, O ye heavens, and give ear O ye earth;
And rejoice ye inhabitants truly again;
For the Lord he is God, and his life never ends,
And besides him there ne'er was a Saviour of men. *(verse 1)*

3. His ways are a wonder; his wisdom is great;
   The extent of his doings, there's none can unveil;
His purposes fail not; from age unto age
   He still is the same, and his years never fail. *(verses 2-3)*

4. His throne is the heavens, his life time is all
   Of eternity *now*, and eternity *then*;
His union is power, and none stays his hand,—
   The Alpha, Omega, for ever: Amen. *(verse 4)*

5. For thus saith the Lord, in the spirit of truth,
   I am merciful, gracious, and good unto those
That fear me, and live for the life that's to come;
   My delight is to honor the saints with repose; *(verse 5)*

6. That serve me in righteousness true to the end;
   Eternal's their glory, and great their reward;
I'll surely reveal all my myst'ries to them,—
   The great hidden myst'ries in my kingdom stor'd— *(verse 6)*

7. From the council in Kolob, to time on the earth.
   And for ages to come unto them I will show
My pleasure & will, what my kingdom will do:
   Eternity's wonders they truly shall know. *(verse 7)*

8. Great things of the future I'll show unto them,
   Yea, things of the vast generations to rise;
For their wisdom and glory shall be very great,
   And their pure understanding extend to the skies: *(verse 8)*

9. And before them the wisdom of wise men shall cease,
   And the nice understanding of prudent ones fail!
For the light of my spirit shall light mine elect,
   And the truth is so mighty 't will ever prevail. *(verses 9-10)*

10. And the secrets and plans of my will I'll reveal;
   The sanctified pleasures when earth is renew'd,
What the eye hath not seen, nor the ear hath yet heard;
   Nor the heart of the natural man ever hath view'd. *(verse 10)*

11. I, Joseph, the prophet, in spirit beheld,
   And the eyes of the inner man truly did see

Eternity sketch'd in a vision from God,
Of what was, and now is, and yet is to be. *(verses 11-12)*

12. Those things which the Father ordained of old,
Before the world was, or a system had run,—
Through Jesus the Maker and Savior of all;
The only begotten, (Messiah) his son. *(verse 13)*

13. Of whom I bear record, as all prophets have,
And the record I bear is the fulness,—yea even
The truth of the gospel of Jesus—*the Christ*,
With whom I convers'd, in the vision of heav'n. *(verse 14)*

14. For while in the act of translating his word,
Which the Lord in his grace had appointed to me,
I came to the gospel recorded by John,
Chapter fifth and the twenty ninth verse, which you'll see. *(verse 15)*

Which was given as follows:

"Speaking of the resurrection of the dead,—
"Concerning those who shall hear the voice of
"the son of man—
"And shall come forth:—
"They who have done good in the resurrection
"of the just.
"And they who have done evil in the resurrec-
"tion of the unjust." *(verses 16-17)*

15. I marvel'd at these resurrections, indeed!
For it came unto me by the spirit direct:—
And while I did meditate what it all meant,
The Lord touch'd the eyes of my own intellect:— *(verses 18-19)*

16. Hosanna forever! they open'd anon,
And the glory of God shone around where I was;
And there was the Son, at the Father's right hand,
In a fulness of glory, and holy applause. *(verse 20)*

17. I beheld round the throne, holy angels and hosts,
And sanctified beings from worlds that have been,

In holiness worshipping God and the Lamb,
Forever and ever, amen and amen! *(verse 21)*

18. And now after all of the proofs made of him,
By witnesses truly, by whom he was known,
This is mine, last of all, that he lives; yea he lives!
And sits at the right hand of God, on his throne. *(verse 22)*

19. And I heard a great voice, bearing record from heav'n,
He's the Saviour, and only begotten of God—
By him, of him, and through him, the worlds were all made,
Even all that career in the heavens so broad, *(verses 23-24)*

20. Whose inhabitants, too, from the first to the last,
Are sav'd by the very same Saviour of ours;
And, of course, are begotten God's daughters and sons,
By the very same truths, and the very same pow'rs. *(verse 24)*

21. And I saw and bear record of warfare in heav'n;
For an angel of light, in authority great,
Rebell'd against Jesus, and sought for his pow'r,
But was thrust down to woe from his Godified state. *(verse 25)*

22. And the heavens all wept, and the tears drop'd like dew,
That Lucifer, son of the morning had fell!
Yea, is fallen! is fall'n, and become, Oh, alas!
The son of Perdition; the devil of hell! *(verses 26-27)*

23. And while I was yet in the spirit of truth,
The commandment was: write ye the vision all out;
For Satan, old serpent, the devil's for war,—
And yet will encompass the saints round about. *(verses 28-29)*

24. And I saw, too, the suff'ring and mis'ry of those,
(Overcome by the devil, in warfare and fight,)
In hell-fire, and vengeance, the doom of the damn'd;
For the Lord said, the vision is further: so write. *(verse 30)*

25. For thus saith the Lord, now concerning all those
Who know of my power and partake of the same;
And suffer themselves, that they be overcome
By the power of Satan; despising my name:— *(verse 31)*

26. Defying my power, and denying the truth;—
    They are they—of the world, or of men, most forlorn,
The Sons of Perdition, of whom, ah! I say,
    'T were better for them had they never been born! *(verses 31-32)*

27. They're vessels of wrath, and dishonor to God,
    Doom'd to suffer his wrath, in the regions of woe,
Through the terrific night of eternity's round,
    With the devil and all of his angels below: *(verse 33)*

28. Of whom it is said, no forgiveness is giv'n,
    In this world, alas! nor the world that's to come;
For they have denied the spirit of God,
    After having receiv'd it: and mis'ry's their doom. *(verses 34-35)*

29. And denying the only begotten of God,—
    And crucify him to themselves, as they do,
And openly put him to shame in their flesh,
    By gospel they cannot repentance renew. *(verse 35)*

30. They are they, who must go to the great lake of fire,
    Which burneth with brimstone, yet never consumes,
And dwell with the devil, and angels of his,
    While eternity goes and eternity comes. *(verse 36)*

31. They are they, who must groan through the great second death,
    And are not redeemed in the time of the Lord;
While all the rest are, through the triumph of Christ,
    Made partakers of grace, by the power of his word. *(verses 37-39)*

32. The myst'ry of Godliness truly is great;—
    The past, and the present, and what is to be;
And this is the gospel—glad tidings to all,
    Which the voice from the heavens bore record to me: *(verse 40)*

33. That he came to the world in the middle of time,
    To lay down his life for his friends and his foes,
And bear away sin as a mission of love;
    And sanctify earth for a blessed repose. *(verse 41)*

34. 'Tis decreed, that he'll save all the work of his hands,
    And sanctify them by his own precious blood;

And purify earth for the Sabbath of rest,
By the agent of fire, as it was by the flood. *(verse 42)*

35. The Savior will save all his Father did give,
Even all that he gave in the regions abroad,
Save the Sons of Perdition: They're lost; ever lost,
And can never return to the presence of God. *(verse 43)*

36. They are they, who must reign with the devil in hell,
In eternity now, and eternity then,
Where the worm dieth not, and the fire is not quench'd;—
And the punishment still, is eternal. Amen. *(verse 44)*

37. And which is the torment apostates receive,
But the end, or the place where the torment began,
Save to them who are made to partake of the same,
Was never, nor will be, revealed unto man. *(verses 45-46)*

38. Yet God shows by vision a glimpse of their fate,
And straightway he closes the scene that was shown:
So the width, or the depth, or the misery thereof,
Save to those that parktake, is forever unknown. *(verses 47-48)*

39. And while I was pondering, the vision was closed;
And the voice said to me, write the vision: for lo!
'Tis the end of the scene of the sufferings of those,
Who remain filthy still in their anguish and woe. *(verse 49)*

40. And again I bear record of heavenly things,
Where virtue's the value, above all that's pric'd—
Of the truth of the gospel concerning the just,
That rise in the first resurrection of Christ. *(verse 50)*

41. Who receiv'd and believ'd, and repented likewise,
And then were baptis'd, as a man always was,
Who ask'd and receiv'd a remission of sin,
And honored the kingdom by keeping its laws. *(verse 51)*

42. Being buried in water, as Jesus had been,
And keeping the whole of his holy commands,
They received the gift of the spirit of truth,
By the ordinance truly of laying on hands. *(verse 52)*

43. For these overcome, by their faith and their works,
    Being tried in their life-time, as purified gold,
And seal'd by the spirit of promise, to life,
    By men called of God, as was Aaron of old. *(verse 53)*

44. They are they, of the church of the first born of God,—
    And unto whose hands he committeth all things;
For they hold the keys of the kingdom of heav'n,
    And reign with the Savior, as priests, and as kings. *(verses 54-56)*

45. They're priests of the order of Melchizedek,
    Like Jesus, (from whom is this highest reward,)
Receiving a fulness of glory and light;
    As written: They're Gods; even sons of the Lord. *(verses 57-58)*

46. So all things are theirs; yea, of life, or of death;
    Yea, whether things now, or to come, all are theirs,
And they are the Savior's, and he is the Lord's,
    Having overcome all, as eternity's heirs. *(verses 59-60)*

47. 'Tis wisdom that man never glory in man,
    But give God the glory for all that he hath;
For the righteous will walk in the presence of God,
    While the wicked are trod under foot in his wrath. *(verse 61)*

48. Yea, the righteous shall dwell in the presence of God,
    And of Jesus, forever, from earth's second birth—
For when he comes down in the splendor of heav'n,
    All these he'll bring with him, to reign on the earth. *(verses 62-63)*

49. These are they that arise in their bodies of flesh,
    When the trump of the first resurrection shall sound;
These are they that come up to Mount Zion, in life,
    Where the blessings and gifts of the spirit abound. *(verses 64-66)*

50. These are they that have come to the heavenly place;
    To the numberless courses of angels above:
To the city of God; e'en the holiest of all,
    And the home of the blessed, the fountain of love: *(verse 67)*

51. To the church of old Enoch, and of the first born:
    And gen'ral assembly of ancient renown'd.

Whose names are all kept in the archives of heav'n,
As chosen and faithful, and fit to be crown'd. *(verse 68)*

52. These are they that are perfect through Jesus' own blood,
Whose bodies celestial are mention'd by Paul,
Where the sun is the typical glory thereof,
And God, and his Christ, are the true judge of all. *(verses 69-70)*

53. Again, I beheld the terrestrial world,
In the order and glory of Jesus, go on;
'Twas not as the church of the first born of God,
But shone in its place, as the moon to the sun. *(verse 71)*

54. Behold, these are they that have died without law;
The heathen of ages that never had hope.
And those of the region and shadow of death,
The spirits in prison, that light has brought up. *(verses 72-73)*

55. To spirits in prison the Savior once preach'd,
And taught them the gospel, with powers afresh;
And then were the living baptiz'd for their dead,
That they might be judg'd as if men in the flesh. *(verse 74)*

56. These are they that are hon'rable men of the earth;
Who were blinded and dup'd by the cunning of men:
They receiv'd not the truth of the Savior at first;
But did, when they heard it in prison, again. *(verses 74-75)*

57. Not valiant for truth, they obtain'd not the crown,
But are of that glory that's typ'd by the moon:
They are they, that come into the presence of Christ,
But not to the fulness of God, on his throne. *(verses 76-79)*

58. Again I beheld the telestial, as third,
The lesser, or starry world, next in its place.
For the leaven must leaven three measures of meal,
And every knee bow that is subject to grace. *(verse 81)*

59. These are they that receiv'd not the gospel of Christ,
Or evidence, either, that he ever was;
As the stars are all diff'rent in glory and light,
So differs the glory of these by the laws. *(verse 82)*

60. These are they that deny not the spirit of God,
    But are thrust down to hell, with the devil, for sins,
As hypocrites, liars, whoremongers, and thieves,
    And stay 'till the last resurrection begins. *(verses 83-85)*

61. 'Till the Lamb shall have finish'd the work he begun;
    Shall have trodden the wine press, in fury alone,
And overcome all by the pow'r of his might:
    He conquers to conquer, and save all his own. *(verses 85 and 107)*

62. These are they that receive not a fulness of light,
    From Christ, in eternity's world, where they are,
The terrestrial sends them the Comforter, though;
    And minist'ring angels, to happify there. *(verse 86)*

63. And so the telestial is minister'd to,
    By ministers from the terrestrial one,
As terrestrial is, from the celestial throne;
    And the great, greater, greatest, seem's stars, moon, and sun. *(verses 86-88)*

64. And thus I beheld, in the vision of heav'n,
    The telestial glory, dominion and bliss,
Surpassing the great understanding of men,—
    Unknown, save reveal'd, in a world vain as this. *(verses 89-90)*

65. And lo, I beheld the terrestrial, too,
    Which excels the telestial in glory and light,
In splendor, and knowledge, and wisdom, and joy,
    In blessings, and graces, dominion and might. *(verse 91)*

66. I beheld the celestial, in glory sublime;
    Which is the most excellent kingdom that is,—
Where God, e'en the Father, in harmony reigns;
    Almighty, supreme, and eternal, in bliss. *(verses 92-93)*

67. Where the church of the first born in union reside,
    And they are as they're seen, and they know as they're known;
Being equal in power, dominion and might,
    With a fulness of glory and grace, round his throne. *(verses 94-95)*

68. The glory celestial is one like the sun;
    The glory terrestr'al is one like the moon;

The glory telestial is one like the stars,
  And all harmonize like the parts of a tune. *(verses 96-98)*

69. As the stars are all different in lustre and size,
  So the telestial region, is mingled in bliss;
From least unto greatest, and greatest to least,
  The reward is exactly as promis'd in this. *(verse 98)*

70. These are they that came out for Apollos and Paul;
  For Cephas and Jesus, in all kinds of hope;
For Enoch and Moses, and Peter, and John;
  For Luther and Calvin, and even the Pope. *(verses 99-100)*

71. For they never received the gospel of Christ,
  Nor the prophetic spirit that came from the Lord;
Nor the covenant neither, which Jacob once had;
  They went their own way, and they have their reward. *(verses 100-1)*

72. By the order of God, last of all, these are they,
  That will not be gather'd with saints here below,
To be caught up to Jesus, and meet in the clouds:—
  In darkness they worshipp'd; to darkness they go. *(verse 102)*

73. These are they that are sinful, the wicked at large,
  That glutted their passion by meanness or worth;
All liars, adulterers, sorc'rers, and proud;
  And suffer, as promis'd, God's wrath on the earth. *(verses 103-4)*

74. These are they that must suffer the vengeance of hell,
  'Till Christ shall have trodden all enemies down,
And perfected his work, in the fulness of times:
  And is crown'd on his throne with his glorious crown. *(verses 105-8)*

75. The vast multitude of the telestial world—
  As the stars of the skies, or the sands of the sea;—
The voice of Jehovah echo'd far and wide,
  Ev'ry tongue shall confess, and they all bow the knee. *(verses 109-10)*

76. Ev'ry man shall be judg'd by the works of his life,
  And receive a reward in the mansions prepar'd;
For his judgments are just, and his works never end,
  As his prophets and servants have always declar'd. *(verse 111)*

77. But the great things of God, which he show'd unto me,
Unlawful to utter, I dare not declare;
They surpass all the wisdom and greatness of men,
And only are seen, as has Paul, where they are. *(verses 114-18)*

78. I will go, I will go, while the secret of life,
Is blooming in heaven, and blasting in hell;
Is leaving on earth, and a budding in space:—
I will go, I will go, with you, brother, farewell.

JOSEPH SMITH.
Nauvoo, Feb. 1843.

## Conclusion

Truly there are many mansions in our Father's house (John 14:2). In his justice and mercy and love he will do all he can do for us—all we will permit him to do—for he "granteth unto men according to their desire" (Alma 29:4, 5; 41:3-8). D&C 76 bears eloquent testimony of this truth. Perhaps the Prophet Joseph Smith said it best.

> Nothing could be more pleasing to the Saints upon the order of the kingdom of the Lord, than the light which burst upon the world through the foregoing vision. Every law, every commandment, every promise, every truth, and every point touching the destiny of man, from Genesis to Revelation, where the purity of the scriptures remains unsullied by the folly of men, go to show the perfection of the theory [of different degrees of glory in the future life] and witnesses the fact that that document is a transcript from the records of the eternal world. The sublimity of the ideas; the purity of the language; the scope for action; the continued duration for completion, in order that the heirs of salvation may confess the Lord and bow the knee; the rewards for faithfulness, and the punishments for sins, are so much beyond the narrow-mindedness of men that every honest man is constrained to exclaim: "It came from God."[31]

## Notes

[1]Charles W. Penrose, *JD* 24:92.

[2]Joseph Fielding Smith, *Church History and Modern Revelation,* 2 vols. (Salt Lake City: The Council of the Twelve Apostles of the Church of Jesus Christ of Latter-day Saints, 1953), 2:50.

[3]Robert J. Matthews, *A Plainer Translation: Joseph Smith's Translation of the Bible, A History and Commentary* (Provo, Ut.: Brigham Young University Press, 1975), p. xxviii.

[4]*HC* 1:245.

[5]*Juvenile Instructor,* vol. 27, pp. 303-4.

[6]"Early Scenes in Church History," *Four Faith Promoting Classics* (Salt Lake City, Ut.: Bookcraft, 1968), p. 81.

[7]*Deseret News*—Extra (Salt Lake City), 14 Sept. 1852, p. 52, as quoted in Robert J. Woodford, "The Historical Development of the Doctrine and Covenants," unpublished Ph.D. Dissertation, Brigham Young University, 1974, p. 929.

[8]*Ibid.,* p. 933.

[9]*HC* 5:402.

[10]Woodford, "The Historical Development of the Doctrine and Covenants," p. 928.

[11]Bruce R. McConkie, *Mormon Doctrine,* 2nd ed. (Salt Lake City: Bookcraft, 1966), p. 65. Cf. McConkie, "Christ and the Creation," *Ensign,* June 1982, p. 10.

[12]*TPJS,* p. 161.

[13]In Orson F. Whitney, *Life of Heber C. Kimball* (Salt Lake City: Bookcraft, 1967), p. 132.

[14]*TPJS,* p. 358.

[15]Spencer W. Kimball, *The Miracle of Forgiveness* (Salt Lake City: Bookcraft, 1969), pp. 122-23.

[16]*HC* 1:366; *TPJS,* p. 24.

[17]See Joseph Fielding Smith, *Doctrines of Salvation,* 3 vols., comp. Bruce R. McConkie (Salt Lake City: Bookcraft, 1954-56), 2:25, 273-78 for statements by Joseph Smith, John Taylor, Joseph F. Smith, George Q. Cannon, and Joseph Fielding Smith.

[18]It is interesting to note that in the earliest available manuscripts and printings of the vision it is rendered "who" (*Kirtland Revelation Book* and *Evening and Morning Star*) and "they" (*Book of Commandments and Law and Covenants*) rather than "for all the rest." See Woodford, "The Historical Development of the Doctrine and Covenants," p. 951.

[19]*TPJS*, p. 357.

[20]*Ibid.*, p. 150.

[21]McConkie, *Mormon Doctrine*, pp. 361-62.

[22]Smith, *Church History and Modern Revelation*, 2:57-58; Heb. 12:22-24.

[23]Smith, *Ibid.*, 2:58.

[24]*TPJS*, p. 348.

[25]"The Three Degrees of Glory," in *Melvin J. Ballard: Crusader for Righteousness* (Salt Lake City: Bookcraft, 1966), p. 221.

[26]Unabridged (Springfield, Mass.: G. & C. Merriam Co., 1969).

[27]Regarding the expression "deny not the Holy Spirit": This may seem like a strange way to speak of wicked souls. The same thing could be said of those who attain terrestrial and celestial glory. As used here (v. 83) it seems to mean that although these people may be very wicked, they did not sink so low as to deny the Holy Spirit and thus become sons of perdition, that they are somewhat above irreconcilable defiance.

[28]Regarding "heirs of salvation": Although the words "save" and "salvation" are generally used in the scriptures to mean exaltation, they are on a few occasions used simply to mean resurrection (e.g., 2 Ne. 2:4), and at other times to mean redemption from the grave *and* from the devil, although those thus redeemed receive different rewards, according to their works (see D&C 76:43-44, 88; 132:16, 17). Hence, by virtue of the atonement, all who have ever lived as mortals on this earth are "saved" from physical death (i.e., resurrected), and all except the sons of perdition are "saved" from death *and* hell or the devil; only those who obey the fulness of the gospel are "saved" (i.e., exalted) in the kingdom of God. The context in which these words are used must be considered carefully.

[29]Regarding "surpasses all understanding": A rather common notion in connection with this verse is that Joseph Smith had taught that if we knew what the telestial kingdom was like, we would commit suicide to get there. What the Prophet said was not in reference to the telestial kingdom, but to life "behind the veil," which may mean a number of things. The Prophet's statement (Charles Walker quoting Wilford Woodruff quoting Joseph Smith) is as follows:

> Br. Woodruff spoke. . . . He refered to a saying of Joseph Smith which he heard him utter (like this) That if the People knew what was behind the vail, they would try by every means to commit suicide that they might get there, but the Lord in his wisdom had implanted the fear of death in every person that they might cling to life and thus accomplish the designs of their creator. (*Diary of Charles Lowell Walker*, ed. by A. Karl Larson

and Katherine M. Larson [Logan, Ut.: Utah State University Press, 1980], vol. 1, pp. 465-66.)

[30]*"Mormon" Doctrine* (Salt Lake City: George Q. Cannon and Sons, 1897), pp. 72, 74, 75.

[31]*HC* 1:252-53.

# 28

# A REVELATION ON PRIESTHOOD

## (D&C 84)

ROBERT L. MILLET

### Introduction

As a result of a conference of the Church held in January 1832, several pairs of elders had been called to missionary service in the eastern United States (D&C 75). They labored for about nine months and began to return to Kirtland. According to the Prophet's history: "The Elders during the month of September began to return from their missions to the Eastern States, and present the histories of their several stewardships in the Lord's vineyard; and while together in these seasons of joy, I inquired of the Lord, and received on the 22nd and 23rd of September, the following revelation on priesthood."[1] Joseph then dictated what has come to be known as section 84 of the Doctrine and Covenants. With regard to the assembled group, one historian has written: "whereas verse 1 indicates that the revelation was received in the presence of six elders (undoubtedly high priests), an unpublished note (dated 23 September 1832) that appears in the 'Kirtland Revelation Book' after verse 42 affirms that the verse (42) was specifically intended for ten high priests, then present."[2]

### The Temple in New Jerusalem (vv. 2-5)

The opening verses of this section contain the word and will of the Lord with regard to the gathering of his Saints to Zion, the center place, and also with regard to the erection of a temple in Independence, the site of the New Jerusalem (D&C 57). In July of 1831 Joseph Smith, Sidney Rigdon, and a number of the elders—together with the Colesville, New York branch—arrived in Independence. A special ceremony was held in early August. The following was recorded by John whitmer in his history of the Church:

> On the 2nd day of August 1831 Brother Sidney Rigdon stood up and asked saying: Do you receive this land for the land of your inheritance with thankful hearts from the Lord? answer from all we do, Do you pledge yourselves to keep the laws of God on

> this land, which you never have kept in your own lands? we do. Do you pledge yourselves to see that others of your brethren who shall come hither do keep the laws of God? we do. After prayer he arose and said, I now pronounce this land consecrated and dedicated to the Lord for a possession and inheritance for the Saints (in the name of Jesus Christ having authority from him.) And for all the faithful Servants of the Lord to the remotest ages of time. Amen.
>
> The day following, eight elders, viz. Joseph Smith Jr., Oliver Cowdery, Sidney Rigdon, Peter Whitmer, Jr., Frederick G. Williams, Wm. W. Phelps, Martin Harris, and Joseph Coe, assembled together where the temple is to be erected. Sidney Rigdon dedicated the ground where the city is to stand: and Joseph Smith, Jr. laid a stone at the Northeast corner of the contemplated Temple in the name of the Lord Jesus of Nazareth. After all present had rendered thanks to the great ruler of the universe, Sidney Rigdon pronounced this spot of ground wholly dedicated to the Lord forever: Amen.[3]

And thus some thirteen months later the Lord revealed to the assembled body of priesthood that "this generation shall not all pass away until an house shall be built unto the Lord" (D&C 84:5). If, in fact, one is to understand the word "generation" to mean a specific period of years (25-30 years, for example), then it might be distressing to learn that a generation has indeed passed without the erection of a temple in Zion. At the same time, it is wise to recognize that prophecy does not always predestinate; people and circumstances and factors contribute to and detract from the fulfillment of prophecy. The hopes and designs of the Saints were frequently shattered by non-believers who did not exactly share the Latter-day Saints' vision; in such cases, the Lord (always allowing for individual exercise of agency) certainly would not hold his people accountable for the accomplishment of his purposes. As stated in a revelation given in Nauvoo in 1841: "Verily, verily I say unto you, that when I give a commandment to any of the sons of men to do a work unto my name, and those sons of men go with all their might and with all they have to perform that work, and cease not their diligence, and their enemies come upon them and hinder them from performing that work, behold, it behooveth me to require that work no more at the hands of those sons of men, but to accept of their offerings" (D&C 124:49).

Who can tell exactly what the Lord had in mind when he spoke of a temple being erected in "this generation?" The Savior explained anciently that "a wicked and adulterous *generation* seeketh after a sign" (Matt. 16:4). In this use of the word generation there seems to be no specific duration or time period intended. To Joseph Smith the Lord explained in 1829: "This *generation* shall have my word through you" (D&C 5:10). Was the Lord only speaking of the Saints in the first half of the 19th century? Were the Saints from 1830 to 1860 the only ones for whom the word of the Lord through Joseph Smith would prove beneficial? Certainly not. This latter use of the word *generation* seems more closely associated with what we would call a *dispensation.* Without question, the people of the dispensation of the fulness of times will receive the knowledge of God and his saving gospel through the instrumentality of Joseph Smith, or they will not receive it. We may rest assured that the prophecy concerning a temple to be constructed by the Church of Jesus Christ of Latter-day Saints in Independence will come to pass in the Lord's due time and will certainly see fulfillment before the final dispensation comes to an end.

## The Higher Priesthood and the Powers of Godliness (vv. 6-22)

Section 84 of the Doctrine and Covenants contains what appears to be Moses' line of priesthood authority. Having begun to speak concerning the "sons of Moses" (v. 6), the Lord interjects significant historical and doctrinal material before returning (v. 31) to his subject. This includes Moses' line of authority. Moses received the priesthood from his father-in-law, Jethro, a priest of the house of Midian. The Midianites were descendants of Abraham through Keturah (Gen. 25:1-4). The line continues through Jethro, Caleb, Elihu, Jeremy, Gad, Esaias, and Abraham. Abraham was ordained by the great high priest, Melchizedek, who received the priesthood "through the lineage of his fathers, even till Noah" (v. 14). The descent of the priesthood from Noah to Adam is given elsewhere, in D&C 107:40-52 and in Moses 6:1-25, 8:1-9.

The priesthood is the power and authority of God, delegated to man on earth, to act in all things for the salvation of man. The higher or

Melchizedek Priesthood "administereth the gospel and holdeth the key of the mysteries of the kingdom, even the key of the knowledge of God" (v. 19). The priesthood is the power by which the blessings of the gospel—the atonement of Christ—are made available and operative in the lives of Church members. The priesthood is a grand channel for revelation and power, a means by which the purposes of God are learned and put into effect. In the words of Joseph Smith, the priesthood is "the channel through which all knowledge, doctrine, the plan of salvation and every important matter is revealed from heaven." Further, the priesthood "is the channel through which the Almighty commenced revealing his glory at the beginning of this earth, through which He has continued to reveal Himself to the children of men to the present time, and through which he will make known His purposes to the end of time."[4]

The Lord makes known through this revelation that it is by means of the authorized ordinances of the priesthood that the "power of godliness" is manifest unto men on earth. It is the power of godliness—the power of righteousness—which enables mortal man to enter into the realm of divine experience. "For without this"—the power of godliness—"no man can see the face of God, even the Father, and live" (v. 22). "In and through the holy priesthood," Elder Bruce R. McConkie has written, "including all the laws and rites that go with it, the power of godliness, or in other words the power of righteousness, is brought to pass in the lives of men. Without these priesthood laws and powers, God's power and glory would not be revealed to man on earth. Without them they would not see the face of God, for if they did, his glory would destroy them. Sinful men cannot see the face of God and live (JST, Exod. 33:20)."[5]

## The Lesser Priesthood and the Preparatory Gospel (vv. 23-28)

Moses knew full well the transcendant powers of the Holy Priesthood. He had tasted of the joys associated with standing in the presence of Jehovah, and sought to make such unspeakable privileges available to the children of Israel. He desired to prepare his people for consummate blessings—to receive the fulness of the powers of the everlasting gospel, and thus become unto God "a kingdom of priests, and an holy nation" (Exod. 19:6). A combination of fear and moral lethargy, however, seemed to preclude an intimate association between Israel and her God. Joseph Smith's inspired revision of Exodus teaches us of the lost opportunities of the people of the house of Israel. Moses returned from speaking with the Lord on Sinai, only to find his people wrapped in idolatry and immorality. Moses thereupon broke the first set of tablets, which had contained the fulness of priesthood ordinances, a divine formula for coming into the presence of God. Note the word of the Lord to Moses:

> And the Lord said unto Moses, Hew thee two other tables of stone, like unto the first, and I will write upon them also, the words of the law, according as they were written at the first on the tables which thou brakest; but it shall not be according to the first, for I will take away the priesthood out of their midst; therefore my holy order, and the ordinances thereof, shall not go before them; for my presence shall not go up in their midst, lest I destroy them. But I will give unto them the law as at the first, but it shall be after the law of a carnal commandment; for I have sworn in my wrath, that they shall not enter into my presence, into my rest, in the days of their pilgrimmage (JST, Ex. 34:1-2; cf. JST, Deut. 10:2).

One of the great evidences of God's infinite mercy and love is his disposition to provide only as much knowledge and power as a people is able to receive. Having all knowledge himself, the Lord is able to discern a nation's "bearing capacity," and thus to make available that amount of light and truth which will bless (rather than curse) its recipients (Alma 29:8; 3 Ne. 26:9-11). This principle is perfectly demonstrated in the Lord's treatment of erring Israel—the introduction of the preparatory gospel, the Law of Carnal Commandments, and the Aaronic Priesthood.

Moses held the keys—the directing powers, the right of presidency—of the Melchizedek Priesthood in his day. In order to remove the Everlasting Gospel from Israel, the Lord needed also to remove the man who held the keys of that priesthood which administered the Everlasting Gospel. When Moses was taken from the people (i.e., was translated) the authorization for subsequent ordination to the Melchizedek Priesthood was taken as well. Elder Bruce R.

McConkie has written:

> We should here observe . . . that when the scripture says the Lord took Moses and the holy priesthood out of the midst of Israel, it means that he took from them the prophet who held the keys and could authorize the priesthood to be conferred upon others. Any who thereafter held either the keys or the Melchizedek Priesthood gained them by special dispensation. The Aaronic Priesthood thus became the priesthood of administration; it was in effect the priesthood of Israel; it handled the affairs of the Church and officiated in the offering of sacrifices. However, there were at many times and may have been at all times prophets and worthy men who held the Melchizedek Priesthood.[6]

In further commenting upon the passage in section 84 which deals with the preparatory gospel (vv. 26-27), Elder McConkie has observed: "In place of the higher priesthood the Lord gave a lesser order, and in place of the fulness of the gospel he gave a preparatory gospel—the law of carnal commandments, the law of Moses—to serve as a schoolmaster to bring them, after a long day of trial and testing, back to the law of Christ in its fulness."[7] When we are eventually able to view our mortal existence from God's perspective, it may well be that we will discover that the number of laws and the amount of structure a generation requires is inversely related to its state of righteousness. That is to say, a righteous generation is perfectly capable of governing itself by principles, and it requires few overt laws and conditions. The intricate system of sacrifices, as well as the complicated dietary code and health laws associated with the law of carnal commandments, represent a profound commentary upon ancient Israel. The myriad ordinances of the law of carnal commandments were not *carnal* in the sense of being vulgar or profane, but rather were temporal, detailed, and regular, part of "a very strict law," a "law of performances and ordinances" which were to be carried out from day to day (Mosiah 13:29-30). The system was a law of *carnal* commandments in the sense that it specified and defined most every action of man. It is as if the Lord had said to the wayward generation: "For behold, it is meet that I command you in all things, inasmuch as you have proven to be slothful and unwise servants" (cf. D&C 58:26-28). At the same time, because of his infinite love, the Lord utilized a negative situation to retrieve whatever was good deep within his erring people. As Paul taught the Galatian Saints, the law was a "schoolmaster" (literally a tutor or guardian) to bring his people to Christ (Gal. 3:24).

In spite of the fact that few of the House of Israel saw behind and beneath the formality to the greater Reality—behind the means to the One who was the End—(Mosiah 13:32); in spite of the fact that darkness and apostasy characterized the Jews—leaders and laymen, publicans and priests—from the time of Moses to the time of Jesus, the Aaronic order of priesthood continued (D&C 84:26-27). In spite of the fact that the sacred office of High Priest (equivalent to the Presiding Bishop in our own day) became sought after and obtained by political means, yet the Aaronic Priesthood continued. Priests still held the Aaronic Priesthood; "they still performed sacrificial rites with all the similitudes and symbols that had always attended these sacred ordinances; and they still directed appropriate worship at the great feasts and made atonement for the people on that one day each year when they entered the Holy of Holies and pronounced the ineffable name ten times."[8] This priesthood continued until the time of John, the son of Zacharias.

John came into mortality under miraculous circumstances, and was from the beginning a child of promise. To aged Zacharias and Elizabeth had been granted the privilege of bringing to earth the one chosen from premortality to prepare the way for the Mortal Messiah (Luke 1:5-80). At the time of John's naming and circumcision—the eighth day after his birth, described briefly in Luke 1:59-66—an angel appeared and gave to John a special blessing. John was set apart at that early age "to overthrow the kingdom of the Jews, and make straight the way of the Lord before the face of his people, to prepare them for the coming of the Lord, in whose hand is given all power" (D&C 84:28). At what point John the Baptist received a formal ordination to the priesthood is not known, though presumably it would have been some time after his baptism, according to the generally understood order of things.[9] Even though Zacharias was a priest after the order of Aaron, there were certainly powers and rights given to John by the angel which even worthy Zacharias did not hold.[10] John was, of course, a forerunner preceding the Messiah. He was also a legal administrator—holding the keys of the Aaronic Priesthood, one who taught doctrine, gave counsel, and took care never to overstep his bounds.[11] In the words of the Master: "Among those that are born of women there is not a greater prophet than John the Baptist" (Luke 7:28).[12]

## The Oath and Covenant of the Priesthood (vv. 33-44)

Bearing the Holy Priesthood is a sacred obligation, a trust that must not be taken lightly. From the beginning of time the Lord has bestowed the rights of priesthood upon his worthy sons, and at the same time he has counseled that the priesthood—like a double-edged sword—is the instrument for blessing as well as cursing. The worthy and pure recipient qualifies himself and his family for transcendent blessings; the man who receives God's authority and then proves unwilling to assume the consequent commitments lays the foundation for unhappiness and punishment. God will not be mocked! God swore to Enoch of old and to his children

> With an oath by himself; that every one being ordained after this order [the Holy Priesthood after the Order of the Son of God] and calling should have power, by faith, to break mountains, to divide the seas, to dry up waters, to turn them out of their course; to put at defiance the armies of nations, to divide the earth, to break every band, to stand in the presence of God; to do all things according to his will, according to his command, subdue principalities and powers; and this by the will of the Son of God which was from before the foundation of the world. And men having this faith, coming up unto this order of God, were translated and taken up into heaven (JST, Gen. 14:30-32).

The above passage makes abundantly clear that the priesthood is the power over the elements, power over men and demons—in short, power over life and death.

In section 84 of the Doctrine and Covenants the Lord reveals anew the terms and conditions pertaining to the reception and utilization of the powers of the Melchizedek Priesthood. The *Oath* which accompanies the reception of the priesthood is an oath that God swears to man. Just as the Father swore that the Beloved Son should be a priest forever (Ps. 110:4), so also does God swear with an oath that every priesthood holder who abides by his part of the two-way promise (the covenant) shall receive incomprehensible blessings.[13] The *Covenant* which accompanies the reception of the Melchizedek Priesthood (there is no oath associated with the Aaronic Priesthood[14]) consists of: (1) those things man promises to do; and (2) those blessings God promises the faithful priesthood bearer. As given in verses 33-44, the Covenant might be represented as follows:

Man Promises

1. Obtain the Priesthood (v. 33)
2. Magnify Callings in the Priesthood (v. 33)
3. Receive the Lord's Servants (v. 36)
4. Beware Concerning Himself (v. 43)
5. Give Diligent Heed to the Words of Eternal Life (v. 43)
6. Live by Every Word of God (v. 44)

God Promises

1. Sanctify Man to the Renewal of the Body (v. 33)
2. Man to Become a Son of Moses and Aaron (v. 34)
3. Man to Become the Seed of Abraham (v. 34)
4. Man to Become a Part of the Church and Kingdom of God (v. 34)
5. Man to Become the Elect of God (v. 34)
6. Man to Receive Christ and the Father (vv. 36-37)
7. Man to Receive All the Father Has (v. 38)

Man's promises to God are penetrating but quite straight-forward. Faithful observance of those promises leads to remarkable blessings. Alma taught the people of Ammonihah that righteous priesthood bearers of the past had magnified their callings to such an extent that they "were sanctified, and their garments were washed white through the blood of the Lamb. Now they, after being sanctified by the Holy Ghost, having their garments made white, being pure and spotless before God, could not look upon sin save it were with abhorrence; and there were many, exceedingly great many, who were made pure and entered into the rest of the Lord their God" (Alma 13:11-12). Faithful priesthood service thus leads to the purification of the soul.

Moses and Aaron were great priesthood figures in their day. Since the priesthoods of Moses and Aaron (Melchizedek and Aaronic, respectively) bless the lives of men everywhere, it is a simple fact that "faithful holders of the Melchizedek Priesthood, no matter what their natural lineage, become by adoption the sons of Moses and Aaron."[15] One writer has described this principle of adoption as follows: "Now, the literal descendants of Moses and Aaron are Levites. But the Lord was not talking about their lineal descendants. . . . In truth, all who will have received both the Aaronic and Melchizedek Priesthoods, who will have magnified their callings in these two priesthoods, will, by adoption, 'become the sons of Moses and of Aaron and the seed of Abraham, and the church and kingdom and the elect of God.'"[16] Worthy priesthood holders are not "adopted" in a legalistic sense into the families of Moses and Aaron. Rather, it is as though they are worthy of being counted as followers—persons who live after the same fashion—of Moses and Aaron. They are worthy of being counted among the noble. Further, those who join the Church, receive the priesthood, and prove faithful to that priesthood are entitled to the name and blessings of Father Abraham—the blessings of the Fathers, foremost of which is eternal life and thus the continuation of the family unit in eternity.[17]

Faithfully enduring to the end in the work of the priesthood eventuates in receiving the promise of eternal life, either here or hereafter. Having arrived at this station, one is appropriately classified as the *elect* of God, having made his calling and *election* sure unto eternal life. Having read verse 34 in section 84 (regarding becoming "the church and kingdom, and the elect of God"), President Marion G. Romney said to the men of the priesthood in 1974: "We talk about making our callings and elections sure. The only way we can do this is to get the priesthood and magnify it."[18] It appears that to become "the church and kingdom of God" is to be entitled to membership in the Church of the Firstborn, the Church of the exalted. In referring to verse 34 (the "church and kingdom of God") President Harold B. Lee taught that such worthy persons "become adopted into the holy family, the church and kingdom of god, the church of the firstborn."[19] "When [a man] has proved himself by a worthy life, having been faithful in all things required of him," wrote Joseph Fielding Smith, "then it is his privilege to receive other covenants and to take upon himself other obligations which will make of him an heir, and he will become a member of the 'Church of the Firstborn.' Into his hands 'the Father has given all things.' He will be a priest and a king, receiving of the Father's fulness and of his glory. . . . And the fulness of these blessings can only be obtained in the temple of the Lord."[20]

All men who receive the Melchizedek Priesthood thus enter into covenant with God. The penalties associated with breaking the covenant are sobering. "Whoso breaketh this covenant after he hath received it, and altogether turneth therefrom, shall not have forgiveness of sins in this world nor in the world to come" (D&C 84:41). Though the language of the above statement is somber, the Lord is not declaring that those who fail to keep the covenant are guilty of the unpardonable sin. Rather, he is teaching that those who receive the priesthood in this life but do not so live as to reap its privileges and blessings on earth, shall not have the right to priesthood hereafter; they forfeit the right to eternal life and eternal associations.[21]

President Wilford Woodruff expressed the power and profundity of the promises given to the faithful priesthood holder in these words: "Who in the name of the Lord can apprehend such language as this? Who can comprehend that, by obeying the celestial law, all that our Father has shall be given unto us—exaltations, thrones, principalities, power, dominion—who can comprehend it? Nevertheless it is here stated."[22]

## The Light of Christ and the Covenant Gospel (vv. 45-61)

Every man born into the world has within him a portion of divinity which has come to be known as the Light of Christ or the Spirit of Jesus Christ. "For behold," Mormon taught, "the Spirit of Christ is given to every man, that he may know good from evil; wherefore, I show unto you the way to judge; for every thing which inviteth to do good, and to persuade to believe in Christ, is sent forth by the power and gift of Christ; wherefore ye may know with a perfect knowledge it is of God" (Moro. 7:16). This spirit and influence is the natural endowment of every mortal. It is a light which, if followed, will lead to do good. In fact, as this section of the revelation instructs, "every one that hearkeneth to the voice of the Spirit cometh unto God, even the Father" (D&C 84:47). That is to say, every person in this life who honestly obeys his or her portion of the inner light will be led to further light and truth, either in this life or in the spirit world.

A later revelation (D&C 88:6-13) instructs us that this Light of Christ is manifest in numerous ways. In the words of Parley P. Pratt: "This is the true light, which in some measure illuminates all men. It is, in its less refined existence, the physical light which reflects from the sun, moon, and stars, and other substances; and by reflection of the eye, makes visible the truths of the outward world. It is, also, in its higher degrees, the intellectual light . . . by which we reason, discern, judge, compare, comprehend and remember the subjects within our reach. Its inspiration constitutes *instinct* in animal life, *reason* in man, *vision* in the Prophets, and is continually flowing from the Godhead throughout all his creations."[23]

Non-Latter-day Saints may be led by the Spirit of Jesus Christ to the higher verities associated with the New and Everlasting Covenant of the Gospel (D&C 84:48). President Joseph F. Smith explained that "it is the Spirit of God which proceeds through Christ to the world, that enlightens every man that comes into the world, and that strives with the children of men, and will continue to strive with them, until it brings them to a knowledge of the truth and the possession of the greater light and testimony of the Holy Ghost."[24] Once at the threshhold of the faith, the individual must arrive at the decision of a lifetime. If he continues faithful and loyal to the directions and promptings of the inner light, he is initiated into the true Church by baptism and made ready to enjoy the "record of heaven; the Comforter; the peaceable things of immortal glory; the truth of all things" (Moses 6:61). If, however, the individual ignores or rejects divine direction, he yields instead to the persuasions of the day and soon becomes enslaved in the ways of the world. "And by this you may know they are under the bondage of sin, because they come not unto me" (D&C 84:50).

In a related way the Lord cautioned Latter-day Saints against treating lightly that which they have received, and thus neglecting the greater light that could be theirs. Specifically, the Lord warned the elders of that day (and by extension, our own day) that their minds had been darkened because of unbelief, and for failing to receive and treasure "the new covenant, even the Book of Mormon" (D&C

84:54-57). Pleading with twentieth-century Saints to avoid similar pitfalls, President Ezra Taft Benson taught:

> Now, we have not been using the Book of Mormon as we should. Our homes are not as strong unless we are using it to bring our children to Christ. Our families may be corrupted by worldly trends and teachings unless we know how to use the Book of Mormon to expose and combat the falsehoods in socialism, organic evolution, rationalism, humanism, etc. Our missionaries are not as effective unless they are "hissing forth" with it. Social, ethical, cultural, or educational converts will not survive under the heat of the day unless their taproots go down to the fulness of the gospel which the Book of Mormon contains. Our Church classes are not as spirit-filled unless we hold it up as a standard. . . .
>
> Do eternal consequences rest upon our response to this book? Yes, either to our blessing or our condemnation.
>
> Every Latter-day Saint should make the study of this book a lifetime pursuit. Otherwise he is placing his soul in jeopardy and neglecting that which could give spiritual and intellectual unity to his whole life. There is a difference between a convert who is built on the rock of Christ through the Book of Mormon and stays hold of that iron rod, and one who is not.[25]

### "Go Ye into All the World" (vv. 62-102)

The Savior gave to the priesthood leaders detailed instructions concerning the preaching of the gospel (D&C 84:62-102). Some of the key principles revealed on this occasion include the following:

1. Missionaries are to preach the gospel and invite all to evidence their faith through repentance and baptism. Those who comply are promised the gifts of the Spirit, the signs which always follow those which believe (cf. Mark 16:15-18; D&C 63:7-12). Recipients of the gifts of the Spirit are to receive them with gratitude and acknowledge the hand of the Lord; they must never "boast themselves of these things, neither speak them before the world (D&C 84:73). Joseph Smith taught that one must receive humbly the gifts of God and never tempt the Almighty: "I took occasion to . . . exhort the brethren never to trifle with the promises of God. I told them it was presumption for any one

to provoke a serpent to bite him, but if a man of God was accidently bitten by a poisonous serpent, he might have faith, or his brethren might have faith for him, so that the Lord would hear his prayer and he might be healed; but when a man designedly provokes a serpent to bite him, the principle is the same as when a man drinks deadly poison knowing it to be such. In that case no man has any claim on the promises of God to be healed."[26]

2. Missionaries are to proceed about their labors with the confidence that they are under the watchcare of the Lord. Those who are faithful have the promise that they "shall not be weary in mind, neither darkened, neither in body, limb, nor joint; and a hair of [their heads] shall not fall to the ground unnoticed. And they shall not go hungry, neither athirst" (D&C 84:80). Like the Savior's disciples of old (in both the Old and New Worlds—Matt. 6 and 3 Ne. 13), these latter-day emissaries are to trust in the Lord as to the appropriate message for given situations. They are to avoid anxiety as to the daily necessities and "let the morrow take thought for the things of itself" (D&C 84:81-86).

3. A missionary effort into the world will continue until the divinely-appointed plagues and pestilences come upon "the nations, to scourge them for their wickedness." The preaching of the gospel will continue into the period of the Millennium, until all shall know the Lord. Those who "remain, even from the least unto the greatest, . . . shall be filled with the knowledge of the Lord, and shall see eye to eye" (D&C 84:96, 98).[27]

## Keeping the System Perfect (vv. 109-10)

Near the end of this great revelation on priesthood the Lord gave timely and timeless counsel which provides a formula for successful priesthood labors and overall effective Church government. The direction is priceless: "Therefore, let every man stand in his own office, and labor in his own calling; and let not the head say unto the feet it hath no need of the feet; for without the feet how shall the body be able to stand? Also the body hath need of every member, that all may be edified together, that the system may be kept perfect" (D&C 84:109-10). At the October 1961 General Conference of the Church, Elder Harold B. Lee addressed the assembled body of priesthood. He quoted D&C 84:108-10 and introduced the Priesthood Correlation Program.[28]

The proper utilization of the Lord's resources and the Lord's personnel is essential in meeting and defeating the problems of the latter days. Priesthood Correlation represents an inspired battle plan for insuring that each officer and member assume and defend his portion of the battle line. Priesthood Correlation is a system of Church administration which seeks to take all of the programs of the Church (e.g., missionary, genealogy, temporal welfare, spiritual welfare), wrap them and operate them as one program, and make them available to all members of the Church. Equally important, it seeks to involve all members in that process.[29] The priesthood is delegated in order that people may be blessed. Priesthood Correlation provides an organized system whereby those blessings are made available in the Lord's own way. Elder Thomas S. Monson taught:

> We are encamped against the greatest array of sin, vice, and evil ever assembled before our eyes. Such formidable enemies may cause lesser hearts to shrink or shun the fight. But the battle plan whereby we fight to save the souls of men is not our own. It was provided . . . by the inspiration and revelation of the Lord. Yes, I speak of that plan which will bring us victory, even the Correlation Program of the Church. And as we do battle against him who would thwart the purposes of God and degrade and destroy mankind, I pray that each of us will stand in his or her appointed place, that the battle for the souls of men may indeed be won."[30]

## Notes

[1]*HC* 1:286-87.

[2]Lyndon W. Cook, *The Revelations of the Prophet Joseph Smith* (Provo: Seventy's Mission Bookstore, 1981), p. 176.

[3]F. Mark McKiernan and Roger D. Launius, eds., *An Early Latter Day Saint History: The Book of John Whitmer, Kept by Commandment* (Indepen-

dence, Mo.: Herald Publishing House, 1980), pp. 79-80.

[4]*HC* 4:207; *TPJS*, pp. 166-67.

[5]*The Promised Messiah* (Salt Lake City: Deseret Book Co., 1978), p. 589.

[6]*Ibid.*, p. 412; see also *TPJS*, pp. 180-81; Joseph Fielding Smith, *Doctrines of Salvation*, 3 vols. (Salt Lake City: Bookcraft, 1954-56), 3:78; McConkie, *The Mortal Messiah*, 4 books (Salt Lake City: Deseret Book Co., 1979-81), 1:60.

[7]*The Mortal Messiah*, 1:60.

[8]*Ibid.*, 1:246.

[9]Bruce R. McConkie, *Doctrinal New Testament Commentary*, 3 vols. (Salt Lake City: Bookcraft Publishers, 1966-73), 1:89.

[10]See Joseph Fielding Smith, *Answers to Gospel Questions*, 5 vols. (Salt Lake City: Deseret Book Co., 1957-66), 5:2.

[11]The finest treatment to date on the life and works of John the Baptist is Robert J. Matthews, *A Burning Light: The Life and Ministry of John the Baptist* (Provo, Ut.: Brigham Young University Press, 1972).

[12]Joseph Smith's explanation of John's greatness is given in *HC* 5:260-61; *TPJS*, pp. 275-76.

[13]See Joseph Fielding Smith, *Conference Report*, April 1970, p. 59; Bruce R. McConkie, *Conference Report*, October 1977, p. 51. A detailed treatment of the elements of the Oath and Covenant of the Priesthood is Robert L. Millet, *Magnifying Priesthood Power* (Bountiful, Ut.: Horizon Publishers, 1974).

[14]Heb. 7:20-21; *HC* 5:555; *TPJS*, p. 323.

[15]Bruce R. McConkie, *Mormon Doctrine*, 2nd ed. (Salt Lake City: Bookcraft, 1966), pp. 745-46.

[16]Lee A. Palmer, *Aaronic Priesthood Through the Centuries* (Salt Lake City: Deseret Book Co., 1964), pp. 319-20.

[17]See a more detailed discussion of the blessings of the Fathers in Milton V. Backman, Jr. and Robert L. Millet, "Heavenly Manifestations in the Kirtland Temple," found herein.

[18]*Conference Report*, April 1974, p. 115.

[19]*Conference Report*, April 1950, p. 99; in *Ye Are the Light of the World* (Salt Lake City: Deseret Book Co., 1974), p. 49.

[20]*The Way to Perfection* (Salt Lake City: Deseret Book Co., 1970), p. 208; see also Smith, *Man: His Origin and Destiny* (Salt Lake City: Deseret Book Co., 1954), p. 272; *Doctrines of Salvation*, 2:41-43.

[21]See statements to this effect by Joseph Fielding Smith in *Doctrines of Salvation*, 3:141-42; Marion G. Romney, *Conference Report*, April 1974, p. 116.

[22]*JD* 22:209.

[23]*Key to the Science of Theology*, 9th ed. (Salt Lake City: Deseret Book Co., 1965), p. 47.

[24]*Gospel Doctrine* (Salt Lake City: Deseret Book Co., 1971), pp. 67-68.

[25]*Conference Report*, April 1975, pp. 96-97.

[26]*HC* 2:95-96; *TPJS*, pp. 71-72.

[27]See Bruce R. McConkie, *The Millennial Messiah* (Salt Lake City: Deseret Book Co., 1982), chapter 52.

[28]*Conference Report*, October 1961, pp. 77-78.

[29]See Bruce R. McConkie, *Let Every Man Learn His Duty* (Salt Lake City: Deseret Book Co., 1976), p. 2.

[30]"Correlation Brings Blessings," *Relief Society Magazine*, April 1967.

# 29

# REVELATIONS CONCERNING ISAIAH
## (D&C 86 and 113)

Kent P. Jackson

Many sections in the Doctrine and Covenants touch on Bible themes and expand both our understanding of the gospel as well as our understanding of important Bible passages. The words of the Lord, as spoken to Isaiah, the eighth-century B.C. prophet of Jerusalem, are reflected in several places in the Doctrine and Covenants.[1] Some of the revelations to the Prophet Joseph Smith deal specifically with Isaianic prophecies. This study will deal with two such passages, D&C 86:8-11 and D&C 113, both of which shed considerable light on Isaiah and teach valuable gospel truths.

### A Latter-day Mission

Section 86 of the Doctrine and Covenants is usually studied for its value in shedding light on Jesus' parable of the wheat and the tares (Matt. 13:24-30).[2] A contribution of equal worth is the insight that it gives into Isaiah 49, one of the most significant revelations of the ancient prophet. Isaiah 49 is a prophecy which deals, among other things, with the role of Ephraim—and perhaps specifically Joseph Smith—in the latter days. Doctrine and Covenants 86 brings Isaiah's words into their Latter-day focus. Isaiah wrote: "Listen, O isles, unto me; and hearken, ye people, from far; The Lord hath called me from the womb; from the bowels of my mother hath he made mention of my name. And he hath made my mouth like a sharp sword; in the shadow of his hand hath he hid me, and made me a polished shaft; in his quiver hath he hid me; And said unto me, Thou art my servant, O Israel, in whom I will be glorified" (Isa. 49:1-3).

The speaker in this passage is called Israel, as is evident in v. 3, who explains his calling (v. 1) and certain manifestations of the divine favor that he has received (v. 2). The Lord called Israel "my servant . . . in whom I will be glorified." That this act of glorification would take place later than Isaiah's day is clear from his use of future tenses throughout the passage. The way in which Israel would glorify the

Lord is specified in vv. 5-6.

Israel pointed out that his labors in the past had been in vain (v. 4). To this the Lord responded with a powerful prophecy of more significant labors that lay ahead: "And now, saith the Lord that formed me from the womb to be his servant, to bring Jacob again to him, Though Israel be not gathered, yet shall I be glorious in the eyes of the Lord, and my God shall be my strength. And he said, It is a light thing that thou shouldest be my servant to raise up the tribes of Jacob, and to restore the preserved of Israel: I will also give thee for a light to the Gentiles, that thou mayest be my salvation unto the end of the earth" (Isa. 49:5-6).

Israel's assigned task, as specified in the passage, can be divided into two parts, each one constituting a major mission to a group of God's children: (1) reestablish Israel and gather it again to the Lord, and (2) serve as "a light to the Gentiles," to make salvation available to them.

## Joseph Smith and Ephraim

Section 86 of the Doctrine and Covenants was revealed to Joseph Smith in December of 1832, only two and one-half years after the organization of the Church. It is one of many revelations that grew out of the Prophet's study of the Bible. In the era in which these revelations were given, heaven-sent communications were unfolding the role that the young prophet and the young Church were to play in accomplishing the Lord's purposes. Perhaps Joseph had never considered the fact that he might have been mentioned in scripture by biblical prophets. Nonetheless he certainly knew by this time that the infant latter-day Church was the kingdom of God and that its continued success was sure. Doctrine and Covenants 86:8-11 made known yet other truths that brought greater emphasis to the mission of the Prophet and his work. Among other things, it brought to light the fact that Joseph Smith and his fellow workers of the lineage of ancient Joseph were the fulfillment of the great revelation recorded in Isaiah 49. It seems, in fact, reasonable to conclude that the "Israel" mentioned in Isaiah's prophecy refers to the specific tribe that was to preside in the last days—the tribe of Ephraim. At the head of that tribe—and presiding under the Lord's direction over latter-day Israel—stands the Prophet

Joseph Smith. Isaiah 49 speaks of him and of the church that was restored through his service.

A few brief comments regarding some key phrases in Isaiah's words will enable us to understand the prophecy and its fulfillment.

**"Called me from the womb" (v. 1):** From the days of the Patriarchs, ancient Joseph and his descendants had been singled out to stand at the head of the house of Israel (see Gen. 37:5-11; 48:13-20; 49:26; Deut. 33:16-17). This was their foreordained calling. An important part of that calling included the challenge to be saviors of their brethren of Israel, just as their forefather Joseph had been a temporal savior in ancient times. Jeremiah prophesied concerning Ephraim's role in the latter-day gathering. As presiding tribe, it would be he who would announce to all that the time of the gathering and return had come (Jer. 31:6).

**"In the shadow of his hand hath he hid me" (v. 2):** At the same time that Joseph's father, Jacob, pronounced the blessing of presidency on Joseph and his posterity, he prophesied that the *government* would be in the hands of the tribe of *Judah* (Gen. 49:8-10). This was fulfilled in the kingship of David and his descendants, and it will be fulfilled to its fullest measure in the millennial kingship of the Lord Jesus Christ. The descendants of Joseph never ruled over the house of Israel, in spite of the fact that they inherited from their ancestor the keys of presidency. Moreover, we have no record that Ephraim ever had the blessings of the gospel from the time of its ancient apostasy to the time of the Restoration. Ephraim's presidency over Israel was to be realized in the last days. With the calling of Joseph Smith, a descendant of Ephraim, the tribe to which he belonged took its rightful position at the head of the family of Israel. Foreordained to a great latter-day service, Joseph's children—both of Ephraim and of Manasseh—have accepted their calling to bring the blessings of the gospel to their brethren.

**"A polished shaft . . . in his quiver" (v. 2):** Joseph Smith himself provided an interpretation that may show the fulfillment of this scripture: "I am like a huge, rough stone rolling down from a high mountain; and the only polishing I get is when some corner gets rubbed off by coming in contact with something else . . . all hell knocking off a corner here and a corner there. Thus I will become a smooth and polished shaft in the quiver of the Almighty."[3] Thus Joseph Smith viewed himself as a polished shaft in the Lord's quiver, perhaps in direct fulfillment of Isaiah's words.

**"To bring Jacob again to him" (v. 5), "to raise up the tribes of Jacob, and to restore the preserved of Israel" (v. 6):** As has been discussed already, it was the commission of the birthright children of Joseph to bring about the gathering of Israel in the last days. Ephraim's leader, Joseph Smith, was the one to whom the keys of the gathering were restored (D&C 110:11),[4] and it will be under the authority of those keys that the gathering will continue. Jeremiah explained that it would be "the watchmen upon the mount Ephraim" that would cry, "Arise ye, and let us go up to Zion unto the Lord our God" (Jer. 31:6). In modern revelation the Lord has affirmed that "they who are in the north countries" will return and receive their blessings under the hand of "the children of Ephraim" (D&C 133:26-34). Today it is, with extremely few exceptions, the children of Ephraim and his brother Manasseh—who constitute the Lord's Church—who are taking the gospel message to the scattered remnants of Israel and who thus are gathering their brethren.

**"A light to the Gentiles" (v. 6):** Nephi and others taught how the great blessings of the last days would be made available not only to the house of Israel, but to the Gentiles as well (see 1 Ne. 22:8-11). Indeed, the gospel is to be taken by Ephraim and his brethren in the dispensation of the fulness of times to *all* people (see JS-M 31; D&C 42:58). Once again, the tribe of Ephraim and Joseph Smith stand out as the main participants in this work. In the fullest sense, Jesus Christ is the "light"—not only to the Gentiles, but to all nations. The Church today has a commission to bear his message; thus it reflects his light.

### "A Savior Unto My People"

Section 86 (vv. 8-11) clarifies Isaiah's prophecy and identifies Joseph Smith and his co-workers of the tribes of Joseph—the members of The Church of Jesus Christ of Latter-day Saints—as the fulfillment of these words from Isaiah. These are they "with whom the priesthood hath continued through the lineage of [their] fathers—For [they] are lawful heirs, according to the flesh, and have been hid from the world with Christ in God" (D&C 86:8-9). Having been foreordained long ago to this calling, and having inherited it through lineal descent, Ephraim's children now are no longer "hid from the world" (D&C 86:9) "in the shadow of [the Lord's] hand" but are at the forefront of the Lord's work in the last days: to restore scattered Israel to the covenant blessings, and to bring the message of the gospel to the Gentiles. The Lord concluded his revelation to Joseph and the Church: "Therefore, blessed are ye if ye continue in my goodness, a light unto the Gentiles, and through this priesthood, a savior unto my people Israel" (D&C 86:11).

### Questions and Answers Concerning Isaiah

Another section of the Doctrine and Covenants that sheds light on the writings of Isaiah is section 113. This section is valuable as an interpretive key to some of Isaiah prophecies, especially those of Isaiah 11. In this section, questions are asked concerning passages in Isaiah, and answers are given. This article will touch briefly on some of the issues brought to light by the statements contained in section 113.

As far as can be determined, the questions and answers were given shortly after the Prophet arrived in Far West, Missouri, in March of 1838.[5] Presumably, the asker of the first three questions was Joseph Smith, though it is not stated specifically. The last two questions were asked by Elias Higbee.

Isaiah 11 is a prophecy with a latter-day orientation. That orientation is not limited to the period of the Restoration, in which we now live, but it includes prophetic insight regarding the Millennium as well. This chapter speaks of the marvelous millennial world in which "the wolf also shall dwell with the lamb, and the leopard shall lie down with the kid" (Isa. 11:6). That will be the day in which "the earth shall be full of the knowledge of the Lord, as the waters cover the sea" (Isa. 11:9). Prior to that day comes the day of Restoration, the period of time in which the Lord would begin the work which would culminate in millennial glory. Three questions regarding this revelation are asked and answered in D&C 113:1-6:

**Q:** "Who is the Stem of Jesse?"

**A:** "It is Christ."

**Q:** "What is the rod . . . that should come of the Stem of Jesse?"

**A:** "It is a servant in the hands of Christ, who is partly a descendant of Jesse as well as of Ephraim, or of the house of Joseph, on whom there is laid much power."

**Q:** "What is the root of Jesse?"

**A:** "It is a descendant of Jesse, as well as of Joseph, unto whom rightly belongs the priesthood, and the keys of the kingdom, for an ensign, and for the gathering of my people in the last days."

These words have been given a variety of interpretations by Latter-day Saint scholars.[6] Since the answer to the first question is quite explicit, the second and third questions are discussed most often. It is my view that D&C 113 teaches that both the "rod out of the stem of Jesse" (Isa. 11:1) and the "root of Jesse" (Isa. 11:10) refer to the same individual—Joseph Smith. This can be demonstrated by comparing the two descriptions given:

| Rod out of the stem of Jesse | Root of Jesse |
|---|---|
| 1. "A servant in the hands of Christ" | |
| 2. "Partly a descendant of Jesse as well as of Ephraim, or of the house of Joseph" | "A descendant of Jesse, as well as of Joseph, unto whom rightly belongs the priesthood, and the keys of the kingdom" |
| 3. "On whom there is laid much power" | "For an ensign, and for the gathering of my people in the last days" |

The two descriptions complement each other; in general, the description of the "root" amplifies that given of the "rod." That the "root" is a servant in the hands of the Lord, as is mentioned concerning the "rod," is clear from the characteristics of his calling mentioned in v. 6. It is most likely that both descriptions refer to the *same* individual, and that the individual in question is Joseph Smith.[7]

It is interesting to note that the "root of Jesse" is called "a descendant of Jesse, as well as of Joseph" (D&C 113:6). We have no evidence in scripture of Joseph Smith's having a heritage from Jesse other than that given in the verses under consideration here. Jesse was the father of David and thus the ancestor of all the kings of Judah, including Jesus Christ. Perhaps the "descent" from Jesse connotes something other than genealogical (i.e., natural) ancestry. As mentioned, Jesse's offspring were the royal line of the house of Israel. Jesus, though not acknowledged as such by his countrymen, was its last king. The Savior conferred the *keys of the kingdom* on his ancient apostles (see Matt. 16:19), whose presidency—Peter, James and John—conferred them on Joseph Smith.[8] Thus, as a priesthood bearer traces the descent of his priesthood authority through the succession of those through whom it came, Joseph Smith's line of authority pertaining to the keys of the kingdom traces back to the line of ancient Jesse. At the council of priesthood leaders and key holders that will yet be held at Adam-ondi-Ahman, Joseph Smith and other leaders of the dispensation of the fulness of times will return the keys of the kingdom to father Adam, who, representing the entire human family, will return the kingdom to its rightful owner, the Lord Jesus Christ. The Savior will then ascend his rightful throne and rule in millennial kingship.

We know of Joseph Smith's descent from Joseph (see 2 Ne. 3:7).[9] In the earlier revelation discussed above (D&C 86:8-11), the Lord had affirmed to his Prophet that he and his co-workers were heirs of the priesthood and had inherited their rights to it through lineal descent. Bearing the priesthood is the right of the birthright sons of Israel, and it becomes their actual inheritance when they prove themselves worthy to receive it. Quoting again: "Thus saith the Lord unto you, with whom the priesthood hath continued through the lineage of your fathers—For ye are lawful heirs, according to the flesh. . . . Therefore your life and the priesthood have remained, and must needs remain through you and your lineage" (D&C 86:8-10). This principle is borne out also in D&C 113:8.

When Moroni appeared to the Prophet Joseph Smith during the night of 21-22 September 1823, he quoted Isa. 11, saying "that it was about to be fulfilled" (JS-H 40). That fulfillment began at that very moment, when the Prophet began to receive the instruction and training that led to the restoration of all things. It will culminate in a glorious fulfillment—in the millennial reign of the Lord Jesus Christ.

The two other questions asked in section 113 concern Isa. 52, a beautiful prophecy of the redemption and restoration of Israel in the last days: "Awake, awake; put on thy strength, O Zion; put on thy beautiful garments, O Jerusalem, the holy city: for henceforth there shall no more come into thee the uncircumcised and the unclean. Shake thyself from the dust; arise, and sit down, O Jerusalem: loose thyself from the bands of thy neck, O captive daughter of Zion" (Isa. 52:1-2). The ultimate redemption of Zion was one of the themes that lay closest to Isaiah's heart, as it did also to the heart of his fellow messenger and kindred spirit Joseph Smith. The latter-day prophet called the establishment of Zion "a theme upon which prophets, priests and kings have dwelt with peculiar delight; they have looked forward with joyful anticipation; . . . and fired with heavenly and joyful anticipations they have sung and written and prophesied of [Zion]."[10] The Lord's modern commentary is befitting a prophecy of such grandeur. In it he brings into sharper focus the crux of Isaiah's message, emphasizing Israel's challenge "to return to the Lord from whence they have fallen" and the restoration of priesthood power to those who are rightful heirs to its blessings.

With these new items of revelation, the Lord once again reminded his Saints of their place in the latter-day work that the ancient prophets foresaw, and which in Joseph Smith's day was beginning to unfold. As the kingdom of God continues to roll forth in the twentieth century, the gradual unfolding of the Lord's purposes becomes increasingly visible.

## Notes

[1]See Monte S. Nyman, *Great Are the Words of Isaiah* (Salt Lake City: Bookcraft, 1980), pp. 289-91.

[2]For a treatment of the New Testament material in D&C 86, see the discussion of section 86 in Robert J. Matthews, "Using the 1981 Edition of the Doctrine and Covenants," found herein.

[3]*TPJS*, p. 304; see also Andrew F. Ehat and Lyndon F. Cook, *The Words of Joseph Smith* (Provo, Ut.: Religious Studies Center, Brigham Young University, 1980), pp. 205, 282.

[4]See Milton V. Backman, Jr., and Robert L. Millet, "Heavenly Manifestations in the Kirtland Temple," found herein.

[5]Lyndon W. Cook, *The Revelations of the Prophet Joseph Smith* (Provo, Ut.: Seventy's Mission Bookstore, 1981), pp. 224-25; cf. *HC* 3:8-10.

[6]See Victor L. Ludlow, *Isaiah: Prophet, Poet, Seer* (Salt Lake City: Deseret Book Co., 1982), pp. 167-78; Nyman, *The Words of Isaiah*, pp. 71-74; Sidney B. Sperry, *The Voice of Israel's Prophets* (Salt Lake City: Deseret Book Co., 1952), pp. 33-37.

[7]Much discussion in Latter-day Saint sources has focussed on the use of the terms "rod" (v. 1) and "root" (v. 10) in Isaiah's tree metaphor. It is not necessary to attempt to juxtapose the two words schematically, that is, to try to determine how the two fit together. The two terms are actually found in separate prophecies: Isa. 11:1-5 comprises one prophecy, vv. 6-9 comprise another, and v. 10 begins a separate prophecy of the gathering. It is sometimes held that the "root" must be the ancestor of the "rod" (twig or stick). This would make it difficult to perceive that both root and rod refer to Joseph Smith. While it is true that the flow of nutrients from the soil follows the order root ⟶ trunk ⟶ twig, at the same time the life-giving nutrients produced through photosynthesis in the leaves flow in the order twig ⟶ trunk ⟶ root. There is no need to assume a genealogical sequence from root to twig. In fact, both the twig and the root stem equally from the trunk. In the Old Testament and in other Near Eastern texts, "root" is often used to mean "offspring," and *not* "ancestor," since it stems from the body of the plant as does the twig (see, for example, J. C. L. Gibson, *Textbook of Syrian Semitic Inscriptions, vol. 3, Phoenician Inscriptions* [Oxford: Clarendon, 1982], pp. 46-47, 57-58 [Azitiwada, line 10]). Thus "root of Jesse" does not necessarily mean Jesse's ancestor, which Joseph Smith clearly was not.

[8]See Kent P. Jackson, "May the Kingdom of God Roll Forth," found herein.

[9]Brigham Young in *JD* 2:269.

[10]*TPJS*, pp. 231-32.

# 30

# A PROPHECY OF WAR

## (D&C 87)

DONALD Q. CANNON

### Historical Setting

The fall and winter of 1832 in the United States was dominated by a political controversy known as the "Nullification Crisis." This crisis grew out of the tensions existing between various geographic sections of the pre-Civil War United States. Specifically, the South felt itself threatened by the North. The state of South Carolina was the center of the unrest generated by this controversy. Southerners, and particularly South Carolinians, felt oppressed and disadvantaged by the high protective tariff of 1828, the so-called "Tariff of Abominations." This tariff imposed heavy duties on foreign manufactured goods, which favored the industrial North, while at the same time it worked against the interest of the agrarian South. In addition to the economic problems, the South was becoming increasingly wary of the nascent antislavery movement in the North. In order to protect itself from these threats, South Carolina passed an Ordinance of Nullification. This ordinance was based on states rights philosophy which claimed the following:

1. Sovereignty resided in the states.
2. The states had created the federal government.
3. The states could decide if a law was constitutional.
4. If it was not, the federal law could be declared null and void in that state.

On 24 November 1832 a special convention in South Carolina declared the Tariff of 1828 null and void. This explosive situation nearly caused a war in 1832.[1]

It was in this historical setting that Joseph Smith had his Prophecy on War. One might ask: how much did the Prophet know about this political controversy? One finds a clue in the *History of the Church*, taken in part from the personal records of the Prophet. For 25 December 1832 we find:

> Appearances of troubles among the nations became more visible this season than they had previously been since the Church began her journey out of the wilderness. The ravages of the cholera were frightful in almost all the large cities on the globe. The plague broke out in India, while the United States, amid all her pomp and greatness, was threatened with immediate dissolution. The people of South Carolina, in convention assembled (in November), passed ordinances, declaring their state a free and independent nation; and appointed Thursday, the 31st day of January, 1833, as a day of humiliation and prayer, to implore almighty God to vouchsafe His blessings, and restore liberty and happiness within their borders. President Jackson issued his proclamation against this rebellion, called out a force sufficient to quell it, and implored the blessings of God to assist the nation to extricate itself from the horrors of the approaching and solemn crisis.[2]

Eleven years later, Joseph Smith was still interested in this subject. In section 130 of the Doctrine and Covenants we read: "I prophesy, in the name of the Lord God, that the commencement of the difficulties which will cause much bloodshed previous to the coming of the Son of Man will begin in South Carolina. It will probably arise through the slave question. This a voice declared to me, while I was praying earnestly on the subject, December 25th, 1832" (D&C 130:12-13). Two items of importance can be seen from this statement. First, the Prophet was aware of the political events of the day. Second, he realized that slavery was emerging as a major issue, as opposed to the earlier concern with the tariff. It is quite understandable that the Prophet would receive revelation and make prophecies in an atmosphere of knowledge. He said that he was deeply concerned about this matter and prayed earnestly about it. He studied and then asked the Lord for revelation.

### Joseph's Prophetic Accuracy

In the *American Heritage Dictionary of the English Language* a prophet is defined as, (a) a person who speaks by divine inspiration, and (b) a predictor. As an example, this dictionary gives Joseph Smith. This revelation of prophecy is certainly a valid and appropriate test of his credibility and authenticity as a prophet.

Let us examine some of Joseph Smith's predictions concerning the

Civil War and then test the truth of those predictions by examining the subsequent historical events. Bear in mind that he made this prophecy 28 years, 3 months and 17 days before the event began.

His first prediction was that war would occur. The spirit of prophecy directed him to say that there definitely would be a war between the states. Of course, this war did take place and is known to us as the Civil War. Between 1861 and 1865 a bitter war raged in the United States.[3]

Joseph Smith prophesied that South Carolina would take the initiative. On 12 April 1861, the Confederate forces laid seige to Fort Sumter. This fort, garrisoned by United States troops, was located in the harbor off Charleston, South Carolina. Indeed, South Carolina did take the initiative.

He further prophesied that this war would bring death to many. As it turned out, the Civil War was one of the bloodiest in history. The number killed or wounded varies considerably depending upon the source. Most Civil War studies give casualty figures in excess of 600,000. This means that the number of casualties, including both North and South, is more than 600,000. One indication of just how high the losses were is shown by a comparison with casualties in other U.S. wars. The aggregate figure for the Civil War is 618, 000 (360,000 North, 258,000 South). The next highest U.S. casualty figure is for World War II, which is 318,000. World War II is followed by World War I with 115,000. U.S. casualty figures for other wars include: The American Revolution: 4,044; War of 1812: 2,200; Mexican War: 13,270; Korean War: 33,000; Vietnam War: 46,616. By overwhelming odds, the casualty figures for the Civil War outnumbered all other U.S. war casualty figures. Two reasons are generally given for the high casualty rate in the Civil War—one medical, the other military. Disease took its toll, but so did the new weapons. Traditional frontal assaults were suicidal in the face of more sophisticated weaponry.[4]

The Prophet foretold the nature of the antagonists in this conflict. He specifically stated that the North would fight the South, as it in fact occurred. This part of the prophecy is especially interesting in view of the fact that the sectional conflict in the early United States pitted the West against the East as well as the North against the South. In the 1830s any number of divisions were possible.

Joseph Smith also prophesied that the Southern states would call upon Great Britain and other nations for aid. Once war broke out the South did send commissioners to various European nations to seek diplomatic recognition and military aid. The South sent representatives to Great Britain, France, Holland and Belgium. Once again, the 1832 prophecy of Joseph Smith was fulfilled with remarkable accuracy.

Joseph Smith's prophecy on war was not limited to the American Civil War. It also included wars in other nations. In fact, the prophecy declared that "war will be poured out upon all nations." Subsequent events have proven that the Latter-day Saint Prophet was accurate in this prediction also. There are admittedly some difficulties associated with documenting this point. One problem is related to the question of determining what constitutes a war. Wars in different centuries vary greatly. Nevertheless, there are studies which have established measuring standards and, furthermore, they conclude that there has been an increase in warfare since the American Civil War. Quincy Wright, for example, maintains that war has occurred with greater frequency and that warfare has become more severe.[5]

Joseph Smith's prophecies on war constitute solid evidence that he was indeed a prophet. His prophecies on the Civil War were fulfilled with remarkable precision and accuracy. Furthermore, his prophecy concerning war being poured out upon the nations has been fulfilled. The number of wars as well as the severity of war has increased dramatically in the century since the Civil War.

Critics of the Prophet Joseph have maintained that this revelation was not published until after the Civil War. It is true that the revelation was not published in the Doctrine and Covenants until 1876. It was published, however, in the Pearl of Great Price in 1851. Furthermore, the leaders of the Church were fully aware of Joseph Smith's prophecy concerning the Civil War as early as the 1830s. Orson Pratt, for example, recalled: "When I was a boy, I traveled extensively in the United States and the Canadas, preaching this restored gospel. I had a manuscript copy of the Revelation, which I carried in my pocket, and I was in the habit of reading it to the people among whom I traveled and preached."[6]

In addition to providing evidence concerning his prophetic gifts, section 87 also provides other doctrinal insights; it discusses the

Lamanites, or the American Indians. These people are referred to in this revelation as "the remnants." The revelation tells us that the Indians would become angry and "vex the Gentiles with a sore vexation" (v. 5).[7]

The Saints are admonished to "stand in holy places." Most commentaries on the Doctrine and Covenants designate the "holy places" as the stakes of Zion. The purpose for stakes is to provide a place of refuge from the world. It is in that sense that stakes are indeed holy places.

## Notes

[1]The best source on the Nullification Crisis is William W. Freehling, *Prelude to Civil War: The Nullification Controversy in South Carolina, 1816-1836* (New York: Harper and Row, 1966).

[2]*HC* 1:301.

[3]The standard one-volume scholarly work on the Civil War is J. G. Randall and David Herbert Donald, *The Civil War and Reconstruction* (Lexington, Mass.: D.C. Health and Company, 1969).

[4]An exhaustive compilation of statistical information on the Civil War is Thomas L. Livermore, *Numbers and Losses in the Civil War in America: 1861-65* (New York: Kraus Reprint Co., 1969).

[5]Quincy Wright, *A Study of War,* 2nd ed. (Chicago: University of Chicago Press, 1965), p. 636.

[7]See Bruce R. McConkie, *The Mortal Messiah,* 4 vols. (Salt Lake City: Deseret Book Co., 1979-81), 4:334-35; and *The Millennial Messiah* (Salt Lake City: Deseret Book Co., 1982), pp. 242, 248.

# 31

# THE OLIVE LEAF

## (D&C 88)

Robert J. Matthews

### Background to the Revelation

As noted in the heading of the 1981 edition of the Doctrine and Covenants, the content of section 88 was received in portions on at least three different dates. Verses 1-126 were received on 27 and 28 December 1832 (how much on the first day is not known), and vv. 127-37 were received on 3 January 1833.[1] The date for vv. 138-41 is not known.

Those present on at least the first two dates were Joseph Smith, Sr., Sidney Rigdon, Orson Hyde, Joseph Smith, Jr., Hyrum Smith, Samuel H. Smith, Newel K. Whitney, Frederick G. Williams, Ezra Thayer, and John Murdock. Brother Williams served as scribe.

This revelation (or collection of revelations) came only two days after the vivid communication now identified as D&C 87, which deals with the wars and destructions about to come upon the earth and which will eventually lead to a "full end of all nations" (D&C 87:6; see also 130:12-17). After the stern warnings and declarations found in the revelation on war, it is interesting that the Prophet identified this revelation as "the olive leaf . . . plucked from the Tree of Paradise, the Lord's message of Peace to us." This document, which has a strong doctrinal content, contains some of the most marvelous instructions we have on record and is calculated not only to inform but also to inspire every person who carefully examines it. To study it is a mind-stretching experience. The language is simple and direct, but the meaning has such depth that a mortal cannot grasp its entirety.

Every reader will notice at the outset that the subject matter of section 88 changes frequently. This increases the difficulty of discussion in a written article, but we are greatly assisted by the voluminous footnotes and cross-references placed in the new edition of the Doctrine and Covenants published in 1981. By following these study aids, we can facilitate our understanding and will need a minimum of other written materials. Moreover, as one's familiarity and understanding increases, he will sense that the revelation flows naturally from one doctrinal concept to another and that the various subjects are vitally related to each other. This revelation, in its many topics, holds out promises and encouragement by giving a glimpse of what the purposes of God are and what our own future can be.

We will, in the pages that follow, present some of the more significant features of section 88 and endeavor to show relationships to the larger doctrinal and historical setting of the Church in this dispensation. Since not every verse can be dealt with in detail, attention will be given to concepts that seem necessary to enable us to grasp, at least to some degree, the depth and sublimity of the revelation. The format is a commentary, intended to be read in connection with the scriptural text. Let it be remembered, moreover, that these are the personal opinions of the writer and not necessarily the official position of the Church.

## Significant Doctrinal Contributions

**Lord of Sabaoth (v. 2).** The term "Lord of Sabaoth" is also found in the New Testament (Rom. 9:29 and James 5:4) and is usually identified as "Lord of Hosts," that is, "Lord of Armies" or as "Ruler over all." The term "Lord of Hosts" (*Yahweh Saba'oth*) is very common in the Old Testament. The Hebrew word *saba'oth* means "hosts," or "armies." The word "Sabaoth" does not appear in the Book of Mormon or the Pearl of Great Price, although "Lord of Hosts" appears in a number of places in both of these works. The title "Lord of Sabaoth" occurs in D&C 87:7; 88:2; 95:7; and 98:2 and has a more extensive meaning than those unfamiliar with the Doctrine and Covenants give to it, with a unique declaration that the Lord of Sabaoth "is by interpretation, the creator of the first day, the beginning and the end" (D&C 95:7). Such a definition far exceeds the concept of just being Lord of many, because it places a time factor of being Lord at the beginning and even being the cause of or initiator of the "first day." This special primacy of Jesus is consistent with other concepts in section 88 that speak of Christ as the creator and the sustainer of the universe in an ultimate and infinite manner. This enlarged definition of Sabaoth enhances its use in 88:2 and is more descriptive than could be obtained from any source outside of the Doctrine and Covenants.

**The Comforter or Promise of Eternal Life (vv. 3-4).** The Comforter here spoken of is identified as the Holy Spirit of Promise and is thus the Holy Ghost. He is the "first Comforter." The second Comforter, as explained by the Prophet Joseph Smith, is the Lord Jesus Christ and has reference to a personal visit.[2] The wording "another Comforter" has led some to wonder if this passage in 88:3-4 has reference to the Second Comforter, and not to the Holy Ghost. However, the personage spoken of is clearly the Holy Spirit of Promise, and "the Holy Spirit of Promise is not the Second Comforter."[3]

**Friends (v. 3).** The close relationship of the Lord to his faithful servants is shown in his greeting them as friends. A servant carries out orders as he is commanded. A "friend" is one with whom the Lord confides his purposes and plans. This subject is touched upon again in D&C 93:45-46 and is more fully explained in John 15:13-15: "Henceforth I call you not servants; for the servant knoweth not what his lord doeth: but I have called you friends; for all things that I have heard of my Father I have made known unto you." The knowledge about to be entrusted to the Saints in this revelation is characteristic of that which would be shared by the Master with his faithful friends.

**Church of the Firstborn (v. 5).** This term occurs in the New Testament (Heb. 12:23) and also in several places in the Doctrine and Covenants (76:54, 67, 71, 94; 77:11; 78:21; 93:22; 107:19). It has reference to those who inherit the fulness of salvation and exaltation. They belong not only to the Church of Jesus Christ (who himself is the Firstborn), but they constitute a church, the membership of which consists only of those who are exalted and thus have the *inheritance* of the firstborn. They are joint heirs with Jesus in all that the Father has and are thus the Church consisting of the firstborn. This is what the gospel does for those who obey it fully; it causes them to be born again and gives them an adoption in the eternal patriarchal family so that they have an inheritance as the firstborn even though they are younger in actual chronology (see also Gal. 3:26-4:7).

**The Light of Christ (vv. 6-13).** In some manner that we do not fully understand, these verses state that the light of Christ is in the sun, moon, stars, and in the earth also, and this light gives life to all things and is the law by which all things are governed. This light shines and is also called the "light of truth" (v. 6) and "is the same light that quickeneth your understandings" (v. 11).

Elder Orson Pratt commented on these verses as follows:

> Who is there in this congregation, or upon the face of the earth, that can tell how that light operates in quickening the understandings of men? . . . Do you know how that is done? I do not; yet this is what God has revealed. He is the light that is in all things. Do you or I comprehend how that light is connected with all things? No. These are lessons which we have got to learn in the future, when we ascend in that scale of knowledge and intelligence now possessed by celestial beings. . . . We are told in this revelation that the light that quickens the understandings of the children of men and that lighteth all things is one and the same and that it is also the life of all things. What are we to understand by this? Have we life? Yes, we certainly have. Where did we obtain this life? When was it created or made? There is a revelation upon this subject which says that intelligence, or the light of truth, was not created, neither indeed can be [93:29]. Is it then eternal? Yes. Then this light that shines is eternal in its nature is it? Yes, because it is the same light that gives light to all things.[4]

**The Redemption of the Soul (vv. 14-17).** The technical definition is that a "soul" consists of a spirit and a physical body. This is helpful in clarifying other passages of scripture dealing with the creation, such as Moses 3:7-9 and Abr. 5:7. The scriptures are not always consistent with the use of the word "soul," and sometimes it is used to mean only the spirit (Alma 40:21). The emphasis in the context of 88:14-17, however, is upon the resurrection and redemption of the soul along with the resurrection and redemption of the earth as a home on which glorified souls will live—and all this by the power of Jesus Christ.

**Purpose and Destiny of the Earth (vv. 17-20, 25-27).** The revelations of God frequently talk about the earth on which we live. In Abr. 3:24-25 we are told that one purpose for the earth is to provide a place where man may dwell and be proved—a probationary place. Section 88 deals with yet another factor—the eternal destiny of the earth is to be a celestial world, "sanctified from all unrighteousness," even worthy of the presence of God the Father (v.18). Those who live on this earth who are meek and are redeemed and sanctified shall live on and possess this earth forever and ever in a resurrected state—resurrected bodies on a resurrected earth. For this intent the earth was made, and will die, and will be quickened.

**The Earth Filleth the Measure of Its Creation (vv. 19, 25).** This phrase appears twice in the revelation (vv. 19, 25). A similar phrase is used in D&C 49:16-17 with the explanation that to answer the purpose of its creation the earth must be filled with man (cf. also 1 Ne. 17:36). These references (combined with Abr. 3:24-25) give the clear scriptural statement that there is divine purpose both to man and to the earth: (1) in their creation, (2) in their present continuance, and (3) in their eternal destiny.

The revelation also reads as though the earth were intelligent. For example: "Verily I say unto you, the earth abideth the law of a celestial kingdom . . . and transgresseth not the law" (v. 25). Furthermore, in Moses 7:48-49 the earth is represented as speaking and experiencing pain because of the wickedness of mankind upon its surface. Many regard these as figurative expressions, but there may be something more literal involved. This factor will be considered further in connection with vv. 34-46.

**Resurrection and Glory According to the Law which Is Obeyed (vv. 21-24, 28-33).** These verses explain that every soul will be resurrected, some to glory and some to no glory, depending upon the law each person chose to obey. The law of Christ—the gospel—leads to a fulness of celestial glory. Any deviation leads to less. In these passages, "quickened" has reference to resurrection, and this quickening comes to all. Verses 24, 32, and 33 clearly indicate that the class of persons known as sons of perdition shall be "quickened," that is, they will be resurrected in their physical body but not to a place of glory, for they failed to receive the only gift (the atonement of Christ) that could have redeemed them. This is a clarification of D&C 76:38-39, which some have misinterpreted to mean that the sons of perdition would not receive the resurrection of the body.[5]

**All Kingdoms are Governed by Law (vv. 34-45).** A key sentence in this passage states that God "hath given a law unto all things, by which they move in their times and seasons; and their courses are fixed, even the courses of the heavens and the earth . . . and all the planets" (vv. 42-43). At least two basic concepts are emphasized here: (1) God is the Author and the Giver of the law, not just a user of it, and (2) there is obedience in the universe. These are both fundamental to the existence of the Lord's kingdoms. Only a limited discussion of these matters is presented here.[6]

As to the "obedience" of the planets and especially of the earth, the question arises whether it is forced obedience or if there is agency and intelligence in nature (other than in man). Elder Orson Pratt felt there was intelligent choice:

> There does not seem to be any agency on the part of these materials [inanimate things], so far as we naturally comprehend it; at least, if there is an agency, it seems to be very obedient instead of disobedient . . . at least we do not know of any disobedience. . . . There are some sayings in this same revelation which seem to indicate that there is a degree of intelligence even in these materials [referring to the earth as in v. 25]. . . . Some . . . might say that the earth is obliged to follow this course. I do not know about this. I am not so sure. I think if we could see a little further, we would understand that, connected with the materials of the earth is a living principle . . . that acts according to certain laws, intelligently, not blindly; and that our earth, in performing its course . . . does so according to law, as much as we do when we go forth and are buried in the waters of baptism.[7]

**Man Shall Eventually Comprehend Even God (vv. 47-50, 66-69).** There are some wonderfully descriptive concepts about God in these verses, such as majesty, power, light, truth, Spirit, wilderness, and the unveiling of his face to man. Concerning our relationship to God, we are told in these verses that as we witness the pattern and order of the cosmos we have already seen him moving in his majesty and power; that eventually righteous men shall comprehend God by "being quickened in him and by him" (v. 49); and that God sustains man by his (God's) light. It is also stated that God's voice is Spirit and that mortal man hears it as a voice in the wilderness—"in the wilderness, because we cannot see him" (v. 66). The Lord continues the instruction by saying that if we have an eye single to his glory, our whole bodies shall be filled with light, and by that means we shall be able to see God and also be able to comprehend all things. These verses are a continuation of the revelation on light given in vv. 6-13 already discussed, and they also add to an earlier exposition about light given in D&C 50:23-30. This is such an important subject that yet a further revelation about light is to be found in D&C 93:26-32. The frequency of the instruction about *light* suggests that it is important for us to know about it; that the Lord wants us to know; and that it is a subject difficult for us to understand in our mortal state.

These passages speak of man seeing the face of God and even comprehending him (which means understanding him), and of man himself knowing all things. Such accomplishments are not by intellectual learning or by research alone, great as these are as aids to arriving at the truth. A careful reading of the above passages shows clearly that man obtains great spiritual heights and privileges only by having an eye single to the glory of God, obeying the commandments, hearing the voice of the Spirit, and being "quickened" by the Lord. This is not secular but spiritual. To obtain these blessings, man must lift his thoughts from nature (the things that are created) up to nature's Author (the Creator). This is the special role of revealed religion and the purpose of the gospel of Jesus Christ, as contrasted with the pursuit of other kinds of truth. Secular learning is an aid, but is separate and distinct from the kind of learning that leads mankind to a full knowledge and acquaintance with God. A study of nature (the earth and all things in the earth or connected with the earth) and the creations beyond the sphere of this earth (that is, a study of the physical things that God has created)—astronomy—is an honorable and necessary pursuit; but to realize his potential, man must do more than that; he must also comprehend even God. The things of God are such that they can be learned only by revelation; therefore, a study of the revelations which make known the character of God and what he requires of man are absolutely essential for salvation (see Mosiah 4:9; Job 11:7). Man will not comprehend God unless he becomes like him, and this is not an easy accomplishment and cannot be obtained outside of the gospel of Jesus Christ. As the Prophet Joseph Smith explained:

> A fanciful and flowery and heated imagination beware of; because the things of God are of deep import; and time, and experience, and careful and ponderous and solemn thoughts can only find them out. Thy mind, O man! if thou wilt lead a soul unto salvation, must stretch as high as the utmost heavens, and search into and contemplate the darkest abyss, and the broad

> expanse of eternity—thou must commune with God. How much more dignified and noble are the thoughts of God, than the vain imaginations of the human heart![8]

And again from the Prophet:

> Let us here observe, that after any portion of the human family are made acquainted with the important fact that there is a God, who has created and does uphold all things, the extent of their knowledge respecting his character and glory will depend upon their diligence and faithfulness in seeking after him, until, like Enoch, the brother of Jared, and Moses, they shall obtain faith in God, and power with him to behold him face to face.[9]

And yet again from the Prophet:

> We consider that God has created man with a mind capable of instruction, and a faculty which may be enlarged in proportion to the heed and diligence given to the light communicated from heaven to the intellect; and that the nearer man approaches perfection, the clearer are his views, and the greater his enjoyments, till he has overcome the evils of his life and lost every desire for sin; and like the ancients, arrives at that point of faith where he is wrapped in the power and glory of his Maker and is caught up to dwell with Him. But we consider that this is a station to which no man ever arrived in a moment: he must have been instructed in the government and laws of that kingdom by proper degrees, until his mind is capable in some measure of comprehending the propriety, justice, equality, and consistency of the same.[10]

Perhaps two further points should be discussed relative to v. 66. The Lord here states that his voice is Spirit and that his Spirit is truth. The revelation says that man hears the voice of the Lord by hearing the Spirit. This is similar to D&C 18:34-36, in which the Lord says that those who have felt and heard his Spirit "can testify that they have heard my voice, and know my words" (18:36). This is an informative definition of what it means to hear the voice of the Lord.

The other point is occasioned by the Lord stating that he is a voice in the wilderness—in the wilderness because we cannot see him (v. 66). These words are followed two verses later by the explanation that if one sanctifies himself so that his mind becomes single to God, the day will come when he will see God. Note the contrast between mortal man being in the wilderness at first, but growing in light until he sees God. That is, when the Lord unveils his face to a friend, that person is in the wilderness no longer. What beautiful imagery!

**A Parable about the Inhabitants of Other Worlds (vv. 51-65).** After declaring the existence, harmony, and relationship of the various bodies that constitute the heavenly machinery, including the sun, moon, stars and planets, the Lord asked: "Unto what shall I liken these kingdoms that ye may understand? Behold, all these are kingdoms" (vv. 46-47). In answer to his own question the Lord gives a parable of a man sending his servants into the field and visiting each of them in turn. He would withdraw from one to visit another. Each servant saw his Lord's countenance and was made glad—"every man in his hour, and in his time, and in his season. . . . Every man in his own order" (vv. 51-60). "Therefore," said the Lord, "unto this parable I will liken all these kingdoms [the worlds he has created], and the inhabitants thereof—every kingdom in its hour, and in its time, and in its season, even according to the decree which God hath made" (v. 61).

This parable is one of the plainest assertions in the scriptures that there are inhabitants on other worlds, and that Jesus Christ is their Savior and Lord, visiting each in its time (cf. D&C 76:23-24).[11]

**The Solemn Assembly; a Great and Last Promise (vv. 69-76).** The Lord instructed the Prophet to call a solemn assembly of the "first laborers in this last kingdom." This was to be held in Kirtland and was to include a spiritual manifestation to those who were worthy. Much needed to be done in anticipation. They were to prepare their hearts and minds, rid themselves of idle thoughts and of excess laughter. Those expecting to be invited to attend were to organize themselves and sanctify their lives, purify their hearts and cleanse their hands and feet, in order that they would be "clean from the blood of this wicked generation" (vv. 69, 74, 75).

The instruction to hold a solemn assembly comes immediately following the promise that the day will come when the faithful will see the face of the Lord, and thus it is clear these two circumstances are related. That the Lord would show himself to his servants and give them the transcendent joy that accompanies a personal visit from their Savior is called "the great and last promise" (vv. 69, 75), and the Lord said he would fulfill it if his people would prepare themselves.

The words "great and last promise" attract our attention, and we wish the revelation provided a direct definition of how the word "last" is used in this instance. Certainly the meaning is not that this was the final (or chronologically last) promise he would make to his servants. The meaning therefore seems to be that this was the *ultimate* promise—that is, that when they were ready, they would see his face and stand in his presence. The feeling is also contained in the passage that this was the last promise until they had accomplished the preparation needed to obtain the promise the Lord had given them.

A few days after receiving section 88, the Prophet Joseph Smith sent a copy of the revelation to the Brethren in Missouri and told them of the anticipated visit of the Savior in the forthcoming assembly. Part of his letter reads:

> [14 January 1833] You will see that the Lord commanded us, in Kirtland, to build a house of God, and establish a school for the Prophets, this is the word of the Lord to us, and we must, yea, the Lord helping us, we will obey: as on condition of our obedience He has promised us great things; yea, even a visit from the heavens to honor us with His own presence. We greatly fear before the Lord lest we should fail of this great honor, which our Master proposes to confer on us; we are seeking for humility and great faith lest we be ashamed in His presence.[12]

Subsequently the Prophet gave repeated instruction to the brethren about the preparation they must make to be ready for the assembly, which would not be held for some years in the future. We note one such instance in the following:

> [12 November 1835] We must have all things prepared, and call our solemn assembly as the Lord has commanded us. . . . The endowment you are so anxious about, you cannot comprehend now . . . but strive to be prepared in your hearts . . . when we meet in the solemn assembly we must be clean every whit. . . . If we are faithful . . . I will venture to prophesy that we will get a blessing that will be worth remembering, if we should live as long as John the Revelator; our blessings will be such as we have not realized before, nor received in this generation. . . .

> All who are prepared, and are sufficiently pure to abide the presence of the Savior will see him in the solemn assembly.[13]

The assembly was not held until the temple was completed. Finally on 30 March 1836, three days after the temple was dedicated, the meeting was convened. It lasted more than a day and a night. The Prophet referred to the spiritual experiences as "a day of Pentecost," and said that "speaking in tongues was manifest, the Savior made his appearance to some, and angels ministered to others."[14]

The term "solemn assembly" is mentioned several times in the Old Testament, one notable occurrence being just after the dedication of the temple by King Solomon (2 Chron. 7:9). Other occurrences had to do with special events and fast days in the history of Israel.

**An Informed Ministry; Knowledge by Study and by Faith (vv. 77-86, 117-18).** In order that the servants of the Lord might effectively carry the message of the restoration to the inhabitants of the earth, the Lord specified that they should study and become acquainted with many branches of knowledge in addition to the doctrines of the kingdom (vv. 77-80). They were to "seek learning, by study and also by faith" (v. 118). What it means to seek learning "by study" we already know something about, but how to seek learning "by faith" requires even more experience and serious contemplation. Whatever else is required in order for one to seek learning by faith, at least two factors have to be recognized. First, the individual seeking the learning must have an eye single to the glory of God—his motives cannot be selfish. Second, he has to trust the revealed word of God as being true. If he wants to gain spiritual knowledge for himself, he has to believe that what the Lord has already revealed in the scriptures is correct, especially the latter-day scriptures. He then proceeds to study, using the scriptures as the standard by which to measure and interpret whatever knowledge he may gain in the other branches of learning. This would seem to be true in all subject matter areas but especially in the study of fields closely related to human behavior and potential.

Although all truth is valuable, some areas are more critical for preparing the elders for their ministry to the nations of the earth and also for their own salvation and spiritual welfare. President Brigham Young spoke of a "perfect celestial science" which he defined as the study of all truth and useful information gained through books, experience and revelation. He emphasized, however, the single importance of theology:

> Do the Elders of Israel understand all that the Lord requires of them? They do not. . . . They can learn from themselves—from the world—from the government of heaven—from the management, government, control, doctrines, and laws of eternity, which will yet be exhibited before us. The Lord has established the world with its varied productions, for the education of his children. . . .
>
> . . . There are a great many branches of education: some go to college to learn languages, some to study law, some to study physic, and some to study astronomy, and various other branches of science. We want every branch of science taught in this place that is taught in the world. But our favourite study is that branch which particularly belongs to the Elders of Israel—namely, theology. Every Elder should become a profound theologian—should understand this branch better than all the world. There is no Elder who has the power of God upon him but understands more of the principles of theology than all the world put together.[15]

The type of individuals which the Lord requires for his ministry are those persons whose garments are clean from the blood of this generation. Those not yet clean were to wait for another time to be called. Those who were called were to labor diligently to warn the people of the judgments to come. The brethren were told in the revelation that not everyone will accept the message, and that one aspect of their teaching was to issue a warning voice so as to leave the world "without excuse"; in this way "their sins are upon their own heads" (vv. 81-82). The number of converts one makes is not the measure of success of the mission. The Prophet Joseph Smith explained:

> It is not the multitude of preachers that is to bring about the glorious millennium! but it is those who are "called, and chosen, and faithful." . . . Remember that your business is to preach the Gospel in all humility and meekness, and warn sinners to repent and come to Christ. . . . If you do your duty, it will be just as well with you, as though all men embraced the Gospel.[16]

**Signs, Earthly Commotions, and Angels Prepare the Way for**

**the Second Coming (vv. 87-116).** This large segment of section 88 bears a striking similarity to chapters 7-22 in the book of Revelation. It is a prophecy of destruction and calamity but also a message of hope. It is, as with all revealed scripture, an assurance that in the end righteousness will triumph over evil; Christ over the devil; the Saints over their oppressors. Ultimate victory will come through the Lord Jesus Christ.

The Prophet had been involved for many months with making an initial draft of an inspired translation of the New Testament, concluding with the book of Revelation in March 1832. In the process of making the translation, many important things were revealed to him about the gospel and in this case about future events to take place on the earth (see D&C 45:60-62). The history of the earth, the ministry of seven angels who play a prominent part in the final judgment scenes, and the opening of the seven seals are significant aspects of the Revelation of John. These were reiterated and partially explained in D&C 77 as a consequence of the translation and were further enlarged upon in these verses from section 88. Thus we regard this part of section 88 as a further clarification and explanation of the Revelation of John. These are eschatological items—the winding-up events to take place on the earth before it is prepared for the celestial glory. All nations must hear the proclamation of the gospel and be informed of the means of redemption. The earth must die and wickedness be cleansed from off its face. There will be a resurrection of all mankind and a final judgment. Through faith in Jesus the Saints will have gained the victory over sin and death and will be crowned with eternal glory (vv. 106-7). The calamities and convulsive quaking of the earth, the wars and the pestilences spoken of in these verses are the "details" involved in the larger concept of the earth being prepared for its eternal celestial destiny.

Before these final things occur, however, the servants of God must prepare themselves for their mission to the world. Therefore, the Lord again took up the subject of the temple and the school, because without these, the missionaries could not be prepared for their ministry. Without the servants of God bearing testimony, the honest in heart would not be gathered and the unrepentant would not be warned and left without excuse.

**A House of Learning; a House of God (vv. 117-37).** In the remaining verses of the revelation, the Lord outlined the procedure for the School of the Prophets and the establishment of a house—a temple—for the School and other sacred purposes. The house is referred to as a place of prayer, fasting, faith, learning, glory, and order, which is therefore "a house of God" (v. 119).

One of the most apparent factors of this part of the revelation is that knowledge, wisdom, books, learning, faith, prayer, glory, and fasting are all closely associated. Learning and wisdom are not solely intellectual pursuits but are linked with faith, prayer and fasting. "The School of the Prophets" thus presents the highest and the best ideal in education. It is a symbol of inspired learning and shows that true education cannot be separated from a spiritual and divine purpose.

In order for mortal men and women to be able to learn essential truths, there has to be a certain mind-set and spiritual preparation. This revelation states that intellectual attainment is inseparably connected with both physical and spiritual characteristics. Thus the instructions are given that those who were to participate in the School were also to cease from lightmindedness, loud laughter, pride, lustful desires, covetousness, idleness, uncleanness, fault finding, and excessive sleep (vv. 122-24). In addition, they were to practice diligence, study, faith, prayer, love for one another, charity, and were to retire to bed early and arise early (vv. 118, 123, 125, 126).

The School of the Prophets called for a mix of hard intellectual effort and inspiration from the Holy Ghost, and characterized a very particular kind of educational process. Learning was to be assisted by the light of the gospel and the light of inspiration. The role the Holy Ghost plays in enabling one to learn was explained dramatically by Elder Orson Pratt:

> What does [the Holy Ghost] do for the education of men? Far more than our academies do. Our children have, by hard study, year after year, to acquire their learning in these human institutions; hard thinking is necessary, reasoning, gaining little by little, and it frequently requires many years of close application to become what is termed a learned man—a man that understands the sciences, that has worked his way through the various departments of mathematics, and perhaps geology, and

> mineralogy, and all the sciences, such as are usually taught in universities. But the man filled with the Holy Ghost has the advantage of students who graduate at our universities. Why? Because he can learn more in ten minutes, in regard to many things, than another, not so favored, can in all his life. Indeed, he can learn some things by the operations of the Holy Ghost, which no natural man or woman could learn, however gifted they might be. You may inquire where they could learn these things? I answer, by the revelations of the Holy Ghost, which brings to light many things that are past, and shows things that are in the future. The Lord . . . opens the past and future to the minds of men, just as Jesus promised his disciples when he was about to leave them. "Howbeit when he, the Spirit of Truth, is come, he will guide you into all truth; and he will show you things to come" (John 16:13).[17]

With v. 126 the original revelation is concluded. The portion from v. 127 onward was added on 3 January 1833, and one notices a change in the literary style in the second part. It is equally inspired and informative but seems less poetic and more prosaic.

The order of the school in the house of God is presented, showing proper greetings of the brethren. The president of the School is to enter the room first and hold a place of honor. With uplifted hands, the president shall greet the members in the name of the Lord in token of the everlasting covenant (vv. 127-37).

The School first met in an upstairs room of the Gilbert and Whitney store in Kirtland. Later it met in a building near the temple, and finally in an upstairs room of the temple (see D&C 95:17). A similar school was held in Missouri for a short time (D&C 97:3-6).[18]

It was while the School was meeting in the store that a question arose about the use of alcohol and tobacco in the School. At the Prophet's inquiry, he received the "Word of Wisdom" on 27 February 1833, which is now known as D&C 89. This section (and section 88) both show that there is a connection between physical things and intellectual and spiritual attainment. One of the promises for obedience to the principles of the Word of Wisdom is to "find wisdom, and great treasures of knowledge, even hidden treasures (D&C 89:19). This information could well have been included in the instruction about the School of the Prophets in section 88, because it is of the same general nature. The guidelines given in section 88 about the School, especially concerning sleep, could be part of the "Word of Wisdom." From this instance, as with many others, we can see that revelations come in a progressive manner, as they are needed and asked for, and as the people are able to bear them, line upon line, here and there a little.

As noted, the School of the Prophets was to include only those who were totally dedicated to the Lord and who were clean from sin. In June 1833, the Lord rebuked the brethren because "contentions arose in the school," which the Lord said was "a very grievous sin" (D&C 95:10). It was also in the School of the Prophets that the excellent lessons known as the seven "Lectures on Faith" were taught.[19]

The Schools were eventually discontinued in Kirtland and in Missouri and revived again in the West under the direction of the First Presidency. The School of the Prophets still exists today but is limited to the First Presidency and the Quorum of the Twelve. It may formally be expanded at some future time to include others, in preparation for their ministry to the nations of the earth.

**The Washing of Feet (vv. 138-41).** Membership in the School was specifically declared to be reserved for those who are "clean from the blood of this generation" (v. 138); they were to be received into the School by the washing of feet, administered by the president of the Church. It was to be preceded by partaking of the sacramental emblems of the Savior's flesh and blood (vv. 139-41). Concerning the washing of feet, the Prophet Joseph Smith said:

> The item to which I wish the more particularly to call your attention to-night, is the ordinance of washing of feet. This we have not done as yet, but it is necessary now, as much as it was in the days of the Savior; and we must have a place prepared, that we may attend to this ordinance aside from the world. . . .
>
> We must have all things prepared, and call our solemn assembly as the Lord has commanded us, that we may be able to accomplish His great work, and it must be done in God's own way. The house of the Lord must be prepared, and the solemn assembly called and organized in it, according to the order of the house of God; and in it we must attend to the ordinance of washing of feet. It was never intended for any but official members. It is calculated to unite our hearts, that we may be one in feeling and sentiment, and that our faith may be strong, so

> that Satan cannot overthrow us, nor have any power over us here.[20]

## Conclusion

It cannot be emphasized too greatly that section 88 is one of the most glorious documents given to man for his spiritual progress and attainment. It speaks of things in a simple, straightforward manner yet deals with concepts so profound and far-reaching that it takes extensive study and contemplation just to appreciate its grandeur. The careful reader is literally bathed in light as a consequence of the experience. One of the things this revelation does for the reader is to lay before him the high priority the Lord has placed on learning and the acquisition of knowledge. Yet it makes unmistakably clear that this is not a cold intellectual pursuit but a spiritual attainment.

Another characteristic that becomes clear from a study of this revelation is the consistency of its content with earlier revelation and an awareness that later revelations continue to expand upon the same themes.

The student of section 88 is rewarded with an enlarged view of the purposes of God, the coming of future events on the earth, and the role of the servants of the Lord in helping to prepare for the Second Coming of the Savior. The reader also senses more fully the promises that are made to individuals. When one begins to understand these things, he is encouraged to prepare himself, by study and by faith, to contribute whatever he can to help the eternal purposes of the Lord roll forward. We thus appreciate a little of what the Prophet had in mind when he named it the "Olive Leaf, . . . the Lord's message of peace to us."[21]

---

## Notes

[1]A discussion of this is found in Robert J. Woodford, "The Historical Development of the Doctrine and Covenants," Ph.D. dissertation, Brigham Young University, 1974, pp. 1127-28.

[2]*TPJS*, pp. 149-51.

[3]Joseph Fielding Smith, *Doctrines of Salvation*, 3 vols., comp. Bruce R.

McConkie (Salt Lake City: Bookcraft, 1954-56), 1:55.

[4]From an address given in Salt Lake City, 14 March 1875, contained in N. B. Lundwall (compiler and publisher), *Wonders of the Universe* (Salt Lake City: 1937), p. 198.

[5]See Larry E. Dahl, "The Vision of the Glories," found herein, note 18; see also the footnote to D&C 76:39, 1981 edition, which also clarifies this point.

[6]See LaMar E. Garrard, "What is Man?," *Hearken, O Ye People: Discourses on the Doctrine and Covenants* (Salt Lake City: Randall Book Co., 1984), pp. 133-49.

[7]*JD* 21:233-34.

[8]*TPJS*, p. 137.

[9]N. B. Lundwall, comp., *Lectures on Faith* (Salt Lake City: N. B. Lundwall, n. d.), Lecture 2, paragraph 55.

[10]*TPJS*, p. 51.

[11]See Joseph Smith's poetic version of the Vision of the Glories, vv. 19-20, in Dahl, "The Vision of the Glories," found herein.

[12]*TPJS*, p. 19.

[13]*Ibid.*, pp. 91-92.

[14]*HC* 2:432-33. For a colorful and informative account of the spiritual manifestations connected with the Kirtland Temple and the solemn assembly, see Milton V. Backman, Jr., *The Heavens Resound* (Salt Lake City: Deseret Book Co., 1983), pp. 284-309. See also Milton V. Backman, Jr. and Robert L. Millet, "Heavenly Manifestations in the Kirtland Temple," found herein.

[15]*JD* 6:317.

[16]*TPJS*, pp. 42-43.

[17]*JD* 19:284.

[18]For a discussion of the School of the Prophets, see Lyndon W. Cook, *The Revelations of the Prophet Joseph Smith* (Provo, Ut.: Seventy's Mission Bookstore, 1981), pp. 185-90.

[19]For a brief account of these "Lectures" see John A. Widtsoe, "Historical Sketch of the Lectures on Faith," pp. 3-6 in Lundwall, comp., *Lectures on Faith.*

[20]*TPJS*, pp. 90-91.

[21]*HC* 1:316.

# 32

# A WORD OF WISDOM (D&C 89)

CATHERINE THOMAS

When the Prophet Joseph Smith recorded the revelation known as the Word of Wisdom, many members of the Church used tobacco, hard liquor, tea and coffee.[1] Brigham Young described the situation that led to the revelation:

> I think I am as well acquainted with the circumstances which led to the giving of the Word of Wisdom as any man in the Church, although I was not present at the time to witness them. The first school of the prophets was held in a small room situated over the Prophet Joseph's kitchen, in a house, which belonged to Bishop [Newel K.] Whitney, and which was attached to his store, which store probably might be about fifteen feet square. In the rear of this building was a kitchen, probably ten by fourteen feet, containing rooms and pantries. Over this kitchen was situated the room in which the Prophet received revelations and in which he instructed his brethren. The brethren came to that place for hundreds of miles to attend school in a little room probably no larger than eleven by fourteen. When they assembled together in this room after breakfast, the first [thing] they did was to light their pipes, and, while smoking, talk about the great things of the kingdom, and spit all over the room, and as soon as the pipe was out of their mouths a large chew of tobacco would then be taken. Often when the Prophet entered the room to give the school instructions he would find himself in a cloud of tobacco smoke. This, and the complaints of his wife at having to clean so filthy a floor, made the Prophet think upon the matter, and he inquired of the Lord relating to the conduct of the Elders in using tobacco, and the revelation known as the Word of Wisdom was the result of his inquiry.[2]

Joseph Smith was not the only one teaching a health rule in the 1830s. Many Americans already recognized that these stimulants were harmful, and a temperance movement was escalating in parts of the United States, including in Ohio.[3] Many reformers of the period taught their own health laws. Some critics have suggested that Joseph created a religion simply by copying from his contemporaries, but the Prophet's health law was distinctive then and is today: (1) it is a revelation from God; (2) it promises to the obedient not only physical and mental health, but spiritual development also; and (3) it warns prophetically of men who will foist upon the public things detrimental to health.[4] Received in a smoke-screen of similar-sounding health codes, the Lord's revelation to Joseph persists today largely substantiated by science.

Thus today the maturation of the Church as well as of medical science makes unnecessary a defense of the Latter-day Saint position on the elements of the Word of Wisdom. No longer need we cite statistics on the destructive consequences of smoking, drinking alcohol, coffee, tea, or using other harmful substances, nor do we need to have revealed the existence of the evil "hearts of conspiring men" (D&C 89:4). These facts are well known throughout the Church. But the history and content of section 89 suggest compelling related questions.

## Two Questions

First, when the Lord revealed the Word of Wisdom, why did he not issue it as a commandment? Second, amid the varieties of Word of Wisdom practice, how should section 89 be interpreted?

### Not by Commandment or Constraint

Saints in the early days of the Church faced the need to make frequent revisions of their lives to harmonize with the prolific revelations of the Lord to the infant Church. Events surrounding section 89 disclose the mercifully gradual process by which members could embrace those teachings that required substantial change in their lives.[5] The Saints understood early that strong drink meant alcoholic beverages, and that hot drinks were tea and coffee. From time to time, between 1834 and 1880, Church leaders exhorted the Saints to obey the Word of Wisdom, but they did not see fit to require obedience.[6] However, in 1880 under John Taylor's presidency, President George Q. Cannon presented to the Church membership a new edition of the Pearl of Great Price and the Doctrine and Covenants and declared: "It has been deemed wise to submit these books with their contents to the conference, to see whether the conference will vote to accept the books and their contents as from God, and binding upon us as a people and as a Church." President Joseph F. Smith seconded the motion, and the conference sustained the proposition by unanimous vote.[7] Here the Saints acknowledged to the Lord their desire to have his "order and will" become commandment. The Prophet Joseph remarked, "When God offers a blessing or knowledge to a man, and he refuses it, he will be damned."[8]

In 1913 President Joseph F. Smith, reviewing the Church's gradual compliance with the Word of Wisdom, wrote: "The reason undoubtedly why the Word of Wisdom was given—as not by 'commandment or restraint' [sic] was that at that time, at least, if it had been given as a commandment, it would have brought every man addicted to the use of these noxious things under condemnation; so the Lord was merciful and gave them a chance to overcome, before he brought them under the law."[9] When the Lord's timetable was fulfilled, it was Heber J. Grant who made this law once and for all binding on the Saints.[10]

Verses 2 and 4 indicate that the revelation is specifically for the Saints of the "last days." Because of advanced techniques in water purification, refrigeration, and food preservation, members of the Church today may live in the only time when a sufficient number of Saints could apply the Word of Wisdom. This law functions very much today as the dietary portions of the Law of Moses did for Old Testament Israel. Thus, in other dispensations, too, the Lord required special dietary observances of the Saints, not only to raise their quality of living, but perhaps also to attract their contemporaries' attention by setting the Saints apart—a valuable function of the Word of Wisdom in our day. In any event, we see that the Lord works sensitively and patiently with his children, not requiring of them what they cannot yet give, nor wishing to lay a "greater burden" on them than necessary (Acts 15:28). In doing so he encourages and prepares them to step up to ever higher laws and development. The Lord does not change, but man's conditions, capacities, and needs do.

## Interpreting the Word of Wisdom

In interpreting section 89, the Latter-day Saint faces the challenge of harmonizing the scriptures, the emphasis of Church leaders, and the Lord's confirmation of personal initiative (D&C 58:26-29). It is helpful to remember that the Church seeks to bring as many souls as possible into God's kingdom and to help each member bear his responsibility in preparing for the Second Coming of the Savior. When these Church goals become individual goals, Latter-day Saints will understand better what the Lord expects of them. Individual compliance with gospel truths has vital implications for the Church's success. The problems caused by one who cannot exercise enough faith to embrace the Word of Wisdom wholly, or who is rebellious, are obvious. But another more subtle problem exists in the Church member who feels that by doing more than the Lord has commanded, he can attain to greater spirituality. Small factions within the Church set up their own standards for worthiness, and in their anxiety to live the highest laws possible, they impede the Lord's work. "Looking beyond the mark," they suffer increasing spiritual blindness (Jacob 4:14); inventing new laws, they cause divisions in the Church at the very time that the Saints are striving to become one for the Savior's appearance.

Elder Mark E. Petersen warned against the "few teachers, who sow seeds of doubt by speculative and unsound doctrines."[11] He reminded the Latter-day Saints of the source of new doctrines: "There is only one man in all the world who has the right to introduce a new doctrine to this Church, and that man is the President of the Church. So, teachers, until you become the President of the Church, will you be willing to content yourselves with the officially accepted doctrines of the Church?"[12]

Elder Bruce R. McConkie warned:

> It is . . . my experience that people who ride gospel hobbies, who try to qualify themselves as experts in some specialized field, who try to make the whole plan of salvation revolve around some field of particular interest to them—it is my experience that such persons are usually spiritually immature and spiritually unstable. This includes those who devote themselves—as though by divine appointment—to setting forth the signs of the times; or, to expounding about the Second Coming; or, to a faddist interpretation of the Word of Wisdom; or, to a twisted emphasis on temple work or any other doctrine or practice. The Jews of Jesus' day made themselves hobbyists and extremists in the field of Sabbath observance, and it colored and blackened their whole way of worship. We would do well

> to have a sane, rounded, and balanced approach to the whole gospel and all of its doctrines.[13]

To those looking for secret knowledge not available to all Latter-day Saints, he wrote:

> All of the doctrines and practices of the Church are taught publicly. There are no secret doctrines, no private practices, no course of conduct approved for a few only. The blessings of the gospel are for all men. Do not be deceived into believing that the General Authorities believe any secret doctrines or have any private ways of living. Everything that is taught and practiced in the Church is open to public inspection, or at least, where temple ordinances are concerned, to the inspection and knowledge of everyone who qualifies himself by personal righteousness to enter the house of the Lord.[14]

Here Elder McConkie gave a critical key to discovering the right path: "The proper course for all of us is to stay in the mainstream of the Church. This is the Lord's Church, and it is led by the spirit of inspiration, and the practice of the Church constitutes the interpretation of the scripture."[15]

## The Practice of the Church

The proscriptions then are clear, as also are those things which the Lord has designated as wholesome food, such as herbs (a term which in Joseph Smith's day included plants and vegetables),[16] grains, every fruit in season, meat of beasts and fowls, and fish. Some questions remain, but Church practice, plus a spirit of reverence for the human body as a divine dwelling, keep faithful Saints on course. This spirit compels one to avoid any harmful substance or action and encourages him to embrace every good principle of physical and spiritual health—to be fit for the Lord.

Latter-day Saints are free to compose their own diets within the Lord's parameters, but not to impose their preferences and opinions on others. Elder Petersen wrote: "I do not believe we should try to establish our personal fads as Church doctrine. I do not believe my eternal salvation will be affected in any way if I eat white bread or white sugar. I do not believe the doctrines of the Church are in any way involved in whether my whole wheat is stoneground or steel-cut."[17]

No one has a guarantee of perfect health on this planet, but obedience to this principle promotes better health and endurance than one could have otherwise. As the Lord stated:

> And all saints who remember to keep and do these sayings, walking in obedience to the commandments, shall receive health in their navel and marrow to their bones; and shall find wisdom and great treasures of knowledge, even hidden treasures; and shall run and not be weary, and shall walk and not faint. And I, the Lord, give unto them a promise, that the destroying angel shall pass by them, as the children of Israel, and not slay them (D&C 89:18-21).

One of the "hidden treasures" may be the realization that the most potent force for health is the power of the Holy Ghost.

Perhaps these treasures are "hidden" because they are communicated not from man to man, but from God to man; only those who have paid the price to receive his revelations will ever know what these treasures are. President Heber J. Grant observed: "No man who breaks the Word of Wisdom can gain the same amount of knowledge and intelligence in this world as the man who obeys that law. I don't care who he is or where he comes from, his mind will not be as clear, and he cannot advance as far and as rapidly and retain his power as much as he would if he obeyed the Word of Wisdom."[18]

The Lord promises to obedient Saints protection from "the destroying angel" (v. 21). If Moses was a prototype of the Savior as he led Israel out of spiritual bondage, the "destroying angel" may well represent spiritual death. Obedience to the Word of Wisdom then is integral to spiritual life.

---

## Notes

[1]Milton V. Backman, Jr., *The Heavens Resound: A History of the Latter-day Saints in Ohio 1830-1838* (Salt Lake City: Deseret Book Co., 1983), p. 234.

[2]*JD* 12:158; Lyndon W. Cook, *The Revelations of the Prophet Joseph Smith* (Provo, Ut.: Seventy's Mission Bookstore, 1981), pp. 191-92.

[3]Backman, *The Heavens Resound*, p. 294.

[4]Roy W. Doxey, *The Word of Wisdom Today* (Salt Lake City: Deseret Book Co., 1975), p. 2.

[5]Backman, *The Heavens Resound*, p. 257.

[6]*Ibid.*, p. 260.

[7]*Journal History*, 10 October 1880.

[8]*TPJS*, p. 322.

[9]*Conference Report*, October 1913, p. 14.

[10]Doxey, *The Word of Wisdom Today*, p. 128.

[11]Mark E. Petersen, *Improvement Era*, June 1953, p. 423.

[12]*Ibid.*, p. 424.

[13]"To Honest Truth Seekers," 1 July 1980, pp. 4-5. (Letter from his office.)

[14]*Ibid.*, pp. 6-7.

[15]"Our Relationship with the Lord," *Brigham Young University 1981-82 Fireside and Devotional Speeches* (Provo, Ut.: Brigham Young University Publications, 1982), p. 103. (Speech delivered at Brigham Young University on 2 March 1982.)

[16]John A. Widstoe and Leah D. Widstoe, *The Word of Wisdom: A Modern Interpretation*, revised ed. (Salt Lake City: Deseret Book Co., 1950), p. 120.

[17]Petersen, *Improvement Era*, p. 424.

[18]*Conference Report*, April 1925, p. 10.

# 33

# THE ORIGIN AND DESTINY OF MAN

## (D&C 93)

LaMar E. Garrard

What is man? Where did he come from? Why is he here on earth? Where is he going? These basic but simple questions have been asked for centuries by philosophers, theologians, and even the common man. How important these questions—and their answers—are to the Latter-day Saints was emphasized by Joseph Smith when he said:

> All men know that they must die. And it is important that we should understand the reasons and causes of our exposure to the vicissitudes of life and death, and the designs and purposes of God in our coming into the world, our sufferings here, and our departure hence. What is the object of our coming into existence,then dying and falling away, to be here no more? It is but reasonable to suppose that God would reveal something in reference to the matter, and it is a subject we ought to study more than any other. We ought to study it day and night, for the world is ignorant in reference to their true condition and relation. If we have any claim on our Heavenly Father for anything, it is for knowledge on this important subject.[1]

### In The Beginning With The Father

One of the great revelations which teach us about the origin and destiny of man is section 93 of the Doctrine and Covenants. By studying this section along with other scriptures and the teachings of Joseph Smith related to this subject, we can follow the admonition of Joseph Smith and consequently gain an understanding of the origin and destiny of man.

This great revelation teaches us about ourselves by first teaching us about Christ and then showing us what our relationship is to him. It states that Christ was "in the beginning with the Father" and was "the Firstborn" (D&C 93:21). This statement could not refer to Christ's birth here upon this earth wherein he took upon himself a body of flesh and blood, since in this case he was the *Only Begotten* of the Father. Rather, it would have to refer to his "beginning" in a premortal state as the firstborn child among a family of spirit children of God the Father. That all men were part of this family of spirit children becomes apparent, for the revelation further states that "ye were also in the beginning with the Father; that which is Spirit, even the Spirit of truth" (D&C 93:23); another verse adds that "man was also in the beginning with God" (D&C 93:29). No doubt this "beginning" refers to our spirit birth, since we are further told that the inhabitants of the world are "begotten sons and daughters unto God" (see D&C 76:24).[2] Furthermore, in his writings Joseph Smith referred to God as the "Father of our spirits,"[3] "our Great Parent,"[4] and "our Father."[5] Modern revelation agrees consistently with references made by Paul in the New Testament on this subject wherein he states: we are "the offspring of God" (Acts 17:28, 29), God the Father is "the Father of spirits" (Heb. 12:9), Christ is "the firstborn of every creature" (Col. 1:15; see also Rev. 3:14), and men are referred to as Christ's "brethren" (see Heb. 2:11-12, 17).

Just what a premortal spirit looks like is revealed to us by an incident wherein a Jaredite prophet (the brother of Jared) was allowed to view the premortal spirit of Christ and was surprised to find out that his (Christ's) spirit resembled a body of flesh and blood (Ether 3:6-20). In fact, the brother of Jared assumed he was looking at a fleshy body until he was corrected by the Savior, who told him that he was not looking at his physical body but rather at his spirit, since he (Christ) had not yet been born upon the earth.

> Seest thou that ye are created after mine own image? Yea, even *all men were created in the beginning* after mine own image.
>
> Behold, this body, which ye now behold, is the body of my spirit; and *man have I created* after the body of my spirit; and even as I appear unto thee to be in the spirit will I appear unto my people in the flesh (Ether 3:15-16, italics added).

In this scripture, the Lord refers to two creations of man: in the second verse it is the *physical* creation of Adam (man), but in the first verse it is the *spirit* creation of all men *in the beginning.*[6] This reference to spirit birth as a "creation" is consistent with a scripture which states that God "*created* all the children of men" before man was upon the earth to till the ground, "for in heaven *created* I them" (Moses 3:5, italics added). The Lord further stated that he "*made* the world, and men before they were in the flesh" (Moses 6:51, italics added). These modern revelations indicate, then, that the "beginning" of man occurred in premortality—in heaven—where we were all "begotten" as spirits, or in other words "created" or "made" in the image of our immortal, resurrected, and exalted parents.[7]

God *designed* or *planned* that the spirit body and physical body of man be made in his image,[8] and it is through his great *creative powers* that we were born or created as spirits as well as mortal beings. Our indebtedness to God for our spirits and mortal bodies was emphasized by King Benjamin when he said:

> O how you ought to thank your heavenly King.
>
> I say unto you, my brethren, that if you should render all the thanks and praise which your whole soul has power to possess, to that God who has *created* you, and has kept and preserved you . . .
>
> I say unto you that if ye should serve him who has *created* you *from the beginning*, and is preserving you from day to day, by lending you breath, that ye may live and move and do according to your own will, and even supporting you from one moment to another—I say, if ye should serve him with all your whole souls yet ye would be unprofitable servants (Mosiah 2:19-21, italics added).

Some have proposed that Joseph Smith taught that the spirit of man was not created but rather has always self-existed. This misunderstanding seems to have arisen as a result of the various meanings associated with the word "create."

In the days of Joseph Smith many theologians believed God created the earth *ex nihilo*, or out of nothing. Joseph Smith refuted that belief and said that the word "create" means to "organize," and that the world was organized by God out of existing element or physical matter which was eternal. Even though the earth had a "beginning" when it was organized, it is still eternal or uncreated in the sense that the elements from which it was organized are eternal and uncreated.

> Now, the word create came from the word *baurau* which does not mean to create out of nothing; it means to organize; the same as a man would organize materials and build a ship. Hence, we infer that God had materials to organize the world out of

> chaos—chaotic matter, which is element, and in which dwells all the glory. Element had an existence from the time he had. The pure principles of element are principles which can never be destroyed; they may be organized and re-organized, but not destroyed. They *had no beginning,* and can *have no end.*[9]

The Doctrine and Covenants teaches that after the earth was created or organized it later fell to a telestial state. In the future it will be changed to a terrestrial state, then die and be resurrected to a celestial state where it will continue throughout eternity as an eternal or immortal home for the righteous.[10]

Similarly, the physical or mortal body of man has "beginning" when it is created or organized in the mother's womb. However, the physical body is also eternal or uncreated in the sense that the elements from which it was organized are eternal and uncreated. Even though the body will undergo a change (reorganization of the elements) at death and again in the resurrection, afterwards it will still continue to exist throughout eternity as an eternal and immortal body (D&C 93:33; cf. Alma 11:45).

In like manner, the spirit of man had a beginning when it was created (begotten) or organized in heaven. Like the earth and our physical bodies, it is also "eternal" with "no beginning" and "no end" in the sense of being organized from "eternal" spirit matter which had "no beginning" and can have "no end.'[11] Evidently Joseph Smith was merely refuting the idea that the spirit was created out of nothing when he said that "the spirit of man is not a created being; it existed from eternity, and will exist to eternity. Anything created cannot be eternal; and earth, water, etc., had their existence in an elementary state, from eternity."[12]

Joseph Smith further explained that this spirit was not immaterial, as some had advocated in his day, but rather was organized from a substance or matter which was quite different from physical matter.

> In tracing the thing to the foundation, and looking at it philosophically, we shall find a very material difference between the body and the spirit; the body is supposed to be organized matter, and the spirit, by many, is thought to be immaterial, without substance. With this latter statement we should beg leave to differ, and state the spirit is a substance; that it is

> material, but that it is more pure, elastic and refined matter than the body; that it existed before the body, can exist in the body; and will exist separate from the body, when the body will be mouldering in the dust; and will in the resurrection, be again united with it.[13]

## Grace for Grace

So we see that section 93 teaches us that mortal man is a dual being composed of a spirit (an offspring of God) which is clothed in a physical body composed of eternal elements. God's great design or plan is to make men happy; as Joseph Smith said, "Happiness is the object and design of our existence."[14] Evidently, gaining a spirit body gives a person a certain amount of happiness (see Job 38:4-7); and gaining a physical body or tabernacle to house that spirit brings still more happiness, for "the great principle of happiness consists in having a body."[15] Man is restricted in his happiness without a physical body,[16] and can only receive a fulness of happiness or joy after the resurrection when the spirit and the physical body are inseparably connected.

> For man is spirit. The elements are eternal, and spirit and element, inseparably connected, receive a fulness of joy;
>
> And when separated, man cannot receive a fulness of joy.
>
> The elements are the tabernacle of God; yea, man is the tabernacle of God, even temples; and whatsoever temple is defiled, God shall destroy that temple (D&C 93:33-35).

Gaining an immortal body in the resurrection is necessary but not sufficient to gain a fulness of joy. Evidently, to gain a fulness of light and truth is the other necessary requirement for gaining a fulness of joy. John tells us that when Christ came on earth to dwell in the flesh, he did not have a fulness of light and truth.[17] He received, however, additional light and truth as he continually obeyed his Father, even though he was subjected to severe opposition in terms of trials and temptations.[18]

> And I, John, bear record that I beheld . . . the Only Begotten of the Father . . . which came and dwelt in the flesh, and dwelt among us.
>
> And I, John, saw that he received not of the fulness at the

> first, but received grace for grace;
>
> And he received not of the fulness at first, but continued from grace to grace, until he received a fulness;
>
> And thus he was called the Son of God, because he received not of the fulness at the first (D&C 93:11-14).

John tells us further that after Christ's resurrection when he received all power in heaven and earth, he also received a fulness of the glory of the Father, which is a fulness of light and truth:[19] "And I, John, bear record that he received a fulness of the glory of the Father; And he received all power, both in heaven and on earth, and the glory of the Father was with him, for he dwelt in him" (D&C 93:16-17; cf. Matt. 28:18).

At that time, as a glorified, perfected, immortal being, Christ experienced a fulness of joy.[20] Not only did Christ receive a fulness of joy, but section 93 reveals to us that men can also attain this great goal if they obey his commandments as he obeyed his Father, while suffering severe trials and temptations.[21]

> The Spirit of truth is of God. I am the Spirit of truth, and John bore record of me, saying: He received a fulness of truth, yea, even of all truth;
>
> And no man receiveth a fulness unless he keepeth his commandments.
>
> He that keepeth his commandments receiveth truth and light, until he is glorified in truth and knoweth all things (D&C 93:26-28).

How is it possible that men can achieve a fulness of light and truth and consequently a fulness of joy? Again, section 93 reminds us that in premortality we sprang from the same source as did Christ. We are also a Spirit of truth or spirit child of God the Father as was Christ: "And now, verily I say unto you, I was in the beginning with the Father, and am the Firstborn. . . . Ye were also in the beginning with the Father; that which is Spirit, even the Spirit of truth" (D&C 93:21, 23).

Once organized or "created," the premortal spirit of man or "Spirit of truth" seems to have inherited from its eternal parents the ability to receive light and truth sent to it by God. The word of God "is truth, and whatsoever is truth is light" (D&C 84:45), and when the spirit of man hearkens to and obeys God by accepting this light and truth, he is enlightened and receives more light.[22] When the spirit of man refuses to accept this light and truth, or in other words disobeys God, he not only loses the light he could have received but may also lose the light already accumulated from prior obedience.[23] That the spirit of man may not have had the ability to be enlightened prior to its organization seems to be implied in the following statement made by Joseph Smith: "We consider that God has created man with a mind capable of instruction, and a faculty which may be enlarged in proportion to the heed and diligence given to the light communicated from heaven to the intellect; and that the nearer man approaches perfection, the clearer are his views, and the greater his enjoyments."[24]

Also, section 93 states that after its "beginning" or organization, the spirit was "innocent" (D&C 93:38). This is no doubt because prior to its organization it had the potential but not the ability to receive light from God. Hence, when there is "no law" given, there is "no sin" (2 Ne. 2:13; Alma 42:17-20).

Modern revelation seems to indicate that two things make it possible for the spirit of man to have the ability to receive or reject light and truth from God: first, the innate, uncreated, and eternal nature of spirit matter itself called "intelligence"; second, the creative and organizing power of God. If God were totally responsible for creating the spirit itself (i.e., responsible for bringing it into existence), then he would be responsible for the basic nature of the spirit, whether it prefers to obey or disobey him. Then it would seem unreasonable and unjust for God to condemn the spirit for disobeying him when he was responsible for the spirit's basic preferences.

Section 93 seems to indicate that the intelligence of spirits (referred to in the parenthetical phrase as "uncreated") is such that after its beginning with the Father (where it was organized or "created" by the power of God and became a "Spirit of truth," or "truth") where it was placed in the proper sphere and *given* agency by God,[25] it could *then* act independently and therefore be accountable for the choices it makes.

> Man was also in the beginning with God. Intelligence, or the light of truth, was not created or made, neither indeed can be.
>
> All *truth* is independent in that sphere in which God has placed it, to act for itself, as all intelligence also; otherwise there is no existence.

> Behold, here is the agency of man, and here is the condemnation of man; because that which was from the beginning is plainly manifest unto them, and they receive not the light.
>
> And every man whose spirit receiveth not the light is under condemnation.
>
> For man is spirit (D&C 93:29-33, italics added).

As the newly-organized spirit of man obeys the laws of God, it gains more light and truth, or knowledge, and advances toward Godhood.[26]

> The first principles of man are self-existent with God. God himself, finding he was in the midst of spirits and glory, because he was more intelligent, saw proper to institute laws whereby the rest could have the privilege to advance like himself. The relationship we have with God places us in a situation to advance in knowledge. He has the power to institute laws to instruct the weaker intelligences, that they may be exalted with himself, so that they might have one glory upon another, and all that knowledge, power, glory, and intelligence, which is requisite in order to save them in the world of spirits.[27]

As mentioned previously, God organized man with one object in mind: to make men happy. In his infinite wisdom and knowledge he knows which pathway is best for us to follow to make us happy. As we obey his commandments or laws (light and truth) he reveals additional commandments which if obeyed, will bring us closer to a fulness of light and truth.[28]

> Happiness is the object and design of our existence; and will be the end thereof, if we pursue the path that leads to it; and this path is virtue, uprightness, faithfulness, holiness, and keeping all the commandments of God. But we cannot keep all the commandments without first knowing them, and we cannot expect to know all, or more than we now know unless we comply with or keep those we have already received. . . .
>
> In obedience there is joy and peace unspotted, unalloyed; and as God has designed our happiness—and the happiness of all His creatures, he never has—He never will institute an ordinance or give a commandment to His people that is not

> calculated in its nature to promote that happiness which He has designed, and which will not end in the greatest amount of good and glory to those who become the recipients of his law and ordinances.[29]

Section 93 reveals to us that "the glory of God is intelligence, or, in other words, light and truth" (D&C 93:36). This indicates that "intelligence" has reference not only to the basic uncreated nature of the spirit, but also to how much light and truth a spirit has accumulated because of its obedience up to that point. John was allowed to see the glory or "intelligence" attained by Christ before this world was organized (D&C 93:7; cf. John 17:5). In another vision Abraham was allowed to see the glory or "intelligence" attained by Christ as well as other premortal spirits at a time when a council was being held to plan the creation of this earth. Just as stars differ from each other in brightness, he saw that some spirits had more glory or were more "intelligent" than others because of their obedience; Christ had gained so much light and truth that he was more intelligent than they all. In fact, Christ had become so intelligent by his obedience that his wisdom excelled above them all, and God chose him to be the Lord God of this earth to rule over all the other spirits or "organized intelligences" (see Abr. 3:19-22). Having gained so much light and truth in premortality, Christ became a source of light and truth (the fountain of all righteousness) for his spirit brothers and sisters.[30] As we listened to him, obeyed him, and became acquainted with his voice, we advanced also in light and truth.[31] Some of the more obedient or noble spirits were chosen to be rulers in mortality (see Abr. 3:22-23; cf. Jer. 1:5). Evidently, the intelligence or amount of light and truth we acquired in premortality affects our tendency to accept light and truth in mortality.[32] Even though we have a fallen mortal body subject to the power or temptations of Satan in this life,[33] to house our spirits (D&C 93:35; cf. 1 Cor. 3:16-17), our spirit (a child of God) can still choose to receive light and truth[34] and obey God. As the spirit accumulates more light and truth it gains the spiritual power to resist and overcome the temptations and trials associated with the fallen body and environment,[35] which are all a part of this fallen mortal world.[36] In other words, as we obey Christ's voice, which comes to us through his Spirit, the redemptive power of the atonement makes it possible for us to overcome the spiritual death which resulted from the fall of man.[37] That is, we are led to the gospel of Jesus Christ (D&C 84:43-48), and if we are obedient and accept it, we will receive the Holy Ghost, and through the redemptive power of Christ we can continue to feast upon the words of Christ and receive additional light and truth.[38] This process of obeying, receiving light and truth, then further obeying that which was revealed to us (going from grace to grace) will continue until sometime after the resurrection when we will receive a fulness of light and truth, becoming like Christ himself, possessing a fulness of the glory of the Father.[39]

> And I, John, bear record that he received a fulness of the glory of the Father;
>
> And he received all power, both in heaven and on earth, and the glory of the Father was with him, for he dwelt in him. . . .
>
> I give unto you these sayings that you may understand and know how to worship, and know what you worship, that you may come unto the Father in my name, and in due time receive of his fulness.
>
> For if you keep my commandments you shall receive of his fulness, and be glorified in me as I am in the Father; therefore, I say unto you, you shall receive grace for grace. . . .
>
> He that keepeth his commandments receiveth truth and light, until he is glorified in truth and knoweth all things (D&C 93:16-17, 19-20, 28).

Worship consists largely in the imitation of the Master.[40] Hence, by knowing what Christ was, what he is now and how he obtained his present position, we can worship God, follow Christ's example, and eventually become a joint heir with him to share eternal life and a fulness of light and truth forever.[41]

---

## Notes

[1] *TPJS*, p. 324.

[2] That this is referring to literal spirit birth and *not* spiritual rebirth is evidenced by the fact that the inhabitants of the world do not all eventually go

through this spiritual rebirth. Also, in many passages of the Doctrine and Covenants, God is referred to as "our" Father as well as the Father of spirits. See D&C 84:83, 92; 88:75; 89:5; 123:6.

[3]*TPJS*, p. 48.

[4]*Ibid.*, p. 55.

[5]*Ibid.*, pp. 56, 353.

[6]Since both creations were made in the image of God, the spirit of man and his physical body should be in the likeness of each other. This agrees with the revelation which states that the "spirit of man" is "in the likeness of his person" (D&C 77:2).

[7]The scriptures state and Joseph Smith taught that exalted persons are capable of having seed eternally (see D&C 131:4; 132:19-20; *TPJS*, pp. 300-1).

[8]See Ether 3:15-16; Moses 2:26-27; Abr. 4:26-27; D&C 77:2.

[9]*TPJS*, pp. 350-52, italics added. Note how the phrases "have no beginning" and "have no end" are similarly used in Abraham 3:18.

[10]D&C 29:22-24; 101:23-25; 88:19-20, 25-26; cf. Rev. 21:1-5.

[11]See D&C 93:29, where the parenthetical phrase "Intelligence, or the light of truth, was not created or made, neither indeed can be," was probably inserted to remind us that the elementary spirit matter or "intelligence" is eternal and uncreated even though the spirit itself had a beginning with God in heaven.

Abr. 3:18 is sometimes used to support the view that the spirits of men never had a beginning and are self-existent. This passage refers to the spirits of men as having "no beginning; they existed before, they shall have no end, they shall exist after, for they are gnolaum, or eternal." Verse 22 in this same context, however, speaks of these spirits as "organized intelligences." Evidently, it is the spirit matter or intelligence that has "no beginning," and can have "no end" for the spirit body or "organized intelligence" definitely had a beginning when it was organized or begotten in heaven. Elder Bruce R. McConkie emphasized this when he said: "Abraham used the name *intelligences* to apply to the spirit children of the Eternal Father. The intelligence or spirit element became intelligences after the spirits were born as individual entities" (*Mormon Doctrine*, 2nd ed. [Salt Lake City: Bookcraft, 1966], p. 387).

Besides Abraham 3:18, statements by Joseph Smith have also been used to propose the idea that spirits are self-existent and were never created (see *TPJS*, pp. 352-54). However, these statements must be taken in context with other statements by Joseph Smith, such as those where he states that it is the "intelligence of spirit" that had no beginning or end and "the mind or intelligence which man possesses is co-equal with God" (*TPJS*, p. 353).

[12]*TPJS*, p. 158.

[13]*Ibid.*, p. 207; cf. D&C 131:7-8.

[14]*Ibid.*, p. 255.

[15]*Ibid.*, p. 181.

[16]*Ibid.*, p. 181; D&C 45:17, 46; cf. Abr. 3:26; Moses 1:39.

[17]The John bearing his testimony here is John the Baptist. See Bruce R. McConkie, *Doctrinal New Testament Commentary*, 3 vols. (Salt Lake City: Bookcraft, 1965), 1:70-71; Sidney B. Sperry, *Doctrine and Covenants Compendium* (Salt Lake City: Bookcraft, 1960), pp. 472-73.

[18]Mosiah 3:7-11; 15:1-9; Heb. 2:9-11, 14-18; 4:14-16; 5:7-9.

[19]"The glory of God is intelligence, or in other words, light and truth" (D&C 93:36). See also D&C 93:6, 26.

[20]After his resurrection when he was perfected (Matt. 5:48; cf. 3 Ne. 12:48), the Savior appeared to his Nephite Twelve and told them that his Father had given him a fulness of joy (3 Ne. 28:10; cf. 3 Ne. 17:20). Christ endured much suffering, temptations, and shame, including death on the cross, "for the joy that was set before him" (Heb. 12:2; cf. 1 Pet. 1:11).

[21]While ministering to the Nephites as a perfected being, Christ promised his Nephite Twelve a future fulness of joy in the kingdom of his Father (3 Ne. 28:10). Man is that he might have joy (2 Ne. 2:25), but that fulness of joy is not to be found in this world (D&C 101:35-38), for we sometimes have to suffer as Christ did (Rom. 8:16-18; 1 Pet. 1:6-7; 2:20-25; 3:17-20; 4:1, 12-18; 5:8-11; Rev. 7:14; D&C 58:1-5; 98:3, 12-15; 101:35-38; 121:7-10; 122:7-9; 123:12-17; 136:30-31; 138:12-14). Eventually, however, we will receive eternal joy for our suffering (D&C 109:76). Those who resist temptation, and endure trials and sufferings while remaining faithful stewards, shall eventually inherit eternal life and "shall enter into the joy of the Lord" (D&C 51:19). Joseph Smith summarized this by saying that "those who have died in Jesus Christ may expect to enter into all the fruitions of joy when they come forth, which they possessed or anticipated here" (*TPJS*, p. 295).

[22]D&C 50:24, 34-35, 40-44; 63:23; 84:43-48; 88:11-13, 66-67; 2 Ne. 31:18-32:5; Alma 12:9-10; 32:27-37, 41-43; *TPJS*, pp. 297-98, 305.

[23]D&C 1:33; 93:39; Alma 12:10-11, 13; 32:38-40; *TPJS*, p. 217. Cf. D&C 10:21; 29:44-45; 45:28-29; 50:25; 57:10; 82:2-4; 84:49-53; 93:39-40; 95:6, 12; John 3:16-21.

[24]*TPJS*, p. 51.

[25]The scriptures indicate that agency comes to us as a gift from God (Moses 4:3-4; D&C 29:36-39; 101:78; 2 Ne. 2:16. Because of *God's power*, men can choose which way to act according to their own desires (Alma 29:4-5), but they will be held accountable for that choice (Alma 3:26-27; cf. *TPJS*, p. 187. In

mortality, there would have been no agency if there had been no atonement provided (2 Ne. 9:5-9; cf. 2 Ne. 2:26-27; 10:23-24; Mosiah 2:21).

[26]There are some who have proposed that we existed as individual entities capable of thinking and *acting* before our spirit birth. However, the scriptures do not seem to warrant such an assumption; the creative and organizing power of God was necessary in order to produce the spirit which could act for itself and be responsible for those actions. Even after spirit birth, the power of God is necessary for us to have free agency and continue to act and be acted upon. See 2 Ne. 2:13-14; Mosiah 2:19-21, 23-25.

[27]*TPJS*, p. 354.

[28]D&C 50:24, 40-44; 63:23; 88:66-67; 2 Ne. 31:20; Alma 12:10; 32:41; John 4:14; *TPJS*, pp. 51, 297-98, 346-48.

[29]*TPJS*, pp. 255-57. C.S. Lewis has said much the same thing: "God made us: invented us as a man invents an engine. A car is made to run on petrol, and it won't run properly on anything else. Now God designed the human machine to run on Himself. He Himself is the fuel our spirits were designed to burn, or the food our spirits were designed to feed on, there isn't any other. That's why it's just no good asking God to make us happy in our own way without bothering about religion. God can't give us a happiness and peace apart from Himself, because it isn't there. There's no such thing" (*The Case for Christianity* [New York City: MacMillan, 1948], p. 43).

[30]Ether 8:26; 12:28. Abinadi refers to Christ as "the light and life of the world; yea, a light that is endless, that can never be darkened" (Mosiah 16:9; see also D&C 6:21; 11:10-14, 28; 3 Ne. 18:16, 24).

[31]In the Joseph Smith Translation, John tells us (John 1:1) that in the beginning before the world was, the gospel was preached through the Son who had become God. See Bruce R. McConkie, *Doctrinal New Testament Commentary*, 1:70-71.

[32]Those who listened to Christ's voice in premortality tend to listen to it in mortality. See John 10:14, 27-29; cf. D&C 84:52; 50:40-44. See also Joseph F. Smith, *Gospel Doctrine* (Salt Lake City: Deseret Book Co., 1971), pp. 12-14.

[33]D&C 29:39-40; 2 Ne. 2:29; 4:17-19, 27; 10:24; 3 Ne. 28:37-39; Rom. 8:1-13; Gal. 5:16-18.

[34]*TPJS*, p. 355; 2 Ne. 2:26-29; 10:23-24; Alma 3:26-27.

[35]Joseph Smith explained that if we listened to God's voice and obeyed, Satan would have no power over us (*TPJS*, pp. 181, 187; cf. Moses 4:4).

[36]Even though we inherit fallen bodies (Ether 3:2) and are born into a wicked world where we are subject to good and evil (Moses 6:55-56), *if we call upon God for help* and then *obey* his voice, he will give us the power to overcome all evil (D&C 50:24, 34-35; Rom. 8:12-14; *TPJS*, p. 51; Alma 13:28).

Christ was subject to all the temptations known to man (Heb. 2:16-18; 4:15; 5:8-9), but he never yielded to temptation because his spirit listened to the voice of the Father and hence ruled over his flesh so that the "will of the Son" was "swallowed up in the will of the Father" (Mosiah 15:1-7).

[37]D&C 29:40-44; Moses 5:9; 6:59-60, 64-65; cf. Mosiah 3:19; Ether 3:2.

[38]2 Ne. 31:17-32:5; cf. John 4:7-15; 6:32-35, 48-63; 7:37-39; 8:12.

[39]D&C 50:24, 34-35, 40-44; 88:66-67; *TPJS*, pp. 346-48, 354.

[40]2 Ne. 31:9-10, 12-13, 16-17; *TPJS*, pp. 347-48.

[41]Rom. 8:14-18; Gal. 4:4-7; D&C 35:2; 50:24, 40-43; 76:56-70; 84:38; 88:49-50, 66-67, 107; 93:20, 26-28; 132:19-21.

# 34
# COUNSEL TO THE EXILES
## (D&C 97-101)

ROBERT A. CLOWARD

In the revelations of the latter months of 1833 we find a most poignant portrayal of the relationship of the Lord to his people. In those times of their extreme need, the veils of formality and habit that too often separate God's people from him were parted. They cried out to him as humbled children. In the urgency of their need, they sought his hiding place. They searched their souls to purge out what might have offended him. They yearned for his response.

He heard their cries, and as an Exalted Father, he answered. This was a teaching moment, and if we are attuned to the Spirit that attends these revelations, we too can learn the lessons of Zion's redemption. As God counseled the exiles, he counsels us as well, for we share their quest. We too must establish Zion.

### Historical Background

The joy of the Saints at learning the revealed location of the land of Zion was all too soon tempered by their dismay at the difficulties which encumbered them. The Lord had designated Jackson County as the place for the city of Zion in July 1831 (D&C 57:1-2), but within two years, vicious mobs were organized to expel the Saints from the county. In addition to the threats from without, a spirit of variance and dissention pervaded much of the Church in Missouri. Writing in January 1833 on behalf of a council of high priests in Kirtland, Hyrum Smith and Orson Hyde said, "we feel more like weeping over Zion than we do like rejoicing over her."[1]

On 20 July 1833 a mob destroyed the printing establishment of William W. Phelps, and three days later Church leaders were forced to sign a pledge that they and the other members of the Church would leave Jackson County. Despite attempts at legal redress, severe persecution continued, and the majority of the Saints had been driven from their homes to take refuge in Clay, Ray, Van Buren, Lafayette, and other counties by November of that year. In sections 97, 98, 100, and 101, the Lord answered their questions and shared with them divine counsel.

## The Saints' Questions

It is not difficult to imagine the kinds of questions that filled the hearts of the Saints as they faced the reality of their exile. This was an Abrahamic test—a test of incongruence, designed to try the foundations of their conviction. Undoubtedly they asked even the most basic questions: "Art thou there?" "Hast thou heard our prayers?" "Hast thou rejected us?" And if they were still found acceptable to the Lord, the flood of questions would continue: "Why have we been forced out of the designated gathering place?" "Is this persecution necessary?" "Will Zion be redeemed?" "Is there to be a new gathering place?" "How can we recover our lands and homes?" "Can we depend upon the law?" "Should we seek revenge upon our persecutors?" "What about thy temple?"[2]

## The Lord's Answers

### Be Still

The Lord gave merciful answers. In one forceful phrase, he assured them of his concern for their plight: "Be still and know that I am God" (D&C 101:16). This command, the first person climax of Psalm 46, invoked the entire psalm, applicable in every way to their situation: "God is our refuge and strength, a very present help in trouble" (Ps. 46:1).[3]

### My People Must Be Tried in All Things

The opening verses of sections 97, 98, and 101 further defined the Saints' standing before the Lord. In section 101, for example, he assured them that they were not rejected, but he clarified his personal role in their affliction: "*I, the Lord,* have suffered the affliction to come upon them, wherewith they have been afflicted, in consequence of their transgressions; Yet I will own them, and they shall be mine in that day when I shall come to make up my jewels" (vv. 2-3, italics added). In an earlier revelation, the blessing of being among the chosen jewels of God was specified as belonging to those who did not incur his anger by failing to be faithful (D&C 60:2-4). It must have been reassuring to the exiles that despite their failings they were not rejected as his chosen people. The Lord made abundantly clear, however, why he had allowed them to be persecuted. They had polluted their inheritances with "jarrings, and contentions, and envyings, and strifes, and lustful and covetous desires among them. . . . They were slow to hearken unto the voice of the Lord their God. . . ." And, he added, "In the day of their peace they esteemed lightly my counsel" (D&C 101:6-8).

The Lord was careful to emphasize his approval of righteous individuals. He was pleased with the humble truth seekers and with the meek (D&C 97:1-2). He was "well pleased" with Parley P. Pratt, who with diligence and personal sacrifice had been directing a school of elders.[4] Those who were honest and contrite and willing to observe their covenants by sacrifice were accepted of the Lord (D&C 97:8). Nevertheless, the Missouri Saints as a whole were not a people worthy of Zion: "Behold, here is wisdom concerning the children of Zion, even many, but not all; they were found transgressors, therefore they must needs be chastened" (D&C 101:41).

## Zion Shall Be Redeemed

While Joseph Smith and Sidney Rigdon were on a mission in New York in October, 1833, their hearts were understandably turned to the troubles of the Saints in Zion. Was the center place to be lost to the mobs of the adversary? The Lord responded, "Zion shall be redeemed, although she is chastened for a little season" (D&C 100:13). It was perhaps to this comforting revelation that the Prophet referred in a letter addressed to the exiled Saints on 10 December 1833:

> I cannot learn from any communication by the Spirit to me, that Zion has forfeited her claim to a celestial crown, notwithstanding the Lord has caused her to be thus afflicted, except it may be some individuals, who have walked in disobedience, and forsaken the new covenant; all such will be made manifest by their works in due time. I have always expected that Zion would suffer some affliction, from what I could learn from the commandments which have been given. But I would remind you of a certain clause in one which says, that after *much* tribulation cometh the *blessing*. By this, and also others, and also one received of late, I know that Zion, in the

due time of the Lord, will be redeemed.[5]

Section 101, dated six days after this letter, answered another significant question. "Zion shall not be moved out of her place, notwithstanding her children are scattered. They that remain, and are pure in heart, shall return, and come to their inheritances, they and their children, with songs of everlasting joy, to build up the waste places of Zion. . . . And, behold, there is none other place appointed than that which I have appointed . . . for the work of the gathering of my saints—Until the day cometh when there is found no more room for them; and then I have other places which I will appoint unto them, and they shall be called stakes, for the curtains of the strength of Zion" (D&C 101:17-18, 20-21).

Jackson County, therefore, was the gathering place. Its redemption was assured. However, it was not the Lord's intention to make clear yet when and how this was to be accomplished. His instructions on the matter in section 101 were all preliminary. First, the Saints were to continue to "gather together, and stand in holy places" (v. 22; cf. v. 64, note the plural in both cases). Second, the gathering was to be "according to the parable of the wheat and the tares" (v. 65). That is, the time of the final separation of the righteous from the wicked had not yet come. Third, the gathering was not to be done with haste, but the Saints were to let all things be prepared before [them]" (v. 68). Fourth, all available land in Jackson County and the surrounding counties was to be purchased by the Saints, including those in the churches of the east, and honorable and wise men were to be appointed to make these purchases (vv. 70-75). Fifth, the Saints were to continue to importune for redress according to the laws and constitution of the people (vv. 76-77).

A sixth recourse was foreshadowed in the Lord's parable concerning Zion (vv. 43-62), i.e., that Zion could be redeemed by an army of warriors from among the Lord's servants.[6] For the time being, however, the Saints were to "renounce war and proclaim peace" (D&C 98:16). The Lord at this point retained for himself the responsibility for Zion's redemption, and he had sworn and decreed and given his promise with an immutable covenant that the Saints' prayers would be answered (D&C 98:2-3). Their responsibility, bitterly underscored by their trials, was to "forsake all evil and cleave unto all good" and to "live by every word which proceedeth forth out of the mouth of God" (D&C 98:11).

### Forgive Others, That Your Father May Forgive You

The Missouri exiles needed answers for their normal and human questions about whether or not to retaliate against their enemies. The Lord's answers included principles that could refine them into a celestial people. At one point, he bluntly taught them that if they and their families did not bear their smitings patiently, their impatience itself would render their smitings just (D&C 98:24)! The Lord's laws of retaliation, war, and revenge in section 98 were ultimately laws of mercy, peace, and reconciliation. While allowing for justice, they encouraged forebearance, kindness, and love.

In several revelations the exiles were taught that concern for their physical well-being was secondary and that death for the Lord's cause brought the promise of life eternal: "Be not afraid of your enemies, for I have decreed in my heart, saith the Lord, that I will prove you in all things, whether you will abide in my covenant, even unto death, that you may be found worthy. For if ye will not abide in my covenant ye are not worthy of me" (D&C 98:14-15; cf. 98:18 and 101:15, 35-38).

### The House of the Lord in Zion

The question of the building of the temple in Zion remained open at this point.[7] The Lord intended his people to be chastened, and leaving them to grieve the loss of the privilege of building a house in which all the pure in heart could see God (D&C 97:16) was chastening indeed. Parley P. Pratt wrote that the revelation given in section 97, which included the command to build the Lord's house "speedily," "was not complied with by the leaders and Church in Missouri, as a whole; notwithstanding many were humble and faithful. Therefore, the threatened judgment was poured out to the uttermost, as the history of the five following years will show."[8]

## Conditions of the Heart

During the Missouri persecutions the Lord made the conditions of the heart a major focus of his counsel to his children. He commanded them to be pure, humble, hopeful, and obedient. They had gone to Jackson County to establish Zion, but "this is Zion—THE PURE IN HEART" (D&C 97:21). The Saints were law-abiding citizens, contrary to the rumors circulated by the mobs,[9] but the Lord required more. In his words, "all among them who know their hearts are honest, and are broken, and their spirits contrite, and are willing to observe their covenants by sacrifice—yea, every sacrifice which I, the Lord, shall command—they are accepted of me" (D&C 97:8).

The Lord expressed his approval for those in Zion who were "truly humble and . . . seeking diligently to learn wisdom and to find truth" (D&C 97:1). Humility is a basic requirement for a proper relationship with the Lord. It is listed first among the requirements for baptism (D&C 20:37). It must accompany confession and repentance (D&C 20:6; 61:2). It is a key to receiving the blessings of prayer (D&C 112:10; 136:32), even to the rending of the veil (D&C 67:10). And humility is essential for those who would be gathered in the last days (D&C 29:1-2).

In the stark face of persecution, loss of property, and even the threat of death, the Lord counseled the Saints to have hope: "Fear not even unto death; for in this world your joy is not full, but in me your joy is full" (D&C 101:36). What godly perspective, compared to the reactions of the natural man! Neither anger nor self-pity were acceptable responses to the Lord's chastening. He was teaching his people to center their focus on him, not on their difficulties.

Zion can only be established among the obedient. So often has the Lord enjoined the principle of obedience in this dispensation that it may justifiably be called the central theme of his revelations and the first law of heaven: "And in nothing doth man offend God, or against none is his wrath kindled, save those who confess not his hand in all things, and obey not his commandments" (D&C 59:21). Obedience is the definition of a godly man. To be acceptable it must not be blind obedience, reluctant obedience, or forced obedience. Proper obedience is more than obeying. It is a condition of the heart. The Lord illustrated this in a commandment to Joseph Smith: "*Prepare thy heart* to receive and obey the instructions which I am about to give unto you" (D&C 132:3, italics added). Hearts unprepared to obey are not worthy before the Lord, and the lesson of proper obedience was crucial for this dispensation, in which Zion cannot fail. It was better that a few should suffer and perish than that a generation should defile the land of Zion by presuming to establish God's holy place in unworthiness.

## Learning About God

The universal worth of the Doctrine and Covenants flows from the breadth of the Lord's perspective. Nineteenth-century events brought revelations of principle that retain significance far beyond their time. In his revelations, the Lord seemed to urge his people to look past the concern of the moment and learn the bigger lesson. For example, when the concern of the moment was a confrontation with lawlessness and mobocracy, the Lord taught in section 98 the value of electing honest and wise men to public office (vv. 9-10), the need for upholding and befriending the constitutional law of the land (vv. 4-7), and the need not just to proclaim peace in Missouri, but to "seek diligently to turn the hearts of the children to their fathers, and the hearts of the fathers to the children; And again, the hearts of the Jews unto the prophets, and the prophets unto the Jews; lest I come and smite the whole earth with a curse, and all flesh be consumed before me" (vv. 16-17). The Second Coming was repeatedly stressed by the Lord as the time of ultimate vengeance on the lawless and of reward for those who had suffered persecution and endured in faith (D&C 97:13-17; 101:23-35).

When the concern of the moment was the building of a temple that would not appear during the lifetime of any of the nineteenth-century Saints, the Lord taught the importance of all such holy places. Temples, he said, are places of thanksgiving, of instruction for those called to the ministry, and places suited for perfecting the Saints in their understanding of theory, principle, and doctrine pertaining to the kingdom of God on the earth (D&C 97:13-14). Furthermore, temples are places where his glory rests, where his presence dwells, and where the pure in heart that come may see him (D&C 97:15-16). The principle of guarding temples against being defiled by unclean things, lest the Lord's presence withdraw (D&C 97:15-17), is so significant that in our day it is to be discussed in every temple recommend interview.

After detailing the reasons for which he had suffered affliction to come upon the Saints in Jackson County, the Lord added, "Verily I say unto you, notwithstanding their sins, my bowels are filled with compassion towards them. I will not utterly cast them off; and in the day of wrath I will remember mercy" (D&C 101:9). To learn this balance of justice and mercy, wrath and love, is to learn about God. He would later teach about "reproving betimes with sharpness, when moved upon by the Holy Ghost; and then showing forth afterwards an increase of love toward him whom thou hast reproved, lest he esteem thee to be his enemy" (D&C 121:43). God is love, but he did not condone partial commitment or intermittent covenant-keeping. He did not mitigate deserved punishment. He spewed the lukewarm Saints out of the center place of Zion. Then, he taught them the depths of his compassion.

We do well to reassess constantly our standing before the Lord. If we are presumptuously arrogant about our chosenness or our righteousness, we may find his reminder of our real status surprisingly stern. Should we not be grateful that, as Alma taught his wayward son Corianton, "there was a time granted unto man to repent, yea, a probationary time, a time to repent and serve God" (Alma 42:4)?

## To Those Who Return

In a much earlier dispensation, a people was rejected by the Lord as unworthy and unprepared to inherit a promised land. They were left to spend forty years in the wilderness. During that time they felt his wrath; they also experienced his love. They were exiles, yet the day came when he judged their children to be an acceptable generation, and through their prophet he gave them instructions to inherit the promised land.

In the due time of the Lord, a latter-day generation will be judged acceptable to establish the center place of Zion and build the temple there. They may well hear words from their prophet like those of Moses—counsel to those who return:

> All the commandments which I command thee this day shall ye observe to do, that ye may live, and multiply, and go in and possess the land which the Lord sware unto your fathers.
>
> And thou shalt remember all the way which the Lord thy God led thee these forty years in the wilderness, to humble thee, and to prove thee, to know what was in thine heart, whether thou wouldest keep his commandments, or no.

> And he humbled thee, and suffered thee to hunger, and fed thee with manna, which thou knewest not, neither did thy fathers know; that he might make thee know that man doth not live by bread only, but by every word that proceedeth out of the mouth of the Lord doth man live.
>
> Thy raiment waxed not old upon thee, neither did thy foot swell, these forty years.
>
> Thou shalt also consider in thine heart, that, as a man chasteneth his son, so the Lord thy God chasteneth thee.
>
> Therefore thou shalt keep the commandments of the Lord thy God, to walk in his ways, and to fear him.
>
> For the Lord thy God bringeth thee into a good land (Deut. 8:1-7).

## Notes

[1]*HC* 1:319.

[2]See Monte S. Nyman, "The Redemption of Zion," found herein.

[3]A reading of the whole psalm is instructive. The Savior similarly invoked an entire psalm with a phrase when he exclaimed on the cross, "My God, my God, why hast thou forsaken me?" See Matt. 27:46 and Ps. 22.

[4]See Parley P. Pratt, *Autobiography of Parley Parker Pratt* (Salt Lake City: Deseret Book Co., 1938), pp. 93-94.

[5]*HC* 1:453-54.

[6]See Richard D. Draper, "Maturing Toward the Millennium," found herein.

[7]The Lord did not resolve this issue for his Saints until five years later in connection with a revelation on the Nauvoo Temple. See D&C 124:45-55, and Robert A. Cloward, "Revelations in Nauvoo," found herein.

[8]*Autobiography*, p. 96.

[9]Alexander Majors, son of a Missouri mobster reported: "There is nothing in the county records to show that a Mormon was ever charged with any misdemeanor in the way of violation of the laws," Alexander Majors, *Seventy Years on the Frontier* (Chicago and New York: Rand, McNally, and Co., 1893), pp. 49-50, cited in Ivan J. Barrett, *Joseph Smith and the Restoration* (Provo, Ut.: Brigham Young University Press, 1973), p. 240.

# 35

# MATURING TOWARD THE MILLENNIUM

## (D&C 101, 103-106)

RICHARD D. DRAPER

### The Young and the Mature Church

The sections of the Doctrine and Covenants considered in this essay reveal two views of the latter-day Church. There is the 19th-century Church: small, weak, vulnerable, and immature. Then there is the future Church: very great, a sanctified body "fair as the sun, and clear as the moon, and . . . terrible unto all nations; [such] that the kingdoms of this world [are] constrained to acknowledge that the kingdom of Zion is in very deed the kingdom of our God and his Christ" (D&C 105:31-32).

At present, we are living in a Church of transition. It is no longer weak and vulnerable and yet it is not the glorious Church of the future. The task of the present is to bring into reality that future Church. Though this will be accomplished through missionary work, temple work, and service in wards and stakes, these are only means to an end. The most important factor and that to which all others move is the true conversion of the individual member of the Church. Only when enough hearts have given themselves to the Savior can the Church of the future become a reality. Until then we will remain a Church in transition.

### The Glory of Zion

One of the most important tasks of the present Church is to prepare the hearts of its people to dwell in the Millennium. The Church will do this by first preparing them "to receive the glory that [the Lord has] for them, even the glory of Zion" (D&C 136:31). Zion is a forerunner to the Millennium. Once the Church members can live the law of Zion they will be able to enjoy her glory and dwell on the sanctified earth, the world-wide expansion of Zion, during the thousand years of its Sabbath. This is because Zion will be built upon the principles of the law of the celestial kingdom. Therefore, the Lord can say of her: "There shall be mine abode, and it shall be Zion, which shall come forth out of all the creations which I have made" (Moses 7:64).

The reason Zion is the abode of God is because she is governed by the laws of the celestial kingdom (D&C 88:28, 29; 105:5). For this reason she endures forever: "And thou hast taken Zion to thine own bosom, from all thy creations, from all eternity to all eternity" (Moses 7:31). Joseph Smith stated:

> The building up of Zion is a cause that has interested the people of God in every age; it is a theme upon which prophets, priests and kings have dwelt with peculiar delight; they have looked forward with joyful anticipation to the day in which we live; and fired with heavenly and joyful anticipations they have sung and written and prophesied of this our day, . . . [which] God and angels have contemplated with delight for generations past; that fired the souls of the ancient patriarchs and prophets; a work that is destined to bring about the destruction of the powers of darkness, the renovation of the earth, the glory of God, and the salvation of the human family.[1]

## Zion is Lost

Joseph was one of those prophets whose souls were fired by the vision of Zion. Of this the Lord said in 1830: "Him have I inspired to move the cause of Zion in mighty power for good, and his diligence I know, and his prayers I have heard. Yea, his weeping for Zion I have seen, and I will cause that he shall mourn for her no longer" (D&C 21:7-8). Shortly after this Joseph received authority to bring Zion into reality, and the process began.[2]

This grand end, however, was never realized during the Prophet's lifetime. Joseph Smith and the Lord were willing, but the Saints were unprepared: "There were jarrings, and contentions, and envyings, and strifes, and lustful and covetous desires among them; therefore, by these things they polluted their inheritances," the Lord said (D&C 101:6). The consequence was that the land of Zion became lost for a time as a possession for the people of God. This loss was due primarily to mob action taken against those Saints living in Missouri; within four years the Saints had lost all their holdings in that State.

Though the Lord had something to say about those who abused and drove out the Saints, he did not allow the Saints to forget that the greater responsibility for failure was theirs. He said, "They were found transgressors, therefore they must needs be chastened" (D&C 101:41). This would be "a sore and grievous chastisement, because they did not hearken altogether unto the precepts and commandments which I gave unto them" (D&C 103:4). The result was made clear by the Lord: they would be "chastened until they learn obedience, if it must needs be, by the things which they suffer" (D&C 105:6).

Initially the suffering the Saints were to endure was not to include the giving up of their Missouri lands. When Oliver Cowdery, who was sent from Missouri in August 1833, reported the outrages which had been committed against the Saints there, the members at Kirtland "concluded with one accord to die with you or redeem you."[3] This was no empty promise. Meetings were held to determine what the best course of action would be. In December a revelation was received (now section 101) in which a parable explained what the Saints were to do about the situation: "Go and gather together the residue of my servants, and take all the strength of mine house, which are my warriors, my young men, and they that are of middle age also among all my servants, . . . and go ye straightway unto the land of my vineyard and redeem my vineyard" (D&C 101:55-56).

In February 1834 the Prophet received another revelation directing that he organize the body of men referred to in the parable (D&C 103:22-26). The group of men who responded to Joseph Smith's call became known as Zion's Camp. The plan was for this body of armed men to work in concert with the state authorities and under state protection in restoring the Saints to their homes. To this end many men left families and farms and traveled over 1,000 miles. Their efforts, however, proved fruitless. The governor of Missouri, Daniel Dunklin, though he had given his promise, decided that he would not help the Saints. This meant that any action of the Saints was futile. In consequence of the concern created by these events, section 105 was given explaining why Zion would not be redeemed at that time, and specifying what the Saints would need to do to redeem it.[4]

Though the expressed purpose of Zion's Camp was not realized, a greater purpose was. The Lord in his economy had more in mind than restoring people to real estate. Joseph Smith, not long after the return to Kirtland of Zion's Camp, explained the purpose of the Lord. He said:

> Brethern, some of you are angry with me, because you did not fight in Missouri; but let me tell you, God did not want you to fight. He could not organize his kingdom with twelve men to open the gospel door to the nations of the earth, and with seventy men under their direction to follow in their tracks, unless he took them from a body of men who had offered their lives, and who had made as great a sacrifice as did Abraham.
>
> Now, the Lord had got his Twelve and his Seventy, and there will be other quorums of Seventies called, who will make the sacrifice, and those who have not made their sacrifices and their offerings now, will make them hereafter.[5]

Out of the attempt to redeem Zion came that power and organization which would redeem the world. The Lord's purposes were indeed met.

## The Church Yet Loved

Though the land of Zion was lost temporarily and the Saints stood rightly condemned, it is important to note that the Saints were not cast off. Indeed the Lord told Joseph Smith: "They have been afflicted, in consequence of their transgressions; yet I will own them, and they shall be mine in the day when I shall come to make up my jewels" (D&C 101:2-3). Through disobedience they had brought troubles upon themselves, yet not the wrath of God. In his eyes they were yet to become his "jewels." This verse is a close parallel of the King James translation of Mal. 3:17. A more literal translation of the Malachi passage would read: "And they will be mine, said Jehovah of hosts, in the day that I make up (my) treasured possession." The Hebrew word translated here as "treasured possession" designates valued property which is deliberately chosen and taken to oneself.[6] The idea is one of a prized possession. Thus the Lord is here stating that his real treasure is not the riches of the earth, but rather the hearts and souls of his children.

How is it, then, that the early Saints could have committed transgressions and yet still be favored by the Lord? In D&C 29:47 the Lord spoke of a time when children begin to become accountable before him. The word "begin" used in that verse may suggest that children do not become accountable all at once but rather grow in accountability. This idea seems to apply to the Church as well. The

Lord is more tolerant with the mistakes of youth than the rebellion of the mature. Though the Church had to suffer the consequences of transgression, still it was not cut off from the influence of the Lord. Time was given for maturation and experience before perfection was demanded.

The early Church, even with its mistakes, was still the infant from which the spiritual giant would eventually grow. For all its weakness, though it lost the land of Zion, it did not lose the capacity to realize its prophetic future and that which it would bring: the Millennium.

## The Millennial Day

In section 101 the Lord speaks of the millennial day being ushered in by the revelation of his glory. This is to be sudden and, for the most part, unexpected. It is a complete break in history such that its flow is totally interrupted and a new course of history is introduced. The new history begins on the basis of the world-shattering revelation given by the Savior as he introduces the new era.

The consequences of that revelation are noted briefly in section 101: all corruption will be consumed and the earth transformed so that the glory of the Lord can dwell upon it; enmity will cease between man and animal; Satan will not be able to tempt mankind; death as we know it will be done away, and revelations will abound (vv. 24-34).

All of the programs of the Church exist to assist men and women to be ready for and enjoy a future day of glory. But before that day can come there is much work to be done. Righteousness must increase. The Church must grow so that it "may become a great mountain and fill the whole earth; that thy church may come forth out of the wilderness of darkness, and shine forth fair as the moon, clear as the sun, and terrible as an army with banners; and be adorned as a bride for that day when thou shalt unveil the heavens, and cause the mountains to flow down at thy presence, and the valleys to be exalted, and the rough places made smooth; that thy glory may fill the earth" (D&C 109:72-74).

Though the earth will rest during the Millennium, there will be a flurry of activity by its inhabitants. Missionary work must continue among those inhabitants of the earth who, though righteous enough to dwell on the sanctified earth, have not accepted the fulness of the Gospel.[7] Work for the righteous dead must be completed, including celestial marriages for those who died before they had this opportunity.

However, this is not all. Men must in that marvelous day use the outpouring of revelation to sanctify themselves and their families, as well as to continue to subdue the earth. It must be remembered that the millennial state is not the final state of the earth, but rather a period of preparation for a yet greater state. For this reason it will be necessary to spend time raising families and preparing both the living and the dead for the fulness of glory which will be revealed from heaven when the millennial period has achieved its purpose.

But all this—missionary work, temple work, raising of families, putting to use the superior knowledge which will be available—is but a part of the work of the Millennium. The real work is that of Christ. It is during this period that he will perfect personally his assigned work so that he can present it to the Father pure, holy, and totally sanctified. Only than can that reconstitution take place so that there can be a new heaven and a new earth where celestial men and women can enjoy the fruits of the tree of life and eat the heavenly manna forever.

If the Church in its immaturity lost the land of Zion, it did not lose the more important keys of preparing the hearts of a people so that they could establish Zion wherever they might be. Surely the heart is more important than real estate, since it is the heart that sanctifies the land and not the land that sanctifies the heart. Therefore, the attempt to claim Zion, including the march of Zion's Camp, was not really futile. Out of it came those leaders who were tried and tested. Through that trial they preserved that faith in God through which purity of heart has come and out of which will come the peace and beauty of the millennial day.

## Notes

[1]*TPJS*, pp. 231-32.

[2]See Richard D. Draper, "To Do the Will of the Lord," found herein.

[3]Letter from Joseph Smith, 10 August 1833, as cited in Lyndon W. Cook, *The Revelations of the Prophet Joseph Smith* (Provo, Ut.: Seventy's Mission Bookstore, 1981), p. 205.

[4]See Monte S. Nyman, "The Redemption of Zion," found herein.

[5]As recalled in Joseph Young, Sen., *History of the Organization of the*

*Seventies* (Salt Lake City: Deseret News Steam Printing Establishment, 1878), p. 14; see also *HC* 2:182, note.

[6]Francis Brown, S. R. Driver, and Charles A. Briggs, eds., *A Hebrew and English Lexicon of the Old Testament* (Oxford: Clarendon Press, 1953), s. v. *segullah.*

[7]Joseph Fielding Smith, *Doctrines of Salvation,* comp. Bruce R. McConkie, 3 vols. (Salt Lake City: Bookcraft, 1954-56), 1:86-87. Bruce R. McConkie, *The Millennial Messiah* (Salt Lake City: Deseret Book Co., 1982), chapters 53, 54.

[8]Smith, *Doctrines of Salvation*, 1:65.

# 36

# THE CHURCH JUDICIAL SYSTEM

## (D&C 102)

JAMES R. MOSS

### A Spiritual Foundation

On 17 February 1834, the Prophet Joseph Smith organized the first stake in this dispensation at Kirtland, Ohio. In conjunction with that organization, he also organized the first stake high council. Section 102 of the Doctrine and Covenants contains the minutes of the meeting at which that high council was organized and the members instructed in their duties. At the time, they were primarily judicial in nature, but they have since been expanded to include several semi-administrative functions in assisting the stake presidency in their duties.

The organization of a stake high council and establishment of procedures for the conduct of high council courts were major steps in the development of the Church judicial system. The development of that system began in April of 1830 when the Church was first organized, and it continued for the next five years. By 1835, the major administrative and judicial structures of the Church were in place, and a judicial system had been developed that has remained essentially unchanged to the present day. It did not develop in a vacuum, but as an integral part of the progressive restoration of the full program of the Church. The history of its development is both a witness to the inspiration of early Church leaders and a testimony to their capacity to adapt themselves and the emerging forms and functions of the Church to judicial concerns.

A Church judicial system became necessary very early for the following reasons: (1) There was need for doctrinal and ecclesiastical clarification in the Church. Definitions of acceptable orthodoxy and ecclesiastical function often came from actual cases handled by early Church courts. This function is similar to "test cases" often taken by secular courts today to clarify legal matters. The Church judicial system thus played an early and important role in dealing not only with individuals, but in helping to refine theological understanding and priesthood procedures. (2) There was need for dealing with both internal and external apostasy in the early days of the Church, when many succumbed to the trials of persecution or temptation. The Church judicial system served a valuable function as an authoritative and effective means of withdrawing fellowship or membership from individuals who were in violation of the law and order of the Church. (3) There was need for a full restoration of correct principles of judicial procedure as a part of the restoration of all things in this dispensation. The Church judicial system thus provides a spiritual foundation and potential role model for secular judicial systems. The judicial structure and procedures outlined in section 102 meet all of these needs.

The major elements of section 102 may be outlined as follows: vv. 1-5: The judicial function of the high council and record of its organization; vv. 6-11: The organization and structure of the high council for judicial purposes; vv. 12-23: The judicial procedures for conducting a high council court; vv. 24-33: The process of appeal and function of other High Priest courts; v. 34: The organization of the first high council court. It should be noted that vv. 30-32 were not part of the minutes of the 17 February 1834 meeting, but were added by Joseph Smith in 1835 when the Doctrine and Covenants was being prepared for publication. These verses deal with the twelve apostles, which were not called until 1835.

The judicial provisions outlined in section 102 are best understood within the context of all the judicial revelations and Church actions taken between 1830 and 1835. The following chart outlines the most important historical developments of that period by relating administrative and judicial procedures established in that period.

## HISTORICAL DEVELOPMENT OF THE CHURCH JUDICIAL SYSTEM—1830-35

| Administrative Development | Judicial Development |
| --- | --- |
| **April 1830**—Offices of Elder and Teacher (D&C 20) | **April 1830**—Teachers' Counsel and Expulsion of Members (D&C 20) |
| **February 1831**—Office of Bishop (D&C 41) | **February 1831**—Elders' Hearing, Church Decision, Bishop Present; Public and Private Confessions; Ecclesiastical Jurisdiction (D&C 42) |
| **June 1831**—Office of High Priest (*HC* 1:175-77) | |
| | **August 1831**—Bishop as Judge (D&C 58) |
| **November 1831**—First Presidency Revealed (D&C 68) | **November 1831**—Bishop or High Priest tried before First Presidency (D&C 68) |
| **January 1832**—President of the High Priesthood (*HC* 1:242-43) | |
| | **February 1833**—Council of High Priests (*HC* 1:327) |
| **March 1833**—First Presidency Organized (D&C 81;90; *HC* 1:334) | |
| | **May 1833**—Appellate Review by First Presidency (*HC* 1:343) |
| **June 1833**—Council of 12 High Priests; Original Jurisdiction of First Presidency; Council of Elders (*HC* 1:354-56) | |
| **December 1833**—Bishop's Court (*HC* 1:469-70) | |
| **February 1834**—High Council Organized (D&C 102; *HC* 2:28-33) | **February 1834**—High Council Court; Council of High Priests Abroad (D&C 102) |
| **February 1835**—Quorum of the Twelve Organized (*HC* 2:187) | |
| | **March 1835**—Bishop and Counselors as Court; First Presidency and 12 High Priests as Appellate Court; Presiding Bishop's Court for First Presidency; General Assembly of Several Quorums (D&C 107) |
| | **August 1835**—Traveling High Council of the Twelve Apostles (Added by Joseph Smith to D&C 102) |

Seen within this historical framework, it is clear that the organization of the stake high council was a major step in the full development of the Church judicial system. It continues today as one of four "standing" courts available for use by the Church and its members to function in judicial matters. Other courts had also been established between 1830 and 1835 of an "extraordinary" nature, courts that are of very limited function in the Church today or not used at all. The following chart shows the structural relationships between these courts and the sequence of their development.

# STRUCTURAL RELATIONSHIPS IN CHURCH JUDICIAL HISTORY

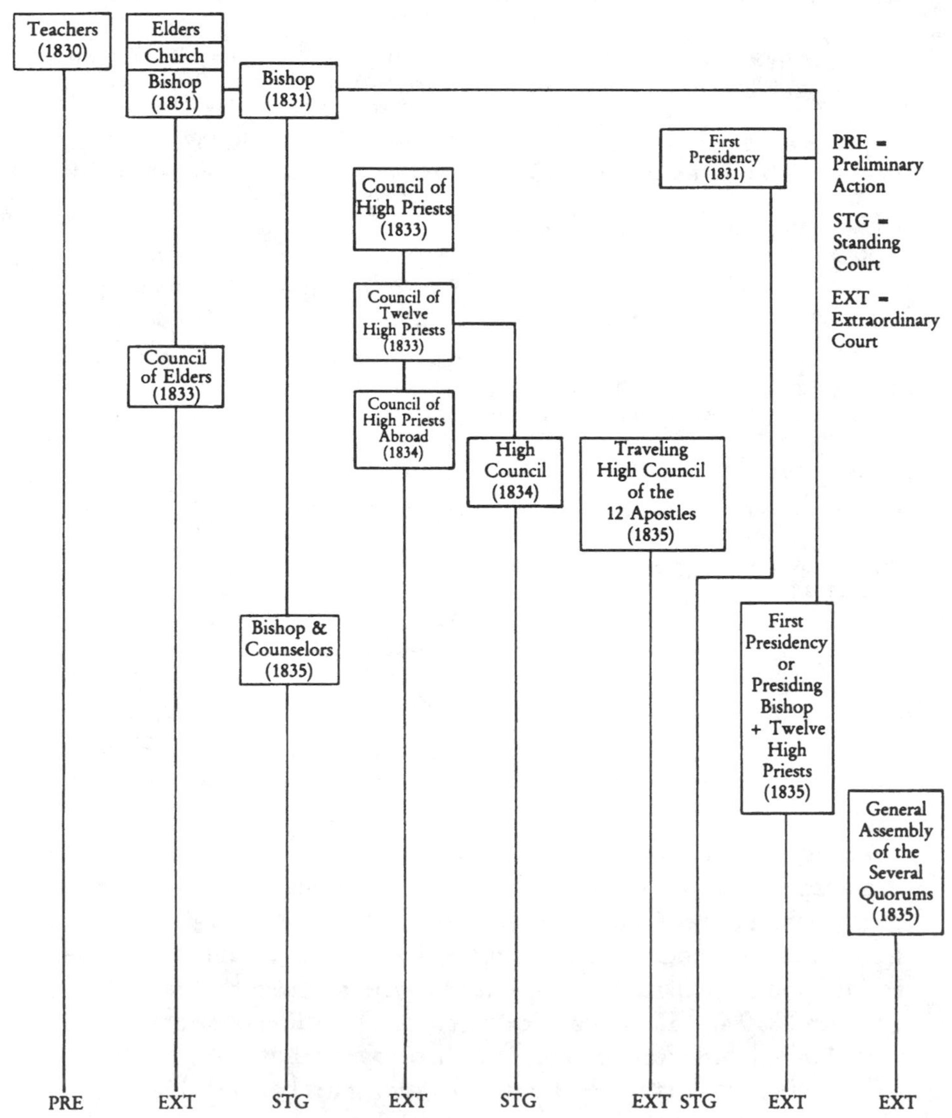

A study of these courts and the procedures outlined for their conduct in the Doctrine and Covenants reveals several important characteristics of the Church judicial system: (1) A judicial philosophy based on gospel principles of justice and mercy, combining individual accountability and free agency with institutional accountability. (2) A flexible yet predictable standard of judicial actions and sanctions that are both just and equitable. (3) An organizational structure that utilizes existing priesthood and ecclesiastical officers, yet at the same time provides universal jurisdiction over all Church members through a system of standing and extraordinary courts, possessing both original and appellate powers. (4) A spiritual procedure in conducting Church courts that places the highest priority on the search for truth, that has the capacity to go beyond the immediate issues and solve the underlying problems of those involved. (5) A stewardship of those judging that greatly strengthens the support of sanctions imposed and helps assure the equity of the penalties applied. (6) A judicial cognizance of extenuating circumstances, but cutting directly opposite prevailing secular practices by requiring a higher, rather than a lower, standard of conduct for those of prominence in the Church. (7) A lack of reliance on judicial precedent, and the incorporation of inspiration rather than the development of a body of canon law as the basis for judicial decisions. (8) A balance of concern for secular requirements and spiritual guidelines in the presentation of evidence and determination of sanctions to be applied.

## Courts of Love

The judicial philosophy reflected in section 102 is that of concern first and foremost for the individual involved. Church courts are courts of love, and all courts are conducted under the inspiration of the Spirit to determine what action will best help an individual to overcome problems and difficulties that stand in the way of progression and reconciliation with God. As Elder Robert L. Simpson has said, "Priesthood courts of the Church are not courts of retribution. They are courts of love. . . . Even excommunication from this Church is not the end of the world; and if this process is necessary in carrying out true justice, I bear you my personal and solemn witness that even this extreme penalty of excommunication can be the first giant step back, provided there follows a sincere submission to the Spirit and faith in the authenticity of God's plan."[1]

A second important purpose of Church courts is to help cleanse the Church and its members of unrighteousness. Elder James E. Talmage taught: "The Lord has no compromise with sin. He has provided that if any man in this Church shall offend, he shall be dealt with as a man who is afflicted with smallpox must be dealt with, with the hope of saving him. . . . The Lord hath declared that there must not be iniquity in his Church."[2] And President Stephen L Richards reminded Church members that "knowingly permitting a serious infraction of divine law to pass unnoticed is no kindness to the offender. He will never gain forgiveness except on the terms the Lord has prescribed."[3]

Fulfilling these two important purposes requires those who serve on high council courts to do so under the inspiration of the Spirit. Those called to the first high council were asked "whether they would act in that office according to the law of heaven, to which they all answered that they accepted their appointments, and would fill their offices according to the grace of God bestowed upon them" (D&C 102:4). When Joseph counseled the early brethren in the Church he taught: "No man is capable of judging a matter, in council, unless his own heart is pure."[4] Brigham Young said, "I would like to see the High Council and the Bishops and all Judges filled with the power of the Holy Ghost, that when a person comes before them they can read and understand that person, and be able to decide a case quickly and justly. . . . I would like the Bishops and other officers to have sufficient power and wisdom from God to make them fully aware of the true nature of every case that may come before them."[5]

The Lord promised spiritual insights in Church courts to those making important decisions: "In case of difficulty respecting doctrine or principle, if there is not a sufficiency written to make the case clear to the minds of the council, the president may inquire and obtain the mind of the Lord by revelation" (D&C 102:23). That spiritual foundation combined with the integrity and dedication of the members of the high council provides for the situation described by President John Taylor: "Men that are disinterested, men who are working for nothing, men who are seeing to adjust difficulties among their brethren, and who meet together from time to time and spend hours and days and weeks in adjusting these difficulties, simply for the love of God and humanity and to correct error and establish the principles of righteousness."[6]

The causes of action that bring individuals before high council courts and the sanctions that may be imposed on them by such courts are most clearly outlined in the Church's general handbook of instructions given to priesthood leaders who are required to participate in such courts. Such causes of action are obviously limited to appropriate ecclesiastical matters, as are the penalties that may be imposed. "We believe that all religious societies have a right to deal with their members for disorderly conduct, according to the rules and regulations of such societies; provided that such dealings be for fellowship and good standing; but we do not believe that any religious society has authority to try men on the right of property or life, to take from them this world's goods, or to put them in jeopardy of either life or limb, or to inflict any physical punishment upon them. They can only excommunicate them from their society, and withdraw from their their fellowship" (D&C 134:10).

Within this limited but all-important function, the stake high council established by Joseph Smith in section 102 has functioned ever since its first organization to bless the Church and its members as part of an inspired Church judicial system. President George Q. Cannon summarized its impact on the Church and its importance to all Church members as follows:

> Many high councils exist in the Church at the present time, there being one in every Stake of Zion. . . . The plan of settling disputes and preventing litigation among brethren, which the Prophet was then inspired to introduce, has grown with the growth of the Church, and the high council has performed an important mission in the years which have followed. It has worked without fees; it has known no coercion; the honesty of its decisions have been beyond question; and often it has been appealed to by men not of the faith, that their disputes might be settled with fairness and economy. It has never usurped the function of the criminal courts; it has never sought to enforce its

judgment by any civil process. It has only decreed according to clear and unmistakable justice and has left the parties to accept the judgment, and if not complied with or appealed from, to have Church fellowship withdrawn from them. The rules which the Prophet established to control its proceedings under divine guidance were delivered to it at the time of organization, and they, speaking of all the high councils which have since been organized, are still governed by them."[7]

## Notes

[1]*Conference Report*, April 1972, pp. 32-33.
[2]*Ibid.*, October 1920, pp. 61-62.
[3]*Ibid.*, April 1954, pp. 11-13.
[4]*HC* 2:25.
[5]*JD* 10:42.
[6]*JD* 26:360.
[7]*The Life of Joseph Smith, The Prophet* (Salt Lake City: Juvenile Instructor Office, 1888), pp. 164-65.

# 37

# REVELATIONS ON PRIESTHOOD, KEYS, AND QUORUMS

## (D&C 107, 108, and 112)

WILSON K. ANDERSEN

### Historical Background

The Lord commanded the Prophet Joseph to call together all of the men who had participated in the Zion's Camp march. These men were to be called to the ministry and from among them twelve were to be called as apostles to carry the word of the Lord and the blessings of his gospel to all nations. This meeting was convened at Kirtland, Ohio on 14 February 1835. Under the hands of Joseph Smith the Three Witnesses to the Book of Mormon had been blessed and authorized to select the Twelve from among the members of the Camp of Zion.

For some it was a call to martyrdom. Little were they aware of the trials, the weight of responsibility, and the great authority they would bear. President George Q. Cannon stated: "Of the disciples chosen then and of those since to keep the quorum complete, not one has escaped the afflictions of time."[1] President Harold B. Lee similarly bore repeated witness that he had been tested and had seen each of those called after him so tested and tried. President Cannon continued:

> With some the pains were too intense to be endured, the burden too heavy to be borne; and they dropped aside from the on-marching ranks to find, as they hoped, repose and safety amidst the cooling shadows of that world from which they had been chosen to be special witnesses of the Son of God. Such are no longer his Apostles.
>
> But the others, with unshaken resoluteness, have gone forward in the fulfilment of their high mission, under the scorching heat of fiery persecution. Joseph is their captain and their fellow soldier in the cause of Christ. With him and after him many of them have, with continuous and unyielding zeal, toiled steadily on until worn out in the performance of the duty assigned them by their Master Jesus; they have passed to the enjoyment of their promised rest.[2]

The first Twelve in this dispensation scarcely knew what to do. They determined in a short while that they would go out to preach the gospel. As they were about to leave, on 28 March 1835, just six weeks after their initial call, they wrote a letter to Joseph containing an interesting request and expressing a choice evidence of their complete faith in their prophet. Signed by the Council of the Twelve by their clerks, Orson Hyde and William E. McLellin, it read in part as follows:

> We therefore feel to ask of him whom we have acknowledged to be our Prophet and Seer, that he inquire of God for us, and obtain a revelation, (if consistent) that we may look upon it when we are separated, that our hearts may be comforted. Our worthiness has not inspired us to make this request, but our unworthiness. We have unitedly asked God our Heavenly Father to grant unto us, through His Seer, a revelation of His mind and will concerning our duty that coming season, even a great revelation, that will enlarge our hearts, comfort us in adversity, and brighten our hopes amidst the powers of darkness.[3]

The Prophet wrote: "In compliance with the above request, I inquired of the Lord, and received for answer the following." Section 107 follows.[4]

The first 58 verses of section 107 were given 28 March, and the other verses were revealed on later occasions.[5]

## Overview of Section 107

Elder John A. Widtsoe has written of section 107:

> On that day the Church of Jesus Christ of Latter-day Saints received a revelation which is one of the most remarkable documents in the possession of man. It stands absolutely unique; there is none like it. . . . It sets forth in plainness and simplicity, the organization of the quorums of the priesthood; the mutual relations of the quorums to one another; the judicial system of the Church is foreshadowed and outlined; and there is a wonderful picture of the early priesthood. I doubt whether any other such documents, of the same small extent, the same few number of words, lies at the foundation of any other great human institution. . . . It is so comprehensive in its brevity, so

magnificent in its simplicity, that we have found no occasion, up to the present, to wish that it might have been more complete.[6]

The contents of this section might be considered as follows:

|  |  |
|---|---|
| Verses 1-7 | The two priesthoods |
| 8-12, 18-19 | Melchizedek Priesthood authority |
| 13-17, 20 | Aaronic Priesthood authority |
| 21-26, 33-36 | The highest presiding quorums |
| 27-31 | The Lord's law for decision-making in priesthood councils |
| 32, 76-78, 82 | Intimations of a Church judiciary |
| 36-37 | The standing (stake) high councils |
| 38-39, 58 | Duties of the Quorum of the Twelve |
| 40-52 | A brief outline of patriarchal priesthood history |
| 53 | The ancient priesthood conference at Adam-ondi-Ahman |
| 59-63 | Presiding offices and priesthood councils |
| 65-67, 91-92 | The Presiding High Priest and President of the church |
| 68-76 | The office of Bishop, and High Priests as Bishops |
| 79-84 | The Council of the First Presidency |
| 85-88 | Aaronic Priesthood presidents |
| 89-90 | Elders and Seventies |
| 93-98 | The order of the Seventy (the vision revealing they are to have seven presidents) |
| 99-100 | Every priesthood bearer to learn his duty and do it |

It may be difficult for us to look back and realize that that occasion (1835) was the beginning of quorums in the Church. It is true that there were a few ordained offices in the priesthoods from the beginning of the Church, but there were no quorums as yet. The First Presidency had only existed in the Church for 23 months, and the office of patriarch for less than 18 months. Church organization developed piecemeal, as the Lord directed. Undoubtedly the entire restoration of priesthood organization is not yet complete. A case in point is the first-time organization of the First Quorum of Seventy as general authorities, by President Spencer W. Kimball, under the Lord's direction in 1975. Even the apostleship itself came in stages. Its fulness did not come until the final keys were restored (see section 110) by Moses, Elias, Elijah, and the Savior in 1836.[7] Those keys and blessings were bestowed on the Twelve some years after that.

## Decision-Making In Priesthood Councils

Beginning at v. 27 of section 107 is the Lord's law for decision-making in priesthood councils. In those early years of the Church in which this revelation was given there was no distinction made between a quorum and a council. Today we would say that most quorums are not councils. In these verses the quorums being referred to (the First Presidency and the Twelve) are also priesthood councils. A priesthood council is an administrative decision-making body of priesthood bearers called together under the direction of a priesthood president or a key holder. All quorum presidencies are priesthood councils. All other priesthood presidencies are priesthood councils. Some councils extend beyond the presidency, as in a stake high council, but must, of course, include the president. There are no priesthood councils without a divinely appointed key holder at its head.

The revelation (vv. 27-31) indicates three requirements for proper, divinely backed, decisions in council: first, unanimity; second (v. 28), the presence of a majority of the council members. Verse 28 means that a majority of the members of a council may function as a council (assuming the presence or authority of its president) when it is impossible for all to be present. Their decisions, if otherwise in accordance with this law, will be "entitled to the same blessings" and "they shall not be unfruitful in the knowledge of the Lord." Evidently these principles should apply in the operations of all priesthood councils. The third requirement—if we may summarize the virtues listed in v. 30 into one phrase—is that the council functions "in all righteousness." The fact that priesthood councils, by the hundreds and thousands, operate this way regularly throughout the Church is truly one of the great evidences of its divinity.

President Stephen L Richards, counselor to President David O. McKay, emphasized the power of Church councils:

> As I conceive it, the genius of our Church government is government through *councils*. The Council of the Presidency, the Council of the Twelve, the Council of the Stake Presidency, . . . the Council of the Bishopric, . . . and the Council of the Quorum Presidency. I have had enough experience to know the value of councils. Hardly a day passes but that I see the wisdom, God's wisdom, in creating councils: to govern his kingdom. In the spirit under which we labor, men can get together with seemingly divergent views and far different backgrounds, and under the operation of that spirit, by counseling together, they can arrive at an accord and that accord (the occasions are so negligible as not to be mentioned), and therefore I say that accord is always right. That accord represents the wisdom of the council, acting under the Spirit.[8]

Section 107, though applicable in principle to quorums, councils, and presidents throughout the entire Church, is particularly relevant to the highest presiding councils, the First Presidency and the Twelve. Concerning these councils President Richards asked: "Now who is entitled to interpret the doctrine of the Church, granting that some items are susceptible of different construction?" In answer to his own question, he stated:

> In the exercise of [the First Presidency's] functions and delegated powers they are controlled by a constitution, a part of which is written and a part of which is not. The written part consists in authenticated scripture, ancient and modern, and in the recorded utterances of our latter-day prophets. The unwritten part is the spirit of revelation and divine inspiration which appertain to their calling.
>
> In formulating their interpretations and decisions they

always confer with the Council of the Twelve Apostles who by revelation are appointed to assist and act with them in the government of the Church. When therefore a judgment is reached and proclaimed by these officers it becomes binding upon all the members of the Church, individual view to the contrary notwithstanding. God's Kingdom is a kingdom of law and order. He is the Lawgiver and the Supreme Judge, but he has delegated authority and the keys of the Kingdom upon these men whom he has chosen. They act for him and, thank the Lord, we accept them. It is the only safe thing to do.

There are some, perhaps, who may feel it is subversive of individual freedom of thought and expression to be controlled by the interpretations of our leaders. I wish to assure them that any feeling of constraint will disappear when once they secure the genius and true merit of this work. Our unanimity of thought and action does not arise, as some suppose, from duress or compulsion in any form. Our accord comes from universal agreement with righteous principles and common response [including common consent] to the operation of the Spirit of our Father. It is actuated by no fear except one. That is the fear of offending God, the Author of our work.[9]

A most beautiful illustration of this function of priesthood councils, under the God-given procedure, was given by Elder Boyd K. Packer. Speaking of the regular weekly meeting of the Council of the First Presidency and the Twelve he said:

Each Thursday morning promptly at eight o'clock, the Council of the Twelve meets in the temple. We meet in the council room on the fourth floor. Chairs for the First Presidency stand against the west wall. Above the chairs are pictures of the Christ. To the left, the first picture, the crucifixion; the center, the resurrected Christ in the Garden; and the picture on the right, Christ calling the Twelve. The Twelve sit in a semicircle facing the Presidency and behind them on the wall are portraits of the Presidents of the Church. For two hours the Council of the Twelve considers matters to be brought before them under the direction of President Kimball. Precisely at ten o'clock, the First Presidency arrives. They have been meeting in their board room in the Church Administration Building. After some sacred ceremonies, including

> prayer at the altar, the meeting of the First Presidency and the Council of the Twelve commences. . . .
>
> There, in that sacred building, where we are literally out of the world, matters relating to the government of the Church are considered carefully and prayerfully. . . .
>
> It may be well for you to know likewise, that *the decisions of this council are not consummated unless they are unanimous. They must be unanimous or there is no decision. Scrupulous care is given to see that these issues have the approval of the Lord.* Many times in that sacred setting, in these meetings, his watch care over the Church has been in evidence.[10]

Truly we should be grateful for the leaders the Lord has chosen, and also for the revealed principles by which they operate.

## Callings in the Priesthood

In vv. 60-63 the Lord speaks of presidents of the various quorums or ordained orders. If we are to exercise priesthood—a power which is not our own, but sent from God—then we must certainly learn to receive his direction. One of the great priesthood lessons is to learn that much of his direction comes through his agents who are appointed principals over us in his priesthood. So much of the Lord's direction, and a prime means of testing the faith and obedience of his children, is not direct but through presiding intermediaries. President Joseph F. Smith summarized the idea in these words: "Every man should be willing to be presided over, and he is not fit to preside over others until he can submit sufficiently to the presidency of *his brethren*."[11]

Perhaps it would be well, in this connection, to look at vv. 8-12 and 89-90 and consider *our brethren* of the priesthood: elders, seventies, high priests, ordained patriarchs, and the ordained apostles. In the early years of the Church there was some difficulty and apparent misunderstanding about the relative authority, roles, and status, of these offices. Each bearer of these offices is called by prophecy and by foreordination (see Alma 13:1-8) to bear the high and holy priesthood after the order of the Son of God.

Elders, seventies, high priests, and ordained patriarchs each hold the high or Melchizedek Priesthood. They each could, with proper authorization, exercise virtually any of the functions of that priesthood.

But normally this is not the case. For example, these officers do not regularly hold any presiding authority—priesthood keys—without a special and temporary conferral of such. They are rather, by ordination and quorum membership, called to be specialists in some broad and basic priesthood responsibilities. The elder, the seventy, the high priest, and the ordained patriarch each have the same parameters of authority, responsibility, and covenant. The ordinations subsequent to elder (i.e., seventy and high priest) bestow no additional priesthood or authority but rather simply a new special focus or responsibility within the Melchizedek Priesthood. We have been consistently taught, under priesthood correlation, that the high priest has no more responsibility for genealogy and temple work than does the elder, though the high priest group leader may have a special role. The elder has no more responsibility for welfare services than does the high priest. Every member should be a missionary, though the seventy has a specific responsibility to serve as a specialist in missionary matters.

The ordained apostle, on the other hand, stands not only as a top executive because of managerial ability, but more importantly as a prophet, seer, and revelator in a most literal and authoritative sense. The knowledge and spiritual gifts the apostle has are available to all the true and faithful. But the apostle stands unique as a holder (by delegation) of the fulness of the keys and of the priesthood, with authority under the President over the entire Church. In this first revelation to them as a body in this dispensation, section 107 was not lacking in specific counsel for their particular calling, as the following demonstrates:

| | |
|---|---|
| Verse 22 | They are to choose (sustain and approve) the First Presidency |
| 23 | They are "to be . . . special witnesses" |
| 24 | They are "a quorum, equal in authority . . . to the three presidents" of the First Presidency |
| 27-31 | Decision-making as a council was to be in unanimity and in righteousness |
| 33 | They are a traveling council and a presiding council under the Presidency |
| 39 | They are "to ordain evangelical ministers |

. . . by revelation"
58 They are "to ordain and set in order all other officers of the Church"
98 They "are . . . under the responsibility to travel among all nations"

## "Let Every Man Learn His Duty"

As indicated earlier, the ordained apostle is unique among all offices in the Church and in the Melchizedek Priesthood. Yet *every* Melchizedek Priesthood holder is called to be one of the Lord's commissioned agents, to bear witness of him, and to speak in his name. The Prophet Joseph Smith said, "No man is a minister of Jesus Christ without being a prophet."[12] In the words of Elder Bruce R. McConkie: "A prophet is one who [regardless of ecclesiastical call or position] has the testimony of Jesus, who knows by the revelations of the Holy Ghost to his soul that Jesus Christ is the Son of God. In addition to this divine knowledge, many [prophets of the ancient times] lived in special situations or did particular things that singled them out as types and patterns and shadows of that which was to be in the life of him who is our Lord."[13]

Section 107 concludes with sublime counsel which is also an admonition that will undoubtedly be a factor in the final judgment of every priesthood holder: "Wherefore, now let every man learn his duty, and to act in the office to which he is appointed, in all diligence. He that is slothful shall not be counted worthy to stand, and he that learns not his duty and shows himself not approved shall not be counted worthy to stand" (D&C 107:99-100). In this connection Elder Francis M. Lyman observed: "The Lord makes no mistakes in calling men; if we fail, it is our own weakness, for the Lord is ready to give strength sufficient to sustain the brethren in the responsibilities that are upon them."[14] President Henry D. Moyle suggested: "It would be more pleasing to our Father in heaven to have us resign our positions—and that is not a practice we commend in the Church—but nonetheless it seems preferable to *neglecting* our duties in the least detail. It gives us an awesome feeling to realize that we are dedicated to the work of the Lord, and having thus committed ourselves, it is not our privilege or our perogative to violate his commandments, even the slightest of them."[15]

Elder Mark E. Peterson stated:

> It is my full belief that whenever any of us accepts a position of any description in the Church, we accept along with it the responsibility of that office, whatsoever it may be. I believe that if a person accepts a position as a teacher in one of our organizations, or if he accepts the responsibility of preaching from the pulpit, such person accepts the responsibility which goes with that call. *He becomes a representative of the Church in that position.* Every teacher and every preacher therefore *is duty bound,* upon accepting such a call, *to represent the official views and doctrines of the Church.*[16]

## Section 108

On that same day that the apostles were first called, Elder Lyman Sherman was called to be one of the presidents of the Seventies.[17] Some months later, in December, President Sherman came to the Prophet Joseph with a request for the word of the Lord through him, "for," he said, "I have been wrought upon to make known to you my feelings and desires, and was promised that I should have a revelation which would make known my duty." Section 108 was then revealed.[18] The brief but pointed piece of prophecy that came commended brother Sherman (vv. 1-2), admonished him (vv. 2-3, 7-8), and then gave him promises (vv. 3-5). Moreover, the Lord told him: "Your sins are forgiven you, because you have obeyed my voice in coming up hither this morning to receive counsel of him whom I have appointed" (v. 1).

As a Church we also receive repeated calls, at least semi-annually, to come up and "receive counsel of him whom [the Lord has] appointed." We are thus admonished to receive the prophet's word "as if from [the Lord's] own mouth" (D&C 21:5) and taught in D&C 112:20 that we cannot presume that we accept the Lord if we do not receive the counsel of his First Presidency.

In relation to the Lord's counsel to "strengthen [our] brethren in all [our] conversation, in all [our] prayers, in all [our] exhortations, and in all [our] doings" (D&C 108:7), we might ponder these words of the great prophet Heber C. Kimball:

> I will give you a key which Brother Joseph Smith used to give in Nauvoo. He said that the very step of apostasy commenced with losing confidence in the leaders of this Church and kingdom, and that whenever you discerned that spirit, you might know that it would lead the possessor of it on the road to apostasy. . . .
>
> No man or woman can have the spirit of prophecy and at the same time do evil and speak evil against their brethren; and you will find that man or that woman barren and unfruitful in the knowledge of God, and filled with disputations.[19]

Note the contrast of that last thought with the Lord's promise in connection with decision-making in priesthood councils: if his agents follow his counsel "they shall *not* be unfruitfull in the knowledge of the Lord" (D&C 107:31, italics added). As with the principles underlying all the words of the Lord, the word to Lyman Sherman is pregnant with implications for each of us.

## Section 112

Section 112 is another revelation to a priesthood president. It might be well to consider it in two lights: as counsel to a quorum president, and as instruction about the Quorum of the Twelve and First Presidency.

|  | |
|---|---|
| Verses 1-13 | Counsel to a quorum president |
| 15-19, 30-34 | The Twelve in relation to the First Presidency |
| 20 | Universal counsel about the teachings of the First Presidency |
| 21-26 | Conditions in the world and where the judgments will begin |

In order to appreciate and fully understand this revelation it is necessary to understand the background. Members of the Church had established "a bank in real estate," the Kirtland Safety Society. Elder George A. Smith stated concerning it: "If they had followed the counsel of Joseph, there is not a doubt it would have been the leading bank in Ohio, probably of the nation. It was founded upon safe principles, and would have been a safe and lasting institution."[20] But a spirit of apostasy gripped some of the leading elders of the Church, including some of the Kirtland Safety Society Officers. One hundred thousand dollars was stolen from the bank, unknown to the president or the cashier. Joseph Smith reported:

> At this time the spirit of speculation in lands and property of all kinds, which was so prevalent throughout the nation, was taking root in the Church. As the fruits of this spirit, evil surmising, fault-finding, disunion, dissension, and apostasy followed in quick succession, and it seemed as though all the powers of earth and hell were combining their influence in an especial manner to over throw the Church at once, and make a final end. . . .
>
> No quorum in the Church was entirely exempt from the influence of those false spirits who were striving against me for the mastery; even some of the Twelve were so far lost to their high and responsible calling as to begin to take sides, secretly, with the enemy. In this state of things, and but a few weeks before the Twelve were expecting to meet in full quorum, (some of them having been absent for some time), God revealed to me that something must be done for the salvation of His Church. And on or about the first of June, 1837, Heber C. Kimball, one of the Twelve, was set apart by the spirit of prophecy and revelation, prayer and laying on of hands, of the First Presidency, to Preside over a mission to England, to be the first foreign mission of the Church of Christ in the last days.[21]

Elder Boyd K. Packer, in pointing out how at times the inspiration of the Lord "may either ignore or contravene the so-called facts concerning an issue," gave as an illustration this statement.

> You remember at the time of Kirtland when the Prophet Joseph Smith was beleaguered on every side. He was harassed by those who should have supported him. In an incredible move he called around him those who were secure to him and whom he trusted and those who might have given him some protection and sent them away on missions to foreign lands. It was a move that certainly was not reasonable, and yet as the pages of history unfolded and the apostates had their day and left the Church, hundreds and thousands and tens of thousands of converts came

forth to fill the ranks that had been abandoned by those who would not listen to the voice of the Prophet."[22]

President Harold B. Lee spoke of the fruits of that same inspiration as follows:

> In one year, 1840 to 1841—one year and fourteen days, to be exact—nine members of the Quorum of the Twelve were called to labor in the British Mission. If you remember the history here at home, those years marked the period of some of the severest persecution that the Church was to undergo in this dispensation. In that one year and fourteen days the nine members of the twelve, with their associates, established churches in every noted town and city in the kingdom of Great Britain. They baptized between 7000 and 8000 converts. They printed 5000 copies of the Book of Mormon, 3000 hymnbooks, 50,000 tracts, and they published 2500 volumes of the *Millennial Star* and emigrated 1000 souls to America.[23]

While Elder Heber C. Kimball was on his mission in England the Lord spoke to his quorum president, Thomas B. Marsh, in Kirtland, Ohio. Section 112 was received on the day that the gospel was first preached in England.[24] President Joseph Fielding Smith noted that through the words of section 112 President Marsh "was instructed to teach the brethren of his council and point out to them their duties and responsibilities in proclaiming the Gospel. Some of the apostles had forsaken their responsibility and had turned their attention to schemes of speculation. . . . This revelation to Thomas Marsh was a warning and a call to him to bring his brethren back into the line of their duty as apostles of Jesus Christ."[25]

## Notes

[1]George Q. Cannon, *The Life of Joseph Smith the Prophet* (Salt Lake City: Juvenile Instructor Office, 1888), p. 193.

[2]*Ibid.*, pp. 193-94.

[3]*HC* 2:210.

[4]*Ibid.*

[5]See Lyndon W. Cook, *The Revelations of the Prophet Joseph Smith* (Provo, Ut.: Seventy's Mission Bookstore, 1981), p. 215.

[6]*Conference Report*, April 1935, pp. 80-81.

[7]See Milton V. Backman Jr., and Robert L. Millet, "Heavenly Manifestations in the Kirtland Temple," found herein.

[8]*Conference Report*, October 1953, p. 86.

[9]*Ibid.*, October 1938, pp. 115-16.

[10]*Fall Faculty Workshop*, Brigham Young University, 1973, pp. 5-6, italics added.

[11]*Improvement Era* 21 (December 1917): 105, italics added.

[12]*TPJS*, p. 160.

[13]*The Promised Messiah* (Salt Lake City: Deseret Book Co., 1978), p. 448.

[14]*Conference Report*, April 1913, p. 69.

[15]*Conference Report*, September 1961, pp. 43-44, italics added.

[16]*Conference Report*, April 1953, p. 83, italics added.

[17]*HC* 2:201-3.

[18]*HC* 2:345.

[19]Cited in Orson F. Whitney, *Life of Heber C. Kimball*, 3rd ed. (Salt Lake City: Bookcraft, 1967), p. 465.

[20]*JD* 11:11.

[21]*HC* 2:487-89; see D&C 110:11.

[22]"A Dedication—To Faith," *Speeches of the Year, 1969* (Provo, Ut.: Brigham Young University, 1969), p. 7.

[23]*Conference Report*, April 1960, p. 108.

[24]*HC* 2:498-99.

[25]*Church History and Modern Revelation*, 4 vols. (Salt Lake City: The Council of the Twelve Apostles of the Church of Jesus Christ of Latter-day Saints, 1953), 3:101.

# 38

# HEAVENLY MANIFESTATIONS IN THE KIRTLAND TEMPLE

## (D&C 109, 110, 137)

Milton V. Backman, Jr.
and Robert L. Millet

### A Season of Spiritual Blessings

One of the most remarkable three-month periods in the early history of the Restoration began on 21 January 1836. During this powerful pentecostal season, the Lord opened the windows of heaven and poured unusual blessings upon Latter-day Saints living in Kirtland, Ohio. While members were receiving a special endowment, or gift, from God and were being blessed with gifts of prophecy, knowledge, faith, healings, and speaking in tongues, the Prophet Joseph Smith received three revelations that are included in the current edition of the Doctrine and Covenants, sections 137, 109, and 110.[1]

For three years Latter-day Saints had sacrificed to build a House for the Lord. In December 1832 they were commanded to build a holy sanctuary or temple, "even a house of prayer, a house of fasting, a house of faith, a house of learning, a house of glory, a house of order, a house of God" (D&C 88:119).

When the revelation was given to build this temple there were only about one hundred members (approximately twenty families) living in Kirtland township. These people were not only few in number, but they lacked land, money, and architectural knowledge. But they united and called upon the Lord for help. Through visions and revelations to the First Presidency (Joseph Smith, Sidney Rigdon, and Frederick G. Williams) the pattern of this building was unfolded, after which these leaders supervised its construction. Meanwhile, missionaries went forth converting others and instructing converts to gather in Kirtland and contribute financially to the temple project. Heeding this call, many faithful Saints migrated to northeastern Ohio. Within three years, membership in Kirtland increased from one hundred to thirteen hundred.[2]

Nearly every member, man, woman, and child, living in Kirtland devoted much of his or her time, talent, and material wealth for the building of the Lord's House. Joseph Smith acted as foreman in the stone quarry and frequently worked on the construction of the temple. "Come, brethren," he would say, "let us go into the stone-quarry and work for the Lord."[3] Meanwhile, the women made stockings, pantaloons, and jackets for the men. The sisters, Heber C. Kimball recalled, "were continually knitting, spinning and sewing, and in fact, I may say doing all kinds of work! They were just as busy as any of us," he added.[4] After sacrificing for three years, Latter-day Saints met in the temple to receive the promised blessings.

As early as January 1831, before the emigration of the New York Saints to Kirtland, the Lord declared that "for this cause I gave unto you the commandment that ye should go to the Ohio; and there I will give unto you my law, and there you shall be endowed with power from on high" (D&C 38:32). While instructing the Saints, the Prophet said that the endowment was a special gift of knowledge derived by revelation and was a gift of power emitted from God. This gift included learning principles of obedience and other laws of God and was in part designed to help missionaries serve with greater effectiveness. Although the Prophet taught that many of the brethren would not comprehend the endowment, he told bearers of the priesthood to prepare for this gift by purifying themselves, by cleansing their hearts and physical bodies. "You need an endowment, brethren," he added, "in order that you may be prepared and able to overcome all things." After instructing the Saints for about three months, the Prophet concluded that the bearers of the priesthood had received "all the necessary ceremonies" relating to that endowment. He then challenged those who had received the gift to "go forth and build the kingdom of God."[5]

Recalling events that transpired during this pentecostal season (which was also the period of the temple's completion and dedication), Orson Pratt declared:

> God was there, his angels were there, the Holy Ghost was in the midst of the people, the visions of the Almighty were opened to the minds of the servants of the living God; the veil was taken from the minds of many; they saw the heavens opened; they beheld the angels of God; they heard the voice of the Lord; and they were filled from the crown of their heads to the soles of their feet with the power and inspiration of the

> Holy Ghost. . . . In that Temple, set apart by the servants of God, and dedicated by a prayer that was written by inspiration, the people were blessed as they never had been blessed for generations.[6]

During a fifteen-week period, extending from 21 January to 1 May 1836, probably more Latter-day Saints beheld visions and received gifts of tongues, interpretation of tongues, and prophecy than during any other period in the history of the Church. Contemporaries reported that members beheld heavenly beings during ten meetings, that many saw visions during eight of these meetings, and that Latter-day Saints beheld the Savior on five occasions.[7]

## A Vision of the Celestial Kingdom

The season of heavenly manifestations was inaugurated by the Prophet's vision of the Father and Son in the celestial glory. On the evening of 21 January 1836, about forty men entered the nearly completed Kirtland Temple. Although the outside plastering had been completed, workers were busy at that time plastering and painting the interior. While climbing the circular staircase, these bearers of the priesthood passed the second floor, which resembled the first with four tiers of pulpits on either end of the room. They continued to the third floor, an attic which had been divided into five classrooms. About sixteen of these men gathered in the west room, which was then being used as a classroom by students studying Hebrew. Accompanying Joseph Smith were his two counselors and his father (who was serving as patriarch), Hyrum Smith, the two bishoprics (one from Missouri and the other residing in Kirtland), and Joseph Smith's scribe, Warren Parrish.[8]

After the Prophet had introduced one of the ordinances connected with the Kirtland endowment—the ordinance of anointing—Joseph Smith testified that "the heavens were opened upon us," and he "beheld the celestial kingdom of God, and the glory thereof." He saw the "blazing throne of God, whereon was seated the Father and Son." He saw "the beautiful streets of that kingdom, which had the appearance of being paved with gold." He also saw in vision in the celestial kingdom "Father Adam and Abraham," his father (who was in the room at the time of the vision), his mother, his deceased brother,

Alvin, and the twelve apostles who had been called in 1835 (D&C 137:1-5).[9] Joseph further declared that his scribe saw some of the same heavenly beings who appeared to him.[10]

Since Joseph Smith did not understand at that time the concept of salvation for the dead, the Prophet was perplexed when he saw his brother Alvin in the celestial kingdom, for Alvin had died before the Church was fully organized. Therefore, during this vision the Prophet asked a question and received the initial revelation on this subject: all, including children, who would have accepted the gospel had they been granted such an opportunity are "heirs of the celestial kingdom of God" (D&C 137:7-10).[11]

Before this remarkable series of visions ended, the high councils from Kirtland and Missouri entered the room, received their anointings, and were blessed with the ministering of angels. The Prophet added that while some of these leaders communed with holy angels, others "saw the face of the Savior" and the spirit of prophecy and revelation was poured out in mighty power. When Oliver Cowdery attempted to describe this unusual meeting, he wrote, the "glorious scene" was "too great to be described." "I only say," he added, "the heavens were opened to many, and great and marvelous things were shown."[12]

## The Dedication of the Temple

Members enjoyed another spiritual feast during the dedication of the temple. On Saturday, 26 March, the day preceding this solemn assembly, Joseph Smith, Oliver Cowdery, Sidney Rigdon, Warren Cowdery (Oliver's brother), and Warren Parrish (Joseph's scribe) met in the president's room on the third floor of the temple to make final preparations for the service. According to Oliver Cowdery, during this meeting he assisted Joseph Smith "in writing a prayer for the dedication" of the Lord's House.[13]

On Sunday, 27 March, approximately eight hundred members (only a portion of those who desired to attend) crowded into the temple to participate in its dedication. During this meeting, which began at nine o'clock and continued until four in the afternoon with only a fifteen or twenty minute intermission, Sidney Rigdon conducted and spoke for two and one-half hours. In the afternoon, Joseph Smith delivered the dedicatory prayer which had been received by revelation (D&C 109). Following this prayer the choir sang a hymn written earlier by William W. Phelps in anticipation of a glorious occasion, "The Spirit of God Like a Fire is Burning." The Prophet then received approval of this prayer from the respective priesthood quorums and the congregation.[14]

The dedicatory prayer was directed to the Father but mentions Jehovah, whose house was being dedicated (D&C 109:4, 34, 68). After thanking God for his mercy, the Prophet asked the Father to accept the house that had been constructed amidst great tribulations and in harmony with his will (D&C 109:1-6, 8). The Prophet then asked God to bless those who worshiped in that temple with faith, wisdom, and obedience and to bless all the Saints and their leaders (D&C 109:13-15, 17-24, 68-72). He prayed that the building would serve as a place for fasting, prayer, and learning (D&C 109:8, 16). He also prayed for the enemies of the Church; for all nations; for leaders of government; for the churches in the world; for the needy, the poor and the afflicted; and for the restoration of Israel (D&C 109:50-55, 58-67).

This prayer set the pattern for subsequent dedicatory prayers. Written by the spirit of inspiration, these prayers are "formal and long and cover many matters of doctrine and petition." They also are read by a Church leader who is appointed to fulfill this assignment. According to President Joseph Fielding Smith, "When we dedicate a house to the Lord, what we really do is dedicate ourselves to the Lord's service."[15]

Following the closing remarks by Hyrum Smith and Sidney Rigdon and Rigdon's closing prayer, the congregation sealed the proceedings with the Hosanna Shout, shouting "Hosanna! Hosanna! Hosanna to God and the Lamb!" three times, and "sealing it each time with amen, amen, and amen."[16]

Some who attended this solemn assembly testified that an angel was present and accepted the proceedings. Others were more specific and declared that the Savior was present and that the apostle Peter had come to accept the dedication.[17]

When Eliza R. Snow recorded her impressions of the dedicatory service, she wrote that "no mortal language" could "describe the heavenly manifestations of that memorable day." The congregation, she added, felt the "sweet spirit of love and union," "a sense of divine presence," and each heart was filled with joy inexpressible."[18] Nancy Alexander Tracy recalled that this was one of the happiest days of her life, for heavenly influences rested upon the Lord's House and heavenly beings appeared to many.[19]

## The Keys of the Priesthood Restored

Approximately six months before his death, Jesus spoke with his disciples at Caesarea Philippi. It was on that occasion that the chief apostle, in response to the Lord's query, declared: "Thou art the Christ, the Son of the living God." Simon was commended for his testimony and assured that such a witness had come from a divine source. "And I say also unto thee," the Master continued, "that thou art Peter, and upon this rock I will build my church; and the gates of hell shall not prevail against it. And I will give unto thee the keys of the kingdom of heaven: and whatsoever thou shalt bind on earth shall be bound in heaven: and whatsoever thou shalt loose on earth shall be loosed in heaven" (Matt. 16:13-19). Within a period of about one week, the Lord's promise was fulfilled. The New Testament Gospels record that Jesus took with him Peter, James, and John—the chief apostles of the church—to a high mountain to pray. While in that setting, these four were transfigured—lifted spiritually to a higher plane—and thus made ready for a transcendent experience.

Moses and Elijah appeared and bestowed upon the meridian apostolic presidency the keys of the kingdom of heaven.[20] *Keys* are directing powers, the right of presidency. These rights would allow the apostles to govern and direct the church in the absence of Jesus Christ, and to make available to the Saints all the powers and blessings of the everlasting gospel. Peter, James, and John had received the Melchizedek Priesthood years earlier and had been given apostolic power and commission at the time of their appointment to the Twelve. Now, however, they had further rights and additional directional responsibilities to bind and seal on earth, that their actions might likewise receive sealing validity in the heavens.

That which transpired in the first century in Palestine was a pattern for the marvelous happenings in Kirtland, Ohio in the nineteenth century. The winter and spring of 1836 proved to be an era of both modern pentecost and modern transfiguration.

By early April bearers of the priesthood had received their washings and anointings, including participating in the ordinance of the washing of feet; they had therefore received a partial endowment. Shortly thereafter, Joseph Smith and Oliver Cowdery knelt in prayer behind drawn curtains adjacent to the large pulpits on the west side of the main floor of the temple. The date was Sunday, 3 April 1836, exactly one week following the dedication of the Lord's House. During the morning hours Elder Thomas B. Marsh (then president of the Twelve) and Elder David W. Patten (also an apostle) spoke to the Saints. In the afternoon the Presidency and the apostles participated in administering and passing the sacrament, after which Joseph Smith and Oliver Cowdery commenced praying privately. At that moment these two men participated in one of the most important visions of the ages.[21] Although temple work as we know it today was not performed in our first temple (members received only a partial endowment at that time), the keys to engage in temple work were unfolded in that House of the Lord (D&C 110). One of the main purposes for the construction of that building was realized on that occasion. Saints who had sacrificed for three years were recipients of one of the most rewarding visions of all time. And the blessings that flowed from that temple "have given literally millions of people great cause to rejoice."[22]

## The Savior Appears

As Jesus and his three Galilean apostles were transfigured anciently, so also were Joseph Smith and Oliver Cowdery—"apostles, and especial witnesses" of the name of Christ (D&C 27:12)—transformed and made ready to see within the veil and receive divine direction and authority. Appropriately, Jesus the Lord appeared first. In ancient days Jehovah had chosen frequently to make his presence known and manifest his glory through a cloud which rested upon his temple. In modern times Jehovah came again to his temple—the first one worthy of his presence in many centuries—and in power and great glory (cf. Exod. 24:9-10; Rev. 1:14-15) accepted the offering of his people. This appearance was a realization of the promise given in 1833: "And inasmuch as my people build a house unto me in the name of the Lord, and do not suffer any unclean thing to come into it, that it be not defiled, my glory shall rest upon it; Yea, and my presence shall be there, for I will come into it, and all the pure in heart that shall come into it shall see God" (D&C 97:15-16).

After announcing that Joseph and Oliver were cleansed from sin, the Lord encouraged the brethren to rejoice in the occasion and to broaden their vision as to the importance of the Kirtland Temple: "Yea the hearts of thousands and tens of thousands shall greatly rejoice in consequence of the blessings which shall be poured out, and the endowment with which my servants have been endowed in this house." Even though the Kirtland temple ceremonies were only a partial endowment (the full endowment would be revealed to the Prophet in Nauvoo in 1842), the keys and powers which were received on 3 April 1836 affect time and the eternities.

**Moses and the Gathering**

Joseph Smith recorded: "After this vision closed, the heavens were again opened unto us; and Moses appeared before us, and committed unto us the keys of the gathering of Israel from the four parts of the earth, and the leading of the ten tribes from the land of the north." The keys or directing power restored by the ancient lawgiver enabled the Saints to accomplish the divine directive delivered in September of 1830: "And ye are called to bring to pass the gathering of mine elect; for mine elect hear my voice and harden not their hearts" (D&C 29:7). To the President of the Church—the man appointed "to preside over the whole church, and to be like unto Moses" (D&C 107:91)—were given keys to gather modern Israel. Even as Moses held keys to lead ancient Israel out of Egyptian bondage, so the President of the Church of Jesus Christ of Latter-day Saints was given keys to call and lead modern Israel out of the bondage of today's world. "These keys empower those who hold them to lead all Israel, the ten tribes included, from all the nations of the earth, coming as the prophetic word affirms, one by one and two by two, to the mountains of the Lord's houses, there to be endowed with power from on high."[23]

People are gathered first spiritually and then temporally. They are gathered first as they accept the true Messiah and are thus "restored to the true church and fold of God" (2 Ne. 9:2); secondly, they are gathered as they go where the Saints of God congregate. In the early days of the restored Church, for example, a convert evidenced his devotion to the faith first by baptism and then by relocating with the "body of Christ," be that in Ohio, Missouri, Illinois, or the Great Basin. It is clear, however, that as early as 1833 the Prophet Joseph understood that the time would come when the concept of gathering would expand, a day "when there is found no more room for them [i.e., when the areas of Missouri or even Utah would no longer be the sole places of gathering]; and then I have other places which I will appoint unto them, and they shall be called stakes, for the curtains or the strength of Zion" (D&C 101:21). By the end of the nineteenth century Saints were told to remain in their native lands and thus to build up the stakes of Zion in all the earth. In August of 1972 Elder Bruce R. McConkie explained to the Saints of Mexico and Central America: "This gathering has commenced and shall continue until the righteous are assembled into the congregations of the Saints in all the nations of the earth." And then, becoming more specific, Elder McConkie added: "The place of gathering for the Mexican Saints is Mexico; the place of gathering for the Brazilian, Brazil; and so it goes throughout the length and breadth of the whole earth. Japan is for the Japanese; Korea is for the Koreans; Australia is for the Australians; every nation is the gathering place for its own people."[24]

Only through the establishment and strengthening of stakes throughout the world could the full concept of Zion be realized; only then could the Lord make it possible for the blessings of the temple to be had universally. Joseph Smith taught: "The main object [of gathering] was to build unto the Lord a house whereby He could reveal unto His people the ordinances of His house and the glories of His Kingdom, and teach the people the way of salvation."[25]

### Elias and the Patriarchal Order

"After this, Elias appeared, and committed the dispensation of the gospel of Abraham, saying that in us and our seed all generations after us should be blessed." The identity of Elias—whether he be Noah,[26] Abraham himself, or a prophet named Elias from the days of Abraham[27]—is not clearly known. This heavenly messenger restored the keys necessary to establish the ancient patriarchal order, making

Joseph Smith and all those who receive celestial marriage through the temple heirs of the blessings and "promises of the fathers"—Abraham, Isaac, and Jacob.[28] The promises to Joseph Smith (and all worthy Latter-day Saints after him) are glorious. The Lord said: "And as I said unto Abraham concerning the kindreds of the earth, even so I say unto my servant Joseph: In thee and in thy seed shall the kindred of the earth be blessed" (D&C 124:58). In addition:

> Abraham received promises concerning his seed, and of the fruit of his loins—from whose loins ye are, namely, my servant Joseph—which were to continue so long as they were in the world; and as touching Abraham and his seed, out of the world they should continue; both in the world and out of the world should they continue as innumerable as the stars. . . . This promise is yours also, because ye are of Abraham, and the promise was made unto Abraham; and by this law [of eternal marriage] is the continuation of the works of my Father, wherein he glorifieth himself. Go ye, therefore, and do the works of Abraham; enter ye into my law and ye shall be saved (D&C 132:30-32).

Elias thus returned and delivered that directing power through which eternal family units may be organized and perpetuated through the new and everlasting covenant of marriage. A modern apostle, Elder Bruce R. McConkie, has written:

> As the crowning cause for wonderment, that God who is no respector of persons has given a like promise [to that of Abraham and Joseph Smith] to every [member] in the kingdom who has gone to the holy temple and entered into the blessed order of matrimony there performed. Every person married in the temple for time and for all eternity has sealed upon him, conditioned upon his faithfulness, all of the blessings of the ancient patriarchs, including the crowning promise and assurance of eternal increase, which means, literally, a posterity as numerous as the dust particles of the earth.[29]

### Elijah and the Sealing Power

The Prophet Joseph wrote concerning the final heavenly ministrant on this occasion: "After this vision had closed, another great and glorious vision burst upon us; for Elijah the prophet, who was taken to heaven without tasting death, stood before us, and said: Behold, the time has fully come, which was spoken of by the mouth of Malachi—testifying that he [Elijah] should be sent, before the great and dreadful day of the Lord come—To turn the hearts of the fathers to the children, and the children to the fathers, lest the whole earth be smitten with a curse." Precisely on the day that Elijah's appearance took place, Jews throughout the world were engaged in the celebration of the Passover, the annual commemoration of the day over three thousand years before when the angel of death had passed over the firstborn of Israel whose dwellings were marked by the blood of lambs. Since the time of Malachi—from about 500 B.C.—Jews world-wide waited with anxious anticipation for the coming of Elijah. Alfred Edersheim has written: "Hence to this day, in every Jewish home [which formally celebrates the Paschal feast], at a certain part of the Paschal service—just after the 'third cup,' or the 'cup of blessing,' has been drunk—the door is opened to admit Elijah the prophet."[30] Elijah did come, but not to Jewish homes. He came rather to the house of the Lord, and to his legal administrators; there he bestowed priesthood keys of inestimable worth and eternal import.

When Moroni appeared to Joseph Smith in 1823 he quoted numerous passages from the Old and New Testaments. The Prophet indicated that he quoted Mal. 4:5-6 but gave a different rendering from that of the King James text. The prophecy began: "Behold, I will reveal unto you the priesthood, by the hand of Elijah the prophet, before the coming of the great and dreadful day of the Lord" (D&C 2:1). Joseph and Oliver had been ordained to the Melchizedek Priesthood and given apostolic power and commission as early as 1829. How was it, then, that Elijah would reveal the Priesthood? Elijah was sent to restore keys—directing powers—of the patriarchal order of priesthood, rights which had not been fully operational in this dispensation. Elijah restored the keys whereby families (organized in the patriarchal order through the keys delivered by Elias) could be bound and sealed for eternity.

Three months before his death, Joseph Smith instructed the Latter-day Saints concerning the mission of Elijah: "The spirit, power, and calling of Elijah is that ye have power to hold the key of the revelations, ordinances, oracles, powers and endowments of the fulness of the Melchizedek Priesthood and of the kingdom of God on the earth."[31] Elijah restored the keys whereby individuals and families may (through the blessings of the holy temple) develop line upon line to the point where they receive the "fulness of the priesthood," and thus become kings and priests, queens and priestesses unto God in the patriarchal order. "Those holding the fulness of the Melchizedek Priesthood," Joseph had taught earlier, "are kings and priests of the Most High God, holding the keys of power and blessings."[32] Through the powers delivered by Elias (via the marriage discipline of the Fathers—Abraham, Isaac, and Jacob) eternal family units—here and hereafter—are created. Through the powers delivered by Elijah, families may be sealed unto eternal life, inasmuch as "the power of Elijah is sufficient to make our calling and election sure."[33]

Because Elijah came, all other ordinances for the living and the dead (e.g., baptisms, confirmations, ordinations, etc.) have real meaning and are thus of efficacy, virtue, and force in eternity.[34] The ordinances associated with the ministry of Elijah (centering in the temples) are the "capstone blessings" of the gospel and the consummation of the work of the Church; they provide purpose and perspective for all other sacred activities.

Elijah came to "plant in the hearts of the children the promises made to the fathers" whereby the "hearts of the children [should] turn to their fathers" (D&C 2:2). The Spirit of the Lord witnesses to faithful Latter-day Saints of the central place of eternal marriage and of the sublime joys associated with the everlasting continuation of the family. Through temples God's promises to the fathers—the promises pertaining to the gospel, the priesthood, and eternal increase (Abr. 2:8-11)—are extended to all God's children. The hearts of the children turn to the ancient fathers because the children are now participants in and recipients of the blessings of the fathers. Being profoundly grateful for such privileges, members of the Church (motivated by the *spirit* of Elijah) also find their hearts turning to their more immediate fathers, and do all within their power (through genealogical research and subsequent temple work) to insure that the blessings of the ancient fathers are enjoyed by ancestry as well as posterity. "If it were not so [that is, if Elijah had not come to restore the powers by which families could be sealed everlastingly], the whole earth would be utterly wasted at [Christ's] coming" (D&C 2:3). Why? Simply because the earth would not have accomplished its foreordained purposes, to establish on its face a family system patterned after the order of heaven. If there were no binding and sealing powers whereby families could be cemented forever, then the plans and designs and schemes of mortal man—being basically purposeless from an eternal perspective—would be revealed at the Second Coming as the empty and superficial substitues which they are. The Lord's purpose is to bring to pass the immortality and eternal life of man (Moses 1:39). Because of Elijah's coming, ancestry and posterity may be grafted together eternally.

"Therefore the keys of this dispensation are committed into your hands; and by this ye may know that the dreadful day of the Lord is near, even at the doors" (D&C 110:16).

## Notes

[1]Parts of this article have been published in Milton V. Backman, Jr., *The Heavens Resound: A History of the Latter-day Saints in Ohio, 1830-1838* (Salt Lake City: Deseret Book Co., 1983), chapters 9 and 16, and appear in this work by permission of the publisher.

[2]*Ibid.*, pp. 140, 147-49.

[3]*Ibid.*, p. 24; *HC* 2:161.

[4]Heber C. Kimball in *JD* 10:165-66. See also "Extracts from Heber C. Kimball's Journal," *Times and Seasons* 6 (15 April 1845): 867.

[5]*HC* 2:309, 432; Diary of Joseph Smith, 1835-36, pp. 34-35, 189, holography, Joseph Smith Collection, Church Archives; see also Dean C. Jessee, *The Personal Writings of Joseph Smith* (Salt Lake City: Deseret Book Co., 1984), p. 82.

[6]*JD* 18:132.

[7]Backman, *The Heavens Resound*, p. 285.

[8]*HC* 2:379-81.

[9]*Ibid.*, pp. 380-81; Jessee, *The Personal Writings of Joseph Smith*, pp. 145-47.

[10]*HC* 2:381; Jessee, *The Personal Writings of Joseph Smith*, p. 147. A description of the events of 1836, including Joseph Smith's revelation on salvation for the dead, was recorded in Joseph Smith's 1835-36 diary. The revelation was included in the 1981 edition of the Doctrine and Covenants

(section 137).

[11]For a discussion of salvation for the dead, specifically relating to D&C 137, see Robert L. Millet, "Salvation Beyond the Grave," found herein.

[12]*HC* 2:382; Oliver Cowdery, Sketch Book, 21 January 1836, Church Archives, published in Leonard J. Arrington, "Oliver Cowdery's Kirtland, Ohio Sketch Book," *BYU Studies* 12 (Summer 1972): 410-26.

[13]Cowdery, Sketch Book, 26 March 1836.

[14]Backman, *The Heavens Resound*, pp. 295-98; *HC* 2:410-27. Official minutes of this meeting, including the dedicatory prayer, appeared in the *Messenger and Advocate* (March 1836). The prayer was initially published in the Doctrine and Covenants in the 1876 edition.

[15]*Church News*, 12 February 1972.

[16]*HC* 2:427-28.

[17]Backman, *The Heavens Resound*, p. 299.

[18]Eliza R. Snow, *Eliza R. Snow: An Immortal—Selected Writings of Eliza R. Snow*, compiled by Nicholas G. Morgan (Salt Lake City: Nicholas G. Morgan Sr. Foundation, 1957), pp. 58, 62.

[19]Autobiography of Nancy Tracy, p. 9, Bancroft Library, University of California, and typescript, LDS Church Archives.

[20]*HC* 3:387; *TPJS*, p. 158.

[21]*HC* 2:434-35; Jessee, *The Personal Writings of Joseph Smith*, pp. 186-87. A description of the vision that is now section 110 in the Doctrine and Covenants was the last entry in Joseph Smith's 1835-36 diary and was first published in the *Deseret News* on 6 November 1852. It was included as section 110 in the 1876 edition of the Doctrine and Covenants.

[22]L. G. Otten and C. M. Caldwell, *Sacred Truths of the Doctrine and Covenants*, 2 vols. (Springville, Utah: LEMB, Inc., 1983), 2:249.

[23]Bruce R. McConkie, *Conference Report*, April 1983, p. 28; *Ensign*, May 1983, p. 22.

[24]Cited by Harold B. Lee in *Conference Report*, April 1973, pp. 6-7; *Ensign*, July 1973, p. 5.

[25]*HC* 5:423; *TPJS*, p. 308.

[26]See Luke 1:19; D&C 27:7; *HC* 3:386 (*TPJS*, p. 157); Joseph Fielding Smith, *Conference Report*, April 1960, p. 72; *Answers to Gospel Questions*, 5 vols. (Salt Lake City: Deseret Book Co., 1960), 3:138-41.

[27]See Bruce R. McConkie, *The Millennial Messiah* (Salt Lake City: Deseret Book Co., 1982), pp. 103, 268.

[28]See Bruce R. McConkie, *Conference Report*, April 1983, p. 28; *Ensign*, May 1983, p. 22.

[29]*The Millennial Messiah*, p. 264.

[30]Alfred Edersheim, *The Temple: Its Ministry and Services as They Were at the Time of Christ* (Grand Rapids, Mich.: Eerdmans, reprinted 1975), p. 230.

[31]*HC* 6:251.

[32]*Ibid.*, 5:555.

[33]Joseph Smith, *HC* 6:252. Why send Elijah? Joseph Smith answered: "Elijah was the last prophet that held the keys of the Priesthood, and who will, before the last dispensation, restore the authority and deliver the keys of the Priesthood, in order that all the ordinances may be attended to in righteousness" (*HC* 4:211).

[34]See Joseph Smith, *HC* 4:211; 6:251; Joseph Fielding Smith, *Doctrines of Salvation*, 3 vols., comp. Bruce R. McConkie (Salt Lake City: Bookcraft, 1954-56), 2:115-28; Bruce R. McConkie, *Mormon Doctrine*, 2nd ed. (Salt Lake City: Bookcraft, 1966), p. 683.

# 39

# JOSEPH SMITH IN SALEM
## (D&C 111)

DONALD Q. CANNON

### Historical Setting

In order to understand the Salem revelation (D&C 111), one must have some knowledge of the financial situation of the Church in 1836. The Church in that period was in debt, or at least had severe shortages of capital. Some of the debt had been incurred in the construction of the Kirtland Temple. This expensive building had taxed the resources of the members. Another source of financial distress was the aid rendered to the Saints in Missouri—both in direct aid and in paying for Zion's Camp.[1]

Give this situation, Church leaders were anxious to find ways to relieve the debt and increase the amount of usable money. When Jonathan Burgess came to Kirtland telling of treasure located in Salem, he found believing listeners. Ebenezer Robinson recalled it this way:

> A brother in the church by the name of Burgess, had come to Kirtland and stated that a large amount of money had been secreted in the cellar of a certain house in Salem, Massachussetts, which had belonged to a widow, and he thought he was the only person now living who had knowledge of it, or to the location of the house. We saw the brother Burgess, but Don Carlos Smith told us with regard to the hidden treasure. His statement was credited by the brethren, and steps were taken to try and secure the treasure.[2]

Concerning the matter of treasure hunting, two points warrant consideration. First, Salem was a prosperous seaport with a world trade. The possibility of treasure being located in Salem was very likely. Second, treasure hunting was widespread among Americans in that era. Consider, for example, the following story from a Salem newspaper during the time when Joseph Smith and his party were in Salem:

> MONEY DIGGING. There are many spots in Long Island where tradition holds that Capt Kidd buried sums of money. A number of men are now engaged making excavations about a

> ledge of rocks in the vicinity of Sand's Point. The ledge is called "Kidd's Rock," and the men are adventures from Boston. More labor has been expended on Long Island in following the delusions of men in regard to buried gold, than if properly bestowed would have sufficed to make many fortunes.—*Long Island Star*.[3]

In addition to treasure seeking in Salem, there is another financial element in the story. En route to Massachussets, the Prophet and his companions visited New York City, where they consulted with creditors concerning their debt.[4]

Joseph Smith, Sidney Rigdon, Hyrum Smith, and Oliver Cowdery left Kirtland 25 July 1836. They traveled by carriage to Fairport and by boat from Fairport to Buffalo, New York. After spending a night at a hotel in Buffalo, they traveled by Erie Canal lineboat to Utica, where they boarded a railroad car bound for Albany. A Hudson River steamer carried them from Albany to New York City. They remained in New York City for four days, taking care of the financial matters previously mentioned. Oliver Cowdery noted, significantly, that they inquired about printing notes for a Church bank. The party traveled by ship from New York to Boston. From Boston to Salem they traveled by rail, arriving 4 August 1836.[5]

Arriving in the wealthy, bustling seaport of Salem, Massachussetts, Joseph Smith was on familiar ground. He had visited with a relative there some years earlier. The occasion for the first visit was a serious leg operation which Joseph had undergone while the family resided in New Hampshire. Hoping that exposure to fresh sea breezes would hasten his recovery, Joseph's parents had arranged for the visit. It may have been during that earlier visit that Joseph gained an appreciation for Salem's resources.[6]

The 1836 visit of Joseph Smith and his companions is verifiable by definitive historical evidence. Several newspapers call attention to the visit, and the party also signed the guest register at the East India Marine Society Museum.[7] The author has examined the register and has, in his possession, both photocopies and colored slides of the guest register and the signatures. Newspapers which carried stories of their visit include: *Salem Observer*, 27 August 1836; *Essex Register*, 25 August 1836; *The Boston Daily Times*, 24 August 1836. The *Salem Observer*, for 27 August

1836, reported, for example:

> MORMONISM. Notices were sent around on Saturday, that Mr. Rigdon, of Ohio, would preach at the Lyceum that afternoon, on the subject of the Christian religion. Having understood that he was a *Mormonite*, we went to the Lyceum, expecting to hear something on the subject of the peculiar doctrines of that sect, and perhaps to get a view of the "Mormon Bible," translated from the Golden Plates said to have been discovered by Jo. Smith, their prophet! The preacher was a man of very respectable appearance, apparently about 40 years of age, and very fluent in his language. He commenced by reading the 1st chapter of the Epistle to the Galatians.

From this article we learn that Sidney Rigdon took a leading role as a spokesman for the Church in this period. It is interesting to note that the Lyceum where he spoke is famous for another reason: from this building the very first long distance phone call was made.

Further documentation of the visit is provided in a letter which Joseph Smith wrote to his wife Emma during his visit to Salem. The letter follows:

> Salem, Mass., August 19th, 1836.
>
> My beloved Wife:—Bro. Hyrum is about to start for home before the rest of us, which seems wisdom in God, as our business here can not be determined as soon as we could wish to have it. I thought a line from me by him would be acceptable to you, even if it did not contain but little, that you may know that you and the children are much on my mind. With regard to the great object of our mission, you will be anxious to know. We have found the house since Bro. Burgess left us, very luckily and providentially, as we had one spell been most discouraged. The house is occupied, and it will require much care and patience to rent or buy it. We think we shall be able to effect it; if not now within the course of a few months. We think we shall be at home about the middle of September. I can think of many things concerning our business, but can only pray that you may have wisdom to manage the concerns that involve on you, and want you should believe me that I am your sincere friend and husband. In haste. Yours &c.,
>
> Joseph Smith, Jr.[8]
>
> Emma Smith

From this letter to his wife it is evident that Joseph Smith was still concerned about finding the treasure, notwithstanding the content of the revelation which he had received nearly two weeks earlier. In fact, they had not been successful in locating the same house that Jonathan Burgess had told them about in Kirtland. They had rented a house on Union Street, which is not far from the Salem Custom House made famous by Nathaniel Hawthorne. Apparently they divided their time between preaching, sightseeing, and looking for the treasure.

Soon after their arrival in Salem, the Prophet Joseph Smith received the revelation currently known as section 111 of the Doctrine and Covenants. On 6 August 1836, Oliver Cowdery, Sidney Rigdon and Hyrum Smith went to visit the East India Marine Society Museum, leaving Joseph Smith in the solitude of the rented house. It was in this setting that he received the revelation.

## Section 111: A Closer Look

Verse one of section 111 constitutes an excellent example of the necessity of understanding the historical background of modern revelation. If one reads v. 1 without any historical awareness, it makes little or no sense. However, the historical information makes perfectly clear what the Lord is talking about. When the Lord says that he is "not displeased with your coming, . . . notwithstanding your follies," the historical facts help us identify those "follies." Their follies included trying to solve their financial problems on their own, without seeking the help of the Lord. The Lord had counseled them earlier in D&C 104:78-80 to humble themselves and seek relief from debt through faith. In August 1836, however, they had relied on the arm of flesh, even to the extent of looking for hidden treasure in Salem. It is no wonder that the Lord used the term "follies."

In his wisdom, however, the Lord refrains from harsh censure and adds positive reinforcement and assurance. In spite of their follies he assured them that he was not displeased with their coming. In a word, coming to Salem was not evil. In subsequent verses he told them how to change the situation into a positive experience.

In v. 2, for example, he referred to the subject of treasure and said that he had much treasure for the benefit of Zion. In that same verse he referred to people as part of the treasure. The brethren in that day evidently believed that the Lord was making reference to converting people to the Church. They set about the task of converting people in Salem in 1836 and in a major missionary effort in the 1840s.

At a special conference held in Philadelphia in 1841, Hyrum Smith and William Law called Erastus Snow and Benjamin Winchester to serve a mission in Salem. They gave Erastus Snow a copy of the Salem Revelation and requested him to fulfill it. Snow and Winchester arrived in Salem in September of 1841. They preached at public meetings, published a pamphlet addressed to the citizens of Salem, and challenged the notorious Mormon apostate, John C. Bennett to debate. Their efforts bore fruit. By March of 1842 they had organized the Salem Branch with 53 members. By the end of that summer, the branch had 90 members.

The success of the Elders did not go unnoticed in the Salem press. Two brief examples will illustrate. On 7 December 1841 the *Salem Gazette* reported: "A very worthy and respectable laboring man, and his wife, were baptized by immersion in the Mormon faith." *The Salem Register* for 2 June 1842 reported: "Mormonism is advancing with a perfect rush in this city." Clearly the Latter-day Saint Elders had found this part of the treasure.

In v. 9 the Lord mentioned another kind of treasure, when he instructed the elders: "Inquire diligently concerning the more ancient inhabitants and founders of this city." Here, perhaps the Lord was challenging the Prophet and his associates to learn of their ancestors while in the area—perhaps as an introduction to genealogical research. Salem is only a few miles from Topsfield, the ancestral home of the Prophet Joseph Smith.[10] Salem had then and still has today excellent library facilities for genealogy, such as the Essex Institute. While we have no evidence that Joseph Smith did genealogical research in Salem in 1836, the opportunity was ideal and the work needed to be done.

Section 111, then, is a revelation which shows the weakness of men, the goodness of God, and the eventual triumph of the Lord's work through the faith and efforts of his Saints.

## Notes

[1]Milton V. Backman, Jr., *The Heavens Resound: A History of the Latter-day Saints in Ohio, 1830-1838* (Salt Lake City: Deseret Book Co., 1983), pp. 142-61, 175-200, 311-14; Marvin S. Hill, C. Keith Rooker, Larry Wimmer, *The Kirtland Economy Revisited: A Market Critique of Sectarian Economics* (Provo, Ut.: Brigham Young University Press, 1977). Although this study stresses the positive aspects of economic conditions in Kirtland, it does point out that lack of capital was a problem. Joseph Smith made frequent reference to problems related to the lack of money in his diaries, letters, etc. See, for example, Dean C. Jessee, ed., *The Personal Writings of Joseph Smith* (Salt Lake City: Deseret Book Co., 1984), pp. 36-37, 58, 98.

[2]Ebenezer Robinson, "Items of Personal History of the Editor," *The Return* (Davis City, Iowa: Church of Christ, 1889-90), pp. 104-5. My own research shows Jonathan Burgess, while Dean Jessee says it is William Burgess.

[3]*The Salem Observer,* 6 August 1836. Note that this article was reprinted from *The Long Island Star.* For an excellent study of the treasure-hunting aspects of the trip to Salem see David R. Proper, "Joseph Smith and Salem," *Essex Institute Historical Collections,* 100 (April 1964): 88-97.

[4]For this information I am indebted to Richard L. Anderson of Brigham Young University. He has graciously shared with me the unpublished manuscript of his forthcoming book *Dear Joseph, Dear Emma* (Salt Lake City: Deseret Book Co., 1985).

[5]*Ibid.*

[6]LeRoy S. Wirthlin, "Nathan Smith, Surgical Consultant to Joseph Smith," *BYU Studies* 17 (Spring 1977): 319-37.

[7]The present name of the museum is the Peabody Museum.

[8]Jessee, *Personal Writings of Joseph Smith,* pp. 349-50.

[9]For a more complete account of the work of Elders Winchester and Snow see Kenneth W. Godfrey, "More Treasures Than One: Section 111" in *Hearken, O Ye People: Discourses on the Doctrine and Covenants* (Salt Lake City: Randall Book Co., 1984).

[10]Donald Q. Cannon, "Topsfield, Massachussets: Ancestral Home of the Prophet Joseph Smith," *BYU Studies* 14 (Fall 1973): 56-76.

# 40
# INSTRUCTIONS AND ASSURANCE FROM FAR WEST
## (D&C 114 and 115)

David F. Boone

The setting for sections 114 and 115 is April 1838 in Far West, Missouri. The Prophet Joseph had recently fled for his life from Kirtland, Ohio, and the Church as a whole was in a state of confusion and chaos. As a result of the spirit of speculation that was running rampant in Ohio and the persecution that became a trademark of Missouri, it was difficult for the Prophet to know exactly who was and who was not still faithful in the Church. Sections 114 and 115 give a measure of assurance to the Prophet as to who was still dependable. Section 114 identifies specific individuals—particularly David W. Patten and the Twelve—as ones in whom Joseph could place his trust. In section 115 the Lord revealed the full name of the restored Church and established a banner or standard of identity for his Latter-day Saints.

### Section 114

The main area of consideration in section 114 is Apostle David W. Patten specifically and later the Twelve Apostles collectively (see D&C 118). Section 114 gives some specific direction to Elder Patten. There is no suggestion that David had sought the instruction, as many of the Elders and Church members were prone to do in the early days of the Church. He was residing in Missouri with Elder Thomas B. Marsh in the midst of acute persecution from both inside and outside of the Church. In fact, being in the area, these two Apostles were the logical choices to steady and preside over the local Church organizations when the presiding officers—David and John Whitmer and W. W. Phelps—lost the confidence and support of the Saints in that area. The Lord directed Brother Patten to "settle up all his business as soon as he possibly can, and make a disposition of his merchandise, that he may perform a mission unto me next spring in company with others, even Twelve" (D&C 114:1).

David Patten's situation was one which holds a great deal of interest and fascination for members of the Church and students of its history. Elder Patten was directed specifically to prepare for a mission to be performed the following spring. The events in Far West, however, were such that by the next spring when the Twelve were to leave from the Temple lot, they had to do so at the peril of their very lives. In fact, by the time of their departure—because of persecution and other factors—at least four of the original members of the Quorum of the Twelve Apostles had become disaffected from the Church. These were William E. McLellin, Luke S. and Lyman E. Johnson, and John F. Boynton.

Elder Patten has become almost legendary in the history of the Church for his courage and personal power in the face of adversity. He was a fearless defender of the faith and also of the Prophet Joseph Smith. Elder Patten stood six feet, one inch tall and weighed over two hundred pounds; he was a man of great physical strength. A biographer recorded that on one occasion he picked up a man bodily and threw him out of the house for continually disturbing a preaching meeting.[1] On another occasion, he went outside to meet a mob bent on doing bodily harm to him and his fellow missionaries. Upon hearing of their intentions, he bared his chest and invited them to shoot him if it would satisfy them. Instead of shooting, they began to fear and ran as if in peril of their own lives.[2]

According to Elder Wilford Woodruff's account of still another situation, he and other elders, including Elder Patten, were asked to appear before a judge on charges of "testifying that Christ would come in this generation and that we promised the Holy Ghost to those whom we baptized." Elder Patten spoke in the missionaries' defense and "delivered a speech of about twenty minutes, holding the audience spell-bound while he told them of their wickedness and the abominations that they were guilty of, also, of the curse of God that awaited them if they did not repent, for taking up harmless, inoffensive men for preaching the Gospel of Christ." At the conclusion of his remarks, the judge indicated that Elder Patten must have been armed with weapons to speak so boldly when all else was against him. To this Elder Patten remarked, "I have weapons that you know not of, and they were given me of God, for He gives me all the power I have."[3] This became a lifelong theme or motto for Elder Patten.

According to the Prophet Joseph Smith, David Patten had confided to him sometime in the early summer of 1838 that he, Patten, had been praying and "had asked the Lord to let him die the death of a martyr." Lycurgus Wilson, who wrote of the life of Elder Patten, suggested that this desire to die as a martyr probably came as a result of the revelation in section 114.[4] The Prophet expressed sorrow at such a request, "for," according to Wilson, the prophet stated, "when a man of your faith asks the Lord for anything, he generally gets it."[5]

David defended the rights of the Saints—their lands and property—as if he really believed he could achieve such an honor. It should be remembered that between the time the revelation was given in April of 1838 and the following April when the Twelve were directed (in section 118) to leave from the Temple lot in Far West, some of the greatest atrocities that the Saints were to know were committed in Missouri. In addition to the persecution, many of the leaders of the Church were losing their places as a result of apostasy, persecution, and their own weakness. For example, in April of 1838 Oliver Cowdery was excommunicated from the Church, and in May, William E. McLellin was cut off. Between August and December of 1838, the Saints were driven from DeWitt County, with some of the Saints dying from persecution and exposure. Likewise, the Saints were being driven from Davies, Caldwell, Roy, and Carroll counties. Members of the Church were involved in skirmishes at Gallatin, Crooked River, and Haun's Mill. The Prophet and other leaders were taken as prisoners to Richmond and were under constant danger and threat of being shot. The situation reached a peak as the Saints were driven from the state of Missouri as a result of the Extermination Order issued by Governor Lilburn W. Boggs.

At one of these confrontations—the Battle of Crooked River in October of 1838—Elder David Patten's unusual desire to die as a martyr was to be granted. A mob of some thirty or forty men had taken three of the Saints prisoners. The vocalized intent of the mob was to kill their captives and then return to burn others of the Saints out of their homes in the Far West area. The Prophet directed Elder Patten, who was characterized as "Captain Fear Not," to take a group of brethren, about seventy-five in number, and in a show of force disperse the mobs and free the captives. In both of these objectives the Saints were successful, but in the process of the charge one of the mobbers, hiding behind a tree, shot Elder Patten in the stomach. Two other Latter-day Saints were killed, and several others were wounded. David was taken back toward Far West where he was met by his wife, the Prophet, and other leading brethren of the Church. Of this sad reunion and parting, Heber C. Kimball reported: "During his removal his sufferings were so excruciating that he frequently desired us to lay him down that he might die; but being desirous to get him out of the reach of the mob, we prevailed upon him to let us carry him among his friends. . . . Although he had medical assistance, his wound was such that there was no hope entertained of his recovery, and this he was perfectly aware of." To his wife, Pheebe Ann, he issued a challenge: "Whatever you do else, oh do not deny the faith." To the brethren who no doubt desired the faith to heal such a willing and capable leader in the cause of truth, he asked: "Brethren you have held me by your faith, but do give me up, and let me go, I beseech you." And then to the Lord he prayed, "I feel that I have kept the faith, I have finished my course, henceforth there is laid up for me a crown, which the Lord the righteous Judge will give me. . . . Father, I ask thee in the name of Jesus Christ, that thou wouldst release my spirit and receive it unto Thyself." According to his request, the elders "committed him to God, and he soon breathed his last, and slept in Jesus without a groan," his noble wish to die as a martyr being fulfilled.[6] The Prophet declared: "Brother Patten was a very worthy man, beloved by all good men who knew him. He was one of the Twelve Apostles, and died as he had lived, a man of God, and strong in the faith of a glorious resurrection, in a world where mobs will have no power or place."[7] Further he said, "There lies a man that has done just as he said he would—he has laid down his life for his friends."[8]

Elder Patten was buried near Far West with full military honors, but because of the persecution in the area and the withdrawal of the Saints, the exact spot of the grave is no longer known. The life and contributions of David Patten, nevertheless, were not nor will be soon forgotten. The Lord in later revelations in the Doctrine and Covenants referred to Elder Patten and the reward that he had gained (see D&C 124:19, 130). As a further illustration of how his brethren of the Twelve felt about the man, in 1876 Orson Pratt, acting under the direction of President Brigham Young, added section 114 to the Doctrine and

Covenants. Later still, President Harold B. Lee recorded: "I have thought it more than mere coincidence that one of the first martyrs in this dispensation, David W. Patten, a member of the Twelve Apostles, lost his life near the valley of Adam-Ondi-Ahman."[9]

The second and concluding verse of section 114 suggests that even though a man such as David W. Patten would lose his life, or others like Marsh, Boynton, or McLellin would lose their places in the leading Quorums of the Church, the work of the Lord would go forward, and others would be chosen to fill the vacancies. More tragic that the loss of one of the Church's stalwart members by death was the loss of one of its members through transgression or apostasy; sad indeed is the plight of those who once shared the confidence of the Prophet and the honor of their God, but who through transgression lost their places in the kingdom.

## Section 115

In section 115 several important historical and doctrinal points are made. Verse 1 concerns the First Presidency of the Church. Several of the early stalwarts served as counselors to the Prophet Joseph. In addition to Oliver Cowdery, Hyrum Smith, Jesse Gause, and Frederick G. Williams, who all had been counselors, Joseph Smith, Sr., Hyrum Smith, and Father John Smith all served as assistant counselors.[10]

In vv. 3 and 4, a doctrinal direction of great significance is given: the name by which the Church should be known. Previous to this time it had been called by several names: The Church of Christ (107:59); The Church of Jesus Christ; the Church of God (84:34); and the Church of the Latter-day Saints. "All these names, however, were by this revelation brushed aside, and since then the official name given in this revelation has been recognized as the true title of the Church. . . . The appropriateness of this title is self-evident, and in it there is a beautiful recognition of the relationship both of the Lord Jesus Christ and of the Saints to the organization. It is 'The Church of Jesus Christ.' It is the Lord's; He owns it, He organized it. It is the Sacred Depository of His truth. It is His instrumentality for promulgating all those spiritual truths with which He would have mankind acquainted."[11]

The name of the Church takes on even greater significance when viewed in relation to the directions given in 3 Nephi. President Marion

G. Romney quoted the Savior: "'How be it my Church save it be called in my name? For if a Church be called in Moses' name then it be Moses' church: or if it be called in the name of a man then it be the church of a man; but if it be called in my name then it is my Church, if it so be that they are built upon my gospel' (3 Ne. 27:8). . . . The restored church thus meets the Savior's two fold-test; it bears His name and it is built upon his gospel."[12]

Verses 7-16 are directed to the commandment from the Lord to build a Temple in Far West, Missouri. This was the third temple commanded in this dispensation. To this point in the history of the Church, however, only one had been built. It appears that the Saints began the work in earnest. The cornerstones of the temple were laid, according to revelation, on 4 July 1838 (v. 10). Other work progressed, too, at a faster pace than had been the case with previous temples. The Saints seem to have been cured of their retitence, perhaps as a result of the Lord's chastening when they were not actively pursuing the construction of the Kirtland Temple. However, when the fury of persecution broke out, the Saints were thwarted once again in realizing the will of the Lord regarding a temple in Far West. The Lord further cautioned the leaders of the Church against going into debt for the purpose of building the Temple, notwithstanding the important structure that it was to be. This was perhaps a foreshadowing of the current Church policy concerning the dedication of Church edifices only after they are fully paid for.

In fulfillment of vv. 17-19 that Far West would become a gathering place of the Saints, a group of approximately 500 of the Kirtland Saints, under the direction of the Seventy's Quorum, made the trip to Far West in the spring and summer of 1838. Most of those who constituted this group had been unable to leave earlier. Most had been compelled to leave Kirtland, Ohio. Far West, Missouri was opening up as a major center for the Saints to gather and settle. Much could be said of a historical nature concerning Kirtland Camp, as the group came to be known, but according to Zerah Pulsipher, one individual in the group, "We suffered the perils of a hard journey for near one thousand miles among hostile people, but the Lord brought [us] to try to see what our faith was made of."[13]

In addition to trying the members (to test their faith), the Far West episode became a "dress rehearsal" of sorts for a larger and more complete exodus. In almost eight years the Saints would be forced to leave their homes again and travel as a group—in search of a new home in the West.

---

## Notes

[1]Lycurgus A. Wilson, *Life of David W. Patten: The First Apostolic Martyr* (Salt Lake City: Deseret News Press, 1904), p. 15.

[2]*Ibid.*, p. 47.

[3]Wilford Woodruff, *Leaves from My Journal* (Salt Lake City: Juvenile Instructor Office, 1881), pp. 22-23.

[4]Wilson, *Life of David W. Patten*, p. 53.

[5]*Ibid.*

[6]Orson F. Whitney, *Life of Heber C. Kimball: An Apostle, The Father and Founder of the British Mission* (Salt Lake City: Bookcraft, 1945), p. 214.

[7]Wilson, *Life of David W. Patten*, p. 70.

[8]*HC* 3:175.

[9]*Conference Report*, April 1948, p. 53.

[10]*HC* 2:509.

[11]*Ibid.*, 3:23-24, n., by Elder B. H. Roberts.

[12]*Ensign*, January 1973, p. 31. See also Daniel H. Ludlow, *A Companion to Your Study of the Doctrine and Covenants*, 2 vols. (Salt Lake City: Deseret Book, 1978), pp. 582-83.

[13]Zerah Pulsipher's Journal, p. 11, typescript, Special Collections, Harold B. Lee Library, Brigham Young University, Provo, Utah.

# 41
# A TIME FOR COMMITMENT
## (D&C 117 and 118)
David F. Boone

Sections 117 and 118 of the Doctrine and Covenants were both received on 8 July 1838, in Far West, Missouri. Historically, the cornerstones of the Temple had been set in place only four days earlier, in keeping with direction by the Lord (see D&C 115:10-16). Far West seemed to be the most obvious gathering place, since the Prophet and Church leaders were there. Perhaps the Saints gathered there out of necessity since there were few other places to go. During the late summer and early fall of 1838 Missouri was the site of increased persecution and opposition to the Latter-day Saints.

Sections 117 and 118 are only two of four revelations that were received by the Prophet Joseph on this date. There is a common theme within the sections. Section 118 is directed to the Quorum of the Twelve Apostles. It was more to the *Quorum* than to the Twelve, because at this time the numbers were being reduced by apostasy and excommunication. Section 117 is the most unique among the four and was the first of the four revelations to be received. It deals with specific individuals and problems.

### Section 117

Verses 1-11 of section 117 contained a rebuke directed toward two individuals who had proven themselves and were called or would be called to positions of authority and responsibility in the Church. It appears that these two brethren had remained behind in Kirtland, Ohio. Newel K. Whitney, it will be recalled, was chosen by the Lord to be the Bishop there (see D&C 72:5-8). William Marks, on the other hand, was called at the conclusion of this experience to serve "in the midst of my people in the city of Far West, and let him be blessed with the blessings of my people" (D&C 117:10).

The Lord's words of confidence should be an indication of how Bishop Whitney and Elder Marks received the chastening from the Lord. Instead of turning against the Lord's work and against the Prophet Joseph personally, they realigned their lives to be in harmony with the program of the Lord and remained useful instruments in the hand of the Almighty. We can contrast their behavior, when they were chastened, with that of others of the early Saints and even Church leaders who took offense personally, and because of pride set about to damage the Church, the Prophet, or both.

In D&C 117 both William Marks and Newel K. Whitney were warned of specific dangers associated with coveting property. This was the same problem that other Saints had been warned of earlier in relation to furthering the work of the Lord (see D&C 19:26). Apparently the direction given to these brethren had to do specifically with their land holdings and business dealings in Kirtland that the Lord directed should be sold to pay for some of the debts of the Church. Further, they were instructed to gather with the Saints. To this point they seem to have been reticent to do so—probably because of these same properties and holdings in Kirtland. The Lord put the ownership of property in a more refined perspective when he declared, "for what is property unto me? . . . For have I not the fowls of heaven, and also the fish of the sea, and the beasts of the mountains? Have I not made the earth? Do I not hold the destinies of all the armies of the nations of the earth? . . . Is there not room enough on the mountains of Adam-ondi-Ahman, and on the plains of Olaha Shinehah [an area near Adam-ondi-Ahman], or the land where Adam dwelt, that you should covet that which is but the drop, and neglect the more weighty matters?"(D&C 117:4, 6, 8).

The Lord was showing that Kirtland had been chosen as a gathering place for the Saints; it had been the site of the building of a temple and many marvelous manifestations for the edification, growth, and development of the Saints. However, that time was now past and the present place of emphasis was Missouri, more specifically in the Far West and Adam-ondi-Ahman areas. These brethren were to give up those things that had little or no eternal worth for those things that mattered most. The Lord strongly encouraged them to correct their priorities and set their lives in order.

In relation to this theme of priorities, Oliver Granger was given special commendations for his work as an agent for the Church and for his representation of the Prophet Joseph Smith in some business matters after the latter was forced to leave the Kirtland area for his own personal safety (D&C 117:12-15). Granger served in behalf of the Prophet Joseph in matters that needed special attention, preferably by the Prophet himself. But the Prophet could not be there, and Oliver Granger was a man who was faithful and who could be trusted to do that which was right. During the Prophet's lifetime Elder Granger was characterized as "a man of faith and business ability—two qualities which form a rare combination."[1] As a result of his faithfulness and integrity, the Lord promised "that his name shall be had in sacred remembrance from generation to generation, forever and ever" (D&C 117:12).

In D&C 117:11, Bishop Whitney was commanded to reject "the Nicolaitane band." What he was to be ashamed of, "all their secret abominations," has reference to the theme suggested earlier as it relates to covetousness and leaving what they had for what the Lord directed them to do. The term "Nicolaitane" specifically related to a group or a secret combination in New Testament times, who perverted true forms of worship to their own purposes, and for their own gratification and pleasure. These Nicolaitans were a group of people who profaned the true worship of the followers of Christ (see Rev. 2:4-6). Elder Bruce R. McConkie has suggested that the Nicolaitans in the ancient Church were "members of the Church who were trying to maintain their church standing while continuing to live after the manner of the world."[2] It was this general caution that the Lord gave to Bishop Whitney and to all members of the Church. He further warned the Bishop in the performance of his official duties as a Bishop and the stewardship he had over the temporal needs of the members of the Church.

## Section 118

Section 118 was received as a result of an inquiry from the Prophet—an appeal for direction: "Show us thy will, O Lord, concerning the Twelve." This inquiry may have been made necessary because of the number of vacancies that had occurred in the Quorum of the Twelve due to persecution, apostasy, and death. By the time this revelation was received, four members of the original Quorum had fallen into disharmony with the Prophet or with the Church in general. These were Elders William E. McLellin, Luke S. Johnson, Lyman E.

Johnson, and John F. Boynton. Each of the four had been excommunicated, and now the Lord was designating replacements for them in the Quorum. The names that the Lord approved for their replacements (D&C 118:6) were Elders John Taylor, John E. Page (who also later left the Church), Wilford Woodruff, and Willard Richards. These four brethren were to "be appointed to fill the places of those who have fallen, and be officially notified of their appointment" (see D&C 118:6).

In fulfillment of the commission to officially notify these brethren and appoint them to their places, Elder John E. Page was ordained an Apostle on 19 December 1838 at the age of thirty-nine. He was afterwards excommunicated, "because of insubordination and rebellion against authority."[3] Elder John Taylor was ordained an apostle the same day as John Page by Brigham Young and Heber C. Kimball. Elder Taylor was thirty years of age at the time of his ordination.

Wilford Woodruff was about a year and a half older than John Taylor and was ordained to the apostleship 26 April 1839. Willard Richards was, at the time of his call, serving a mission in Great Britain. It was necessary for the brethren to wait until the principal parts of this revelation were fulfilled before he could be ordained properly. By the time he was added officially to the Quorum, another individual, George A. Smith, was ordained at Far West, Missouri, on 26 April, 1838. Willard Richards was ordained a year later in Preston, Lancashire, England—the only person to be added to the Quorum and ordained outside of the United States. At the time of their ordinations Elder Richards was thirty-five years of age and George A. Smith was but twenty-one.[4]

## The Return to Far West

The apostles took seriously the direction to take up a mission as the Lord had instructed. The instructions given in the Doctrine and Covenants regarding their mission are significant for several reasons. First, this would be the second in a long line of missions to England that would prove in a very literal sense to be the salvation of the Church. Second, this revelation was given at a time when, although persecution raged around them, Far West was an area of Latter-day Saint concentration. The departure of the Twelve from there would be a hardship for the other Saints. And third, between the time of the revelation (8 July 1838) and the time for the apostles to depart (26 April 1839) the Saints were forced to leave the area and their homes, and their places were taken by those who were very antagonistic toward the Church. It was very unusual for an exact date and place to be specified for such a mission, because in addition to the Saints knowing when and where the mission was to begin, the mobs were privy to the same information and warned the Saints against returning to that area.

In early April the mob faction met, and under the leadership of a Protestant minister, Samuel Bogart, they reviewed the revelation; oaths were made that the revelation would not be fulfilled. They also approached Elder Theodore Turley, a Latter-day Saint who had remained behind because of his business affairs, and berated him for his continued faith in the Prophet and the Twelve. Bogart challenged Brother Turley's faith by saying, "The Twelve are now scattered all over creation; let them come here if they dare; if they do, they will be murdered. As that revelation cannot be fulfilled, you will now give up your faith." Elder Turley jumped to his feet and exclaimed, "In the name of God that revelation will be fulfilled."[5] The mobsters laughed at him, believing that this was one prophecy that they could avert, and that in doing so they would foil the works of "Mormonism." Within three weeks another meeting was held. This gathering was at Quincy, Illinois and was composed of the leadership of the Church. The Prophet and some members of the Twelve had only days before "escaped" from their guards. A vote was taken among those assembled; these knew fully the danger and the consequences if they should be detected trying to return to an area from which they had been expelled by Executive Order of the Governor of the State of Missouri. Brigham Young provided this insight:

> Many of the authorities considered, in our present persecuted and scattered condition, the Lord would not require the Twelve to fulfill his words to the letter, and, under our present circumstances, he would take the will for the deed; but I felt differently and so did those of the Quorum who were with me. I asked them, individually, what their feelings were upon the subject. They all expressed their desires to fulfill the revelation. I told them the Lord God has spoken, and it was our

> duty to obey and leave the event in his hands and he would protect us.[6]

Apparently the Brethren did not try to keep their plans a secret, because on the morning of 26 April 1839, when they arrived at the Temple Lot at Far West, they were accompanied and met by a number of the Saints who remembered the significance of that date. Five members of the Quorum of the Twelve met and ordained two others who had been called previously. This made a majority; with such they were able to transact the business of the Church.

Those members of the Quorum who were in attendance were Elders Brigham Young, Heber C. Kimball, Orson Pratt, John Taylor, and John E. Page. The two who were ordained at the time were Elders Wilford Woodruff and George A. Smith. The business of the occasion included the following: "Some ordinations to the Priesthood were attended to. Some persons who had proved false to the Church were excommunicated. The Twelve prayed in the order of their standing in the Quorum; and a song was sung. A stone near the southeast corner of the Lord's house was rolled into place under the direction of Alpheus Cutler, the master workman. When the business at hand had been disposed of, they departed for Quincy, taking their families with them."[7] With that they officially began their mission "to go over the great waters," as commanded (D&C 118:4-5).

## The Mission to Great Britain

It is significant that the families are mentioned in conjunction with the business of the meeting, because the Lord had directed in section 118 that if the Brethren were obedient in the directions and instructions that he had given them he would bless them. "I, the Lord, give unto them a promise that I will provide for their families; and an effectual door shall be opened for them, from henceforth" (D&C 118:3). It was every bit as much a test of faith for the families to have their husbands, fathers, and bread winners leave them as it was for the brethren to go into inhospitable areas to fulfill the requirements of the revelation. Journalist Edward Stevensen recorded the plight of Sister Young and her family:

> Brigham Young started from Montrose, Iowa on his

> mission to England, leaveing her [Sister Young] with 50 cts and no home, and he had been sick and was now weak and poorly clad to start on a foreign mission and his wife had to do all kinds of work to make a liveing sometimes cleaning hogs intrals to get soap grease . . . which in turn she sold and bought bread and she was not alone in his trial, poverty and humiliating sircumstances.[8]

As Elder Stevenson indicated, Sister Young had plenty of company in her afflictions, but not all of the sickness, disease, and setbacks came to the families after the missionaries left. The missionaries were also affected. Elder Wilford Woodruff recorded:

> Inasmuch as the devil had been thwarted in a measure by the Twelve going to Far West and returning without harm, it seemed as though the destroyer was determined to make some other attempt upon us to hinder us from performing our missions; for as soon as any one of the Apostles began to prepare for starting he was smitten with chills and fever, or sickness of some kind. Nearly all of the Quorum of the Twelve or their families began to be sick, so it still required the exercise of a good deal of faith and perseverance to start off on a mission.[9]

When they did start each of the individuals had his own problems that restricted his progress. Brigham Young had no money, Wilford Woodruff had no means of conveyance; Brigham paddled him across the river in a canoe. Others of the missionaries had similar problems, but for now they had started. Elder Woodruff was so ill that when he reached the east side of the Mississippi River, he lay down to rest, being too weak and sick to continue on. He recorded that the Prophet Joseph Smith found him there and said to him, "Well, Brother Woodruff, you have started upon your mission." Elder Woodruff in reply responded, "Yes, but I feel and look more like a subject for the dissecting room than a missionary." The Prophet chided him and directed him to be on his way and gave him a blessing that he would be able to continue.[10]

He was able to proceed, as were the others. After they overcame the opposition they were able to fulfill spectacular missions in compliance with the Lord's command. At the April 1841 conference of the British Mission, for example, nine members of the Quorum of the Twelve Apostles were present. Eight of that number were at that time serving in the British Isles, while one, Orson Hyde, was making contacts among the distinguished Jewish citizens of the area in preparation for, and on his way to, his mission to dedicate the land of Palestine for the return of the Jews. Each of the members of the Twelve that were in the area made significant contributions while serving. Brigham Young, for example, served chiefly as an administrator over the Mission. While most of his time and energy was spent in that regard, he also gathered hymns for the compilation of the first hymnal for the British Saints.

A part of Elder Young's reputation while in Great Britain came as a result of his gift of healing. He was noted far and wide for his power, under the influence of the Spirit, in restoring health and vitality to those who were ill or incapacitated. As assistants and counselor in his administrative duties, Elder Young used Heber C. Kimball, a lifelong friend and companion, and also Willard Richards. In later years when Brigham Young succeeded the Prophet Joseph Smith in the Presidency of the Church, President Young chose these same two men as his counselors. Their beginnings in England were the making of a compatible working relationship.

In addition to their administrative duties, Elders Kimball and Richards both had time for proselyting activites. Elder Kimball returned to the areas of Chatburn and Downham, where he had served as a missionary in 1837-38. He also was one of the first to take the Gospel to London. Elder Richards, on the other hand, had been doing missionary work since Heber C. Kimball had departed from the earlier mission. Brother Richards had remained behind, had met and married his wife, and had continued with the administrative duties in the absence of any of the members of the Twelve. Upon their return he was ordained to be one of the Quorum.

Elder Parley P. Pratt's duties were also somewhat administrative in nature. He was a writer and an editor. His major duties were with the *Millennial Star*, the Church's publication for the constantly growing Latter-day Saint membership in Britain. Being close to the activities of leadership, Elder Pratt was the likely candidate and was chosen to remain in the mission after the other members of the Twelve departed for their homes in 1841. His brother, Orson, was greatly involved in the opening of new areas for proselyting activites. He went to Scotland and stayed there almost for the duration of his missionary term.

Others who had very spiritual experiences were Elders John Taylor and Wilford Woodruff. John Taylor worked in the Liverpool area; it was there that he converted a family by the name of Cannon to the restored Gospel. The mother, Ann Quale, readily received the message. But her husband, George, was more reticent. After the family joined the Church they emigrated to America where a young son, George Q. Cannon, later became prominent in Church affairs and served for many years in the First Presidency of the Church.

Wilford Woodruff during this same period was having incredible success of his own. Being led by the Spirit he traveled to an area where a major congregation was waiting, studying, and praying that the Lord would send them the truth of the restored gospel that they believed would come. Elder Woodruff found some 600 former Methodists, who by a common bond had come together to study the scriptures and worship as they understood they should. Of this group more than 45 were licensed ministers who had left their own congregations for the same purpose of seeking after truth. All but one of this congregation joined the restored Church, and many of them made up a group that gathered with the Saints to Nauvoo. After the arrival of the Saints in Utah, Elder Woodruff once again referred to this group and indicated that never in the history of the Church had such a large group of converts remained as active and supportive of the leadership of the Church as did this group from England. This group of 600 from the United Brethren made up only a third of the 1800 baptisms that Elder Woodruff reported during his stay in the British Isles.

Another successful missionary—and the youngest of the group—Elder George A. Smith was also blessed with unusual success. Elder Smith suffered from bleeding lungs and was for the most part restricted to the more rural regions of the mission. However, he accompanied Heber C. Kimball and others to London where he preached the first sermon by a Latter-day Saint in the famed Tabernacle Square. He was not able to witness much success from his efforts, but in the London area the Church grew under the administration of a later apostle, Lorenzo Snow, and still later—in 1956—a temple was built near London.

In retrospect, the feeling and prophecy that was made by the Prophet Joseph Smith that "something new must be done for the salvation of the Church" has equal applicability to the mission of the Twelve to England in 1840, as it did when he said it prior to the mission to that land in 1837-38. Whereas in the earlier mission the Elders were fighting for a meager foothold among an unyielding and highly tradition-steeped people, in the later mission they established a solid and permanent foundation, upon which missionaries have successfully harvested for generations since. An illustration of this principle is supplied when it is understood that between 1840 and 1850, between five and six thousand converts came to America and bolstered the number of Latter-day Saints in the Nauvoo area. These numbers are even more impressive when one knows that most of these converts went West with the main body of the Saints. Their descendants have likewise contributed much to the Church since then.

## Conclusion

There are two major lessons to be learned from the experience of the Twelve on their mission to Great Britain. First, the mission molded, strengthened, and educated the future leaders of the Church. Of the nine apostles who went at great personal and family sacrifice to Far West to begin their mission to England, all nine eventually went west with the Saints. That is amazing in light of the number of the general Church leaders who fell into apostasy in the earlier days of the Church. All three of the apostles who remained in America later left the Church.

In addition to the leadership training that the mission to England gave to those who would later preside over the Church, it also taught the Saints the principle of "followership." That is, they were converted to principles rather than personalities. When the Prophet Joseph and his brother were martyred, one of the great tests which confronted the membership of the Church was to commit themselves to follow the Twelve, those who had been directed in the early part of 1844 to lead out in spiritual matters. Many of those who were present on the occasion of the meetings in August of 1844 and who chose to support and uphold the Twelve were those who had been contacted, taught, converted, and baptized by those very men in England. These Saints knew the leadership capabilities of the Twelve and were willing to support them even if it meant moving another two thousand miles farther west. They had already left their homes once, possessed little in the Illinois area, and were willing to move on if that was required. They had been educated in large measure to follow the direction of the Twelve from the time they first were introduced to the gospel in their native lands, and a majority remained faithful when the test of leadership came to the Saints as a body.

The mission was a test for the Twelve—from the courage to return to Far West to the trial of their faith to leave their families in destitute and impoverished conditions to go to England. After the trial of their faith, which did not end with their arrival in England, they were further blessed; the blessings had a ripple effect until the whole Church was affected. Theirs was not only a mission for the Twelve, it was a mission for the survival and continued growth of the whole Church.

## Notes

[1]Hyrum M. Smith and Janne M. Sjodahl, *Doctrine and Covenants Commentary* (Salt Lake City: Deseret Book Co., 1951), p. 746.

[2]Bruce R. McConkie, *Doctrinal New Testament Commentary,* 3 vols. (Salt Lake City: Bookcraft, 1966-73), 3:446.

[3]Joseph Fielding Smith, *Essentials in Church History,* 27th ed. (Salt Lake City: Deseret Book Co., 1974), p. 381.

[4]*Ibid.*, p. 591.

[5]*HC* 3:306-7.

[6]In Elden Jay Watson, ed., *Manuscript History of Brigham Young, 1801-1844* (Salt Lake City: Elden Jay Watson, 1968), p. 35.

[7]Richard L. Evans, *A Century of "Mormonism" in Great Britain* (Salt Lake City: Deseret News Press, 1937), p. 88.

[8]J. Grant Stevenson, "The Life of Edward Stevenson, Member of the First Council of Seventy, Friend of the Prophet Joseph Smith and the Three Witnesses," Unpublished Master's Thesis, Brigham Young University, 1955, p. 146, original spelling retained.

[9]Matthias F. Cowley, *Wilford Woodruff: History of His Life and Labors As Recorded in His Daily Journals* (Salt Lake City: Bookcraft, reprint 1964), p. 108.

[10]*Ibid.*, p. 109.

# 42
# "A STANDING LAW FOREVER"
## (D&C 119 and 120)

STEPHEN D. RICKS

In response to Joseph Smith's prayer, "O Lord, show unto thy servants how much thou requirest of the properties of thy people for a tithing,"[1] he received on 8 July 1838 at Far West, Missouri what is now section 119 of the Doctrine and Covenants. Here the Lord directed the Saints to place their surplus property "into the hands of the bishop of my church in Zion" (D&C 119:1). Thereafter, "those who have thus been tithed shall pay one-tenth of all their interest annually; and this shall be a standing law unto them forever" (D&C 119:4). Ten days later, on 18 July 1838, Joseph Smith received a further revelation (the current section 120 of the Doctrine and Covenants) directing that the tithes collected "be disposed of by a council, composed of the First Presidency of my Church, and of the bishop and his council, and by my high council; and by mine own voice unto them." Such payment of one-tenth of one's increase for the support of the community or the maintenance of its religious institutions is a well-attested practice, both among Christians as well as in Ancient Israel.[2]

### Tithing In The Latter-day Church

The words "tithing," "tithe," and "tithed" are mentioned several times in the Doctrine and Covenants prior to section 119. In section 64, for example (revealed 11 September 1831 at Kirtland, Ohio), the following is recorded: "Behold, now it is called today until the coming of the Son of Man, and verily it is a day of sacrifice, and a day for the tithing of my people; for he that is tithed shall not be burned at his coming" (D&C 64:23). Similarly, in D&C 97:11-12 (received 2 August 1833) we read: "Yea, let it [i.e., the Kirtland Temple] be built speedily by the tithing of my people. Behold this is the tithing and the sacrifice which I, the Lord, require at their hands, that there may be a house built unto me for the salvation of Zion" (cf. also D&C 85:3). In all of these instances the word tithing seems to be used not in its etymological sense of "tenth," but rather in the more general sense of "contribution" or "offering."[3] Even in D&C 119:4, the word "tithed" seems to be used in other than its root sense: "Those who have thus been tithed [i.e., by having placed their surplus property into the hands of the bishop] shall pay one-tenth of all their interest annually." But this verse makes equally clear that from this time on it is required of the Saints to "tithe" (i.e., to pay one-tenth) of their yearly increase.

Already before the giving of D&C 119, Joseph and Oliver had promised (in a manner not altogether unlike the patriarch Jacob in Gen. 28:20-22) to give a tenth to the Lord in fulfillment of a vow. While suffering because of their debts in 1834, Joseph and Oliver vowed in solemn prayer to the Lord:

> That if the Lord will prosper us in our business and open the way before us that we may obtain means to pay our debts; that we be not troubled nor brought into disrepute before the world, nor His people; after that, of all that He shall give unto us we will give a tenth to be bestowed upon the poor of His Church, or as He shall command; and that we will be faithful over that which He has entrusted to our care, that we may obtain much; and that our children after us shall remember to observe this sacred and holy covenant; and that our children and our children's children, may know of the same.[4]

This vow was, however, personal, and not binding on the membership of the Church as a whole.

There are similarities between the Law of Consecration and certain stipulations in the revelation on tithing in D&C 119:1-2 (which was revealed in 1838). In the revelation on tithing, the Saints were directed to place their surplus property "into the hands of the bishop of my church in Zion" (D&C 119:1). The Law of Consecration, on the other hand (which was revealed in 1831), had required that each member consecrate his property to the Church and receive in return a stewardship based on his wants and needs (D&C 42:30-32). In both cases, however, one's residue or surplus would have remained entrusted to the Church.[5] Still, as Brigham Young noted, this new principle "seemingly was not fully understood or practiced."[6] With his characteristic rhetorical flair and keen insight into the foibles of human nature, Brigham described in 1855 his experiences in seeing to the carrying out of the requirements of the revelation.

> I found the people said they were willing to do about as they

> were counselled, but upon asking them about their surplus property, most of the men who owned land and cattle would say, "I have got so many hundred acres of land, and I have got so many boys, and I want each of them to have eighty acres, therefore this is not surplus property." Again, "I have got so many girls, and I do not believe I shall be able to give them more than forty acres each." "Well, you have got two or three hundred acres left." "Yes, but I have a brother-in-law coming on, and he will depend on me for a living; my wife's nephew is also coming on, he is poor, and I shall have to furnish him a farm after he arrives here." I would go on to the next one, and he would have more land and cattle than he could make us of to advantage. It is a laughable idea, but is nevertheless true, men would tell me they were young and beginning in the world, and would say, "We have no children, but our prospects are good, and we think we shall have a family of children, and if we do, we want to give them eighty acres of land each; we have no surplus property." "How many cattle have you?" "So many." "How many horses, &c?" "So many, but I have made provisions for all these, and I have use for everything I have got."
>
> Some were disposed to do right with their surplus property, and once in a while you would find a man who had a cow which he considered surplus, but generally she was of the class that would kick a person's hat off, or eyes out, or the wolves had eaten off her teats. You would once in a while find a man who had a horse that he considered surplus, but at the same time he had the ringbone, was broken-winded, spavined in both legs, and had the pole evil at one end of the neck and a fistula at the other, and both knees sprung.[7]

In a similar vein, Orson Pratt said, "Who in the world among all the Latter-day Saints would have any surplus property if it is left ot his own judgment?"[8] Although some may not have understood or obeyed the principle, the *History of the Church* records some three weeks after D&C 119 was revealed that "many of the brethren . . . consecrated their surplus property according to the revelation."[9]

Perhaps because many of the Saints had difficulty in determining what was "surplus property," thereafter the "Law of Tithing" (as it was referred to in the "Eleventh General Epistle of the Presidency of the Church of Jesus Christ of Latter-day Saints" in 1854) was given, "which required that all should in the first instance pay one-tenth of their entire property into the Church, and thereafter pay one-tenth of all their increase; which was for the poor, to promote the spread of the Gospel among the nations of the earth, support the ministry, and building of Temples unto the Most High."[10] In "An Epistle of the Twelve Apostles to the Saints of the Last Days," dated 13 December 1841, the Twelve wrote with regard to the proposed temple at Nauvoo that it should "be built by tithing and consecration, and every one is at liberty to consecrate all they find in their hearts so to do; but the tithings required, is one-tenth of all anyone possessed at the commencement of the building, and one-tenth part of all his increase from that time until the completion of the same, whether it be money, or whatever he may be blessed with."[11] Those who had nothing else to tithe were expected to donate every tenth day of labor on the temple. Franklin D. Richards, recounting his experiences in the building of the Nauvoo temple, said that "the tithing of the people on that Temple was mostly in labor as I well recollect—for I worked in the quarry every tenth day when I was not absent on missionary service."[12]

While the Saints are no longer required to deed their surplus propery to the Church, and are no longer generally expected to tithe their entire property at the outset, the principle of tithing has remained a significant part of the Church's economic organization. Whereas today the majority of tithing is given in the form of cash payments, there were several means of payment in the early years following the receipt of the revelation in section 119, each of which comprised a significant percentage of the total tithing contribution. Leonard Arrington, former Church Historian, has described these various means of donating tithing in fair detail in *Great Basin Kingdom;*[13] here each of the major categories will be mentioned only briefly.

1. **Property Tithing.** As has been noted above, this consisted of a ten percent assessment on all property owned by the member at the time that he began to pay and ten percent of his annual increase afterwards. This was first required of the Saints in connection with the construction of the temple at Nauvoo and was reinvoked at the General Conference in Salt Lake City on 7 September 1851.[14]

2. **Labor Tithing.** Saints were expected to donate one day of labor in ten for work on various projects, such as temples and other

church buildings, as well as forts, roads, and the like. As the "Epistle of the Twelve Apostles to the Saints of the Last Days" noted above makes clear, even if members had insufficient means to pay other forms of tithing, no able-bodied Saint was to be exempted from labor tithing.[15] However, at least after the removal of the Saints to the West, those who wished to and had the means could have labor tithing performed by others if proper compensation were made and the animals used for the work were maintained. In 1863, when there was difficulty in obtaining sufficient labor tithing for work on the temple in Salt Lake, Brigham Young noted in an address in that year that "I immediately put on the work two good mule teams with a good man to manage each, then I put on two good common laborers to work on this block; I feed, clothe and pay the men, sustain the teams and keep the wagons in repair."[16]

3. **Produce and Stock Tithing.** Somewhat in the tradition of Lev. 27:30-33, tithes were to be paid on all increase in products of the household, farm, ranch, or mine.

4. **Institutional Tithing.** Concerns such as stores and factories were expected to pay a tenth on their earned profits to the Church. Arrington refers to this tithing as "a kind of forerunner of the modern corporate profits tax."[17]

5. **Cash Tithing.** During the nineteenth century, cash payments of tithing represented only a fraction of the Church's total tithing income. However, cash tithing was particularly encouraged at that time because of the relative infrequency of its payment and its easy liquidity outside of the Great Basin.[18]

In what is now section 120 of the Doctrine and Covenants, the distribution of tithes is made the responsibility of "a council, composed of the First Presidency of my Church, and of the bishop and his council, and by mine own high council." Although the "high council" no longer plays a role in the disbursement of tithes, both the First Presidency and "the bishop and his council" (more recently, the Presiding Bishopric) have retained their responsibilities in this regard. They constitute the Council on the Disposition of Tithes.

## Conclusion

The revelation in the Doctrine and Covenants directs that tithing be "a standing law unto them forever" (D&C 119:4). Without attempting to determine whether the practice of tithing is an eternal principle—the position which Brigham Young seems to take[19]—or whether it might be abroagated in favor of a "higher law," such as the Law of Consecration and Stewardship—the position of Joseph F. Smith[20]—this phrase may, I think, be understood in the sense that, just as tithing has been observed in previous dispensations, it remains the minimum which the Lord requires, or will require, of his Saints in this dispensation. It would be incorrect to assume (as happened in the Christian church in postapostolic times) that by paying tithes the Christian had fully discharged his obligation to the Lord and his kingdom.[21] The Lord frequently exhorted his followers to forsake all in order to gain eternal life. While the payment of tithes remains a significant part of building the Lord's kingdom, it does not exhaust the ways in which the Saint may expend his means, energy, time, and talents in serving the Lord's cause.

## Notes

[1]*HC* 3:44.

[2]See Stephen D. Ricks, "Tithing in Ancient and Modern Israel," pp. 205-17 in *Hearken, O Ye People: Discourses on the Doctrine and Covenants* (Salt Lake City: Randall Book Co., 1984).

[3]The Modern English word "tithe" derives from the Old English *teogotha*, "tenth." A similar use of "tithing" in the general sense of "contribution" can be found in Donald Q. Cannon and Lyndon W. Cook, eds., *Far West Record* (Salt Lake City: Deseret Book Co., 1983), pp. 129-31.

[4]*HC* 2:175.

[5]Leonard J. Arrington, Feramorz Y. Fox, and Dean L. May, *Building the City of God* (Salt Lake City: Deseret Book Co., 1976), p. 34.

[6]"Eleventh General Epistle of the Presidency of the Church of Jesus Christ of Latter-day Saints," *Millennial Star* 16:27 (8 July 1854), p. 427; for a convenient source for the epistle, see James R. Clark, ed., *Messages of the First Presidency*, 6 vols. (Salt Lake City: Bookcraft, 1965-75), 2:139.

[7]*JD* 2:306-7.

[8]*JD* 16:157; cf. *JD* 17:110.

[9]In the entry under the date of Thursday, 26 July 1838, in *HC* 3:47.

[10]"Eleventh General Epistle," Clark, *Messages of the First Presidency*, 2:139.

[11]"An Epistle of the Twelve Apostles to the Saints of the Last Days," *HC* 4:473.

[12]*JD* 23:314.

[13]The following discussion is heavily dependent on the description of the various categories of tithing in Leonard J. Arrington's *Great Basin Kingdom* (Lincoln, Neb.: University of Nebraska Press, 1958), pp. 133-37.

[14]"Sixth General Epistle of the Presidency of the Church of Jesus Christ of Latter-day Saints," *Millennial Star* 14:2 (15 January 1852), p. 25.

[15]*HC* 4:473-74.

[16]*JD* 10:205.

[17]Arrington, *Great Basin Kingdom,* p. 137.

[18]*Ibid.,* 136-37.

[19]Thus, Brigham Young declared, "The Lord Almighty never had his kingdom on the earth without the law of tithing being in the midst of his people, and he never will. It is an eternal law that God has instituted for the benefit of the human family, for their salvation and exaltation," *JD* 14:89; cf. *JD* 15:163.

[20]See, e.g., *Millennial Star* 56 (29 October 1893): 386; see also *Conference Report,* April 1900, pp. 47-48; Lorenzo Snow, *Conference Report,* October 1900, pp. 61-62; *JD* 20:368; Orson Pratt, *JD* 17:109-10. For further discussion of this topic, see Robert L. Millet, "The Development of the Concept of Zion in Mormon Theology," Ph.D. Dissertation, Florida State University, April 1983, pp. 106-8.

[21]Lukas Vischer, *Tithing in the Early Church* (Philadelphia: Fortress Press, 1966), pp. 10, 30.

# 43

# A RAY OF LIGHT IN AN HOUR OF DARKNESS

## (D&C 121-123)

JAMES R. CHRISTIANSON

### Introduction

There are various plausible ways to analyze or explain events in the life of Joseph Smith. One of these might be appropriately called "the scheduling of a prophet."

Joseph's life prior to 1820 was crucial to events that followed that date. Those fifteen years saw him born into the right family and the correct lineage; living in a pre-determined location at the proper moment in history, and facing telling circumstances while immersed in just the right environmental mix. All of these brought him as scheduled to his appointment with destiny.

The decade after 1820 was equally vital. These were the formative years. Beginning with the First Vision, his course in life was remarkably endowed with experiences intended to heighten his spiritual sensitivity, deepen his understanding of the ways of the Lord, broaden his grasp of things past, present and future, and increase his capacity to assimilate truth while warding off evil and enhancing his appreciation of his role and purpose in life. To accomplish this, the heavens were opened to a degree perhaps unknown to any other mortal. Among his teachers and learning models during this period were the Savior; the prophets Moroni, John the Baptist, Peter, James, and John; the messengers Gabriel and Raphael; and a whole array of Book of Mormon characters about whom he could discourse in detailed and tireless fashion.

### The Lord's Spokesman

Aided by Urim and Thummim, an effective teaching device, this was truly a time of abundant learning for the boy who metamorphosed into a prophet, the Lord's spokesman. It was this role that characterized the next period of Joseph's story. From 1830 to 1838, his life and the lives of his followers were enriched by his words as they flowed forth, the product of practically every form of revelation or inspiration.

With but few exceptions, the drama of the twenties was past, but a wide variety of questions were asked and needs arose, to which Joseph voiced the word and will of the Lord. With the Book of Mormon published and the priesthood restored, he took action to establish the Kingdom, firm up its foundation, and expand its borders. "Thus saith the Lord" was an awaited preamble to much of what the Prophet had to say. It preceded injunctions as common as where his disciples were to live, how they were to serve, what they should eat and drink, how they were to teach and rear their children, and made plain their responsibilities one to another. It introduced awe-inspiring declarations that defined the eternities both past and future, detailed dramatic events to precede and accompany the Second Coming, and described the glorious appearances of such personages as the Savior, Moses, Elias, and Elijah.

During these years it was the Lord speaking through Joseph on numerous occasions that fills the pages of much of the Doctrine and Covenants. It was a time rich with reassurance that he was the Lord's prophet and that his words and those of no other represented the word and will of God (D&C 43:1-5).

## A Spokesman for the Lord

The next and final phase of Joseph's mortal experience unfolded during the years 1839 to 1844. As the Lord's spokesman, Joseph essentially relayed those things seen, heard and felt as the Spirit directed. It was as though the Lord himself had spoken through Joseph Smith; hence the words "Thus saith the Lord" or something akin to them prefaced almost all scriptural statements during the years 1830 to 1839. The fourth and final period of his life was clearly distinct from the other three. As a mature, confident prophet, Joseph knew the mind and will of the Lord and, therefore, spoke *for* him and his words were as though they had come directly from Diety. His declarations and writings, were spoken as "one having authority." Those that have been preserved, both the ones that do not and some that do appear in the Doctrine and Covenants, are considered among the most profound, significant, and far-reaching of his teachings. Among such are the King Follett Discourse,[1] the 16 June 1844 discourse on the Godhead[2] and the Temple Endowment. Available as part of the Standard Works are sections 121, 122, 123, 127, 128, 130, and 131 of the Doctrine and

Covenants.

The latter references, considered scripture by the Church, were a significant departure from previously acknowledged revelations. They are essentially answers to gospel questions in the case of 130 and 131, while the remainder are letters to the Saints written during times when Joseph could not communicate directly with them. It is in these "epistles" that Joseph expressed himself in the full measure of his calling and was, indeed, the spokesman for the Lord.

The historical setting for three of these sections (121, 122, and 123) was a cold, wet, dark jail cell in Liberty, Missouri. Joseph, his brother Hyrum, and his counselor in the presidency of the Church, Sidney Rigdon, along with three of their brethren, were confined there for nearly four months, beginning 1 December 1838. The cause of their arrest and imprisonment was a charge of treason brought against them by the State of Missouri.

Forced to flee Kirtland, Ohio, in January 1838, due to a wave of apostasy which led to threats on his life, Joseph made his way to Far West, Missouri.[3] His arrival in March 1838 was followed by several quiet but prosperous months during which a number of other settlements were established, crops were planted, additional Saints gathered, and a spirit of optimism was engendered.

Once again, however, as their numbers increased, misunderstandings arose and conflict soon followed. The battle of Crooked River, which resulted in bloodshed and death on both sides and in the subsequent charge of treason, was followed by the infamous Extermination Order of Missouri Governor Boggs and by an attack on the settlement of Haun's Mill. The resultant deaths of seventeen men and boys, plus the seizure through deception of Joseph and other Church leaders by the state militia, took the heart out of Latter-day Saint resistance and led to the expulsion of the Saints from the state.

During the five weeks that passed, from the time he was taken into custody until his confinement at Liberty Jail, Joseph, along with his fellow prisoners, was subjected to conditions and circumstances that were both humiliating and degrading. All attempts at securing a fair hearing were a distortion of justice. This experience, followed by the long winter months spent in Liberty, were distressing to the Prophet. His own miseries were compounded by reports that both his family and the Saints in general were suffering greatly. Joseph's letters during these months reflected anxiety for the well-being of his loved ones and for his followers, scattered as they were over parts of Illinois and Missouri. But they also portray transcendant expressions of confidence in and total awareness of the mission and doctrine of the kingdom which were beautifully poetic and insightful.[4] It was during these months, while helplessly separated from family and friends, that Joseph experienced some of the highest highs and lowest lows of his life. It was here in the unmerciful fires of persecution that he was steeled and molded into the role of one who confidently and powerfully spoke for Deity.

In a letter penned just two weeks after his arrival in Liberty, Joseph gave vent to the hurt and frustration spawned by the defection to the enemy of some who in better times had been his closest associates. There were, he stated, "Renegadoes, Mormon dissenters . . . running through the world and spreading various foul and libelous reports against us thinking thereby to gain the friendship of the world because they knew that we are not of the world and that the world hates us; therefore they make a tool of these fellows by them they do all the injury they can and after that they hate them worse than they do us because they find them to be base traitors and sycophants. Such characters God hates we cannot love them the world hates them and we sometimes think the devil ought to be ashamed of them."[5] This said, he went on to explain the nature of their betrayal and villainy. Among other things it was noted:

> And now brethren we say unto you, what can we enumerate more; is not all manner of evil of every description spoken against us falsely, yea, we say unto you falsely; we have been misrepresented and misunderstood and belied and the purity of our hearts have not been known. And it is through ignorance, yea, the very depth of ignorance is the cause of it, and not only ignorance but gross wickedness on the part of some and hypocrisy also who by a long face and sanctified prayers and very pious sermons had power to lead the minds of the ignorant and unwary and thereby obtain such influence that when we approached their iniquities the devil gained great advantage and would bring great sorrow upon our heads and in fine we have waded through an ocean of tribulation, and mean abuse practiced upon us by the ill bred and ignorant such as Hinkle,

> Corrill, and Phelps, Avard, Reed Peck, Cleminson, and various others who are so very ignorant that they cannot appear respectable in any decent and civilized society, and whose eyes are full of adultery and cannot cease from sin. Such characters as McLellin, John Whitmer, D. Whitmer, O. Cowdery, Martin Harris, who are too mean to mention and we had liked to have forgotten them. Marsh and Hyde whose hearts are full of corruption, whose cloak of hypocrisy was not sufficient to shield them or to hold them up in the hour of trouble, who after having escaped the pollutions of the world through the knowledge of God and become again entangled and overcome the latter end is worse than the first. But it has happened unto them according to the words of the savior, the dog has returned to his vomit, and the sow that was washed to her wallowing in the mire.[6]

As days blended into weeks and weeks into months, Joseph's naturally forgiving nature reasserted itself, and the rancur that accompanied his initial period of incarceration faded away. Visits from loved ones lightened the prisoners' burdens if the news they sometimes brought did not. By March, the Saints, those free of Missorui, were well received in Illinois. Though their future was still in doubt, they were safe from further persecution. This news must have gladdened the heart of the Prophet but did not erase questions as to why so much suffering was required.

## A Prophetic Letter

It was under these circumstances on 19 March 1839, that Joseph received letters from Emma, from brothers Don Carlos and William, and from Edward Partridge.[7] Each of the four reported favorably concerning the welfare of his family and the remainder of the Saints and expressed hope that they would soon be reunited. Emma's words, especially, must have touched his heart. Noting her feelings regarding their long separation and his confinement, she wrote:

> Was it not for conscious innocence, and the direct interposition of divine mercy, I am very sure I never should have been able to have endured the scenes of suffering that I have passed through, since what is called the Militia, came into

> Far West, under the ever to be remembered Governor's notable order. . . . We are all well at present, except Frederick, who is quite sick. Little Alexander who is now in my arms is one of the finest little fellows, you ever saw in your life, he is so strong that with the assistance of a chair he will run all round the room . . . No one but God, knows the reflections of my mind and the feelings of my heart when I left our house and home, and almost all of everything that we possessed excepting our little children, and took my journey out of the State of Missouri, leaving you shut up in that lonesome prison. But the recollection is more than human nature ought to bear . . . The daily sufferings of our brethren in travelling and camping out nights, and those on the other side of the river would beggar the most lively description. The people in this state are very kind indeed, they are doing much more than we ever anticipated they would; I have many more things I could like to write but have not time and you may be astonished at my bad writing and incoherent manner, but you will pardon all when you reflect how hard it would be for you to write, when your hands were stiffened with hard work, and your heart convulsed with intense anxiety. But I hope there is better days to come to us yet.[8]

The following day, the Prophet composed a long letter addressed to his scattered proselytes in general and to Bishop Partridge in particular. The writing was sent to Emma with instructions that she and his extended family should read it first and then share a copy of it with the Church. Joseph recognized that the document, containing all of what became sections 121, 122, and 123 of the Doctrine and Covenants, was no ordinary missive. He felt the inspiration of its wording, as well as the confidence and power of its message. Hence the instructions on how it was to be received and shared.[9]

The first two pages of the letter briefly but explicitly detail the sufferings of the Saints at the hands of some Missourians. "They practise these things upon the saints," he declared, "who have done them no rong who are inocent and virtuous who loved the Lord their god and were willing to forsaik all things for Christ sake these things are awfull to relait but they are verily true it must needs bee that offences come, but WO! to them by whom they come. O God where art thou and where is the pavilion that covereth thy hiding place. . . ."[10] The letter continues with vv. 1-6 of section 121. To the reader it appears that Joseph, deeply pained by the memories made fresh through his letter's review of the Missouri experience, turned to one whom he knew and asked, "Why has this thing happened?" and "Wilt Thou not stand with us?" Having relieved his pent-up anguish due in part to his own inability to respond to the needs of his people, the Prophet counseled that their sufferings were but an expression of the times leading to the Second Coming and, in time, their detractors would answer for all that they had done.

Following a brief summary of the fruitless and ill-advised attempts by their lawyers to have their case reviewed and the recounting of an attempted escape, Joseph noted his joy in receiving letters from Emma and others, all of which breathed

> . . . a kind and consoling spirit we were much gratified with there contence we had been a long time without information and when we read those letters they were to our souls as the gentle air, is refreshing but our joy was mingled with greaf because of the suffering of the poor and much injured saints and we need not say to you that the flood gates of our harts were hoisted and our eyes were a fountain of tears but those who have not been inclosed in the walls of a prison without cause or provication can have but a little ideah how sweat [sweet] the voice of a friend is one token of friendship from any sorce whatever a wakens and calles into action evry simpathetick feeling it brings us in an instant evry thing that is pased it sesses [siezes] the present with a vivasity of lightning it grasps after the future with the fearsness of a tiger it rhetrogrades from one thing to an other untill finally all enmity malice and hatred and past diferances misunderstandings and mis managements be slain victoms at the feet of hope and when the hart is sufficiently contrite than the voice of inspiration steals along and whispers "my son peace be unto thy soul."[11]

Verses 7-24 comprise the next portion of the letter. This inspired and inspiring response, intended as reassurance for the Saints, clearly assuaged Joseph's troubled spirit as well. His words following v. 25 convey a degree of understanding not previously evident. God, he noted, required a tried and purged people. Like Abraham, they had passed through the refiner's fire.

The Prophet allowed that in his absence decisions had to be made but warned against the sophistry of aspiring, foolish, and prideful individuals. "The things of God," he wrote, "are of deep import; and time, and experience, and careful and ponderous and solom thought can only find them out. Thy mind, O man! if thou wilt lead a soul unto salvation, must stretch as high as the utmost heavens, and search into and contemplate the darkest abyss, and the broad expanse of eternity—thou must commune with God."[12]

Joseph pursued this theme, instructing the Saints as to what the Lord expects of those, "called to hold the keys of the mysteries of those things that have been kept hid from the foundation of the world until now." He admonished them that "honesty, and sobriety, and candor, and solemnity, and virtue, and pureness, and meekness, and simplicity crown our heads in every place; and in fine become as little children, without malice, guile, or hypocrisy." If after all they had suffered they would do these things, he wrote, exercising faith and prayer in the sight of God, "He shall give unto you knowledge by His Holy Spirit."[13] This citation introduces vv. 26-32, which are in turn followed by a brief statement describing the futility of those whose actions temporarily misrepresent or distort an accurate reflection of the truth in the same manner that flood waters pollute the pure and crystal-clear quality of a stream.

In v. 33 Joseph asked, "How long can rolling waters remain impure? What power shall stay the heavens?" He then went on to answer these questions, declaring that Governor Boggs of Missouri and other "renegados, liars, priests, thieves, and murderers" had "poured down, from their spiritual wickedness in high places, and from their strongholds of the devil, a flood of dirt and mire and filthiness and vomit upon our heads."[14] This, however, did not signal the closing of the heavens, but would rather effect a purging and cleansing of the Church. All Hell, he testified,

> may poor forth its rage like the burning lavy of mount versuvias or of Etna or of the most terible of the burning mountains and yet shall mormonism stand. watter, fire, truth, and god are all the same truth is [as] mormonism God is the author of it he is our shield it is by him we received our birth, it was by his voice that we were called to a dispensation of his gospel in the

> begining of the fullness of times it was by him we received the book of mormon and it was by him that we remain unto this day and by him we shall remain if it shall be for our glory and in his almighty name we are determined to indure tribulation as good soldiers unto the end.[15]

With this, plus a request for news from various Church leaders and any who cared to write, the letter was concluded and signed by each of the prisoners: Joseph, Hyrum, Lyman Wight, Caleb Baldwin, and Alexander McRae.

Having apparently reviewed and corrected his epistle and possibly after re-reading the correspondence from Emma and others, Joseph determined that he had more to say. After once again enlisting the services ofAlexander McRae as scribe, he proceeded to dictate several additional pages.

Addressing himself to the desperate need for a site where his people might gather, Joseph encouraged Bishop Partridge and other leading brethren to pursue the land offer extended by Isaac Galland. He was impressed that Galland was genuinely interested in the welfare of the Church members. He was likewise hopeful that the Governor, Attorney General, and United States Surveyor for the State of Iowa might act in ways that would benefit the Saints.

It was, he noted, deeply impressed upon his and his companions' minds that any door opened might be viewed as an act of providence for which the Church must be both ready and worthy. The "terrible storms" and "thick darkness" as spoken of by the prophets were not far off and great care must be taken "lest you grieve the holy spirit which shall be poured out at all times upon your heads when you are exercised with those principals of ritiousness that are agreeable to the mind of God."[16]

These principles would be violated, Joseph warned, should "there be any among you who aspire after their own aggraundisement and seek their own oppulance while their brethren are groning in poverty." Care should be given, he wrote that their hearts not be open to "such high mindedness." Otherwise a condition would prevail wherein "there are many called but few are chosen."[17]

At this point, the letter proclaimed the exquisite discourse that comprises the last twelve verses of section 121. Here Joseph speaks with an authority and clarity that is distinctive and sets this segment of his epistle apart from the thoughts which introduce it. It has been said of the Prophet that at times he out-transcended the prominent transcendentalists of his day: Emerson, Thoreau, Alcott, and Parker. Surely this was one of those occasions.

Section 122 takes up where 121 ends, and though directed to the Saints, it is given as an individual experience—most likely a burst of insight or comprehension which came as he dictated the letter, all the while pondering past events that made it necessary and the circumstances from which it was emerging. It is, nevertheless, stated in a manner that each member upon reading it or hearing it read could identify with its message in a personal way. Though included here, it is closely identified with those parts of the letter which now appear as vv. 1-25 of section 121. The following lines appear immediately after the last verse of section 122:

> Now Brotheren, I would sejest for the concideration of the conferance of its being carefully and wisely understod by the council or conference that our brethren scattered abroad who understand the spirit of the gethering that they fall into the places of refuge and safty that God shall open unto them betwean Kirtland and Far West. . . . And again we further sejest for the concideration of the council that there be no organizations of large bodies upon common stock princepals in property or of large companies of firms untill the Lord shall signify it in a proper maner as it opens such a dredfull field of the avericious and the indolent and corrupt hearted to pray upon the inocent and virtious and honest we have reason to believe that many things were introduced among the saints before God had signified the times and not withstanding the principles and plans may have been good yet aspiring men or in other words men who had not the substance of Godliness about them perhaps undertook to handle edge tools children you know are fond of tools while they are not yet able to use them. Time and experiance however is the only safe remidy against such evils.[18]

This passage is valuable not only for what it contains but also for the stark comparison it reveals between the words of the Prophet when, as on this occasion, he addressed a highly spiritual matter and then turned to one of more secular significance. Extracted from the original it also exposes the weakness that characterized the language and writing skills of both Joseph and his scribe, Alexander McRae. The letter was edited before it was published in the *Times and Seasons* in May, 1840. The excerpting of those portions that became sections 121, 122, and 123 was by Orson Pratt in 1876.

Section 123 follows the above excerpt. The letter is then concluded with an appeal to the Saints to avoid secret oaths and organizations of every kind. Referring to the "wickedness of Doctor Avard," he asked that "our covenant be that of the everlasting covenant" and added that "pure friendship always becomes weakened the very moment you undertake to make it stronger by penal oaths and secrecy."[19]

In closing, Joseph declared that the allegiance of the Saints should be to God and to the Constitution. On this subject after all that he and the Saints had endured, he testified boldly:

> We say that the constitution of the Unit[ed] States is a glorious standard it is founded [in] the wisdom of God it is a heavenly banner it is to all those who are privilaged with the sweats of its liberty like the cooling shades and refreshing watters of a greate rock in a thirsty and a weary land it is like a greate tree under whose branches men from every clime can be shielded from the burning raies of an inclemant sun. We bretheren are deprived of the protection of this glorious principal by the cruelty of the cruele by those who only look for the time being for pasterage like the beasts of the field only to fill themselves and forget that the mormons as well as the pr[e]sbitareans and those of every other class and discription have equal rights to partake of the fruit of the great tree of our national liberty but notwithstanding we see what we see and we feel what [we] feel and know what we know yet that fruit is no les presious and delisious to our taist we cannot be weaned from the milk nether can we be drawn from the breast neither will we deny our relegeon because of the hand of oppresion but we will hold on untill death we say that God is true that the constitution of the United States is [true] that the Bible is true that the book of [mor]m[on] is true and [that we know] that we have an house not made [with hands] eternal in the heavens, whose [builder and m]aker is God.[20]

Hence in one of the darkest moments of his life, the Prophet Joseph Smith wrote a letter that has lighted the way and has enlightened the lives of generations of individuals who, while they honor his name and cherish his memory, more fully worship their God and his Christ because of what he shared with them from a cold and forbidding jail cell in Missouri.

## Notes

[1]*HC* 6:303-17.

[2]*Ibid.*, pp. 473-79.

[3]*Ibid.*, 3:1.

[4]Dean C. Jessee, ed., *The Personal Writing of Joseph Smith* (Salt Lake City: Deseret Book Company, 1984), pp. 360-430. Sources cited in this collection retain original spelling and punctuation. Built in 1833 at a cost of $600, the jail at Liberty, Missouri, was a two-story structure approximately twenty-two feet square built of rough-hewn limestone. Inside the outer wall was another wall of oak logs. The two walls were separated by a twelve-inch space filled with loose rock, the whole presenting a formidable barrier four feet thick. The interior of the jail was divided into upper and lower rooms, the lower, or dungeon, lighted by two small windows grated with heavy iron bars. It was here on 1 December 1838, that Joseph Smith began four months and five days of confinement.

[5]"Joseph Smith to the Church in Caldwell County," 16 December 1838, as cited in Jessee, *The Personal Writings of Joseph Smith*, p. 379.

[6]*Ibid.*, pp. 380-81.

[7]*Ibid.*, p. 389. Also *HC* 3:272-74.

[8]"Emma Smith to Joseph Smith," 7 March 1839, L.D.S. Church Archives. As cited in Jessee, *The Personal Writings of Joseph Smith*, pp. 388-89.

[9]"Joseph Smith to Emma Smith," 21 March 1839, L.D.S. Church Archives. As cited in Jessee, *The Personal Writings of Joseph Smith*, pp. 408-9.

[10]"Joseph Smith to the Church of Latter-day Saints at Quincy, Illinois and scatter abroad and to Bishop Partridge in particular." 20 March 1839, *Ibid.*, p. 391. This letter is in the handwriting of Caleb Baldwin and Alexander McRae.

[11]*Ibid.*, pp. 393-94.

[12]*HC* 3:295.

[13]*Ibid.*, p. 296.

[14]*Ibid.*, p. 297.

[15]Jessee, *The Personal Writings of Joseph Smith*, pp. 398-99.

[16]*Ibid.*, p. 401.

[17]*Ibid.*

[18]*Ibid.*, p. 403-4.

[19]*Ibid.*, p. 405. Samson Avard was founder of the variously named Danite Band in Missouri. Using secrecy, oaths, and binding covenants, its members acted briefly as a group bent on resisting and, if necessary, destroying the enemies of the Church.

[20]*Ibid.*, pp. 406-7.

# 44
# REVELATIONS IN NAUVOO
## (D&C 124-126)

Robert A. Cloward

The three sections labeled revelations from the Nauvoo period all came in 1841. By the summer of that year, the little town of Commerce, Illinois, laid out by land speculators on a horseshoe bend of the Mississippi River, had witnessed an influx of between 8,000 and 9,000 Latter-day Saints.[1] They were of mixed origin, the largest number composed of exiles fleeing the Extermination Order of Governor Lilburn W. Boggs of Missouri, to which were added many converts from the eastern United States, Canada, and the British Isles. Some had already left behind a string of homes. Undoubtedly they were dismayed at the extent to which the Lord required the trial of their faith. But the determination and perseverance of these Saints demonstrated their convictions.

After escaping from oppressive captors during a change of venue from Daviess County to Boone County, Missouri in April of 1839, Joseph Smith had chosen Commerce as the new gathering place.[2] To some the location seemed quite undesirable, and many of the Saints suffered from malarial fever carried by mosquitoes which bred in the swampy land. Joseph Smith commented, "Commerce was so unhealthful, very few could live there; but believing that it might become a healthful place by the blessing of heaven to the Saints, and no more eligible place presenting itself, I considered it wisdom to make an attempt to build up a city."[3]

On 29 October 1839, the Prophet left Commerce with Sidney Rigdon and Judge Elias Higbee to seek redress from the Federal Government for the wrongs committed against the members of the Church in Missouri. Their appeal was reluctantly received by the President of the United States, Martin Van Buren, who remarked to Joseph and Judge Higbee, "Gentlemen, your cause is just, but I can do nothing for you."[4]

The Saints, however, were doing something for themselves. Their industry and determination were making of Commerce, renamed Nauvoo by the Prophet, a prosperous city, soon to be the largest in

Illinois. Swamps were drained, land cleared, and wide streets laid out at right angles. Comfortable homes were constructed of stone and brick, and Joseph Smith wrote to the Saints abroad in January, 1841: "The name of our city (Nauvoo) is of Hebrew origin, and signifies a beautiful situation, or place, carrying with it, also, the idea of rest; and is truly descriptive of the most delightful location."[5]

This scene of vigorous activity was the backdrop for the revelations known as sections 124, 125, and 126. They contain the Lord's instructions on a wide variety of topics of concern to the Prophet and to the Church. Section 124, received 19 January 1841, is the longest of all the published revelations. Before discussing it, I will briefly comment on sections 125 and 126, which contain just four and three verses respectively.

## A Revelation for the Saints in Iowa

Shortly after the purchase of Illinois land in 1839, the Church had purchased large tracts on the opposite side of the Mississippi River in the Territory of Iowa.[6] At the general conference held in October of that year, John Smith was appointed president over the Iowa Saints.[7] However, the increasing emphasis on Nauvoo as a gathering place naturally caused many to wonder whether they should leave their settlements and join the Saints at Nauvoo. In direct answer to this question, the Lord revealed in March 1841: "Let them gather themselves together unto the *places* which I shall appoint unto them by my servant Joseph, and build up *cities* unto my name" (D&C 125:2, italics added). Nauvoo was to be the cornerstone of Zion (D&C 124:2), but the Lord intended that other stakes be strengthened, including the one in Iowa.

In August, 1841, a stake conference was held at Zarahemla, "and the branches in Iowa, so far as represented, consisted of 750 members."[8] By the time of the exodus in 1846, the Saints had exerted a major influence on the growth of the territory, and cities had been developed at Montrose, Zarahemla, Ambrosia, Augusta, Nashville, and Keokuk.

## A Revelation for Brigham Young

Section 126 was received by the Prophet in the house of Brigham

Young at Nauvoo.[9] With the other members of the Quorum of the Twelve, Brigham Young had been called by revelation in 1838 to preach the gospel in England (see D&C 118). Illness and persecution did not prevent their responding to this commandment, and in scarcely more than a year of missionary work, they converted literally thousands to the Church.[10]

On 1 July 1841, President Young, with Heber C. Kimball and John Taylor, returned to Nauvoo from their labors. The revelation, given a little over a week later on 9 July, began with the Lord's tender address, "Dear and well-beloved brother, Brigham Young" (D&C 126:1). "My servant Brigham," the Lord continued, "it is no more required at your hand to leave your family as in times past, for your offering is acceptable to me" (D&C 126:1). As President of the Quorum of the Twelve, Brigham Young was directed to remain in Nauvoo and to "send" the Lord's word abroad (D&C 126:3).

The significance of the command to remain at Nauvoo became clear in the general conference of the following month. Prior to this time, the Twelve had served mainly as a traveling council. At the afternoon conference session of 16 August 1841, Joseph Smith announced "that the time had come when the Twelve should be called upon to stand in their place next to the First Presidency, and attend to the settling of emigrants and the business of the Church at the stakes, and assist to bear off the kingdom victoriously to the nations, and as they had been faithful, and had borne the burden in the heat of the day, that it was right that they should have an opportunity of providing something for themselves and families."[11] By setting them "in their place next to the First Presidency," the Prophet was preparing the way for the Twelve, with Brigham Young as President to preside over the Church at the time of his death.

### Make a Solemn Proclamation

In his preface to the Doctrine and Covenants, the Lord announced in 1831 that the weak and simple would proclaim the fulness of the gospel "unto the ends of the world, and before kings and rulers" (D&C 1:23). Ten years later, he commanded that such a proclamation be made in writing. The time had come to call upon rulers and governments to give heed to the light and glory of Zion (D&C 124:6).

The fact that the Lord had given a commandment by no means guaranteed the facilitation of its fulfillment. Robert B. Thompson, named to help Joseph Smith with the writing (D&C 124:12), died before the end of the year,[12] and John C. Bennett, named to assist in the promulgation of the proclamation (D&C 124:16), fell into apostasy.[13] The completion of the project continued to concern the Prophet until the time of his death.[14]

A year after the martyrdom, Parley P. Pratt composed a document under the direction of the Twelve Apostles entitled, "PROCLAMATION of the Twelve Apostles of the Church of Jesus Christ of Latter-day Saints. To all the Kings of the World; To the President of the United States of America; To the Governors of the several States; And to the Rulers and People of all Nations." It was published in New York on 6 April 1845. The spirit of this proclamation is manifest in its opening line: "KNOW YE:—That the kingdom of God has come: as has been predicted by ancient prophets, and prayed for in all ages; even that kingdom which shall fill the whole earth, and shall stand for ever."[15] The command was issued to leaders of nations and kingdoms to repent, be baptized for the remission of sins and contribute to the establishment of the kingdom of God.

The Lord's command to make a solemn proclamation has had a continuing fulfillment. The bold missionary thrust of the Church for more than one and one-half century, spreading the message of the restored gospel throughout the world, is a response to the Lord's instruction. At the One Hundred Fiftieth Annual General Conference, commemorating the Sesquicentennial anniversary of the organization of the Church, Elder Gordon B. Hinckley read a new proclamation, entitled, "Proclamation From the First Presidency and the Quorum of the Twelve Apostles of The Church of Jesus Christ of Latter-day Saints." Broadcast from the reconstructed Peter Whitmer, Sr. farmhouse at the site of the organization of the Church, this bold statement recounted the events of the restoration and witnessed to the divine destiny of the Church, inviting all to heed the message of the missionaries and accept the truth. It concluded:

> We call upon all men and women to forsake evil and turn to God; to work together to build that brotherhood which must be recognized when we truly come to know that God is our

> Father and we are his children; and to worship him and his Son, the Lord Jesus Christ, the Savior of mankind. In the authority of the Holy Priesthood in us vested, we bless the seekers of truth wherever they may be and invoke the favor of the Almighty upon all men and nations whose God is the Lord, in the name of Jesus Christ, amen.[16]

## Many Are Called, But Few Are Chosen

Throughout section 124, the Lord revealed his will and counsel to individuals at Nauvoo. Even a brief consideration of the blessings offered these men and their subsequent lives provides a lesson on the contingent nature of the Lord's promises. "When we obtain any blessing from God, it is by obedience to that law upon which it is predicated" (D&C 130:21). Many of these men were commended by the Lord and received great promises, but they subsequently forfeited them through sin and apostasy.[17]

For example, John C. Bennett was assigned by the Lord to stand by Joseph Smith in the hour of affliction, "and his reward shall not fail if he receive counsel. And for his love he shall be great, for he shall be mine if he do this, saith the Lord. I have seen the work which he hath done, which I accept if he continue, and will crown him with blessings and great glory" (D&C 124:16-17). Bennett's apostasy has already been mentioned above. The two "if" statements defined the contingent nature of the Lord's promises to him: "if he receive counsel" and "if he continue." He did neither, and his blessing was lost.

Similarly, the Lord extended to Lyman Wight a beautiful blessing: "And I will bear him up as on eagles' wings; and he shall beget glory and honor to himself and unto my name. That when he shall finish his work I may receive him unto myself" (D&C 124:18-19). Faithful for a time, and even called to the Apostleship, Lyman Wight later rejected the leadership of the Twelve and published a pamphlet in 1848 denying their authority. He was excommunicated from the Church. Likewise, George Miller, Isaac Galland, William Law, Robert D. Foster, and Sidney Rigdon did not endure in their faith.

Of those who remained true to the church, mention may be made of Vinson Knight and Hyrum Smith. To Vinson Knight the Lord said, "and I will accept of his offerings, for they shall not be unto me as the offerings of Cain, for he shall be mine, saith the Lord. Let his family rejoice and turn away their hearts from affliction; for I have chosen him and anointed him, and he shall be honored in the midst of his house, for I will forgive all his sins, saith the Lord" (D&C 124:74-76). And to Hyrum Smith, "blessed is my servant Hyrum Smith; for I, the Lord, love him because of the integrity of his heart, and because he loveth that which is right before me, saith the Lord" (D&C 124:15). Both of these men later met death in Illinois, faithful to their callings and hopeful of the fulfillment of their profferred blessings.

## Priesthood Organization

Verses 123-45 of section 124 list the officers of the Church. Deaths, apostasy, and other developments had made some reorganization necessary. Of great significance among these changes was the call of Hyrum Smith to serve as patriarch in the place of his deceased father, Joseph Smith, Sr. (v. 124).[18] The First Presidency, as revealed earlier in this revelation, was to consist of Joseph Smith, Jr., Sidney Rigdon, and William Law, with William Law filling the vacancy left by the calling of Hyrum Smith to be patriarch. Brigham Young was named president over the Twelve, and the vacancy in that quorum brought about by the death of David Patten at the Battle of Crooked River in 1838 remained open for the time being.

It is significant to note that the language of the Lord in this revelation concerning callings was: "I give unto you [name] to be [calling]." In all cases, two principles were upheld by the Lord: (1) the agency of the person called (note the phrase "if he will receive it" in the naming of Shadrach Roundy for the bishopric), and (2) the law of common consent (note v. 144: "And a commandment I give unto you, that you should fill all these offices and approve of those names which I have mentioned, or else disapprove of them at my general conference").

## The Lord's Boarding House

Much of section 124 deals with the building of a boarding house in Nauvoo (vv. 22-24, 56-83, 111-22). To some it may seem curious that the plans for a hotel, complete with trustees, investment policy, and a list of potential stockholders would be received by revelation from

God, but the Nauvoo House was intended to play an important role in his work.

The revelation is clear as to the sacred nature of this hotel. The Lord commanded that it be built "unto his name" (vv. 22, 24, 56). He called it "my boarding house," and added, "let my name be named upon it" (v. 56). The governor of the house was not to allow it to be polluted: "It shall be holy, or the Lord your God will not dwell therein" (v. 24).[19] This is an excellent example of the principle revealed in D&C 29:34: "Wherefore, verily I say unto you that all things unto me are spiritual." In an earlier dispensation, Zechariah had prophesied of sacred things in another holy city: "In that day shall there be upon the bells of the horses, HOLINESS UNTO THE LORD; and the pots in the Lord's house shall be like the bowls before the altar. Yea, every pot in Jerusalem and in Judah shall be holiness unto the Lord of hosts" (Zech. 14:20-21).

The building of a hotel must be associated with the command given to Joseph Smith to make a proclamation to kings and governors. The Lord indicated that the hearts of many of them would be softened, and his challenge to them was stirring: "Awake, O kings of the earth! Come ye, O, come ye, with your gold and your silver, to the help of my people, to the house of the daughters of Zion" (D&C 124:11). A place had to be provided to receive such visitors: "And let it be a delightful habitation for man, and a resting-place for the weary traveler, that he may contemplate the glory of Zion, and the glory of this, the corner-stone thereof" (D&C 124:60).

The Nauvoo House was also intended as a residence for Joseph Smith and his descendants (the right of stockholders would be passed to their heirs), and as a place where people who came to the city could receive counsel from those whom the Lord had designated as "plants of renown" (see Ezek. 34:29; cf. Isa. 60:21; 61:3) and as "watchmen upon her walls" (see Isa. 62:6). All this was part of the far-ranging plan for the gathering place of the Church.

Joseph Smith continually urged the Saints to complete the construction of the Nauvoo House. He, more than many, envisioned the significance of the project. Typical of his exhortations on the matter is the reference in a sermon given at the General Conference meeting of 6 April 1843: "It is not right that all the burden of the Nauvoo House should rest on a few individuals; and we will now consider the propriety of sending the Twelve to collect means for it. There has been too great a solicitude in individuals for the building of the Temple to the exclusion of the Nauvoo House."[20] Ultimately, the press of increased persecutions and the desire to complete the Temple prevailed, and on 4 March 1844 the completion of the Nauvoo House was postponed.[21] The building was never completed, and the property and partially constructed walls remained in the hands of Emma Smith with the settlement of the Prophet's estate.

Two principles of the Lord's work may be learned from the Nauvoo House revelation. First, there is a permanence of perspective in the Lord's work. He knew, of course, that the Saints would soon be driven from Nauvoo, yet he required of them undertakings which looked forward "from generation to generation." His kingdom is not a temporary one. Second, to establish his kingdom, the Lord requires temples, but he also requires hotels. Spiritual principles and ordinances are complemented by temporal affairs in his work.

## The Nauvoo Temple

Beginning with Moroni's quotation from Mal. 4 in 1823 (JS-H 37-39), The Church of Jesus Christ of Latter-day Saints has increasingly focused on the importance of temples. Our great mission in mortality is to discover the way to eternal life and to walk in that way: "And this is life eternal, that they might know thee the only true God, and Jesus Christ, whom thou hast sent" (John 17:3). A temple is the House of the Lord—a place where his mortal children go to make contact with him and a place where he may reveal himself to them. In addition, it is a place where sacred priesthood ordinances are performed.[22]

The first command to build a temple had come to the Prophet Joseph Smith in July 1831 (D&C 57:1-3). This was to be the temple in the center place of Zion in Jackson County, Missouri. The site for this temple was dedicated on 3 August 1831, but before the construction began, mobs had expelled the Saints from the county. Just two months after the first mob gathered, the Prophet was commanded to tarry in Kirtland, Ohio and build a temple there (D&C 95:8-9).[23] The Lord had promised the Prophet that in Ohio he would "be endowed with power from on high" (see D&C 38:32), and it was in the Kirtland Temple that the restoration of the sacred keys occurred as described in D&C 110.

The Kirtland Temple was not intended as a place for the performance of endowment ceremonies for the general Church membership or for ordinances for the dead. Speaking of the Kirtland Temple, Brigham Young said, "And those first Elders who helped to build it, received a portion of their first endowments, or we might say more clearly, some of the first, or introductory, or initiatory ordinances, preparatory to an endowment. The preparatory ordinances there administered, though accompanied by the ministrations of angels, and the presence of the Lord Jesus, were but a faint similitude of the ordinances of the house of the Lord in their fulness."[24]

Section 124 contains instructions on the building of the temple in Nauvoo (vv. 25-48, 55). The Lord promised Joseph Smith: "And verily I say unto you, let this house be built unto my name, that I may reveal mine ordinances therein unto my people; For I deign to reveal unto my church . . . things that pertain to the dispensation of the fulness of times. And I will show unto my servant Joseph all things pertaining to this house, and the priesthood thereof, and the place whereon it shall be built" (D&C 124:40-42).

Perhaps sensing that he would not live to see the Nauvoo Temple completed,[25] Joseph Smith began on 4 May 1842 to administer the ordinances revealed to him in fulfillment of the Lord's promise. He spent that day with several church leaders in the upper part of his red brick store "instructing them in the principles and order of the Priesthood, attending to washings, anointings, endowments and the communication of keys pertaining to the Aaronic Priesthood, and so on to the highest order of the Melchisedek Priesthood, setting forth the order pertaining to the Ancient of Days, and all those plans and principles by which any one is enabled to secure the fullness of those blessings which have been prepared for the Church of the First Born, and come up and abide in the presence of the Eloheim in the eternal worlds."[26] He wrote of the occasion that it was the first time this order was instituted in the latter days and that the things received by a few that day would be made available to all the Saints of the last days when they were prepared to receive them and when a proper place was prepared for them to be communicated.[27]

The construction of the Nauvoo Temple required a prodigious

effort. Even before section 124 was received, the First Presidency had sent an address to the Saints abroad declaring that the time had come to gather to Nauvoo and to make the sacrifices necessary to build a house for the ordinances of God.[28] This request was heightened by the word of the Lord: "Send ye swift messengers" (D&C 124:26) and "Let all my saints come from afar" (D&C 124:25). In 1843, the Prophet taught the meaning of the principle of gathering as follows: "What was the object of gathering the Jews, or the people of God in any age of the world? . . . The main object was to build unto the Lord a house whereby He could reveal unto His people the ordinances of His house and the glories of His kingdom, and teach the people the way of salvation; for there are certain ordinances and principles that, when they are taught and practiced, must be done in a place or house built for that purpose."[29] The Lord intended to gather a chosen people at Nauvoo and make them a covenant people through the ordinances of the temple.

In section 124, the Lord taught a principle by which the Saints could know if their work was acceptable to him. "Verily, verily, I say unto you, that when I give a commandment to any of the sons of men to do a work unto my name, and those sons of men go with all their might and with all they have to perform that work, and cease not their diligence, and their enemies come upon them and hinder them from performing that work, behold, it behooveth me to require that work no more at the hands of those sons of men, but to accept of their offerings" (v. 49). On this basis, the Lord said that he had accepted the offerings of the faithful people whom he had first commanded to build the temple at Jackson County, Missouri. They could be consoled that the Lord would not hold them responsible for failing to build the temple there in the midst of their persecutions.

Enemies of the Church were determined to halt or prevent the work on the Nauvoo Temple as well. After a brief lull following the martyrdom of Joseph and Hyrum Smith, pressure intensified upon the Saints to leave Nauvoo. This pressure "propelled Brigham Young toward two main objectives: first, to complete the temple and other unfinished projects in Nauvoo; and second, to find and prepare to depart for a new place of settlement."[30] President Young was anxious to see the people spiritually strengthened by the temple ordinances, and despite preparations to leave the city, the Saints redoubled their work on the temple. On 10 December 1845, the first endowment work was begun in the attic story, and during the next eight weeks before the temple closed on 8 February 1846, nearly 5,600 members received their endowments.[31]

Before leaving Nauvoo, Brigham Young and the Twelve Apostles met in the still uncompleted structure. Brigham Young wrote of that occasion: "I met with the Council of the Twelve in the southeast corner room of the attic of the Temple. We knelt around the altar, and dedicated the building to the Most High. We asked his blessing upon our intended move to the west; also asked him to enable us some day to finish the Temple, and dedicate it to him, and we would leave it in his hands to do as he pleased; and to preserve the building as a momument to Joseph Smith. We asked the Lord to accept the labors of his servants in this land. We then left the Temple."[32]

A special crew of workers remained behind in Nauvoo to complete the construction. Orson Hyde, representing the Twelve, was to oversee this work. By mid-April 1846, public dedications were announced for the first three days of May. On 30 April, the day before the public dedications began, a private dedication was held, which Wilford Woodruff described in his journal as follows: "In the evening of this day I repaired to the Temple with Elder Orson Hyde and about twenty other elders of Israel. There we were all clothed in our priestly robes and dedicated the Temple of the Lord, erected to His most holy name by the Church of Jesus Christ of Latter-day Saints. Notwithstanding the predictions of false prophets and the threat of mobs that the building should never be completed nor dedicated, their words had fallen to the ground. The Temple was now finished and dedicated to Him. After the dedication, we raised our voices in a united shout of 'Hosanna to God and the Lamb!'"[33]

Their offering was acceptable to God, and the workmen joined the remainder of the Saints in Iowa. The temple was left behind, but it had fulfilled its purpose. Erastus Snow later commented: "The Spirit, Power, and Wisdom of God reigned continually in the Temple, and all felt satisfied that during the two months we occupied it in the endowment of the Saints, we were amply paid for all our labors in building it."[34] Brigham Young, in a spirit of rejoicing during the period the endowments were being performed, said: "This church has obtained already all they have labored for in building this Temple, but after we leave here (I feel it in my bones) there will be thousands of men that can go into any part of the world and build up the kingdom, and build temples."[35]

Considering the Nauvoo Temple in retrospect, a modern apostle has observed: "Those who look back on Church history sometimes grind their teeth at the injustice of the persecutions or weep over the loss of temples. They were taken from us. But those who took the temples and defiled them have nothing, comparatively, and we have everything. They have a building or a site or two; we have the keys, we have the ordinances, we have the authority."[36]

## Notes

[1]B. H. Roberts, *A Comprehensive History of The Church of Jesus Christ of Latter-day Saints.* 6 vols. (Salt Lake City: Deseret News Press, 1930), 2:84-85.

[2]*HC* 3:319-21. Of this escape from their intoxicated guard, Hyrum Smith poignantly said, "we took our change of venue for the state of Illinois." (*HC* 3:423.)

[3]*Ibid.*., 3:375.

[4]*Ibid.*, 4:80.

[5]*Ibid.*, 4:268.

[6]*HC* 3:378. See also Lyndon W. Cook, "Isaac Galland—Mormon Benefactor," *Brigham Young University Studies* 19.3 (Spring 1979): 268-84.

[7]*HC* 4:12.

[8]*Ibid.*, p. 399.

[9]*Ibid.*, p. 382.

[10]See James B. Allen and Malcolm R. Thorp, "The Mission of the Twelve to England, 1840-41: Mormon Apostles and the Working Class," *Brigham Young University Studies* 15.4 (Summer 1975): 499-526. See also David A. Boone, "A Time for Commitment," found herein.

[11]*HC* 4:403.

[12]*Ibid.*, p. 411.

[13]*Ibid.*, 5:71-82.

[14]*Ibid.*, 4:483-84; 6:79-80, 176-77.

[15]James R. Clark, comp., *Messages of the First Presidency,* 6 vols. (Salt Lake City: Bookcraft, 1965-75), 1:252-53.

[16]*Conference Report*, April 1980, p. 77; *Ensign*, May 1980, p. 53.

[17]For helpfuls biographical information on each man named in section 124, see Lyndon W. Cook, *The Revelations of the Prophet Joseph Smith* (Provo: Seventy's Mission Bookstore, 1981), pp. 251-81.

[18]Note that in v. 95 Hyrum Smith was also to be "crowned with the same blessing, and glory, and honor, and priesthood, and gifts of the priesthood, that once were put upon him that was my servant Oliver Cowdery." Oliver Cowdery had been excommunicated for apostasy 12 April 1838 at Far West, Missouri. See *HC* 3:17.

[19]Compare the similar injunction for temples in D&C 97:15-17.

[20]*HC* 5:329.

[21]*Ibid.*, 6:230.

[22]See approaches to the definition of "temple" in Richard O. Cowan, "Temple Building Ancient and Modern" (Provo: Brigham Young University Press, 1971); and James E. Talmage, *The House of the Lord* (Salt Lake City: Deseret Book Co., 1968).

[23]The revelation in D&C 95:8-9 was given on 1 June 1833. The mob in April (see *HC* 1:342). On 23 July 1833, the cornerstones of the Kirtland Temple were laid, the very day that another mob served notice of expulsion on the Missouri Saints (see *HC* 1:400).

[24]*JD* 2:31.

[25]In remarks to the Relief Society on 28 April 1842, Joseph Smith "spoke of delivering the keys of the Priesthood to the Church, and said that the faithful members of the Relief Society should receive them in connection with their husbands, that the Saints whose integrity has been tried and proved faithful, might know how to ask the Lord and receive an answer; for according to his prayers, *God had appointed him elsewhere*" *HC* 4:604 (italics added); see also *TPJS*, p. 226.

[26]*HC* 5:2; *TPJS*, p. 237.

[27]*Ibid.*

[28]*Ibid.*, 4:186, see also *ibid.*, 4:205.

[29]*Ibid.*, 5:423.

[30]Francis M. Gibbons, *Brigham Young, Modern Moses, Prophet of God* (Salt Lake City: Deseret Book Co., 1981), p. 109.

[31]Lyndon W. Cook, *The Revelations*, p. 250.

[32]*HC* 7:580.

[33]Matthias F. Cowley, *Wilford Woodruff* (Salt Lake City: Bookcraft, 1964), p. 247.

[34]Andrew K. Larsen, *Erastus Snow* (Salt Lake City: University of Utah Press, 1971), p. 96, cited in Lisle G Brown, "The Sacred Departments for

Temple Work in Nauvoo: The Assembly Room and the Council Chamber," *Brigham Young University Studies* 19.3 (Spring 1979): 361-74.

[35]Quoted in Helen Mar Whitney, "Scenes in Nauvoo, and Incidents from H. C. Kimball's Journal" (entry for "Friday, January 2nd, 1846") *Woman's Exponent* 12.8 (15 September 1883): 58, cited in Don F. Colvin, "A Historical Study of the Mormon Temple at Nauvoo, Illinois," unpublished master's thesis, Brigham Young University, 1962, p. 160.

[36]Boyd K. Packer, *The Holy Temple* (Salt Lake City: Bookcraft, 1980), p. 176.

# 45

# INSTRUCTIONS ON BAPTISM FOR THE DEAD

## (D&C 127 and 128)

Richard O. Cowan

Sections 127 and 128 are unlike any other sections in the Doctrine and Covenants. Both are letters, written by Joseph Smith during the first week of September, 1842. During the previous May, Missouri's governor, Lilburn W. Boggs, who had issued the extermination order against the Saints, was shot and wounded. The Latter-day Saints were immediately suspected, and Joseph Smith was specifically accused of being an accessory to the crime. During August the Prophet was arrested on these charges but was soon released. At this point some Missourians threatened to take the law into their own hands by crossing the river into Illinois and seizing the Prophet by force. Joseph therefore went into hiding for the sake of his own and the Church's safety.

In the first of these letters (section 127), dated 1 September, the Prophet set forth several topics on which he elaborated at greater length in the more lengthy epistle (section 128) five days later. These included an exhortation to continue the work of the temple (D&C 127:4), instructions to provide a recorder (v. 6), a reference to the power to bind or loose (v. 7), a promise to reveal more pertaining to the priesthood (v. 8), and a command to have the archives in order (v. 9). Even though these ideas reached the Saints in the form of a letter, the Prophet clearly prefaced them with "thus saith the Lord" (see vv. 4 and 6).

### Beginnings of Temple Work

Temple ordinances as we know them today had been restored during the two years preceding the time when these two letters were written. The first baptisms for the dead were performed in the Mississippi River beginning in September of 1840. On 19 January 1841, however, the Lord explained that "this ordinance belongeth to my house" but indicated that he would give the Saints a "sufficient time" to build the temple and in the meantime would accept the baptisms being performed in the river (D&C 124:29-33). The Nauvoo Saints took these words very seriously so immediately set to work excavating for the temple's basement. By fall this lower story was enclosed and a temporary font provided. On 30 October, the Prophet declared: "There shall be no more baptisms for the dead, until the ordinance can be attended to in the Lord's House . . . for thus saith the Lord!"[1] On 8 November the font and temple basement were dedicated, and baptisms were commenced there two weeks later.[2]

On 5 May 1842, Joseph Smith presented the temple endowment for the first time. The *History of the Church* records that he had spent the day in his private office instructing his brethren "in the principles and order of the Priesthood, attending to washings, anointings, endowments, and the communication of keys pertaining to the Aaronic Priesthood, and so on to the highest order of the Melchizedek Priesthood, setting forth the order pertaining to the Ancient of Days, and all those plans and principles by which any one is enabled to secure the fullness of those blessings which have been prepared for the Church of the First Born, and come up and abide in the presence of the Eloheim in the eternal worlds." The Prophet explained that these truths were "to be received only by the spiritual minded," and by any of the Saints "so soon as they are prepared" and a "proper place" is provided. He therefore exhorted them to "be diligent in building the temple."[3] Sealings of husbands and wives were also performed during this period. It was concerning these matters that Joseph Smith gave further instructions in his two epistles to the Saints.

## Importance of Accurate Records

In both of his epistles, the Prophet stressed the importance of having a recorder present whenever ordinances were performed (D&C 127:6 and 128:3). Not only would he preserve an accurate record, but he would also see and hear that each ordinance is performed properly. In section 128 we find the first reference to the ward as a key Church unit; the city of Nauvoo had been divided into wards for both political and ecclesiastical purposes. Although the instructions in v. 3 were related to baptisms for the dead, the standards of accuracy mentioned here can appropriately be applied to any records kept by ward clerks or others. The provision in v. 4 for a general Church recorder anticipated the work now being done by the genealogical, historical, membership, and other departments at Church headquarters. As the Church has grown in size worldwide and as new technology has become available, the methods of keeping records as outlined in these early instructions has been superceded. Likewise, for example, the intimate system of local leaders coming together to exchange membership data, as outlined at the time the Church was organized (D&C 20:81-84), has been superceded in the twentieth century by a computerized system for keeping membership records.

The Prophet Joseph Smith stressed the importance of all these records as he commented on the meaning of Rev. 20:12, explaining that the "books" out of which we will be judged are "the records which are kept on the earth" (D&C 128: 6-7). These earthly records, Elder Bruce R. McConkie explained, include the "Standard Works of the Church" which teach "how men should walk in this mortal probation," together with "the records of the Church wherein are recorded the faith and good works of the Saints." The "book of life," Elder McConkie continued, is "figuratively . . . our own life, and being, the record of our acts transcribed in our souls, an account of our obedience or disobedience written in our bodies. Literally, it is the record kept in heaven of the names and righteous deeds of the faithful."[4]

### The Power to Bind and Loose

In his instructions, the Prophet linked the keeping of accurate records to the power to bind or loose on earth and have this action recognized in heaven (D&C 128:8). At least four requirements must be met for an ordinance performed on earth to be binding in heaven: (1) It must be performed "in authority"—priesthood and specific authorization. (2) All saving ordinances must be done "in the name of the Lord" Jesus Christ. (3) They must be performed "truly and faithfully"—precisely as the Lord has instructed. (4) "A proper and faithful record of the same" must be kept (D&C 128:9). If these conditions are not met, the action is not recorded in heaven.

Joseph Smith acknowledged that the idea of being able to bind or loose on earth and have it bound or loosed in heaven "may seem to some to be a very bold doctrine." Nevertheless, he insisted, this power has always been given whenever the Lord has given a dispensation of the gospel to men on earth. As an illustration, he cited the Lord's promise to Peter to give him "the keys of the kingdom of heaven" which included this binding and loosing power (Matt. 16:18-19 and D&C 128:9-10).

These "sealing keys" had been restored six years earlier by Elijah, just one week following the dedication of the Kirtland Temple (D&C 110:13-16). Through these keys, all ordinances—both for the living and for the dead—may be of "efficacy, virtue, or force in and after the resurrection from the dead" (D&C 132:7). By these same powers and through ordinances available in holy temples, individuals may achieve their maximum potential and receive the fullness of priesthood blessings, and families may be organized eternally in the patriarchal order.[5]

## The Role of Priesthood Ordinances

In his epistle, the Prophet next turned specifically to the ordinance of baptism. Elder Boyd K. Packer related the terms "ordinance," "ordain," and "order," suggesting that "ordinances" are a ceremony "by which things are put in proper order."[6] These ordinances are a source of power by which we can place our lives in order according to God's eternal principles. An earlier revelation had declared: "This greater priesthood administereth the gospel and holdeth the key of the mysteries of the kingdom, even the key of the knowledge of God. Therefore, *in the ordinances thereof,* the power of godliness is manifest" (D&C 84:19-20, emphasis added). Not only do gospel ordinances communicate needed divine power, but they are also designed to teach important concepts. The laying on of hands, for example, is a tangible representation of the link necessary to transmit a blessing, gift, or priesthood authority from one person to another.

In section 128 the Prophet reminded the Saints that baptism by immersion was a visible representation of death and burial, and then a coming forth from the grave and resurrection into a new life. Hence the font symbolizes the grave and should be "underneath where the living are wont to assemble" (D&C 128: 12-13). In Latter-day Saint temples the baptismal font is customarily found in the lower part of the building. Even in recent smaller one-story temples, the font is situated in a step-down area.

## The Importance of Work for the Dead

Expanding on Paul's teachings in Heb. 11:40, the Prophet Joseph Smith declared that "they [the fathers] without us cannot be made perfect—neither can we without our dead be made perfect," and that "their salvation is necessary and essential to our salvation" (D&C 128:15). Just a year earlier, the Prophet had warned the Saints that those who neglect seeking out their dead "do it at the peril of their own salvation."[7] Why is this so? In the celestial kingdom we will be organized as God's family according to the patriarchal order. Turning again to a tangible symbol, the Prophet taught that there must be "a welding link of some kind or other between the fathers and the children" (D&C 128:18). Unless we are welded to our forebears who in turn are welded into God's family, we cannot be saved. On the other hand, they cannot be saved without the ordinances which we, who are living upon the earth, must perform in their behalf. Hence neither we nor they can be saved without the other. Joseph Smith specifically linked the accomplishment of this to baptism for the dead. What he said about baptism should be applied to other necessary ordinances, such as the endowment, which we may perform in behalf of those who have died. At the time the Prophet wrote his epistle, baptisms were the only ordinances being performed for the dead; vicarious endowments, for example, were not inaugurated until 1877.

Joseph Smith quoted Malachi's prophecy that Elijah would come and turn the hearts of the fathers and children to one another. Joseph indicated that he could have given a plainer translation, but that it was sufficient to know that the earth would be wasted were it not to take place (D&C 128: 17-18). In March of 1844 he provided a plainer translation, explaining that Elijah's keys would make it possible for the children to be "sealed" to their fathers, and the fathers "sealed" to the children.[8] In 1823 the Angel Moroni had provided a similar clarification as he paraphrased Malachi's prophecy: "Behold, I will reveal unto you the Priesthood, by the hand of Elijah the prophet" (D&C 2:1)[9]

What would bring this uniting of generations to pass? Moroni's paraphrase explained that Elijah "shall plant in the hearts of the children the promises made to the fathers, and the hearts of the children shall turn to their fathers" (D&C 2:2). The worldwide upsurge of interest in genealogy and tracing one's roots attests to the fulfillment of this prophecy. Because, as the Prophet had already explained, keeping an accurate record of ordinances performed is essential, he now urged the Saints to prepare a complete record. "Let us, therefore," he challenged, "as a church and people, and as Latter-day Saints, offer unto the Lord an offering in righteousness; and let us present in his holy temple, when it is finished, a book containing the records of our dead, which shall be worthy of all acceptation" (D&C 128:24). Such a record would provide evidence that necessary ordinances had been performed to establish the required welding links from generation to generation. Modern technology has made it possible more than ever before to comply with the Prophet's challenge. We as individual families are responsible for preparing our own records for the first four generations. Beyond that point, through the name-extraction program and using the computer, "as a church and a people," we are compiling the "International Genealogical Index" which is a record of our common ancestry.

### Glad Tidings for the Living and the Dead

The Prophet Joseph Smith concluded the second of his two epistles with a review of events in the restoration of the gospel, which brought "glad tidings of great joy" for both the living and the dead. As he reviewed these events, he provided details of information not made known elsewhere. For example, he reported that Peter, James, and John had restored the Melchizedek Priesthood between the towns of Colesville and Harmony. Likewise, there is no other record of the incident when Michael or Adam detected the devil when he attempted to appear as an angel of light (D&C 128:20). The identity of Raphael is not known, nor is more information available concerning the appearances of Michael or Adam and of Gabriel or Noah as mentioned in v. 21.

"Brethren, shall we not go on in so great a cause?", the Prophet challenged as he finished his letter. "Go forward and not backward. Courage, brethren; and on, on to the victory!" (D&C 128:22).

## Notes

[1]*HC* 4:426.

[2]*Ibid.*, p. 446.

[3]*Ibid.*, 5:1-2.

[4]Bruce R. McConkie, *Doctrinal New Testament Commentary*, 3 vols. (Salt Lake City: Bookcraft, 1966-73), 3:578.

[5]See Milton V. Backman, Jr., and Robert L. Millet, "Heavenly Manifestations in the Kirtland Temple," found herein.

[6]Boyd K. Packer, *The Holy Temple* (Salt Lake City: Bookcraft, 1980), p. 145.

[7]*HC* 4:426; *TPJS*, p. 193.

[8]*TPJS*, p. 337.

[9]See Charles R. Harrell, "Turning the Hearts of the Fathers and the Children," found herein.

# 46

# IMPORTANT ITEMS OF INSTRUCTION

## (D&C 129-131)

Bruce A. Van Orden

### "Instructions" from the Prophet in 1843

Nearly all sections of the Doctrine and Covenants are "revelations" given to (or through) Joseph Smith the Prophet. More than half of those revelations were given to the Prophet during the formative Kirtland period of the Church. Interestingly, the Nauvoo period of Church history (1839-46) produced only three "revelations" that are found in the Doctrine and Covenants (section 124, 125, and 126). Sections 127 and 128 are "epistles" from the Prophet to the Saints while he was hiding from harassing law enforcement officers in September 1842.

Sections 129-31 fall into yet another category, that of inspired "instructions." On four separate occasions in 1843, Joseph Smith, accompanied by his loyal scribe, William Clayton, instructed either individuals or groups on significant points of doctrine unique to Mormonism. These instructions eventually made their way into the official history of Joseph Smith (now known as the *History of the Church*), a project headed first by Willard Richards, and following his death, by George A. Smith. Portions of the history containing these instructions were published in the *Deseret News* in 1856, the first time they were to appear in print. Under the direction of Brigham Young. these "instructions" were included in the 1876 edition of the Doctrine and Covenants. They were officially canonized when that edition was presented before the conference of the Church in 1880.

### Setting for Section 129

Doctrine and Covenants 129 contains instructions given to Elder Parley P. Pratt on 9 February 1843, on the occasion of his return from his mission to Great Britain. Parley had remained over a year and one-half longer in Britain than his brethren of the Twelve, to preside over the Church there and to edit the *Millennial Star.* He had just arrived in Nauvoo two days previously. Joseph Smith was eager to hear the report of the British Mission from Elder Pratt and spent the better part of the next two days with him.[1] It was a pleasant reunion for the two noble warriors in the Lord's kingdom, who had spent both seasons of peace and also moments of severe hardship in prison bonds together.

Among other things, Parley was eager to learn more about the doctrine of angels and the keys to distinguish angels of the Lord from the angels of the devil. The Prophet had discussed similar matters about angels with the Quorum of the Twelve on two separate occasions in late June and early July of 1839, prior to the apostles' leaving for their mission to England.[2] Parley had not been in attendance at either of those two meetings, because he was still incarcerated in Richmond, Missouri at the time. When he finally arrived in England and spoke with the other brethren, he evidently learned something of these instructions from them, and then sought clarification about the instructions directly from the Prophet upon his arrival in Nauvoo.

The Prophet compiled and rehearsed these "grand keys" by which the correct nature of ministering angels may be distinguished. The version of the instructions given to Elder Pratt is the source for D&C 129, rather than the earlier 1839 version given to members of the Quorum of the Twelve.

### Setting for Section 130

After two years of hiding from enemies, Joseph Smith finally experienced a period of peace in the spring of 1843. The Prophet, never known for inactivity, was constantly on the move during this period. Because he could move about without concern that he might be apprehended by his enemies, Joseph directed much of his attention that spring to visiting numerous outlying settlements from Nauvoo where many members of the Church had gathered. The most frequently visited village was Ramus, the site for the inspired instructions found in sections 130 and 131.

Ramus was located on Crooked Creek, twenty miles east of Nauvoo and eight miles northeast of Carthage in Hancock County. The town was laid out entirely by Latter-day Saints and nearly all of its eventual five hundred inhabitants were Church members. Joel H. Johnson, an early friend of the Prophet in Kirtland and a missionary in the Crooked Creek area in 1838 and 1839, founded the community in

April 1839. Several Saints gathered to the area and by 1840 the town was officially laid out, a stake was organized, and the name Ramus, meaning "branch" from the Latin word, was given to the community.[3] Joel Johnson, called as the stake president, published notices in the *Times and Seasons* urging all Saints gathering to Illinois to consider settling in Ramus.[4] He was successful in his efforts, and soon Ramus became the largest and most prosperous of the several outlying settlements outside of Nauvoo.

Ramus Stake grew rapidly during its first year, and harmony seemed to prevail. Late in 1841, however, a secret clan was organized by some of the community leaders to steal from the enemies of the church, and a serious fissure developed among the leadership of the stake. The leaders argued bitterly for several weeks. At length those individuals who advocated and practiced stealing left town, were caught by the law and prosecuted, and were cut off from the Church. Hyrum Smith of the First Presidency and four members of the Council of the Twelve came to Ramus in November 1841, dissolved the stake, and kept only a branch. The community then settled back into more normal activities.[5]

On 1 March 1843 (the same year D&C 130 and 131 were given), Brigham Young, representing the Twelve Apostles, wrote to the Ramus Branch requesting provisions to assist Joseph Smith with temporal means. Elder Young indicated that the lack of provisions for Joseph Smith's family was all that hindered the Prophet from bringing to publication the revelations, the inspired translation of the Bible, and his official history. "We call on you for immediate relief in this matter," Brother Brigham urged. "We invite you to bring our President as many loads of wheat, corn, beef, pork, lard, tallow, eggs, poultry, venison, and everything eatable at your command. . . . The measure you mete shall be measured to you again. If you give liberally to your President in temporal things, God will return to you liberally in spiritual and temporal things too. . . . Brethren, will you do your work, and let the President do his for you before God? We wish an immediate answer by loaded teams or letter."[6]

The response of the Ramus Saints to this plea was immediate. Two days later Joseph Smith recorded, "Bishop Newell K. Whitney returned from Ramus this evening, with five teams loaded with provisions and grain, as a present to me, which afforded me very seasonable relief. I pray the Lord to bless those who gave it abundantly; and may it be returned upon their heads an hundred fold!"[7] The promises of Brigham Young that the Ramus Saints would be blessed spiritually for this assistance and the blessing pronounced upon them by the Prophet were realized in ample measure during the next two months with the wonderful items of instruction (found in D&C 130 and 131) that they received at the feet of the Prophet.

One of the leading citizens of Ramus was Benjamin F. Johnson, who was twenty-four years old in 1843 and the younger brother of Joel H. Johnson, founder of the community. Benjamin or "Bennie," as he was called by Joseph Smith, was one of the Prophet's closest friends. Whenever Joseph visited Ramus, he stayed at the Benjamin Johnson home. Because of his closeness to the Prophet, Benjamin and his family were dubbed "the Royal Family" by the other Saints in Ramus. Joseph delivered many of his now famous instructions found in D&C 130 and 131 in the Johnson home.[8]

Sunday, 2 April 1843, is the date for the instructions contained in section 130. Joseph Smith, together with Orson Hyde of the Twelve and his scribe William Clayton, had arrived on Saturday.[9] Early Sunday morning the Prophet took Benjamin Johnson with him for a private talk in the nearby woods. Joseph introduced Benjamin to the principle of plurality of wives which he had received earlier through revelation. He asked Benjamin to help him convince Almira, Benjamin's sister, that she should become one of Joseph's plural wives. All this was shocking to Benjamin, even though he was a close friend to the Prophet. Joseph calmed the young man's fears and prophesied that soon he would receive a testimony of the "principle."[10]

A public meeting was held that morning at 10 a.m. Elder Orson Hyde was the first speaker. He preached from John 14:23 regarding the Second Coming of the Savior, saying, "He will appear on a white horse as a warrior, and maybe we shall have some of that same spirit. Our God is a warrior." Elder Hyde also gave as his opinion, "It is our privilege to have the Father and Son dwelling in our hearts."[11]

The Prophet could not allow this teaching of false doctrine to go unattended, so at lunch Joseph told Orson that he was going to offer some correction to the latter's morning sermon. Orson replied, "They shall be thankfully received." These corrections of Elder Hyde's sermon were the beginning of the "important items of instruction" found in D&C 130.[12]

Joseph preached at the afternoon and evening meetings. His words were recorded by his dutiful scribe, William Clayton. In time the contents of these sermons were included in Joseph Smith's official history. But only portions of his words that day in Ramus have been included in the Doctrine and Covenants.[13]

## Setting for Section 131

On Tuesday, 16 May 1843, Joseph Smith arrived in Ramus for another visit. The Prophet made several social calls in the afternoon before going to Benjamin Johnson's home for the evening. "Before retiring, I gave Brother and Sister Johnson some instructions on the priesthood," Joseph recorded later in his history.[14] Brother Johnson's memoirs reveal even more about what those instructions were like: "In the evening he called me and my wife to come and sit down, for he wished to marry us according to the Law of the Lord. I thought it was a joke, and said, I should not marry my wife again, unless she *courted* me, for I did it all the first time. He chided my levity, told me he was in earnest, and so it proved, for we stood up and were sealed by the Holy Spirit of Promise."[15]

The same eventful evening Joseph placed his hand on the knee of his devoted scribe, William Clayton, and said, "Your life is hid with Christ in God." Joseph proceeded to seal Brother Clayton unto eternal life and to explain more details about the new and everlasting covenant of marriage similar to those found in D&C 132:16-17, 26.[16] Joseph concluded his instructions to Clayton by referring to the three heavens or degrees in the celestial kingdom and certifying that entrance into the highest only would come through participation in the new and everlasting covenant of marriage (see D&C 131:1-4). This last ordinance had just been performed that evening for Benjamin Johnson and his wife Melissa.

Still later that evening Joseph Smith and Benjamin Johnson were conversing privately in a bedroom. Benjamin recorded that Joseph "gave me such ideas pertaining to endowments as he thought proper."[19]

The next morning, Wednesday, the 17th of May, Joseph preached in a public morning meeting. Doctrine and Covenants 131:5-6, concerning the more sure word of prophecy, was part of that sermon. Joseph also stated in the same speech that salvation means a man's being placed beyond the powers of his enemies and that Paul had seen the third heavens, but that he (Joseph) had seen more than that. Joseph also stated that Peter had penned the most sublime language of any of the apostles.[18]

That evening the Prophet and the town residents had another interesting experience. A Methodist preacher, Samuel Prior, who was visiting Ramus, was called upon to speak to the congregation. This surprised Prior, who had expected no religious toleration among the Mormons. After Prior closed his remarks, Joseph politely asked Prior for permission to make comments on the latter's speech. In Prior's words, Joseph "mildly" spoke "like one who was more desirous to disseminate truth and expose error, than to love the malicious triumph of debate over me."[19] Doctrine and Covenants 131:7-8, regarding all spirit being matter, is part of Joseph's comments in response to Reverend Prior's remarks. Reverend Prior later called on the Prophet in Nauvoo.

## Doctrinal Gems in Sections 129-131

These "instructions" of the Prophet in 1843, now found in D&C 129-131, contain numerous doctrinal gems that in some instances are related, but in other cases bear hardly any relationship to each other. In any event all of these revealed doctrines are unique to the Latter-day Saints and serve to extend vastly our vision of eternity. For purposes of clarity and space, we will deal with only three of these key doctrinal areas, drawing from all three instructional sections of the Doctrine and Covenants and other useful interpretive sources.

### The Ministry of Angels

The Restoration of the gospel and the Church is largely based on the visitations of angels to the Prophet Joseph Smith and a few selected others. Early in his role as a prophet, Joseph became acquainted with the nature of angels, having been visited by Moroni, John the Baptist, Peter, James, John, Michael, Gabriel, Raphael (see D&C 128:20-21), as well as such Book of Mormon personages as Mormon, Nephi, and

Alma.[20] On the other hand, Joseph also became acquainted with Satan and his innumerable train of associates when he first was shown the Book of Mormon plates by the Angel Moroni.[21] Somewhere in these early experiences he became acquainted with what he called the "grand keys" to distinguish good angels from evil angels. Thus he gave as instructions to Elder Parley P. Pratt the instructions contained in D&C 129:4-9.

That Joseph understood something about these keys as early as the 1829-30 period or even earlier may be drawn from his statement in D&C 128:20: "The voice of Michael on the banks of the Susquehanna, detecting the devil when he appeared as an angel of light!" Since the Prophet did not return to the Susquehanna River area near Harmony, Pennsylvania after 1830, this experience with Michael and the devil disguised as an angel of light would have occurred by that year.

Joseph Smith certainly was thoroughly acquainted with these "grand keys" by 1839, because he instructed members of the Twelve concerning them prior to the apostles' leaving for their monumental mission to Great Britain. The Prophet was eager to counsel the Twelve in many matters of the kingdom prior to their leaving and hence spent a week with them in private meetings from 27 June to 2 July 1839. Some of his profound instructions dealt with the ministry of angels. Elder Wilford Woodruff penned the following in his journal of 27 June 1839:

> Among the vast number of the Keys of the Kingdom of God Joseph presented the following one to the Twelve for their benefit in there experience & travels in the flesh as follows:
>
> In order to detect the devel when he transforms himself nigh unto an angel of light. When an angel of God appears unto man face to face in personage & reaches out his hand unto the man & he takes hold of the angels hand & feels a substance the same as one man would in Shaking hands with another he may then know that it is an angel of God, & he should place all Confidence in him. Such personages or angels are Saints with there resurrected Bodies.
>
> But if a personage appears unto man & offers him his hand & the man takes hold of it & he feels nothing or does not sens any substance he may know it is the devel, for when a Saint whose body is not resurrected appears unto man in the flesh he will not offer him his hand for this is against the law given him

> & in keeping in mind these things we may detec the devil that he deceived us not.[22]

The connection between these instructions and those in section 129 is unmistakable. Hence these "grand keys" were known by at least some members of the Twelve three and one-half years before they were revealed again in 1843.

A few days after the above discourse, on 2 July 1839, Joseph Smith was still instructing the Twelve. "We may look for angels and receive their ministrations," he told them, "but we are to try the spirits and prove them, for it is often the case that men make a mistake in regard to these things. . . . Lying spirits are going forth in the earth. There will be great manifestations of spirits, both false and true."[23] These instructions and keys concerning angels became very useful for the Twelve in Britain, for in addition to being ministered to by righteous angels in the course of their missionary work, they were likewise plagued by evil spirits.

The Prophet apparently was also thoroughly acquainted with the appropriate appearance of angels. For one thing, he explained in 1839 that an angel of God never has wings.[24] In 1842 he recalled an experience where Satan had appeared as an angel of light. "A sister in the state of New York had a vision," he wrote,

> who said it was told her that if she would go to a certain place in the woods an angel would appear to her.—she went at the appointed time and saw a glorious personage descending arrayed in white, with sandy coloured hair; he commenced and told her to fear God and said that her husband was called to do great things, but that he must not go more than one hundred miles from home or he would not return; whereas God had called him to go to the ends of the earth: and he has since been more than one thousand miles from home, and is yet alive. Many true things were spoken by this personage and many things that were false.—How it may be asked was this known to be a bad angel? by the color of his hair; that is one of the signs that he can be known by, and by contradicting a former revelation.[25]

In the same instructions given to Parley P. Pratt on 9 February 1843 (but which were not included in D&C 129), Joseph related, "A man came to me in Kirtland, and told me he had seen an angel, and described his dress. I told him he had seen no angel, and that there was no such dress in heaven."[26]

Joseph Smith also delineated two different types of heavenly beings in his instructions to Parley P. Pratt: (1) "Angels, who are resurrected personages, having bodies of flesh and bones" (D&C 129:1) and (2) "the spirits of just men made perfect, they who are not resurrected, but inherit the same glory" (D&C 129:3). Several months later, while preaching at a funeral sermon, Joseph indicated that the spirits of just men made perfect "can only be revealed in flaming fire, or glory" and that angels "have advanced farther—their light and glory being tabernacled, and hence [they] appear in bodily shape."[27] The spirits of just men made perfect are interpreted as the spirits of individuals who have worked out their salvation, but are awaiting the day of their resurrection.[28]

President George Q. Cannon broadened this Doctrine and Covenants definition of angels when he wrote in 1891:

> In the broadest sense, any being who acts as a messenger for our Heavenly Father, is an angel, be he a God, a resurrected man, or the spirit of a just man; and the term is so used in all these senses in the ancient scriptures. In the stricter and more limited sense, an angel is, as the Prophet Joseph Smith states, a resurrected personage, having a body of flesh and bones; but it must be remembered that none of the angels who appeared to men before the death of the Savior could be of that class, for none of them was resurrected.[29]

This idea of various appointments and stations of angels was further clarified by President Charles W. Penrose in 1912: "Angels are God's messengers, whether used in the capacity as unembodied spirits, selected according to their capacities for the work required, or as disembodied spirits, or as translated men, or as resurrected beings. They are agents of Deity of different degrees of intelligence, power and authority, under the direction of higher dignitaries, and subject to law and order in their respective spheres."[30]

Regarding the dwelling place of these angels, the Prophet explained to the Ramus Saints in April 1843 that angels "reside in the presence of God" where "all things for their glory are manifest, past, present, and future" (D&C 130:7). Joseph also pointed out that all the angels that minister or have ministered to this earth have belonged to this earth (D&C 130:5). Presumably this means that all the resurrected beings, translated beings, or spirits who have served as heavenly messengers were once mortal beings on this earth, or will yet take a body and live on earth.

## Christ's Second Coming

Nothing seemed to attract the attention of the Prophet and the early Saints as much as the subject of the prophesied coming of the Savior. After all, Joseph Smith had learned in his earliest heavenly manifestations that the restoration of the gospel and the true Church were but a necessary prelude to the Second Coming of the Son of Man and his millennial reign on the earth. Many of the early revelations to the Prophet in the Doctrine and Covenants were dedicated wholly or in large measure to the signs of the times and to warning of the great calamities and destructions that must occur prior to the Second Coming.[31]

Joseph's "instructions" to the Saints in Ramus as found in D&C 130 contribute to our understanding of the Second Coming in two general areas: (1) the actual appearance of the Savior when he comes again, and (2) the time of his coming.

As previously mentioned, Orson Hyde accompanied the Prophet to Ramus in early April 1843 and propounded some incorrect doctrine in his sermon there. Elder Hyde had claimed that the Savior would appear "on a white horse as a warrior."[32] Joseph kindly corrected Orson before the Saints by declaring, "When the Savior shall appear we shall see him as he is. We shall see that he is a man like ourselves" (D&C 130:1). The Prophet actually was doing no more than sustaining the Apostle John's statement in his first general epistle, wherein he wrote, "When he shall appear, we shall be like him; for we shall see him as he is" (1 John 3:2). We also read from Luke that an angel said, as the Lord ascended to heaven in full view of his apostles, "This same Jesus, which is taken up from you into heaven, shall so come in like manner as ye have seen him go into heaven" (Acts 1:11).

Joseph Smith's teachings as to the time of the Second Coming in these "instructions" were particularly useful to the Saints in the Nauvoo period when speculation was rife concerning the date of the

Lord's appearance. Many millennialistic prophecies were in the air in the United States in the 1840s. Foremost among those in America who were predicting actual dates was William Miller, who had predicted—according to his biblical interpretation—that Christ would appear on 3 April 1843. So much of America was caught up in Miller's calculations and predictions that Horace Greeley's *New York Tribune* published an extra edition on 2 March 1843, to refute Miller's mathematics. Many of the Latter-day Saints also expected the Savior to return soon and saw signs in the heavens in 1843 that they took to be evidences of the Savior's imminent return.[33] The Prophet often referred to William Miller in his conversations and was obviously eager to obtain the Lord's will on the subject of when Christ would come again.

"I was once praying very earnestly to know the time of the coming of the Son of Man" (D&C 130:14), explained the Prophet to the members in Ramus just the day before Miller's projected date of 3 April 1843. Joseph went on to tell how the Lord informed him that if he (Joseph) lived until he was eighty-five years old, he would see the face of the Son of Man (D&C 130:15). Joseph was left wondering whether this appearance referred to the beginning of the Millennium or to some previous appearing, or whether he would die and thus see Christ's face (D&C 130:16). In any event the Prophet was convinced that the Savior would not come again prior to 1890 (the year when Joseph would have been 85). This prophecy and another which he gave four days later in general conference,[34] were held in high esteem by the Latter-day Saints for the next several years and served as effective counterpoints to the false views of William Miller. On 3 April Joseph observed, "Miller's day of judgment has arrived, but it is too pleasant for false prophets."[35]

As far as we in the present are concerned, we must be satisfied with the biblical explanation that no one knows the day or the hour when the Savior will return (see Matt. 24:36). Our main objective should be to stand in holy places (D&C 87:8) and to have the Holy Spirit as our guide (D&C 45:57) rather than laboring to ascertain the exact date of the Lord's reappearing.

## More Sure Word of Prophecy

Joseph Smith used 2 Peter chapter 1 as his text when he instructed the Saints in Ramus on 17 May 1843. When he came across the phrase, "the more sure word of prophecy" in v. 19, he defined it as follows: "a man's knowing that he is sealed up unto eternal life, by revelation and the spirit of prophecy, through the power of the Holy Priesthood" (D&C 131:6).

This was not the first time the Prophet had discoursed on this subject, one which he considered vital in one's quest for eternal life. Speaking to the Twelve Apostles on 17 June 1839 (the same occasion when he gave the apostles the "grand keys" to distinguish angels), the Prophet spoke about two comforters, the first being the Holy Ghost, and the second being the actual ministration of Christ to a mortal person.

> After a person has faith in Christ, repents of his sins, and is baptized for the remission of his sins and receives the Holy Ghost, (by laying on of hands), which is the first Comforter, then let him continue to humble himself before God, hungering and thirsting after righteousness, and living by every word of God, and the Lord will soon say to him, son, thou shalt be exalted. When the Lord has thoroughly proved him, and finds that the man is determined to serve Him at all hazards, then the man will find his calling and his election made sure, then it will be his privilege to receive the other Comforter, which the Lord hath promised the Saints.[36]

The phrase, "to make your calling and election sure," also comes from 2 Peter 1, this time from v. 10. It appears from Joseph Smith's foregoing description that at this date (1839) the Prophet was closely tying together the concepts of *making one's calling and election sure* and *the more sure word of prophecy.*

Just three days before Joseph Smith gave his instructions in Ramus that are now found in D&C 131, he was speaking to a similar gathering of outlying Saints in Yelrome (named after Isaac Morley; Yelrome is Morley spelled backwards with an additional *e*). As he would do later in the week, the Prophet took as his text 2 Peter chapter 1. Pertaining to the need for obtaining the more sure word of prophecy, the Prophet declared, "The apostle [Peter] exhorts them to add to their faith, virtue, knowledge, temperance, &c., yet he exhorts them to make their calling and election sure. And though they had heard an audible voice from heaven bearing testimony that Jesus was the Son of God, yet he says we have a more sure word of prophecy, whereunto ye do well that ye take heed as unto a light shining in a dark place."[37] The Prophet then proceeded to define the more sure word of prophecy: "[The assurance] that they were sealed in the heavens and had the promise of eternal life in the kingdom of God. Then, having this promise sealed unto them, it was an anchor to the soul, sure and steadfast. Though the thunders might roll and lightnings flash, and earthquakes bellow, and war gather thick around, yet this hope and knowledge would support the soul in every hour of trial, trouble and tribulation. Then knowledge through our Lord and Savior Jesus Christ is the grand key that unlocks the glories and mysteries of the kingdom of heaven."[38] Thus the Prophet in effect defined *the more sure word of prophecy* as the *knowledge* that one has *made his calling and election sure.* Hence Joseph's statement, "It is impossible for a man to be saved in ignorance" (D&C 131:6), when taken in its proper context, has reference to *the more sure word of prophecy*, and not simply to the acquisition of intellectual knowledge. Rather it means that a person must receive the assurance from the Lord that his calling and election is made sure. No man can be saved ultimately in ignorance of this *knowledge.*[39]

As previously mentioned, the instructions about the three degrees in the celestial kingdom and that a person must have entered the new and everlasting covenant of marriage to obtain the highest of those three degrees (D&C 131:1-4) were given in private conversation to Joseph Smith's scribe, William Clayton, in Benjamin Johnson's home in Ramus, Illinois. Virtually in the same breath, Joseph proclaimed to William that his "life was hid with Christ in God," and "that nothing but the unpardonable sin can prevent [him] from inheriting eternal life." Joseph assured William further that he was "sealed up by the power of the Priesthood unto eternal life."[40] Once again, noting the context and the selection of words, we can safely conclude that *having one's life hid with Christ in God* (see Col. 3:3) is synonymous with *having one's calling and election made sure.* Furthermore, eternal marriage sets one on a course which may eventuate in these consummate blessings.

## Conclusion

Joseph Smith was a man who took on many roles. He was able to express himself clearly and forcefully during the spring of 1843, a period of unusual peace for him. He showed himself at his best as a profound theologian, a loyal friend, a charismatic teacher, a kind person to strangers, and a revealer of new and (to the world) unusual doctrine and religious practices.

Doctrine and Covenants 129-31 have long been loved and widely quoted by Latter-day Saints. Most members of the Church have been inspired to greater religious application by the content of these three sections. While the doctrines and prophecies of these three sections are profound and singularly interesting, they did not arise from a whim of Joseph Smith. There is strong evidence of previous thought and revelation on all of the subjects in these important items of instruction.

## Notes

[1]*HC* 5:265-67.

[2]Scott G. Kenney, ed., *Wilford Woodruff's Journal,* 9 vols. (Midvale, Ut.: Signature Books, 1983-84), 1:341 (27 June 1839); and *HC* 3:391-92.

[3]Joel Hills Johnson Diary, Church Archives, Historical Department of The Church of Jesus Christ of Latter-day Saints, Salt Lake City, Ut. (hereafter referred to as Church Archives).

[4]*Times and Seasons* 2 (15 November 1840):223; 2 (15 October 1841):573.

[5]Joel Hills Johnson Diary; and Macedonia Branch, Ramus Stake, *Minutes,* pp. 1-8, Church Archives.

[6]*HC* 5:293.

[7]*Ibid.,* pp. 294-95.

[8]Benjamin F. Johnson, *My Life's Review* (Independence, Mo.: Zion's Printing and Publishing Co., 1941), pp. 85-93.

[9]*HC* 5:318.

[10]Johnson, *My Life's Review,* pp. 94-95.

[11]*HC* 5:323.

[12]*Ibid.*

[13]Andrew E. Ehat and Lyndon W. Cook, eds., *The Words of Joseph Smith* (Provo, Ut.: Religious Studies Center, Brigham Young University, 1980), pp. 169-73, 267-70.

[14]*HC* 5:391.

[15]Johnson, *My Life's Review,* p. 96.

[16]*HC* 5:391-92.

[17]Johnson, *My Life's Review*, p. 96.

[18]*HC* 5:392.

[19]*Times and Seasons* 4 (15 May 1843):197-98.

[20]According to George Q. Cannon in *JD* 13:47; and John Taylor in *JD* 21:161-64.

[21]According to Oliver Cowdery in *Messenger and Advocate* 2 (October 1835):198.

[22]*Wilford Woodruff's Journal* 1:341, original spelling and punctuation retained.

[23]*HC* 3:391-92.

[24]Ehat and Cook, *The Words of Joseph Smith*, p. 12.

[25]*Times and Seasons*, 3 (1 April 1842):747.

[26]*HC* 5:267.

[27]*Times and Seasons* 4 (15 September 1843):331.

[28]Ehat and Cook, *The Words of Joseph Smith*, p. 14.

[29]"Editorial Thoughts," *Juvenile Instructor*, 15 January 1891, p. 53.

[30]*Improvement Era* 15 (August 1912):950.

[31]See Kent P. Jackson, "The Signs of the Times: 'Be Not Troubled,'" found herein.

[32]*HC* 5:323.

[33]*Ibid.*, pp. 300-1, 309-10.

[34]See *HC* 5:336-37; and Ehat and Cook, *The Words of Joseph Smith*, pp. 179-81.

[35]*HC* 5:326.

[36]*Ibid.*, 3:380.

[37]*Ibid.*, 5:388.

[38]*Ibid.*, pp. 388-89.

[39]See Bruce R. McConkie, *Doctrinal New Testament Commentary*, 3 vols. (Salt Lake City: Bookcraft, 1966-73), 3:325-39 for a thorough discussion of the correlation between making one's calling and election sure and the more sure word of prophecy.

[40]*HC* 5:391.

# 47

# A NEW AND EVERLASTING COVENANT (D&C 132)

Robert L. Millet

President Brigham Young spoke eloquently concerning the infinite scope of marriage:

> The whole subject of the marriage relation is not in my reach, nor in any other man's reach on this earth. It is without beginning of days or end of years: it is a hard matter to reach. We can tell some things with regard to it: it lays the foundation for worlds, for angels, and for the Gods; for intelligent beings to be crowned with glory, immortality and eternal lives. In fact, it is the thread which runs from the beginning to the end of the holy Gospel of Salvation—of the Gospel of the Son of God; it is from eternity to eternity.[1]

The profound truths contained in section 132 of the Doctrine and Covenants (when read in conjunction with other revelations, particularly section 131) constitute the scriptural authority for the unique and exalted concept of marriage and family among the Latter-day Saints. In a day when iniquity abounds and the love of many has begun to wax cold (D&C 45:27), the revelations of God through his prophets provide an anchor to the troubled soul. D&C 132 is a message which is both peaceful and penetrating, a revelation which can bring order and organization to things on earth, as well as point man toward his infinite possibilities among the Gods.

## Backgrounds

The fulness of the gospel is called by the Lord his "new and everlasting covenant." In a revelation given in October, 1830 Joseph Smith was told: "Verily I say unto you, blessed are you for receiving mine everlasting covenant, even the fulness of my gospel, sent forth unto the children of men, that they might have life and be partakers of the glories which are to be revealed in the last days, as it was written by the prophets and apostles in days of old" (D&C 66:2; cf. 39:11; 45:9; 133:57). Elder Bruce R. McConkie has written:

> The gospel is the *everlasting* covenant because it is ordained by Him who is Everlasting and also because it is everlastingly the same. In all past ages salvation was gained by adherence to its terms and conditions, and that same compliance will bring the same reward in all future ages. Each time this everlasting covenant is revealed it is *new* to those of that dispensation. Hence the gospel is the *new and everlasting covenant.*[2]

Eternal Marriage, the ordinance by which couples enter into the Patriarchal Order (D&C 131:1-2), is *a* new and everlasting covenant within the fulness of the gospel. In our day it is a crucial element in the restitution of all things (D&C 132:40, 45). Eternal Marriage is the ordinance and covenant which leads to the consummate blessings of the gospel of Jesus Christ; it is that order of the priesthood which, when put into effect, will bind ancestry to posterity and thus prevent the earth from being utterly wasted at the time of the Savior's Second Coming (D&C 2).

As the introductory material to section 132 states, the basic doctrines of this revelation were received as early as 1831, yet the full application and historical context reflect its 1843 recording. A statement from Joseph Noble, a close associate of Joseph Smith the Prophet, is instructive. Noble observed that the revelation on eternal marriage was given to Joseph "while he was engaged in the work of translation of the Scriptures."[3] The opening verse of the revelation suggests that Joseph had inquired concerning Old Testament personalities and their participation in plural marriage. The Prophet would have been involved in the study of Abraham, Isaac, and Jacob—the book of Genesis—in 1830 and 1831.[4] Elder B. H. Roberts has given the following extended explanation:

> There is indisputable evidence that the revelation making known this marriage law was given to the Prophet as early as 1831. In that year, and then intermittently up to 1833, the Prophet was engaged in a revision of the English Bible text under the inspiration of God, Sidney Rigdon in the main acting as his scribe. As he began his revision with the Old Testament, he would be dealing with the age of the Patriarchs in 1831. He was doubtless struck with the favor in which the Lord held the several Bible Patriarchs of that period, notwithstanding they

> had a plurality of wives. What more natural than that he should inquire of the Lord at that time, when his mind must have been impressed with the fact—Why, O Lord, didst Thou justify Thy servants, Abraham, Isaac, and Jacob; as also Moses, David and Solomon, in the matter of their having many wives and concubines (see opening paragraph of the Revelation)? In answer to that inquiry came the revelation, though not then committed to writing.[5]

The Prophet Joseph Smith shared many of the details of the revelation with intimate associates, particularly when he felt one could be trusted to value and preserve a sacred matter. Between 1831 and 1843 a number of the leaders of the Church were instructed concerning the eternal marriage covenant (including the plurality of wives) and were told that eventually many of the faithful would be called upon to comply with the will of the Lord. In speaking to a gathering of the Reorganized Church of Jesus Christ of Latter Day Saints in Plano, Illinois in 1878, Orson Pratt

> explained the circumstances connected with the coming forth of the revelation on plural marriage. Refuted the statement and belief of those present that Brigham Young was the author of the revelation; showed that Joseph Smith the Prophet had not only commenced the practice of that principle himself, and taught it to others, before President Young and the Twelve had returned from their mission in Europe, in 1841, but that Joseph actually received revelations upon that principle as early as 1831.[6]

As one might expect, the doctrine of plural marriage was not easily received, even by those who were otherwise counted as faithful. President John Taylor, known to be one of the purest men who ever lived, explained that "when this system [polygamy] was first introduced among this people, it was one of the greatest crosses that was ever taken up by any set of men since the world stood."[7] Helen Mar Whitney, one of Joseph Smith's plural wives, recalled that Joseph "said that the practice of this principle would be the hardest trial the Saints would ever have to test their faith."[8] One of those for whom the principle was particularly difficult was Emma Smith, wife of the Prophet. It appears, therefore, that one of the major reasons for the formal recording of the revelation in 1843 was to assist Emma to recognize the divine source of this doctrine. William Clayton, private secretary to Joseph Smith, recorded the following:

> On the morning of the 12th of July, 1848, Joseph and Hyrum Smith came into the office of the upper story of the "Brick-store," on the bank of the Mississippi River. They were talking of the subject of plural marriage, [and] Hyrum said to Joseph, "If you will write the revelation of celestial marriage, I will take and read it to Emma, and I believe I can convince her of its truth, and you will hereafter have peace." Joseph smiled and remarked, "You do not know Emma as well as I do." Hyrum repeated his opinion, and further remarked, "The doctrine is so plain, I can convince any reasonable man or woman of its truth, purity, and heavenly origin," or words to that effect. . . . Joseph and Hyrum then sat down, and Joseph commenced to dictate the Revelation on Celestial Marriage, and I wrote it, sentence by sentence, as he dictated. After the whole was written, Joseph asked me to read it through slowly and carefully, which I did, and he pronounced it correct.[9]

The following entry from William Clayton's diary for 12 July 1843 is interesting: "This A.M. I wrote a Revelation consisting of 10 pages on the order of the priesthood, showing the designs in Moses, Abraham, David and Solomon having many wives & concubines &c. After it was wrote Prests. Joseph & Hyrum presented it and read it to E[mma]. who said she did not believe a word of it and appeared very rebellious."[10]

D&C 132 is a revelation dealing with celestial marriage. It also contains information and explanations concerning the practice of plural marriage. One Latter-day Saint historian, Danel Bachman, has suggested that section 132 consists largely of the Lord's answers to three critical questions posed by the Prophet Joseph Smith.[11] We will consider the questions and answers more carefully as we come to them in the text of the revelation.

## The Lord's Justification (vv. 1-6)

The first question asked by the Prophet Joseph was simply why the polygamous actions of notable Old Testament prophet-leaders had received divine approval. Why was it, the Prophet wanted to know, that prophets, patriarchs, and kings could have many wives and concubines?[12] In the Lord's response, Joseph was told to prepare his heart for the instructions about to be given (v. 3); in this instance the explanation for the ancient phenomenon was to be accompanied by a commandment to institute the practice in modern times. Seeking further light and knowledge had led the Prophet to further and greater obligations; much was about to be given, and much would soon be required (cf. D&C 82:3). Salvation in the highest heaven was at stake. Those who received this new and everlasting covenant (and thereafter chose to abide by its terms and conditions) qualified themselves—through the eternal principle of obedience (cf. D&C 130:20-21)—for the fulness of the glory of the Father, "which glory shall be a fulness and a continuation of the seeds forever and ever" (v. 19). These are they who shall be *enlarged*, that is, have an *increase*—spirit children into the eternities. They enjoy *eternal lives* (D&C 131:1-4; 132:17, 24). Joseph had taught these principles only two months earlier: "Except a man and his wife enter into an everlasting covenant and be married for eternity, while in this probation, by the power and authority of the Holy Priesthood, they will cease to increase when they die; that is, they will not have any children after the resurrection. But those who are married by the power and authority of the priesthood in this life, and continue without committing the sin against the Holy Ghost, will continue to increase and have children in the celestial glory."[13]

Salvation consists in the blessing of eternal lives, the continuation of the family unit in eternity. Damnation is the result of rejecting this new and everlasting covenant and is due largely to pursuing the broad and wide ways of the world; the punishment is "the deaths," the dissolution of the family unit beyond the grave (D&C 132:17, 24-25).

## Marriage in the Lord: Sealed by the Holy Spirit of Promise (vv. 7-27, 49-50)

The second question posed by the Prophet Joseph Smith seems to be associated with the cryptic statement by Jesus in response to a Sadduceean trap: "Ye do err, not knowing the scriptures, nor the power of God. For in the resurrection they neither marry, nor are given in marriage, but are as the angels of God in heaven" (Matt. 22:29-30; cf.

Luke 20:34-36). This expression, little understood in the days of the Prophet, is repeatedly given today as scriptural evidence against the Latter-day Saint doctrine of eternal marriage. Joseph Smith's question concerning its meaning led to a modern revealed commentary upon the passage and pointed us to the reality that Jesus Christ had taught the doctrine of eternal marriage during his mortal ministry.[14]

From section 132 we learn that THEY who neither marry nor are given in marriage in eternity are they who choose not to enter in by the strait gate and partake of the new and everlasting covenant of marriage. Even persons who qualify in every other way for the glories of the celestial kingdom, but who for selfish reasons reject opportunities for celestial marriage, cannot attain unto the highest degree of the celestial glory (cf. D&C 131:1-4). Such persons are "appointed angels in heaven, which angels are ministering servants, to minister for those who are worthy of a far more, and an exceeding, and an eternal weight of glory." The Lord continued: Because they did not abide by his law, "they cannot be enlarged, but remain separately and singly, without exaltation, in their saved condition, to all eternity; and from henceforth are not gods, but are angels of God forever and ever" (D&C 132:16-17). In commenting upon the status of *angels*, Joseph Smith said: "Gods have an ascendency over the angels, who are ministering servants. In the resurrection, some are raised to be angels, others are raised to become Gods."[15]

The Holy Spirit of Promise is the Holy Ghost, the Holy Spirit promised to the faithful. The Holy Ghost is a member of the Godhead with vital and important roles in the salvation of the people of the earth. He is a *revelator* and a testator, the means by which a witness of the truth is obtained. He is a *sanctifier*, the means by which filth and dross are burned out of the human soul as though by fire. One of the highest functions the Holy Ghost serves is to be a *sealer*, as the Holy Spirit of Promise. In this capacity he searches the heart, certifies a person is just, and thereafter seals an exaltation upon that person. That is to say, to be sealed by the Holy Spirit of Promise is to be sealed unto eternal life. In commenting on v. 7 in section 132 (regarding all covenants, contracts, bonds, etc. having the seal of the Holy Spirit of Promise), Elder Bruce R. McConkie has written:

> By way of illustration, this means that baptism, partaking of

> the sacrament, administering to the sick, marriage, and every covenant that man ever makes with the Lord . . . must be performed in righteousness by and for people who are worthy to receive whatever blessing is involved, otherwise whatever is done has no binding and sealing effect in eternity.
>
> Since "the Comforter knoweth all things" (D&C 42:17), it follows that it is not possible "to lie to the Holy Ghost" and thereby gain an unearned or undeserved blessing, as Ananias and Sapphira found out to their sorrow (Acts 5:1-11). And so this provision that all things must be sealed by the Holy Spirit of Promise, if they are to have "efficacy, virtue, or force in and after the resurrection from the dead" (D&C 132:7), the Lord's system for dealing with absolute impartiality with all men, and for giving all men exactly what they merit, neither adding to nor diminishing from.
>
> When the Holy Spirit of Promise places his ratifying seal upon a baptism, or a marriage, or any covenant, except that of having one's calling and election made sure, the seal is a conditional approval or ratification; it is binding in eternity only in the event of subsequent obedience to the terms and conditions of whatever covenant is invoved.
>
> But when the ratifying seal of approval is placed upon someone whose calling and election is thereby made sure—because there are no more conditions to be met by the obedient person—this act of being sealed up unto eternal life is of such transcendent import that of itself it is called being sealed by the Holy Spirit of Promise, which means that in this crowning sense, being so sealed is the same as having one's calling and election made sure.[16]

Without question, one of the most misunderstood (and misquoted) verses of scripture is D&C 132:26. Some members of the Church have wrested the scriptures to the point where they have concluded that a temple marriage alone (which they equate with being sealed by the Holy Spirit of Promise) will assure them of an exaltation, in spite of "any sin of the new and everlasting covenant whatever, and all manner of blasphemies." When it is fully understood, however, that the marriage ceremony performed in the House of the Lord—though performed by worthy priesthood bearers granted sacred sealing powers—is a conditional ordinance, a rite whose eventual blessings are contingent upon the faithfulness (in years to come) of the participants, then v. 26 is recognized as being consistent with other related principles—obedience, endurance to the end, and appropriate reward. Verse 26 has reference to those who have received the new and everlasting covenant of marriage, have complied with all its conditions, and have passed the tests of mortality. These are they who, paraphrasing Joseph Smith, have lived by every word of God, and are willing to serve the Lord at all hazards. They have made their callings and elections sure to eternal life.[17] Persons who attain to this level of righteousness "are sealed up against all manner of sin and blasphemy except the blasphemy against the Holy Ghost and the shedding of innocent blood."[18]

The Prophet Joseph Smith extended the challenging invitation to the Saints: "I would exhort you to go on and continue to call upon God until you make your calling and election sure for yourselves, by obtaining this more sure word of prophecy, and wait patiently for the promise until you obtain it."[19] Latter-day Saints who are married in the temple may thus press forward in the work of the Lord and with quiet dignity and patient maturity seek to be worthy of the certain assurance of eternal life before the end of their mortal lives. But should one not formally receive the more sure word of prophecy in this life, he has the scriptural promise that faithfully enduring to the end—keeping the covenants and commandments from baptism to the end of his life (Mosiah 18:8-9)—eventuates in the promise of eternal life, whether that promise be received here or hereafter (D&C 14:7; cf. 2 Ne. 31:20; Mosiah 5:15).

All men are subject to temptation and mortal weaknesses and therefore commit some sin, even those whose callings and elections have been made sure (see D&C 20:32-34; 124:124). Though the disposition to commit grievous sin would certainly be less among such individuals, yet the principles of repentance and forgiveness are as highly treasured by these as by any of our Father's children. At the same time, where much is given, much is expected and required. Joseph Smith taught: "If men sin wilfully after they have received the knowledge of the truth, there remaineth no more sacrifice for sin."[20] In the words of a modern apostle: "Suppose such persons become disaffected and the spirit of repentance leaves them—which is a seldom and almost unheard of eventuality—still, what then? The answer is—and the revelations and teachings of the Prophet Joseph Smith so recite!—they must then pay the penalty of their own sins, for the blood of Christ will not cleanse them."[21]

When one is guilty of serious transgression and loses the right to the Spirit and the protective blessings of the priesthood, he is essentially "delivered unto the buffetings of Satan" (D&C 132:26), such that "Lucifer is free to torment, persecute, and afflict such a person without let or hindrance. When the bars are down, the cuffs and curses of Satan, both in this world and in the world to come, bring indescribable anguish typified by burning fire and brimstone"[22] (cf. D&C 78:12; 82:20-21; 104:9-10; 1 Cor. 5:1-5).

Once one has been sealed by the Holy Spirit of Promise, he is in a position to either rise to exaltation or (through rebellion and apostasy) fall to perdition. Verse 27 has specific reference to those who have received the new and everlasting covenant of marriage and proven faithful enough to have the final stamp of approval from the Holy Ghost. One who has been sealed up unto eternal life and thereafter proves to be a total enemy to the cause of righteousness is guilty of "shedding innocent blood," the innocent blood of Christ, and assenting unto his death.[23] Such a vicious disposition would lead the transgressor to reject and crucify the Son of God afresh (cf. Heb. 6:4-6).

Among the most beautiful and touching verses in section 132 are vv. 49 and 50, wherein the Lord seals an exaltation upon the head of Joseph the Seer. What a comfort to a troubled and weary mind to hear such words as these: "Verily I seal upon you your exaltation, and prepare a throne for you in the kingdom of my Father, with Abraham your father." The reader of this revelation is also given a meaningful insight into how to qualify for such a transcendent promise: "Behold I have seen your sacrifices, and will forgive all your sins; I have seen your sacrifices in obedience to that which I have told you. Go, therefore, and I make a way for your escape, as I accepted the offering of Abraham of his son Isaac." The key element in obtaining the promise of exaltation is *sacrifice*. It was to the School of the Prophets in the Winter of 1834-35 that Joseph had given profound counsel: only through the sacrifice of all things could one come to the point of faith or confidence wherein he could have an actual knowledge that the course in life he was pursuing was according to the divine will. "Those, then, who make the sacrifice," the Prophet had taught, "will have the testimony that their course is pleasing in the sight of God; and those who have this testimony will have faith to lay hold on eternal life."[24] That principle of truth was now realized and confirmed directly upon the head of the one who had declared it less than ten years earlier; no matter what the eventuality, nothing could separate the man of God from the love of his God.[25]

### Marriage Among the Ancients (vv. 28-40)

As a type of follow-up on his first question, Joseph Smith was given additional insights into requirements made of individuals in ancient times. The Patriarch Abraham was instructed to take Hagar, the servant of Sarah, as a second wife, in order to bring to pass the promises made earlier to the Father of the Faithful—that his posterity would be as numerous as the stars in the heavens or the sands upon the seashore (Gen. 22:17; Abr. 3:14). This modern revelation helps to clarify the Old Testament story considerably (see Gen. 16), and shows that the decision to take an additional wife was a God-inspired directive, and not simply a desperate move by Sarah to insure posterity for her grieving husband. Joseph Smith was told that because of Abraham's perfect obedience he was granted the privilege of eternal increase. The Lord then said to Joseph: "This promise is yours also, because ye are of Abraham, and the promise was made unto Abraham." Then came the command to Joseph Smith, who had in 1836 received the keys necessary to become a modern Faither of the Faithful (D&C 110:12): "Go ye, therefore, and do the works of Abraham; enter ye into my law and ye shall be saved" (D&C 124:31-32; cf. 124:58).

The Lord further explained that Abraham, Isaac, and Jacob had attained godhood because of their implicit obedience. More specifically, because they only took additional wives as those wives were given by God, they have entered into their exaltation. David and Solomon were also given directions (through the legal administrators of their day) to take additional wives, and enjoyed the approbation of the heavens as they stayed within the bounds the Lord had set. When they moved outside the divinely given channel, however, and began to acquire wives and concubines for selfish or lustful reasons (e.g., David in the case of

Bathsheba, 2 Sam. 11; Solomon in the case of taking "strange women" as wives, women who "turned away his heart" from the things of righteousness, 1 Kgs. 11), they offended God and forfeited the eternal rewards that might have been theirs. Jacob in the Book of Mormon, speaking in behalf of the Lord, warned his people: "Behold, David and Solomon truly had many wives and concubines, which thing was abominable before me, saith the Lord" (Jacob 2:24). When both scriptural passages are read together (Jacob 2 and D&C 132), it becomes clear that the Lord was condemning—in no uncertain terms—*unauthorized* plural marriages, and not the principle of plurality of wives per se. Later in that same chapter of Jacob the word of the Lord came: "For if I will, saith the Lord of Hosts, raise up seed unto me [through plural marriage] I will command my people; otherwise they shall hearken unto these things" (Jacob 2:30). Note the words of Joseph Smith as late as October of 1843: "[I] Gave instructions to try those persons who were preaching, teaching, or practicing the doctrine of plurality of wives; for, according to the law, I hold the keys of this power in the last days; for there is never but one on earth at a time on whom the power and its keys are conferred; and I have constantly said no man shall have but one wife at a time, unless the Lord directs otherwise."[26]

## Concerning Adultery (vv. 41-48, 58-62)

Verse 41 of section 132 suggests the third question that Joseph Smith must have asked of the Lord. In essence, the question of the Prophet was: "Why were not such polygamous relationships violations of the law of chastity? Why was this not considered adultery?" The Lord's answer was simple and forthright, although considerable space was devoted to the issue in the revelation: any action inspired, authorized, or commanded of God is moral and good. More specifically, marriages approved of the Almighty are recognized and acknowledged as sacred institutions, despite the values or opinions of earth or hell. Joseph wrote in 1839: "How much more dignified and noble are the thoughts of God, than the vain imaginations of the human heart!"[27] Verse 36 of this section sheds light on this principle, the idea that whatever God requires is right: "Abraham was commanded to offer his son Isaac; nevertheless, it was written: Thou shalt not kill.

Abraham, however, did not refuse, and it was accounted unto him for righteousness." In a letter written to Nancy Rigdon in 1842, Joseph sought to explain (albeit in veiled language) the appropriateness of plural marriage when divinely sanctioned:

> Happiness is the object and design of our existence, and will be the end thereof if we pursue the path that leads to it; and this path is virtue, uprightness, holiness, and keeping all the commandments of God. But we cannot keep all the commandments without first knowing them, and we cannot expect to know all, or more than we now know, unless we comply with or keep those we have already received. That which is wrong under one circumstance, may be and often is, right under another. God said thou shalt not kill,—at another time he said thou shalt utterly destroy. This is the principle on which the government of heaven is conducted—by revelation adapted to the circumstances in which the children of the kingdom are placed. Whatever God requires is right, no matter what it is, although we may not see the reason thereof till long after the events transpire. If we seek first the kingdom of God, all good things will be added. So with Solomon—first he asked wisdom, and God gave it him, and with it every desire of his heart, even things which may be considered abominable to all who do not understand the order of heaven only in part, but which, in reality, were right, because God gave and sanctioned by special revelation. . . . Every thing that God gives us is lawful and right, and 'tis proper that we should enjoy his gifts and blessings whenever and wherever he is disposed to bestow; but if we should seize upon these same blessings and enjoyments without law, without revelation, without commandment, those blessings and enjoyments would prove cursings and vexations in the end, and we should have to go down in sorrow and wailings of everlasting regret. . . . Blessings offered, but rejected are no longer blessings, but become like the talent hid in the earth by the wicked and slothful servant—the proffered good returns to the giver, the blessing is bestowed upon those who will receive.[28]

In section 132 Emma Smith was encouraged to submit to the will of the Lord pertaining to her husband—to yield her heart to the mind of God with regard to the matter of plural marriages. Obedience would lead to glorious blessings; disobedience would lead to damnation, for the covenant people are to abide by this "law of the priesthood" whenever it is specifically given to them by new revelation through the living prophet.

## Summary

We may rest assured that whatever God reveals is given for the benefit and fulfillment of his children—for their happiness. Celestial or eternal marriage has been given to man, according to the word of the Master, in order that man might "multiply and replenish the earth, according to my commandment, and . . . fulfill the promise which was given by my Father before the foundation of the world, and for their exaltation in the eternal worlds, that they may bear the souls of men; for herein is the work of my Father continued, that he may be glorified" (D&C 132:63; cf. v. 31). One of the most popular and important scriptural passages in the Church is found in the Pearl of Great Price. The Lord explained to Moses the purpose of creation and existence: "For behold, this is my work and my glory—to bring to pass the immortality and eternal life of man" (Moses 1:39). That the Prophet understood early in his ministry that God's progression and development was accomplished through the exaltation of his children, is evident from an early recording of Moses 1:39. Note a variant rendering of this statement in the Prophet's first draft of the Bible translation: "Behold, this is my work TO my glory, to the immortality and eternal life of man."[29] In short, God's work—creating worlds without number, peopling them with his spirit sons and daughters, and providing the truths of the gospel for their edification and salvation (Moses 1:27-38)—not only benefits his children, but further glorifies himself. In speaking by the inspiration of the Lord, Joseph the Prophet explained the following in the famous King Follett Sermon on 7 April 1844:

> What did Jesus do? Why; I do the things I saw my Father do when worlds came rolling into existence. My Father worked out his kingdom with fear and trembling, and I must do the same; and when I get my kingdom, I shall present it to my Father, so that he may obtain kingdom upon kingdom, and it will exalt him in glory. He will then take a higher exaltation, and I will

take his place, and thereby become exalted myself. So that Jesus treads in the tracks of his Father, and inherits what God did before; and God is thus glorified and exalted in the salvation and exaltation of all his children.[30]

## Notes

[1]*JD* 2:90.

[2]*Mormon Doctrine*, 2nd ed. (Salt Lake City: Bookcraft, 1966), pp. 529-30.

[3]See minutes of the Davis Stake Conference, published under "Plural Marriage," in *Millennial Star* 16:454; cited by Danel Bachman in "New Light on an Old Hypothesis: The Ohio Origins of the Revelation on Eternal Marriage," *Journal of Mormon History* 5 (1978): 22.

[4]See Robert J. Matthews, *A Plainer Translation: Joseph Smith's Translation of the Bible, A History and Commentary* (Provo: Brigham Young University Press, 1975), pp. 96, 257.

[5]*HC* 5:xxix-xxx.

[6]*Millennial Star,* 9 December 1878, p. 788; cited in Matthews, *A Plainer Translation*, p. 258.

[7]*JD* 11:221.

[8]"Scenes and Incidents in Nauvoo," *Woman's Exponent* 10 (1 November 1881): 83.

[9]*The Historical Record*, pp. 225-26; cited in Hyrum M. Smith and Janne M. Sjodahl, *Doctrine and Covenants Commentary* (Salt Lake City: Deseret Book Company, reprint 1965), pp. 820-21.

[10]Cited in Lyndon W. Cook, *The Revelations of the Prophet Joseph Smith* (Provo, Ut.: Seventy's Mission Bookstore, 1981), p. 294.

[11]See "New Light on an Old Hypothesis," pp. 19-32.

[12]A concubine was a wife who came from a position of lower social standing, and who thus did not enjoy the same status as one of higher birth. Under ancient practice, where caste systems were much more common than at present, a man could take a slave or non-citizen as a legal wife, but it was understood that she was of a lower status. This was the case with Sarah (the first wife) and Hagar (the servant who became a concubine).

[13]*TPJS*, pp. 300-1.

[14]See Bruce R. McConkie, *Doctrinal New Testament Commentary,* 3 vols. (Salt Lake City: Bookcraft, 1966-73), 1:604-6; *The Mortal Messiah,* 4 books (Salt Lake City: Deseret Book Co., 1979-81), 3:374-81.

[15]*TPJS*, p. 312.

[16]*Doctrinal New Testament Commentary*, 3:335-36.

[17]*TPJS*, pp. 149-50.

[18]McConkie, *Mormon Doctrine*, p. 110.

[19]*TPJS*, p. 299.

[20]*Ibid.*, p. 128.

[21]*Doctrinal New Testament Commentary*, 3:343.

[22]*Mormon Doctrine*, p. 108.

[23]McConkie, *Doctrinal New Testament Commentary*, 3:161, 345; *The Mortal Messiah*, 2:216.

[24]Lectures on Faith, Lec. #6, Par. 10.

[25]For detail concerning Joseph Smith receiving the fulness of the priesthood, see Ronald K. Esplin, "Joseph, Brigham, and the Twelve: A Succession of Continuity," *Brigham Young University Studies* 21.3 (Summer 1981): 301-41; Andrew F. Ehat, "Joseph Smith's Introduction of Temple Ordinances and the 1844 Mormon Succession Question," Unpublished Master's Thesis, Brigham Young University, 1982.

[26]*TPJS*, p. 324.

[27]*Ibid.*, p. 137.

[28]From Dean C. Jessee, *The Personal Writings of Joseph Smith* (Salt Lake City: Deseret Book Co., 1984), pp. 507-9; see also *HC* 5:134-36; *TPJS*, pp. 255-57.

[29]See Old Testament Manuscript #2 in Matthews, *A Plainer Translation*, p. 222, emphasis added.

[30]*TPJS*, pp. 347-48.

# 48
# CHURCH AND STATE
## (D&C 134)

JAMES R. MOSS

### Obey, Honor, and Sustain

As Latter-day Saints, "We claim the privilege of worshiping Almighty God according to the dictates of our own conscience, and allow all men the same privilege, let them worship how, where, or what they may." Further, "We believe in being subject to kings, presidents, rulers, and magistrates, in obeying, honoring, and sustaining the law" (Articles of Faith, 11 and 12).

These two fundamental beliefs—freedom of worship, and support of secular government—are basic to our understanding of the gospel. Yet historically the relationship between church and state has been one of tension and great difficulty, both in America and throughout the world. Section 134 of the Doctrine and Covenants is a declaration on "government and laws in general" adopted by the Church 17 August 1835, "that our belief with regard to earthly governments and laws in general may not be misinterpreted nor misunderstood."[1] The document was authored by Oliver Cowdery.[2] Although not originally received as a revelation, it has since been accepted and sustained as scripture and therefore claims the same authority and power as other sections in the Doctrine and Covenants.

Section 134 may conveniently be divided into the following: vv. 1, 3, 5-6, 8: Support of secular government; vv. 2, 5, 11: Support of inherent rights and individual freedoms; vv. 4, 7, 10, 12: Support of religious freedom; v. 9: Support of separation of church and state. The section strikes a reasoned, careful, and inspired balance between the concerns of organized society and individuals, between church and state, and between freedom and appropriate social restraints.

As Latter-day Saints, we support the concept that secular governments are appropriate and legitimate forms of social organization here on earth, and that we should honor and obey the laws that come from them to govern us when they conform with gospel principles. President David O. McKay taught, "The three significant words used in the 12th Article of Faith express the proper attitude of the membership of the Church toward law. These words are—obey, honor, and sustain. . . . We obey law from a sense of right. We honor law because of its necessity and strength to society. We sustain law by keeping it in good repute."[3] This same attitude was expressed earlier in this dispensation by Brigham Young when he wrote to the Saints in the British Isles: "Sustain the government of the nation wherever you are, and speak well of it, for this is right, and the government has a right to expect it of you so long as that government sustains you in your civil and religious liberty, in those rights which inherently belong to every person born on the earth."[4]

The rule of law among men, rather than personal rule, is also supported by section 134. Joseph Smith taught that law is good and from God, and that we should use it in society: "If, then, we admit that God is the source of all wisdom and understanding, we must admit that by His direct inspiration He has taught man that law is necessary in order to govern and regulate His own immediate interest and welfare; for this reason, that law is beneficial to promote peace and happiness among men. And as before remarked, God is the source from whence proceeds all good; and if man is benefitted by law, then certainly law is good; and if law is good, then law, or the principle of it eminated from God; for God is the source of all good; consequently, then, he was the first Author of law, or the principle of it, to mankind."[5]

Section 134 teaches, however, that there is a limit to the allegience owed secular governments. God holds governments accountable for making and administering laws "for the good and safety of society" (D&C 134:1). Governments are to frame laws that "secure to each individual the free exercise of conscience, the right and control of property, and the protection of life" (D&C 134:2). Governmental officers are to enforce and administer laws "in equity and justice" (D&C 134:3). Governments are to protect individuals "in their inherent and inalienable rights" and are to hold "sacred the freedom of conscience" (D&C 134:5). Governments are therefore to use their power and authority not to coerce individuals but to support them in their divine, inherent individual rights.

President Joseph F. Smith taught that as long as governments serve their citizens in righteousness, those citizens should support their government:

> The law of the land, which all have no need to break, is that law which is the constitutional law of the land, and that is as God himself has defined it. . . . Now it seems to me that this makes this matter so clear that it is not possible for any man who professes to be a member of the Church of Jesus Christ of Latter-day Saints to make any mistake, or to be in doubt as to the course he should pursue under the command of God in relation to the observance of the laws of the land. . . .
>
> The Lord Almighty requires this people to observe the laws of the land, to be subject to "the powers that be," so far as they abide by the fundamental principles of good government, but He will hold them responsible if they will pass unconstitutional measures and frame unjust and proscriptive laws. . . . If lawmakers have a mind to violate their oath, break their covenants and their faith with the people, and depart from the provisions of the Constitution, where is the law, human or divine, which binds me, as an individual, to outwardly and openly proclaim my acceptance of their acts?[6]

## Actively Involved

In order to insure that the laws of government are both constitutional and acceptable to God and man in preserving inherent individual rights, section 134 also teaches that we should be actively involved in the process of selecting those who lead us in government: "Civil officers and magistrates" who "administer the law in equity and justice should be sought for and upheld" (D&C 134:3). Joseph Smith led the way in becoming actively involved in civic affairs in his time, even running for President of the United States in 1844. He taught, "It is our duty to concentrate all our influence to make popular that which is sound and good, and unpopular that which is unsound. 'Tis right, politically, for a man who has influence to use it, as well as for a man who has no influence to use his. From henceforth I will maintain all the influence I can get."[7] President John Taylor echoed Joseph's counsel some years later when he counseled, "As we have progressed the mist has been removed, and in relation to these matters, the Elders of Israel begin to understand that they have something to do with the world politically as well as religiously, that it is as much their duty to study correct political principles as well as religious, and to seek to know and comprehend the social and political interests of man, and to learn and be able to teach that which would be best calculated to promote the interest of the world."[8] More recently, President Ezra Taft Benson has asked, "What about our citizenship responsibility—our obligation to safeguard our freedom and preserve the Constitution? . . . The enemy is amongst and upon us. Zion must awake and arouse herself. We, the elders of Israel can be and should be, the leaven in the loaf of freedom."[9]

The duty of Latter-day Saints to become involved in political activity is one that has been outlined many times by Church leaders. We are to register and vote in elections, become aware of the important issues confronting the people, search out and support individuals of integrity who will represent us well in public office, and make wise decisions on matters presented for our vote. But Church leaders have also counseled repeatedly that we should do this as individuals, not as representatives of the Church. President Harold B. Lee referred to this caution in an address at Brigham Young University:

> All through the last political campaign [Church members] were saying, "Why doesn't the Church tell us how we should vote?" If the Church had done that, we would have a lot of Democrats or Republicans who would have wanted to apostatize. We believe in being subject to kings, presidents, rulers, and magistrates. We are told to obey the laws of God and we will have no need to break the laws of the land. When they would ask me who to vote for in the coming election, I would tell them to read Mosiah 29 and section 134 of the Doctrine and Covenants, pray about that, and any Latter-day Saint could know who to vote for in any given election. It is just as simple as that."[10]

President Ezra Taft Benson has also provided direction in seeking to make correct decisions regarding the various election issues that confront voters.

> Not only should we seek humble, worthy, courageous leadership; but we should measure all proposals having to do with our national or local welfare by four standards:
>
> First, is the proposal, the policy or the idea being promoted, right as measured by the Gospel of Jesus Christ? I assure you it is much easier for one to measure a proposed policy by the

> Gospel of Jesus Christ if he has accepted the Gospel and is living it.
>
> Second, is it right as measured by the Lord's standard of constitutional government, wherein He says: "And that law of the land which is constitutional, supporting that principle of freedom in maintaining rights and privileges, belongs to all mankind, and is justifiable before me" (D&C 98:5)? . . .
>
> Third, we might well ask the question: Is it right as measured by the counsel of the living oracles of God? . . .
>
> Fourth, what will be the effect upon the morale and the character of the people if this or that policy is adopted?[11]

In addition to the responsibility of seeking and encouraging good people to become involved in secular government, section 134 outlines a major responsibility of each individual to "step forward and use their ability in bringing offenders against good laws to punishment" (D&C 134:8). In addition, it teaches that "all men are justified in defending themselves, their friends, and property, and the government, from the unlawful assaults and encroachments of all persons in times of exigency, where immediate appeal cannot be made to the laws, and relief afforded" (D&C 134:11). We are not to be passive citizens, but are to be actively involved in helping governments accomplish their necessary and appropriate responsibilities and are to take the lead ourselves in situations where government cannot act.

## Freedom of Religion

Section 134 teaches that a major right is that of religious freedom. "We believe that religion is instituted of God; and that men are amenable to him, and to him only, for the exercise of it," and that no "human law has a right to interfere in prescribing rules of worship to bind the consciences of men, nor dictate forms for public or private devotion," that government should "never suppress the freedom of the soul" (D&C 134:4). The section also teaches that governments do not have the right to "proscribe" citizens in their religious opinions but should "enact laws for the protection of all citizens in the free exercise of their religious belief" (D&C 134:7). This exercise of religious freedom, sustained by the Bill of Rights in the U.S. Constitution and by appropriate provisions in many other nations, is one of the most fundamental and important rights secular governments should sustain. As Elder John A. Widtsoe said, "A good government must secure for every citizen the free exercise of conscience. Matters of belief or religious practice should not be interfered with, unless they oppose laws formulated for the common good. There should be no mingling of religious influence with trespassing upon each others' field."[12]

But given the right of religious freedom and the responsibility to sustain secular government, what should we do if there is a conflict between church and state? Section 134 addresses that issue directly. "We do not believe it is just to mingle religious influence with civil government, whereby one religious society is fostered and another proscribed in its spiritual privileges, and the individual rights of its members, as citizens, denied" (D&C 134:9). As the First Presidency of the church has since stated,

> The Church of Jesus Christ of Latter-day Saints holds to the doctrine of the separation of church and state; the non-interference of church authority in political matters; and the absolute freedom and independence of the individual in the performance of his political duties. We declare that from principle and policy, we favor: the absolute separation of church and state; no domination of the state by the church; no church interference with the functions of the state; no state interference with the functions of the church, or with the free exercise of religion; the absolute freedom of the individual from the domination of ecclesiastical authority in political affairs; the equality of all churches before the law.[13]

Although the Church teaches the necessity for an institutional separation between church and state, it is, nevertheless, important that a unity and relationship remain between the gospel and law, between correct doctrinal principles and governmental action. As President Ezra Taft Benson has said:

> I support the doctrine of separation of church and state as traditionally interpreted to prohibit the establishment of an official national religion. But I am opposed to the doctrine of separation of church and state as currently interpreted to divorce government from any formal recognition of God. The current trend strikes a potentially fatal blow at the concept of

> the divine origin of our rights and unlocks the door for an easy entry of future tyranny. If Americans should ever come to believe that their rights and freedoms are instituted among men by politicians and bureaucrats, then they will no longer carry the proud inheritance of their forefathers, but will grovel before their masters seeking favors and dispensations—a throwback to the feudal system of the Dark Ages.[14]

It is obvious to perceptive observers of the political scene both today and in past times that a strong spiritual influence from the Almighty is an absolute necessity for effective secular government. As President J. Reuben Clark said, "where any matter touched by the State has to do with our spiritual welfare, our religion, the Church (meaning all churches) not only may but must be concerned."[15] The separation between church and state, as required by the U.S. Constitution and by the fundamental laws of many nations, must therefore not lead to a separation of law and gospel. All men should strive to promote sound principles of government that are built on the doctrines taught by the Lord.

Section 134 of the Doctrine and Covenants contains much wise counsel that can help all mankind recognize the legitimate role of secular governments and their responsibilities in promoting and maintaining both individual freedoms and religious belief and practice, within an appropriate division between church and state. As Latter-day Saints who look to the return of the divine Lawgiver who will rule and reign on earth, we can yet remain in submission to earthly governments as we strive to expand and implement the gospel principles that will provide the best possible laws and lawgivers in society. And we, as Brigham Young taught, can continue to look for the day when "the world will be revolutionized by the preaching of the gospel and the power of the priesthood, and this work we are called to do. In its progress every foolish and unprofitable custom, every unholy passion, every foolish notion in politics and religion, every unjust and oppressive law, and whatever else that is oppressive to man, and that would impede his onward progress to the perfection of the Holy Ones in eternity, will be removed until everlasting righteousness prevails over the whole earth."[16] In the words of a modern revelation, "Wherefore, be subject to the powers that be, until he reigns whose right it is to reign, and subdues all enemies under his feet" (D&C 58:22).

## Notes

[1]*HC* 2:247.

[2]See Lyndon W. Cook, *The Revelations of the Prophet Joseph Smith* (Provo, Ut.: Seventy's Mission Bookstore, 1981), p. 296.

[3]*Conference Report,* April 1937, p. 28.

[4]*Millennial Star* 14 (17 July 1852): 321.

[5]*HC* 2:12-13.

[6]*JD* 23:70-71.

[7]*HC* 5:286.

[8]*JD* 9:340.

[9]*Conference Report,* April 1963, p. 113.

[10]"Doing the Right Things For the Right Reasons," *Selected Speeches* (Provo, Ut.: Brigham Young University, 1961), p. 9 (address at Brigham Young University, 19 April 1961).

[11]Quoted in *Our Prophets and Principles* (Salt Lake City: *The Instructor*, 1956), pp. 69-70.

[12]Quoted in Daniel H. Ludlow, *A Companion to Your Study of the Doctrine and Covenants*, 2 vols. (Salt Lake City: Deseret Book Co., 1978), 1:684.

[13]*Conference Report,* April 1907, p. 14.

[14]*God, Family, Country* (Salt Lake City: Deseret Book Co., 1974), pp. 283-84.

[15]*Church News*, 16 June 1945.

[16]*JD* 9:309.

# 49

# THE MARTYRDOM OF JOSEPH SMITH
## (D&C 135)

SUSAN W. EASTON

Penned by John Taylor, an eyewitness of the brutal assassination of Joseph Smith and his brother Hyrum, D&C 135 uniquely conveys the inestimable worth of the seal affixed by the fallen testators. Elder Taylor acknowledged that through their tragic death a firm seal was placed on the divinity of the Doctrine and Covenants and the Book of Mormon: "To seal the testimony of this book and the Book of Mormon we announce the martyrdom of Joseph Smith the Prophet, and Hyrum Smith the Patriarch" (D&C 135:1).

These noble brothers bound their testimony with family blood, portraying through sacrifice that Joseph Smith was the Lord's anointed prophet, seer, revelator and translator. Jointly they magnified their sacred responsibility, together they suffered a martyr's fate, and forever they unite to "stand at the judgment seat as a witness against all men who have rejected their words of eternal life."[1] John Taylor wrote, "Henceforward their names will be classed among the martyrs of religion; and the reader in every nation will be reminded that the Book of Mormon, and this book of Doctrine and Covenants of the church, cost the best blood of the nineteenth century to bring them forth for the salvation of a ruined world" (D&C 135:6). The reader will with poignancy concur that "Joseph Smith . . . has done more, save Jesus only, for the salvation of men" (D&C 135:3). From his first youthful utterance in the Palmyra woods to his manly cry at Carthage, Joseph sought to do the will of God. His search, coupled with committed obedience, enabled sacred truths from the dispensations past to be revealed. Revelations, translations, covenants, eternal truths were the continuum of his life's labor.

Joseph's devotion to God brought accolades "and left a fame and name that cannot be slain" (D&C 135:3). John Taylor said of him, "I think he was one of the greatest Prophets that ever lived, Jesus himself excepted."[2] Josiah Quincy, a visitor to Nauvoo, wrote in 1880 in his book *Figures of the Past,* "It is by no means improbable that some future textbook . . . will contain a question . . . What historical American of the nineteenth century has exerted the most powerful influence upon the destinies of his countrymen? And it is by no means impossible that the answer to that interrogatory may be thus written: Joseph Smith, the Mormon Prophet."[3]

Of those who knew Joseph as the Prophet, no one was closer in the sharing of responsibility and in the assistance of the furtherance of the Lord's work than his brother, Hyrum. "In life they were not divided, and in death they were not separated!" (D&C 135:3). Joseph once said, "I could pray in my heart that all my brethren were like unto my beloved brother Hyrum, who possesses the mildness of a lamb, and the integrity of a Job, and in short, the meekness and humility of Christ; and I love him with that love that is stronger than death."[4] Joseph's opinion of Hyrum was also shared by John Taylor. "If ever there was an exemplary, honest, and virtuous man, an embodiment of all that is noble in the human form, Hyrum Smith was its representative."[5]

Hyrum was chosen by the Lord to take the witness position once held by Oliver Cowdery (D&C 124:94-95). As a witness it was necessary that he conjointly suffer the martyr's fate. Despite the necessity of this sacrifice, Joseph in his last direct narrative in the *History of the Church* stated, "I told Stephen Markham that if I and Hyrum were ever taken again we should be massacred, or I was not a prophet of God. I want Hyrum to live to avenge my blood, but he is determined not to leave me."[6] The determination, combined with the need of divine testament, resulted in the brothers' unification in death. As the hymn laments: "But Oh they're gone from my embrace, from earthly scenes their spirit fled. Two of the best of Adam's race now lie entombed among the dead."[7]

### Events that Led to the Incarceration at Carthage

It is difficult to analyze exactly what were the events that led to the death of the Prophet and Patriarch. Persecution was the lot of Joseph and his brother since boyhood in Palmyra. Ridicule, arrest warrants, and evil speaking were their common foes. Enemies, mobbers, and traitors sought to thwart the plans of God. Doctrines held sacred by the brothers (e.g., plural marriage, temple ordinances, the nature of God) were distorted by apostates to disprove their claims of divine revelation and arouse public sentiment against them. Despite heavenly protection throughout their ordeals, Joseph in June of 1844 was filled with premonitions of his impending death. "All the enemies upon the face of the earth may roar and exert all their power to bring about my death, but they can accomplish nothing, unless some who are among us and enjoy our society, have been with us in our councils, participated in our confidence . . . join with our enemies, turn our virtues into faults, and, by falsehood and deceit, stir up their wrath and indignation against us, and bring their united vengeance upon our heads."[8]

This premonition became a reality as William and Wilson Law, Chauncey and Francis Higbee, Robert and Charles Foster and William Marks, bound together by an oath of conspiracy, sought the destruction of Joseph Smith.[9] Their evil plans ignited public sentiment as they divulged their intent in the *Nauvoo Expositor*. The first and only issue charged Joseph Smith with indulging in whoredoms, abusing political power, and claiming power to seal men up to eternal life. They branded him as a base seducer, a liar and a murderer.

Swift action by the Nauvoo city council resulted in the *Expositor* being declared a public nuisance. Orders were given and carried out which resulted in the press and type being moved to the street and destroyed. The oath-bound publishers, seeing their opportunity to bring charges against Nauvoo public officials, fled to Carthage. While in Carthage they swore out a warrant for the arrest of Joseph Smith, a leading public official of Nauvoo. The charge against Joseph was that of rioting.

Public sentiment against the Latter-day Saints was at a feverish pitch in Carthage. The incidents surrounding the *Expositor* provided the fuel to fan the fires of prejudice and hatred. Thomas Sharp, the editor of the *Warsaw Signal*, wrote: "War and extermination is inevitable! Citizens, Arise, One and All!!! Can you stand by, and suffer such Infernal Devils! to rob men of their property and rights, without avenging them? We have no time to comment: every man will make his own. *Let it be made with powder and ball!!!*"[10]

Joseph was arrested and then discharged. He was again arrested with the same result. The legal process, however, did not pacify the Prophet's enemies. They clamored for his blood. Carthage became a scene of mobbed insurrection and rebellion toward justice and liberty. Governor Thomas Ford yielded to public outcries and demanded not just Joseph but the Smith brothers (meaning Joseph and Hyrum) to appear in a Carthage courtroom. The Prophet, previously acquitted of the charges, exclaimed, "There is no mercy—no mercy here."[11]

"No," rejoined Hyrum, "just as sure as we fall into their hands we are dead men."[12]

An attempt was made by Joseph and Hyrum to escape the martyr's fate by fleeing to the West. The attempt was abated after Joseph was entreated by friends to return to Nauvoo and give himself up to the law as ascribed in Carthage. At this point a downcast Prophet exclaimed, "If my life is of no value to my friends it is of none to myself."[13]

Early on a Monday morning the Prophet, accompanied by Hyrum and other brethren, left Nauvoo for Carthage. He left behind a devoted family, thousands who recognized him as the Lord's anointed, and a beautiful city which he helped create. As he turned to gaze upon Nauvoo for the final time he said, "This is the loveliest place and the best people under the heavens; little do they know the trials that await them."[14]

Four miles outside of Carthage, Joseph and his brethren were met by sixty mounted militia. Turning to the men accompanying him, Joseph stated, "I am going like a lamb to the slaughter; but I am calm as a summer's morning; I have a conscience void of offense towards God, and towards all men. I shall die innocent, and it shall yet be said of me—He was murdered in cold blood" (D&C 135:4).

Hyrum also must have known for himself his impending death. As he made ready to leave for Carthage he was reading in the twelfth chapter of Ether: "I . . . bid farewell unto the Gentiles, yea, and also unto my brethren whom I love, until we shall meet before the judgment-seat of Christ, where all men shall know that my garments are not spotted with your blood" (Ether 12:38).

For Joseph and Hyrum, Carthage was a scene of broken promises, conspiracy oaths, illegal arraignment, and eventual incarceration. Accusations of riot were turned to treason. Rumors once whispered in secret now were shouted. The throngs unabashedly declared that the Smith brothers would not leave Carthage alive. The Warsaw mobs sang: "Where now is the Prophet Joseph? Where now is the Prophet Joseph? Where now is the Prophet Joseph? Safe in Carthage jail!"[15] Even the governor, though not in boisterous song, joined with the chorus of conspirators, mobbers, and militia in abetting the deaths of Joseph and Hyrum.

## Final Scenes in Carthage

After Governor Thomas Ford's departure for Nauvoo on June 27th the spirits of Joseph and his friends were downcast. One evidence is found in the correspondence Joseph wished sent to Emma. In the letter he wrote, "I am very much resigned to my lot, knowing I am justified and have done the best that could be done. Give my love to the children and all my friends . . . May God bless you all."[16]

That afternoon, while incarcerated in Carthage, Joseph was visited by many friends. However, as the day waned, his only companions in the jail were Hyrum and two members of the Quorum of the Twelve—John Taylor and Willard Richards.

John was asked to sing. The desired song seemed to harmonize with the feelings of an ominous foreboding.

In prison I saw him next, condemned
    To meet a traitor's doom at morn;
The tide of lying tongues I stemmed,
    And honored him 'mid shame and scorn.
My friendship's utmost zeal to try,
He asked if I for him would die;
The flesh was weak; my blood ran chill;
But the free spirit cried, "I will!"[17]

Around five in the afternoon, Willard Richards noticed a hundred or more men running around the corner of the jail. John Taylor described them as "an armed mob—painted black—of from 150 to 200 persons" (D&C 135:1). Despite early attempts to protect themselves against mob violence the four were no match for the brutal assassins.

Hyrum was the first to fall. He backed away from the door of the jail to the center of the room. One ball pierced the upper panel of the door and struck him on the left side of the nose. He fell back crying, "I am a dead man!" (D&C 135:1). Bending over the body of his lifeless brother, Joseph sobbed, "Oh dear, brother Hyrum!"[18] Hyrum was hit by three other balls. One ball entered his left side, another his head, via his throat, and the other lodged in his left leg.

John Taylor became the second victim of the murderous mob. He decided to leap out the east window of the jail. As he attempted to do so, a ball fired from the doorway and struck his thigh. As he began to fall out the window, a bullet from the outside hit the watch in his vest and knocked him back into the room. Crawling, he moved under the bed. While lying under the bed he was hit by three more balls: one below the left knee, which was never extracted, another in his hip, and a third in the fore-part of his left arm.

Joseph then moved toward the east window. As he did so two bullets hit him from the door-way, and two struck him from the outside. He fell to the ground exclaiming, "O Lord, My God" (D&C 135:1).

Willard Richards miraculously escaped the bullets of the assassins as Joseph had prophesied "without even a hole in his robe" (D&C 135:2).[19]

The message sent from Willard to the people of Nauvoo on that June day in 1844 was "Joseph and Hyrum are dead. Taylor wounded. . . . I am well. . . . The citizens here are afraid of the Mormons attacking them. I promise them no!"[20]

## The Witnesses Reflect on The Martyrdom

"John Taylor and Willard Richards, two of the Twelve, were the only persons in the room at the time" (D&C 135:2). John Taylor recalled just shortly before the death of Joseph and Hyrum speaking to Joseph saying, "Brother Joseph if you will permit it, and say the word, I will have you out of this prison in five hours, if the jail has to come down to do it."[21] John's plan was to travel to Nauvoo and gather brethren to assist in Joseph's and Hyrum's release. He considered Joseph's incarceration "a flagrant outrage upon . . . liberty and rights."[22] Joseph, seemingly resigned to his fate, refused.

After the death of the Prophet, John wrote, "I felt a dull, lonely, sickening sensation. . . .When I reflected that our noble chieftain, the prophet of the living God, had fallen, and that I had seen his brother in the cold embrace of death, it seemed as though there was a void or vacuum in the great field of human existence to me, and a dark gloomy chasm in the kingdom, and that we were left alone. Oh, how lonely was that feeling!"[23]

Willard Richards recalled Joseph speaking to him, "If we go into the cell, will you go in with us?"[24] Willard replied, "Brother Joseph . . . you did not ask me to come to Carthage—you did not ask me to come to jail with you—and do you think I would forsake you now? But I will tell you what I will do; if you are condemned to be hung for treason, I will be hung in your stead, and you shall go free."[25] Once again the resigned Prophet acknowledged his friend but replied in the negative. As Joseph fell to the ground below the east window of the jail, Willard, with no thought for his own safety, rushed to the window in a determined effort to see the man he loved. As John Taylor wrote, "Ye men of wisdom, tell me why, no guilt, no crime in them were found, their blood doth now so loudly cry from prison walls and Carthage ground."[26]

Without realization the assassins of destruction left behind much more than the corpses of two men. They left "a broad seal affixed to 'Mormonism' that cannot be rejected by any court on earth" (D&C 135:7). They left "truth of the everlasting gospel that all the world cannot impeach" (D&C 135:7). They left two martyr's crowns that they helped forge with their senseless brutality.

The testators are dead; yet, their testament lives on. Their seal is affixed to the truthfulness of the Book of Mormon and the Doctrine and Covenants. Throughout eternity they will be numbered with the sanctified and the religious martyrs of all ages.

"Prophet and Patriarch, farewell!"[27]

## Notes

[1]Joseph Fielding Smith, "The Martyrs," *Improvement Era*, June 1944, p. 365.

[2]*JD* 18:326-27.

[3]Joseph F. Merrill, *Conference Report*, April 1947, pp. 134-35.

[4]Pearson H. Corbett, *Hyrum Smith, Patriarch* (Salt Lake City: Deseret Book Co., 1976), p. xiii.

[5]B. H. Roberts, *The Life of John Taylor* (Salt Lake City: George Q. Cannon and Sons, 1892), p. 42.

[6]*HC* 6:546.

[7]John Taylor, "Oh Give Me Back My Prophet Dear," *Hymns* (Salt Lake

City: The Church of Jesus Christ of Latter-day Saints, 1948), no. 137, v. 1.

[8]*HC* 6:152.

[9]"You solemnly swear, before God and all holy angels, and those your brethren by whom you are surrounded, that you will give your life, your liberty, your influence, your all, for the destruction of Joseph Smith, so help you God!" (*The Contributor* 5.7 [April 1884]; see Ivan J. Barrett, *Joseph Smith and the Restoration* [Provo, Ut.: Brigham Young University Press, 1973], p. 590).

[10]Brigham H. Roberts, *A Comprehensive History of the Church of Jesus Christ of Latter-day Saints,* 6 vols. (Salt Lake City: The Church of Jesus Christ of Latter-day Saints, 1930), 2:236.

[11]*HC* 6:545. For further references see Dallin H. Oaks and Marvin S. Hill, *Carthage Conspiracy: The Trial of the Accused Assassins of Joseph Smith* (Chicago: University of Illinois Press).

[12]*HC* 6:545.

[13]*Ibid.,* p. 549.

[14]*Ibid.,* p. 554.

[15]Brigham H. Roberts, *A Comprehensive History,* 2:281.

[16]*Ibid.*, 2:268-69.

[17]Montgomery, "A Poor Wayfaring Man of Grief," *Hymns,* no. 153, v. 6.

[18]*HC* 6:618.

[19]*Ibid.*, 6:619, "Dr. Richards' escape was miraculous; he being a very large man, and in the midst of a shower of balls, yet he stood unscathed, with the exception of a ball which grazed the tip end of the lower part of his left ear. His escape fulfilled literally a prophecy which Joseph made over a year previously, that the time would come that the balls would fly around him like hail, and he should see his friends fall on the right and on the left, but that there should not be a hole in his garment."

[20]*Ibid..*, 6:621-22.

[21]Daniel Tyler, *A Concise History of the Mormon Battalion in the Mexican War, 1846-1847* (Chicago: The Rio Grande Press, Inc., 1964), pp. 46-47.

[22]*Ibid.*

[23]*Ibid.,* pp. 51-52. For further reference see Lawrence R. Flake, *Mighty Men of Zion: General Authorities of the Last Dispensation* (Salt Lake City: Karl D. Butler, 1974), p. 15.

[24]*HC* 6:616.

[25]*Ibid.*

[26]John Taylor, "Oh Give Me Back My Prophet Dear," v. 2.

[27]*Ibid.*, v. 4.

# 50

# THE WORD AND WILL OF THE LORD

## (D&C 136)

Richard D. Draper

### Prelude to the Revelation

The majority of the Latter-day Saints, after leaving Nauvoo, had settled at Winter Quarters during the fall and winter of 1846-47. There were still, however, many scattered at other locations. While they were waiting in these temporary camps for the weather to break, much attention was given to the means and organization necessary for the contemplated move to the Rocky Mountains. This, however, was not the first time the subject had been the center of attention for the Saints and their leaders. Even before Joseph Smith's martyrdom some two and one-half years earlier, the West had been seen as the future hope of the Saints. Indeed, as early as 1834 the Prophet had told the Saints:

> I want to say to you before the Lord, that you know no more concerning the destinies of this Church and Kingdom than a babe upon its mother's lap. You do not comprehend it. It is only a little handful of Priesthood you see here tonight, but this Church will fill North and South America—it will fill the Rocky Mountains. There will be tens of thousands of Latter-day Saints who will be gathered in the Rocky Mountains and there they will open the door for the establishing of the Gospel among the Lamanites. . . . This people will go into the Rocky Mountains; they will there build temples to the Most High. They will raise up a posterity there, and the Latter-day Saints who dwell in these mountains will stand in the flesh until the coming of the Son of Man. The Son of Man will come to them while in the Rocky Mountains.[1]

That this idea continued to press itself upon the minds of the Saints is evident in a blessing which was given to Lorenzo Dow Young by Hyrum Smith and others in 1836. In the report of this blessing the following is stated: "Brother Hyrum led. The spirit rested mightily upon him and he was full of blessing and prophecy. He said that I should regain my health, live to go with the Saints into the bosom of the Rocky Mountains to build up a place there."[2]

## The Organization of the General Council

As pressure mounted against the Saints from both governmental and private sources in Illinois, the Prophet set in motion the machinery for accomplishing the move. Meeting with a select group of men on 20 February 1844, Joseph Smith "instructed the Twelve Apostles to send out a delegation and investigate the locations of California and Oregon, and hunt out a good location, where we can remove to after the temple is completed."[3] The matter continued to be discussed in meetings that took place during the next few weeks. A council was organized on 11 March 1844 which was referred to as the "Special Council" and later as the "General Council."[4] This has also been referred to as the "Council of Fifty" because of the approximate number of men which composed its ranks. Part of the duties of this council was to plan and carry out the westward trek.

There has been much discussion about the importance of the "Council of Fifty" and its role in Latter-day Saint history. It should be noted that most, if not all, of the Mormon leadership was involved in this body (though it did have other men associated with it). Because of the close association of the Church leaders it cannot be determined to what degree the two bodies should be viewed as separate. However, it would be well to view the "Council of Fifty" as an organization of Latter-day Saint leaders whose duty it was to take care of the temporal needs of the Saints, and in this instance, the move to the Rocky Mountains.[5]

## The Background of D&C 136

As the spring of 1847 approached there was need for a formal pattern of organization for the companies which would make the move to the new home for the Latter-day Saints in the West. Much time was devoted to this matter. "Thought upon it finally so crystallized in the mind of Brigham Young," said B. H. Roberts, "that on the 14th of January, 1847, at Winter Quarters, he was prepared to announce 'The Word and Will of the Lord' upon the march of the camps of Israel to the West."[6] Years before, Joseph Smith had instructed some of the brethren on the principles of receiving the mind and will of the Lord. To that group he had stated: "It was necessary to have our minds on

God and exercise faith and become of one heart and of one mind." Then he turned the attention of the group to receiving a revelation. The result was section 88 of the Doctrine and Covenants. This revelation was given over the course of three days.[7] Just how it was received is not noted in the minutes, but it seems that time was necessary to get it in final form, and more than one hand was responsible in its final preparation. So too it seems to be with the reception and recording of section 136.

On 14 January 1847 Brigham Young met with a number of the leading brethren. They discussed the best methods for organizing companies and who should be responsible. After the discussion Brigham began to give the revelation. This took most of the afternoon and evening to complete, with a number of people assisting in the production of the final form of the revelation and also enjoying the endowment of the Spirit which accompanied the manifestation of the Lord's will.[8]

The next day it was decided to read the revelation to members of the Church in the various locations. Individuals were assigned to take it to the camps. The urgency felt by the leaders to get the revelation out to the Saints is indicated by the fact that though the temperatures ranged to below zero, men mounted buckboards and horses, taking copies to be read to their assigned camps. The response was excellent.

## General Outline of the Revelation

The revelation can be divided into two sections. The first deals with the nature of the organization and responsibilities of the companies which were to be created for the western trek. The second deals with the social and religious requirements of the individuals who were to compose the various companies. The revelation shows how the practical blends with the spiritual to produce harmony and order. It also shows that in the Lord's eyes there is no division between spiritual and temporal. The trek west was to be undertaken with a covenant and a promise. This meant that the move was essentially a spiritual affair designed for the exaltation of the individual as well as for the preservation of the Church. Therefore, it is not surprising that specific modes of behavior were expected of those who participated in the migration. As with ancient Israel, with whom God established his covenant and *then* led them into the promised land, the Saints were expected to live a covenant law in order to reap blessings both temporally and spiritually.

Before examining what the Lord expected of his Saints as far as spiritual and social behavior was concerned, a few remarks concerning the responsibilities and organization of the camps seem in order.

One interesting fact about this revelation is that it was given to a specific group of people living at a specific time with a specific mission to carry out. Though there are timeless elements in it, the revelation is basically designed to meet important needs felt at a given time, thus showing that the Lord does not only direct affairs dealing with eternity but also with time.

Each company was to be composed of approximately one hundred families. Over these a captain was placed. He was called appropriately a "captain of one hundred." Assisting him were two captains, each responsible for fifty of the families. Under these served captains who were each responsible for ten families. Presiding over each company was to be a president and two counselors (v. 3). What the relationship was between the captains of fifty and the president of the company is not given.

Each company was not only to provide for its families but also for its share of the poor, fatherless, widows and families of those men who had joined the Mormon Battalion. Pioneers were to be sent out ahead of the bodies to prepare ground and crops for those coming after. Those who for one reason or another had to be left behind for a time were to have houses prepared and crops put in by the company (vv. 5-9). In this way all were to be cared for, not merely by their own effort but also by the resources and manpower of a whole company. With all sharing the burden and contributing what each could, all would be benefited and the tremendous task would be accomplished.

Through this organization, the Lord turned the thoughts of the Saints to others, during a period when it would have been very easy to think only of self. But this is not all. The Lord also turned the Saints toward himself. A covenant was required, "that we will walk in all the ordinances of the Lord" (v. 4). Through the entire long, wearisome, and dangerous trek the people were to remember to behave as saints. The savageness of the country was not to be mimicked in the camps of

Israel.

Through the requirement of a covenant the Lord placed his people in a position where he could bless them. This was in accordance with the divine law which stated that all blessings were predicated on obedience to law, "For all who will have a blessing at my hands shall abide the law which was appointed for that blessing, and the conditions thereof, as were instituted from before the foundations of the world" (D&C 132:5; see also 131:20, 21). By tailoring a law to meet the needs of a specific moment, the Lord made it possible for the people to reap great blessings from that moment. However, obedience was absolutely necessary.

Though the Lord organized all according to company, he made it clear that the individual was to feel responsible for the general welfare of the whole (D&C 136:10). Thus the laws he reiterated for the purpose of the present necessity were to govern the behavior of the individual as one with responsibility for the whole. Language was to be kept pure and used for edifying—never for evil speaking. Material goods of another were to be carefully guarded and that which was borrowed quickly returned or compensated for (vv. 20-26). In all things the people were to remember the Lord. In this way they could be instructed by him and thus learn true wisdom (vv. 32, 33). In this way all obstacles could be overcome, all people provided for, and each individual edified, sanctified, and perfected.

Through this great revelation we can see once again how the Lord turns all things to the advantage of those who are his. Nineteen years earlier he had assured his Saints, "God doth not walk in crooked paths, neither doth he turn to the right hand nor to the left, neither doth he vary from that which he hath said, therefore his paths are straight, and his course is one eternal round. Remember, remember that it is not the work of God that is frustrated, but the work of men" (D&C 3:2-3). As his people are faithful the Lord will turn all things to their favor. With this assurance the future for the faithful is bright and secure, for nothing will be allowed to impede the work of God.

## Notes

[1]Wilford Woodruff, *Conference Report,* 8 April 1897, p. 57, quoting a speech given by Joseph Smith on 26 April 1834 in Kirtland, Ohio.

[2]James Amasa Little, "Biography of Lorenzo Dow Young," *Utah Historical Quarterly* 14 (1946): 46.

[3]*HC* 6:222.

[4]*Ibid.,* 224, 260-61, 264.

[5]Two treatments of the role of the Council of Fifty in Mormon History are Hyrum L. Andrus, *Joseph Smith and World Government* (Salt Lake City: Deseret Book Co., 1958), and Klaus J. Hansen, *Quest for Empire: The Political Kingdom of God and the Council of Fifty in Mormon History* (East Lansing: Michigan State University Press, 1970). A more recent approach to this council (and one which takes issue with Andrus and Hansen) is D. Michael Quinn, "The Council of Fifty and Its Members, 1844 to 1945," *BYU Studies* 20 (Winter, 1980): 163-97.

[6]B. H. Roberts, *Comprehensive History of the Church of Jesus Christ of Latter-day Saints, Century I,* (Salt Lake City: Deseret News Press, 1930), 3:154-55.

[7]Lyndon W. Cook, *The Revelations of the Prophet Joseph Smith* (Provo, Ut.: Seventy's Mission Bookstore, 1981), p. 181.

[8]*Ibid.,* pp. 297-99.

# 51

# SALVATION BEYOND THE GRAVE

## (D&C 137 and 138)

ROBERT L. MILLET

Elder Boyd K. Packer, in speaking to a group of Church educators, remarked: "We live in a day of great events relating to the scriptures. It has been only a short time since two revelations were added to the standard works." Then, after making brief reference to what are now sections 137 and 138 of the Doctrine and Covenants, he continued: "I was surprised, and I think all of the Brethren were surprised, at how casually that announcement of two additions to the standard works was received by the Church. But we will live to sense the significance of it; we will tell our grandchildren and our great-grandchildren, and we will record in our diaries, that we were on the earth and remember when that took place."[1]

### The Vision of the Celestial Kingdom

The historical setting of Joseph Smith's Vision of the Celestial Kingdom (D&C 137) is both inspiring and informative. The headquarters of the Saints had moved from New York and Pennsylvania to Ohio. By 1831 two Church centers were organized, one in Kirtland and the other in Missouri (Zion). Joseph Smith and his people received a commandment as early as 1833 to build a temple in Kirtland and were given profound promises. The Lord instructed that they "should build a house, in the which house I design to endow those whom I have chosen with power from on high" (D&C 95:8). Truly the sacrifices of the Saints brought forth the blessings of heaven as God rewarded the works of his chosen people with a marvelous outpouring of light and truth.[2]

Joseph and the early leaders of the Church had begun to meet in the temple before its completion, and had participated in washings, anointings, and blessings, all in preparation for what came to be known as the Kirtland Endowment. On Thursday evening, 21 January 1836, the Prophet and a number of Church leaders from Kirtland and Missouri had gathered in the third or attic floor of the Kirtland Temple (in the translating or "President's Room"). After anointings and after all the presidency had laid their hands upon the Prophet's head and pronounced many glorious blessings and prophecies, a mighty vision burst upon the assembled leadership.[3]

> The heavens were opened upon us, and I beheld the celestial kingdom of God, and the glory thereof, whether in the body or out I cannot tell.
>
> I saw the transcendent beauty of the gate through which the heirs of that kingdom will enter, which was like unto circling flames of fire;
>
> Also the blazing throne of God, whereon was seated the Father and the Son.
>
> I saw the beautiful streets of that kingdom, which had the appearance of being paved with gold (vv. 1-4).

Joseph had learned by vision in February of 1832 the nature of those who would inherit the highest heaven, the celestial. These persons are they who "overcome by faith, and are sealed by the Holy Spirit of Promise," they "into whose hands the Father has given all things" (D&C 76:53, 55). The Prophet's Vision of the Celestial Kingdom was not unlike John the Revelator's vision of the holy city, the earth in its sanctified and celestial state. "The foundations of the wall of the city," writes John, "were garnished with all manner of precious stones." Further, "the street of the city was pure gold, as it were transparent glass" (Rev. 21:19, 21).

Joseph's account of the Vision continues: "I saw Father Adam and Abraham; and my father and my mother; my brother Alvin, that has long since slept; And marveled how it was that he had obtained an inheritance in that kingdom, seeing that he had departed this life before the Lord had set his hand to gather Israel the second time, and had not been baptized for the remission of sins" (D&C 137:5-6). Joseph Smith's brief view of the celestial kingdom permitted him to witness specific personalities who had proven true and faithful in all things, and thus had qualified for exaltation. Adam, the first man and father of the race, had sought the Lord and found him. "Abraham received all things," a revelation stated, "whatsoever he received, by revelation and commandment, . . . and hath entered into his exaltation and sitteth upon his throne" (D&C 132:29). That Joseph's vision was a glimpse into the future celestial realm is evident from the fact that he saw his parents—Joseph Sr. and Lucy Mack—in the kingdom of the just, when in fact both were still living in 1836. Father Smith was, interestingly, in the same room with his son at the time the vision was received.

Alvin Smith was born on 11 February 1798 in Tunbridge, Vermont, the first-born of Joseph Sr. and Lucy Mack Smith. His was a pleasant and loving disposition, and he always sought out opportunities to aid the family in their continual financial struggles. Joseph Jr. later described his oldest brother as one in whom there was no guile.[4] "He was a very handsome man, surpassed by none but Adam and Seth."[5] Lucy Mack writes that on the morning of 15 November in 1823, "Alvin was taken very sick with the bilious colic." One physician hurried to the Smith home and administered calomel to Alvin. The dose of calomel "lodged in his stomach," and on the third day of sickness, Alvin became aware of the fact that death was near. He asked that each of the Smith children come to his bedside for his parting counsel and final expression of love. As his mother later recalled, "When he came to Joseph, he said, 'I am going to die, the distress which I suffer, and the feelings that I have, tell me my time is very short. I want you to be a good boy, and do everything that lies in your power to obtain the Record [Joseph had been visited by Moroni less than three months before this time]. Be faithful in receiving instruction, and in keeping every commandment that is given you.'"[6] Alvin died on 19 November. Lucy Mack Smith wrote of the pall of grief surrounding his passing: "Alvin was a youth of singular goodness of disposition—kind and amiable, so that lamentation and mourning filled the whole neighborhood in which he resided."[7] Alvin's brother Joseph wrote many years later: "I remember well the pangs of sorrow that swelled my youthful bosom and almost burst my tender heart when he died. He was the oldest and noblest of my father's family. . . . He lived without spot from the time he was a child. . . . He was one of the soberest of men, and when he died, the angel of the Lord visited him in his last moments."[8]

Inasmuch as Alvin had died some seven years before the formal organization of the Church (and thus had not been baptized by proper authority), Joseph wondered how it was possible for Alvin to have attained the highest heaven. Alvin's family had been shocked and saddened at his funeral when they heard the Presbyterian minister announce that Alvin would be consigned to hell, having never officially been baptized or involved in the church. William Smith, Alvin's younger brother, recalls: "Hyrum, Samuel, Katherine, and mother were members of the Presbyterian Church. My father would not join. He did not like it because of Rev. Stockton had preached my brother's funeral sermon and intimated very strongly that he had gone to hell, for Alvin was not a church member, but he was a good boy and my father did not like it."[9] What joy and excitement must have filled the souls of both Joseph Jr. and Joseph Sr. as they heard the voice of an omniscient and omni-loving God: "Thus came the voice of the Lord unto me, saying: All who have died without a knowledge of this gospel, who would have received it if they had been permitted to tarry, shall be heirs of the Celestial kingdom of God; Also all that shall die henceforth without a knowledge of it, who would have received it with all their hearts, shall be heirs of that kingdom; For I, the Lord, will judge all men according to their works, according to the desire of their hearts" (D&C 137:7-9).

God does not and will not hold anyone accountable for a gospel law of which he was ignorant. Every person will have opportunity—here or hereafter—to accept and apply the principles of the gospel of Jesus Christ. Only the Lord, the Holy One of Israel, is capable of "keeping the gate" and thus discerning completely the hearts and minds of mortal men; he alone knows when a person has received sufficient knowledge or impressions to constitute a valid opportunity to receive the Plan of Salvation. Joseph had reaffirmed that the Lord will judge men not only by their actions, but also by their attitudes—the desires of their hearts (cf. Alma 41:3).

One of the most profoundly beautiful of doctrines is that enunciated in the Vision of the Celestial Kingdom regarding the status of children who die before the time of accountability: "And I also beheld that all children who die before they arrive at the years of accountability are saved in the Celestial Kingdom of heaven" (D&C 137:10). King Benjamin had learned from an angel that "the infant perisheth not that dieth in his infancy" (Mosiah 3:18). After having described the nature of those who will come forth in the first resurrection, Abinadi said simply: "And little children also have eternal life" (Mosiah 15:25). A revelation given to Joseph Smith in September of 1830 specified that "little children are redeemed from the foundation of the world through mine Only Begotten" (D&C 29:46; cf. JST, Matt. 19:13-15). Joseph Smith taught in 1842 that "the Lord takes many away even in infancy, that they may escape the envy of man, and the sorrows and evils of this present world; they were too pure, too lovely, to live on earth; therefore, if rightly considered, instead of mourning we have reason to rejoice as they are delivered from evil, and we shall soon have them again."[10] By virtue of his infinite understanding of the human family, "we may assume that the Lord knows and arranges beforehand who shall be taken in infancy and who shall remain on earth to undergo whatever tests are needed in their cases."[11] These children will come forth from the grave as they lie down—as children—[12] and will grow to maturity in the Millennium. They will not be expected to face tests or temptations in their resurrected state, but will go on to enjoy the highest and grandest blessings of exaltation associated with the everlasting continuation of the family unit.[13]

Four and one-half years after Joseph Smith's Vision of the Celestial Kingdom the Prophet delivered his first public discourse on the subject of baptism for the dead at the funeral of Seymour Brunson, a member of the Nauvoo High Council. One man who was in attendance at the funeral has left us the following account:

> I was present at a discourse that the Prophet Joseph delivered on baptism for the dead 15 August 1840. He read the greater part of the 15th chapter of Corinthians and remarked that the Gospel of Jesus Christ brought glad tidings of great joy. . . . He also said the apostle [Paul] was talking to a people who understood baptism for the dead, for it was practiced among them. He went on to say that people could now act for their friends who had departed this life, and that the plan of salvation was calculated to save all who were willing to obey the requirements of the law of God. He went on and made a very beautiful discourse.[14]

One month later, on 14 September 1840, Joseph Smith, Sr. passed away. Just before his death, Father Smith requested that someone be baptized for and in behalf of his oldest son, Alvin. Hyrum Smith complied with his father's last wishes, and was baptized by proxy for Alvin in 1840 and again in 1841.[15] Alvin received the endowment by proxy on 11 April 1877, and was sealed to his parents on 25 August 1897.[16]

**The Vision of the Redemption of the Dead (D&C 138)**

The knowledge of a universal salvation revealed initially through the Prophet Joseph continued to be expanded and elaborated as the ongoing Restoration made further truths available "line upon line." It is to the Prophet's nephew—Joseph F. Smith—that we now turn for precious insights into the manner in which the gospel is preached in the world of spirits.

During the last six months of his life, President Joseph F. Smith suffered from the effects of advancing years (he was in his 80th year) and spent much of his time in his personal study in the Beehive House. President Smith did manage to garner enough strength to attend the 89th semi-annual conference of the Church (October 1918). At the opening session of the conference (Friday, October 4th) he arose to welcome and address the Saints, and with a voice filled with emotion, spoke the following:

> As most of you, I suppose, are aware, I have been undergoing a siege of very serious illness for the last five months. It would be impossible for me, on this occasion, to occupy sufficient time to express the desires of my heart and my feelings, as I would desire to express them to you. . . .
>
> I will not, I dare not, attempt to enter upon many things that are resting upon my mind this morning, and I shall postpone until some future time, the Lord being willing, my attempt to tell you some of the things that are in my mind, and that dwell in my heart. *I have not lived alone these last five months. I have dwelt in the spirit of prayer, of supplication, of faith and of determination; and I have had my communication with the Spirit of the Lord continuously.*[17]

According to the President's son, Joseph Fielding Smith, the Prophet was here expressing (albeit in broadest terms) the fact that during the past half-year he had been the recipient of numerous manifestations, some of which he had shared with his son, both before and following the conference. One of these manifestations, the Vision of Redemption of the Dead, had been received just the day before, on 3

October, and was recorded immediately following the close of the conference.[18]

The aged Prophet's attention was drawn to the world beyond mortality by his frequent confrontation with death. His parents, Hyrum and Mary Fielding Smith, both died while he was a young man. Among the great trials of his life none was more devastating than the passing of many of his children into death. President Smith was possessed of an almost infinite capacity to love, and thus the sudden departure of dear ones brought extreme anguish and sorrow. Joseph Fielding Smith later wrote: "When death invaded his home, as frequently it did, and his little ones were taken from him, he grieved with a broken heart and mourned, not as those who mourn who live without hope, but for the loss of his 'precious jewels' dearer to him than life itself."[19]

On 20 January 1918 Hyrum Mack Smith, oldest son of Joseph F. and then a member of the Council of the Twelve Apostles, was taken to the hospital for a serious illness, where the physicians diagnosed a ruptured appendix. Despite constant medical attention and repeated prayers, Hyrum M.—then only 45 years of age and at the time with a pregnant wife—died on the night of 23 January. This was a particularly traumatic affliction for the President. Hyrum had been called as an apostle at the same conference wherein his father had been sustained as the Church's sixth president (October 1901). Hyrum Mack was a man of depth and wisdom beyond his years, and his powerful sermons evidenced his unusual insight into gospel principles. "His mind was quick and bright and correct," remarked President Smith. "His judgment was not excelled, and he saw and comprehended things in their true light and meaning. When he spoke, men listened and felt the weight of his thoughts and words." Finally, the Prophet observed: "He has thrilled my soul by his power of speech, as no other man ever did. Perhaps this was because he was my son, and he was filled with the fire of the Holy Ghost."[20] Already in a weakened physical condition due to age, the Prophet's sudden sense of loss caused him "one of the most severe blows that he was ever called upon to endure."[21]

Even though President Smith indicated in October of 1918 that the preceding six months had been a season of special enrichment, in fact it may be shown that the last thirty months of his life (specifically, from

April 1916 to October 1918) represent a brief era of unusual spiritual enlightenment, in which he delivered to the Church some of the most important and inspiring insights of this dispensation.

At the April 1916 general conference President Smith delivered a remarkable address, the thrust of which established a theme for the next thirty months of his life, and most important for this discussion, laid the foundation for his final doctrinal contribution—the Vision of the Redemption of the Dead. In his opening sermon entitled "In the Presence of the Divine," Joseph F. spoke of the nearness of the world of spirits, and of the interest and concern for us and our labors exercised by those who have passed beyond the veil. He stressed that those who labored so diligently in their *mortal* estate to establish the cause of Zion would not be denied the privilege of "looking down upon the results of their own labors" from their *post-mortal* estate. In fact, the President insisted, "they are as deeply interested in our welfare today, if not with greater capacity, with far more interest, behind the veil, than they were in the flesh." Perhaps the keynote statement of the Prophet in this sermon was the following: *"Sometimes the Lord expands our vision from this point of view and this side of the veil, so that we feel and seem to realize that we can look beyond the thin veil which separates us from that other sphere."*[22] This remark, both penetrating and prophetic, set the stage for the next two and one-half years.

In June of 1916 the First Presidency and the Twelve released a doctrinal exposition in pamphlet form entitled "The Father and the Son." This document was delivered to alleviate doctrinal misunderstandings concerning the nature of the Godhead, and specifically the role and scriptural designation of Jesus Christ as "Father."[23]

One of the most significant fruits of this segment of time was a talk delivered by President Joseph F. Smith at a Temple Fast Meeting in February of 1918, entitled "The Status of Children in the Resurrection." In this address we gain not only an insight into the power and prophetic stature of one schooled and prepared in doctrine; in addition, we are allowed a brief glimpse into the heart of a noble father who—having lost little ones to death and having mourned their absence—rejoices in the sure knowledge that: (1) mortal children are immortal beings, spirits who continue to live and progress beyond the veil; and (2) as taught by the Prophet Joseph Smith, children will come forth from the grave as they lie down—as children—and such persons will thereafter be nurtured and reared to physical maturity by worthy parents. "O how I have been blessed with these children," exulted President Smith, "and how happy I shall be to meet them on the other side!"[24]

Further evidence that the veil had become thin for Joseph F. is to be found in his recording (on 7 April 1918) of a dream/vision he had received many years earlier, while on his first mission to Hawaii. The dream had served initially to strengthen the faith and build the confidence of a lonely and weary fifteen-year-old on the slopes of Haleakala on the island of Maui; it had, through the years that followed, served to chart a course for Joseph F. and give to him the assurance that his labors were acceptable to the Lord, and that he also had the approbation of his predecessors in the presidency of the restored Church. In the dream young Joseph F. encountered his uncle, the Prophet Joseph, and was fortified in his desire to remain free from the taints of the world. In addition, he learned at an early age that the separation between mortality and immortality is subtle, and that the Lord frequently permits an intermingling of the inhabitants of the two spheres.[25]

As finite man stands in the twilight of life, he is occasionally able to view existence with divine perspective and is thus capable of opening himself to the things of infinity. "If we live our holy religion," President Brigham Young taught in 1862, "and let the Spirit reign," the mind of man "will not become dull and stupid, but as the body approaches dissolution *the spirit takes a firmer hold on the enduring substance behind the veil*, drawing from the depths of that eternal Fountain of Light sparkling gems of intelligence which surround the frail and sinking tabernacle with a halo of immortal wisdom."[26] This poignant principle was demonstrated beautifully in the life of President Joseph F. Smith. Here was a man who met death and sorrow and persecution with a quiet dignity, and thus through participating in the fellowship of Christ's sufferings was made acquainted with the things of God. On Thursday, 3 October 1918, President Smith, largely confined to his room because of illness, sat meditating over matters of substance. On this day the Prophet specifically began to read and ponder upon the universal nature of the Atonement, and the Apostle Peter's allusions to Christ's post-mortal ministry. The stage was set: preparation of a lifetime and preparation of the moment were recompensed with a heavenly endowment—the Vision of the Redemption of the Dead. In the words of the President: "As I pondered over these things which are written, the eyes of my understanding were opened, and the Spirit of the Lord rested upon me, and I saw the hosts of the dead, both small and great" (D&C 138:11).

Joseph F. Smith saw in vision "an innumerable company of the spirits of the just," the righteous dead from the days of Adam to the meridian of time. These all were anxiously awaiting the advent of the Christ into their dimension of life, and were exuberant in their anticipation of an imminent resurrection (vv. 12-17). Having consummated the atoning sacrifice on Golgotha, the Lord of the living and the dead passed in the twinkling of an eye into the world of the departed. The dead, having "looked upon the long absence of their spirits from their bodies as a bondage" (v. 50; cf. D&C 45:17), were, in a sense, in prison. Yes, even the righteous sought "deliverance" (vv. 15, 18); the Master came to declare "liberty to the captives who had been faithful" (v. 18). As Peter had said, Christ went beyond the veil to preach "unto the spirits in prison" (1 Pet. 3:19). Joseph Smith had taught: "Hades, Sheol, paradise, spirits in prison, are all one; it is a world of spirits."[27] And as Elder Bruce R. McConkie has explained, in this vision "it is clearly set forth that the whole spirit world, and not only that portion designated as hell, is considered to be a spirit prison."[28]

To the congregation of the righteous the Lord appeared, and "their countenances shone, and the radiance from the presence of the Lord rested upon them" (v. 24). President Smith observed as the Lord taught "the everlasting gospel, the doctrine of the resurrection and the redemption of mankind from the fall, and from individual sins on conditions of repentance" (v. 19). In addition, Christ extended to the righteous spirits "power to come forth, after his resurrection from the dead, to enter into his Father's kingdom, there to be crowned with immortality and eternal life" (v. 51).

It is while pondering the question of how the Savior could have taught the gospel to so many in the spirit world in so short a time (the time intervening between his death on Friday and his rise from the tomb on Sunday morning) that President Smith received what may well be the most significant doctrinal insight of the entire vision. The President came to understand "that the Lord went not in person among the wicked and disobedient"—those in hell—but rather "organized his forces and appointed messengers, clothed with power and authority," that such representatives might carry the message of the gospel "unto whom he [the Lord] could not go personally, because of their rebellion and transgression" (vv. 20-22, 25-30, 37). The chosen messengers "declare the acceptable day of the Lord." They carry the gospel message to those who had no opportunity in mortality to accept or reject the truth, and also to those who rejected the message on earth. These (who are visited by messengers) are taught the first principles and ordinances of the gospel (including the vicarious nature of the ordinances), in order that the inhabitants of the world of spirits might be judged and rewarded by the same divine standards as those who inhabit the world of mortals (vv. 31-34). The insight that Christ did not personally visit the disobedient is a doctrinal matter introduced to the Church for the first time in October of 1918 and does much to broaden our scope and answer questions with regard to the work within that sphere.

By the power of the Holy Ghost President Smith perceived the identity of many of the noble and great from the beginning of time, including Adam, Seth, Noah, Abraham, Isaiah, the Nephite prophets before Christ, and many more. In addition, the President recognized Mother Eve and many of her faithful daughters. Joseph F. had taught a number of years earlier that women minister to women in the spirit world, even as they do in holy places on earth.[29]

It would appear at this point that President Smith's vision shifted in time—from a first century A.D. gathering to a scene of workers in the spirit world during the final gospel dispensation. A change in time-frame is common in visions, as can be seen from the experiences of Nephi (1 Ne. 13-14), John the Apostle (Rev. 11-12), and Joseph Smith (D&C 76). President Smith saw in the spirit world his predecessors in the presidency of the restored Church, and other noble leaders who played such a critical role "in laying the foundations of the great latter-day work" (vv. 53-54).

It may be that the vision shifted again in time, allowing President Smith a glimpse into the pre-mortal world. He observed that the great leaders of the latter-day Church were "among the noble and great ones who were chosen in the beginning to be rulers in the Church of God," and he became aware of their pre-mortal lessons, preparation, and foreordination (vv. 55-56).

President Joseph F. Smith's vision confirms another doctrine that had been taught by Joseph Smith: the faithful in this life continue to teach and labor in the world of spirits in behalf of those who know not God (v. 57). As recorded in George Laub's Journal under date of 12 May 1844, the Prophet Joseph declared: "Now all those die in the faith goe to the prison of Spirits to preach to the ded in body, but they are alive in the Spirit & those Spirits preach to the Spirits that they may live according to god in the Spirit and men do minister for them in the flesh" (sic).[30] Joseph F. had taught this doctrine on a number of occasions;[31] here he became an eyewitness of the same.

Having laid before us his remarkable vision—"a complete and comprehensive confirmation of the established doctrine of the Church where salvation for the dead is concerned"[32]—President Smith climaxed his doctrinal contribution with testimony: "Thus was the vision of the redemption of the dead revealed to me, and I bear record, and I know that this record is true, through the blessing of our Lord and Savior, Jesus Christ, even so. Amen" (v. 60).

The Vision of the Redemption of the Dead was dictated by President Smith to his son—Joseph Fielding Smith—at the close of the October 1918 conference. The vision was presented to the First Presidency, Twelve, and Patriarch in a Council Meeting on Thursday, 31 October 1918. Because of his weakened condition, the President was not able to be in attendance but asked Joseph Fielding to read the revelation to the gathered general authorities. Note the following from the journal of Anthon H. Lund, first counselor to President Smith: "In our Council Joseph F. Smith, Jr. read a revelation which his father had had in which he saw the spirits in Paradise and he also saw that Jesus organized a number of brethren to go and preach to the spirits in prison, but did not go himself. It was an interesting document and the apostles accepted it as true and from God."[33] Elder James E. Talmage of the Council of the Twelve Apostles recorded the following in his personal journal:

> Attended meeting of the First Presidency and the Twelve. Today President Smith who is still confined to his home by

> illness, sent to the Brethren the account of a vision through which, as he states, were revealed to him important facts relating to the work of the disembodied Savior in the realm of departed spirits, and of the missionary work in progress on the other side of the veil. By united action the Council of the Twelve, with the Counselors in the First Presidency, and the Presiding Patriarch accepted and endorsed the revelation as the word of the Lord. President Smith's signed statement will be published in the next issue (December) of the Improvement Era, which is the organ of the Priesthood quorums of the church.[34]

The text of the vision first appeared in the 30 November edition of the *Deseret News*. It was printed in the December *Improvement Era*, and in the January 1919 editions of the *Relief Society Magazine*, the *Utah Genealogical and Historical Magazine*, the *Young Women's Journal*, and the *Millennial Star*.

President Smith's physical condition worsened during the first weeks of November, 1918. On Sunday, 17 November he was taken with an attack of pleurisy, which finally developed into pleuro-pneumonia. Tuesday morning, 19 November 1918 his work in mortality was completed. It was fitting that at the April 1919 general conference Elder James E. Talmage should deliver the following touching and appropriate tribute to the President. Elder Talmage asked: "Well, where is he now?" The apostle answered: *"He was permitted shortly before his passing to have a glimpse into the hereafter, and to learn where he would soon be at work.* He was a preacher of righteousness on earth, he is a preacher of righteousness today. He was a missionary from his boyhood up, and he is a missionary today amongst those who have not yet heard the gospel, though they have passed from mortality into the spirit world. I cannot conceive of him as otherwise than busily engaged in the work of the Master."[35]

## Conclusion

The Lord loves all of his children and desires that every soul have the privilege of participating in the principles and ordinances of the gospel of Jesus Christ. The doctrine of salvation for the dead, given by revelation through Joseph Smith, and expanded through a remarkable vision of Joseph F. Smith, broadens our own perspective and points us toward the eternities. Joseph Smith's Vision of the Celestial Kingdom opens us to the reality of an omniscient and omni-loving God. Joseph F. Smith's Vision of the Redemption of the Dead sets forth with remarkable clarity the manner in which the Savior "declared liberty to the captives" in the meridian of time, and also unfolds the pattern by which the doctrines of salvation continue to be made known in the world beyond the grave. And so it is that the work of redemption goes forward on both sides of the veil. "Because of this," Peter taught the Saints, "is the gospel preached to them who are dead, that they might be judged according to men in the flesh, but live in the spirit according to the will of God" (JST, 1 Pet. 4:6.)

---

## Notes

[1]"Teach the Scriptures," in *Charge to Religious Educators*, 2nd ed. (Salt Lake City: Church Educational System, 1982), p. 21; this is the text of a talk delivered to CES personnel 14 October 1977, Salt Lake City.

[2]See Milton V. Backman, Jr. and Robert L. Millet, "Heavenly Manifestations in the Kirtland Temple," found herein.

[3]*Ibid.*; see also *HC* 2:378-80.

[4]*HC* 5:126.

[5]*Ibid.*, p. 247.

[6]Lucy Mack Smith, *History of Joseph Smith*, Preston Nibley, ed. (Salt Lake City: Bookcraft, 1958), pp. 86-89.

[7]*Ibid.*, p. 88.

[8]*HC* 5:126-27.

[9]See an interview with William Smith by E. C. Briggs and J. W. Peterson, published in the *Deseret News* (Salt Lake City), 20 January 1894.

[10]*HC* 4:553.

[11]Bruce R. McConkie, expressing the sentiments of President Joseph Fielding Smith, in "The Salvation of Little Children," *Ensign*, April 1977, p. 6.

[12]*HC* 4:555-56.

[13]McConkie, "The Salvation of Little Children," pp. 5-6; see also Joseph Fielding Smith, *Doctrines of Salvation*, 3 vols. (Salt Lake City: Bookcraft, 1954-56), 2:54-57.

[14]A report by Simon Baker in *Journal History*, under date of 15 August 1840, LDS Church Archives; also in Andrew F. Ehat and Lyndon W. Cook,

*The Words of Joseph Smith* (Provo, Ut.: Religious Studies Center, Brigham Young University, 1980), p. 49; see also *HC* 4:231.

[15]"Nauvoo Baptisms for the Dead," Book A, Church Genealogical Society Archives, pp. 145, 149.

[16]From Joseph Smith, Sr. Family Group Sheet, Church Genealogical Society Archives.

[17]Joseph F. Smith, *Conference Report*, October 1918, p. 2.

[18]Joseph Fielding Smith, *The Life of Joseph F. Smith* (Salt Lake City: Deseret Book Company, 1969), p. 466.

[19]*Ibid.*, p. 455.

[20]*Ibid.*, p. 474.

[21]*Ibid.*

[22]*Conference Report*, April 1916, pp. 1-8.

[23]See *Improvement Era*, August 1916, pp. 934-42; James R. Clark, comp., *Messages of the First Presidency*, 6 vols. (Salt Lake City: Bookcraft, 1971), 5:23-34.

[24]*Improvement Era*, May 1918, pp. 567-74; Clark, *Messages of the First Presidency*, 5:90-98.

[25]*Improvement Era*, November 1919, pp. 16-17; Clark, *Messages of the First Presidency*, 5:99-101; Smith, *Life of Joseph F. Smith*, pp. 445-47.

[26]*JD* 9:288.

[27]*HC* 5:425.

[28]Bruce R. McConkie, "A New Commandment: Save Thyself and Thy Kindred," *Ensign*, August 1976, p. 11.

[29]See Joseph F. Smith, *Young Women's Journal* 23 (1911): pp. 128-32; *Gospel Doctrine* (Salt Lake City: Deseret Book Co., 1971), p. 461.

[30]Ehat and Cook, *The Words of Joseph Smith*, p. 370.

[31]See *Gospel Doctrine*, pp. 134-35, 460-61.

[32]Bruce R. McConkie, "A New Commandment: Save Thyself and Thy Kindred," *Ensign*, August 1976, p. 11.

[33]Anthon H. Lund Journal, LDS Church Archives, Salt Lake City; under date of 31 October 1918.

[34]James E. Talmage Journal, LDS Church Archives, Salt Lake City; under date of 31 October 1918.

[35]*Conference Report*, April 1919, p. 60.

# 52

# OFFICIAL DECLARATIONS 1 AND 2

Richard O. Cowan

Some students of the Doctrine and Covenants have wondered why Official Declarations 1 and 2 did not become numbered sections like the balance of the material in this book of scripture. As this article will show, these documents are not the actual records of the revelations themselves but rather are inspired announcements that the revelations had been received. Each of these declarations is related to a major turning point in the history of the Church. Because their subjects are so different, these two documents will be treated independently.

## Official Declaration 1

To appreciate fully the significance of the "Manifesto," as Official Declaration 1 is popularly known, one must have some knowledge of the history of plural marriage as practiced among the Latter-day Saints. As early as the 1830s Joseph Smith first learned of this principle by revelation, but he was not permitted to teach it at that time. In 1841, after the Saints had settled in Nauvoo, the practice was introduced secretly and on a limited basis among selected members of the Church. The first public announcement of the doctrine came in 1852, after the Saints had made their trek to the relative isolation of the Rocky Mountain West. Recent research has shown that by the 1880s approximately fifteen percent of all Church members belonged to plural families. Although there were some abuses which attracted widespread notoriety, many other families enjoyed rich spiritual blessings if they were willing to put forth the effort required for successful living in this unique order of marriage.

Congress passed the first anti-bigamy law in 1862, but preoccupation with the Civil War and its aftermath delayed enforcement for nearly two decades. In 1882 the Edmunds Law enlarged the definition of offenses to be punished: Marrying a plural wife continued to be regarded as a felony, while living or "co-habiting" with a plural wife became a misdemeanor. Bitter anti-Mormon agitation during the next few years led to the passage of yet harsher legislation. The Edmunds-Tucker Law of 1887 not only punished those convicted of polygamy, but also limited the Saints' participation in the political process, disincorporated the Church as a legal institution, and provided for the seizure of its assets. The Latter-day Saints continued to seek help from the courts, fully expecting that these laws would be declared unconstitutional because they infringed freedom of religion. Early in 1889 arguments concerning the Edmunds-Tucker Law were presented to the United States Supreme Court; much to the Saints' disappointment, the high court upheld even this harshest law in May of 1890.

**President Woodruff's Dilemma**

Even before the Supreme Court handed down its final decision, Church leaders fully expected that the anti-polygamy laws would once again be upheld. These developments posed a difficult dilemma for President Wilford Woodruff and for the Latter-day Saints as a whole. Their choice was not between a law of God and a law of man, but rather between what appeared to be two divinely sanctioned precepts. They regarded the practice of plural marriage as revealed by God (section 132), but they also had been instructed to obey "that law of the land which is constitutional" (D&C 98:5). In November of 1889 the Lord gave by revelation a message of assurance to President Woodruff and his counselors: "Thus saith the Lord, unto my servants . . . I the Lord hold the destiny of this nation, and all other nations of the earth in mine own hands; all that I have revealed, and promised and decreed . . . shall come to pass, and no power shall stay my hand."[1] Nevertheless, while President Woodruff was praying for guidance, the Lord showed him "by vision and revelation exactly what would take place" if the practice of plural marriage was not stopped. He foresaw that all the temples would be lost and ordinances for the living and the dead would cease, the First Presidency and the Twelve as well as other leaders would be imprisoned, and that under these conditions the Church and its work would be destroyed. President Woodruff's description of this revelation was published in the Doctrine and Covenants for the first time in the 1981 edition (see "Excerpts from Three Addresses by President Wilford Woodruff Regarding the Manifesto," following OD 1). In the light of these instructions, the First

Presidency in 1889 withdrew authorization for further plural marriages.

The Endowment House, an adobe structure on Temple Square which had been built as a place where sacred ordinances could be performed until the Salt Lake Temple was finished, was torn down during November of 1889, when President Woodruff learned that unauthorized plural marriages were being performed there. Following the Supreme Court's decision in 1890, charges intensified to the effect that the Church was still sanctioning plural marriages. In response, President Woodruff issued the "Manifesto" (Official Declaration 1) just before the October general conference: "Inasmuch as laws have been enacted by Congress forbidding plural marriages, which laws have been pronounced constitutional by the court of last resort, I hereby declare my intention to submit to those laws, and . . . publicly declare that my advice to the Latter-day Saints is to refrain from *contracting* any marriage forbidden by the law of the land" (Official Declaration 1, emphasis added). Concerning the circumstances in which this statement was prepared, President Woodruff testified: "I went before the Lord, and I wrote what the Lord told me to write."[2] Thus Official Declaration 1 is an inspired announcement of the fact that a revelation, previously received, had ended the practice of plural marriages. Some wondered how these instructions applied to those who had already entered plural marriage. Within a short time Church leaders and U. S. Government officials agreed that new polygamous marriages would be permitted to continue living with and supporting them without fear of prosecution. Under these terms Utah was finally admitted as one of the United States in 1896. For a time the Church allowed plural marriages to be performed outside of the United States, particularly in the Mormon colonies of northern Mexico. In 1904, however, President Joseph F. Smith again upheld the principles set forth in the Official Declaration of 1890 and stressed that the Church henceforth would not sanction plural marriages anywhere in the world.[3] President Smith also directed that the 1890 Manifesto be included in the Doctrine and Covenants, and this was done with copies printed beginning in 1908.

Two members of the Twelve, John W. Taylor and Matthias F. Cowley, could not accept President Smith's expanded application of the prohibition against polygamous marriages. In 1905 the First Presidency had to take the unusual step of asking for these Apostles' resignation. Since that time several small "fundamentalist" groups have continued to insist that plural marriage is an essential doctrine, and have gained public notoriety by performing such marriages. These persons, however, have been denounced by Church leaders and are subject to excommunication. All this has served to demonstrate the importance of following the living prophet through whom revelation continues to guide the Church in each era of its history.

## Official Declaration 2

Few things have had a greater impact on the gospel's worldwide progress than did the revelation received in 1978 through President Spencer W. Kimball extending the blessing of the priesthood to members of all races. Over the years, Blacks had been free to join the Church and were welcomed at its activities, but they could not receive the priesthood. Latter-day Saints accepted this ban as inspired, but it increasingly became the subject of criticism and attacks, especially during the widespread agitation for civil rights in the 1960s. A few, even within the Church, tauntingly suggested that the Prophet should "receive a revelation" to change the policy. Significantly, however, the revelation did not come in the face of these pressures, but it came in due course over a decade later when such agitation had largely ceased. Just as had been the case in 1890, divine revelation rather than external pressures brought the important change.

Over a period of several months the General Authorities discussed at length in their regular temple meetings the matter of extending the blessings of the priesthood. In addition to these deliberations, President Kimball frequently went to the temple, particularly on Saturdays and Sundays when he could be in that holy place alone in order to plead for guidance. "I want to be sure," he later reflected. In recalling the events associated with this time period, President Kimball explained:

> I remember very vividly that day after ay I walked to the temple and ascended to the fourth floor where we have our solemn assemblies and where we have our meetings of the Twelve and

> the First Presidency. After everybody had gone out of the temple, I knelt and prayed. I prayed with much fervency. I knew that something was before us that was extremely important to many of the children of God. I knew that we could receive the revelations of the Lord only by being worthy and ready for them and ready to accept them and put them into place. Day after day I went alone and with great solemnity and seriousness in the upper rooms of the temple, and there I offered my soul and offered my efforts to go forward with the program. I wanted to do what he wanted. I talked about it to him and said, "Lord, I want only what is right. We are not making any plans to be spectacularly moving. We want only the thing thou dost want, and we want it when you want it and not until.[4]

On 1 June 1978, nearly all the General Authorities gathered, fasting, for their regular monthly meeting in the temple. After this three-hour session which was filled with spiritual uplift and enlightenment, President Kimball invited his counselors and the Twelve to remain while the other General Authorities were excused. When the First Presidency and the Twelve were alone, he again brought up the possibility of conferring the priesthood on worthy brethren of all races. He expressed the hope that there might be a clear answer received one way or the other. "At this point," Elder Bruce R. McConkie recalled, "President Kimball asked the brethren if any of them desired to express their feelings and views as to the matter at hand. We all did so, freely and fluently and at considerable length, each person stating his views and manifesting the feelings of his heart. There was a marvelous outpouring of unity, oneness, and agreement in the council."[5] After a two-hour discussion, President Kimball asked the group to unite in formal prayer and modestly suggested that he act as voice. He recalled:

> I told the Lord if it wasn't right, if He didn't want this change to come in the Church that I would be true to it all the rest of my life, and I'd fight the world . . . if that's what He wanted. . . . I had a great deal to fight, myself largely, because I had grown up with this thought that Negroes should not have the priesthood and I was prepared to go all the rest of my life till my death and fight for it and defend it as it was. But this

> revelation and assurance came to me so clearly that there was no question about it.[6]

Elder McConkie further described the occasion:

> It was during this prayer that the revelation came. The Spirit of the Lord rested mightily upon us all; we felt something akin to what happened on the day of Pentecost and at the dedication of the Kirtland Temple. From the midst of eternity, the voice of God, conveyed by the power of the Spirit, spoke to his prophet. . . . And we all heard the same voice, received the same message, and became personal witnesses that the word received was the mind and will and voice of the Lord.[7]

Reflecting on this experience, President Spencer W. Kimball and President Ezra Taft Benson and others of the Twelve concurred that none "had ever experienced anything of such spiritual magnitude and power as was poured out upon the Presidency and the Twelve that day in the upper room in the house of the Lord."[8]

During the following week, an official announcement of this revelation was prepared under President Kimball's direction. On 9 June 1978, this inspired announcement was approved by the General Authorites and was issued to the public. "As we have witnessed the expansion of the work of the Lord over the earth," the Brethren declared, "we have been grateful that people of many nations have responded to the message of the restored gospel, and have joined the Church in ever-increasing numbers. This, in turn, has inspired us with a desire to extend to every worthy member of the Church all of the privileges and blessings which the gospel affords." Witnessing "the faithfulness of those from whom the priesthood has been withheld," Church leaders pleaded "long and earnestly" in behalf of these people. "He [the Lord] has heard our prayers," the Brethren affirmed, "and by revelation has confirmed that the long-promised day has come when every faithful, worthy man in the Church may receive the holy priesthood, with power to exercise its divine authority, and enjoy with his loved ones every blessing that flows therefrom, including the blessings off the temple" (Official Declaration 2). This revelation was approved at the fall general conference that year, and was added to the Doctrine and Covenants as "Official Declaration 2" in the new 1981 edition.

The impact of this revelation was far-reaching. Faithful black Latter-day Saints rejoiced as they received long-hoped-for ordination to the priesthood, mission calls, calls to serve in bishoprics or stake presidencies, and, of course, the eternal blessings of the temple. In November 1978, just five months after the revelation came, the First Presidency called two experienced couples to open missionary work in the black nations of Nigeria and Ghana.

Like sections 137 and 138, Official Declaration 2 was added to the scriptural canon at a particularly appropriate time in the Church's history. The introductory statement in the 1981 edition explains that sections 137 and 138 both set forth "the fundamentals of salvation for the dead." Within a decade of their being added to the Standard Works, the number of temples in service or under construction more than doubled. Similarly, Official Declaration 2 was added to the canon at a time of unprecedented international Church growth. In this setting, the 1978 revelation paved the way for the Church more than ever before to fulfill its worldwide mission. Sections 137 and 138 bolstered the Latter-day Saints' efforts to extend gospel blessings to the dead in a greater way than ever before. Official Declaration 2 likewise opened the door to reach all the living (as well as the dead) with the privileges and opportunities of the Lord's plan for eternal progress and joy.

## Notes

[1]James R. Clark, comp., *Messages of the First Presidency*, 6 vols. (Salt Lake City: Bookcraft, 1965-75), 3:175.

[2]Statement of 1 November 1891, published with Official Declaration 1 in the 1981 edition of the Doctrine and Covenants.

[3]Clark, *Messages of the First Presidency*, 4:84-85.

[4]Spencer W. Kimball in a missionary meeting, 23 October 1978 at the Johannesburg, South Africa Area Conference; in Edward L. Kimball, ed., *The Teachings of Spencer W. Kimball* (Salt Lake City: Bookcraft, 1982), pp. 450-51.

[5]Bruce R. McConkie, "The New Revelation on Priesthood," *Priesthood*

(Salt Lake City: Deseret Book Co., 1981), pp. 126-27; see also McConkie, "All Are Alike Unto God," *The Second Annual Church Educational System Religious Educators' Symposium: The Book of Mormon* (Salt Lake City: The Church of Jesus Christ of Latter-day Saints, 1978), pp. 3-5.

[6]*Church News*, 6 Januarry 1979, p. 4.

[7]McConkie, "The New Revelation on Priesthood," p. 128.

[8]*Ibid.*

# Notes on Contributors

**WILSON K. ANDERSEN** is Associate Professor of Church History and Doctrine at Brigham Young University. He received his B.S. and M.Ed. degrees from BYU and has taught religion courses at that institution since 1962. Brother Andersen has authored and prepared numerous manuals and courses of study in the area of Church History and Doctrine and is an acknowledged specialist in the area of priesthood and Church government. He and his wife Margaret are the parents of five children.

**A. GARY ANDERSON** is Associate Professor of Church History and Doctrine at Brigham Young University. He obtained his Ed.D. from Brigham Young University with a major in Educational Administration and a minor in Religious Education. He served as Director of the LDS Institute of Religion at Dixie College in St. George, Utah for nine years before joining the faculty at BYU. Brother Anderson and his wife Annette are the parents of nine children.

**RICHARD LLOYD ANDERSON** is Professor of Ancient Scripture at Brigham Young University. He received his M.A. degree in Greek from BYU, his J.D. from Harvard University, and his Ph.D. from the University of California-Berkeley in Roman and Greek History. Professor Anderson is a recognized scholar in both ancient studies and LDS Church history. In 1981 he published a major work on the lives of the witnesses of the Book of Mormon. In 1983 he published *Understanding Paul*, an important book on the life and message of the apostle to the Gentiles. A forthcoming volume on the letters between the Prophet Joseph Smith and his wife, Emma, has been eagerly anticipated by Latter-day Saints for a number of years. Brother Anderson and his wife, the former Carma de Jong, are the parents of four children.

**MILTON V. BACKMAN, JR.** is Professor of Church History and Doctrine at Brigham Young University. Brother Backman received his Bachelors and Masters degrees from the University of Utah, and his Ph.D. from the University of Pennsylvania in History. A recognized authority on the Kirtland period in LDS Church history, Professor Backman recently published a major work on the subject entitled *The*

*Heavens Resound.* He and his wife Kathleen are the parents of three children.

**DAVID F. BOONE** is the Faculty Support Center Supervisor for Religious Education and part-time instructor of Church History and Doctrine at Brigham Young University. David obtained his Master's Degree from BYU in History, with special emphasis in the frontier American West and LDS Church History. He and his wife Mary are the parents of five children.

**DONALD Q. CANNON** is Professor of Church History and Doctrine at Brigham Young University. Brother Cannon obtained his B.A. and M.A. degrees from the University of Utah, and his Ph.D. from Clark University, specializing in U.S. and European history. Before coming to BYU he worked as Assistant and Associate Professor of History at the University of Southern Maine. Brother Cannon has recently co-edited the *Far West Record* and also co-authored a textual study of Joseph Smith's famous King Follett Sermon. He and his wife Jo Ann are the parents of six children.

**JAMES R. CHRISTIANSON** is Associate Professor of Church History and Doctrine at Brigham Young University. He received his Ph.D. from the University of Kansas in History and Anthropology. Brother Christianson has worked for the Church Educational System as a seminary and institute instructor, and also as a division coordinator in the midwestern U.S., Europe, and the Southern States. He joined the faculty at BYU in 1977. Brother Christianson and his wife Helen have nine children.

**ROBERT A. CLOWARD** is the Church Educational System Coordinator in Knoxville, Tennessee and Director of the Institute of Religion at the University of Tennessee. Brother Cloward received his Bachelors and Masters degrees in Spanish from Brigham Young University and the Indiana University, respectively. His Ph.D. was taken at the University of Illinois. He has taught Spanish in public schools, as well as being involved in the growth of the Church Educational System programs in the southern United States and the islands of the Caribbean. Robert and his wife Kathleen are the parents of two children.

**RICHARD O. COWAN** is Professor of Church History and Doctrine at Brigham Young University. Brother Cowan received his Ph.D. from Stanford University in History and joined the BYU faculty in 1961. He is a popular and beloved teacher and is the author of numerous books on LDS history, particularly the period of the twentieth century. Brother Cowan and his wife Dawn are the parents of six children.

**LARRY E. DAHL** is Associate Professor of Church History and Doctrine at Brigham Young University. He received his Ed.D. from BYU in 1971 in Public School Administration and Religious Education. Brother Dahl worked for many years for the Church Educational System as an instructor, curriculum writer, and district and division coordinator. He was for a time employed by the Church in Instructional Development and as a staff member of the Melchizedek Priesthood committee. Brother Dahl and his wife Roberta are the parents of nine children.

**RICHARD D. DRAPER** is an instructor at the Institute of Religion adjacent to the Utah Technical College in Orem, Utah. Brother Draper has been associated with the Church Educational System for a number of years as a seminary and institute instructor, as well as a member of the College Curriculum staff. He received his M.A. degree from Arizona State University and concentrated on the American Westward Movement. He is completing a Ph.D. at BYU in Ancient History, with an emphasis on early Christianity. Richard and his wife Barbara are the parents of six children.

**SUSAN WARD EASTON** is Assistant Professor of Church History and Doctrine at Brigham Young University. She received her Ed.D. in Educational Psychology and Counseling from Brigham Young University and for a time worked as an Assistant Professor in the College of Family, Home, and Social Science at that institution. Susan is the mother of three boys.

**LAMAR E. GARRARD** is Professor of Church History and Doctrine at Brigham Young University. Brother Garrard has had a wide background and varied professional career. He received training in such fields as Engineering, Philosophy, Psychology, and Religion, obtaining the Ph.D. from Brigham Young University in Psychology in 1968. He has worked for seven years as an engineer, and a total of sixteen years as a professor of psychology, philosophy, and religion. Brother Garrard and his wife Agnes are the parents of six children.

**CHARLES R. HARRELL** is Assistant Professor of Engineering Technology at Brigham Young University. He received his B.S. from BYU and his M.E.A. degree from the University of Utah in Production Planning and Factory Automation. Brother Harrell worked for four years in Methods and Systems Analysis with Ford Motor Company, and for two years as Account Manager for Eaton-Kenway. Charles is married to the former Yvonne Hendrickson, and they have four children.

**LEON R. HARTSHORN** is Professor of Church History and Doctrine at Brigham Young University. Brother Hartshorn received his Bachelors and Masters degrees from BYU in the History and Philosophy of Religion, his Ed.D. from Stanford University in Educational Administration. He worked for a number of years for the Department of Seminaries and Institutes and taught for a time at the BYU-Hawaii campus. Brother Hartshorn and his wife Bea have five children.

**GEORGE A. HORTON, JR.** is Associate Professor of Ancient Scripture at Brigham Young University. He received his Bachelors and Masters degrees from BYU and his Ed.D. from the University of California at Los Angeles in Curriculum, Programmed Instruction, and Pupil Personnel. Brother Horton has worked as Curriculum Director of the Church Educational System and has served as dean or director of numerous tours to the Holy Land. He and his wife Norma are the parents of seven children.

**KENT P. JACKSON** is Assistant Professor of Ancient Scripture at Brigham Young University. Brother Jackson obtained his B.A. from BYU and his M.A. and Ph.D. degrees from the University of Michigan in Near Eastern Studies. He has published a major work on Ammonite inscriptions, as well as numerous articles on both LDS and non-LDS topics. He joined the BYU faculty in 1980. Brother Jackson and his wife Nancy are the parents of five children.

**JOSEPH FIELDING McCONKIE** is Associate Professor of Ancient Scripture at Brigham Young University. He obtained his Ed.D. from BYU in 1973 and has worked with the Church Educational System as a seminary instructor and institute director. Brother McConkie has also worked as an Army Chaplain. He is the author of a number of excellent LDS works now in print. Brother McConkie and his wife Brenda are the parents of eight children.

**ANN N. MADSEN** is an Instructor in the Department of Ancient Scripture at BYU, where she has taught since 1977. Subsequent to receiving a B.S. from the University of Utah, she received her M.A. in Ancient Studies from BYU, where she concentrated in Old Testament and Hebrew. Her thesis was a comprehensive treatment of Melchizedek in the scriptures and other ancient literature. She and her husband Truman are the parents of three children.

**ROBERT J. MATTHEWS** is Dean of Religious Education and Professor of Ancient Scripture at Brigham Young University. Brother Matthews obtained his Ph.D. from BYU in 1968, his doctoral dissertation representing a major textual study of Joseph Smith's translation of the Bible. Dean Matthews was associated for a number of years with Seminaries and Institutes, and worked as a seminary and institute instructor, as well as director of academic research. Brother Matthews and his wife Shirley are the parents of four children.

**KEITH H. MESERVY** is Associate Professor of Ancient Scripture at Brigham Young University, where he joined the faculty in 1958. Brother Meservy received his B.A. from BYU and his M.A. from Johns Hopkins University. An acknowledged scholar in Old and New Testament studies, he has inspired students for many years with his depth of insight into scriptural passages. Brother Meservy and his wife Arlene have four children.

**ROBERT L. MILLET** is Assistant Professor of Ancient Scripture at Brigham Young University. Brother Millet received his Ph.D. from Florida State University in Biblical Studies, 19th-20th Century Religious Thought, and Psychology. Before joining the faculty at BYU in 1983, he worked with the Church Educational System as a seminary instructor, institute director, and teaching support consultant. Brother Millet and his wife Shauna are the parents of five children.

**JAMES R. MOSS** is Associate Professor of Church History and Doctrine at Brigham Young University. He obtained his B.S. from the University of Utah in Political Science and his J.D. from the Stanford University School of Law. He has worked as a Division Coordinator for the Church Educational System in both Southern California and in the British Isles. Brother Moss has also been a member of the Utah state legislature. He and his wife LaVelle are the parents of seven children.

**MONTE S. NYMAN** is Associate Dean of Religious Education and Professor of Ancient Scripture at Brigham Young University. Brother Nyman is a recognized authority on the Book of Mormon and for years wrote the institute course of study. He has also written a major work on the life and message of Isaiah the Prophet. He received his Ed.D. from Brigham Young University in 1965 and joined the faculty at BYU in 1966. Before coming to BYU Brother Nyman taught in the public schools and also worked with the Church Educational System as a seminary and institute instructor. He and his wife Mary Ann are the parents of eight children.

**LEAUN G. OTTEN** is Associate Professor of Church History and Doctrine at Brigham Young University. A popular teacher, Brother Otten received his Master of Education degree from BYU and worked for a number of years as instructor at the Institute of Religion at Utah State University. He joined the faculty at BYU in 1972. He is the co-author of a two-volume work on the Doctrine and Covenants. Brother Otten and his wife Ella Rae are the parents of seven children.

**KEITH W. PERKINS** is Chairman of the Department of Church History and Doctrine at Brigham Young University. He worked with the Church Educational System as the Principal of the Granite LDS Seminary in Salt Lake City, as well as an instructor at the Institute of Religion adjacent to Arizona State University. Brother Perkins received his M.A. and Ph.D. degrees from BYU in Church History and Doctrine. He and his wife Vella are the parents of four children.

**MELVIN J. PETERSON** is Professor of Church History and Doctrine at Brigham Young University. He received his B.S., M.S., and Ed.D. degrees from BYU, where he has taught since 1964. Brother Peterson's Master's Thesis, written in 1955, was entitled "A Comparison of the Book of Commandments and Subsequent Editions of the Doctrine and Covenants." He and his wife Jeneal are the parents of eight children.

**STEPHEN D. RICKS** is Assistant Professor of Hebrew and Semitic Languages at Brigham Young University. Stephen received his Ph.D. in Near Eastern Religions at the University of California-Berkeley and Graduate Theological Union, and has been employed at BYU since 1981. He and his wife Shirley have five children.

**CATHERINE THOMAS** is a part-time instructor in the Department of Ancient Scripture at Brigham Young University. Her baccalaureate degree was in English, and she is presently pursuing a Ph.D. in Ancient History from BYU, her area of concentration being the Intertestamental Period. Sister Thomas and her husband Gordon are the parents of six children.

**RODNEY TURNER** is Professor of Ancient Scripture at Brigham Young University. Brother Turner received his A.B. and M.A. degrees at Brigham Young University, his areas of concentration being the Bible, Modern Scripture, and Theology. He received his Ed.D. from the University of Southern California in Educational Administration and Philosophy. In addition to his many years at BYU, Brother Turner has worked with the Department of Seminaries and Institutes of Religion for the Church and is the author of two major doctrinal works. He and his wife Bonnie are the parents of six children.

**BRUCE A. VAN ORDEN** is a curriculum writer for the Church Educational System and part-time instructor of Church History and Doctrine at Brigham Young University. He is presently completing a Ph.D. at BYU in American, Latter-day Saint, and Modern European History. Bruce and his wife Karen have four children.

**ROBERT J. WOODFORD** is an Instructor at an LDS Institute of Religion in Salt Lake City. Brother Woodford received his Ph.D. from Brigham Young University with a major in Bible and Modern Scripture and a minor in Religious Education. His doctoral dissertation, "The Historical Development of the Doctrine and Covenants," is the definitive textual study of the history and development of the Doctrine and Covenants. Brother Woodford and his wife Narda are the parents of eight children.

# SCRIPTURE INDEX

## The Old Testament

## The New Testament

## The Book of Mormon

## The Doctrine & Covenants

## The Pearl of Great Price

# SUBJECT INDEX

# ABOUT THE EDITORS

**Robert L. Millet,** professor of ancient scripture and former dean of Religious Education at Brigham Young University, taught in the Church Educational System before joining the faculty at BYU in 1983. He earned a master's degree in psychology from BYU and a Ph.D. in religious studies from Florida State University. Brother Millet and his wife, Shauna, are the parents of six children.

**Kent P. Jackson** is a professor of ancient scripture at Brigham Young University, where he has taught since 1980. He earned his Ph.D. in ancient Near Eastern and biblical studies from the University of Michigan. Brother Jackson and his wife, Nancy, are the parents of five children and the grandparents of three.